Funny You Should Say That

Funny You Should Say That

Amusing Remarks from Cicero to the Simpsons

Andrew Martin

THE OVERLOOK PRESS
Woodstock & New York

First published in the United States in 2006 by
The Overlook Press, Peter Mayer Publishers, Inc.
Woodstock & New York

WOODSTOCK:
One Overlook Drive
Woodstock, NY 12498
www.overlookpress.com
[for individual orders, bulk and special sales, contact our Woodstock office]

NEW YORK:
141 Wooster Street
New York, NY 10012

The paper used in this book meets the requirements for paper
permanence as described in the ANSI Z39.48-1992 standard.

Cataloging-in-Publication Data is available from the Library of Congress

Manufactured in the United States of America
1 2 3 4 5 6 7 8 9 10
ISBN-10 1-58567-833-3
ISBN-13 978-1-58567-833-4

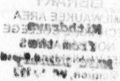

Contents

5 **Arts and Culture**

Literature

Film

Theatre and Performance

Visual Art

Music

Newspapers, Radio and Television

6 **Sport and Recreation**

Sport

Recreation

Introduction

It is a privilege to be allowed to make your own selection of humour especially if, as I do, you admire funny people probably more than you ought. But it is also very hard work.

I remember that, in my first week of compiling this book, I was gazing at the appropriate shelves at the London Library when a passing librarian called out, 'There's nothing funny in our humour section.' 'Well, thanks for letting me know,' I thought. It was not a good start, and there followed three years in which I hardly ever read a book or watched a film without a pen and paper in hand just in case I should come across something good. Typically, I would find a funny quote just before deciding to turn the lights out while reading in bed and then, in reaching for my pen, I would accidentally knock the book shut, causing me to spend the next hour looking for the right page, and sometimes, I'm afraid, never finding it, which could leave me with a disconnected feeling for most of the next day.

I would like to mention here that this is not one of those books where you'll read, 'It is a truth universally acknowledged, that a single man in possession of a good fortune must be in want of a wife', followed by a breezy ' – Jane Austen'. No, you are told that the quote occurs in chapter one of *Pride and Prejudice*, and you are given a potted biography of Jane Austen, alongside the 1,300 other authors (I think it is) of the 5,000 quotes in the book.

The aim is that the book might be read for pleasure as well as reference, so the quotes are arranged in thematic clusters. Anyone reading about 'Marriage', for example, might stray into 'The Battle of the Sexes', which is the next category. 'Charm and Flattery' is next to 'Jealousy', because that's how I think it works in life.

Within their thematic categories, the quotes are also arranged, as far as possible, chronologically, so that the reader can trace the steady stream of complaints about, say, the telephone or British railways, from the moment of invention to the present day; or so the reader can see that, in telling mother-in-law jokes, Les Dawson was only following on from Lord Byron. It is interesting to read what a Helen Simpson character thought of the marriage bed in 1990, 'no escaping the mildmint breath toothpasting its way across the pillows', and compare what Laurence Sterne thought of it in 1759, when he observed that married man would 'never . . . lie *diagonally* in his bed again as long as he lives'. And it is strange to see how the most unlikely subjects have attracted humorists. I'm proud of my little run of quotes on buttonholes, for example, or cheese.

With reference to the subtitle of this dictionary, I'll not deny that there are a few more quotes here from the Simpsons than there are from Cicero. A. J. P. Taylor said that 'history gets thicker as it approaches recent times', and so does humour. Probably, there is too much humour now, a consequence of the entertainment boom, the higher quality of material life, not to mention *longer* life. Humour has replaced formality and manners as the social lubricant, and it seems to be the job of modern politicians to smile all the time, but here I am really talking about purported humour – hollow humour. How often do any of us experience the real jolt of something genuinely funny? Jonathan Swift said that he had laughed only twice in his entire life, and if a book reviewer writes that a book 'made me laugh out loud four times', it's considered a great endorsement and will certainly be printed on the jacket.

That said, I don't claim that every quote here is laugh-out-loud funny. Some of them, now that I come to think of it, are extremely depressing, including one of my favourites of all, spoken by Ted Turner: 'Life is like a B-movie. You don't want to leave in the middle of it, but you don't want to see it again.' Proper humour, as opposed to the sort that ends in exclamation marks, is closely allied with gloom, especially if you're from the north of England as I am.

This book is my selection, qualified by the consideration that most people looking under 'Hunting', for instance, will want to know what Oscar Wilde said about it – a remark that they can almost but not quite remember. The question of whether not to include a very famous funny quote that is in fact not funny at all is one of many I've wrestled with. It's a question of balance. I've also tried to avoid being too politically correct or too offensive or, then again, too compromising. I don't want to bleat about it, but I have lost sleep over many such editorial matters. Is it strictly right and proportionate, for example, that the potted biography of Terry Venables has come out twice as long as the one for Leo Tolstoy?

But it's done now. I would like to thank Ellie Smith, Georgina Laycock, Martin Toseland, Sue Phillpott, Deirdre Clark, Lydia Darbyshire and Caroline Sheard, and I hope there are more than four proper laughs in it for most readers.

Andrew Martin
April 2005

1

Being Human

Appearance
Beauty and Ugliness

1 **Brian O'Linn was a gentleman born,/ His hair it was long and his beard unshorn,/ His teeth were out and his eyes far in –/ 'I'm a wonderful beauty,' says Brian O'Linn!**
Anon. First verse of 'Brian O'Linn', collected in *The Faber Book of Nonsense Verse* ed. Geoffrey Grigson (1979). According to Grigson, 'There are many versions, English, Irish and Scottish, with the hero variously named Brian, Tommy and Tam.' A form of the final stanza is quoted in W. Wager's 'The longer thou livest, the more foole thou art' (1569).

2 **I could not endure a husband with a beard on his face:/ I had rather lie in the woollen.**
William Shakespeare Beatrice in *Much Ado About Nothing*, act 2, sc. 3 (1598–9)

3 **Go up, thou bald head . . .**
II Kings 2:23, the Bible, Authorized Version (1611)

4 **Thy teeth are like a flock of sheep that are even shorn . . .**
Song of Solomon 4:2, ibid.

5 **Bring us the mirror, you ignoramus! And take care you don't dirty the glass by letting your reflection get in it!**
Molière Cathos in *Such Foolish Affected Ladies*, sc. 6 (1659)

6 **If to her share, some female errors fall,/ Look on her face, and you'll forget 'em all.**
Alexander Pope *The Rape of the Lock*, canto 2, line 17 (1714)

7 **Tell me, Constance, how do I look this evening? Is there anything whimsical about me? Is it one of my well-looking days, child? Am I in face today?**
Oliver Goldsmith Miss Hardcastle in *She Stoops to Conquer*, act 1, sc. 1 (1773)

8 **I like large features. People with**

small features and *squeeny* noses never do anything.

Lord Melbourne To Queen Victoria in the mid 1830s. Quoted in *Lord M.*, ch. 5, by David Cecil (1954)

9 This I set down as a positive truth. A woman with fair opportunities and without a positive hump, may marry whom she likes.

William Makepeace Thackeray *Vanity Fair*, ch. 4 (1847–8)

10 Anything to me is sweeter/ Than to see Shock-headed Peter.

Heinrich Hoffmann *Shock-Headed Peter* (1848), originally in German as *Struwwelpeter*

11 Plain women he regarded as he did the other severe facts of life, to be faced with philosophy and investigated by science.

George Eliot Of Tertius Lydgate in *Middlemarch*, bk 1, ch. 11 (1871–2)

12 The moment one sits down to think, one becomes all nose, or all forehead, or something horrid. Look at the successful men in any of the learned professions. How perfectly hideous they are!

Oscar Wilde Lord Henry Wotton in *The Picture of Dorian Gray*, ch. 1 (1891)

13 It is only shallow people who do not judge by appearances.

Lord Henry Wotton in ibid., ch. 2

14 The youth of the present day are quite monstrous. They have absolutely no respect for dyed hair.

Oscar Wilde Mr Dumby in *Lady Windermere's Fan*, act 3 (1893)

15 The only two general maxims in which I have much belief are 'Carpe Diem' and 'never have your hair cut outside Bond St.'

Raymond Asquith Letter to H. T. Baker of 21 September 1898, collected in *Raymond Asquith: Life and Letters* ed. John Jolliffe (1980). He had just had a 'villainous' haircut – in Bond Street.

16 Beauty is all very well at first sight; but who ever looks at it when it has been in the house three days?

George Bernard Shaw Ann Whitfield in *Man and Superman*, act 4 (1903)

17 I always say beauty is only sin deep.

Saki *Reginald in Russia*, 'The Baker's Dozen' (1910). In *Mr Norris Changes Trains* by Christopher Isherwood, ch. 3 (1935), Arthur Norris says '. . . Anni's beauty is only sin-deep. I hope that's original.'

18 Constance is one of those strapping, florid girls that go well with the autumn scenery or Christmas decorations in church.

Ibid. 'The Mouse'

19 Look at the woebegone walk of him. Eaten a bad egg. Poached eyes on ghost.

James Joyce *Ulysses*, ch. 8 (1922). Bloom spies John Howard Parnell, brother of James Stewart Parnell MP.

20 She said she always believed in the old addage, 'Leave them while you're looking good.'

Anita Loos *Gentlemen Prefer Blondes*, ch. 1 (1925). This is the view of the narrator, Lorelei Lee's maid Lulu. Lorelei Lee is not a good speller.

21 Men seldom make passes/ At girls who wear glasses.

Dorothy Parker *Enough Rope*, 'News Item' (1926)

22 My wife's the ugliest woman in the world – I'd sooner take her with me than kiss her goodbye.

Max Miller Recorded at the Holborn Empire, London, October 1938, reissued in *Max Miller: The Cheeky Chappie – All His Live Shows in the Late 30s, Early 40s* (CD, 2000)

23 Here's Nijinsky doing the rhumba/ Here's her social security numbah.

Groucho Marx From 'Lydiah, the Tattooed Lady', a song sung by Groucho in *At the Circus* (film, 1939, screenplay by Irving Brecher, directed by Edward Buzzell)

24 My beard looks very horrible at present . . . Anyway it gives me a hobby sadly needed during the voyage, like a pet or a pot plant

whose progress I watch day by day.

Evelyn Waugh Letter to Laura Waugh of 18 February 1941, collected in *The Letters of Evelyn Waugh* ed. Mark Amory (1980). Waugh was sailing to Egypt.

25 **The bosom can be passing fair/ That apes the apple or the pear:/ I do not itch to lay my head/ On melons or on loaves of bread.**

A. P. Herbert 'Vital Statistics (2)', *Punch* 16 January 1957, repr. in *Look Back and Laugh*, 'The Fifties' (1960). The poem begins: 'I do not find that I am fond/ Of this too celebrated blonde,/ So photographed, so much discussed/ Because of her enormous bust.'

26 **I'm tired of all this nonsense about beauty being only skin deep. That's deep enough.**

Jean Kerr *The Snake Has All the Lines*, 'Mirror, Mirror on the Wall' (1958). She adds: 'What do you want – an adorable pancreas?'

27 **Dave, I'm not so blond. I'm nearly back to my own colour, more red. I'm going all plain an sertificated.**

Nell Dunn Joy in *Poor Cow*, 'More Trouble' (1967)

28 **He looks as if he's escaped off the side of Notre Dame.**

Christopher Hampton Celia in *The Philanthropist*, sc. 3 (1970)

29 **Beautiful: Adjective applied to the daughter of any woman prominent in the weekly illustrated newspapers.**

Beachcomber *Beachcomber: The Works of J. B. Morton*, 'A Dictionary for Today', ed. Richard Ingrams (1974)

30 **It's been said that a pretty face is a passport. But it's not, it's a visa, and it runs out fast.**

Julie Burchill *Sex and Sensibility*, 'Kiss and Sell' (1992)

31 **I've gone out with some of those guys – the ones who are short, fat and ugly – and it doesn't make any difference. They're just as unappreciative and self-centered as the good-looking ones.**

Candace Bushnell *Sex and the City*, ch. 4 (1996)

32 **Ugliness is superior to beauty, because ugliness lasts.**

Serge Gainsbourg *GQ* magazine, January 2000. Gainsbourg refused to have mirrors in his home.

33 **It costs a lot to make a person look this cheap.**

Dolly Parton Quoted in *Women's Wicked Wit* ed. Michelle Lovric (2000)

34 **Hair matters.**

Hillary Clinton *The Times*, 'Quotes of the Week', 2 June 2001. Clinton was addressing students: 'This,' she said, 'was a lesson Wellesley and Yale Law School failed to instil.'

35 **[Of plastic surgery] It would have been cheaper to have my DNA changed.**

Joan Rivers Quoted in the *Independent* 18 April 2002

36 **My secret for staying young is good food, plenty of rest and a make-up man with a spray gun.**

Bob Hope Quoted in the *Independent* 16 May 2003

37 **You cannae polish a turd.**

Anon. The actually reasonably good-looking Sam Leith employing 'the ancient Scottish saying' in the *Spectator* 3 January 2004, to explain why he had for a long time resisted the temptation to have a facial

Size

1 **Troth, and your bum is the greatest thing about you; so that in the beastliest sense you are Pompey the Great.**

William Shakespeare Escalus to Pompey in *Measure for Measure*, act 2, sc. 1 (1603–4)

2 **I do think better of womankind than to suppose they care whether Mr John Keats five feet high likes them or not.**

John Keats Letter to Benjamin Bailey of 18 July 1818, collected in *The Letters of John Keats* ed. H. E. Rollins, vol. 1 (1958)

3 **To conclude, the only fault of the Spanish beauty is that she too soon**

indulges in the magnificence of the en bon point.

Benjamin Disraeli Letter to Maria D'Israeli of 1 August 1830, collected in *Benjamin Disraeli Letters: 1815–1834* ed. J. A. W. Gunn, John Matthews, Donald M. Schurman (1982). The letter was written from Granada.

4 There was once a young man of Oporta/ Who daily got shorter and shorter,/ The reason he said/ Was the hod on his head,/ Which was filled with the *heaviest* mortar.

Lewis Carroll *Melodies* (1845)

5 O fat white woman whom nobody loves,/ Why do you walk through the fields in gloves,/ when the grass is soft as the breast of doves/ And shivering sweet to the touch?

Frances Cornford 'To a Fat Lady Seen from a Train' (1910). In 1933 G. K. Chesterton responded to this poem, attacking the poet: 'Why do you rush through the fields in trains?/ . . . fat-head poet that nobody reads.' Arthur Marshall, in his book *Smile Please* (1982), speculated that the gloves were 'possibly a sensible precaution against midge bites'.

6 I was skating one day at full swing and came clash against a man of my own stature who was going at the same time. We both fell asunder – got up – and *laughed*. Had we been short men we might have resented.

Alfred, Lord Tennyson Quoted in *Tennyson and His Friends*, 'Some Recollections of Tennyson's Talk from 1835 to 1853', ed. Hallam, Lord Tennyson (1911)

7 The Right Hon. was a tubby little chap who looked as if he had been poured into his clothes and had forgotten to say 'When!'

P. G. Wodehouse *Very Good, Jeeves*, 'Jeeves and the Impending Doom' (1930)

8 This Englishwoman is so refined/ She has no bosom and no behind.

Stevie Smith 'This Englishwoman', publ. in *A Good Time Was Had by All* (1937). This is the entire poem; it is accompanied by a drawing.

9 'Tall aren't you?' she said./ 'I didn't mean to be.'

Raymond Chandler *The Big Sleep*, ch. 1 (1939).

The question is asked of Philip Marlowe by Carmen Sternwood.

10 I'm fat but I'm thin inside. Has it ever struck you that there's a thin man inside every fat man, just as they say there's a statue in every block of stone?

George Orwell *Coming up for Air*, pt 1, ch. 3 (1939). In *The Unquiet Grave*, pt 2 (1944), Cyril Connolly said: 'Imprisoned in every fat man a thin one is wildly signalling to be let out.'

11 He was about six feet two, and not much of it soft.

Raymond Chandler Of Mr Derace Kingsley in *The Lady in the Lake*, ch. 1 (1944)

12 When Mrs Frederick C. Little's second son was born, everybody noticed that he was not much bigger than a mouse.

E. B. White *Stuart Little*, ch. 1, 'In the Drain' (1945). The opening sentence of the book.

13 'Corky,' he said earnestly, 'the advice I would give to every young man starting out in life is that if you are going to yield to impulse, be careful before you do so that there isn't a blighter eight feet high and broad in proportion standing behind you.'

P. G. Wodehouse Ukridge in *A Few Quick Ones*, 'A Tithe for Charity' (1959)

14 Two mortuarial men entered the room. One was taller than the other, as is often the case in Ireland.

Spike Milligan *Puckoon*, ch. 4 (1963)

15 [Of William Conrad] Whereas nowadays Conrad is very fat indeed, in those days he was simply very fat.

Clive James *Observer* 11 May 1975. James was comparing the appearance of the American actor William Conrad in *The Naked Jungle* (film, 1954), with his appearance by the time of *Cannon*, a police drama which ran through the 1970s and in which Conrad played the title role.

16 [Eric, of his wife] I'm not saying she's fat but we've been married six

years, and I still haven't seen all of her.

Eric Morecambe and Ernie Wise *The Morecambe and Wise Jokebook*, skit 26 (1979). Ernie protests: 'But I thought you said she had a million-dollar figure', to which Eric replies: 'She has, but it's all in loose change.'

17 I wouldn't say that my wife is fat, but . . . she's got a fat butt!

Les Dawson *The Malady Lingers On*, 'A Word to the Reader' (1982)

18 Most men wear their belts low here, there being so many outstanding bellies, some big enough to have names of their own and be formally introduced.

Garrison Keillor *Lake Wobegon Days*, 'Home' (1985)

19 My God, if her bum was a bungalow she'd never get a mortgage on it.

Victoria Wood 'Turkish Bath', sketch from *Victoria Wood as Seen on TV* (TV series 1985), collected in *Up to You, Porky – The Victoria Wood Sketch Book* (1985). The speaker is Thelma, an attendant in a Turkish bath. But in the *Daily Telegraph* 7 January 2003 Wood said: 'There's nothing wrong with wodgy arms and a big bum.'

20 **JOURNALIST: How tall are you?**
RINGO STARR: Two feet, nine inches.

Ringo Starr *The Q/ Omnibus Press Rock 'n' Roll Reader*, 'The Beatles Press Conferences' (1994). The remark dates from the early 1960s.

21 Mmm . . . Am I wrong or did it just get fatter in here?

Matt Groening Patty, Homer Simpson's sister-in-law, as Homer enters the room in *The Simpsons*, 'Homer vs Patty and Selma', first broadcast 26 February 1995

22 My mother kept telling me I would 'shoot up'. I was still asking her, at the age of twenty: 'What's all this about me shooting up?'

Martin Amis *The Information*, pt 2 (1995). The speaker is Richard Tull, 'a man who stands five-feet-six-inches tall (or 5' 6½", according to a passport I once had)'.

23 I think when men tell women to lose weight, it's a diversion from their own lack of size in certain areas.

Candace Bushnell Comment made by anonymous woman in *Sex and the City*, ch. 3 (1996)

24 I don't look fatter. I can fasten the button, though not, alas, the zipper on my '89 jeans. So maybe my whole body is getting smaller but denser.

Helen Fielding *Bridget Jones's Diary* (1996), entry for Tuesday 7 March

25 [Of fat girls] The rule was that you were allowed them – to practise on, as it were, like rough paper – so long as you weren't seen with them.

Howard Jacobson *No More Mister Nice Guy*, ch. 5 (1998)

26 When I walk around the West End these days, it seems to me that outside every thin girl is a fat man, trying to get in.

Katharine Hepburn Quoted in *Women's Wicked Wit* ed. Michelle Lovric (2000)

27 My feet are small for the same reason my waist is small – things don't grow in the shade.

Dolly Parton Quoted in ibid.

28 When I was a child, I was so fat I was the one chosen to play Bethlehem in the school Nativity play.

Jo Brand *The Penguin Book of Modern Humorous Quotations* ed. Fred Metcalf (2nd edn 2001)

29 There are perks to being flat-chested. I can pass for fourteen in a blackout.

Jenny Éclair *The Times*, 'Quotes of the Week', 18 August 2001

Peculiarities of Appearance

1 Though one eye may be very agreeable, yet as the prejudice has always run in favour of two, I would not

wish to affect a singularity in that article.

Richard Brinsley Sheridan Captain Absolute in *The Rivals*, act 3, sc. 1 (1774)

2 [Remark to an irritating thin man] **Sir, you are like a pin, but without either its head or its point.**

Douglas Jerrold Attributed

3 **'A literary man – *with* a wooden leg – and all print is open to him!'**

Charles Dickens Mr Boffin in *Our Mutual Friend*, 'Book the First: The Cup and the Lip', ch. 5 (1864–5). He is marvelling at the one-legged Silas Wegg, a fruit-seller he has engaged to teach him literature.

4 *Rouge* and *esprit* used to go together. That is all over now. As long as a woman can look ten years younger than her own daughter, she is perfectly satisfied.

Oscar Wilde Lord Henry Wotton in *The Picture of Dorian Gray*, ch. 4 (1891)

5 **Bah! The thing is not a nose at all, but a bit of primordial chaos clapped on to my face.**

H. G. Wells *Select Conversations with an Uncle*, 'The Man with a Nose' (1895)

6 **... Any dreams I had/ Of being loved have always ended poorly/ Because this nose arrived ten minutes early ...**

Edmond Rostand Cyrano in *Cyrano de Bergerac*, act 1 (1897), from the translation (1975) by Christopher Fry

7 **'It ain't a 'ump, and it don't look like kervicher of the spine,'** observed the voluble young lady to herself. 'Blimy if I don't believe 'e's taking 'ome 'is washing up his back.'

Jerome K. Jerome *The Passing of the Third Floor Back*, ch. 1 (1907)

8 **For though poets may sing of the romance of the sea/ And the mountains and rivers and tide-ways,/ There is nothing so strange – you may take it from me –/ As the look of one's face when it's sideways.**

A. P. Herbert *Wisdom for the Wise*, 'The Tailor' (1930)

9 **Roderick Spode? Big chap with a small moustache and the sort of eye that can open an oyster at sixty paces?**

P. G. Wodehouse *The Code of the Woosters*, ch. 2 (1938)

10 **He had rather bloodshot eyes of that pure Cambridge blue associated by Daniel with people who were a little mad.**

Pamela Hansford Johnson *The Unspeakable Skipton*, ch. 2 (1960)

11 **Flat back of head, untrustworthy.**

Lynn Barber Typical of the notes she made on men while at Oxford University in the 1960s, quoted in *Mostly Men*, Introduction (1991)

12 **'Look at him,' my friend Ivan remarked over the breakfast table. 'It is really difficult to decide whether he is an Englishman or only a funny drawing of an Englishman.'**

George Mikes *How to Unite Nations*, 'Twice Lucky' (1963). The man in question was in a hotel in Bayswater, London, wearing flannels and a tweed jacket, reading *The Times* and smoking a pipe. But he turned out to be Hungarian.

13 **His face is small but then he's got quite a small head. It's the rest of him. Somebody the other day said he looked like a polythene bag full of water.**

Alan Ayckbourn Marge, speaking of her husband Gordon, in *Absent Friends*, act 1 (1974)

14 [Of Donny Osmond] **The star, of course, is Donny. He is a cow-eyed, fine-boned lad of the type you see languishing angelically in a Botticelli *tondo*. His acreage of gum is a testimonial to the stimulating properties of the electric toothbrush.**

Clive James *Observer* 18 August 1974. James was reviewing a BBC programme called *The Osmonds*, which he described as 'utter corn ... laborious mimes to playback, sub-Motown choreography and mirthless humour'.

15 **Certain people are born with natural false teeth.**

Robert Robinson Spoken on *Stop the Week* (BBC radio programme) in 1977, quoted in *Collins Dictionary of Quotations* ed. A. Norman Jeffares and Martin Gray (1995)

16 **I had buck teeth ... I could find no redeeming example of what later became known as a role model; buck-teeth people in comics and films were sometimes brainy ('Hi, prof') but always risible. Even today I find it hard to forgive Walt Disney for his buck-toothed hound called Goofy.**

Ian Jack *Before the Oil Ran Out*, 'Finished with Engines' (1986)

17 **When I talk about the giants of show business, I can't overlook Jimmy Durante's nose.**

George Burns *All My Best Friends*, ch. 1 (1989). Durante was known as 'The Schnozz'.

18 **My body, on the move, resembles in sight and sound nothing so much as a bin-liner full of yoghurt.**

Stephen Fry *The Hippopotamus*, ch. 3 (1995)

19 **I've no regrets other than a really awful haircut in the mid-Eighties – the haircut that launched a thousand Third Division soccer players.**

Bono Remark made in February 1997, quoted in *People on People: The Oxford Dictionary of Biographical Quotations* ed. Anne Ratcliffe (2001). He also wore sunglasses indoors.

20 *Add interest to your personality*: **Do people ignore you? Why not cultivate a handlebar moustache?/ It could provide an invaluable talking point.**

Craig Brown *The Little Book of Chaos* (1998)

21 **I wouldn't like to be as bald as he is. You'd never know where to stop washing your hair.**

Alan Bennett Typical remark of Alan Bennett's mother, as recalled in *Telling Tales*, 'Days Out' (2000)

22 **[Of Clark Gable] Ears too big.**

Anon. Attributed remark of a 'Hollywood executive' on watching a screen test by the actor, quoted in *Cassell's Movie Quotations* ed. Nigel Rees (2nd edn 2002)

Clothes and Fashion

1 **Thou look'st like Antichrist in that lewd hat.**

Ben Jonson Ananias to Kastril in *The Alchemist*, act 4, sc. 4 (1605)

2 **God sends cold according to Cloathes.**

George Herbert *Outlandish Proverbs*, no. 33 (1640)

3 **Then to Whitehall ... and among other things met with Mr Townsend, who told of his mistake the other day, to put both his legs through one of his knees of his breeches, and went so all day.**

Samuel Pepys Diary entry for 6 April 1661, *Everybody's Pepys* ed. Henry B. Wheatley (1926). Mr Townsend was an official of the Wardrobe department.

4 **Good God! To what an Ebb of Taste are Women fallen, that it should be in the power of a lac'd Coat to recommend a Gallant to 'em.**

Sir John Vanbrugh The observation of a character called Young Fashion, in *The Relapse*, act 1, sc. 3 (1696)

5 **Button-holes! – there is something lively in the very idea of 'em – and trust me, when I get amongst 'em – You gentry with great beards – look as grave as you will – I'll make merry work with my button-holes – I shall have 'em all to myself – 'tis a subject – I shall run foul of no man's wisdoms or fine sayings in it.**

Laurence Sterne *Tristram Shandy* (1759–67), vol. 4. ch. 15, on the origin of button-holing

6 **Formerly, indeed, the buckle was a sort of machine, intended to keep on the shoe; but the case is now quite reversed, and the shoe is of no earthly use, but to keep on the buckle.**

Richard Brinsley Sheridan *A Trip to Scarborough*, act 1, sc. 1 (1777)

7 O Lord, Sir – when a heroine goes mad she always goes into white satin.

Richard Brinsley Sheridan *The Critic*, act 3, sc. 1 (1779)

8 As with my hat upon my head/ I walked along the Strand,/ I there did meet another man/ With his hat in his hand.

Samuel Johnson From 'Anecdotes by George Steevens', *European Magazine* January 1785. Steevens was an associate of Dr Johnson and a Shakespearian scholar.

9 Damn braces: Bless relaxes.

William Blake *The Marriage of Heaven and Hell*, 'Proverbs of Hell' (1790–3)

10 All this buttoning and unbuttoning.

Anon. An eighteenth-century suicide note, quoted in *The Oxford Dictionary of Quotations* ed. Angela Partington (4th edn 1996)

11 I bought some Japan Ink likewise, & next week shall begin my operations on my hat, on which You know my principal hopes of happiness depend.

Jane Austen Letter to Cassandra Austen of 27–28 October 1798, collected in *Jane Austen's Letters* ed. Dierdre Le Faye (1995)

12 Some folks in the street by the Lord make me stare,/ So comical droll is the dress that they wear;/ For the gentlemen's waist is at top of their back,/ And their large Cossack trowsers, that fit like a sack.

Anon. 'The Fashions' from *Oliver's Comic Songs* (1825?). This is the song of a 'poor country lad . . . come up to London to see what's what'.

13 When you have seen a man in a nightcap, you lose all respect for him.

Charles Dickens *Sketches by Boz*, 'Scenes', ch. 16, 'Omnibuses' (1836)

14 Beware of all enterprises that require new clothes.

Henry David Thoreau *Walden; or, Life in the Woods*, 'Economy' (1854)

15 No one knows how ungentlemanly he can look, until he has seen himself in a shocking bad hat.

R. S. Surtees *Mr Facey Romford's Hounds*, ch. 9 (1865)

16 Wheeare es-ta been sin Ah saw thee/ On Ilkla Mooar baht 'at?

Anon. Traditional Yorkshire song, usually sung to the tune of the hymn 'Cranbrook' (1805, by Thomas Clark), and thought to be an account of a choir outing from Halifax in 1886 – a member of the choir went on to Ilkley Moor without a hat, but with Mary Jane, who is mentioned in the song. The words are quoted in *Basic Broad Yorkshire Sayings and Traditions* by Arnold Kellett (1991).

17 They say – people who ought to be ashamed of themselves do – that a consciousness of being well dressed imparts a blissfulness to the human heart that religion is powerless to bestow. I am afraid these cynical persons are sometimes correct.

Jerome K. Jerome *The Idle Thoughts of an Idle Fellow*, 'On Dress and Deportment' (1886)

18 Where did you get that hat?/ Where did you get that tie?

James Rolmaz 'Where Did You Get That Hat?' (song, 1888)

19 A really well made buttonhole is the only link between Art and Nature.

Oscar Wilde 'Phrases and Philosophies for the Use of the Young', *Chameleon* December 1894

20 One should either be a work of art, or wear a work of art.

Ibid.

21 She was a curious woman, whose dresses always looked as though they had been designed in a rage and put on in a tempest.

Oscar Wilde *The Picture of Dorian Gray*, ch. 4 (1891). The woman described is Lady Henry Wotton.

22 The chin a little higher, dear. Style largely depends on the way the chin is worn. They are worn very high, just at present.

Oscar Wilde Lady Bracknell in *The Importance of Being Earnest*, act 4 (1895)

23 There have been dandies, like
D'Orsay, who were nearly painters;
painters, like Mr Whistler, who
wished to be dandies; dandies, like
Disraeli, who afterwards pursued
some less arduous calling.

Max Beerbohm *Works*, 'Dandies and
Dandies' (1896)

24 I wear no gloves? My hands are
bare!/ I did have *one*, one of an
ancient pair,/ But carelessly I threw
the thing away/ In an insolent face
which had too much to say.

Edmond Rostand Cyrano in *Cyrano de
Bergerac*, act 1 (1897), in Christopher Fry's
translation (1975)

25 Last night I dreamed that I wore
sandals and was ashamed.

Arnold Bennett Entry for 7 September 1898,
The Journals of Arnold Bennett (1896–1910)
ed. Newman Flower (1932)

26 I think it terribly sad that woman,
the loveliest object we have in the
world – the most beautiful thing
that God has created – should go
about tricked out and disfigured by
all the barbaric acts of the milliner.

W. T. Stead Interviewed for *The World of
Dress* June 1905, repr. in *The Penguin Book of
Interviews* ed. C. Silvester (1993). His other
'pet aversions' were the wasp-waist and the
trained walking-skirt. Trousers, he believed,
'should be capable of being patched'.

27 His shoes exhaled the right
soupçon of harness-room; his socks
compelled one's attention without
losing one's respect.

Saki *The Chronicles of Clovis*, 'Ministers of
Grace' (1911)

28 I'm Burlington Bertie/ I rise at ten
thirty and saunter along like a
toff,/ I walk down the Strand with
my gloves in my hand,/ Then I
walk down again with them off.

W. F. Hargreaves 'Burlington Bertie from
Bow' (song, 1915)

29 Jeeves lugged my purple socks out of
the drawer as if he were a vegetarian
fishing a caterpillar out of his salad.

P. G. Wodehouse *My Man Jeeves*, 'Jeeves and
the Chump Cyril' (1919)

30 An Oxford man! . . . Like hell he is!
He wears a pink suit.

F. Scott Fitzgerald Tom Buchanan speaking
of Gatsby in *The Great Gatsby*, ch. 7 (1925)

31 You have got to be a queen to get
away with a hat like that.

Anita Loos *Gentlemen Prefer Blondes*, ch. 4
(1925)

32 Gentlemen, it was necessary to abol-
ish the fez, which stands on the
heads of our nation as an emblem
of ignorance, negligence, fanaticism
and hatred of progress and civilization, to accept in its place the hat,
the headgear worn by the whole civilized world.

Kemal Ataturk Speech to the Turkish
Assembly, October 1927. In 'The Fez', by contrast, in 1976, the rock group Steely Dan
sang: 'You'll never do it without the fez on.'

33 Then he wrote . . . to the laundry to
say would they send back two
buttonholes that were missing from
his blue shirt.

Norman Hunter *The Incredible Adventures of
Professor Branestawm*, ch. 5 (1933)

34 Looks like a well-kept grave.

W. C. Fields His reaction to the appearance
of a flirtatious overdressed widow in an enormous complicated hat in *You're Telling Me*
(film, 1934, screenplay by Walter de Leon and
Paul M. Jones)

35 Brevity is the soul of lingerie.

Dorothy Parker Attributed

36 That's quite a dress you almost
have on.

Alan Jay Lerner Jerry Mulligan (Gene Kelly) to
Lise Bouvier (Leslie Caron) in *An American in
Paris* (film, 1951, directed by Vincente
Minnelli)

37 I won't take me coat off – I'm not
stopping.

Ken Platt His catchphrase from 1951 onwards

38 Have you heard about 'The Edwardians'? They are a gang of
proletarian louts who dress like
Beaton with braided trousers & vel-
vet collars & murder one another in
'Youth Centres'.

Evelyn Waugh Letter to Nancy Mitford of

5 May 1954, collected in *The Letters of Evelyn Waugh* ed. Mark Amory (1980). Waugh was referring to Teddy Boys. He added that Cecil Beaton 'was always being stopped now by the police and searched for knuckle-dusters'.

39 **The trick of wearing mink is to look as though you are wearing a cloth coat. The trick of wearing a cloth coat is to look as though you are wearing mink.**

Pierre Balmain Quoted in the *Observer*, 'Sayings of the Week', 25 December 1955

40 **Do you remember those old stockings? The black ones and the blue ones, and those horrible khaki ones . . . Oh, I was glad when *they* came to an end.**

Eric Morecambe and Ernie Wise Eric Morecambe to Ernie Wise in *Two of a Kind*, a video selection (1992) from the best of their first major TV series *Two of a Kind* (1962)

41 **I am trying to think of my panama hat as an investment. It certainly has no other role to play.**

Philip Larkin Letter to Barbara Pym of 29 September 1963, collected in *Selected Letters of Philip Larkin (1940–85)* ed. Anthony Thwaite (1992)

42 **Top hats look like very sensible containers, suitable for holding almost everything with the exception of the human head.**

George Mikes *How to Unite Nations*, 'A Day at the Races' (1963)

43 **Hats divide generally into three classes: offensive hats, defensive hats, and shrapnel.**

Katherine Whitehorn *Shouts and Murmurs*, 'Hats' (1963)

44 **One of the few lessons I have learnt in life is that there is invariably something odd about women who wear ankle socks.**

Alan Bennett *The Old Country* (1978)

45 **While clothes with pictures and/or writing on them are not entirely an invention of the modern age, they are an unpleasant indication of the state of things.**

Fran Lebowitz *Metropolitan Life*, 'Clothes

with Pictures and/or Writing on Them: Yes – Another Complaint' (1978)

46 **My latest tie commemorates the centenary of railway catering (1879–1979). I admired it in a bar & the chap took it off and gave it to me . . . It's only when you get close you see it's a crossed knife & fork, BR arrows, sausage rolls rampant & so on.**

Philip Larkin Letter to Winifred Bradshaw of 23 August 1979, collected in *Selected Letters of Philip Larkin (1940–85)* ed. Anthony Thwaite (1992)

47 **The softer a man's head the louder his socks.**

Helen Rowland Quoted in *Violets and Vinegar*, 'If the Devil Dress Her Not', ed. Jilly Cooper and Tom Hartman (1980)

48 **Few/ articles of attire/ Arouse my ire,/ Get my goat/ Or generally ruffle/ Me/ To the same degree/ As the duffel/ Coat.**

Mark Bevan 'Hold My Coat', *Punch* February 1982, collected in *Punch Lines* ed. Amanda-Jane Doran (1992)

49 **'It's years,' said an Oxford friend of mine the other day – and he said it with a sigh – 'It's years since I've seen the back of a young man's neck.'**

John Sparrow *Words on the Air*, 'Beards' (1981)

50 **A sweater is a garment worn by a child when his mother feels chilly.**

Anon. Quoted in *Laughter Lines: Family Wit and Wisdom*, 'One-eyed Parents', ed. James A. Simpson (1986)

51 **I lost a buttonhole.**

Steven Wright *I Have a Pony* (CD, 1986)

52 **[On formal wear] I'm so self-conscious. Every single thing on me is rented.**

Woody Allen Cliff Stern (Woody Allen) in *Crimes and Misdemeanors* (film, 1989, directed by Woody Allen)

53 **I never cared for fashion much. Amusing little seams and**

witty little pleats. It was the girls I liked.

David Bailey Remark made in November 1990, quoted in *People on People: The Oxford Encyclopaedia of Biographical Quotations* ed. Susan Ratcliffe (2001)

54 A gentleman approached me in the street earlier and asked, 'Have you got a light mac?' to which I replied, truthfully, 'No, but I've got a dark brown overcoat.'

Stephen Fry *Paperweight*, 'Trefusis's Postcard from America' (1992)

55 You cannot enjoy Mozart and choose to wear an anorak.

Giles Gordon *Aren't We Due a Royalty Statement?*, ch. 27 (1993)

56 'The thing that really drives me crazy,' said the artist, 'is when I see a woman wearing one of those tartan skirts with high knee socks. I can't work all day.'

Candace Bushnell *Sex and the City*, ch. 2 (1996)

57 Up early, and waistcoat for an interesting day.

Alan Clark Entry for Wednesday 10 December 1997, collected in *The Last Diaries: In and Out of the Wilderness* ed. Ion Trewin (2002)

58 Never trust anyone who wears a bow tie. A cravat's supposed to point down and accentuate the genitalia. Why would you trust anyone whose tie points *out* to accentuate his ears?

David Mamet A doctor in *State and Main* (film, 1999, written and directed by David Mamet)

59 You mean those clothes of hers are intentional?

Dorothy Parker Quoted in *Women's Wicked Wit* ed. Michelle Lovric (2000)

60 Is it possible to wear a beret back to front?

Anon. Quoted in *The Times*, 'Quotes of the Week', 29 April 2000, and ascribed to 'Letter to *The Times*'

61 I always compare models to supermodels in the way I compare

Tampax to Super Tampax: supermodels cost a bit more and they are a lot thicker.

Jo Brand Quoted in *Women's Wicked Wit* ed. Michelle Lovric (2000)

62 Q: What do you call a Frenchman in sandals? A: Philippe Philoppe.

Anon. 'Kid's joke' told by Jade Jagger to *Q* magazine September 2003

Vanity

1 There was never yet fair woman but she made mouths in a glass.

William Shakespeare The Fool in *King Lear*, act 3, sc. 2 (1605)

2 Vanity of vanities, saith the Preacher, vanity of vanities; all is vanity.

Ecclesiastes 1:2, the Bible, Authorized Version (1611)

3 The more women looke in their glasse, the lesse they looke to their house.

George Herbert *Outlandish Proverbs*, no. 250 (1640)

4 'Your colours are beautiful,' said a deeply rouged lady, as she sat for her picture. The painter answered, 'Your ladyship and I deal at the same shop.'

Anon. *The New London Jest Book*, 'Choice Jests', no. 392, ed. W. C. Hazlitt (1871)

5 Most women are not so young as they are painted.

Max Beerbohm *The Works of Max Beerbohm*, 'A Defence of Cosmetics' (1896)

6 A bald man is a desperate man; but a bald *vain* man is a hairless Greek Tragedy.

Spike Milligan *Puckoon*, ch. 5 (1963)

7 A narcissist is someone better looking than you are.

Gore Vidal *New York Times* 12 March 1981

8 Actors marrying actors play a dangerous game. They're always fighting over the mirror.

Burt Reynolds *Sunday Today* 24 May 1987

Sex and Gender

Love

1 Cupid is a knavish lad,/ Thus to make poor females mad.

William Shakespeare Puck in *A Midsummer Night's Dream*, act 3, sc. 2 (1595)

2 We that are true lovers run into strange capers; but as all is mortal in nature, so is all nature in love mortal in folly.

William Shakespeare Touchstone in *As You Like It*, act 2, sc. 4 (1599)

3 Love is the fart/ Of every heart:/ It pains a man when 'tis kept close,/ And others doth offend, when 'tis let loose.

Sir John Suckling 'Love's Offence' (1646)

4 Love gilds us over and makes us show fine things to one another for a time, but soon the gold wears off, and then again the native brass appears.

George Etherege Mr Dorimant in *The Man of Mode*, act 2, sc. 2 (1676)

5 Love .../ That cordial drop heaven in our cup has thrown/ To make the nauseous draught of life go down.

Earl of Rochester 'Letter from Artemisia in the Town to Chloe in the Country' (1679)

6 How happy could I be with either,/ Were t'other dear charmer away!

John Gay Macheath, on the subject of Lucy Lockit and Polly Peachum, in *The Beggar's Opera*, act 2, sc. 13, air 35 (1728)

7 What is commonly called love, namely the desire of satisfying a voracious appetite with a certain quantity of delicate white human flesh.

Henry Fielding *Tom Jones*, bk 6, ch. 1 (1749)

8 It hath been observed by wise men or women, I forget which, that all persons are doomed to be in love once in their lives.

Ibid., bk 1, ch. 11

9 Friendship is a disinterested commerce between equals; love, an abject intercourse between tyrants and slaves.

Oliver Goldsmith *The Good Natured Man*, act 1 (1768)

10 I have followed Cupid's Jack-a-lantern, and find myself in a quagmire at last.

Richard Brinsley Sheridan Acres in *The Rivals*, act 3, sc. 4 (1774)

11 In love, everything is both true and false; it's the one subject on which it's impossible to say anything absurd.

Nicolas-Sébastien Roch de Chamfort Written c. 1785, collected in *Chamfort: Reflections on Life, Love and Society*, 'Reflections and Anecdotes', ed. Douglas Parmee (2003)

12 Did you ever hear of Captain Wattle?/ He was all for love, and a little for the bottle.

Charles Dibdin *Captain Wattle and Miss Roe* (1797)

13 As to *Love*, that is done in a week . . .

Lord Byron Letter of 18 September 1812 to Lady Melbourne, collected in *Letters and Journals*, vol. 3, *Alas! The Love of Women!* (1813–1814), ed. Leslie A. Marchand (1974)

14 There cannot be a better practical illustration of the wise saw and ancient instance, that there may be too much of a good thing, than is presented by a loving couple.

Charles Dickens *Sketches by Boz*, 'Sketches of Young Couples', 'The Loving Couple' (1836)

15 The course of true love is not a railway.

Charles Dickens *The Pickwick Papers* (1836–7), part of the title of ch. 8

16 'There are strings,' said Mr Tappertit, '. . . in the human heart that had better not be wibrated.'

Charles Dickens *Barnaby Rudge*, ch. 22 (1841)

17 Barkis is willin'.

Charles Dickens Barkis's proposal of marriage to Peggotty, *David Copperfield*, ch. 5 (1850)

18 Love's like the measles – all the worse when it comes late in life.

Douglas Jerrold *The Wit and Opinions of Douglas Jerrold*, 'A Philanthropist', ed. Blanchard Jerrold (1859)

19 Lady Angela, tell me two things. Firstly, what on earth is this love that upsets everybody; and, secondly, how is it to be distinguished from insanity?

W. S. Gilbert Patience in *Patience*, act 1 (1881)

20 'Tis better to have loved and lost, than never to have lost at all.

Samuel Butler *The Way of All Flesh*, ch. 77 (1903). A play on Tennyson's *In Memoriam A. H. H.*, canto 27 (1850), ''Tis better to have loved and lost/ Than never to have loved at all.' Compare also Mrs Marwood in William Congreve's *The Way of the World*, act 2, sc. 1 (1700): 'Say what you will, 'tis better to be left than never to have loved.'

21 Women who love the same man have a kind of bitter freemasonry.

Max Beerbohm *Zuleika Dobson*, ch. 4 (1911)

22 Scratch a lover, and find a foe.

Dorothy Parker *Enough Rope*, 'Ballade of a Great Weariness' (1926)

23 Oh, life is a glorious cycle of song,/ A medley of extemporanea;/ And love is a thing that can never go wrong;/ And I am Marie of Roumania.

Dorothy Parker 'Inventory' (1937)

24 As a rule, when he fell in love at first sight, his primary impulse was a desire to reach out for the adored object and start handling her like a sack of coals, but the love which this girl inspired in him was a tender, chivalrous love.

P. G. Wodehouse *Uncle Fred in the Springtime*, ch. 7 (1939). The subject is Pongo Twistleton.

25 Love is the delusion that one woman differs from another.

H. L. Mencken *Chrestomathy*, ch. 30 (1949)

26 Birds do it, bees do it,/ Even educated fleas do it./ Let's do it, let's fall in love.

Cole Porter 'Let's Do It' (song, 1954). But in 'Most Gentlemen Don't Like Love' (song, 1938), Porter wrote: 'Most gentlemen don't like love/ They just kick it around.'

27 A youth with his first cigar makes himself sick; a youth with his first girl makes other people sick.

Mary Wilson Little Quoted in *Violets and Vinegar*, 'Kiss Me and Be Quiet', ed. Jilly Cooper and Tom Hartman (1980)

28 When people say, 'You're breaking my heart', they do in fact usually mean that you're breaking their genitals.

Jeffrey Bernard *Spectator* 31 May 1986

29 1. Don't see him. Don't phone or write a letter./ 2. The easy way: get to know him better.

Wendy Cope *Serious Concerns*, 'Two Cures for Love' (1992)

30 Love is what happens to a man and woman who don't know each other.

Somerset Maugham Quoted in *And I Quote*, 'Love', ed. Ashton Applewhite and others (1992)

31 When was the last time you heard someone announce, 'I am truly, madly in love', without thinking, Just wait until Monday morning.

Candace Bushnell *Sex and the City*, ch. 1 (1996)

32 When you start having lunch and actually eating, it's already over.

Erica Jong Quoted in *Women's Wicked Wit* ed. Michelle Lovric (2000)

33 Remember, love is like a garden. It needs to be watered regularly. With tears.

Jeff Green *The A–Z of Living Together*, 'Crying' (2002)

34 I find it very hard to tell someone I love them – especially when I don't.

Ivor Dembina Line used in his stand-up routine during 2003

Marriage

1 A young man married is a man that's marred.

William Shakespeare Parolles in *All's Well that Ends Well*, act 2, sc. 3 (1603–4)

2 . . . It is better to marry than to burn.

I Corinthians 7: 9, The Bible, Authorized Version (1611)

3 DUCHESS: What do you think of marriage?
ANTONIO: I take 't, as those that deny purgatory,
It locally contains or heaven or hell;
There's no third place in 't.

John Webster *The Duchess of Malfi*, act 1, sc. 1 (1623)

4 What is it then to have or have no wife,/ But single thralldom, or a double strife?

Francis Bacon *The World* (1629)

5 Waking this morning out of my sleep of a sudden, I did with my elbow hit my wife a great blow over her face and nose, which waked her with pain, at which I was sorry, and to sleep again.

Samuel Pepys Diary entry for 1 January 1662, *Everybody's Pepys* ed. Henry B. Wheatley (1926)

6 And strange to see what delight we married people have to see those poor fools decoyed into our condition.

Samuel Pepys Diary entry for 25 December 1665, ibid. Pepys had been watching a Christmas Day wedding.

7 I love to be envied, and would not marry a wife that I alone could love; loving alone is as dull as eating alone.

William Wycherley Mr Sparkish in *The Country Wife*, act 3, sc. 2 (1675)

8 No man worth having is true to his wife, or can be true to his wife, or ever was, or ever will be so.

Sir John Vanbrugh Berinthia in *The Relapse*, act 3, sc. 2 (1696)

9 Two years' marriage has debauched my five senses. Everything I see, everything I hear, everything I feel, everything I smell, and everything I taste, methinks has wife in't.

Sir John Vanbrugh Sir John Brute in *The Provok'd Wife*, act 1, sc. 1 (1697)

10 These articles subscrib'd, if I continue to endure you a little longer, I may by degrees dwindle into a wife.

William Congreve Lady Wishfort in *The Way of the World*, act 5, sc. 1 (1700)

11 What they do in heaven we are ignorant of; what they do *not* we are told expressly, that they neither marry, nor are given in marriage.

Jonathan Swift *Thoughts on Various Subjects* (1711). The reference is to Matthew 22:30: 'For in the resurrection they neither marry, nor are given in marriage.'

12 Not louder shrieks to pitying heav'n are cast,/ When husbands, or when lapdogs breathe their last.

Alexander Pope *The Rape of the Lock*, canto 3, line 157 (1714)

13 From marrying in haste, and repenting at leisure;/ Not liking the person, yet liking his treasure:/ Libera nos.

Elizabeth Thomas 'A New Litany, occasioned by an invitation to a wedding' (1722). The phrase 'Married in haste, we may repent at leisure' occurs in *The Old Bachelor*, act 5, sc. 1 (1693), by William Congreve.

14 Do you think your mother and I should have lived comfortably so long together, if ever we had been married?

John Gay Mr Peachum in *The Beggar's Opera*, act 1, sc. 8 (1728)

15 His designs were strictly honourable, as the phrase is; that is, to rob a lady of her fortune by way of marriage.

Henry Fielding *Tom Jones*, bk 11, ch. 4 (1749). Mrs Fitzpatrick is speaking of Mr Fitzpatrick, and his earlier intentions towards her aunt.

16 My brother Toby, quoth she, is going to be married to Mrs Wadman./ Then he will never, quoth my father, lie *diagonally* in his bed again as long as he lives.

Laurence Sterne *Tristram Shandy* (1759–67) bk 6, ch. 39

17 O! how short a time does it take to put an end to a woman's liberty!

Fanny Burney Journal entry concerning a

wedding, 20 July 1768. *The Early Journals and Letters of Fanny Burney*, vol. 1, ed. L. E. Troide (1988).

18 'Tis now six months since Lady Teazle made me the happiest of men – and I have been the most miserable dog ever since!

Richard Brinsley Sheridan Sir Peter Teazle in *The School for Scandal*, act 1, sc. 2 (1777)

19 One asked his friend, why he, being so proper a man himself, had married so small a wife. 'Why, friend,' said he, 'I thought you had known that of all evils we should chuse the *least*.'

Anon. *The Glasgow Magazine of Wit* (1803)

20 It is a truth universally acknowledged, that a single man in possession of a good fortune must be in want of a wife.

Jane Austen *Pride and Prejudice*, ch. 1 (1813), the opening sentence of the book. Compare *Mansfield Park*, ch. 1: 'There are certainly not so many men of large fortune in the world, as there are pretty women to deserve them.'

21 When a man takes the field,/ If to woman he yield,/ Be sure he's a slave all his life –/ For if she's a Jade,/ While yet only a maid,/ Only think what she'll be when a wife.

Anon. 'Zounds, My Lad', from *Oliver's Comic Songs* (1825?)

22 Yes, Bob, the fever goes but the wife doesn't.

William Makepeace Thackeray *Travels in London*, 'On Love, Marriage, Men and Women' pt 3, (1853). These essays are presented as letters from a Mr Brown to his young nephew Bob.

23 Do not adultery commit;/ advantage rarely comes of it.

Arthur Hugh Clough 'The Latest Decalogue' (1862)

24 A gentleman rode up to a public house in the country, and asked, 'Who is the master of this house?' 'I am, sir,' replied the landlord; 'my wife has been dead about three weeks.'

Anon. *The New London Jest Book*, 'Choice Jests', no. 462, ed. W. C. Hazlitt (1871)

25 You seem to forget that I am married, and that the one charm of marriage is that it makes a life of deception absolutely essential for both parties.

Oscar Wilde Lord Henry Wotton in *The Picture of Dorian Gray*, ch. 1 (1891)

26 Always! That's a dreadful word. It makes me shudder when I hear it. Women are always using it. They spoil every romance by trying to make it last for ever.

Lord Henry Wotton in ibid., ch. 2

27 When a woman marries again it is because she detested her first husband. When a man marries again, it is because he adored his first wife. Women try their luck; men risk theirs.

Lord Henry Wotton in ibid., ch. 15

28 To speak frankly, I am not in favour of long engagements. They give people the opportunity of finding out each other's characters before marriage, which I think is never advisable.

Oscar Wilde Lady Bracknell in *The Importance of Being Earnest*, act 4 (1895)

29 The hardest task in a girl's life is to prove to a man that his intentions are serious.

Helen Rowland *Reflections of a Bachelor Girl* (1903)

30 What God hath joined together no man ever shall put asunder: God will take care of that.

George Bernard Shaw Preface to *Getting Married* (1908)

31 'Can you break off an engagement slowly?'

E. M. Forster Margaret Schlegel in *Howards End*, ch. 2 (1910)

32 He pictured marriage as a perpetual afternoon tea alone with an elegant woman, amid an environment of ribboned muslin.

Arnold Bennett Of Denry Machin in *The Card*, ch. 3 (1911)

33 LADY ASTOR: If you were my husband, I'd poison your coffee.
WINSTON CHURCHILL: If you were my wife I'd drink it.
Winston Churchill The scene is Blenheim Palace, 1912 – but it's probably apocryphal

34 Adultery is the application of democracy to love.
H. L. Mencken *A Book of Burlesques*, 'Sententiae' (1920)

35 A husband is what is left of a lover, after the nerve has been extracted.
Helen Rowland *A Guide to Men*, 'Prelude' (1922)

36 So it seems that Gerry has had quite a lot of trouble himself and he can not even get married on account of his wife.
Anita Loos *Gentlemen Prefer Blondes*, ch. 1 (1925)

37 'You're too young to marry,' said Mr McKinnon, a stout bachelor./ 'So was Methuselah,' said James, a stouter.
P. G. Wodehouse *Meet Mr Mulliner*, 'Honeysuckle Cottage' (1927)

38 Marriage isn't a word – it's a *sentence*!
King Vidor Caption in *The Crowd* (silent film, 1928, written and directed by King Vidor)

39 By God, D. H. Lawrence was right when he had said there must be a dumb, dark, dull, bitter belly-tension between a man and a woman, and how else could that be achieved save in the long monotony of marriage?
Stella Gibbons *Cold Comfort Farm*, ch. 20 (1932)

40 All right, have it your way – you heard a seal bark.
James Thurber Cartoon caption in the *New Yorker* 30 January 1932, repr. in *The Thurber Carnival*, pt 8 (1945). It is the most famous of Thurber's cartoons. The remark is addressed by a husband to a wife in bed – they have not yet noticed the seal behind the headboard.

41 Holy Deadlock
A. P. Herbert Title of a novel (1934)

42 You might think about me a bit and whether . . . you could bear the idea of marrying me . . . I can't advise you in my favour because I think it would be beastly for you, but think how nice it would be for me.
Evelyn Waugh Letter to Laura Herbert of spring 1936, collected in *The Letters of Evelyn Waugh* ed. Mark Amory (1980). He did marry her.

43 [My wife's father] said if you marry my daughter I'll give you three acres and a cow . . . I'm still waiting for the three acres.
Max Miller Recorded at the Holborn Empire, London, October 1938, reissued in *Max Miller: The Cheeky Chappie – All His Live Shows in the Late 30s, Early 40s* (CD, 2000)

44 We sat in the car park till twenty to one/ And now I'm engaged to Miss Joan Hunter Dunn.
John Betjeman *A Subaltern's Love Song* (1945)

45 My husband and I . . .
Elizabeth II Opening words of her first Christmas message, delivered in 1953. The phrase became a staple for imitators of the Queen, and on her twenty-fifth wedding anniversary she implicitly acknowledged the fact by saying: 'I think everybody will concede that on this, of all days, I should begin my speech with the words, "My husband and I".'

46 A man is incomplete until he has married. Then he's finished.
Zsa Zsa Gabor *Newsweek* 28 March 1960

47 I believe in every marriage there should be give and take. I've practised this principle throughout eighty-four perfect marriages.
Marty Feldman and Barry Took Betty Marsden in *Around the Horne* (BBC radio series), 10 April 1966. She is impersonating the much-married Zsa Zsa Gabor. This line was cut from the original broadcast but restored in *The Best of Round the Horne* by Barry Took and Mat Coward.

48 your finger/ sadly/ has a familiar ring/ about it . . .
Roger McGough *Summer with Monika*, 'Summer with Monika' (1967)

49 [On how to deal with divorced

friends] **Treat them as attractive people for social purposes; don't just ask them round to tea with the children.**

Katherine Whitehorn *Whitehorn's Social Survival*, 'Work' (1968)

50 **The concerts you enjoy together/ Neighbours you enjoy together/ Children you destroy together/ That make marriage a joy**

Stephen Sondheim 'The Little Things You Do Together' (song), *Company* (stage musical, 1970)

51 **I've been in love with the same woman for forty-one years. If my wife finds out, she'll kill me.**

Henny Youngman *Henny Youngman's Greatest One-Liners* (1970)

52 **A brigand demands your money *or* your life; a woman demands both.**

Samuel Butler Quoted by Kenneth Tynan in a diary entry for 24 January 1971, *The Diaries of Kenneth Tynan* ed. John Lahr (2001)

53 **You've got to get married, haven't you? You can't go through life being happy.**

Colin Crompton *Laugh with the Comedians* (LP, 1971)

54 **I married beneath me, all women do.**

Nancy Astor Attributed remark quoted in the *Dictionary of National Biography (1961–70)* (1981) – in fact, she married a viscount

55 **Monogamy leaves a lot to be desired.**

Anon. Graffito seen in London, 1982, quoted in *The Penguin Dictionary of Modern Humorous Quotations* ed. Fred Metcalf (2nd edn 2001)

56 **Last year, my wife ran off with the fellow next door, and I must admit I still miss him.**

Les Dawson *The Malady Lingers On*, 'The Art of a Pun . . . or How to Lose an Audience Fast' (1982), quoted as a preface to Tim Lott's novel *White City Blue* (1999), where it is attributed to Jerry Springer

57 **Marriage is nothing like being in prison! Women are let out every day to go to the shops and stuff, and quite a lot go to work.**

Sue Townsend *The Secret Diary of Adrian Mole Aged 13¾* (1982)

58 **I'm not going to make the same mistake once.**

Warren Beatty Attributed. *Was It Good for You Too?* by Bob Chieger (1983). On 27 October 1991 Beatty was quoted in the *Observer* as saying: 'The highest level of sexual excitement is in a monogamous relationship.'

59 **Dolores, I am making a citizen's divorce.**

Steve Martin and Carl Reiner Dr Hfuhruhurr to his wife in *The Man with Two Brains* (film, 1983, directed by Carl Reiner)

60 **Men are easy to get but hard to keep.**

Mae West Interviewed by Charlotte Chandler for her book *The Ultimate Seduction* (1984), quoted in *The Penguin Book of Interviews* ed. C. Silvester (1993). Mae West offered this advice on how to keep a man: 'You have to keep your eye on the balls. If you don't take good care of your man, someone else will.'

61 **My mother said it was simple to keep a man. You must be a maid in the living room, a cook in the kitchen, and a whore in the bedroom. I said I'd hire the other two and take care of the bedroom bit.**

Jerry Hall *Observer* 6 October 1985

62 **I've never yet met a man who could look after me. I don't need a husband. What I need is a wife.**

Joan Collins Quoted in the *Sunday Times* 27 December 1987

63 **Sex was for men, and marriage, like lifeboats, was for women and children.**

Carrie Fisher *Surrender the Pink*, ch. 1 (1990)

64 **You don't even have a right to your own bed when you're married. There is no escaping the mildmint breath toothpasting its way across the pillows.**

Helen Simpson *Four Bare Legs in a Bed and Other Stories*, 'Four Bare Legs in a Bed' (1990)

65 **Don't torture yourself, Gomez. That's my job.**
Caroline Thompson and Larry Wilson Morticia Addams (Anjelica Huston) to her husband Gomez Addams (Raul Julia) in *The Addams Family* (film, 1991, directed by Barry Sonnenfeld). The film was inspired by the cartoons of Charles Addams.

66 **It's pretty easy. Just say 'I do' whenever anyone asks you a question.**
Richard Curtis Carrie (Andie MacDowell), in *Four Weddings and a Funeral* (film, 1994, directed by Mike Newell, written by Richard Curtis)

67 **The only really happy folk are married women and single men.**
H. L. Mencken Attributed. Quoted in *Collins Dictionary of Quotations* ed. A. Norman Jeffares and Martin Gray (1995).

68 **His divorce had been so vicious that even his lawyers had panicked.**
Martin Amis *Yellow Dog*, pt 1, ch. 1, sect. 1 (2003)

69 **Love and marriage is like a horse and carriage; obsolete for a hundred years.**
Ivor Dembina Line used in his stand-up performances during 2003

70 **Why buy a book when you can join a lending library?**
Benny Hill Habitual response of Benny Hill when asked why he was not married, quoted in *Word* magazine June 2003. But this is certainly not Hill's coinage – in his autobiography *Nobody Hurt in Small Earthquake* the humorist Michael Green attributes the remark to a colleague of his on the *Northampton Chronicle and Echo* in the 1950s.

The Battle of the Sexes

1 **'Tis not a year or two shows us a man:/ They are all but stomachs, and we all but food;/ To eat us hungerly, and when they are full,/ They belch us.**
William Shakespeare Emilia in *Othello*, act 3, sc. 4 (1604)

2 **These are rare attainments for a damsel, but pray tell me, can she spin?**
James I On being introduced in 1610 to a young girl who knew Latin, Greek and Hebrew. Attributed.

3 **A continual dropping in a very rainy day and a contentious woman are alike.**
Proverbs 27:15, the Bible, Authorized Version (1611)

4 **We lay our souls to pawn for the devil for a little pleasure, and a woman makes the bill of sale.**
John Webster Flamineo in *The White Devil*, act 5, sc. 6 (1612)

5 **If all men are born free, how is it that all women are born slaves?**
Mary Astell *Some Reflections on Marriage*, Preface (1706)

6 **Man has his will, – but woman has her way.**
Oliver Wendell Holmes *The Autocrat of the Breakfast Table*, ch. 1 (1858)

7 **There was a young lady of station,/ 'I love man' was her sole exclamation;/ But when men cried, 'You flatter,'/ She replied, 'Oh! No matter,/ Isle of Man is the true explanation.'**
Lewis Carroll Fragment of a song, *The Lewis Carroll Picture Book*, 'The Legend of Scotland', ed. S. D. Collingwood (1899)

8 **I doubt if any man could tell how any woman was dressed ten minutes after he had left her.**
Jerome K. Jerome *Three Men on the Bummel*, ch. 2 (1900)

9 **'Papa, what is a bicycle built for two?'/ 'Your mother's, my child. She rides it, and I have to clean it.'**
Anon. *Humours of Cycling*, 'Spokelets', ed. Jerome K. Jerome (1905)

10 **Women must come off the pedestal. Men put us up there to get us out of the way.**
Lady Rhondda *Observer*, 'Sayings of the Week', 12 December 1920

11 **Woman suffrage: I will vote for it when women have left off making**

a noise in the reading-room of the British Museum, when they leave off wearing high head-dresses in the pit of a theatre, and when I have seen as many as twelve women in all catch hold of the strap or bar on getting into an omnibus.

Samuel Butler *Selections from the Note-Books of Samuel Butler* ed. A. T. Bartholomew (1930)

12 Woman lives but in her lord;/ Count to ten, and man is bored./ With this the gist and sum of it,/ What earthly good can come of it?

Dorothy Parker 'General Review of the Sex Situation' (1937)

13 I never hated a man enough to give him his diamonds back.

Zsa Zsa Gabor *Observer* 28 August 1957

14 Sometimes I think if there was a third sex men wouldn't get so much as a glance from me.

Amanda Vail *Love Me Little*, ch. 6 (1957)

15 Whatever women do they must do twice as well as men to be thought half as good. Luckily, this is not difficult.

Charlotte Whitton *Canada Month* June 1963

16 You silly moo.

Johnny Speight Catchphrase of the ever-fulminating reactionary Alf Garnett (Warren Mitchell) in the TV sitcom *Till Death Us Do Part* (1966–8, and 1972–5). It was addressed to his wife Else.

17 Is it too much to ask that women be spared the daily struggle for super-human beauty in order to offer it to the caresses of a superhumanly ugly mate?

Germaine Greer *The Female Eunuch*, 'Loathing and Disgust' (1970)

18 Please understand, I respect and admire the frailer sex/ And I honour them every bit as much as the next/ Misogynist

Jake Thackray 'On Again! On Again!' (song), transcribed in *Jake's Progress* (1977). The song begins: 'I love a good bum on a woman, it makes my day.'

19 Of course I'm a feminist. You have to be these days – it's the only way to pull the chicks.

Ben Elton, Rick Mayall and Lise Meyer Rick in *The Young Ones* (TV, sitcom 1982–4), quoted in *The Penguin Dictionary of Modern Humorous Quotations* ed. Fred Metcalf (2nd edn 2001)

20 A man is designed to walk three miles in the rain to phone for help when the car breaks down – and a woman is designed to say 'you took your time' when he comes back dripping wet.

Victoria Wood 'Dotty on Women's Lib', a sketch from *Wood and Walters* (TV series, 1982), collected in *Up to You, Porky – The Victoria Wood Sketch Book* (1985)

21 How much fame, money, and power does a woman have to achieve on her own before you can punch her in the face?

P. J. O'Rourke *Modern Manners*, p. viii (1983)

22 I like to daydream, but I have my two feet firmly planted on my husband.

Woody Allen Julie Kavner (mother) to Dianne Wiest (Aunt Bea) in *Radio Days* (film, 1986, written and directed by Woody Allen)

23 If men were shouted down for being sexist when they used the word 'postman', then asking if there was any chance of a quick shag seemed like a bit of a non-starter.

John O'Farrell On life in the early 1980s. *Things Can Only Get Better*, 'Political Animals' (1998).

24 Don't argue with your mate in the kitchen. Because we know where everything is and you don't.

Diane Amos Quoted in *The Penguin Dictionary of Modern Humorous Quotations* ed. Fred Metcalf (2nd edn 2001)

25 On one issue at least, men and women agree: they both distrust women.

H. L. Mencken Attributed. Quoted in ibid.

26 I only know people call me a feminist whenever I express sentiments
that differentiate me from a door-
mat and/or a prostitute.

Rebecca West Quoted by Julie Burchill in the
Guardian 21 June 2003

27 *Making love* – that's what my girlfriend does when I'm fucking her.

Anon. Slogan on a T-shirt for sale in Camden
Market, London, September 2003

28 I once asked the wife why it takes
half a million sperm to fertilize one
egg. She said, 'Because they're men,
and they won't ask for directions.'

Bob Monkhouse *Sun* 30 December 2003

29 A woman without a man is like a
fish without a bicycle.

Gloria Steinem Attributed

Men on Women

1 Once a woman has given you her
heart you can never get rid of the
rest of her.

Sir John Vanbrugh Lord Foppington in *The
Relapse*, act 2, sc. 1 (1696)

2 When lovely woman stoops to
folly/ And finds too late that men
betray,/ What charm can soothe her
melancholy,/ What art can wash
her guilt away?

Oliver Goldsmith *The Vicar of Wakefield*,
ch. 29 (1766)

3 Women, then, are only children of a
larger growth.

Lord Chesterfield *Letters to His Son* (1774),
from a letter of 5 September 1748

4 [Of *Don Juan*] The truth is that it is
too true – and the women hate
every thing which strips off the
tinsel of *Sentiment* – & they are
right – or it would rob them of their
weapons.

Lord Byron Letter to John Murray II of
12 October 1820, collected in *Letters and Journals*, vol. 7, *Between Two Worlds (1820)*, ed.
Leslie A. Marchand (1977)

5 I expect that Woman will be the last
thing civilized by Man.

George Meredith *The Ordeal of Richard
Feverel*, ch. 1 (1859)

6 Women – one half of the human
race at least – care fifty times more
for a marriage than a ministry.

Walter Bagehot *The English Constitution*,
'The Monarchy' (1867)

7 There is no such thing as a shy
woman, or, at all events, I have
never come across one.

Jerome K. Jerome *The Idle Thoughts of an
Idle Fellow*, 'On Being Shy' (1889)

8 Women have no appreciation of
good looks; at least, good women
have not.

Oscar Wilde Lord Henry Wotton in *The Picture of Dorian Gray*, ch. 1 (1891)

9 MRS ALLONBY: Define us as a sex.
LORD ILLINGWORTH: Sphinxes
without secrets.

Oscar Wilde *A Woman of No Importance*,
act 1 (1894)

10 All women become like their
mothers. That is their tragedy. No
man does. That's his.

Oscar Wilde Algernon Moncrieff in *The Importance of Being Earnest*, act 1 (1895)

11 What, sir, would the people of the
earth be without woman? They
would be scarce, sir, almighty
scarce.

Mark Twain Speech to the Washington Corre-
spondents' Club *c.* 1900, collected as
'Woman – An Opinion', *Mark Twain:
Speeches* ed. Shelley Fisher Fishkin (1996)

12 The female of the species is more
deadly than the male.

Rudyard Kipling 'The Female of the Species'
(1919)

13 Remember, you're fighting for this
woman's honour, which is probably
more than she ever did.

Groucho Marx Rufus T. Firefly (Groucho
Marx) referring to Mrs Teasdale (Margaret
Dumont) in *Duck Soup* (film, 1933, screenplay
by Bert Kalmar, Arthur Sheekman, Nat Perrin
and Harry Ruby, directed by Leo McCarey). In
his book *Groucho* Stefan Kanfer states that

Groucho insisted, against some opposition, on the inclusion of 'probably' in this line.

14 **Women are like elephants to me. I like to look at them, but I wouldn't want to own one.**

W. C. Fields Commodore Orlando Jackson (W. C. Fields) in *Mississippi* (film, 1935, directed by A. Edward Sutherland, screenplay by W. C. Fields and others)

15 **I am interested to see how many young women share the illusion that a woman goes any faster when she runs than she does walking.**

George Lyttelton Letter to Rupert Hart-Davis of 21 March 1956, collected in *The Lyttelton–Hart-Davis Letters*, vols 1 and 2, *1955–1957*, ed. Rupert Hart-Davis (1978)

16 **Have you ever had a letter, and on it is franked 'Please give your blood generously'? Well, the Postmaster-General does that, on behalf of all the women in the world.**

John Osborne Jimmy Porter in *Look Back in Anger*, act 2 (1956)

17 **Rose was the sweetest girl in a world where sweet girls are rather rare, but experience had taught him that, given the right conditions, she was capable of making her presence felt as perceptibly as one of those hurricanes which become so emotional on reaching Cape Hatteras.**

P. G. Wodehouse *Plum Pie*, 'Bingo Bans the Bomb' (1966)

18 **[Of women] I mean, damn it all, one minute you're having a perfectly good time and the next you suddenly see them there like – some old sports jacket or something – literally beginning to come apart at the seams.**

Alan Ayckbourn Ronald in *Absurd Person Singular*, act 3 (1971)

19 **A woman wouldn't make a bomb that kills you. A woman would make a bomb that makes you feel bad for a while. That's why there should be a woman President. There'd never be any wars, just**

every twenty-eight days there'd be very intense negotiations.

Robin Williams *Robin Williams: Live at the Met* (video, 1987)

20 **I do not understand how you can pour wax on your upper thigh, rip the hair out by the root, and still be afraid of a spider.**

Jerry Seinfeld *I'm Telling You for the Last Time* (live CD, 1998)

21 **If they ever invent a vibrator that can open pickle jars, we've had it.**

Jeff Green *Mail on Sunday*, 'Quotes of the Week', 21 March 1999

22 **My wife has a black belt in body language.**

Daren King *Jim Giraffe*, 'Stretch Armlong' (2004)

Women on Men

1 **CLEOPATRA: Thou eunuch Mardian. MARDIAN: What's your Highness' pleasure? CLEOPATRA: Not to hear thee sing. I take no pleasure In aught a eunuch has . . .**

William Shakespeare *Antony and Cleopatra*, act 1, sc. 5 (1606–7)

2 **You men are unaccountable things; mad till you have your mistresses, and then stark mad till you are rid of 'em again.**

Sir John Vanbrugh Belinda in *The Provok'd Wife*, act 4, sc. 4 (1697)

3 **I concluded that, like other men I knew, his mind had been receptive up to a certain age, and had then snapped shut on what it possessed, like a replete crustacean never reached by another high tide.**

Edith Wharton *The Spark*, ch. 3 (1924)

4 **An archaeologist is the best husband a woman can have; the older she gets, the more interested he is in her.**

Agatha Christie Attributed. Quoted in a news report of 9 March 1954 and later denied by Christie. Her second husband Sir

Max Mallowan, whom she married in 1930, was an archaeologist.

5 A little old lady once said to me, 'I have known a great many men. All of them had to be carried every step of the way.'

Quentin Crisp *The Naked Civil Servant*, ch. 21 (1968)

6 The cocks may crow, but it's the hen that lays the egg.

Margaret Thatcher Quoted in the *Sunday Times* 9 April 1989. In 1975 she had said: 'In politics, if you want anything said, ask a man. If you want anything done, ask a woman.'

7 A friend of ours terminated her liaison with an apparently god-like boyfriend when he used the word 'vehicle'.

Mary Killen *How to Live with Your Husband*, 'Triggers for Arguments' (1996)

Women on Women

1 You thought, miss! I don't know any business you have to think at all – thought does not become a young woman.

Richard Brinsley Sheridan Mrs Malaprop in *The Rivals*, act 1, sc. 2 (1774)

2 A woman especially, if she have the misfortune of knowing any thing, should conceal it as well as she can.

Jane Austen *Northanger Abbey*, ch. 14 (1818)

3 Men don't know women, or they would be harder to them.

Anthony Trollope Lady Ongar in *The Claverings*, ch. 15 (1867)

4 Many a woman has a past, but I am told that she has at least a dozen, and they all fit.

Oscar Wilde The Duchess of Berwick speaking of Mrs Erlynne in *Lady Windermere's Fan*, act 1 (1893)

5 I couldn't give advice to a woman unless I knew her, and I don't know any.

Mae West Quoted in *The Ultimate Seduction*, 'Mae West', by Charlotte Chandler (1984)

6 Feminine intuition, a quality perhaps even rarer in women than in men.

Ada Leverson Quoted in *The Feminist Companion to Literature in English* ed. Virginia Blain and others (1990)

7 I hate women. They get on my nerves.

Dorothy Parker Quoted in *Women's Wicked Wit* ed. Michelle Lovric (2000)

Homosexuality and Bisexuality

1 The 'homo' is the legitimate child of the suffragette.

Wyndham Lewis *The Art of Being Ruled*, pt 8, ch. 4 (1926)

2 Army always queer in best regiments, hence decent appearance.

Evelyn Waugh Postcard to Penelope Betjeman of 3 July 1956, collected in *The Letters of Evelyn Waugh* ed. Mark Amory (1980)

3 I became one of the stately homos of England.

Quentin Crisp *The Naked Civil Servant*, ch. 24 (1968)

4 By heterosexuals the life after death is imagined as a world of light, where there is no parting. If there is a heaven for homosexuals, which doesn't seem very likely, it will be very poorly lit and full of people they can feel pretty confident they will never have to meet again.

Ibid., ch. 22

5 My dear fellow, buggers can't be choosers.

Maurice Bowra On being warned not to marry his plain fiancée. Quoted by Francis King in *Maurice Bowra: A Celebration*, 'Pray You, Undo This Button', ed. Hugh Lloyd-Jones (1974).

6 [Of bisexuality] It immediately doubles your chances for a date on Saturday night.

Woody Allen *New York Times* 1 December 1975

7 **There is no indication that he was in any way troubled by the Apostle Paul's strictures on homosexual practices.**

Malcolm Muggeridge Review in the *Observer* of *Ruling Passions* by Tom Driberg (1977), quoted in *Tom Driberg: His Life and Indiscretions*, Introduction, by Francis Wheen (1990)

8 [Of homosexuality]
BENNETT: Tommy, when you come down to it, it's as simple as knowing whether or not you like spinach.
JUDD: I can never make up my mind about spinach.
BENNETT: Then perhaps you're ambidextrous.

Julian Mitchell *Another Country*, act 2, sc. 6 (1981)

9 [Of his 'vague schoolboy homosexuality'] **Our homosexuality was dictated by necessity rather than choice. We were like a generation of diners condemned to cold cuts because the steak and kidney was 'off'.**

John Mortimer *Clinging to the Wreckage*, ch. 5 (1982)

10 **'I'm a lesbian,' Inge said, '. . . you're supposed to say something like, "What a waste."'**

Ed McBain Inge Turner to Steve Carella in *Eight Black Horses*, ch. 2 (1985)

11 **Oranges Are Not the Only Fruit**

Jeanette Winterson Title of a novel about lesbianism (1985)

12 **No man is so boring, or so unpleasant or so unattractive that he cannot find an equally boring, unpleasant or unattractive woman to be his life's companion if he sets his mind to it, and I have no doubt that the same must be true in the homosexual world.**

Auberon Waugh *Another Voice: The Nilsen Millennium* (1986). Dennis Nilsen is a homosexual murderer, currently imprisoned. He was once a trade union official and, according to Waugh, who was no socialist, 'offers a paradigm of the relationship between personal inadequacies, left-wing views and bureaucratic sadism'.

13 **For those of you who don't know what a friend of Dorothy is: ask a policeman or one in five Tory MPs.**

Stephen Fry *Paperweight*, 'Friends of Dorothy' (1992)

14 **I have never been attracted to another man, but I like to touch myself around my penis when I masturbate. As a result, I am worried that I may be homosexual. What do readers think?**

Viz Fake reader's letter, signed 'Big Straight Jock, Glasgow', May 2003

15 **Being gay was a bit like the Olympics; it disappeared in ancient times, and then they brought it back in the twentieth century.**

Nick Hornby Maureen in *A Long Way Down*, p. 29 (2005)

Lust and Promiscuity

1 **'Tis no sin love's fruits to steal,/ But the sweet thefts to reveal:/ To be taken, to be seen,/ These have crimes accounted been.**

Ben Jonson From Volpone's song, *Volpone*, act 3, sc. 2 (1605)

2 **MACDUFF: What three things does drink especially provoke?**
PORTER: Marry, sir, nose-painting, sleep, and urine. Lechery, sir, it provokes, and unprovokes; it provokes the desire, but it takes away the performance.

William Shakespeare *Macbeth*, act 2, sc. 3 (1606)

3 **A mistress should be like a little country retreat near the town, not to dwell in constantly, but only for a night and away.**

William Wycherley Mr Dorilant in *The Country Wife*, act 1, sc. 1 (1672–3)

4 [Of *Don Juan*] **Could any man have written it – who has not lived in the world – and tooled in a post-chaise?**

in a hackney coach? in a gondola?
against a wall? in a court carriage?
in a vis a vis? – on a table? – and
under it?

Lord Byron Letter to Hon. Douglas Kinnaird
of 26 October 1819?, collected in *Letters and
Journals*, vol. 6, *The Flesh Is Frail (1818–19)*,
ed. Leslie A. Marchand (1976)

5 My feelings, Mrs Todgers, will not
consent to be entirely smothered,
like the young children in the
Tower. They are grown up, and the
more I press the bolster on them,
the more they look round the
corner of it.

Charles Dickens Pecksniff declaring his affections in *Martin Chuzzlewit*, ch. 9 (1843–4)

6 I've taken my fun where I've found
it,/ An' now I must pay for my fun,/
For the more you 'ave known o' the
others/ The less you will settle to
one.

Rudyard Kipling 'The Ladies' (1896)

7 On Friday night Mrs Devereaux told
me a fine retort of a pressing lover
to a refusing mistress. 'Bah!' she
said. 'With people like you, love
only means one thing.' 'No,' he
replied. 'It means twenty things,
but it doesn't mean nineteen.'

Arnold Bennett Entry for 22 November 1904,
The Journals of Arnold Bennett, vol. 1, *1896–
1910*, ed. Newman Flower (1932)

8 Brought up in an epoch when ladies
apparently rolled along on wheels,
Mr Quarles was peculiarly susceptible to calves.

Aldous Huxley *Point Counter Point*, ch. 20
(1928)

9 Is that a gun in your pocket, or are
you just glad to see me?

Mae West Lady Lou (Mae West) in *She Done
Him Wrong* (film, 1933, screenplay by Harvey
Thew and John Bright, based on Mae West's
play *Diamond Lil*, directed by Lowell
Sherman)

10 Why don't you come up sometime,
see me?

Mae West Invariably quoted as 'Why don't

you come up and see me sometime?' From
ibid.

11 And there was that wholesale libel
on a Yale prom. If all the girls
attending it were laid end to end,
Mrs Parker said, she wouldn't be at
all surprised.

Dorothy Parker Quoted in *While Rome Burns*,
'Our Mrs Parker' (1934), by Alexander
Woollcott

12 I can honestly say that I always
look on Pauline as one of the nicest
girls I was ever engaged to.

P. G. Wodehouse *Thank You Jeeves*, ch. 6
(1934)

13 A man's sexual aim, as he had often
said to himself, is to convert a creature who is cool, dry, calm, articulate, independent, purposeful into a
creature that is the opposite of
these; to demonstrate to an animal
which is pretending not to be an
animal that it is an animal.

Kingsley Amis *One Fat Englishman*, ch. 11
(1963). The author of these thoughts is Roger
Micheldene, the fat Englishman.

14 In the spring a young man's fancy
lightly turns to thoughts of love;/
And in summer,/ and in autumn,/
and in winter –/ See above.

E. Y. Harburg 'Tennyson Anyone?' (1965). The
first line is from Tennyson's poem *Locksley
Hall* (1842).

15 You were born with your legs apart.
They'll send you to your grave in a
'Y'-shaped coffin.

Joe Orton Prentice in *What the Butler Saw*,
act 1 (1969)

16 ... The graveyards of Leeds 2/
Were hardly love nests but they had
to do –/ Through clammy mackintosh and winter vest/ And rumpled
jumper for a touch of breast.

Tony Harrison 'Allotments', publ. in *The
Loiners* (1970)

17 She wore a short skirt and a tight
sweater and her figure described
parabolas that could cause cardiac
arrest in a yak.

Woody Allen *Getting Even*, 'Mr Big' (1971)

18 **Bigamy is having one husband too many. Monogamy is the same.**

Anon. Epigraph to Erica Jong's *Fear of Flying*, ch. 1 (1973)

19 **My mother used to say, 'Delia, if S-E-X ever rears its ugly head, close your eyes before you see the rest of it.'**

Alan Ayckbourn *Bedroom Farce* (1977). In his review in the *Daily Telegraph* of the 2002 West End revival of the play, Charles Spencer describes this as 'one of the all-time great sex lines'.

20 **[Of men] That's why we're driven to find Miss Right. Or at least Miss Right Now.**

Robin Williams *Robin Williams: Live at the Met* (video, 1987)

21 **Do you really feel, Clemency, m'dear, that it's worth leaving a tolerant husband, three lovely children and nine hundred acres for the sake of six inches of angry gristle?**

Jilly Cooper *Polo*, ch. 3 (1991)

22 **Women need a reason to have sex. Men just need a place.**

Lowell Ganz and Babaloo Mandel Mitch Robbins (Billy Crystal) in *City Slickers* (film, 1991, screenplay by Lowell Ganz and Babaloo Mandel, directed by Ron Underwood)

23 **Philanderers: Avoid the embarrassment of shouting out the wrong name in bed by only having flings with girls who have the same name as your wife.**

Viz 'Top-Tips', August 2003

24 **A hard man's good to find.**

Mae West Attributed

The Sex Act

1 **One day Cunegonde was walking near the castle, in the little copse which was known as 'the park', when through the bushes she saw Dr Pangloss giving a lesson in applied physics to her mother's maid, a pretty and obliging little brunette.**

Voltaire *Candide*, ch. 1 (1759)

2 **Not tonight, Josephine.**

Anon. Satirizes Napoleon's indifference towards the ardency of his wife. Occurs in 'I Cover the Waterfront' (song, 1933), but may have originated in vaudeville early in the twentieth century. Quoted in *Cassell's Dictionary of Catchphrases* ed. Nigel Rees (1995).

3 **He said it was artificial respiration, but now I find I am to have his child.**

Anthony Burgess *Inside Mr Enderby*, pt 1, ch. 4 (1963)

4 **I wasn't kissing her, I was just whispering in her mouth.**

Chico Marx *Marx Brothers Scrapbook*, ch. 24, by Richard J. Anobile (1973)

5 **The pleasure is momentary, the position ridiculous, and the expense damnable.**

Lord Chesterfield Attributed. Quoted in *Kiss Hollywood Goodbye*, ch.21, by Anita Loos (1974).

6 **Sexual intercourse began/ In nineteen sixty-three/ (Which was rather late for me) –/ Between the end of the *Chatterley* ban/ And the Beatles' first LP.**

Philip Larkin *Annus Mirabilis* (1974)

7 **Have you ever tried lifting your father's corpse off your living mother?**

Julian Mitchell Bennett in *Another Country*, act 1, sc. 1 (1981). Bennett, whose father died in coitus, continues: 'He was like a huge sack of – of wet mud.'

8 **No one has sex in the morning.**

John Junor Quoted in *Brief Lives: Sir John Junor* by Alan Watkins (1982)

9 **Perhaps men could be divided into two kinds – those who take their watches off, and those who leave them on.**

Charlotte Chandler Charlotte Chandler came out with this while interviewing Mae West, mainly on the subject of sex, for her book *The Ultimate Seduction* (1984). West approved of the remark: 'Say – I like that.'

10 Q: What's the worst thing about oral sex? A: The view.

Anon. Joke quoted by Maureen Lipman in *How Was It for You?*, 'A Joking Aside' (1985)

11 CONNIE: Our next-doors had sex again last night.
BEATTIE: Not again!
CONNIE: I mean, I like a joke, but that's twice this month. I could not think what the noise was. I thought our central heating had come on a month early.

Victoria Wood 'In the Office', a sketch from *Victoria Wood as Seen on TV* (1985), collected in *Up to You, Porky – The Victoria Wood Sketch Book* (1985)

12 Men couldn't fake an orgasm. Who wants to look that dumb, you know?

Robin Williams *Robin Williams: Live at the Met* (video, 1987)

13 You then make sure you make the woman in question feel both lovely and desirable; I've always found that saying 'You look both lovely and desirable' can usually be depended upon to do the trick.

Joseph Connolly *Summer Things*, ch. 6 (1998)

14 Infatuation fizzled through them, their kiss burned on, glowed inside them, her head, his loins. A temporary eternal flame.

Carrie Fisher *Surrender the Pink*, ch. 9 (1990)

15 Making love within a marriage means that if the phone goes you sometimes answer it.

Mavis Cheek *The Sex Life of My Aunt*, ch. 5 (2002)

16 If you want a healthy sex life, the key word is communication. If you're making love to your partner, for heaven's sake tell them.

Ivor Dembina Line used in his stand-up performances during 2003

17 Attempting sex in this [drunken] state is like trying to play snooker with a piece of rope.

Jeff Green *The A–Z of Living Together*, 'Alcohol'

Pregnancy and Contraception

1 Maternity has never been an incident in my life.

Oscar Wilde Miss Prism in *The Importance of Being Earnest*, act 4 (1895). She adds: 'The suggestion, if it were not made before such a large group of people, would be almost indelicate.'

2 Good work, Mary. We all knew you had it in you.

Dorothy Parker Telegram to Mrs Robert Sherwood, who had given birth after a long pregnancy, quoted in *While Rome Burns*, 'Our Mrs Parker' (1934), by Alexander Woollcott

3 It is now quite lawful for a Catholic woman to avoid pregnancy by a resort to mathematics, though she is still forbidden to resort to physics and chemistry.

H. L. Mencken, *Notebooks*, 'Minority Report' (1956)

4 The Pope has made a fortune out of his new book: *The Pill's Grim Progress*.

Frank Carson *Laugh with the Comedians* (LP, 1971)

5 Do you remember Edna? The one you called a human contraceptive?

Simon Gray Ben Butley in *Butley*, act 1 (1971)

6 There was an old woman who lived in a shoe. She had so many children she didn't know what to do ... obviously.

Barry Cryer *I'm Sorry I Haven't a Clue* (BBC radio series, 1972 onwards) – from *I'm Sorry I Haven't a Clue: Five* (cassette, 1999)

7 He no playa da game, he no maka da rules.

Anon. Supposedly a generic Italian woman's attitude to the Pope and contraception. Quoted in *How to Survive Children*, 'What Size Cup Does He Take?', by Katherine Whitehorn (1975).

8 You ought to have your vasectomy done before it goes up again.

Anon. Remark 'overheard in Great Sutton',

quoted in *Word of Mouth*, 'Eavesdroppings', ed. Nigel Rees (1983)

9 **A diaphragm is a little tiny trampoline for the sperm. It doesn't stop them, but it keeps them amused for a while.**

Robin Williams *Robin Williams: Live at the Met* (video, 1987)

10 **It's like being grounded for eighteen years.**

Anon. New York City Board of Education poster warning against teenage pregnancy, quoted in *And I Quote*, 'Parents', ed. Ashton Applewhite and others (1992)

11 **A lot of what I dreaded about pregnancy are the things that actually occur.**

Carrie Fisher *Delusions of Grandma*, p. 46 (1994 paperback edn)

12 **Whenever I hear people discussing birth control, I always remember that I was the fifth.**

Clarence Darrow Quoted in *The Penguin Dictionary of Modern Humorous Quotations* ed. Fred Metcalf (2nd edn 2001)

13 **I claim an absolute right to be interested in the condition of the human foetus because . . . well, I used to be one myself.**

Christopher Hitchens Opening of an article on abortion, *Vanity Fair* February 2003

14 **It is often said that safe sex in North Wales means branding the sheep that kicks.**

Victor Lewis-Smith London *Evening Standard* 21 August 2003. Lewis-Smith added: 'But the people of Gwynedd were a model of propriety during my recent visit.'

15 **I remember when safe sex was a padded headboard.**

Bob Monkhouse *Sun* 30 December 2003

16 **Pro-lifers murdering people. It's irony on a base level, but I like it. It's a hoot. It's a fuckin' hoot.**

Bill Hicks Quoted in the *Guardian* 14 February 2004

Sexual Perversion

1 **[Of Oedipus] Of all ideals they hail as good/ the most sublime is motherhood/ There was a man though who it seems/ took this idea to extremes.**

Tom Lehrer 'Oedipus Rex', *An Evening Wasted with Tom Lehrer* (LP, 1960)

2 **Assistant masters came and went. By no means all of them had university degrees. Some liked little boys too little and some too much.**

Evelyn Waugh *A Little Learning*, ch. 4 (1964)

3 **Afterthought on de Sade's view of sexual enjoyment: a pleasure shared is a pleasure halved.**

Kenneth Tynan Entry for 22 April 1977, *The Diaries of Kenneth Tynan* ed. John Lahr (2000)

4 **I knew a woman, and her singing coach, eighty-four years old, the last guy you'd have thought was weird. Well, listen to this . . . he kept wanting to sing *from her diaphragm*. I mean, it would take years to learn that, wouldn't it?**

Steve Martin *A Wild and Crazy Guy*, 'An Exposé' (LP, 1978)

5 **Normal intercourse and customary caresses should be enough if you are really in love with your sexual partner. But, since no one is, sexual experimentation and even perversion have gained a sort of general social acceptance like using the same size glasses for red and white wine.**

P. J. O'Rourke *Modern Manners*, ch. 13 (1983)

6 **I believe there's only one recorded instance of incest being practised outside a family and that turned out not to be incest after all.**

Stephen Fry *Paperweight*, 'The Family Curse' (1992)

7 **Am I the only person in Britain who was not sexually abused as a child?**

Victor Lewis-Smith *Inside the Magic*

Rectangle, 'Minders' (1995). Lewis-Smith complained: 'Scout masters, vicars, little old ladies in tea shops – not one of them offered me so much as a sweetie or muttered, "It's our little secret." '

8 **'Paedophiles' is a bit impartial for my liking: it makes it sound a harmless hobby such as stamp collecting or liking France, and it gets paediatricians' houses burned down, which is bad.**
Julie Burchill *Guardian* 12 July 2003

9 **For sale, rubber sheets, £45; clean, £40.**
Jimmy Carr Proposed small-ad for *Loot*, the weekly London advertising paper – to be placed in the 'Water Sports' section. Quoted in the *Daily Telegraph* 4 August 2003.

Prostitution

1 **Prisons are built with stones of Law, brothels with bricks of religion.**
William Blake *The Marriage of Heaven and Hell*, 'Proverbs of Hell' (1790–3)

2 **I've never had a whore under this roof before. Ever since your mother died.**
Harold Pinter Max in *The Homecoming*, act 1 (1965)

3 **If anyone offered me money in exchange for sex, I accepted it gladly, and by money I mean 7s. 6d.**
Quentin Crisp *The Naked Civil Servant*, ch. 3 (1968)

4 **You can lead a horticulture, but you can't make her think.**
Dorothy Parker On being challenged to make a sentence using the word 'horticulture'. Quoted in *You Might As Well Live* ed. John Keats (1970).

5 **Mind you, I take off my hat to prostitutes.**
Anon. Overheard remark, quoted in *Word of Mouth*, 'Eavesdroppings', ed. Nigel Rees (1983)

6 **Whores: Necessary in the nineteenth century for the contraction**

of syphilis, without which no one could claim genius.
Julian Barnes *Flaubert's Parrot*, ch. 12 (1984)

7 **FATHER: I'm sad because, my darling, our poverty has now reached such extremes that I can no longer afford to keep us and must look to my own dear tiny darling to sustain me in my frail dotage.**
KATE: But Father, surely . . .
FATHER: Yes, Kate . . . I want you to become a prostitute.
Richard Curtis and Ben Elton *Blackadder 2* (TV series, 1985), 'Bells'

8 **[Of British prostitutes] Few even pretend to enjoy the job, they make no secret of despising their customers and being in it only for the money . . . If a job is worth doing at all, it is worth doing well, and these women are a disgrace.**
Auberon Waugh *Spectator* 25 May 1985

9 **Wherever he has lived Frank [Ritz] has known where the whores are. Call it instinct; like a squirrel knowing the whereabouts of emergency rations.**
Howard Jacobson *No More Mr Nice Guy*, ch. 6 (1998)

Pornography

1 **We live in far too permissive a society. Never before has pornography been this rampant. And those films are so badly lit!**
Woody Allen *Side Effects*, 'My Speech to the Graduates' (1981)

2 **Looked at *Big and Bouncy*. It is Passion Sunday, after all.**
Sue Townsend Entry for Sunday 5 April, *The Secret Diary of Adrian Mole Aged 13¾* (1982)

3 **The only thing pornography has been known to cause is solitary masturbation; as for corruption, the only immediate victim is English prose.**
Gore Vidal Quoted in the *Observer* 28 January 1996

4 **There's so much darn porn, I never get out of the house.**

Jack Nicholson *Sunday Times* 7 March 1999, explaining why he was disconnecting from the Internet

5 **[On what to say on being caught looking at pornography on the Internet] Can you believe that? Someone has hacked on to the Salvation Army website and put rude pictures up.**

Jeff Green *The A–Z of Living Together*, 'Excuses' (2000)

6 **'I don't watch pornography.'/ 'You mean you *say* you don't watch pornography.'**

Martin Amis Xan Meo to pornography impresario Karla White in *Yellow Dog*, pt 2, ch. 7, sect. 6 (2003)

Masturbation

1 **In an incorrigible fantasist, auto-eroticism soon ceases to be what it is for most people – an admitted substitute for sexual intercourse. It is sexual intercourse that becomes the substitute – and a poor one – for masturbation.**

Quentin Crisp *The Naked Civil Servant*, ch. 16 (1968)

2 **Masturbation is the thinking man's television.**

Christopher Hampton Braham in *The Philanthropist*, sc. 3 (1970)

3 **Because he spills his seed on the ground.**

Dorothy Parker On why she named her canary 'Onan', quoted in *You Might As Well Live* by John Keats (1970)

4 **COUNTESS ALEXANDROVNA (Olga Georges-Picot): 'Boris, you are the greatest lover that I have ever had.'**
BORIS (Woody Allen): 'Well, I practise a lot when I'm on my own.'

Woody Allen From *Love and Death* (film, 1975, written and directed by Woody Allen)

5 **Hey, don't knock masturbation! It's sex with someone I love.**

Woody Allen Alvy Singer (Woody Allen) in *Annie Hall* (film, 1977, screenplay by Woody Allen and Marshall Brickman, directed by Woody Allen)

6 **The persecution [of Cyril Connolly] started when, on rereading *Enemies of Promise* one day, I came upon the passage where he claims never to have masturbated at the age of eighteen and a half. Was this a record, I asked, and wrote off to the editor of the *Guinness Book of Records*.**

Auberon Waugh *Will This Do?*, ch. 14 (1991). The answer was 'no'.

The Single Life

1 **Single women have a dreadful propensity for being poor – which is one very strong argument in favour of matrimony.**

Jane Austen Letter to Fanny Knight of 13 March 1817, *Jane Austen's Letters* ed. R. W. Chapman (1952)

2 **Five showy girls – but Thirty is an age/ When girls may be *engaging* but they somehow don't *engage*.**

Lewis Carroll *Phantasmagoria*, 'A Game Of Fives' (1869)

3 **Somehow, a bachelor never quite gets over the idea that he is a thing of beauty and a boy forever!**

Helen Rowland *A Guide to Men*, 'Bachelors' (1922). The allusion is to Keats's *Endymion*: 'A thing of beauty is a joy for ever.'

4 **Bachelors are always very keen on hifi – care more about the reproduction of their records than the reproduction of their species, haw haw.**

Philip Larkin Letter to Norman Isles of 26 February 1967, collected in *Selected Letters of Philip Larkin 1940–85* ed. Anthony Thwaite (1992)

5 **Even a marriage with oneself may not last for ever.**

Quentin Crisp *The Naked Civil Servant*, ch. 24 (1968). Crisp was middle-aged and 'deflated', which 'occurred prematurely because I had subjected a shallow and horribly articulate personality to a lifetime of unflagging scrutiny'.

6 **I know it's over/ And it never really began.**
Morrissey 'I Know It's Over', *The Queen Is Dead* (LP, 1986). One critic described it as 'a candidate for Morrissey's most bleak work'.

7 **A married man's home gives him something to come back to. But a bachelor's home does better than that – it gives him something to leave.**
P. J. O'Rourke *The Bachelor Home Companion*, ch. 2 (1987)

8 **The last time I was inside a woman was when I visited the Statue of Liberty.**
Woody Allen Cliff Stern (Woody Allen) in *Crimes and Misdemeanors* (film, 1989, directed by Woody Allen)

9 **What is a date really, but a job interview that lasts all night?**
Jerry Seinfeld *I'm Telling You for the Last Time* (CD, 1998)

10 **No man wanted me. Rapists would tap me on the shoulder and say, 'Seen any girls?'**
Joan Rivers Quoted in *Women's Wicked Wit* ed. Michelle Lovic (2000)

Human Aspiration
Ambition

1 **And he that strives to touch the stars,/ Oft stumbles at a straw.**
Edmund Spenser *The Shepheardes Calender*, 'July' (1579)

2 **Thou art not for the fashion of the times,/ Where none will sweat for promotion.**
William Shakespeare Orlando to his faithful servant Adam, in *As You Like It*, act 2, sc. 3 (1599)

3 **Ambition often puts men upon doing the meanest offices; so climb-**
ing is performed in the same posture with creeping.
Jonathan Swift *Miscellanies in Prose and Verse*, 'Various Thoughts Moral and Diverting' (1711)

4 **Petty souls are more susceptible to ambition than great ones, just as straw or thatched cottages burn more easily than palaces.**
Nicolas-Sébastien Roch de Chamfort Written c. 1785, collected in *Chamfort: Reflections on Life, Love and Society*, 'Reflections and Anecdotes', ed. Douglas Parmee (2003)

5 **It is odd I never set myself seriously to wishing without attaining it – and repenting.**
Lord Byron Entry for 17 November 1813, collected in *Letters and Journals*, vol. 3, *Alas! The Love of Women! (1813–14)*, ed. Leslie A. Marchand (1974)

6 **In this world there are only two tragedies. One is not getting what one wants, and the other is getting it.**
Oscar Wilde Mr Dumby in *Lady Windermere's Fan*, act 3 (1893). He adds: 'The last is much the worst: the last is a real tragedy!'

7 **Ambition is the last refuge of the failure.**
Oscar Wilde 'Phrases and Philosophies for the Use of the Young', *Chameleon* December 1894

8 **I shall have more to say when I am dead.**
Edward Arlington Robinson Last line of the poem 'John Brown', publ. in *The Three Taverns* (1920)

9 **An Englishman's real ambition is to get a railway compartment to himself.**
Ian Hay *Observer*, 'Sayings of the Week', 29 April 1923

10 **Ducking for apples – change one letter and it's the story of my life.**
Dorothy Parker Attributed

11 **At the age of six I wanted to be a cook. At seven I wanted to be Napoleon. And my ambition has been growing ever since.**
Salvador Dali *The Secret Life of Salvador Dali*, Prologue (1948)

12 **I want to be what I was when I wanted to be what I am now.**

Anon. *And I Quote*, 'Identity', ed. Ashton Applewhite and others (1992)

Success and Failure

1 **The higher the Ape goes, the more he shewes his taile.**

George Herbert *Outlandish Proverbs*, no. 745 (1640)

2 **Yes, I have climbed to the top of the greasy pole.**

Benjamin Disraeli On returning on 27 February 1868 from an audience with Queen Victoria, and the kissing of hands that formally made him Prime Minister for the first time. Quoted in *Disraeli* by Robert Blake, ch. 22 (1966).

3 **Heroing is one of the shortest-lived professions there is.**

Will Rogers Syndicated article, 15 February 1925. In his *Autobiography* (1949) he said that the key thing for a hero is knowing when to die.

4 **Whom the gods wish to destroy they first call promising.**

Cyril Connolly *Enemies of Promise*, ch. 3 (1938)

5 **Complete silence surrounds that book. It might have sailed into the blue and been lost. 'One of our books did not return', as the BBC puts it.**

Virginia Woolf Entry for 2 August 1940, *A Writer's Diary, Being Extracts from the Diary of Virginia Woolf* ed. Leonard Woolf (1953). The reference is to her recently published biography of Roger Fry, which had not gathered many reviews.

6 **There are no second acts in American lives.**

F. Scott Fitzgerald *The Last Tycoon, Hollywood Etc* ed. Edmund Wilson (1941)

7 **[Of Tommy Bowles, journalist and politician] Towards the end of his career, he said to a friend . . . sadly and rather pompously, 'I regard myself as the greatest failure of the Nineteenth Century.' And the friend**
said, 'O, come, Tommy! Say rather, the smallest success.'

Max Beerbohm Speech given at his seventieth birthday party, 24 August 1942, quoted in *The Letters of Max Beerbohm 1892–1956*, Appendix, ed. Rupert Hart-Davis (1988)

8 **The penalty of success is to be bored by people who used to snub you.**

Nancy Astor *Sunday Express* 12 January 1956

9 **Few thought he was even a starter/ There were many who thought themselves smarter/ But he ended PM/ CH and OM/ An earl and a Knight of the Garter.**

Clement Attlee Quoted in *Attlee*, ch. 29, by Kenneth Harris (1982). Attlee is describing himself in a letter of 8 April 1956 to his brother Tom, just before he was made a Knight of the Garter.

10 **Success has not changed them, they are still the same arrogant, self-opinionated pair they always were.**

Michael Flanders and Donald Swann From the sleeve notes to *At the Drop of a Hat* (LP, 1957)

11 **What is a cult? It just means not enough people to make a minority.**

Robert Altman Interview in the *Guardian* 11 April 1981

12 **Show me a good loser and I'll show you a loser.**

Paul Newman Spoken in 1982, collected in *Sayings of the Eighties* ed. Jeffrey Care (1989). Compare the quote attributed to Knute Rockne, the American football player and coach: 'Show me a good and gracious loser, and I'll show you a loser.'

13 **There's nothing the British like more than a bloke who comes from nowhere, makes it, and then gets clobbered.**

Melvyn Bragg *Guardian* 23 September 1988. Bragg was thinking of Richard Burton, whose biography by Bragg, *Rich*, appeared that year. But Bragg, a media success from a humble background, might have been speaking of himself.

14 **It is sobering to consider that when**

Mozart was my age he had already been dead for a year.

Tom Lehrer Quoted in *And I Quote*, 'Achievement', ed. Ashton Applewhite and others (1992)

15 I had thought of calling my life's work 'A Slight Improvement' after my best school report.

Hugo Williams *Freelancing*, 'A Slight Improvement' (1995)

16 Winning doesn't really matter as long as you win.

Vinnie Jones Spoken in 1996, quoted in *The Book of Football Quotations*, 'Philosophers United', ed. Phil Shaw (1999)

17 I don't think we have failed, we have just found another way that doesn't work.

Anon. Attributed to 'pilot of the failed around-the-world balloon flight', *The Times* 13 March 1999

18 I take the view that any self-respecting cat does not tie a tin can to its tail.

Professor Albert Henry Halsey Explaining on Radio 4, 4 May 2003, why he'd always refused an honour

Competition

1 No one – absolutely no one – tries to delve into his heart;/ everyone watches the pack on the back of the man in front.

Persius Satire 4 (30s BC), *Horace: Satires and Epistles; Persius: Satires* trans. and ed. Niall Rudd (1973)

2 THIRD FISHERMAN: Master, I marvel how the fishes live in the sea.
FIRST FISHERMAN: Why, as men do a-land; the great ones eat up the little ones.

William Shakespeare *Pericles*, act 2, sc. 1 (1608)

3 Sir, there is no settling the point of precedency between a louse and a flea.

Samuel Johnson *The Life of Samuel Johnson*

by James Boswell, vol. 4, p. 193 (1791); in G. B. Hill's edition of 1887, rev. L. F. Powell (1934). The debate concerned the relative merits of two poets called Derrick and Smart, or possibly Derrick and Boyce.

4 For what do we live, but to make sport for our neighbours, and laugh at them in our turn?

Jane Austen Mr Bennet in *Pride and Prejudice*, ch. 59 (1813)

5 Well, people on their own are different from people in crowds. People on their own are all right, but in crowds something comes over them. They just want to be on the winner.

Lester Piggott Interview in the *Observer* 7 June 1970, repr. in *The Penguin Book of Interviews* ed. C. Silvester (1993)

6 Whenever a friend succeeds, a little something in me dies.

Gore Vidal TV interview with David Frost, quoted in the *Sunday Times* 16 September 1973. A parallel remark, 'It is not enough to succeed, others must fail', has been attributed to Vidal.

Luck and Fate

1 Necessity with her imperial law picks out by lot/ both high and humble./ All names are shaken in that capacious urn.

Horace *Odes*, bk 3, no. 1 (c.23 BC), *Horace: The Complete Odes and Epodes* trans. David West (1997)

2 And if I perish, I perish.

Esther 6:16, the Bible, Authorized Version (1611)

3 And of all axioms this shall win the prize, –/' 'Tis better to be fortunate than wise.'

John Webster Flamineo in *The White Devil*, act 5, sc. 6 (1612)

4 Astrologie is true, but the Astrologers cannot finde it.

George Herbert *Outlandish Proverbs*, no. 641 (1640)

5 The best of men cannot suspend

their fate:/ The good die early, and the bad die late.

Daniel Defoe 'Character of the Late Dr S. Annesley' (1697)

6 The power of fortune is confessed only by the miserable; for the happy impute all their success to prudence or merit.

Jonathan Swift *Miscellanies in Prose and Verse*, 'Various Thoughts Moral and Diverting' (1711)

7 Some people are so fond of ill-luck that they run half-way to meet it.

Douglas Jerrold *Wit and Opinions of Douglas Jerrold*, 'Meeting Troubles Half-way', ed. Blanchard Jerrold (1859)

8 See how the Fates their gifts allot,/ For A is happy – B is not./ Yet B is worthy, I dare say,/ Of more prosperity than A!

W. S. Gilbert Mikado in *The Mikado*, act 2 (1885)

9 Unseen, in the background, Fate was quietly slipping the lead into the boxing gloves.

P. G. Wodehouse *Very Good, Jeeves* (1930)

10 A self-made man is one who believes in luck and sends his son to Oxford.

Christina Stead *The House of All Nations*, 'Credo' (1938)

11 Luck is always important, especially in Las Vegas.

Hunter S. Thompson *Fear and Loathing in Las Vegas*, pt 2, ch. 6 (1971)

12 I'm a very unlucky person. Treets melt in my hand, and Lord Longford once mugged me.

Les Dawson *The Malady Lingers On*, 'The Malady Lingers On . . .' (1982). Treets were sweets that were supposed to 'melt in your mouth, not in your hand', and Lord Longford was famously pacifistic.

13 For you're a Leo, same as me/ (Isn't it comforting to be/ So lordly, selfish, vital, strong?/ Or do you think they've got it wrong?)

Philip Larkin *Poems for Charles Causley*, 'Dear CHARLES, My Muse, asleep or dead' (1982)

14 I broke a mirror, and my house is supposed to get seven years' bad luck, but my lawyer thinks he can get me five.

Steven Wright *I Have a Pony* (CD, 1986)

15 'What do you think I was born under?' asked Bart./ Chessie laughed. 'A pound sign, I should think.'

Jilly Cooper *Polo*, ch. 3 (1991)

16 You can tell a lot about someone's personality if you know his star sign: Jesus, born on 25 December – fed the five thousand, walked on water – typical Capricorn.

Harry Hill Said during his stage act at the Edinburgh Fringe Festival, 1995

17 To what do I attribute my longevity? Bad luck.

Quentin Crisp *Spectator* 20 November 1999. Crisp also wrote, 'Is not the whole world a vast house of assignation to which the filing system has been lost?'

Optimism and Pessimism

1 To fear the worst oft cures the worst.

William Shakespeare Cressida in *Troilus and Cressida*, act 3, sc. 2 (1601–2)

2 He that lives in hope danceth without music.

George Herbert *Outlandish Proverbs*, no. 1006 (1640)

3 He that lives on hope will die fasting.

Benjamin Franklin *Poor Richard's Almanac*, Preface (1758)

4 In this best of all possible worlds . . . all is for the best.

Voltaire Dr Pangloss in *Candide*, ch. 1 (1759). From this derives the phrase popularly associated with Pangloss: 'All is for the best in the best of all possible worlds.'

5 All tragedies are finished by a death,/ All comedies are ended by a

marriage;/ The future states of both are left to faith . . .

Lord Byron *Don Juan*, canto 3, st. 9 (1819–24)

6 'Hope is said by the poet, sir,' observed the gentleman, 'to be the nurse of Young Desire.'/ Martin signified that he had heard of the cardinal virtue in question serving occasionally in that domestic capacity.

Charles Dickens Colonel Driver in *Martin Chuzzlewit*, ch. 16 (1843–4)

7 Hope. It's that as animates you. Hope is a buoy, for which you overhaul your Little Warbler, sentimental diwision, but Lord, my lad, like any other buoy, it only floats; it can't be steered nowhere.

Charles Dickens Captain Cuttle to Walter Gay in *Dombey and Son*, ch. 50 (1847–8)

8 A man, hearing that a raven would live two hundred years, bought one to try.

Anon. *The New London Jest Book*, 'Choice Jests', no. 710, ed. W. C. Hazlitt (1871)

9 The reason we like to think well of others is that we are all afraid for ourselves. The basis of optimism is sheer terror.

Oscar Wilde Lord Henry Wotton in *The Picture of Dorian Gray*, ch. 6 (1891)

10 Cheer up! The worst is yet to come!

Philander Chase Johnson *Everybody's Magazine* May 1920

11 The latest definition of an optimist is one who fills up his crossword puzzle in ink.

Clement King Shorter *Observer*, 'Sayings of the Week', 22 February 1925

12 An optimist is a guy/ that has never had/ much experience.

Don Marquis *archy and mehitabel*, 'certain maxims of archy' (1927)

13 'Supposing a tree fell down, Pooh, when we were underneath it?'/ 'Supposing it didn't,' said Pooh after careful thought.

A. A. Milne Piglet to Pooh in *The House at Pooh Corner*, ch. 8 (1928)

14 I long ago came to the conclusion that life is six to five against.

Damon Runyon Sam the Gonoph in 'A Nice Price', publ. in *Collier's* 8 September 1934, repr. in *Money from Home* (1935). In *Rosencrantz and Guildenstern Are Dead* (1966) Tom Stoppard put into the mouth of the Player the words 'Life is a game at terrible odds – if it was a bet you wouldn't take it.'

15 The man who is a pessimist before 48 knows too much; if he is an optimist after it, he knows too little.

Mark Twain *Notebook*, ch. 33 (1935). In the London Library edition, somebody has noted 'poor and very old' alongside.

16 Even today the indoctrination goes on. China. Russia. Our own democracies corrupt with pornography and media violence. As my father once said, 'It will only last for ever.'

Spike Milligan Diary entry for 15 October 1943, *Mussolini: My Part in His Downfall* (1978)

17 I'm an optimist alright, and I know everything will come out alright in the end. But I'll be on the other end.

Arthur 'Bugs' Baer *New York Journal-American* 12 January 1944

18 You've got to ac-cent-tchu-ate the positive/ Elim-my-nate the negative/ Latch on to the affirmative/ Don't mess with Mister In-between.

Johnny Mercer 'Ac-cent-tchu-ate the Positive' (song, 1944)

19 The optimist proclaims that we live in the best of all possible worlds; and the pessimist fears this is true.

James Branch Cabell *The Silver Stallion*, bk 4, ch. 26 (1953)

20 The world lay all before me – like a trapdoor.

Quentin Crisp *The Naked Civil Servant*, ch. 5 (1968)

21 You've got your whole life ahead of you. You're just at the dawn of your disasters.

Dick Clement and Ian La Frenais Terry Collier (James Bolam) to Bob Ferris (Rodney Bewes) in *Whatever Happened to the Likely Lads?*

(TV series, 1973–4). Bob has just been temporarily left by Thelma, to whom he is engaged.

22 **There was an attack by 'Cross Bencher' in the *Sunday Express* today saying I was finished – historically such comments have always preceded a tremendous advance of one kind or another!**
Tony Benn Diary entry for Sunday 31 August (1980), *Tony Benn: The End of an Era, Diaries 1980–90*, ch. 1 (1994)

23 **Odd that we call the end of a rope or chain, the *end*; while in Greek it is the *beginning*.**
Geoffrey Madan *Geoffrey Madan's Notebooks*, 'Beauty, Point and Charm', ed. J. A. Gere and John Sparrow (1981)

24 **I am an optimist, but I am an optimist who takes his raincoat.**
Harold Wilson Quoted in *Political Rhubarb, A Rose by Any Other Name* ed. Adam Shaw (1987)

25 **I don't know, Marge, trying is the first step towards failure.**
Matt Groening Homer Simpson in *The Simpsons*, 'Reality Bites', first broadcast 7 December 1997

26 **Matt was an eternal optimist. In 1968 he still hoped Glenn Miller was just missing.**
Pat Crerand Quoted in *The Book of Football Quotations*, 'The Grey Hair and Dreadlocks Club', ed. Phil Shaw (1999). Matt Busby was the manager of Manchester United from 1945. Glenn Miller, the big-band leader, was presumed dead after an air crash in 1944.

Fame

1 **The philosophers who write treatises 'on despising glory' actually inscribe their own names on those very books! In the actual writings in which they scorn publicity and fame they want to be publicized and named!**
Cicero *Pro Archia*, pt 26 (62 BC), collected in *Cicero: Defence Speeches* trans. D. H. Berry (2000)

2 **Fame is like a river, that beareth up things light and swollen, and drowns things weighty and solid.**
Francis Bacon *Essays*, 'Of Praise' (1625)

3 **Censure is the tax a man pays to the public for being eminent.**
Jonathan Swift *Miscellanies in Prose and Verse*, 'Various Thoughts Moral and Diverting' (1711)

4 **It is charming to totter into vogue.**
Horace Walpole Letter to George Selwyn of 2 December 1765, collected in *Horace Walpole: Correspondence*, vol. 30 (1973)

5 **Celebrity: The advantage of being known by people who don't know you.**
Nicolas-Sébastien Roch de Chamfort Written c. 1785, collected in *Chamfort: Reflections on Life, Love and Liberty*, 'Reflections and Anecdotes', ed. Douglas Parmee (2003)

6 **[To a man who approached him and said, 'Mr Jones, I believe?'] If you believe that, you'll believe anything.**
Duke of Wellington Attributed

7 **In these days a man is nobody unless his biography is kept so far posted up that it may be ready for the national breakfast table on the morning after his demise.**
Anthony Trollope *Doctor Thorne*, ch. 25 (1858)

8 **It is silly of you, for there is only one thing in the world worse than being talked about, and that is not being talked about.**
Oscar Wilde Lord Henry Wotton in *The Picture of Dorian Gray*, ch. 1 (1891)

9 **I was sorry to have my name mentioned as one of the great authors, because they have a sad habit of dying off. Chaucer is dead, Spenser is dead, so is Milton, so is Shakespeare, and I am not feeling very well myself.**
Mark Twain Speech to the Savage Club, 9 June 1899, collected as 'Statistics' in *Mark Twain: Speeches* ed. Shelley Fisher Fishkin (1996)

10 Private faces in public places/ Are wiser and nicer/ Than public faces in private places.

W. H. Auden 'Shorts, 1929–31', *W. H. Auden: Collected Poems*, ed. Edward Mendelson (1976)

11 To try to live in posterity is like an actor who leaps over the footlights and talks to the orchestra.

Samuel Butler *Selections from the Note-Books of Samuel Butler*, ch. 13, ed. A. T. Bartholomew (1930)

12 So a boring neighbour said could I get a 'celebrity' to judge the beauty competition for the village fête. Not so easy because those who are madly famous in London, Paris & New York are unheard of in Stinchcombe.

Evelyn Waugh Letter to Nancy Mitford of 10 August 1948, collected in *The Letters of Evelyn Waugh* ed. Mark Amory (1980)

13 Fame was a claim of Uncle Ed's,/ Simply because he had three heads,/ Which, if he'd only had a third of,/ I think he would never have been heard of.

Ogden Nash *The Private Dining Room and Other Verses*, 'A Caution to Hillbilly Singers, Harpists, Harpoonists, Channel-Swimmers, and People First in Line for World Ticket Series' (1952)

14 Who he?

Harold W. Ross Quoted in *The Years with Ross* by James Thurber (1957). Ross, as editor of the *New Yorker*, would scribble this in the margin of the copy whenever he struck a name he'd never heard of.

15 In the future, everybody will be world famous for fifteen minutes.

Andy Warhol From a catalogue for an exhibition of his photographs held in Stockholm in 1968

16 Fourteen heart attacks and he had to die in my week. In MY week.

Janis Joplin Ex-President Eisenhower had finally died, preventing her photograph appearing on the front of *Newsweek*. Quoted in *New Musical Express* 12 April 1969.

17 *The Rutles* are a living legend that will live on long after most other living legends have died.

Eric Idle Opening caption in *The Rutles: All You Need Is Cash* (film, 1978, written by Eric Idle, directed by Eric Idle and Gary Weis)

18 At Seattle Airport the man at the desk asked, when to pay the bill I produced my credit card, whether I was related to the poet Stephen Spender. So I said, 'That's me.' He looked pleased and said, 'Gee, a near-celebrity.'

Stephen Spender Diary entry for 9 April 1980, *Journals 1939–83* ed. J. Goldsmith (1985). Spender was very conscious of his fame, or lack of it. In a diary entry for 26 January 1979, he wrote that he had been walking down Long Acre having seen *Götterdämmerung* at Covent Garden, when he farted loudly. Some children cheered, and Spender fretted: 'Supposing they knew that this old man walking along Long Acre and farting was Stephen Spender?'

19 Being on the telly, you're in a funny position – not famous, just current.

Robert Robinson *The Dog Chairman*, 'The Dog Chairman' (1982)

20 INTERVIEWER: Do you think you'll always be famous?
    DAVID ST HUBBINS: No, but *we'll* always remember us.

Anon. Quoted in the Preface to *Inside Spinal Tap* by David Occhiogrosso (1985)

21 You're not a star until they can spell your name in Karachi.

Humphrey Bogart Quoted in *Star Billing* by David Brown (1985). Also attributed to Roger Moore.

22 The Victorians, of course, had an obsession about souvenirs of the famous . . . An elderly friend of the family used to keep what looked like a small dog turd under a glass dome on his mantelpiece. It was proudly labelled: 'Cigar butt thrown away by His Royal Highness, the Prince of Wales, outside the Café Royal, London, November 14, 1893'.

Michael Green *The Boy Who Shot Down an Airship*, ch. 1 (1988)

23 The media overestimates its own

importance. I was on the cover of everything for three years but I still only had half a bottle of milk in the fridge.

Mark E. Smith Said in 1990, quoted in the *New Musical Express* 4 February 1995

24 I am a cult figure – people have often told me 'You're one of the biggest cults around here.'

Kenneth Williams Williams often said this, and can be heard doing so on *Silver Minutes* (cassette, 1992), the best of the radio panel game *Just a Minute*

25 The best fame is a writer's fame: it's enough to get a table at a good restaurant, but not enough that you get interrupted when you eat.

Fran Lebowitz *Observer* 30 May 1993

26 The nice thing about being a celebrity is that when you bore people they think it's their fault.

Henry Kissinger *Reader's Digest* (1995), quoted in *The Penguin Dictionary of Modern Humorous Quotations* ed. Fred Metcalf (2nd edn 2001)

27 In the spring of 1989, shortly after my twenty-seventh birthday, as I stood in the sleet at a bus stop in Colchester, it dawned on me that I had probably, all things considered, failed in my mission to become Sting.

Giles Smith *Lost in Music*, Introduction (1995). He adds: 'At least for the time being.'

28 There was talk of a testimonial match, of a stand being named after me, but there was nothing, not even a toilet. They could have had a Brian Clough bog, or something like that.

Brian Clough Moaning, in 1997, about the lack of appreciation of his seventeen years as manager of Nottingham Forest football club. Quoted in *The Book of Football Quotations*, 'The Grey Hair and Dreadlocks Club', ed. Phil Shaw (1999).

29 Being effective is more important than being recognized.

Margaret Beckett Remark made in January 2000, quoted in *People on People: The Oxford Dictionary of Biographical Quotations*

ed. Susan Ratcliffe (2001). Beckett is one of the least famous ministers of the Blair government. Outside politics she has attracted attention mainly for her habit of going on holiday in a caravan.

30 There is Alvar Liddell, for instance, who reads the news; no one I know is called Alvar, which in any case is pronounced Elvar and runs so smoothly off its namesake's tongue ... that I take it to be one name not two – Elvarliddell, someone like Geraldo, say, or Mantovani, so famous that his two names have melted into one as tends to happen in the world of entertainment.

Alan Bennett *Telling Tales*, 'Our War' (2000). When Bennett met the pop singer Morrissey he was unable to call him anything at all, such was his embarrassment at meeting someone with only one name.

31 I had that Christopher Marlowe in my boat once.

Tom Stoppard Boatman to Shakespeare in *Shakespeare in Love* (film, 2000, directed by Tom Stoppard and Marc Norman)

32 [Of T. E. Lawrence] He's always backing into the limelight.

Lord Berners Attributed. Quoted in *People on People: The Oxford Dictionary of Biographical Quotations* ed. Susan Ratcliffe (2001). In 2002 Alex Games called his biography of the reticent yet prolific Alan Bennett *Backing into the Limelight*.

33 Fame is like a big piece of meringue – it's beautiful and you keep eating it, but it doesn't really fill you up.

Pierce Brosnan *The Times*, 'Quotes of the Week', 19 January 2002

34 When you see someone famous you stiffen like a whippet on a leash.

Philip O'Connor Said to Andrew Barrow in *Quentin and Philip*, ch. 21, by Andrew Barrow (2002)

35 Nonebrity: Someone famous for no apparent reason, e.g. Tara Palmer Tomkinson.

Anon. 'The Jargon Bulletin', a dictionary of jargon, *Word* magazine, June 2003

36 It is hard to imagine any smart restaurant admitting someone who

looks and behaves like Keith Richards, unless of course he actually is Keith Richards, in which case it's free meals all round, the management only too anxious to commemorate the visit of the great man with a signed photograph, elaborately framed.

Craig Brown *This Is Craig Brown*, 'Celebrities on the Wall' (2003)

37 I noticed that Tony Blackburn has an almost orangey complexion. A lot of showbusiness celebrities have this almost orangey complexion. It is as if this sun is not ours, or as if they sunbathe by moonlight.

Ibid., 'There Yego: A Day with Tony Blackburn'

38 Grey, thirty-eight years old that summer, had been quite famous once, when he was thirty-seven.

Daisy Waugh *Ten Steps to Happiness*, ch. 1 (2003)

39 There's this statistic that 95 per cent of autographs are lost a week after they're signed.

Jack White He of the Red Stripes duo, interviewed in *Q* magazine June 2003

Accidents

1 Hee that stumbles and falles not, mends his pace.

George Herbert *Outlandish Proverbs*, no. 7 (1640)

2 Humpty Dumpty sat on a wall,/ Humpty Dumpty had a great fall./ All the king's horses,/ And all the king's men,/ Couldn't put Humpty together again.

Anon. The root of the rhyme is supposedly an incident in the Civil War, when Charles I and his men attempted to bridge the River Severn at Gloucester with a huge contraption nicknamed by the troops 'Humpty Dumpty'. The thing collapsed into the water.

3 A man may surely be allowed to take a glass of wine by his own fireside.

Richard Brinsley Sheridan Attributed. On

being seen in 1780 drinking a glass of wine in the street while watching the Drury Lane theatre, of which he was principal director and proprietor, burning fiercely. (It had been set alight in the Gordon Riots.)

4 There are very few moments in a man's existence when he experiences so much ludicrous distress, or meets with so little charitable commiseration, as when he is in pursuit of his own hat.

Charles Dickens *The Pickwick Papers*, ch. 4 (1837). Dickens concludes that the best way is 'to keep gently up with the subject of the pursuit, to be wary and cautious, to watch your opportunity well, get gradually before it, then make a rapid dive, seize it by the crown, and stick it firmly on your head: smiling pleasantly all the time, as if you thought it as good a joke as anybody else'.

5 It is no use crying over spilt milk, because all the forces of the universe are bent on spilling it.

Somerset Maugham *Of Human Bondage*, ch. 67 (1915)

6 I was just thinking by the side of the river – thinking, if any of you know what that means – when I received a loud BOUNCE.

A. A. Milne Eeyore, having been bounced into the river by Tigger. *The House at Pooh Corner*, Ch. 6 (1928).

7 Perhaps 'ablaze' is too strong a word.

Stella Gibbons *Cold Comfort Farm*, ch. 16 (1932). This actually relates to lights burning in a house.

8 He's fallen in the water!

Spike Milligan Regular cry of the tremulous schoolboy Bluebottle (Peter Sellers) in *The Goon Show* (BBC radio series 1951–60)

9 My very photogenic mother died in a freak accident (picnic, lightning) when I was three . . .

Vladimir Nabokov *Lolita*, pt 1, sect. 1 (1955). In a profile of Tom Stoppard in the *New Yorker* 19 December 1977, Ken Tynan quoted Stoppard as saying that this was his 'favourite parenthesis'.

10 Knocked down a doctor? With an

ambulance? How could she? It's a
contradiction in terms.

N. F. Simpson *One Way Pendulum*, act 1 (1960)

11 'I must begin by saying that last
night I jumped on your uncle's
stomach.'/ 'Jumped on his
stomach?' whispered Gladys, finding speech./ 'Oh, purely inadver-
tently, but I could tell by his
manner that he was annoyed.'

P. G. Wodehouse *Plum Pie*, 'A Good Cigar Is a
Smoke' (1966)

12 When you get hit by a car in Brooklyn they don't call an ambulance . . .
it's showtime to the Brooklyn folks!

Eddie Murphy *Eddie Murphy* (CD, 1982)

13 Where there's smoke, there's toast.

Anon. *And I Quote*, 'Cooking', ed. Ashton
Applewhite and others (1992)

14 Sometimes he attempted to tap-
dance on the cracked linoleum floor.
Once he had slipped on something,
looked down angrily to see what it
was and couldn't help smiling when
he found it was a banana skin.

Andrew Barrow *The Tap Dancer*, ch. 1 (1992).
The reference is to the narrator's father.

15 When the big red bus knocked him
down in Fitzjohn's Avenue, the first
thing that floated into Eric's mind
was that it was a funny thing – you
think you know a street well, walk
down it every day, but it's not till
you're flat on your back in the
middle of it that you realize how
terribly broad it is, how very tall
the houses are.

Joseph Connolly *This Is It*, ch. 1 (1996), the
book's opening sentence

16 Avoid chip pan fires by suspending
a plastic bag full of water over the
pan each time you cook. If a fire
occurs, the bag will melt and the
water will extinguish the flames.

Viz 'Top Tips', April 2003

17 Deeply hurt – the man who walked
into the open coal hole.

Anon. 'News Items', *Pearson's Book of Fun*,
'Sundry Siftings', ed. Mr X (n.d.)

Awards

1 The cross of the Legion of Honour
has been conferred upon me. However, few escape that distinction.

Mark Twain *A Tramp Abroad*, ch. 8 (1880)

2 [On being made Poet Laureate in
1850] In the end I accepted the
honour, because during dinner Venables told me that, if I became Poet
Laureate, I should always when I
dined out be offered the liver-wing
of a fowl.

Alfred, Lord Tennyson *Alfred Lord Tennyson:
A Memoir by His Son*, vol. 1 (1897)

3 Thank you, Mr President. I feel very
humble, but I think I have the
strength of character to fight it.

Bob Hope On being awarded a Congressional Gold Medal in 1963 by President
Kennedy

4 You're looking at an actor whose
price has just doubled.

Art Carney On winning an Oscar for his performance as an elderly widower in *Harry and
Tonto* (1974). Quoted in the *Daily Telegraph*
14 November 2003.

5 [On accepting an Oscar for her role
in *L. A. Confidential*] I just want to
thank everyone I met in my entire
life.

Kim Basinger *Observer*, 'Sayings of the
Week', 29 March 1998

6 My career must be slipping. This is
the first time I've been available to
pick up an award.

Michael Caine At the Golden Globe Awards,
Beverly Hills, California, 24 January 1999

7 Awards are like piles. Sooner or
later, every bum gets one.

Maureen Lipman *Independent* 31 July 1999

8 Watch out – both my kids have
Oscars.

Anon. Quoted in the *Independent on Sunday*
20 April 2003, slogan on a T-shirt worn by
Kathlyn Beatty, mother of Warren Beatty
and Shirley MacLaine

Human Characteristics

Melancholia

1 [Of life] . . . a tale/ told by an idiot, full of sound and fury,/ Signifying nothing.
William Shakespeare Macbeth in *Macbeth*, act 5, sc. 5 (1606)

2 The pencil of the Holy Ghost hath laboured more in describing the afflictions of Job than the felicities of Solomon.
Francis Bacon *Essays*, 'Of Adversity' (1625)

3 As our life is very short, so it is very miserable,/ and therefore it is well it is short.
Jeremy Taylor *The Rule and Exercise of Holy Dying*, ch. 1 (1651)

4 Life is an incurable disease . . .
Abraham Cowley 'To Dr Scarborough', st. 6 (1656)

5 Men should be bewailed at their birth, and not at their death.
Montesquieu *Lettres persanes* (Persian Letters), no. 40 (1721)

6 Nothing is more hopeless than a scheme of merriment.
Samuel Johnson *The Idler*, no. 58, 26 May 1759

7 It was a Sunday afternoon, wet and cheerless: and a duller spectacle this earth of ours has not to show than a rainy Sunday in London.
Thomas De Quincey *Confessions of an English Opium Eater*, pt 2 (1822)

8 We're all in the dumps,/ For diamonds are trumps,/ The kittens are gone to St Paul's,/ The babies are bit,/ The moon's in a fit/ And the houses are built without walls.
Anon. 'We're all in the Dumps', thought to have first appeared in *Blackwood's Edinburgh Magazine* July 1824

9 'Dinner is on the table!'/ Thus the melancholy retainer, as who should say, 'Come down and be poisoned, ye unhappy children of men!'
Charles Dickens *Our Mutual Friend*, 'Book the First: The Cup and the Lip', ch. 2 (1864–5)

10 I never had a piece of toast/ Particularly long and wide,/ But fell upon the sanded floor,/ And always on the buttered side.
James Payn *Chambers Journal* 2 February 1884

11 Nothing to do but work,/ Nothing to eat but food,/ Nothing to wear but clothes,/ To keep one from going nude.
Benjamin Franklin King First verse of 'The Pessimist' *Ben King's Verses* (1894)

12 I tell you, we're in a blessed drainpipe, and we've got to crawl along it till we die.
H. G. Wells *Kipps*, bk 1, ch. 2 (1905). Said by Minton, 'a gaunt, sullen-faced youngster' and a colleague of Kipps's in drapery.

13 Life has a way of overgrowing its achievements as well as its ruins.
Edith Wharton *The Spark*, ch. 5 (1924)

14 Men who are unhappy, like men who sleep badly, are always proud of the fact.
Bertrand Russell *The Conquest of Happiness*, ch. 1 (1930)

15 The tree has four or five leaves.
Samuel Beckett Stage direction at the beginning of *Waiting for Godot*, act 2 (1954)

16 I have been spending this evening in a way that bodes ill – like the sewing of a shroud.
Philip Larkin Letter to Pat Strang of 3 February 1954, collected in *Selected Letters of Philip Larkin (1940–85)* ed. Anthony Thwaite (1992). In fact, Larkin had been 'writing a talk on modern poetry'.

17 But Jesus, when you don't have money, the problem is food. When you have money, it's sex. When you have both, it's health.
J. P. Donleavy O'Keefe in *The Ginger Man*, ch. 5 (1955). 'If everything is simply jake then you're frightened of death,' he concludes.

18 Nothing, like something, happens everywhere.

Philip Larkin *I Remember, I Remember* (1955)

19 Term, holidays, term, holidays, till we leave school, and then work, work, work till we die.

C. S. Lewis *Surprised by Joy*, ch. 4 (1955)

20 I always get the fuzzy end of the lollipop.

Marilyn Monroe Sugar Kane (Marilyn Monroe) in *Some Like It Hot* (film, 1959, screenplay by Billy Wilder and I. A. L. Diamond, directed by Billy Wilder)

21 Soon we'll be out, amid the cold world's strife/ Soon we'll be sliding down the razor blade of life.

Tom Lehrer 'Bright College Days' *An Evening Wasted with Tom Lehrer* (LP, 1960)

22 If there wasn't death, I think you couldn't go on.

Stevie Smith *Observer* 9 November 1969

23 A man once said he knew it was time to get up when he heard his wife scraping the burnt toast.

Katherine Whitehorn *Observations*, 'Mistakes of the Season' (1970)

24 What better way to end a day? Listening to the rain gushing through our roof . . .

Alan Ayckbourn Delia in bed with her husband Ernest in *Bedroom Farce*, act 1 (1974). She has identified damp patches on the ceiling.

25 It is the first day of spring. The council have chopped all the elms down in Elm Tree Avenue.

Sue Townsend *The Secret Diary of Adrian Mole Aged 13¾* (1982), entry for Friday 20 March

26 The world is not black and white. More like black and grey.

Graham Greene *Observer* 2 January 1983

Happiness

1 Living well is the best revenge.

George Herbert *Outlandish Proverbs*, no. 524 (1640)

2 Life would be very pleasant if it were not for its enjoyments.

R. S. Surtees *Mr Facey Romford's Hounds*, ch. 32 (1865)

3 Be happy while y'er leevin,/ For y'er a lang time dead.

Anon. 'Scottish homily for a house', *Notes & Queries*, 9th series, vol. 8 (7 December 1901)

4 'And yet,' demanded Councillor Barlow, 'What's he done? Has he ever done a day's work in his life? What great cause is he identified with?'/ 'He's identified,' said the first speaker, 'with the great cause of cheering us all up.'

Arnold Bennett Of Denry, or Edward Henry Machin, the card himself, *The Card*, ch. 12 (1911). Closing words of the book.

5 Happiness makes up in height for what it lacks in length.

Robert Frost Title of a poem collected in *A Witness Tree* (1942)

6 Happy is the man with a wife to tell him what to do and a secretary to do it.

Lord Mancroft Quoted in *The Penguin Dictionary of Modern Humorous Quotations* ed. Fred Metcalf (2nd edn 2001)

7 Happiness is the sublime moment when you get out of your corsets at night.

Joyce Grenfell Attributed

Humour

1 As the crackling of thorns under a pot, so is the laughter of a fool.

Ecclesiastes 5:12, the Bible, Authorized Version (1611)

2 Look, he's winding up the watch of his wit, by and by it will strike.

William Shakespeare Sebastian speaking of Gonzalo in *The Tempest*, act 2, sc. 1 (1611)

3 Satire is a kind of glass, wherein beholders do generally discover everybody's face but their own.

Jonathan Swift *The Battle of the Books*, Preface (1697). In the Preface to *A Tale of a*

Tub (1704) Swift wrote: 'Satire, being levelled at all, is never resented for an offence by any.'

4 **All human race would fain be wits,/ And millions miss, for one that hits.**

Jonathan Swift *On Poetry: a Rhapsody*, written 1732, collected in *Jonathan Swift: The Selected Poems* ed. Roland A. Jeffares (1992)

5 **The man who chuses never to laugh, or whose becalm'd passions know no motion, seems to me only in the quiet state of a green tree; he vegetates, 'tis true, but shall we say he lives?**

Colley Cibber *An Apology for the Life of Mr Colley Cibber, Comedian*, ch. 1 (1739)

6 **'Tis no extravagant arithmetic to say, that for every ten jokes, – thou hast got an hundred enemies.**

Laurence Sterne *Tristram Shandy* bk 1, ch. 12 (1759)

7 **A joke's a very serious thing.**

Charles Churchill *The Ghost*, bk 4 (1763)

8 **In my mind there is nothing so illiberal and ill-bred, as audible laughter.**

Lord Chesterfield *Letters to His Son* (1774), letter of 9 March 1748

9 **There's no possibility of being witty without a little ill nature: the malice of a good thing is the barb that makes it stick.**

Richard Brinsley Sheridan Lady Sneerwell in *The School for Scandal*, act 1, sc. 1 (1777)

10 **What is an epigram? A dwarfish whole,/ Its body brevity, and wit its soul.**

Samuel Taylor Coleridge 'Epigram' (1809)

11 **Laughter is pleasant, but the exertion is too much for me.**

Thomas Love Peacock *Nightmare Abbey*, ch. 5 (1818)

12 **Wit is the salt of conversation, not the food.**

William Hazlitt *Lectures on English Comic Writers*, 'On Wit and Humour' (1819)

13 **[A pun] is a pistol let off at the ear; not a feather to tickle the intellect.**

Charles Lamb *Last Essays of Elia*, 'Popular Fallacies', no. 9 (1833)

14 **We wonder Mr Babbage does not invent a punning-engine; it is just as possible as a calculating one.**

Walter Bagehot 'The First Edinburgh Reviewers', *National Review* (1855), collected in *The Complete Works of Walter Bagehot* (1966–86), vol. 1, ed. Norman St John-Stevas

15 **It requires a surgical operation to get a joke well into Scotch understanding. Their only idea of wit ... is laughing immoderately at stated intervals.**

Sydney Smith *A Memoir of the Reverend Sydney Smith* by Lady Holland, vol. 1, ch. 2 (1855)

16 **A gentleman observed one day to Erskine, that punning is the lowest sort of wit. 'It is so,' answered he, 'and therefore the *foundation* of all wit.'**

Anon. *The New London Jest Book*, 'Choice Jests', no. 690, ed. W. C. Hazlitt (1871)

17 **A difference in taste in jokes is a great strain on the affections.**

George Eliot *Daniel Deronda*, bk 2, ch. 15 (1876)

18 **Well, one must be serious about something if one wants to have any amusement in life.**

Oscar Wilde Algernon Moncrieff in *The Importance of Being Earnest*, act 3 (1895). 'I,' he adds, 'happen to be serious about Bunburying.'

19 **That boy will make his way in this country: he has no sense of humour.**

George Bernard Shaw Charteris speaking of the Page in *The Philanderer*, act 2 (1893)

20 **It is one of the most trying things about this life, this necessity of laughing uproariously when vinous old men say things that are dirty but not funny; else one is written down as a prig.**

Raymond Asquith Letter to H. T. Baker of 25 August 1899, collected in *Raymond*

Asquith: Life and Letters ed. John Jolliffe (1980). Someone had just told him 'a coarse story about Dizzy [Disraeli]'.

21 **We are not amused.**

Queen Victoria Attributed to a journal entry for 2 January 1900, in *Notebooks of a Spinster Lady*, ch. 21, by Caroline Holland (1919). She notes that the Queen has 'a good deal of humour and a most musical laugh ... But her remarks can freeze as well as crystallise'. This particular remark was prompted by an anecdote, told by an 'unfortunate equerry', that contained 'a spice of scandal or impropriety'.

22 **Impropriety is the soul of wit.**

Somerset Maugham *The Moon and Sixpence*, ch. 17 (1919)

23 **Everything is funny as long as it's happening to someone else.**

Will Rogers *The Illiterate Digest*, 'Warning to Jokers: Lay Off the Prince' (1924)

24 **Men will confess to treason, murder, arson, false teeth, or a wig. How many of them will own up to a lack of humour?**

Frank Moore Colby *The Colby Essays* vol. 1, *Satire and Teeth* (1926)

25 **If Jesus Christ were to come to-day, people would not even crucify him. They would ask him to dinner, and hear what he had to say, and make fun of it.**

Thomas Carlyle Quoted in *Carlyle at His Zenith*, p. 238, by D. A. Wilson (1927)

26 **What do you mean, funny? Funny-peculiar or funny ha-ha?**

Ian Hay *The Housemaster*, act 3 (1938)

27 **I haven't laughed so much since auntie caught her tits in the mangle.**

Anon. Popular expression, quoted in *The Cassell Dictionary of Catchphrases* ed. Nigel Rees (1995). Rees believes that it may originate from British service life in the 1950s. 'Laugh? I nearly bought my own beer' serves the same function.

28 **Good taste and humour ... are a contradiction in terms, like a chaste whore.**

Malcolm Muggeridge *Time* 14 September 1953

29 **Humour is emotional chaos remembered in tranquility.**

James Thurber *New York Post* 29 February 1960. In *Lyrical Ballads* (1802) Wordsworth defined poetry as 'emotion recollected in tranquility'.

30 **I cannot see much future for Russian humorists. They have a long way to go before they can play the Palladium.**

P. G. Wodehouse *Plum Pie*, 'A Note on Humour' (1966). Wodehouse believed that Khrushchev 'was probably considered Russia's top funny man – at least if you were domiciled in Moscow and didn't think so, you would have done well to keep it to yourself'.

31 **I am all for incest and tortured souls in moderation, but a good laugh from time to time never hurt anybody.**

Ibid. Wodehouse was speaking of 'playwrights *nowadays* who are writing nothing but that grim stark stuff'.

32 **Say I make a 'joke' and it doesn't appeal to you, you are annoyed rather than amused. Annoyed, simply because you haven't yet found out how to unlaugh.**

Flann O'Brien *The Best of Myles*, 'Miscellaneous' (1968)

33 **Comedy, like sodomy, is an unnatural act.**

Marty Feldman *The Times* 9 June 1969

34 **He's about as funny as a baby's open grave.**

Sir Laurence Olivier Quoted by Kenneth Tynan in an entry for 28 September 1971, *The Diaries of Kenneth Tynan* ed. John Lahr (2000)

35 **The good thing about Evelyn – and she has a good side, although she is most careful to hide it from strangers – is that she has absolutely no sense of humour. Which is very useful since it means you never have to waste your time trying to cheer her up.**

Alan Ayckbourn John in *Absent Friends*, act 2 (1974)

36 [Of Alastair Burnet] **NBC came through on vision and CBS came through on sound. Then neither came through on anything. Alastair celebrated by dropping his phone. A jest and a smile might have helped, but he reserves these for inappropriate moments.**

Clive James *Observer* 11 August 1974. Burnet was reporting on the resignation of Richard Nixon. As well as being the anchor man of ITV's News at Ten in the 1970s and 80s, Burnet edited the *Economist* and the *Daily Express.*

37 **To many people Victorian wit and humour is summed up by *Punch*, when every joke is supposed to end with 'collapse of stout party', though this phrase tends to be as elusive as 'Elementary, my dear Watson' in the Sherlock Holmes sagas.**

R. Pearsall *Collapse of Stout Party*, Introduction (1975)

38 **Words with a 'K' are funny.**

Neil Simon Willy Clark (Walter Matthau) drawing on his vaudeville experience in *The Sunshine Boys* (film, 1975, screenplay by Neil Simon (from his play), directed by Herbert Ross)

39 **It's funny – there's nothing that stops you laughing like the sight of other people laughing about something else.**

Michael Frayn The Rev. R. D. Sainsbury in *Donkey's Years*, act 2 (1976)

40 **To err is humour.**

Anon. *The Dictionary of Puns*, 'Humour', ed. John S. Crosbie (1977)

41 **The marvellous thing about a joke with a double meaning is that it can only mean one thing.**

Ronnie Barker *Sauce*, 'Daddie's Sauce' (1977)

42 **The Art of a Pun . . . or How to Lose an Audience Fast . . .**

Les Dawson Chapter heading in *The Malady Lingers On* (1982). Dawson also writes: 'I firmly believe that the art of punning needs a swift mind, high intelligence, and raw courage, especially if you're in a strange pub.'

43 **Irony: The modern mode: either the devil's mark or the snorkel of sanity.**

Julian Barnes *Flaubert's Parrot*, ch. 12 (1984)

44 **Men think a gal with good lines is better than one with a good line.**

Mae West Quoted in *The Ultimate Seduction*, 'Mae West', by Charlotte Chandler (1984)

45 **If there's to be a special award for Best Comedy Performance as distinct from Best Actor or Actress, then let's have an award for Best *Serious* Performance.**

Maureen Lipman *How Was It for You?* 'A Joking Aside' (1985)

46 **OSCAR WILDE: I wish I had said that.**
   WHISTLER: You will, Oscar, you will.

James McNeill Whistler Quoted in *Oscar Wilde* by Richard Ellman, pt 2, ch. 5 (1987)

47 **Q: Who was the funniest man in the Bible? A: Samson, he brought the house down.**

Anon. Quoted in *Bishop's Brew (An Anthology of Clerical Humour)*, ch. 4, ed. Ronald Brown (1989)

48 **Do not dabble in paradox, Edward, it puts you in danger of fortuitous wit.**

Tom Stoppard Lady Croome in *Arcadia*, act 1, sc. 1 (1993)

49 **Analysing humour is like dissecting a frog – few people are interested, and the frog dies.**

Victor Lewis-Smith *Inside the Magic Rectangle*, 'Arena: The Peter Sellers Story' (1995)

50 **I'm thinking of compiling a list of commonly used phrases that mean exactly the opposite of what they appear to be saying. The first one will be, 'Look, I can take a joke as well as the next man.' The second, 'You've got to laugh, haven't you?', followed by 'Here, this'll make you laugh.'**

A. A. Gill *Spectator* 14 August 1999

51 **As I said in *Money*, if you had a fully active sense of humour in America you would be sobbing with**

laughter all the hours there are. It would incapacitate you entirely.

Martin Amis *Writers in Conversation*, 'In Conversation with Martin Amis' (2000), by Christopher Bigsby. Amis did concede that his novel *Money* – about greed and egotism in the 1980s – 'went down much more easily there than it did here'.

52 A joke isn't yours. It's used and you don't know where it's been.

Ricky Gervais Interview in the *Guardian* 7 September 2002. Gervais is also quoted as saying: 'Why can't people have their own thoughts? Why not just tell something amusing that happened, make a story of it, a story with soul?'

53 We're all humorists now.

Craig Brown *Daily Telegraph* 18 January 2003

54 There are three rules of comedy: 1. No puns. 2. No puns. 3. No puns.

John Cleese Attributed

Wisdom

1 Blend a little foolishness into your plans./ Folly is delightful in its place.

Horace *Odes*, bk 4, no. 12 (*c.* 13 BC), *Horace: The Complete Odes and Epodes* trans. David West (1997)

2 Great men are not always wise . . .

Job 32:9, the Bible, Authorized Version (1611)

3 To me the fatigue of being upon a continual Guard to hide them [his follies], is more than the reputation of being without them can repay.

Colley Cibber *An Apology for the Life of Mr Colley Cibber, Comedian*, ch. 1 (1739)

4 Some men are wise and some are otherwise.

Tobias Smollett *Roderick Random*, ch. 6 (1748)

5 If the fool would persist in his folly he would become wise.

William Blake *The Marriage of Heaven and Hell*, 'Proverbs of Hell' (1790–93)

6 My only books/ Were women's

looks,/ And folly's all they've taught me.

Thomas Moore *Irish Melodies*, 'The Time I've Lost in Wooing' (1807)

7 I'll not listen to reason . . . Reason always means what someone else has got to say.

Elizabeth Gaskell *Cranford*, ch. 14 (1853)

8 Why level downward to our dullest perception always, and praise that as common sense?

Henry David Thoreau *Walden: Or, Life in the Woods*, Conclusion (1854)

9 Nowadays most people die of a sort of creeping common sense, and discover when it is too late that the only things one never regrets are one's mistakes.

Oscar Wilde Lord Henry Wotton in *The Picture of Dorian Gray*, ch. 3 (1891)

10 DUMBY: Experience is the name everyone gives to their mistakes.
CECIL GRAHAM: One shouldn't commit any.
DUMBY: Life would be very dull without them.

Oscar Wilde *Lady Windermere's Fan*, act 3 (1893)

11 I always pass on good advice. It is the only thing to do with it. It is never of any use to oneself.

Oscar Wilde Lord Goring in *An Ideal Husband*, act 1 (1895)

12 It is a far, far better thing to have a firm anchor in nonsense than to put out on the troubled seas of thought.

J. K. Galbraith *The Affluent Society*, ch. 11, sect. 4 (1958)

13 If there's one thing I can't bear, it's people who are wise *during* the event.

Kenneth Tynan Entry for 4 August 1974, *The Diaries of Kenneth Tynan* ed. John Lahr (2000)

14 George, what do Wise Men never do?

Joyce Grenfell Question addressed by his

teacher/director to a small boy during rehearsal for the school nativity play. From 'Nativity Play' (sketch), collected in *Turn Back the Clock* (1977).

15 **Experience is something you don't get until just after you need it.**
Steven Wright Line used in his stage act of the 1980s.

16 **The process of ripening in cheese is a little like the human acquisition of wisdom and maturity; both processes involve a recognition, or incorporation, of the fact that life is an incurable disease with a hundred per cent mortality rate – a slow variety of death.**
John Lanchester *The Debt to Pleasure*, 'Winter', 'Another Winter Menu' (1996)

17 **Common sense is the little man in a grey suit who never makes a mistake in addition, but it's always someone else's money he's adding up.**
Raymond Chandler Quoted in *Raymond Chandler: A Biography*, ch. 2, by Tom Hiney (1997)

Anger

1 **I am the mildest man in the world, yet I have already killed three men – and two of them were priests.**
Voltaire Candide in *Candide*, ch. 15 (1759)

2 **A sharp tongue is the only edged tool that grows keener with constant use.**
Washington Irving *The Sketch Book of Geoffrey Crayon, Gent.*, 'Rip Van Winkle' (1820)

3 **As savage as a bear with a sore head.**
Frederick Marryat *The King's Head*, vol. 2, ch. 6 (1830)

4 **Those straw-coloured women have dreadful tempers.**
Oscar Wilde Mrs Erlynne in *Lady Windermere's Fan*, act 2 (1893). Lady Plymdale is the straw-coloured woman.

5 **I know of no more disagreeable sensation than to be left feeling gener-** ally angry without anybody in particular to be angry at.
Frank Moore Colby *The Colby Essays*, vol. 1, *The Literature of Malicious Exposure* (1926)

6 **Great fury, like great whisky, requires long fermentation.**
Truman Capote *Music for Chameleons*, 'Hand-carved Coffins' (1980)

7 **Never go to bed mad. Stay up and fight.**
Phyllis Diller *Phyllis Diller's Housekeeping Hints*, quoted in *Violets and Vinegar*, 'Stay Up and Fight', ed. Jilly Cooper and Tom Hartman (1980)

8 **Angry wife to husband: 'You are being deliberately calm.'**
Anon. *Laughter Lines: Family Wit and Wisdom*, 'For Better or Worse', ed. James A. Simpson (1986)

Boastfulness and Modesty

1 **The sovereign'st thing that any man may have/ Is little to say, and much to hear and see.**
John Skelton *The Bowge of Courte*, line 211 (1499)

2 **An affected modesty is very often the greatest vanity, and authors are sometimes prouder of their blushes than of the praises that occasioned them.**
George Farquhar Preface to *The Constant Couple* (1699)

3 **An impudent fellow may counterfeit modesty; but I'll be hanged if a modest fellow can ever counterfeit impudence.**
Oliver Goldsmith Sir Charles Marlow in *She Stoops to Conquer*, act 2, sc. 1 (1773)

4 **I believe I forgot to tell you I was made a Duke.**
Duke of Wellington Postcript to a letter to his nephew Henry Wellesley, 22 May 1814

5 **It is going to be fun to watch and see how long the meek can keep the earth after they inherit it.**
Kin Hubbard Quoted in *Abe Martin's Wisecracks* ed. E. V. Lucas (1930)

6 I occasionally swank a little because people like it; a modest man is such a nuisance.
George Bernard Shaw *Observer*, 'Sayings of the Week', 7 March 1937

7 I run a couple of newspapers – what do you do?
Herman J. Mankiewicz and Orson Welles Kane (Orson Welles) in *Citizen Kane* (film, 1941, directed by Orson Welles). Kane also says: 'I don't know how to run a newspaper, Mr Thatcher. I just try everything I can think of.'

8 Modesty is the art of encouraging people to find out for themselves how wonderful you are.
Anon. *And I Quote*, 'Modesty', ed. Ashton Applewhite and others (1992)

9 Vic is like me, only more so.
Daren King Scott Spec in *Jim Giraffe*, 'Golden Showers' (2004)

Self-esteem

1 I must make use of this opportunity to thank you, dear Sir, for the very high praise you bestow on my other Novels – I am too vain to wish to convince you that you have praised them beyond their Merit.
Jane Austen Letter to James Stanier Clarke of 11 December 1815, collected in *Jane Austen's Letters* ed. Dierdre Le Faye (1995)

2 My belief is that in life people will take you very much at your own reckoning.
Anthony Trollope *The Small House at Allington*, ch. 32 (1864). In ch. 22 of *Orley Farm* Trollope wrote: 'Nobody holds a good opinion of a man who has a low opinion of himself.'

3 Self-evident, adj.: Evident to one's self and to nobody else.
Ambrose Bierce *The Devil's Dictionary* (compiled 1881–1906)

4 To love oneself is the beginning of a lifelong romance, Phipps.
Oscar Wilde Lord Goring to his manservant in *An Ideal Husband*, act 3 (1899)

5 The Queen and the Ladies-in-waiting/ Sat at the window and sewed./ She cried, 'Look! Who's that *handsome* man?'/ They answered, 'Mr Toad.'
Kenneth Grahame 'The Song of Mr Toad', *The Wind in the Willows*, ch. 10 (1908)

6 The affair between Margot Asquith and Margot Asquith will live as one of the prettiest love stories in all literature.
Dorothy Parker Observation on Margot Asquith's *Lay Sermons* made in a review in the *New Yorker* October 1927. Quoted in *People on People: The Oxford Dictionary of Biographical Quotations* ed. Susan Ratcliffe (2001).

7 I suppose flattery hurts no one, that is, if he doesn't inhale.
Adlai Stevenson TV broadcast, 30 March 1952

8 There goes Mrs Twenty-Three, important, the sun gets up and goes down in her dewlap, when she shuts her eyes it's night.
Dylan Thomas *Under Milk Wood* (1954). The thought is Captain Cat's.

9 He settled himself in one of the tubular chairs and crossed his hands benignly over his stomach, like Father Christmas in a big shop waiting for the children to be let in.
Pamela Hansford Johnson *The Unspeakable Skipton*, ch. 20 (1960)

10 A fair share of everything is starvation diet to an egomaniac.
Quentin Crisp *The Naked Civil Servant*, ch. 1 (1968)

11 If my wife is committing adultery my position would be intolerable. Being completely without sin myself I'd have to cast the first stone. And I am dead against violence.
Joe Orton Pringle in *Funeral Games*, pt 1, sc. 2 (TV play, 1968)

12 An egoist is a person who is always me-deep in conversation.
Anon. *The Dictionary of Puns*, 'Me', ed. John S. Crosbie (1977)

13 YALE [Michael Murphy]: You are so self-righteous. We're just people, we're just human. You think you're God!
ISAAC DAVIS [Woody Allen]: I've got to model myself after someone!

Woody Allen *Manhattan* (film, 1979, written by Woody Allen and Marshall Brickman, directed by Woody Allen)

14 We have become a grandmother.

Margaret Thatcher Quoted in *The Times* 4 March 1989

15 'Ere's ti ye an me,/ An ti mah wife's husband,/ Nut forgettin missen.

Anon. Traditional Yorkshire toast, quoted in *Basic Broad Yorkshire: Sayings and Traditions* by Arnold Kellett (1991)

16 When I put my hand on my knee I don't mind.

Dillie Keane 'I Like Me' (song), quoted in the London *Evening Standard* 15 December 1994

17 [Questionnaire question]: With which historical figure do you most identify?
KEITH RICHARDS: Myself.

Keith Richards Responding to 'The Proust Questionnaire', *Vanity Fair* January 2003

Self-control

1 'Ah dear! When Gamp was summoned to his long home, and I see him a-lying in Guy's Hospital with a penny-piece on each eye, and his wooden leg under his left arm, I thought I should have fainted away. But I bore up.'

Charles Dickens Mrs Gamp in *Martin Chuzzlewit*, ch. 19 (1843–4)

2 When angry, count four; when very angry, swear.

Mark Twain 'Pudd'nhead Wilson's Calender', *The Tragedy of Pudd'nhead Wilson*, ch. 10 (1894). In his *Notebook* (1935), Twain wrote: 'If I cannot swear in heaven I shall not stay there.'

3 Moderation is a fatal thing, Lady Hunstanton. Nothing succeeds like excess.

Oscar Wilde Lord Illingworth in *A Woman of No Importance*, act 3 (1894)

4 Her self-possession was complete, the only exterior indication that her life was at crisis point being an aura of happiness which transformed her whole aspect.

Nancy Mitford *Love in a Cold Climate*, ch. 14 (1949)

5 Your sense of detachment is terrifying, lad. Most people would at least flinch upon seeing their mothers' eyes and teeth handed around like nuts at Christmas.

Joe Orton Truscott in *Loot*, act 2 (1966). Actually, the teeth are dentures, and there is only one eye – a glass one.

Boredom and Boringness

1 God is in heaven, and thou upon the earth: therefore let thy words be few.

Ecclesiastes 5:2, the Bible, Authorized Version (1611)

2 'Tis a very hard thing to be rid of him, for he's one of those nauseous offerers at wit who, like the worst fiddlers, run themselves into all companies.

William Wycherley *The Country Wife*, act 1, sc. 1 (1672–3). The reference is to Mr Sparkish.

3 The secret of being a bore . . . is to tell everything.

Voltaire *Discours en vers sur l'homme* (Poetic Discourse on Man), 'De la nature de l'homme' (On the Nature of Man) (1737)

4 Society is now one polish'd hord,/ Formed of two mighty tribes, the *Bores* and/ *Bored*

Lord Byron *Don Juan*, canto 13, st. 95 (1819–24)

5 Every hero becomes a bore at last.

Ralph Waldo Emerson *Representative Men*, 'Uses of Great Men' (1850)

6 The essence of civilisation, as we know, is dullness.

Walter Bagehot 'Matthew Arnold's Empedocles on Etna', *The Inquirer* (1853), collected in *The Complete Works of Walter Bagehot*

(1966–86), vol. 14 p. 179, ed. Norman St John-Stevas

7 When a man fell into his anecdotage it was a sign for him to retire from the world.

Benjamin Disraeli *Lothair*, ch. 28 (1870). The opinion of Mr Pinto.

8 According to Mr Burnand, the Queen of the Iceni used to greet her army thus: 'I'm Boadicea! Are you bored to see her!'

O. P. Q. Philander Smiff *Smiff's History of England*, 'The Romans in Britain' (1876)

9 Bore, n.: A person who talks when you wish him to listen.

Ambrose Bierce *The Devil's Dictionary* (compiled 1881–1906)

10 I suppose he bored you. If so, he never forgave you. It's a habit bores have.

Oscar Wilde Lord Henry Wotton to Dorian Gray in *The Picture of Dorian Gray*, ch. 19 (1891)

11 If only people had the gift of knowing when they were bored and the courage to admit the fact openly when it was discovered, how many novelists, poets, playwrights, musicians, and entertainers would be compelled to join the ranks of the unemployed!

Arnold Bennett Entry for 13 October 1896, *Journals of Arnold Bennett, 1896–1910*, ed. Newman Flower (1932)

12 He is an old bore; even the grave yawns for him.

Sir Herbert Beerbohm Tree Speaking of Israel Zangwill, writer and noted Zionist. Quoted in *Herbert Beerbohm Tree*, Appendix 4, by Max Beerbohm (1920).

13 A bore is a man who, when you ask him how he is, tells you.

Bert Leston Taylor *The So-Called Human Race*, p. 163 (1922)

14 A platitude is simply a truth repeated until people get tired of hearing it.

Stanley Baldwin Speech to the House of Commons, 29 May 1924

15 There is no greater bore than the travel bore.

Vita Sackville-West *Passenger to Tehran*, ch. 1 (1926)

16 Everybody is somebody's bore.

Edith Sitwell *Observer* 3 July 1927

17 The effect of boredom on a large scale in history is underestimated. It is the main cause of revolutions, and would soon bring to an end all the static Utopias and the farmyard civilizations of the Fabians.

William Ralph Inge *End of an Age*, ch. 6 (1948)

18 I won't bore you with the story of how we finally located the King's tomb – oh, I don't know, I might as well.

Spike Milligan Peter Sellers in the first programme in the series *Crazy People*, forerunner of *The Goons*, broadcast on BBC radio 28 May 1951

19 I don't know about bores. Maybe you shouldn't feel too sorry if you see some swell girl getting married to them. They don't hurt anybody, most of them, and maybe they're all terrific whistlers or something. Who the hell knows? Not me.

J. D. Salinger Narrator Holden Caulfield in *The Catcher in the Rye*, ch. 17 (1951)

20 It is very odd how completely unable so many men are to put themselves in the place of their own audience – so very unlike the old Duke of Devonshire, who yawned during his own maiden speech because, as he told somebody, 'it was so damned dull'.

George Lyttelton Letter to Rupert Hart-Davis of 24 October 1956, collected in *The Lyttelton –Hart-Davis Letters*, vols 1 and 2, ed. Rupert Hart-Davis (1978)

21 HAMM: What time is it?
CLOV: The same as usual.

Samuel Beckett *Endgame* (1957)

22 Dylan talked copiously, then stopped. 'Somebody's boring me,' he said, 'I think it's me.'

Dylan Thomas Quoted in *Four Absentees* ch. 16, by Rayner Heppenstall (1960)

23 **The office of works! Do tell me about it.**
Ronald Searle 'The Female Approach' – which Katherine Whitehorn, in her book *Whitehorn's Social Survival* (1968) describes as 'the key to the question' of how to behave in society

24 **When I first met her she was one of the jumpiest girls you could ever hope to meet. Still, as I say, she's much calmer since she's been with me. If I've done nothing else for her, I've acted as a sort of sedative.**
Alan Ayckbourn Ronald, talking of his wife Marion, in *Absurd Person Singular*, act 3 (1972)

25 **It's a real problem to decide whether it's more boring to do something boring than to pass along everything boring that comes in to somebody else and then have nothing to do at all.**
Joseph Heller *Something Happened*, 'The Office in which I Work' (1974)

26 **There are certain phrases that, when you hear them, strike dread in your heart. One of these is: 'Do you mind if I say something?' And another is the patent lie: 'I'm not going to make a speech.'**
Joyce Grenfell Note prefacing 'Speeches', *Turn Back the Clock* (1977)

27 **ERIC OLTHWAITE: Irene – guess who's got a new shovel, then? IRENE OLTHWAITE: Oh, *shut up*, you boring little tit . . . !**
Terry Jones and Michael Palin *Ripping Yarns*, 'The Testing of Eric Olthwaite' (BBC TV; 1978). Eric is the son of a Yorkshire coalminer who pretends to be French so as to avoid speaking to his extremely boring son. Eric's main interest, apart from shovels, is rainfall indices.

28 **Two clergymen talking:/ 'When I preach, I have the congregation glued to their seats.'/ 'Now, why didn't I think of that!'**
Anon. Quoted in *Bishop's Brew, An Anthology of Clerical Humour*, ch. 4, ed. Ronald Brown (1989)

29 **Most speakers don't need an introduction, just a conclusion.**
Anon. *And I Quote*, Introduction, ed. Ashton Applewhite and others (1992)

30 **According to legend, Telford is so dull that the bypass was built before the town.**
Victor Lewis-Smith Quoted in the London *Evening Standard* 9 December 1994

31 **Some speakers electrify their listeners, others only gas them.**
Anon. Quoted in *A Gentleman Publisher's Commonplace Book*, 'The Core', by John G. Murray (1996)

32 **Not everyone was captivated by the England–Argentina match. My wife fell asleep during the penalty shoot-out.**
Anon. Letter to the *Daily Telegraph* 1998, quoted in *The Book of Football Quotations*, 'This Supporting Life', ed. Phil Shaw (1999)

33 **Ann talks of culture, long and deep,/ Though Ann, indeed, is not magnetic;/ She talks until I fall asleep/ A sort of gentle Ann aesthetic . . .**
Anon. 'Some Girls I Know', *Pearson's Book of Fun*, 'Capital Verses', ed. Mr X (n.d.)

Patience and Impatience

1 **Hee puls with a long rope, that waits for anothers death.**
George Herbert *Outlandish Proverbs*, no. 25 (1640)

2 **Patience: A minor form of despair, disguised as a virtue.**
Ambrose Bierce *The Devil's Dictionary* (compiled 1881–1906)

Decisiveness and Indecision

1 **Nothing is so perfectly amusing as a total change of ideas.**
Laurence Sterne *Tristram Shandy* (1760–67), bk 9, Dedication

2 **Sir Stafford has a brilliant mind, until it is made up.**

Margot Asquith Attributed. Of Sir Richard Stafford Cripps, Labour Chancellor of the Exchequer 1947–50.

3 **My Indecision Is Final**

Jake Eberts Title of a book about the travails of Goldcrest Films (1990)

4 **I think therefore I am. I think.**

Anon. T-shirt slogan spotted in Bruton, Somerset, in 2000. Quoted in *The Penguin Dictionary of Humorous Quotations* ed. Fred Metcalf (2nd edn 2001)

5 **I'll give you a definite maybe.**

Sam Goldwyn Quoted in *Postmaster and the Merton Record*, p. 105 (2003)

Competence and Incompetence

1 **To err is human; to forgive, divine.**

Alexander Pope *An Essay on Criticism*, line 525 (1711)

2 **Errors look so very ugly in persons of small means – one feels they are taking quite a liberty in going astray; whereas people of fortune may naturally indulge in a few delinquencies.**

George Eliot *Scenes of Clerical Life*, ch. 25 (1858)

3 **There was an old man of Thermopylae,/ Who never did anything properly;/ But they said, 'If you choose/ To boil eggs in your shoes,/ You shall never remain in Thermopylae.'**

Edward Lear *More Nonsense: One Hundred Nonsense Pictures and Rhymes* (1862)

4 **BETTER DROWNED THAN DUFFERS IF NOT DUFFERS WON'T DROWN.**

Arthur Ransome *Swallows and Amazons*, ch. 1 (1930). Telegram from the children's father, allowing them to go sailing.

5 **I might give my life for my friend, but he had better not ask me to do up a parcel.**

Logan Pearsall Smith *Afterthoughts*, ch. 6, 'Myself' (1931)

6 **Never assume that habitual silence means ability in reserve.**

Anon. *Livres sans nom* (Books without a Name; 1930), 'Twelve Reflections', collected in *Geoffrey Madan's Notebooks* ed. J. A. Gere and John Sparrow (1981)

7 **A motto: Do it tomorrow; you've made enough mistakes today.**

Dawn Powell Entry for 23 August 1956, *The Diaries of Dawn Powell 1931–65* ed. T. Page (1995)

8 **Just like that!**

Tommy Cooper Catchphrase of the deliberately incompetent magician and comedian, and title of his autobiography (1975)

9 **Incompetence: Always 'utter'.**

Henry Root *Henry Root's World of Knowledge* (1982)

10 **This slip has been inserted by mistake.**

Alasdair Gray Erratum slip inserted in *Unlikely Stories, Mostly* (1983)

11 **D'oh!**

Matt Groening Homer Simpson in *The Simpsons* (TV cartoon, 1989 onwards). He says it whenever he makes a mistake, which is often.

12 **No one is completely worthless – they can always serve as a bad example.**

Anon. *And I Quote*, 'Example', ed. Ashton Applewhite and others (1992)

Childishness

1 **When I am grown to man's estate/ I shall be very proud and great./ And tell the other girls and boys/ Not to meddle with my toys.**

Robert Louis Stevenson *A Child's Garden of Verses*, 'Looking Forward' (1885)

2 **He was of the childish order of men who ignore children, lest the dividing rampart fall.**

Philip O'Connor *Memoirs of a Public Baby*, pt 1, ch. 3 (1958)

Affectation

1 **Affectation is catching, I find; from your grave bow I got it.**
Sir George Etherege Harriet in *The Man of Mode*, act 4, sc. 2 (1676)

2 **I hate a straightforward fellow . . . If every man were straightforward in his opinions, there would be no conversations.**
Benjamin Disraeli St Aldegonde in *Lothair*, ch. 28 (1872)

3 **I'm so affected, even my lungs are affected.**
Aubrey Beardsley Remark made *c.* 1894. Quoted in *Aubrey Beardsley: A Biography*, ch. 6 by Matthew Hurgis (1998), and literally true, since Beardsley was consumptive.

4 **Nothing gives such weight and/ dignity to a book as a good appendix.**
Herodotus Quotation preceding the Appendix to *A Tramp Abroad* (1912) by Mark Twain

5 **The fine flower of stupidity blossoms in the attempt to appear less stupid.**
Anon. *Livres sans Nom* (Books without a Name; 1930), 'Twelve Reflections', collected in *Geoffrey Madan's Notebooks* ed. J. A. Gere and John Sparrow (1981)

6 **A good general rule is to state that the bouquet is better than the taste, and vice versa.**
Stephen Potter On wine-tasting. *One-Upmanship*, ch. 14 (1952)

7 **So Harry says, 'You don't like me any more. Why not?' And he says, 'Because you've got so terribly pretentious.' And Harry says, 'Pretentious? Moi?'**
John Cleese A Mr Johnson chatting to Sybil Fawlty in 'The Psychiatrist', *Fawlty Towers*, (TV series co-written with Connie Booth, 1975 and 1979)

8 **Pretension and imposture can carry a heavy charge of sexuality. Whose pulses ever race for what is natural?**
Howard Jacobson *Redback*, ch. 13 (1986)

9 **Before you advise anyone 'Be yourself!' reassess his character.**
Anon. Twentieth-century proverb quoted in *The Columbia Dictionary of Quotations* ed. Robert Andrews (1993)

10 **[Of 'the chattering classes when confronted with the incomprehensible'] They remember the first night of *The Rite of Spring*, and want to be remembered as the ones who cheered, not rioted; so they applaud everything they see, just to be on the safe side.**
Victor Lewis-Smith *Inside the Magic Rectangle*, 'Omnibus: Freeze' (1995)

Mind
Intelligence and Stupidity

1 **He has not so much brain as earwax.**
William Shakespeare Thersites speaking of Agamemnon in *Troilus and Cressida*, act 5, sc. 1 (1602)

2 **A knowledgeable fool is a greater fool than an ignorant fool.**
Molière Clitandre in *The Learned Ladies*, act 4, sc. 2 (1672)

3 **For fools rush in where angels fear to tread.**
Alexander Pope *An Essay on Criticism*, line 625 (1711)

4 **When a true genius appears in the world, you may know him by this sign, that the dunces are all in confederacy against him.**
Jonathan Swift *Thoughts on Various Subjects* (1711). In 1718 in 'To Mr Delany' Swift wrote: 'Hate by Fools, and fools to hate,/ Be that my motto and my fate.' In 1980 John Kennedy Toole's novel *A Confederacy of Dunces* appeared several years after he had committed suicide, and it won a Pulitzer Prize in 1981.

5 **A man may be very entertaining and instructive upon paper (said he), and exceedingly dull in common discourse. I have observed, that those who shine most in pri-**

vate company, are but secondary stars in the constellation of genius – A small stock of ideas is more easily managed, and sooner displayed, than a great quantity crowded together.

Tobias Smollett Letter from Jerry Melford to Sir Watkin Phillips dated 10 June, *The Expedition of Humphry Clinker* (1771)

6 Ignorance, madam, pure ignorance.

Samuel Johnson Asked why he had defined *pastern* as the 'knee' of a horse. (A pastern is part of a horse's foot.) From *The Life of Samuel Johnson* by James Boswell, vol. 1, p. 293 (1791); in G. B. Hill's edition of 1887, rev. L. F. Powell (1934). Boswell also notes that Johnson defined 'Windward' and 'Leeward' identically, even though they mean the opposite of each other.

7 The Cardinal [of Ravenna] is at his wits' end – it is true that he did not have far to go.

Lord Byron Letter to John Murray II of 22 July 1820, collected in *Letters and Journals*, vol. 8, *Born for Opposition* (1821), ed. Leslie A. Marchand (1978)

8 Major Yammerton was rather a peculiar man, inasmuch as he was an ass, without being a fool.

R. S. Surtees *Ask Mamma*, ch. 25 (1858)

9 A quaint fellow once said that he wondered much who that great scholar Mr Finis could be, whose name was almost to every book.

Anon. *The New London Jest Book*, 'Choice Jests', no. 872, ed. W. C. Hazlitt (1871)

10 'Excellent,' I cried. 'Elementary,' said he.

Sir Arthur Conan Doyle *The Memoirs of Sherlock Holmes*, 'The Crooked Man' (1894). In none of the Conan Doyle Holmes stories does Holmes say the words with which he is most associated, 'Elementary, my dear Watson', although in *Sherlock Holmes*, the play Conan Doyle wrote with William Gillette in 1902, he exclaims: 'Elementary, the child's play of deduction.'

11 MABEL CHILTERN: What sort of a woman is she?
LORD GORING: Oh! A genius in the daytime and a beauty at night.

Oscar Wilde *An Ideal Husband*, act 1 (1899)

12 James's uncle had just about enough brain to make a jay-bird fly crooked.

P. G. Wodehouse *The Man Upstairs*, 'Out of School' (1914)

13 Mediocrity knows nothing higher than itself, but talent instantly recognizes genius.

Sir Arthur Conan Doyle *The Valley of Fear*, ch. 1 (1915)

14 [Of Hercule Poirot] He tapped his forehead. 'These little grey cells. It's "up to them".'

Agatha Christie *The Mysterious Affair at Styles*, ch. 10 (1920) – the story in which Christie's detective Poirot first appears. He often referred to his 'little grey cells'. In *The Mystery of the Spanish Chest* (1960) we are told that he 'enjoyed making incomprehensible statements'.

15 He was good natured, obliging and immensely ignorant, and was endowed with a stupidity which by the least little stretch would go around the globe four times and tie.

Mark Twain *Autobiography*, ch. 46 (1924). Said of 'a lawyer from Dunkirk, New York', who drew up the contract by which Charles Webster would represent, as agent, Huckleberry Finn.

16 I am a Bear of Very Little Brain, and long words Bother me.

A. A. Milne Winnie-the-Pooh in *Winnie-the-Pooh*, ch. 1 (1926)

17 Owl hasn't exactly got Brain, but he Knows Things.

Ibid., ch. 9 (1926)

18 'Rabbit's clever,' said Pooh thoughtfully./ 'Yes,' said Piglet, 'Rabbit's clever.'/ 'And he has Brain.' 'Yes,' said Piglet, 'Rabbit has Brain.'/ There was a long silence. 'I suppose,' said Pooh, 'that's why he never understands anything.'

A. A. Milne *The House at Pooh Corner*, 'A Very Grand Thing' (1928)

19 I see the happy moron,/ He doesn't give a damn,/ I wish I were a moron,/ My God! Perhaps I am!

Anon. *Eugenics Review* July 1929

20 **Gentlemen, Chicolini here may talk like an idiot, and look like an idiot, but don't let that fool you. He really is an idiot.**
Groucho Marx Rufus T. Firefly (Groucho Marx) addressing a courtroom in *Duck Soup* (film, 1933, screenplay by Bert Kalmar, Arthur Sheekman, Nat Perrin and Harry Ruby, directed by Leo McCarey)

21 **[Schooboy, asked to define a vacuum] I have it in my head but can't express it.**
Anon. Quoted in *The Cheltenham Flyer* by W. G. Chapman, ch. 13, 'Vacuum Brake – Emergency Signal – Slip Coaches' (1934)

22 **'I guess you think I'm dumb,' Brody said./ 'Just average, for a grifter.'**
Raymond Chandler *The Big Sleep*, ch.3 (1939). The response is Philip Marlowe's.

23 **Her eyes were wide set and there was thinking room between them.**
Raymond Chandler Of Miss Harriet Huntress in *Trouble Is My Business* (1950)

24 **Affection's contempt for intelligence being well-known, the British heart being the solvent of the British brain.**
Philip O'Connor *Memoirs of a Public Baby*, pt 1, ch. 4 (1958)

25 **Rita was a natural for every beauty contest where personality was not a factor.**
Keith Waterhouse *Billy Liar*, ch. 3 (1959). She had won the title 'Miss Stradhoughton' and been voted by some American airmen 'The Girl We Would Most Like To Crash The Sound Barrier With'.

26 **You stupid boy!**
Jimmy Perry and David Croft Customary response of Captain Mainwaring (Arthur Lowe) to the naïve suggestions of seventeen-year-old Private Pike (Ian Lavender) in *Dad's Army* (TV series 1968–77, written by Jimmy Perry and David Croft)

27 **For a penguin to have the same size of brain as a man the penguin would have to be over sixty-six feet high.**
Monty Python team Dr Peaches Bartowicz (Michael Palin) in *Monty Python's Flying Circus* (episode 12, 3rd series, broadcast 11 January 1973)

28 **'There Ain't Half Been Some Clever Bastards'**
Ian Dury Song (1978)

29 **BALDRICK: Have you got a plan, my lord?**
BLACKADDER: Yes, I have, and it's so cunning you could brush your teeth with it.
Richard Curtis and Ben Elton *Blackadder 2* (TV series, 1985), 'Money'

30 **Genius is an infinite capacity for giving pain.**
Anon. Quoted in *A Gentleman Publisher's Commonplace Book*, 'Core', by John G. Murray (1996)

31 **The difference between genius and stupidity is that genius has its limits.**
Anon. *Away an' Ask Yer Mother (Your Scottish Father's Favourite Sayings)*, ch. 2, ed. Allan Morrison (2003)

States of Mind

1 **It's dogged as does it. It ain't thinking about it.**
Anthony Trollope Giles Hoggett, 'an old man from Hoggle End', in *The Last Chronicle of Barset*, ch. 61 (1867)

2 **Ask yourself whether you are happy, and you cease to be so.**
John Stuart Mill *Autobiography*, ch. 5 (1873)

3 **Everyone is more or less mad on one point.**
Rudyard Kipling *Plain Tales from the Hills*, 'On the Strength of a Likeness' (1888)

4 **A very weak-minded fellow I'm afraid, and, like the feather pillow, bears the marks of the last person who has sat on him!**
Earl Haig Referring to the 17th Earl of Derby in a letter to Lady Haig of 14 January 1918. Quoted in *Private Papers of Douglas Haig*, ch. 16, ed. Robert Blake (1952).

5 **There is only one difference**

between a madman and me. I am not mad.

Salvador Dali Entry for 15 July 1952, *The Diary of a Genius* (1966)

6 **Mental: Non-U for U *mad*.**

Nancy Mitford *Noblesse Oblige*, 'The English Aristocracy', ed. Nancy Mitford (1956)

7 **There's a rule saying I have to ground anyone who's crazy ... There's a catch. Catch-22. Anyone who wants to get out of combat duty isn't really crazy.**

Joseph Heller Doc Daneeka in *Catch-22*, ch. 5 (1961). The narrator explains: 'Orr was crazy and could be grounded. All he had to do was ask; and as soon as he did, he would no longer be crazy and would have to fly more missions.'

8 **I must be crazy to be in a looney bin like this.**

Jack Nicholson R. P. McMurphy (Jack Nicholson) in *One Flew over the Cuckoo's Nest* (film, 1975, directed by Milos Forman, screenplay by Lawrence Hauben and Bo Goldman, from the novel by Ken Kesey)

9 **This pig does not weigh as much as I believed, but I never thought it would.**

Matthew Parris 'An Irishman', quoted by Matthew Parris in *The Times* 13 April 1994, collected in *I Couldn't Possibly Comment* (1997)

Psychology

1 **Ful wys is he that kan hymselven knowe!**

Geoffrey Chaucer *The Canterbury Tales*, 'The Monk's Tale', (c.1387)

2 **A lunatic in Bedlam was asked how he came there. He answered, 'By a dispute.' 'What dispute?' The Bedlamite replied: 'The world said I was mad! I said the world was mad, and they outvoted me.'**

Anon. *The New London Jest Book*, 'Choice Jests', no. 580, ed. W. C. Hazlitt (1871)

3 **[Sir Roderick Glossop] is always called a nerve specialist, because it sounds better, but everybody knows** he's really a sort of janitor to the looney-bin.

P. G. Wodehouse *The Inimitable Jeeves*, ch. 7 (1923)

4 **Neurosis is the way of avoiding non-being by avoiding being.**

Paul Tillich *The Courage to Be*, pt 2, ch. 3 (1952)

5 **The discovery of phobias by psychiatrists has done much to clear the atmosphere. Whereas in the old days a person would say: 'Let's get the heck out of here!' today she says: 'Let's get the heck out of here! I've got claustrophobia!'**

Robert Benchley *Benchley or Else*, 'Phobias' (1958)

6 **A psychiatrist is a man who goes to the Folies Bergère and looks at the audience.**

Mervyn Stockwood Quoted in the *Observer* 15 October 1961

7 **The trouble with Freud is that he never played the Glasgow Empire Saturday night.**

Ken Dodd Quoted in *The Times* 7 August 1965. As Dodd understood it, 'Freud's theory was that when a joke opens a window and all those bats and bogeymen fly out, you get a marvellous feeling of relief and elation.'

8 **Any man who goes to a psychiatrist should have his head examined.**

Sam Goldwyn Quoted in *Moguls* by Norman Zierlod (1969)

9 **A fellow walks into the psychiatrist's with a poached egg on his head and a rasher of bacon on each foot, and he says: 'It's about my brother ...'**

Mike Burton *Laugh with the Comedians* (LP, 1971)

10 **He's done a great job on you. Your self-esteem is a notch below Kafka's.**

Woody Allen Isaac Davis (Woody Allen) speaking to Mary Wilke (Diane Keaton) of her therapist in *Manhattan* (film, 1979, written by Woody Allen and Marshall Brickman, directed by Woody Allen)

11 **Just think of me as one you never figured.**

Neil Young 'Powderfinger', *Rust Never Sleeps* (LP, 1979)

12 **Suzanne sighed . . . 'I think it was Freud who said that the way they determined if people were crazy was whether their insanity interfered with love and work. Those are the two areas. And we have no love and no work.'**

Carrie Fisher *Postcards from the Edge*, 'Dysphoria' (1987)

13 **A neurosis is a secret you don't know you're keeping.**

Kenneth Tynan *The Life of Kenneth Tynan*, ch. 19, by Kathleen Tynan (1987)

14 **There's nowt so queer as fowk.**

Anon. Traditional Yorkshire saying quoted in *Basic Broad Yorkshire: Sayings and Traditions* by Arnold Kellett (1991). A variant is 'Fowks is queer. The'r all queer b[a]r thee an me – / an' sometimes Ah'm nut so sewr abaht thee!'

15 **By handing over character analysis entirely to psychoanalysts and psychologists, we neglect the accumulated worldly wisdom of, say, GPs or prostitutes or clergymen, or even, dare I say it, palmists and astrologers, bookies and casino staff (who are often amazingly perceptive), hairdressers and restaurateurs.**

Lynn Barber *Mostly Men*, Introduction (1991)

16 **Q: How many psychiatrists does it take to change a lightbulb? A: One. But the lightbulb has to really want to change.**

Anon. *And I Quote*, 'Psychiatrists and Psychology', ed. Ashton Applewhite and others (1992)

17 **Psychiatry is the disease of which it claims to be the cure.**

Anon. Quoted in *A Gentleman Publisher's Commonplace Book*, 'Core', by John G. Murray (1996)

Memory

1 **Absent-minded professor to exstudent: 'Remind me, was it you or your brother who was killed in the war?'**

Anon. Quoted by Craig Brown in the *Daily Telegraph* 18 January 2003. Brown said that he came across this joke in various forms 'every few years', but believed that it first appeared, in essence, in *Wit and Mirth*, a collection of 1630 by John Taylor. The remark has also been attributed to William Archibald Spooner.

2 **Spent the afternoon in casting up my accounts, and do find myself to be worth £40 and more, which I did not think, but afraid that I have forgot something.**

Samuel Pepys Diary entry for 29 February 1660, *Everybody's Pepys* ed. Henry B. Wheatley (1926)

3 **Johnson had said that he could repeat a complete chapter of 'The Natural History of Iceland', from the Danish of Horrebow, the whole of which was exactly thus: – CHAP. LXXII *Concerning Snakes*. There are no snakes to be met with throughout the whole island.**

Samuel Johnson *The Life of Samuel Johnson* by James Boswell, vol. 3, p. 279 (1791); in G. B. Hill's edition of 1887, rev. L. F. Powell (1934)

4 **There is a wicked inclination in most people to suppose an old man decayed in his intellects. If a young or middle aged man, when leaving a company, does not recollect where he laid his hat, it is nothing; but if the same inattention is discovered in an old man, people will shrug up their shoulders, and say, 'His memory is going.'**

Ibid., vol. 4, p. 181

5 **I cannot sing the old songs now!/ It is not that I deem them low;/ 'Tis that I can't remember how/ They go.**

C. S. Calverley A version of 'The Old Songs', a ballad of 1865 by Claribel (or Mrs C. A. Barnard): 'I cannot sing the old songs/ I sang long year ago,/ For heart and voice would fail me,/ And foolish tears would flow.'

6 'It's a poor sort of memory that only works backwards,' the Queen remarked.

Lewis Carroll *Through the Looking Glass*, ch. 5 (1872)

7 I've a grand memory for forgetting, David.

Robert Louis Stevenson Alan Stewart in *Kidnapped*, ch. 18 (1886)

8 That is just the way with memory; nothing that she brings to us is complete. She is a wilful child; all her toys are broken. I remember tumbling into a huge dusthole, when a very small boy; and, if memory were all we had to trust to, I should be compelled to believe I was there still.

Jerome K. Jerome *The Idle Thoughts of an Idle Fellow*, 'On Memory' (1889)

9 'Tisn't beauty, so to speak, nor good talk necessarily. It's just It. Some women'll stay in a man's memory if they once walked down a street.

Rudyard Kipling *Traffics and Discoveries*, 'Mrs Bathurst' (1904)

10 [Of Mrs Disraeli] She is an excellent creature, but she can never remember which came first, the Greeks or the Romans.

Benjamin Disraeli *Collections and Recollections*, ch. 1, by G. W. E. Russell (1908)

11 The pellet with the poison's in the vessel with the pestle; the chalice from the palace has the brew that is true.

Danny Kaye Hawkins (Danny Kaye) in *The Court Jester* (film, 1956, directed and written by Norman Panama and Melvin Frank). He is making a doomed attempt to remember how to avoid drinking a poisoned drink. After some mishaps the instructions are changed to 'The pellet with the poison's in the flagon with the dragon; the vessel with the pestle has the brew that is true.'

12 We met at nine/ We met at eight. I was on time/ No, you were late/ Ah yes! I remember it well.

Alan Jay Lerner 'I Remember It Well' (song, 1957)

13 One always forgets the most important things. It's the things one can't remember that stay with you.

Alan Bennett Matron (impersonating Moggie) in *Forty Years On*, act 1 (1968)

14 Introduce yourselves, I can smell something burning.

Katherine Whitehorn Recommended formula for hostesses who have forgotten guests' names, *Whitehorn's Social Survival*, 'The Social Scene' (1968)

15 It is a lucky thing for the American moralist that our country has always existed in a kind of time-vacuum: we have no public memory of anything that happened before last Tuesday.

Gore Vidal *New York Times* 26 September 1970, collected in *The Essential Gore Vidal*, 'Drugs', ed. Fred Kaplan (1999)

16 . . . It being as hard to think of one season when you're in another as to remember one tune while whistling another.

Katherine Whitehorn *Observations*, ch. 34, 'Their Blessed Plots' (1970)

17 Sir, I have been commissioned by Michael Joseph to write an autobiography and I would be grateful to any of your readers who could tell me what I was doing between 1960 and 1974.

Jeffrey Bernard Letter in the *New Statesman* 18 July 1975

18 ERIC: I went to see the specialist last week about my loss of memory.
ERNIE: What did he do?
ERIC: He made me pay him in advance.

Eric Morecambe and Ernie Wise *The Morecambe and Wise Jokebook*, skit 21 (1979)

19 Am in Market Harborough. Where ought I to be?

G. K. Chesterton Telegram sent by G. K. Chesterton to his wife, quoted in *Words on the Air*, 'Memory', by John Sparrow (1981)

20 About four years ago, I was . . . No, it was yesterday . . .

Steven Wright *I Have a Pony* (CD, 1986)

21 **Critical member of congregation to preacher who read his sermon from notes: 'If *you* can't remember it, how do you expect us to?'**

Anon. Quoted in *Bishop's Brew (An Anthology of Clerical Humour)*, ch. 4, ed. Ronald Brown (1989)

22 **Q: What's good about having Alzheimer's? A: You can hide your own Easter eggs.**

Anon. *And I Quote*, 'Age and Ageing', ed. Ashton Applewhite and others (1992)

23 **Bill has cooked me some French toast. His family sends him maple syrup in gallon bottles and he is very generous with it. I must remember to like him.**

Daisy Waugh *A Small Town in Africa*, pt 3 (1994)

24 **I tried the all-whisky diet. I lost three days.**

Anon. Quoted in *Whisky Wit and Wisdom*, 'Drinking It', ed. Gavin D. Smith (2000)

Sleep and Dreams

1 **And so to bed.**

Samuel Pepys Diary entry for 29 May 1667, *Everybody's Pepys* ed. Henry B. Wheatley (1926). Pepys's habitual sign-off.

2 **It is probable that a trivial degree of indigestion will give rise to very fantastic dreams in a fanciful mind; while, on the other hand, a good orthodox repletion is necessary towards a fanciful creation in a dull one.**

Leigh Hunt 'Of Dreams', *The Indicator* 18 October 1820, collected in *Leigh Hunt as Poet and Essayist* ed. Charles Hunt (1891). He goes on to: 'The inspirations of veal in particular are accounted extremely Delphic: Italian pickles partake of the spirit of Dante.'

3 **Early to bed and early to rise/ Is the way to feel stupid and have red eyes.**

Shirley Brooks 'New Proverb', *Shirley Brooks' Wit and Humour* (1875)

4 **I hate a man who goes to sleep at once; there is a sort of indefinable**

something about it which is not exactly an insult, and yet is an insolence; and one which is hard to bear, too.

Mark Twain *A Tramp Abroad*, ch. 13 (1880)

5 **There ain't no way to find out why a snorer can't hear himself snore.**

Mark Twain *Tom Sawyer Abroad*, ch. 10 (1894)

6 **Don't wake him up. He's got insomnia. He's trying to sleep it off.**

Chico Marx Chico Marx in *A Night at the Opera* (film, 1935, written by George S. Kaufman and Morrie Ryskind, directed by Sam Wood)

7 **Q: Why do people go to bed? A: Because the bed won't come to them.**

Anon. *The Crack-a-Joke Book*, 'Leg Pullers', ed. Jane Nissen (1978)

8 **Life is something to do when you can't get to sleep.**

Fran Lebowitz *Observer* 21 January 1979

9 **ERNIE: For a start, I've got this terrible insomnia.
ERIC: Well, I wouldn't lose any sleep over it.**

Eric Morecambe and Ernie Wise *The Morecambe and Wise Jokebook*, skit 19 (1979)

10 **It was like one of those dreams you have when you're a child and you dream someone's given you a toy motorcar that can fly, and you wake up and it isn't even Saturday.**

Robert Robinson *The Dog Chairman*, 'How Not to Write Books' (1982)

11 **I knew a woman, she asked me if I slept good. I said, 'No, I made a few mistakes.'**

Steven Wright *I Have a Pony* (CD, 1986)

12 **Sleep is for wankers.**

Keith Moon Quoted in *Q* magazine February 2004

The Artistic Mind

1 **The poet ranks far below the painter in the representation of vis-**

ible things, and far below the musician in the representation of invisible things.

Leonardo da Vinci *Selections from the Notebooks of Leonardo da Vinci 1452–1519* ed. Irma A. Richter, p. 198 (1952)

2 If I cannot take a Pentonville omnibus and show it to be fine then I am not a fully equipped artist.

Arnold Bennett Letter to Frank Harris of 30 November 1908

3 As my poor father used to say/ In 1863,/ Once people start on all this Art/ Good-bye, moralitee!

A. P. Herbert *Lines for a Worthy Person* (1930)

4 Art – the one achievement of Man which has made the long trip up from all fours seem well advised.

James Thurber *Forum and Century* June 1939

5 There is only one position for an artist anywhere: and that is, upright.

Dylan Thomas *Quite Early One Morning*, pt 2, 'Wales and the Artist' (1954)

6 My dear Tristan, to be an artist *at all* is like living in Switzerland during a world war.

Tom Stoppard Henry Carr in *Travesties* (1975)

7 I believe entertainment can aspire to be art, and can become art, but if you set out to make art you're an idiot.

Steve Martin *Today*, 17 May 1989

Imagination and Inspiration

1 The names of all these places you have probably heard of, and you have only not to look in your Geography books to find out all about them.

Edward Lear The places being the dwelling places of the Seven Families of the Land of Gramblamable, including Lake Pipple-Popple, and the outskirts of the City of Tosh. *Nonsense Songs, Stories, Botany and Alphabets* (1871), ch. 1, 'The History of the Seven Families of the Lake Pipple-Popple'.

2 We know that the nature of genius is to provide idiots with ideas twenty years later.

Louis Aragon *Treatise on Style*, 'The Pen' (1928). He also said: 'Geniuses are like ocean liners: they should never meet.'

3 But it isn't easy. Because Poetry and Hums aren't things which you get, they're things which get *you*. And all you can do is to go where they can find you.

A. A. Milne Winnie the Pooh in *The House at Pooh Corner*, ch. 9 (1928)

4 Christopher Robin had spent the morning indoors going to Africa and back, and he had just got off the boat and was wondering what it was like outside, when who should come knocking at the door but Eeyore.

Ibid., ch. 1

5 Imagination can do any bloody thing, almost.

Samuel Butler *Selections from the Note-Books of Samuel Butler*, ch. 7, ed. A. T. Bartholomew (1930)

6 Genius is one per cent inspiration and ninety-nine per cent perspiration.

Thomas Alva Edison *Harper's Monthly* September 1932

7 The human imagination is much more capable than it gets credit for. This is why Niagara is always a disappointment when one sees it for the first time.

Mark Twain *Notebook*, ch. 26 (1935). 'One's imagination,' he goes on, 'has long ago built a Niagara to which this one is a poor, dribbling thing.'

8 Deprivation is for me what daffodils were for Wordsworth.

Philip Larkin *Required Writing*, p. 47 (1938)

9 Lying in bed, I abandoned the facts again and was back in Ambrosia.

Keith Waterhouse Narrator Billy Fisher, who lives in a fantasy world, in *Billy Liar*, ch. 1 (1959). Opening sentence of the book.

10 What I do is make people up and

then write songs about them.
They're much more interesting like
that and also you meet a better
class of person.

Jake Thackray *Jake's Progress*, 'Before I Was a
Performing Man . . .' (1977)

11 **Reality leaves a lot to the
imagination.**

John Lennon Attributed. Possibly spoken late
on in his life.

12 **We try not to have ideas, preferring
accidents.**

Gilbert and George *Independent* 17 April 1989

13 **He may have come up with the idea
for the recipe, but I came up with
the idea of charging $6.95 for it.**

Matt Groening Moe, the barkeeper in *The
Simpsons*, 'Flaming Moe's', first broadcast
21 January 1991. Homer Simpson has
invented a flaming cocktail that attracts a
lot of business to Moe's bar.

14 **He shows great imagination . . .
which should be curtailed at all
costs.**

Peter Ustinov Remark in a school report of
Peter Ustinov's, quoted in the London
Evening Standard 21 April 1994

Life and Death

*The Body and Its
Functions*

1 **My lord, we make use of you, not
for your bad legs, but for your good
head.**

Elizabeth I Remark addressed to William
Cecil, who had gout. Quoted in *Sayings of
Queen Elizabeth I* ed. Frederick Chamberlin
(1923)

2 **. . . I am escaped with the skin of
my teeth.**

Job 19:20, the Bible, Authorized Version (1611)

3 **. . . the very hairs of your head are
all numbered.**

Matthew 10:30, ibid.

4 **[At the theatre] . . . and here I sitting
behind in a dark place, a lady spit**

backward upon me by a mistake,
not seeing me; but after seeing her
to be a very pretty lady, I was not
troubled at it at all.

Samuel Pepys Diary entry for 28 January
1661, *Everybody's Pepys* ed. Henry B. Wheatley (1926)

5 **At thunder now no more I start,/
Than at the rumbling of a cart:/
Nay what's incredible, alack!/ I
hardly hear a woman's clack.**

Jonathan Swift 'On His Own Deafness', written 1734, collected in *Jonathan Swift: Selected
Poems* ed. Roland A. Jeffares (1992)

6 **Since everything is made for a purpose, everything must be for the
best possible purpose. Noses, you
observe, were made to support spectacles: consequently, we have spectacles.**

Voltaire *Candide*, ch. 1 (1759), part of the
highly optimistic 'metaphysico-theologo-
cosmolonigological' teachings of Dr
Pangloss

7 **I'm actually afraid of his lungs.**

Oliver Goldsmith Mrs Hardcastle in *She
Stoops to Conquer*, act 1, sc. 1 (1773), of her
son Tony Lumpkin. She probably means she
is afraid *for* his lungs – that he may be consumptive. Her husband Mr Hardcastle is
afraid *of* them, though, because Tony 'sometimes whoops like a speaking trumpet'.

8 **Mr Long's character is very *short*. It
is nothing. He fills a chair. He is a
man of genteel appearance, and
that is all.**

Samuel Johnson *The Life of Samuel Johnson*
by James Boswell, vol. 4, p. 81 (1791); in G. B.
Hill's edition of 1887, rev. L. F. Powell (1934).
The reference is to Mr Dudley Long, highly
rated as a wit by others.

9 **I have only one eye, – I have a right
to be blind sometimes . . . I really do
not see the signal!**

Lord Nelson Said in 1801 at the Battle of
Copenhagen, quoted in *The Life of Nelson*,
ch. 7 (1839), by Robert Southey

10 **A gentleman happening to turn up
against a house to make water, did
not see two young ladies looking
out of a window close by, until he**

heard them giggling; then looking towards them, he asked, what made them so merry? O! Lord, said one of them, a very *little thing* will make us laugh.

Anon. *Glasgow Magazine of Wit* (1803)

11 And so reversed the go is now, from what was once the gig, sir,/ That his lordship wears his hair, and my lady wears a wig, sir.

Anon. 'The Hobbies of the Times', *Oliver's Comic Songs* (1825?)

12 'If either of you saw my ankles,' she said, when she was safely elevated, 'say so, and I'll go home and destroy myself.'

Charles Dickens Miss Mowcher in *David Copperfield*, ch. 22 (1849), having just climbed on to a table top (she is a dwarf). Nobody did see them.

13 It is the entire man that writes and thinks, and not merely his head. His leg has often as much to do with it as his head – the state of his calves, his vitals and his nerves.

Leigh Hunt *Stories in Verse*, Preface (1855)

14 A person being asked what made him bald, said, *My hair*.

Anon. *The New London Jest Book*, 'Choice Jests', no. 35, ed. W. C. Hazlitt (1871)

15 Being kissed by a man who *didn't* wax his moustache was – like eating an egg without salt.

Rudyard Kipling *The Story of the Gadsbys*, 'Poor Dear Mama' (1889)

16 Tim Turpin he was gravel blind,/ And ne'er had seen the skies;/ For nature when his head was made,/ Forgot to dot his eyes.

Thomas Hood 'Tim Turpin', *Humorous Poems* (1893)

17 When he looked straight at you, you didn't know where you were yourself, let alone what he was looking at.

G. K. Chesterton James Welkin, a man with a squint, in *The Innocence of Father Brown*, 'The Invisible Man' (1911)

18 I'll thcream and thcream until I'm thick!

Richmal Crompton Violet Elizabeth Bott in

Still William, ch. 8 (1925). She had wanted William to play 'houth' with her. She was known for her scream. In *William in Trouble* Crompton tells us that it would 'have put a factory siren to shame'.

19 The body is but a pair of pincers set over a bellows and a stewpan and the whole fixed upon stilts.

Samuel Butler *Selections from the Note-Books of Samuel Butler*, ch. 1, ed. A. T. Bartholomew (1930)

20 What is man, when you come to think upon him, but a minutely set, ingenious machine for turning, with infinite artfulness, the red wine of Shiraz into urine?

Isak Dinesen *Seven Gothic Tales*, 'The Dreamers' (1934)

21 A good thing I brought my legs, huh?

Groucho Marx Line delivered by Groucho on being handed a load of books by Chico. *A Day at the Races* (film, 1937, screenplay by George Seaton, Robert Pirosh, George Oppenheimer).

22 Haven't I got big eyes, look? That's from my mother, looking all over England for my father.

Max Miller Recorded at the Finsbury Park Empire, London, 12 October 1942, reissued in *Max Miller: The Cheeky Chappie – All His Live Shows in the Late 30s, Early 40s* (CD, 2000)

23 I test my bath before I sit,/ And I'm always moved to wonderment/ That what chills the finger not a bit/ Is so frigid on the fundament.

Ogden Nash 'Samson Agonistes' (1942)

24 He's got one very poor eye but the other's got double vision it's so good.

Anon. Said by a 'comedy violinist' of her husband, Herbert, quoted in a letter of 20 August 1943 from Joyce Grenfell to Virginia Graham, collected in *Joyce and Ginnie: The Letters of Joyce Grenfell and Virginia Graham* ed. Janie Hampton (1997)

25 I'll dispose of my teeth as I see fit, and after they've gone I'll get along. I started off living on gruel, and by

God, I can always go back to it
again.

S. J. Perelman *Crazy Like a Fox*, 'Nothing but
the Tooth' (1944)

26 **God gave us eyelids: we can hide
the eyes/ From what is hideous or
horrifies./ I wonder greatly that in
recent years/ We've not grown little
flaps to close the ears.**

A. P. Herbert *Anywhere* (c.1948), quoted in
Look Back and Laugh, 'The Forties' (1960)

27 **The back of a head, seen at a ball,
can have a most agitating effect
upon a young girl, so different from
the backs of other heads that it
might be surrounded by a halo.**

Nancy Mitford *Love in a Cold Climate*, ch. 9
(1949)

28 **He watched his restless hands, surprised they had remembered to
come with him.**

V. S. Pritchett *Mr Beluncle*, ch. 15 (1951)

29 **I must admit my eyes ain't what
they used to be . . . No, they used to
be my ears.**

Spike Milligan Henry Crun in *The Goon Show*,
'The Mysterious Punch-up-the-Conker', first
broadcast 7 February 1957

30 **Your right leg I like. I like your
right leg. A lovely leg for the role.
That's what I said when I saw you
come in. I said, 'A lovely leg for the
role.' I've got nothing against your
right leg. The trouble is – neither
have you.**

Peter Cook From the sketch 'One Leg Too
Few' first performed by Peter Cook and
Dudley Moore in 1960, quoted in *Peter Cook:
A Biography*, ch. 3, by Harry Thompson
(1997). Moore was playing Mr Spiggott, a
one-legged man eagerly auditioning for the
role of Tarzan; Cook was a diplomatic theatrical agent. In 1993 Cook said of this sketch:
'I've never written anything better.' In 1990
Jonathan Miller noted 'the sudden leakage
that occurs between the figurative, on the
one hand, and the concrete meaning.
Through Peter's comic timing what happens
is a catastrophic and sudden and abrupt per-
meability between these previously completely separate categories.'

31 **You're nothing else but a wild animal, when you come down to it.
You're a barbarian. And to put the
old tin lid on it, you stink from
arse-hole to breakfast time.**

Harold Pinter Mick speaking to Davies in *The
Caretaker*, act 3 (1960)

32 **Webster was short and handsomish,
with ill-cut straight brown hair and
grey eyes, all in all a bit of a ladies'
man, one bit in particular.**

Spike Milligan *Puckoon*, ch. 3 (1963)

33 **'Don't worry 'bout yer old genitals,
lad,' said the old man, 'they'll stand
up fer themselves.'**

Ibid., ch. 2

34 **You never heard such silence.**

Harold Pinter Max in *The Homecoming*, act 1
(1965)

35 **It's a funny thing – I cut my
fingernails all the time, and every
time I think to cut them, they need
cutting. Now, for instance. And yet,
I never, to the best of my knowledge, cut my toenails.**

Tom Stoppard Rosencrantz in *Rosencrantz
and Guildenstern Are Dead*, act 1 (1967)

36 **All legs leave *something* to be
desired, do they not? That is part of
their function and all of their charm.**

Alan Bennett Lady D in *Forty Years On*, act 1
(1968)

37 **It's not your teeth that are decay-
ing. It's you.**

Anon. Quentin Crisp's dentist, quoted in *The
Naked Civil Servant*, ch. 29 (1968)

38 **I use the sauna from time to time.
I'm fortunate in being blessed with
the ability to sweat in the everyday
course of events.**

David Mamet Danny Shapiro in *Sexual Perver-
sity in Chicago* (1974). In another Mamet play,
Duck Variations, '3rd Variation', George says:
'The purpose of sweat is, in itself, not clear.'

39 **She did *look* deaf, didn't she?**

Ibid.

40 **The ear may be a dust trap, but
when it comes to keeping your sun-**

glasses on, it has clear advantages over a drawing-pin pressed into the side of your head.

Alan Coren *Punch* September 1975

41 I can't think of anything more repulsive than the sight of a man with nothing on. All that hideous bundle.

Ben Travers *The Bed before Yesterday*, act 1, sc. 3 (1975)

42 Long-legged girls are fascinating – built for walking through grass.

Laurie Lee *Observer*, 'Sayings of the Week', 10 July 1977

43 Did you know there's no proper name for the back of the knees?

Viv Stanshall Reg Smeaton, boring news-agent in *Sir Henry at Rawlinson End* (LP, 1978). 'Did you know that the elephant shrew never closes its eyes?' is another one of his.

44 She had more legs than a bucket of chicken.

Steve Tyler Of a teenage girl sometime in the 1970s, quoted in *Q* magazine April 2000

45 Brown tits ¾ on show'll/ scotch the lies they're not her own/ Death's the only gigolo'll/ rumble that they're silicone.

Tony Harrison *The Bonebard Ballads, Continuous*, 'Flying Down to Rio: A Ballad of Beverly Hills' (1981)

46 Is there such a thing as a smelling aid?

Arthur Marshall *Smile Please*, 'Through the Nose' (1982). His sense of smell had 'completely atrophied'.

47 Take your cap off, Patrick, so that the wind can blow the dandruff from your hair.

Anon. Quoted in *Word of Mouth*, 'Eavesdroppings', ed. Nigel Rees (1983)

48 There's no such thing as bad pussy. Ladies might think they've got a bad pussy . . . I'd like to see them after the show, to give them a second opinion.

Richard Pryor *Here and Now* (live video, 1983)

49 Oh God! This place stinks like a pair

of armoured trousers after the Hundred Years War.

Richard Curtis and Ben Elton Blackadder (Rowan Atkinson) in *Blackadder 2* (TV series, 1985), 'Money'

50 For many years my father kept a chart on how to eliminate the waste of time. If your hair is short you don't have to brush it. I calculate that at the end of the day you've saved a day over people with long hair.

Tony Benn *Spectator* October 1987, repr. in *The Penguin Book of Interviews* ed. C. Silvester (1993). Benn described himself as 'a short-haired socialist rather than a long-haired one'. The interview was conducted by Susan Barnes in April 1965 for the *Sun*. She submitted it to Benn, who deemed it 'the bitchiest, most horrible thing I've ever read', and asked her not to publish. The article then lay dormant for twenty-two years.

51 Remember to look both ways before crossing your eyes.

Roger McGough 'The Stowaways', collected in *Funny Stories* ed. Michael Rosen (1991)

52 Funny noises are not funny.

Matt Groening Bart Simpson's punishment is to write this many times on the blackboard in *The Simpsons*, 'Black Widower', first broadcast 8 April 1992

53 HANNAH: Chaps sometimes wanted to marry me, and I don't know a worse bargain. Available sex against not being allowed to fart in bed.

Tom Stoppard Hannah Jarvis in *Arcadia*, act 2, sc. 5 (1993)

54 Isn't the scrotum an ugly bugger? It's like a hairy brain.

Billy Connolly Delivered during his twenty-two-night run at the Hammersmith Apollo, London, in 1994

55 Seeing an X-ray is like seeing a photograph of the future. I had met my skeleton for the first time . . .

Hugo Williams *Freelancing*, 'Lucky to Be Alive' (1995)

56 Q: What is funny about legs? A: The bottom is at the top.

Anon. 'A riddle from a lady of 92', *A Gentle-*

man *Publisher's Commonplace Book*, 'Delightful Oddities', by John G. Murray (1996)

57 **Being a woman is worse than being a farmer – there is so much harvesting and crop spraying to be done: legs to be waxed, underarms shaved, eyebrows plucked, feet pumiced, skin exfoliated and moisturized, spots cleansed, roots dyed . . .**
Helen Fielding *Bridget Jones's Diary* (1996), entry for Sunday 15 January

58 **Mort was interested in lots of things. Why people's teeth fitted together so neatly, for example. He'd given that one a lot of thought.**
Terry Pratchett *The Death Trilogy*, 'Mort', p. 14 (1998; first publ. 1988)

59 **I went to the dentist. He said my teeth were all right, but my gums had to come out.**
Tommy Cooper *The Very Best of Tommy Cooper*, vol. 1 (cassette, 1999)

60 **The length of the film should be directly related to the endurance of the human bladder.**
Sir Alfred Hitchcock Attributed remark, cited in *Cassell's Movie Quotations* ed. Nigel Rees (2nd edn 2002)

61 **Men are judged as the sum of their parts while women are judged as some of their parts.**
Julie Burchill Quoted in *Women's Wicked Wit* ed. Michelle Lovric (2000)

62 **If I ever met Keith Richards again, I'd say, 'Listen, I don't want to talk to you, I want to interview your liver!'**
Nick Kent *Vogue* May 2003. Keith Richards is sometimes known as 'two livers'.

63 **Other people's house smells hit you harder when you're not supposed to be there.**
D. B. C. Pierre *Vernon God Little*, act 2, ch. 13 (2003)

Health and Illness

1 **To cure the mind's wrong bias, spleen,/ Some recommend the bowling green;/ Some hilly walks: all exercise/ Fling but a stone, the giant dies.**
Matthew Green 'The Spleen' (1737), collected in *Wit and Humour of the Poets* ed. Leigh Hunt (1882)

2 **But let not little men triumph upon knowing that Johnson was an HYPOCHONDRIACK . . .**
James Boswell *The Life of Samuel Johnson* by James Boswell, vol. 1, p. 65 (1791); in G. B. Hill's edition of 1887, rev. L. F. Powell (1934)

3 **My sore throats are always worse than anyone's.**
Jane Austen Mary Musgrove in *Persuasion*, ch. 18 (1818)

4 **'The gout, sir,' replied Mr Weller, 'the gout is a complaint as arises from too much ease and comfort. If ever you're attacked with the gout, sir, jist you marry a widder as has got a good loud woice, with a decent notion of usin' it, and you'll never have the gout agin.'**
Charles Dickens Tony Weller in *The Pickwick Papers*, ch. 20 (1837)

5 **'What's the reason,' said Mr Squeers, deriving fresh facetiousness from the bottle; 'what's the reason of rheumatics? What do they mean? What do people have 'em for – eh?'**
Charles Dickens *Nicholas Nickleby*, ch. 57 (1838–9)

6 **A person seldom falls sick, but the bystanders are animated with a faint hope that he will die.**
Ralph Waldo Emerson *The Conduct of Life*, 'Considerations by the Way' (1860)

7 **The loikes of us is always wat [wet] – that is barring the insides of us. It comes to us natural to have the rheumatics.**
Anthony Trollope Giles Hogget, 'an old man from Hoggle End', in *The Last Chronicle of Barset*, ch. 61 (1867)

8 'Don't give me any more emetics,' said Pat to his physician; 'they do me no good; I have taken two already, and neither of them would stay upon my stomach.'

Anon. *The New London Jest Book*, 'Choice Jests', no. 609, ed. W. C. Hazlitt (1871)

9 To get back my youth I would do anything in the world, except take exercise, get up early, or be respectable.

Oscar Wilde Lord Henry Wotton in *The Picture of Dorian Gray*, ch. 19 (1891)

10 No gentleman ever takes exercise.

Oscar Wilde Algernon Moncrieff in *The Importance of Being Earnest*, act 2 (1895)

11 Lost: A troublesome cough. Last heard of about six o'clock on Wednesday night, when the owner purchased a box of Koffnot Lozenges.

Anon. Advertisement, *Halifax Evening Courier* 2 May 1905

12 'Ye can call it influenza if ye like,' said Mrs Machin. 'There was no influenza in my young days. We called a cold a cold.'

Arnold Bennett *The Card*, ch. 8 (1911)

13 'There is no such thing as rheumatism,' said Miss Gilpet.

Saki *The Chronicles of Clovis*, 'The Quest' (1911)

14 Also said to be dying is Ronnie Knox. I went to visit him at a hospital in the City Road, EC1, which had without compromise painted across the front in enormous letters 'St Mark's Hospital for Diseases of the Rectum'.

Evelyn Waugh Letter to Katherine Asquith of June? 1936, collected in *The Letters of Evelyn Waugh* ed. Mark Amory (1980). Knox was a writer, and the Catholic chaplain at Oxford University 1926–39. Waugh wrote his biography in 1959.

15 Early to rise and early to bed/ Makes a male healthy and wealthy and dead.

James Thurber *New Yorker* 18 February 1939

16 One of the minor pleasures in life is to be slightly ill.

Harold Nicolson *Observer* 1950, quoted in *The Penguin Dictionary of Modern Humorous Quotations* ed. Fred Metcalf (2nd edn 2001)

17 Old remedies were the best. Had not the leeks sewn in the waistband of his long underwear staved off leprosy?

Spike Milligan *Puckoon*, ch. 11 (1963)

18 Piles is piles, and you'll know soon enough when you catch them because your insides'll drop out and you'll die and then where will you be?

Alan Bennett Nanny in *Forty Years On*, act 1 (1968). Her charge, Boy, has been sitting on hot pipes.

19 It was a cough that carried her off,/ It was a coffin they carried her off in.

Anon. Untitled poem collected in *The Faber Book of Nonsense Verse* ed. Geoffrey Grigson (1979)

20 A child that has a cold we may suppose/ Like wintry weather – Why? – It blows its nose.

Thomas Dibdin 'Last Days of the Last of the Three Dibdins', collected in ibid.

21 Exercise: Cures all illnesses except those it causes.

Henry Root *Henry Root's World of Knowledge* (1982)

22 DR LEECH: Mmm, I think you're in luck, though. An extraordinary new cure has just been developed for exactly this kind of sordid problem.
BLACKADDER: It wouldn't have anything to do with leeches, would it?

Richard Curtis and Ben Elton 'Bells', *Blackadder* 2 (TV series, 1985). Blackadder continues: 'Just, I've never had anything you doctors didn't try to cure with leeches.' (*Blackadder* 2 was set in Elizabethan times.)

23 I do have to be careful about my health, because I have a grumbling ovary which once flared up in the middle of *The Gondoliers*.

Victoria Wood 'Kitty: One', sketch from *Victoria Wood as Seen on TV* (TV series, 1985), collected in *Up to You, Porky – The Victoria Wood Sketch Book* (1985). Kitty is described as 'fifty-three, from Manchester and proud of it'.

24 **We 'need' cancer because, by the very fact of its incurability, it makes all other diseases, however virulent, *not* cancer.**
Gilbert Adair *Myths and Memories*, 'Under the Sign of Cancer' (1986)

25 **This Week's Cause of Cancer in the *Sunday Times* is bracken, the spores of which are said to affect the lungs.**
Alan Bennett Diary entry for 15 November 1987, publ. in *Writing Home: Diaries 1980– 1990* (1994)

26 **A friend of mine said, 'You want to go to Margate, it's good for rheumatism.' So I did, and I got it.**
Tommy Cooper TV show, collected in *Tommy Cooper: Just Like That!* (video, 1993)

27 **ME, that pernicious disease which cruelly attacks the well-to-do, rendering them incapable of physical effort (curiously, ME never seems to strike, say, subsistence farmers in the poorer parts of Africa).**
Victor Lewis-Smith *Inside the Magic Rectangle*, 'Natural Neighbours' (1995)

28 **Paul McGrath limps on water.**
Anon. Banner waved in 1997 by Derby fans, referring to their frequently injured Irish defender. Quoted in *The Book of Football Quotations*, 'This Supporting Life', ed. Phil Shaw (1999).

29 **You show me something that doesn't cause cancer, and I'll show you something that isn't on the market yet.**
George Carlin *Brain Droppings* (1997)

30 **[Of medicines] This one is quick acting, but this one is long lasting. When do I need to feel good: now or later? That's a tough question.**
Jerry Seinfeld *I'm Telling You for the Last Time* (CD, 1998)

31 **I went to the doctor, and I said: 'It hurts me when I do that.' He said, 'Well don't do it.'**
Tommy Cooper Perennial Cooper favourite, in *The Very Best of Tommy Cooper*, vol. 1 (cassette, 1999)

32 **The only exercise I get these days is walking behind the coffins of my friends who take exercise.**
Peter O'Toole Quoted in the *Observer* 1 August 1999

33 **You don't have cancer, it has you.**
Ian Dury *The Times*, 'Quotes of the Week', 1 April 2000. It was the week Dury died.

34 **So I went to the doctor's and he said 'You've got hypochondria.' I said, 'Not that as well!'**
Tim Vine *Loose Ends* (BBC radio series, 2000), quoted in *The Penguin Dictionary of Modern Humorous Quotations*, ed. Fred Metcalf (2nd edn 2001)

35 **Health nuts are going to feel stupid someday, lying in hospital dying of nothing.**
Redd Foxx Quoted in ibid.

36 **The time was that malignant fivishness to which the flu sufferer awakens after late-afternoon fever dreams.**
Jonathan Franzen *The Corrections*, 'At Sea' (2001)

37 **What's the worst thing about having a lung transplant? . . . Having to bring up someone else's phlegm.**
Jeff Green *The A–Z of Living Together*, 'Xmas' (2002)

38 **Polio fucked up my body a little bit . . . If I close my eyes, my left side, I really don't know where it is – but over the years I've discovered that almost one hundred per cent for sure it's gonna be very close to my right side . . . probably.**
Neil Young Quoted in *Shakey – Neil Young's Biography*, 'Mr Blue and Mr Red', by Jimmy McDonough (2002)

39 **Hypochondria's the only disease I haven't got.**
Anon. Joke overheard in a South Devon pub, September 2003

Birth and Babies

1 What a strange thing is the propagation of life! – A bubble of Seed which may be spilt in a whore's lap – or in the Orgasm of a voluptuous dream – might (for aught we know) have formed a Caesar or a Buonaparte.

Lord Byron 'Detached Thoughts', no. 102, collected in *Letters and Journals*, vol. 9, *In the Wind's Eye (1821–22)*, ed. Leslie A. Marchand (1979)

2 [Of his birth] I was annoyed when I saw the way they treated me. Instead of turning me over and over, and upside down, and playing lawn tennis with me on the bed quilt, I think father might at least have lent me a pair of trousers to go on with.

Dan Leno *Dan Leno Hys Booke*, Chapter First (1899)

3 All the way home on the boat he was moaning that when he got to England he would have to go and see his sisters, and he didn't know how he was going to face it, because all of them were knee-deep in babies which he would be expected to kiss.

P. G. Wodehouse *Uncle Dynamite*, ch. 6 (1948). Bill Oakshott is speaking of Major Brabazon-Plank, who had once been severely injured whilst judging a bonny baby competition.

4 I was born because it was a habit in those days, people didn't know anything else.

Will Rogers *The Autobiography of Will Rogers*, ch. 1 (1949)

5 I was born at a very early age. As a matter of fact, I was two when I was born, I remember it very well.

Gerard Hoffnung Delivered during a series of radio interviews with Charles Richardson in 1951, collected in *Hoffnung – A Last Encore* (cassette, 1973)

6 Indeed it is clear that babies are by nature one-up. Whatever they do it is your fault and your fault only.

Stephen Potter *Supermanship*, ch. 2 (1958)

7 [Fletcher (Ronnie Barker) reassuring McLaren (Tony Osoba) on the matter of his illegitimacy]
FLETCHER: Plenty of famous people have been born out of wedlock: William the Conqueror, Leonardo da Vinci, Lawrence of Arabia, Napper Wainwright.
MCLAREN: Napper Wainwright?
FLETCHER: He was a screw at Brixton. Mind you he *was* a bastard.

Dick Clement and Ian La Frenais *Porridge* (TV series, 1974–7)

8 Birth was the death of him.

Samuel Beckett Opening words of *A Piece of Monologue* (1979)

9 Ballads and babies. That's what happened to me.

Paul McCartney 'On Turning Fifty' *Time* 8 June 1992

10 It goes without saying that you should never have more children than you have car windows.

Erma Bombeck Quoted in *Women's Wit and Wisdom* (1991)

11 With the birth of each child, you lose two novels.

Candida McWilliam *Guardian* 5 May 1993

12 I described in exquisite detail the twenty-hour labour, the progression from planned water birth with Vivaldi playing to lying in stirrups, fanny to the wind, all hope and dignity gone as I pleaded for anyone with a steady hand to give me an epidural and/or kill me quickly.

Meera Syal *Life Isn't All Ha Ha Hee Hee*, ch. 5 (1999)

13 They say that men can never experience the pain of childbirth. They can if you hit them in the goolies with a cricket bat for fourteen hours.

Jo Brand Quoted in *Women's Wicked Wit* ed. Michelle Lovric (2000)

14 When I had my baby, I screamed and screamed. And that was just during conception.

Joan Rivers Quoted in ibid.

15 I had no idea how traumatic the whole process of childbirth is . . . and it's tough on the women as well.

Jack Dee Observation made in a trailer for a TV programme about childbirth, 15 May 2003

16 [Definition of a baby] A loud noise at one end and no sense of responsibility at the other.

Ronald Knox Attributed

Parenthood

1 He that hath children, all his morsels are not his owne.

George Herbert *Outlandish Proverbs*, no. 423 (1640)

2 I wish either my father or my mother, or indeed both of them, as they were in duty both equally bound to it, had minded what they were about when they begot me.

Laurence Sterne The opening lines of *Tristram Shandy* (1759–67), bk 1, ch. 1

3 Illness apart, parental anxieties begin when a child begins to walk; for beginning to walk is beginning to tumble. It is defiance of gravitation, and Newton is sometimes avenged.

Samuel Palmer Letter to Mrs Julia Robinson of 9 December 1872

4 They fuck you up, your mum and dad./ They may not mean to, but they do./ They fill you with the faults they had/ And add some extra just for you.

Philip Larkin 'This Be the Verse' (1974)

5 Cleaning your house while your kids are still growing is like shovelling the walk before it stops snowing.

Phyllis Diller Quoted in *Violets and Vinegar*, 'I Liked You Better Smaller', ed. Jilly Cooper and Tom Hartman (1980)

6 I'm sorry you are wiser,/ I'm sorry you are taller;/ I liked you better foolish/ And I liked you better smaller.

Aline Kilmer 'For the Birthday of a Middle-aged Child', quoted in ibid.

7 There's something about getting married and having children that turns ordinary people into . . . parents. Here's a young man and a young woman who have been putting their feet up on furniture all their lives. They have one child, and suddenly feet on furniture is a crime worse than arson.

P. J. O'Rourke *The Bachelor Home Companion*, ch. 9 (1987)

8 Q MAGAZINE: Who's the better father, you or your dad?
   HOMER SIMPSON: I'm a better dad, cos when I strangle my son, the marks don't show.

Matt Groening Cartoon character Homer Simpson 'interviewed' in *Q* magazine June 2003

9 It suddenly occurs to me what parenthood has most in common with: childhood. The defining experience of both parenthood and childhood is the same: helplessness.

Tim Lott *The Love Secrets of Don Juan*, ch. 7 (2003)

Childhood and Youth

1 I don't know what Scrope Davies meant by telling you I liked Children, I abominate the sight of them so much that I have always had the greatest respect for the character of *Herod*.

Lord Byron Letter to Augusta Leigh in *Letters and Journals*, vol. 2, *Famous in My Time (1810–12)*, ed. Leslie A. Marchand (1973)

2 I never see any differences in boys. I only know two sorts of boys. Mealy boys and beef-faced boys.

Charles Dickens Mr Grimwig in *Oliver Twist*, ch. 4 (1838)

3 [Of youth] **Far too good to waste on children.**

George Bernard Shaw Attributed

4 **He was, for a start, only about twenty-five years old, although grown old with quick experience, like forced rhubarb.**

Keith Waterhouse Of Mr Shadrack the under-taker in *Billy Liar*, ch. 2 (1959)

5 **Like so many infants of tender years he presented to the eye the aspect of a mass murderer suffering from an ingrowing toenail.**

P. G. Wodehouse *A Few Quick Ones*, 'Leave it to Algy' (1959). In a similar vein, the follow-ing from *Eggs, Beans and Crumpets*, 'Sonny Boy' (1940): 'The infant was looking more than ever like some mass-assassin who has been blackballed by the Devil's Island Social and Outing Club as unfit to associate with the members.'

6 **It is still quite possible to stand in a throng of children without once detecting even the faintest whiff of an exciting, rugged after-shave or cologne.**

Fran Lebowitz *Metropolitan Life*, 'Children: Pro or Con?' (1979)

7 **Remember that as a teenager you are at the last stage in your life when you will be happy to hear that the phone is for you.**

Fran Lebowitz *Social Studies*, 'Tips For Teens' (1981)

8 **The smile of a child as he starts for school,/ Is a bit restrained as a gen-eral rule./ The teacher's smile, in the same way tends/ To droop a bit as the holiday ends./ But the smile much wider than the others,/ As the summer riot ends, is Mother's.**

Anon. Quoted in *Laughter Lines: Family Wit and Wisdom*, 'Angels or Devils', ed. Rev. James A. Simpson (1987)

9 **The real truth about children is they don't speak the language very well.**

P. J. O'Rourke *The Bachelor Home Com-panion*, ch. 9 (1987)

10 **It is only rarely that one can see in a little boy the promise of a man, but one can almost always see in a little girl the threat of a woman.**

Alexandre Dumas Attributed. Quoted in *Who Said What* ed. John Daintith and others (1988)

11 **Don't be cool. It's very boring.**

Stephen Fry Advice to pupils at his old school, Uppingham. *The Times*, 'Quotes of the Week', 17 October 1998, collected in *The Times Quotes of the Week*, introduced by Philip Howard (2002).

12 **Adults may only enter with a child. If you see an adult who happens to be on their own please contact a member of Coram's staff.**

Anon. Sign outside Coram's Fields, a park in London WC1

Growing Up

1 **At twenty years of age, the will reigns; at thirty, the wit; at forty, the judgement.**

Benjamin Franklin *Poor Richard's Almanac* (1758), entry for June 1741

2 **Youth is a blunder; Manhood a struggle; Old Age a regret.**

Benjamin Disraeli *Coningsby*, bk 3, ch. 1 (1844)

3 **A greenery-yallery, Grosvenor Gal-lery, foot-in-the-grave young man!**

W. S. Gilbert Bunthorne in *Patience*, act 2 (1881)

4 **The post on her left was occupied by Mr Erskine of Treadley, an old gentleman of considerable charm and culture, who had fallen, how-ever, into bad habits of silence, hav-ing, as he explained once to Lady Agatha, said everything he had to say before he was thirty.**

Oscar Wilde *The Picture of Dorian Gray*, ch. 3 (1891). He is to the left of the Duchess of Harley.

5 **The only excuse I can make for him is that he was very young – not yet four and twenty – and that in mind as in body, like most of those who**

in the end come to think for themselves, he was a slow grower.

Samuel Butler *The Way of All Flesh*, ch. 61 (1903). The 'he' is Ernest Pontifex, hero of the novel.

6 At my time of life I really ought to be able to rely on myself to say, 'I don't read French; and I have never ridden a horse.'

Max Beerbohm Letter of 23 July 1906 to Reggie Turner, collected in *Letters to Reggie* ed. Rupert Hart-Davis (1964). Beerbohm was thirty-four.

7 I have measured out my life with coffee spoons.

T. S. Eliot 'The Love Song of J. Alfred Pru-frock' (1917)

8 Every one should keep a mental waste-paper basket and the older he grows the more things he will consign to it – torn up to irrecoverable tatters.

Samuel Butler *Selections from the Note-Books of Samuel Butler*, ch. 7, ed. A. T. Bartholomew (1930)

9 I should never keep a diary, it is too much numbering one's days.

Robert Robinson *Landscape with Dead Dons*, ch. 16 (1956)

10 Do engine drivers, I wonder, eternally wish they were small boys?

Flann O'Brien *The Best of Myles*, 'Waama, etc.' (1968)

11 When I was a child, what I wanted to be when I was grown up was an invalid.

Quentin Crisp *The Naked Civil Servant* (1968)

12 Maturity is a high price to pay for growing up.

Tom Stoppard Gale in *Where Are They Now?* (BBC radio play, 1973). He also says: 'Childhood is Last Chance Gulch for Happiness.'

13 I used to be Snow White – but I drifted.

Mae West Quoted in *Peel Me a Grape*, p. 47, by Joseph Weintraub (1975)

14 **WORKMAN 1:** He'll be starting shaving next.
WORKMAN 2: Then spend the rest

of his life trying to stop the bleeding.

Jack Rosenthal *P'Tang, Yang, Kipperbang* (TV play, 1983). The subject is fourteen-year-old Alan.

15 Inside every human being in my opinion is a twelve- to fourteen-year-old.

Jeffrey Katzenberg *Observer*, 'Sayings of the Week', 17 December 1989. Katzenberg was President of Walt Disney at the time.

16 A critical faculty is a terrible thing. When I was eleven there were no bad films, just films that I didn't want to see, there was no bad food, just Brussels sprouts and cabbage, and there were no bad books – everything I read was great.

Nick Hornby *Fever Pitch*, 'England!' (1992)

17 I don't seem to have been a useful age since I was eight and finally old enough to have my own bicycle. After that it seems to have been pretty much downhill.

Sandi Toksvig *Flying under Bridges*, ch. 1 (2001)

18 The older I get, the better I was.

Anon. T-shirt slogan spotted in Ibiza and quoted in *The Times* 28 September 2002

The Generation Gap

1 Age is deformed, youth unkind,/ We scorn their bodies, they our mind.

Thomas Bastard *Chrestoleros*, bk 7, epigram 9 (1598)

2 What can a young lassie, what shall a young lassie,/ What can a young lassie do wi' an auld man?

Robert Burns 'What Can a Young Lassie Do wi' an Auld Man?' (1792)

3 And sigh that one thing only has been lent/ To youth and age in common – discontent.

Matthew Arnold 'Youth's Agitations' (1852)

4 Every generation laughs at the old

fashions, but follows religiously the new.

Henry David Thoreau *Walden; or, Life in the Woods*, 'Economy' (1854)

5 **I am fond of children (except boys).**

Lewis Carroll Letter of 1879 to Kathleen Eschwege, aged twelve. Quoted in *Lewis Carroll*, ch. 28, by Michael Bakewell (1996).

6 **When I was a boy of fourteen, my father was so ignorant I could hardly stand to have the old man around. But when I got to be twenty-one, I was astonished at how much he had learned in seven years.**

Mark Twain Attributed

7 **Children are like jam: all very well in the proper place, but you can't stand them all over the shop – eh, what?**

E. Nesbit *The Wouldbegoods*, ch. 1 (1901). The opinion of the Bastable children's Indian uncle.

8 **The denunciation of the young is a necessary part of the hygiene of older people, and greatly assists in the circulation of their blood.**

Logan Pearsall Smith *Afterthoughts*, 'Age and Death' (1931). Pearsall Smith also said: 'What music is more enchanting than the voices of young people, when you can't hear what they say?'

9 **Children aren't happy with nothing to ignore,/ And that's what parents were created for.**

Ogden Nash *Happy Days*, 'The Parent' (1973)

10 **I think children shouldn't be seen or heard.**

Jo Brand Quoted in *Women's Wicked Wit* ed. Michelle Lovric (2000)

11 [Of the similarity between teenage children and their grandparents] **They're both on drugs, they both detest you, and neither of them have got a job.**

Jasper Carrott *Daily Telegraph* 7 January 2004

12 **Tonight we honor a man old enough to be his own father.**

George Burns Attributed

Middle Age

1 **I am past thirty, and three parts iced over.**

Matthew Arnold Letter of 12 February 1853, *The Letters of Matthew Arnold to Hugh Clough* ed. Howard Foster Lowry (1932)

2 **As an old buck is an odious sight, absurd, and ridiculous before gods and men; cruelly, but deservedly, quizzed by you young people, who are not in the least duped by his youthful airs or toilette artifices, so an honest, good-natured, straight-forward, middle-aged, easily pleased Fogy is a worthy and amiable member of society.**

William Makepeace Thackeray *Travels in London* 'On the Pleasures of Being a Fogy', pt 2 (1853)

3 **From forty to fifty a man is at heart either a stoic or a satyr.**

Arthur Pinero *The Second Mrs Tanqueray*, act 1 (1893)

4 **Thirty-five is a very attractive age. London society is full of women of the very highest birth who have, of their own free choice, remained thirty-five for years.**

Oscar Wilde Lady Bracknell in *The Importance of Being Earnest*, act 4 (1895)

5 **Mr Salteena was an elderly man of forty-two.**

Daisy Ashford *The Young Visiters*, ch. 1 (1919)

6 **I'm like a backward berry/ Unripened on the vine,/ For all my friends are fifty/ And I'm only forty-nine.**

Ogden Nash *The Private Dining-room and Other Verses*, 'The Calendar-Watchers' (1952)

7 **After fifty, one ceases to digest; as someone once said, 'I just ferment my food now.'**

Henry Green *Now Dig This: The Unspeakable Writings of Terry Southern, 1990–95*, 'Writers at Work: Henry Green', ed. Nile Southern and Josh Alan Friedman (2001). Southern's conversation with Green was published originally in the *Paris Review* in 1958.

8 A man shouldn't fool with booze until he's fifty; then he's a damn fool if he doesn't.

William Faulkner *William Faulkner of Oxford*, p. 110 (1965)

9 Middle age is when wherever you go on holiday you pack a sweater.

Denis Norden *Observer*, 'Sayings of the Week', 18 January 1976, collected in *The Observer Sayings of the Week* ed. Valerie Ferguson (1978)

10 I have always loved jokes. I loved them when I was very young and I still love them now that I'm . . . well, now that I'm . . . er . . . still very young.

Tim Brooke-Taylor *The Crack-a-Joke Book*, Introduction, ed. Jane Nissen (1978)

11 I'm forty-two, she's seventeen. I'm older than her father. I'm dating a girl wherein I can beat up her father – that's the first time that phenomenon's ever occurred.

Woody Allen Isaac Davis (Woody Allen) to Yale (Michael Murphy) in *Manhattan* (film, 1979, screen play by Woody Allen and Marshall Brickman, directed by Woody Allen)

12 It now takes me all night to do what I used to do all night.

Anon. Attributed to a photographer on a local newspaper married to 'a pretty woman thirty years his junior'. *Nobody Hurt in Small Earthquake*, ch. 3, by Michael Green (1990).

13 I'm aiming by the time I'm fifty to stop being an adolescent.

Wendy Cope *Daily Telegraph* 9 December 1992

14 Do you think we ought to get some hormone replacement packs in for emergencies, darling? One day you could come home, sweety, and find me just a toothless old wad of gum on the floor.

Jennifer Saunders 'Birthday', first broadcast 1992, *Absolutely Fabulous* (BBC TV sitcom, 1992–6)

15 [After meeting a female fan] She said she was approaching forty, and I couldn't help wondering from what direction.

Bob Hope Quoted in the *Independent* 26 July 2003

Old Age

1 A good old man, sir; he will be talking: as they say, 'when the age is in, the wit is out.'

William Shakespeare Said of Verges by Dogberry, in *Much Ado About Nothing*, act 3, sc. 5 (1598)

2 Thou shouldst not have been old till thou hadst been wise.

William Shakespeare The Fool in *King Lear*, act 1, sc. 5 (1605)

3 Every man desires to live long; but no man would be old.

Jonathan Swift *Miscellanies in Prose and Verse*, 'Various Thoughts Moral and Diverting' (1711)

4 When folks git ole en strucken wid de palsy, dey mus spec ter be laff'd at.

Joel Chandler Harris *Nights with Uncle Remus*, ch. 23 (1883)

5 There's many a good tune played on an old fiddle.

Samuel Butler Mrs Jupp in *The Way of All Flesh*, ch. 61 (1903)

6 Nothing really wrong with him – only anno domini, but that's the most fatal complaint of all, in the end.

James Hilton Said of Mr Chips by Dr Merivale in *Goodbye, Mr Chips*, ch. 1 (1934)

7 All I have to live on now is macaroni and memorial services.

Margot Asquith Entry for 16 September 1943, quoted in *Chips: The Diaries of Sir Henry Channon* ed. Robert Rhodes James (1993)

8 A man in his eightieth year does not want to do things.

Winston Churchill To Lord Moran (Churchill's doctor) in 1954, quoted in *Churchill: A Brief Life*, ch. 14, by Piers Brendon (2001)

9 MINNIE BANNISTER: Did you take your male hormone pills?
HENRY CRUN: Yes Min, they give me the strength to go to sleep, Min.

Spike Milligan *The Goon Show* (BBC radio

series), 'I Was Monty's Treble', first broadcast 10 November 1958. The quavery geriatrics living in sin converse in bed.

10 **In a dream you are never eighty.**

Anne Sexton *All My Pretty Ones*, 'Old' (1962)

11 **Will you still need me, will you still feed me,/ When I'm sixty-four?**

John Lennon and Paul McCartney 'When I'm Sixty-Four' (song, 1967, from the LP *Sergeant Pepper's Lonely Hearts Club Band*)

12 [Explanation of the cause of Groucho Marx's death] **Too many birthdays.**

Andy Marx Groucho died 19 August 1977, aged eighty-seven. This remark, made by his grandson, was quoted in *The Essential Groucho* by Stefan Kanfer, ch. 17, 'Everybody Has a Temperature' (2000).

13 **The wrinkled retainer hung up his greasy fez on a peg, and with joints crackling like the screwing up of plastic egg cartons hacked and ooh-arhh-thricketed his way out into the hall.**

Viv Stanshall *Sir Henry at Rawlinson End* (LP, 1978)

14 **'Oh to be eighty again!'**

Anon. Remark made by 'a really very ancient male American', quoted in *Smile Please*, 'Cheese It, Sly Boots!' (1982) by Arthur Marshall

15 **I am no longer young. You might have suspected that.**

Ronald Reagan Address to students at St John's University, New York, 28 March 1985. Quoted in *Ronald Reagan: The Wisdom and Humour of the Great Communicator*, 'Visions of America', ed. Frederick J. Ryan Junior (1995).

16 **Believe me, at my age it's hard to find anything I haven't done before. And even harder to do it.**

George Burns *All My Best Friends*, ch. 1 (1989)

17 **Surely nothing could be that funny.**

George Melly On being told by Mick Jagger that his wrinkles were laughter lines. Quoted in the *Independent on Sunday* 1 January 1995, but many dates have appeared for this.

18 **I recently turned sixty. Practically a third of my life is over.**

Woody Allen *Observer*, 'Sayings of the Week', 10 March 1996

19 **I have been asked to pose for *Penthouse* on my hundredth birthday. Everybody is going to be sorry.**

Dolly Parton Quoted in *Women's Wicked Wit* ed. Michelle Lovric (2000)

20 **DOCTOR: You're going to live to be eighty.**
PATIENT: I am eighty!
DOCTOR: What did I tell you?

Anon. Quoted in *The Penguin Dictionary of Humorous Quotations* ed. Fred Metcalf (2nd edn 2001)

21 **Growing old is compulsory. Growing up is optional.**

Bob Monkhouse *Sun* 30 December 2003

22 [On being asked whether he felt his life had gone by quickly] **Honey, it's been like smoke through a keyhole.**

Jack Nicholson *Daily Telegraph* 4 February 2004

23 **Dover for the continent, Eastbourne for the incontinent.**

Anon. Quoted in *Inside the Magic Rectangle*, 'Without Walls: Heigh Ho!' by Victor Lewis-Smith

Death

1 **Thus march we, playing, to our latest rest,/ Only we die in earnest – that's no jest.**

Sir Walter Raleigh 'On the Life of Man' (1612)

2 **One dies only once, and it's for such a long time!**

Molière Mascarille in *The Amorous Quarrel*, act 5, sc. 4 (1662)

3 **And when we're worn,/ Hack'd, hewn with constant service, thrown aside/ To rust in peace, or rot in hospitals.**

Thomas Southerne Arbanes in *The Loyal Brother*, act 1 (1682)

4 **Life is a jest; and all things show it./ I thought so once; but now I know it.**

John Gay 'My Own Epitaph' (1720)

5 **It is impossible that anything so natural, so necessary, and so univer-**

sal as death, should ever have been designed by Providence as an evil to mankind.

Jonathan Swift *Works*, vol. 15, *Thoughts on Religion* (1765)

6 Let him go abroad to a distant country; let him go to some place where he is *not* known. Don't let him go to the devil where he *is* known!

Samuel Johnson After Boswell had asked whether a man should commit suicide if he knows he is about to be detected in a fraud. *The Journal of a Tour to the Hebrides* (1785) entry for 18 February 1773.

7 This is no time for making new enemies.

Voltaire On being asked, on his deathbed in 1778, to renounce the devil. Attributed.

8 I have seen a thousand graves opened – and always perceived that whatever was gone – the *teeth and hair* remained of those that had died with them – Is not this odd? – they go the very first things in youth – & yet last the longest in the dust.

Lord Byron Letter of 18 November 1820 to John Murray II, collected in *Letters and Journals*, vol. 7, *Between Two Worlds* (1820), ed. Leslie A. Marchand (1977)

9 Men talk of killing time while time quietly kills them.

Dion Boucicault *London Assurance*, act 2, sc. 1 (1841)

10 Thou shalt not kill; but need'st not strive/ Officiously to keep alive.

Arthur Hugh Clough 'The Latest Decalogue' (1862)

11 Die, my dear Doctor, that's the last thing I shall do!

Lord Palmerston Attributed last words

12 When you're wounded and left on Afghanistan's plains/ And the women come out to cut up what remains/ Just roll to your rifle and blow out your brains/ And go to your Gawd like a soldier.

Rudyard Kipling 'The Young British Soldier' (1892)

13 To lose one parent may be regarded as a misfortune . . . to lose both seems like carelessness.

Oscar Wilde Lady Bracknell in *The Importance of Being Earnest*, act 1 (1895)

14 The report of my death was an exaggeration.

Mark Twain *New York Journal* 2 June 1897. This usually appears as 'Reports of my death have been greatly exaggerated.'

15 To die would be an awfully big adventure.

J. M. Barrie *Peter Pan*, act 3 (1904). A film called *An Awfully Big Adventure* was made in 1994 – it had nothing to do with death.

16 Waldo is one of those people who would be enormously improved by death.

Saki *Beasts and Super Beasts*, 'The Feast of Nemesis' (1914)

17 They ought to have some law to pierce the heart and make sure or an electric clock or a telephone in the coffin and some kind of canvas airhole. Flag of distress.

James Joyce *Ulysses*, ch. 6 (1922). As the gravediggers throw the earth on to the coffin, Bloom reflects that Paddy Dignam may not be dead after all.

18 Razors pain you;/ Rivers are damp;/ Acids stain you;/ And drugs cause cramp./ Guns aren't lawful;/ Nooses give;/ Gas smells awful;/ You might as well live.

Dorothy Parker *Enough Rope*, 'Résumé' (1926)

19 It's a funny old world – a man's lucky if he can get out of it alive.

W. C. Fields *You're Telling Me* (film, 1934, screenplay by Walter de Leon, Paul M. Jones, directed by Erle C. Kenton)

20 So here it is at last, the distinguished thing!

Henry James On experiencing his first stroke. Quoted in *A Backward Glance* by Edith Wharton, ch. 14 (1934).

21 Death must be distinguished from dying, with which it is often confused.

Sydney Smith Quoted in *The Smith of Smiths* by H. Pearson, ch. 11 (1934)

22 **Either he's dead or my watch has stopped.**

Groucho Marx Dr Hackenbush (Groucho Marx) in *A Day at the Races* (film, 1937, screenplay by Robert Pirosh, George Seaton and George Oppenheimer, directed by Sam Wood). According to Stefan Kanfer in his book *The Essential Groucho* (2000), the line was originally 'Is he dead or is my watch stopped?'; but the Marx Brothers changed it, having learned that 'statements were often funnier than investigations'.

23 **It is never necessary to commit suicide, especially when you may live to regret it.**

Winston Churchill Remark addressed to Harold Macmillan c.1952, in which Churchill conceded his willingness to make political concessions in order to stay in office. Quoted in *Winston Churchill, A Brief Life*, ch. 12, by Piers Brendon (2001).

24 **In reality, killing time/ Is only the name for another of the multifarious ways/ By which Time kills us.**

Sir Osbert Sitwell 'Milordo Inglese' (1958)

25 **[Of death:] Nature's way of telling you to slow down.**

Anon. American life insurance slogan quoted in *Newsweek* 25 April 1960

26 **There are a small army of men living in London today, who spend their time studying the columns of *The Times* so as to be sure to turn up at the right Memorial Services. They are safe: the dead cannot protest against their friendship.**

Duke of Bedford *The Duke of Bedford's Book of Snobs*, 'On Illness' (1965), written in collaboration with George Mikes

27 **If this is dying, then I don't think much of it.**

Lytton Strachey Deathbed comment, quoted in *Lytton Strachey* by Michael Holroyd, vol. 2, pt 2, ch. 6 (1968)

28 **Alas, Peacock, I'd love to come but I'm committing suicide on Friday.**

Derek (Deacon) Lindsay Response to a party invitation from Kenneth Tynan ('Peacock'), recorded by Tynan in a diary entry for 22 May 1972, *The Diaries of Kenneth Tynan* ed. John Lahr (2001). Tynan thought this was a joke, but when Lindsay failed to appear at the party, Tynan telephoned him. Lindsay groggily stated that he had taken ten Seconal, adding, 'Picture my surprise when, an hour ago, my eyes opened on yet another grey London afternoon.'

29 **Dying is a very dull, dreary affair. And my advice to you is to have nothing whatever to do with it.**

Somerset Maugham Quoted in *Escape from the Shadows*, ch. 5, by Robin Maugham (1972)

30 **It's not that I'm afraid to die, I just don't want to be there when it happens.**

Woody Allen Kleinman in 'Death (A Play)', publ. in *Without Feathers* (1976)

31 **Death, where is thy victory?/ Grave, where is thy sting?/ When I snuff it bury me quickly/ Then let carousels begin . . .**

Jake Thackray 'The Last Will and Testament of Jake Thackray' (song), *Jake's Progress* (1977). The first two lines are based on I Corinthians 15:55.

32 **Death has got something to be said for it:/ There's no need to get out of bed for it;/ Wherever you may be/ They give it to you, free.**

Kingsley Amis 'Delivery Guaranteed' (1979). In *Getting Even* (1972) Woody Allen said: 'On the plus side, death is one of the few things that can be done as easily lying down.'

33 **Suicide is no more than a trick played on the calendar.**

Tom Stoppard Purvis in *The Dog It Was That Died* (BBC radio play, 1982). The sentiment is expressed in a posthumous letter.

34 **She's dead! My God, I'd better get her to a cemetery right away!**

Steve Martin and Carl Reiner Dr Hfuhruhurr in *The Man with Two Brains* (film 1983, directed by Carl Reiner)

35 **There is nothing like a morning funeral for sharpening the appetite for lunch.**

Arthur Marshall *Life's Rich Pageant*, 'Scene One' (1984). It was his father's funeral.

36 **Good career move.**

Gore Vidal After the death in 1984 of

Truman Capote, who'd long since run out of steam as a writer. Attributed.

37 **I could never bear to be buried with people to whom I had not been introduced.**

Norman Parkinson Quoted in his obituary in the *Guardian* 16 February 1990

38 **So You're Going to Die**

Matt Groening Title of a pamphlet given to Homer Simpson by Dr Hibbert in *The Simpsons*, 'One Fish, Two Fish, Blowfish, Blue Fish', first broadcast 24 January 1991

39 **'Do you remember finding out about that?' he asked earnestly. 'That you were going to die? Not you, particularly – everyone.'/ Cora raised her eyebrows in mock astonishment. 'Am I? God, if I'd known that, I would've worn something completely different.'**

Carrie Fisher *Delusions of Grandma*, p. 17 (1994 paperback edn)

40 **Have the good taste to die.**

Anon. Harvey Two-Face (Tommy Lee Jones) to Batman (Val Kilmer) in *Batman Forever* (film, 1995, directed by Joel Schumacher, screenplay by too many to mention). Two-Face is bailing out of a blazing helicopter in which Batman remains.

41 **Indecisive about committing suicide? Then hang yourself with a bungee rope.**

Viz *Viz – The Full Toss (A Corking Compendium of Issues 70 to 75)* (1997)

42 **DEATH RULED 'UNAVOIDABLE'**

Anon. Headline from the *Seattle Times* 9 July 1997, cited in *The Fortean Times*, issue 177 (2003)

43 **My own view during the deepest and darkest night-time of the soul was to end it all, but the usual irritating thought that I wouldn't be there to see the effect curtailed enthusiasm.**

Mavis Cheek *Getting Back Brahms*, ch. 1 (1997)

44 **It's worth remembering that in practice you can't fall any faster than terminal velocity, which for a human being is about 130mph, which is, history shows, fast enough.**

John Lanchester *Mr Phillips*, 2.1 (2000)

45 **We're all cremated equal.**

Goodman Ace Quoted in *The Penguin Dictionary of Modern Humorous Quotations* ed. Fred Metcalf (2nd edn 2001)

46 **My favourite piece of information is that Branwell Brontë, brother of Emily and Charlotte, died standing up leaning against a mantelpiece, in order to prove it could be done.**

Douglas Adams *The Salmon of Doubt*, 'The Universe', 'The Little Computer That Could' (2002)

47 **Death is a terrible thing. The trouble is, the next day you're so bloody stiff.**

Bob Monkhouse Bob Monkhouse discussing his cancer on *Parkinson* (TV series), 19 October, 2002

48 **[Asked whether he'd prefer burial or cremation] Surprise me.**

Bob Hope Quoted in the *Independent* 26 July 2003. Hope also said: 'Dying is to be avoided – it can ruin your whole career.'

49 **I told you I was ill.**

Spike Milligan This was Milligan's idea, mentioned throughout his career, of a good inscription for a tombstone. Quoted in the *Daily Telegraph* 21 April 2003 in a news story about what appeared to be a family dispute over the headstone of Milligan's grave in St Thomas's Church, Winchelsea, East Sussex.

50 **The best way to commit suicide is Russian roulette: that way you make an enjoyable game of it.**

Simon Nye Ken Morley (Rex) in *Hardware* (ITV comedy series, March 2003 onwards)

51 **Mr S. Hussein seems to have resigned to spend more time with his ancestors.**

Mark Steyn Suspecting that Saddam Hussein had been killed during the early stages of the Second Gulf War. *Spectator* 5 April 2003.

2

Society

Social Relations
Friendship and Enmity

1 It's very much *your* affair when the house next door is ablaze.

Horace *Epistles*, bk 1, no. 18 (*c.* 20 BC), *Horace: Satires and Epistles; Persius: Satires* trans. and ed. Niall Rudd (1973)

2 I always fight with a man before I make him my friend; and if once I find he will fight, I never quarrel with him afterwards.

George Farquhar Captain Brazen in *The Recruiting Officer*, act 3, sc. 2 (1706)

3 Malice is of a low stature but it hath very strong arms.

George Savile, 1st Marquess of Halifax *Political, Moral, and Miscellaneous Thoughts and Reflections*, 'Of Prerogative, Power and Liberty' (1750)

4 This is Liberty-hall, gentlemen.

Oliver Goldsmith Mr Hardcastle in *She Stoops to Conquer*, act 2, sc. 1 (1773)

5 Mrs Montagu had dropt me. Now, sire, there are people one should like very well to drop, but would not wish to be dropped by.

Samuel Johnson *The Life of Samuel Johnson* by James Boswell, vol. 4, p. 73 (1791); in G. B. Hill's version of 1887, rev. L. F. Powell (1934)

6 I was angry with my friend;/ I told my wrath, my wrath did end./ I was angry with my foe:/ I told it not, my wrath did grow.

William Blake *Songs of Experience*, 'A Poison Tree' (1794)

7 Business, you know, may bring money, but friendship hardly ever does.

Jane Austen *Emma*, ch. 34 (1816)

8 Give me the avowed, erect and manly foe;/ Firm I can meet, perhaps return the blow;/ But of all the plagues, good Heaven, thy wrath can send,/ Save me, oh, save me, from the candid friend.

George Canning 'New Morality', collected in *The British Satirist* (1826)

9 **My idea of an agreeable person is a person who agrees with me.**
Benjamin Disraeli Hugo Bohun in *Lothair*, ch. 41 (1870)

10 **If there is one person I do despise more than another, it is the man who does not think exactly the same on all topics as I do.**
Jerome K. Jerome *The Idle Thoughts of an Idle Fellow*, 'On Eating and Drinking' (1889)

11 **A man cannot be too careful in the choice of his enemies. I have not got one who is a fool.**
Oscar Wilde Lord Henry Wotton in *The Picture of Dorian Gray*, ch. 1 (1891)

12 **The holy passion of friendship is of so sweet and steady and loyal and enduring a nature that it will last through a whole lifetime, if not asked to lend money.**
Mark Twain *The Tragedy of Pudd'nhead Wilson*, ch. 8, 'Pudd'nhead Wilson's Calender' (1894)

13 **If you value a man's regard, *strive* with him. As to *liking*, you like your newspaper – and despise it.**
George Bernard Shaw Letter to Ellen Terry of 25 September 1896

14 **The more people one knows, the easier it becomes to replace them.**
E. M. Forster Margaret Schlegel in *Howards End*, ch. 15 (1910)

15 **Here's another nice mess you've gotten me into.**
Oliver Hardy Ollie (Oliver Hardy) in *The Laurel–Hardy Murder Case* (film, 1930, directed by James Parrott). 'My candidate for the worst of their short films,' wrote Charles Barr in his filmography of 1967 *Laurel and Hardy*, but it featured the first use of the catchphrase that would later occur in various of their films, always uttered by the pompous Oliver to the eternally bumbling Stan. The words are usually misquoted as 'another fine mess', which was the title of a Laurel and Hardy short released in 1930 – 'a film which deserves to be better known', according to Barr.

16 **My sad conviction is that people can only agree about what they're not really interested in.**
Bertrand Russell *New Statesman* 1 July 1939,
quoted in *Geoffrey Madan's Notebooks*, 'Aphorisms and Reflections', ed. J. A. Gere and John Sparrow (1981)

17 **Ooh, you are awful . . . but I like you!**
Dick Emery This was Emery's catchphrase, which he always delivered while dressed as a big-busted dolly-bird called Mandy stopped in the street by a TV reporter. Mandy would always detect some double entendre in her interlocutor's words, at which she would affectionately shove him to the ground as she said the line. It was used on Emery's TV shows throughout the 1960s and 70s.

18 **It was announced that the trouble was not 'malignant' . . . It was a typical triumph of modern science to find the only part of Randolph [Churchill] that was not malignant and remove it.**
Evelyn Waugh Entry for March 1964, publ. in *The Diaries of Evelyn Waugh* ed. Michael Davie (1976)

19 **[Of friends] God's apology for relations.**
Hugh Kingsmill *The Best of Hugh Kingsmill*, Introduction, by Michael Holroyd (1970)

20 **The friends of the born nurse/ Are always getting worse.**
W. H. Auden 'Shorts, 1929–31', *W. H. Auden: Collected Poems* ed. Edward Mendelson (1976)

21 **I do not believe that friends are necessarily the people you like best, they are merely the people that got there first.**
Peter Ustinov *Dear Me*, ch. 5 (1977)

22 **I wrote this book called *How to Get Along with Everyone*. I didn't write it by myself, I wrote it with this other asshole jerk.**
Steve Martin 'Language', *A Wild and Crazy Guy* (LP, 1978). His other books, he claimed, include *How to Make Money off the Mentally Ill* and *How I Turned A Million in Real Estate into Twenty-five Dollars in Cash*.

23 **Champagne for my real friends, real pain for my sham friends.**
Francis Bacon Quoted in *Francis Bacon: Anatomy of an Enigma*, ch. 9 (1996), by Michael

Peppiatt. This was, according to Peppiatt, Bacon's habitual cry when ordering drinks at the Colony Club, Soho, from its opening in 1948 onwards. In his autobiography *Life's Rich Pageant* Arthur Marshall recalls being bullied in the 1920s at school by a boy who would pull down on his side-whiskers crying 'Sham pain', then yank them upwards crying 'Real pain!'

24 **It's nice to get stabbed in the front for a change.**

Terry Venables As manager of the Australian national football team, he received a generally hostile press. Line delivered in 1997, quoted in *The Book of Football Quotations*, 'Just about Managing', ed. Phil Shaw (1999).

25 **You only need four friends to carry your coffin.**

Sir Alex Ferguson Remark made on it being suggested to him that the footballing hero Kenny Dalglish didn't have many friends. Quoted in the *Daily Telegraph* 2 September 2003.

26 **My friend he comes to borrow cash,/ I often lend him tin,/ So if he finds me in, I'm out;/ But if I'm out, I'm in.**

Anon. 'In and Out', *Pearson's Book of Fun*, 'Capital Verses', ed. Mr X (n.d.)

Domesticity

1 **The House shewes the owner.**

George Herbert *Outlandish Proverbs*, no. 8 (1640)

2 **Love and a cottage! Eh, Fanny! Give me indifference and a coach and six!**

George Colman the Elder and David Garrick *The Clandestine Marriage*, act 1 (1766)

3 **Thus first necessity invented stools,/ Convenience next suggested elbow-chairs,/ And luxury the accomplish'd sofa last.**

William Cowper *The Task*, bk 1, 'The Sofa' (1785)

4 **I did not think he ought to be shut up. His infirmities were not noxious to society. He insisted on people praying with him; and I'd as lief pray with Kit Smart as anyone**

else. **Another charge was that he did not love clean linen; and I have no passion for it.**

Samuel Johnson *The Life of Samuel Johnson* by James Boswell, vol. 1, p. 397 (1791); in G. B. Hill's edition of 1887, rev. L. F. Powell (1934). Christopher Smart, the poet, had been locked up for being mad.

5 **Whenever we visit a man for the first time, we contemplate the features of his knocker with the greatest curiosity, for we all know, that between the man and his knocker, there will be a greater or less degree of resemblance and sympathy.**

Charles Dickens *Sketches by Boz*, ch. 7, 'Our Next Door Neighbour' (1836)

6 **Woman alone can organize a drawing room; man sometimes succeeds in a library.**

Benjamin Disraeli *Coningsby*, bk 3, ch. 2 (1844)

7 **A man is . . . so in the way in the house!**

Elizabeth Gaskell *Cranford*, ch. 1 (1853)

8 **A man, who wanted to get rid of his house, carried about a stone of it as a specimen.**

Anon. *The New London Jest Book*, 'Choice Jests', no. 182, ed. W. C. Hazlitt (1871)

9 **A home without a cat – and a well-fed, well-petted, and properly revered cat – may be a perfect home, perhaps, but how can it prove title?**

Mark Twain *The Tragedy of Pudd'nhead Wilson*, ch. 1 (1894)

10 **The General was essentially a man of peace, except in his domestic life.**

Oscar Wilde Lady Bracknell in *The Importance of Being Earnest*, act 4 (1895)

11 **I want a house that has got over all its troubles; I don't want to spend the rest of my life bringing up a young and inexperienced house.**

Jerome K. Jerome *They and I*, ch. 11 (1909)

12 **Addresses are given to us to conceal our whereabouts.**

Saki *Reginald in Russia*, 'Cross Currents' (1910)

13 **Home is the place where, when you have to go there,/ They have to take you in.**
Robert Frost 'The Death of the Hired Man' (1914)

14 **Well, you've got some nick-nacks here all right, I'll say that. I don't like a bare room.**
Harold Pinter Davies in *The Caretaker*, act 1 (1960)

15 **In domestic life space is all.**
Evelyn Waugh Letter to Ann Fleming of 5 September 1960, collected in *The Letters of Evelyn Waugh* ed. Mark Amory (1980)

16 **. . . staying at home broadens the mind.**
George Mikes *How to Unite Nations*, 'Down with Travel' (1963)

17 **There was no need to do any housework at all. After the first four years the dirt doesn't get any worse.**
Quentin Crisp *The Naked Civil Servant*, ch. 15 (1968). Squalor was Crisp's 'natural setting . . . I slid out of bed in the morning like a letter from an envelope.'

18 **Yellow checkers for the kitchen/ Climbing ivy for the bath/ She is lost in *House and Gardens*/ He's caught up in *Chief of Staff* . . .**
Joni Mitchell 'Harry's House – Centerpiece', *The Hissing of Summer Lawns* (LP, 1975)

19 **I hate housework! You make the beds, you do the dishes – and six months later you have to start all over again.**
Joan Rivers Quoted in *Woman Talk*, 'Work', ed. Michele Brown and Ann O'Connor (1984)

20 **A home gives you something to do around the house.**
P. J. O'Rourke *The Bachelor Home Companion*, ch. 2 (1987)

21 **A real cowboy has a five-dollar house and a forty-dollar saddle.**
Anon. *And I Quote*, 'Cowboys', ed. Ashton Applewhite and others (1992)

22 **I got home the other night, and the wife was crying her eyes out. I said, 'What's the matter?' She said, 'I'm homesick.' I said, 'This *is* your home.' She said, 'I know, I'm sick of it.'**
Tommy Cooper *The Very Best of Tommy Cooper*, vol. 1 (cassette, 1999)

23 **A man who is slovenly and untidy is considered normal.**
Germaine Greer *The Times* 27 February 1999

24 **The [Neighbourhood] Watch generally see themselves as the armed wing of the parish council.**
Guy Browning *Guardian*, 'How to . . .' column, 16 November 2002

25 **A bonfire will give off smoke in direct proportion to the irritability of your neighbours.**
Ibid., 28 December 2002

26 **If you have a combined toilet and bathroom, your partner may, occasionally, ask to pee while you're cleaning your teeth . . . let it happen, but don't be alarmed when she says she just needs a 'tinkle' and then makes a noise like an elephant jet-washing a milk tanker.**
Jeff Green *The A–Z of Living Together*, 'Bonding' (2002)

27 **It's not an apartment. It's a fucking *comp*artment. I should have read the fucking ad better.**
Bill Hicks 'New York Apartment', *Love Laughter and Truth* (CD, 2002)

28 **If we moved in next door to you, your lawn would die.**
Lemmy Remark made *c.* 1975, quoted in the *Daily Telegraph* 11 October 2002. In the same interview Lemmy recalled that Motorhead had been cited in the *Guinness Book of Records* as 'the loudest band ever'.

29 **Q: How many men does it take to change a loo roll? A: Nobody knows, it's never been done.**
Anon. Women's joke heard somewhere in Canada in 2003

Family

1 **My son – and what's a son? A thing begot/ Within a pair of minutes,**

thereabout,/ A lump bred up in darkness.

Thomas Kyd Hieronimo in *The Spanish Tragedy*, act 3, sc. 11 (1592)

2 Now that you are become an Aunt, you are a person of some consequence & must excite great Interest whatever You do. I have always maintained the importance of Aunts as much as possible, & I am sure of your doing the same now.

Jane Austen Letter to Caroline Austen of 30 October 1815, collected in *Jane Austen's Letters* ed. Dierdre Le Faye (1995)

3 I should, many a good day, have blown my brains out, but for the recollection that it would have given pleasure to my mother-in-law.

Lord Byron Letter to Thomas Moore of 28 January 1817. He had recently been left by Annabella Milbanke, whom he had married in 1815. The depression referred to arose from the stress of composing *Childe Harold*.

4 There was an old soldier of Bicester/ Was walking one day with his sister,/ A bull, with one poke,/ Toss'd her into an oak,/ Before the old gentleman miss'd her.

Anon. Untitled. Collected, dated 1822, in *The Faber Book of Nonsense Verse*, ed. Geoffrey Grigson (1979).

5 No one likes his dependants to be treated with respect, for such treatment forms an unpleasant contrast to his own conduct.

Benjamin Disraeli *Vivian Grey*, bk 3, ch. 7 (1826–7)

6 A poor relation – is the most irrelevant thing in nature.

Charles Lamb *Last Essays of Elia*, 'Poor Relations' (1833)

7 'Dom-bey and son,' ... Those three words conveyed the one idea of Mr Dombey's life.

Charles Dickens *Dombey and Son*, ch. 1 (1848)

8 It is a melancholy truth that even great men have their poor relations.

Charles Dickens *Bleak House*, ch. 28 (1852–3)

9 You must see my daughters. I have a blue-eyed daughter who is my Beauty daughter. I have a Sentimental daughter, and I have a Comedy daughter. You must see them all.

Charles Dickens Harold Skimpole in ibid., ch. 43. His daughters are Arethusa, Laura and Kitty.

10 But wait a bit. I object to pirates as sons-in-law.

W. S. Gilbert Major-General Stanley in *The Pirates of Penzance* (1879), to which the Pirate King replies: 'We object to major-generals as fathers-in-law. But we waive the point. We do not press it.'

11 But there, everything has its drawbacks, as the man said when his mother-in-law died, and they came down upon him for the funeral expenses.

Jerome K. Jerome *Three Men in a Boat*, ch. 3 (1889)

12 I'm Charley's aunt from Brazil – where the nuts come from.

Brandon Thomas *Charley's Aunt*, act 1 (1892). The basis of a repeated joke in the play.

13 Lizzie Borden took an axe/ And gave her mother forty whacks;/ When she saw what she had done/ She gave her father forty-one!

Anon. Folk rhyme. Lizzie Borden was acquitted of murdering her parents on 4 August 1892 in Fall River, Massachusetts.

14 Good families are generally worse than any others.

Anthony Hope *The Prisoner of Zenda*, ch. 1 (1894)

15 Some aunts are tall, some aunts are not tall. That is a matter that surely an aunt may be allowed to decide for herself.

Oscar Wilde Jack in *The Importance of Being Earnest*, act 1 (1895)

16 Relations are simply a tedious pack of people, who haven't got the remotest knowledge of how to live, nor the smallest instinct about when to die.

Algernon Moncrieff in ibid., act 1. Later he

says relations are 'a sort of aggravated form of the public'.

17 I need hardly tell you that in families of high position strange coincidences are not supposed to occur. They are hardly considered the thing.

Lady Bracknell in ibid., act 4

18 A mother-in-law is not a simple idea. She is a very subtle idea. The problem is not that she is big and arrogant; she is frequently little and quite extraordinarily nice. The problem of the mother-in-law is that she is like the twilight: half one thing and half another.

G. K. Chesterton *Alarms and Discursions*, 'The Three Kinds of Men' (1910)

19 [On being shown the Grand Canyon] What a marvellous place to drop one's mother-in-law.

Marshal Foch Attributed

20 To my daughter Leonora without whose never-failing sympathy and encouragement this book would have been finished in half the time.

P. G. Wodehouse Dedication to *The Heart of a Goof* (1926). In the *Bloomsbury Book of Dedications* ed. Adrian Room (1990), this is described as 'a traditional dedication that has occurred many times since and may not have been original to Wodehouse in the first place'. The dedicatee was in fact Wodehouse's stepdaughter.

21 It is not at all *chic* to live in a suburb with an aunt.

Stevie Smith *Novel on Yellow Paper* (1936), p. 65 (1980 edn)

22 This morning, Baxter was forgotten, and he was experiencing that perfect happiness which comes from a clear conscience, absence of loved ones, congenial society and fine weather.

P. G. Wodehouse *Uncle Fred in the Springtime*, ch. 2 (1939)

23 Big sisters are the crab grass in the lawn of life.

Charles Schulz The melancholic Linus in *Peanuts* (strip cartoon, 1950 onwards)

24 Yes, of course I remember you. Didn't your father have a son?

Spike Milligan Hercules Grytpype-Thynne's inquiry of Neddie Seagoon in *The Goon Show*, 'The Yehti', first broadcast 8 March 1955

25 There was a knock on the door. I knew it was the mother-in-law because the mice were throwing themselves on the traps.

Les Dawson Staple line of his live act from the 1960s onwards

26 MOTHER: Do you love me Albert?
ALBERT: Yes.
MOTHER: Yes – what?
ALBERT: Yes, please.

Tom Stoppard *Albert's Bridge* (BBC radio play, 1967)

27 First things first, second things never.

Shirley Conran Family motto quoted in *Superwoman: How to be a Working Wife and Mother* (1975)

28 I'm beginning to lose patience/ With my personal relations:/ They are not deep,/ And they are not cheap.

W. H. Auden 'Shorts, 1929–31', *Collected Poems* ed. Edward Mendelson (1976)

29 There is a kind of algebra about courtship. It goes like this: On the one hand: the more beautiful the girl is that you fall in love with. On the other hand: the more peculiar her parents turn out to be.

Jake Thackray *Jake's Progress*, 'Before I Was a Performing Man . . .' (1977)

30 Maynards? So much incest in that family even the bulldog's got a club foot.

Viv Stanshall Sir Henry in *Sir Henry at Rawlinson End* (LP, 1978)

31 The six years that I lived with that family were very happy ones, although there is also much to be said for working on a chain gang.

Woody Allen *Side Effects*, 'Confessions of a Burglar' (1980)

32 Everyone has a family tree; the

Dawsons have one, it's a weeping willow.

Les Dawson *The Malady Lingers On*, 'The Art of a Pun . . . Or How to Lose an Audience Fast' (1982)

33 There is usually something odd about sisters that come in triplicate.

Arthur Marshall *Life's Rich Pageant*, sc. 3 (1984). He cites, among others, Cinderella and her ugly relations, and 'Macbeth's friends'.

34 I am the son and heir/ of nothing in particular.

Morrissey 'How Soon Is Now?' (song, 1984, by Johnny Marr and Morrissey)

35 'A grandmother', said one little girl, 'is that old lady who sits in the corner of the room and keeps your mother from hitting you.'

Anon. Quoted in *Laughter Lines: Family Wit and Wisdom*, 'The Afternoon Snoozers', ed. Rev. James A. Simpson (1987)

36 At every party there are two kinds of people – those who want to go home and those who don't. The trouble is, they are usually married to each other.

Ann Landers *International Herald Tribune* 19 June 1991

37 The Oggs were what is known as an extended family – in fact not only extended but elongated, protracted and persistent.

Terry Pratchett *Witches Abroad*, p. 31 (1991)

38 Happy families – is that what you're telling me they're all playing out there! Is that the only game in town suddenly – happy families? Everyone else is shuffling the happy family deck and there's just me, Frank Ritz, playing snakes and ladders.

Howard Jacobson *No More Mr Nice Guy*, ch. 8 (1998)

39 I haven't spoken to my mother-in-law for eighteen months – I don't like to interrupt her.

Ken Dodd Delivered at the Empire Theatre, Sunderland, May 2000

40 They say the definition of ambivalence is watching your mother-in-law drive over a cliff in your new Cadillac.

David Mamet *Guardian* 19 February 2000

41 I've got a theory of relatives, too: don't hire them.

Jack L. Warner Quoted in *Halliwell's Who's Who in the Movies* ed. John Walker (2001)

42 Money – the one thing that keeps us in touch with our children.

Gyles Brandreth *The Times* 'Quotes of the Week', 2 February 2002

43 We were not a close family. There were too many thistles in the salad.

Scott Young Quoted in *Shakey – Neil Young's Biography*, 'Mr Blue and Mr Red', by Jimmy McDonough (2002). Scott Young is Neil's father.

44 A dad is a man who has photos in his wallet where his money used to be.

Anon. *Away an' Ask Yer Mother (Your Scottish Father's Favourite Sayings)*, Introduction, ed. Allan Morrison (2003)

45 A lot of people have been tracing their family histories on the Internet. I'm no exception, and what I've discovered is that I come from a very long line of dead people.

Pat Condell Joke told on *The Store* (BBC Radio 4), 4 August 2003

46 There were so many people in my family, I was eight years old before it was my turn in the bathroom.

Bob Hope Quoted in the *Independent* 16 May 2003

47 My brother is straight with me. He always says, 'Britney, your ass is huge right now.' But I suppose it's good he's totally honest.

Britney Spears *Daily Star* 21 December 2003

Festive Occasions

1 They talke of Christmas so long, that it comes.

George Herbert *Outlandish Proverbs*, no. 840 (1640)

2 'If I could work my will,' said Scrooge indignantly, 'every idiot who goes about with "Merry Christmas" on his lips, should be boiled with his own pudding, and buried with a stake of holly through his heart.'

Charles Dickens *A Christmas Carol*, Stave 1 (1843)

3 What ought to be done to the man who invented the celebrating of anniversaries? Mere killing would be too light.

Mark Twain *Notebook*, ch. 26 (1935)

4 [Of Christmas] Oh well it is all over now and thank Xt too. The presents I got were – as always – far inferior in every way to the ones I gave, that is annoying. The parties I went to didn't have any nice young ladies at them, and everybody had a much smaller brain than mine.

Kingsley Amis Letter to Philip Larkin of 27 December 1945, collected in *The Letters of Kingsley Amis* ed. Zachary Leader (2000)

5 It was the week before Christmas – now don't get excited. This isn't going to be a story about Santa Claus.

Groucho Marx Opening words of an article for *This Week* 12 December 1948, quoted in *The Essential Groucho*, 'Freelancing', ed. Stefan Kanfer (2000)

6 The stores along Hollywood Boulevard were already beginning to fill up with overpriced Christmas junk, and the daily papers were beginning to scream about how terrible it would be if you didn't get your Christmas shopping done early. It would be terrible anyway; it always is.

Raymond Chandler *The Long Goodbye*, ch. 2 (1954)

7 The Grinch hated Christmas! The whole Christmas season!/ Now, please don't ask why. No one quite knows the reason./ It could be his head wasn't screwed on just right./ It could be, perhaps, that his shoes were too tight./ But I think the most likely of all/ May have been his heart was two sizes too small.

Dr Seuss 'How the Grinch Stole Christmas' (1957)

8 [Of Christmas] The one thing that really needs remembering is that it's the attempt to blow the balloon too big that results in the limp rag at the end.

Katherine Whitehorn *Observations*, 'Mistakes of the Season' (1970)

9 One quick drink, that's all they're getting. Then it's happy Christmas and out they bloody well go.

Alan Ayckbourn Geoffrey in *Absurd Person Singular*, act 2 (1972)

10 I'm extremely sentimental about Christmas, actually. Every Christmas I still take my socks off and stand them in front of the fireplace.

Eric Morecambe and Ernie Wise *The Morecambe and Wise Jokebook*, skit 10 (1979)

11 If Christmas is about one particular thing . . . it's about sitting in front of the telly, falling asleep, and finding you've missed close-down.

Miles Kington *Moreover*, 'The Moreover Advice Service' (1982)

12 All the balloons have shrivelled up. They look like old women's breasts shown on television documentaries about the Third World.

Sue Townsend *The Secret Diary of Adrian Mole Aged 13¾* (1982), entry for Thursday 30 December

13 Be sure to remember when Hallowe'en is. Answering the door when you're three-quarters crocked and finding a pack of midget He-Men, Master of the Universes on the front porch can be a scary experience if you're not expecting it.

P. J. O'Rourke *The Bachelor Home Companion*, ch. 10 (1987)

14 Bloody Christmas, here again/ Let us raise a loving cup:/ Peace on earth, goodwill to men,/ And make them do the washing up.

Wendy Cope 'Another Christmas Poem', *Serious Concerns* (1992)

15 Christmas, the time of year when people descend into the bunker of the family.

Byron Rogers *Daily Telegraph* 27 December 1993

16 Tomorrow is Twelfth Night. Hooray. It is a marvellous occasion, when we find our sitting-rooms festooned with charming little pieces of sticky tape, which were used to hold up the decorations.

Oliver Pritchett *The Dogger Bank Saga: Writings 1980–95*, 'The Rain It Raineth Every Day – Official' (1995)

17 Aren't we forgetting the true meaning of this day – the birth of Santa?

Matt Groening Bart Simpson in *The Simpsons*, 'Miracle on Evergreen Terrace', first broadcast 21 December 1997

18 Every year on Christmas day I like to tell my mother that I'm a lesbian, even though I'm not. It just gets everything going.

Jenny Éclair Quoted in *The Virago Book of Christmas*, 'Mischief and Malfeasance at Christmas', ed. Michelle Lovric (2002)

19 I forget the derivation of Boxing Day, but the feeling of wanting to invite your loved ones outside one at a time and punch them in the face, does that come into it somewhere?

Allison Pearson *I Don't Know How She Does It*, ch. 5 (2002)

20 Birthdays are the one day in the year when you can guarantee that everyone who knows you – your family, friends and colleagues at work – will completely forget about you.

Guy Browning *Guardian*, 'How to . . .' column, 8 March 2003

21 How you elect to spend New Year's Eve will depend upon your/ a. Age/ b. Remaining levels of optimism/ c. Threshold of pain.

Joseph Connolly *Christmas and How to Survive It*, 'The Last Hurrah' (2004)

Class and Snobbery

1 Writing, Madam, 's a mechanic part of wit! A gentleman should never go beyond a song or a billet.

Sir George Etherege Sir Fopling Flutter in *The Man of Mode*, act 4, sc. 1 (1676). He has just been urged to write a novel.

2 I am apt to conceive, that one reason why many English writers have totally failed in describing the manners of upper life, may possibly be that, in reality, they know nothing of it. This is a knowledge unhappily not in the power of many authors to arrive at.

Henry Fielding *Tom Jones*, bk 14, ch. 1 (1749)

3 [Of Lord Chesterfield] This man I thought had been a wit among Lords; but, I find, he is only a Lord among wits.

Samuel Johnson *The Life of Samuel Johnson* by James Boswell, vol. 1, p. 266 (1791); in G. B. Hill's edition of 1887, rev. L. F. Powell (1934)

4 Respectable means rich, and decent means poor. I should die if I heard my family called decent.

Thomas Love Peacock *Crotchet Castle*, ch. 3 (1831)

5 It is odd enough, but certain people seem to have as great a pleasure in pronouncing titles as their owners have in wearing them.

Charles Dickens John Willet in *Barnaby Rudge*, ch. 35 (1841)

6 Nothing like blood, sir, in hosses, dawgs and men.

William Makepeace Thackeray James Crawley in *Vanity Fair*, ch. 34 (1847–8). Crawley has earlier said: 'See the chaps in a boat race; look at the fellers in a fight; ay, look at a dawg killing rats – which is it wins? The good-blooded ones.'

7 The aristocrat is the democrat ripe, and gone to seed.

Ralph Waldo Emerson *Representative Men*, 'Napoleon, the Man of the World' (1850)

8 The only infallible rule we know is, that the man who is always talking

about being a gentleman never is one.

R. S. Surtees *Ask Mamma*, ch. 1 (1858)

9 Mr and Mrs Veneering were bran-new people in a bran-new house in a bran-new quarter of London.

Charles Dickens *Our Mutual Friend*, 'Book the First: The Cup and the Lip' ch. 2 (1864–5). Hamilton Veneering is a self-made rich man, having risen through the ranks of Chicksey, Veneering and Stobbles, druggists.

10 One has often wondered whether upon the whole earth there is anything so unintelligent, so unapt to perceive how the world is really going, as an ordinary young Englishman of our upper class.

Matthew Arnold *Culture and Anarchy*, ch. 2 (1869)

11 I'm as cheerful as a poor devil can be expected to be who has the misfortune to be a duke, with a thousand a day!

W. S. Gilbert The Duke of Dunstable in *Patience*, act 1 (1881)

12 Ah! Hopper is one of Nature's gentlemen, the worst type of gentleman I know.

Oscar Wilde Cecil Graham in *Lady Windermere's Fan*, act 2 (1893)

13 'Bourgeois,' I observed, 'is an epithet which the riff-raff apply to what is respectable, and the aristocracy to what is decent.'

Anthony Hope *The Dolly Dialogues*, ch. 17 (1894)

14 It gives one position, and prevents one from keeping it up. That is all that can be said about land.

Oscar Wilde Lady Bracknell in *The Importance of Being Earnest*, act 1 (1895)

15 Really, if the lower orders don't set us a good example, what on earth is the use of them?

Algernon Moncrieff in ibid.

16 [Of life as a salesman] You're just superior enough to feel that you're not superior.

H. G. Wells Mr Hoopdriver in *The Wheels of Chance*, ch. 36 (1896)

17 Godolphin Horne was nobly born;/ He held the human race in scorn.

Hilaire Belloc 'Godolphin Horne', *Cautionary Tales* (1907)

18 A fully equipped duke costs as much to keep up as two dread-noughts; and dukes are just as great a terror and they last longer.

David Lloyd George Speech delivered in Newcastle, 9 October 1909

19 The man who notices nothing about the clerk except his cockney accent would have noticed nothing about Simon de Montfort except his French accent.

G. K. Chesterton *Alarms and Discursions*, 'The Philosophy of Sight-seeing' (1910)

20 It is impossible for an Englishman to open his mouth without making some other Englishman despise him.

George Bernard Shaw *Pygmalion*, Preface (1912)

21 I am fond of digging in the garden and I am parshial to ladies if they are nice I suppose it is my nature. I am not quite a gentleman but you would hardly notice it but cant be helped anyhow.

Daisy Ashford *The Young Visiters*, ch. 1 (1919). The socially aspiring Mr Salteena responds to an invitation.

22 Gentlemen do not take soup at luncheon.

Lord Curzon An observation made when, as Chancellor of Oxford University, he was shown the menu of a lunch intended for the King. Quoted by E. L. Woodward in *Short Journey*, ch 7 (1924), and by Evelyn Waugh in *Noblesse Oblige*, 'An Open Letter to the Honourable Mrs Peter Rodd [Nancy Mitford] on a Very Serious Subject, from Evelyn Waugh', ed. Nancy Mitford (1956)

23 Like many of the upper class/ He liked the sound of breaking glass.

Hilaire Belloc 'About John', publ. in *New Cautionary Tales* (1930)

24 Unlike the male codfish, which, suddenly finding itself the parent of

three million five hundred thousand little codfish, cheerfully resolves to love them all, the British aristocracy is apt to look with a somewhat jaundiced eye on its younger sons,

P. G. Wodehouse *Blandings Castle and Elsewhere*, 'The Custody of the Pumpkin' (1935)

25 He had all the cosmopolitan charm and elegance of a man who has been determined, over a period of years, to conceal from the world the dreadful facts that his father was a large Dunfermline grocer, and was still a large Dunfermline grocer, and that his grandfather had been a very, very small Dunfermline grocer.

A. G. Macdonell *Lords and Masters*, ch. 13 (1936). The subject is a Mr Andrew Hay.

26 She never reads a paper, and she seldom sees a book,/ She is worshipped by her butler, tolerated by her cook./ And her husband treats her nicely, and she's *mostly* on her horse,/ While the children are entirely in the nursery of course.

Joyce Grenfell 'The Countess of Cotelely' (song/poem, music by Richard Addinsell), *Tuppence Coloured* (revue, 1947), collected in *Turn Back the Clock* (1977). In 1956 Grenfell performed this on the *Ed Sullivan Show*, Sullivan believing it would make a good contrast to his other guest, Elvis Presley.

27 Phone for the fish knives, Norman/ As cook is a little unnerved;/ You kiddies have crumpled the serviettes/ And I must have things daintily served.

John Betjeman 'How to Get on in Society', publ. in *A Few Late Chrysanthemums* (1954). The poem is a list of social solecisms.

28 You can be in the Horse Guards and still be common, dear.

Terence Rattigan *Separate Tables*, 'Table Number Seven' (1955)

29 When drunk, gentlemen often become amorous or maudlin or vomit in public, but they never become truculent.

Alan S. C. Ross *Noblesse Oblige*, 'U and non-U. An essay in sociological linguistics', ed. Nancy Mitford (1956)

30 When they win at bingo in Lytham they don't shout 'House!', they shout 'Bungalow!'

Les Dawson A staple of Dawson's routines from the 1950s onwards. He lived for a long time in Lytham St Anne's, a resort immediately south of, and more genteel than, Blackpool.

31 Will the people in the cheaper seats clap your hands? All the rest of you, if you'll just rattle your jewellery.

John Lennon To the audience of the Royal Command Performance, London, 4 November 1963, quoted in *Shout! The True Story of the Beatles*, pt 2, 'November 1963', by Philip Norman (1981). The original plan had been to say: 'Rattle your *fuckin'* jewellery.'

32 This lair of old Bassett's was one of the fairly stately homes of England – not a show place like the joints you read about with three hundred and sixty-five rooms, fifty-two staircases and twelve courtyards, but definitely not a bungalow.

P. G. Wodehouse *Stiff Upper Lip, Jeeves*, ch. 5 (1963)

33 The real mountaineer has a tremendous advantage over the social climber: once he has arrived at the summit, he looks around, fixes his flag – and comes down again. The social climber, however, must stay up on top.

Duke of Bedford *The Duke of Bedford's Book of Snobs*, 'On Downstarts' (1965), written in collaboration with George Mikes

34 As a father, I have certain responsibilities towards my daughter, and I have to find out certain things about you. For example, where you went to school. Not that it matters, but it is important.

Peter Cook *Not Only . . . But Also* (episode 3, 1st series, 1965). Peter Cook is a middle-class father vetting his daughter's oikish boyfriend (Dudley Moore).

35 No writer before the middle of the nineteenth century wrote about the

working classes other than as grotesques or pastoral decorations.
Then when they were given the
vote certain writers started to suck
up to them.

Evelyn Waugh Interview in the *Paris Review*,
Summer/Fall 1963, repr. in *The Penguin Book
of Interviews* ed. C. Silvester (1993)

36 Please accept my resignation. I
don't care to belong to any club that
will have me as a member.

Groucho Marx Quoted in *The Groucho Letters*, Introduction, ed. Arthur Sheekman
(1967). The letter was to the Friar's Club,
Hollywood.

37 My personal ancestor was Lord Cra-
pologies Fel de Minge . . . Came over
with William the Conqueror, first-
class of course . . .

Spike Milligan Lord Fortnum in *The Bed-
Sitting Room*, act 1 (1969)

38 [Of the 11th Duke of Devonshire] The
decisive gulf separating the duke
from his horny-palmed employees,
in my view, is that while they wear
baggy clothes bought off the hook,
his baggy clothes are tailor-made.

Clive James *Observer* 8 July 1973. James was
reviewing a BBC programme, *The World of
the 11th Duke*.

39 When I want a peerage, I shall buy
it like an honest man.

Lord Northcliffe Quoted in *Swaff*, ch. 2, by
Tom Driberg (1974)

40 She recalled the time Mr Cumber-
patch the gardener . . . had fallen
badly in the the orchard. Why,
Henry had fairly raced back for his
pistol. He couldn't bear to see the
humblest creature in pain.

Viv Stanshall *Sir Henry at Rawlinson End* (LP,
1978)

41 I've always felt it was the car which
went down to the showroom to
choose the man, not the other way
round, and Volvos liked to pick a
dentist who sent his son to a not
quite first-rate public school.

Robert Robinson *The Dog Chairman*, 'The Place
of the Volvo in Old Norse Mythology' (1982)

42 Common criminals are 'at large';
Lord Lucan is merely 'missing'.

Henry Root *Henry Root's World of Knowledge*
(1982)

43 The place was packed – but there
was no one there.

Ann Barr and Peter York The Sloane's lament
on having turned up at the wrong sort of
party. *The Official Sloane Ranger Diary* (1983),
line quoted on the back cover.

44 Q: Why did the chicken cross the
road? A: To see the duchess lay a
foundation stone.

Maureen Lipman *How Was It for You?* 'A Joking Aside' (1985). The first joke that Maureen
Lipman ever heard.

45 There's a certain part of the contented majority who love anybody
who is worth a billion dollars.

J. K. Galbraith *Guardian* 23 May 1992. He was
thinking in particular of the plutocrat presi-
dential candidate Ross Perot.

46 Snobbery is merely a deprecatory
synonym of discrimination.

Jonathan Meades On being asked whether
he was a snob. *The Times*, 'Quotes of the
Week' 2 February 2002.

47 'The class war is obsolete,' Harold
Macmillan announced after winning the 1959 general election. He
then formed a government whose
members included a duke, three
earls and a marquess.

Francis Wheen *Hooh-Hahs and Passing Frenzies*, 'Dispatches from the Class War', 'Baying
for Broken Glass' (2002)

48 People lived on the right side of the
tracks or the wrong side of the
tracks. We lived under the tracks.

Bob Hope Of his childhood in Cleveland.
Quoted in the *Independent* 16 May 2003.

49 I'm middle class, but I'm hard – al
dente.

Jimmy Carr *Daily Telegraph*, 20 April 2004

Town and Country

1 Rus in urbe.

Martial *Epigrammata*, bk 12, no. 57 (c.AD 90)

2 I nauseate walking; 'tis a country diversion, I loathe the country.

William Congreve Millamant in *The Way of the World*, act 4, sc. 1 (1700)

3 Walls have tongues, and hedges ears.

Jonathan Swift 'A Pastoral Dialogue between Richmond Lodge and Marble Hill' (1727)

4 London is literally new to me; new in its streets, houses, and even in its situation; as the Irishman said, 'London is now gone out of town.'

Tobias Smollett Letter from Matt Bramble to Dr Lewis, dated 20 May, in *The Expedition of Humphry Clinker* (1771)

5 Give me fresh air, and Islington!

George Colman the Elder Mrs Rubrick in *The Spleen (or Islington Spa)*, act 1 (1776)

6 We do not look in great cities for our best morality.

Jane Austen *Mansfield Park*, ch. 9 (1814)

7 The two divinest things this world has got,/ A lovely woman in a rural spot!

Leigh Hunt *The Story of Rimini*, canto 3 (1816)

8 There is nothing good to be had in the country, or if there is, they will not let you have it.

William Hazlitt 'Observations on Mr Wordsworth's "Excursion" ' (1817)

9 I have no relish for the country; it is a kind of healthy grave.

Sydney Smith Letter of 1838 to Miss G. Harcourt, collected in *Letters of Sydney Smith* (1953)

10 It is my belief, Watson, founded upon my experience, that the lowest and vilest alleys in London do not present a more dreadful record of sin than does the smiling and beautiful countryside.

Sir Arthur Conan Doyle *The Adventures of Sherlock Holmes*, 'The Five Orange Pips' (1892)

11 When one is in town one amuses oneself. When one is in the country one amuses other people. It is excessively boring.

Oscar Wilde Jack in *The Importance of Being Earnest*, act 1 (1895)

12 Nothing ages a woman like living in the country.

Colette *Music Hall Sidelights*, 'On Tour' (1913)

13 'Nonsense, Mary!' cried Flora, paling. 'Of course there will be a bathroom. Even in Sussex – it would be *too much*.'

Stella Gibbons *Cold Comfort Farm*, ch. 2 (1932)

14 She soon made herself take an interest in country things, and now she tries to make the country people interested in them too.

Dodie Smith Of Miss Marcy in *I Capture the Castle*, ch. 2 (1949)

15 It is an important general rule to always refer to your friend's country establishment as a 'cottage'.

Stephen Potter *Lifemanship*, ch 2 (1950)

16 I'll never forget the day I met Neddie. The golden morning sunlight was bathing the Devon hills as he made his way through a reeking slum alley off Lisle Street.

Spike Milligan Grytpype Thynne in *The Goon Show*, 'The Mystery of the Fake Neddie Seagoons' (episode 9, 7th series, first broadcast 29 November 1956). Collected in *The Essential Spike Milligan* compiled by Alex Games (2002). Lisle Street is in London WC2.

17 The country is laid out in a haphazard, sloppy fashion, offensive to the tidy mind.

Alan Brien *Punch* 22 March 1979

18 I met a girl once, she was walking across the Pennines with a sack of wheat on her back. She said, 'Excuse me, do you know where there's an all-night windmill?'

Les Dawson *The Malady Lingers On*, 'The Art of a Pun . . . Or How to Lose an Audience Fast' (1982)

19 I saw a pair of stout knickerbockers in a shop in Oxford, and the ticket

pinned to them said they were guaranteed by the Country Gentlemen's Association, or some such name, and underneath it said 'Ferretproof'.

Robert Robinson *The Dog Chairman*, 'Ferretproof' (1982)

20 **Rural England has been dying for as long as anyone can remember ... It was dying because of the Enclosures Act. Then it died when the railways opened and it died when the railways closed. It died when everyone left and it died when everybody came back.**

Stephen Pile *Punch* April 1990, collected in *Punch Lines* ed. Amanda-Jane Doran (1992)

21 **I can see from here that those running shoes wouldn't support your ankles if you slipped into a rabbit hole. A bap could tide you over until the air ambulance arrived.**

Mary Killen *How to Live with Your Husband*, 'Perma-Fawltyism' (1996)

Manners, or Lack of

1 **O tempora, O mores!**

Cicero (Oh, the times! Oh, the manners!). *In Catilinam*, speech 1, ch. 1 (63 BC)

2 **My Lord, I had forgot the fart.**

Elizabeth I *Brief Lives* by John Aubrey (n.d.). Spoken to Edward de Vere on his return from seven years' self-imposed exile triggered by the embarrassment of having farted in the presence of the Queen.

3 **Prithee don't screw your wit beyond the compass of good manners.**

Colley Cibber Narcissa in *Love's Last Shift*, act 2, sc. 1 (1696)

4 **Drunkenness, Sir Harry, is the worst pretence a gentleman can make for rudeness: for the excuse is as scandalous as the fault.**

George Farquhar Angelica in *The Constant Couple*, act 5, sc. 1 (1699)

5 **Why, brother Wilfull of Salop, you** may be as short as a Shrewsbury cake, if you please.

William Congreve Sir Wilfull Witwoud in *The Way of the World*, act 3, sc. 3 (1700)

6 **How civilly the People of Quality hate one another.**

Sir Richard Steele Betty in *The Lying Lover*, act 3, sc. 1 (1703)

7 **He is the very pineapple of politeness.**

Richard Brinsley Sheridan Mrs Malaprop in *The Rivals*, act 3, sc. 3 (1774). She is referring to Captain Absolute, and she means 'pinnacle'.

8 **Introduce [an author] to a party of milliners' girls, and they are ready to split their sides laughing at him: over his bottle, he is dry: in the drawing-room, rude or awkward: he is too refined for the vulgar, too clownish for the fashionable.**

William Hazlitt 'On the Conversation of Authors', *London Magazine* September 1820, collected in *The Essays of William Hazlitt* ed. Catherine Macdonald Maclean (1949). Hazlitt himself was noted among his friends for his strangeness.

9 **'English is an expressive language,' said Mr Pinto, 'but not difficult to master. Its range is limited. It consists, as far as I can observe, of four words: "nice", "jolly", "charming", and "bore"; and some grammarians add "fond".'**

Benjamin Disraeli *Lothair*, ch. 28 (1870). Mr Pinto is 'a little, oily Portuguese'.

10 **Curtsey while you're thinking what to say. It saves time.**

Lewis Carroll The Red Queen to Alice in *Through the Looking-Glass*, ch. 2 (1872)

11 **It is a very ungentlemanly thing to read a private cigarette case.**

Oscar Wilde Jack in *The Importance of Being Earnest*, act 1 (1895)

12 **Lady Bracknell, I hate to seem inquisitive, but would you kindly inform me who I am?**

Jack in ibid., act 4. Having been left as a baby in a bag in a station waiting-room, he is uncertain about his origins.

13 The English are busy; they don't have time to be polite.

Montesquieu *Pensées et fragments inédits*, vol. 2, no. 1428 (1901)

14 Are you lost daddy I arsked tenderly./ Shut up he explained.

Ring Lardner *The Young Immigrants*, ch. 10 (1920)

15 I met Curzon in Downing Street, and received the sort of greeting a corpse would give an undertaker.

Stanley Baldwin Attributed remark, supposedly made in 1923. Lord Curzon became Baldwin's rival for the prime-ministership upon the death of Andrew Bonar Law. When Baldwin did become PM, Curzon opined that he was 'Not even a public figure. A man of no experience. And of the utmost insignificance.'

16 [Of gentlemanliness] This old-fashioned trade is more wretchedly paid/ Than any profession I know,/ For although the supply is undoubtedly high/ The demand is undoubtedly low.

A. P. Herbert *Wisdom for the Wise*, 'The Gentleman' (1930)

17 JUDGE: You are extremely offensive, young man.
F. E. SMITH: As a matter of fact, we both are, and the only difference between us is that I am trying to be, and you can't help it.

F. E. Smith *Frederick Elwin, Earl of Birkenhead*, vol. 1, ch. 9, by the 2nd Earl of Birkenhead (1933)

18 What's up, Doc?

Tex Avery Bugs Bunny's habitual inquiry of (Dr) Elmer Flood in Warner Bros' *Bugs Bunny* cartoon series (1937–63). Tex [Fred] Avery is thought to have been the originator.

19 The English never smash in a face. They merely refrain from asking it to dinner.

Margaret Halsey *With Malice toward Some*, pt 3 (1938)

20 I don't mind if you don't like my manners. I don't like them myself. They're pretty bad. I grieve over them long winter evenings.

Raymond Chandler Marlowe in *The Big Sleep*, ch. 3 (1939)

21 I have written a tremendous homily on the nature of the English gentleman who always protects the weaker & unpopular. Can't say I've ever noticed it much myself.

Evelyn Waugh Letter to Nancy Mitford of 9 November 1949, collected in *The Letters of Evelyn Waugh* ed. Mark Amory (1980)

22 To Americans, English manners are far more frightening than none at all.

Randall Jarrell *Pictures from an Institution*, pt 1, ch. 4 (1954)

23 'Excuse me' is only one of the phrases current today which has lost its meaning. Today it means 'Get out of my way.' 'Can I help you, sir?' means 'What the hell are you doing here?' 'With due respect' . . . means 'I have no respect for your opinions at all.'

John Betjeman *Spectator* 11 October 1957, collected in *The Wit of the Spectator* ed. Christopher Howse (1989). Betjeman adds that when someone says to him 'Excuse me' he always answers 'No.'

24 I suppose it would be a breach of hospitality if I socked my hostess's sister in the eye?

P. G. Wodehouse *Service with a Smile* (1962)

25 The English are polite by telling lies. The Americans are polite by telling the truth.

Malcolm Bradbury Dr Bernard Froelich in *Stepping Westward*, bk 1, ch. 1 (1965)

26 I don't *want* to behave like a civilized yuman bein'.

Richmal Crompton William Brown in *William and the Masked Avenger*, 'William and the Masked Avenger' (1966)

27 The Chinese word for cocktail party means, literally, 'two-hours-standing-up' and goes, characteristically, to the root of the matter.

C. Northcote Parkinson *Mrs Parkinson's Law*, 'Hosts and Guests' (1968)

28 It is the first duty of a gentleman to remember in the morning who he went to bed with the night before.

Dorothy L. Sayers Quoted in *Whitehorn's*

Social Survival, 'Awkward Questions', by
Katherine Whitehorn (1968)

29   **We walked on the moon, you be
polite.**
Joni Mitchell 'Don't Interrupt the Sorrow',
The Hissing of Summer Lawns (LP, 1975). By
'We' she means Americans.

30   **A rose has no back.**
Geoffrey Madan *Geoffrey Madan's Note-
books*, 'Humorous and Memorable', ed. J. A.
Gere and John Sparrow (1981). He explains
that this is 'the Chinese reply if you apologize for turning your back'.

31   **I don't like stand-offishness, but on
the other hand there are women of
sixty-five touring the West Country
cathedrals, travelling always in
pairs and driving Triumph Sodomite motorcars, who insist on saying
good morning to everyone at break-
fast-time in hotels – one total
stranger in a twin-set asked me
how I'd slept.**
Robert Robinson *The Dog Chairman*, 'The
Middle-Aged Philistine Abroad' (1982). The
cars in question are Triumph Dolomites.

32   **Boz offered me a sniff of his glue
today, but I declined it with thanks.**
Sue Townsend *The Secret Diary of Adrian
Mole Aged 13¾* (1982), entry for 13 March

33   **Old Cary Grant fine. How you?**
Cary Grant Attributed telegram message,
quoted in *Cary Grant* by R. Schickel (1983).
The line is supposedly in response to another
telegram, sent to Grant's agent and inquir-
ing 'How old Cary Grant?'

34   **Good manners can replace morals.
It may be years before anyone
knows if what you are doing is
right. But if what you are doing is
nice, it will be immediately evident.**
P. J. O'Rourke *Modern Manners*, ch. 1 (1983)

35   **[Example of conduct unbecoming a
gentleman or a lady, elicited in a
Spectator competition] Upsetting
your glass and appropriating your
host's while he mops up.**
Anon. Submitted by C. P. F. to the *Spectator*
7 April 1984, collected in *The Wit of the Spectator* ed. Christopher Howse (1989). Other

examples included 'Lighting a pipe while pro-
posing marriage' and 'Belonging to Mensa'.

36   **He said do you want a drink or do
you want a kick up the bum with
an open-toed sandal?**
Victoria Wood Kelly in 'He Didn't: One',
Barmy: The New Victoria Wood Sketch Book
(1987)

37   **When a man opens the car door for
his wife, it's either a new car or a
new wife.**
Prince Philip, Duke of Edinburgh *Today*
2 March 1988

38   **When people *ask* you to do something, all you can say is no.**
Miles Davis Quoted in *Profiles*, 'Miles Davis',
by Kenneth Tynan (1989)

39   **Eat my shorts!**
Matt Groening Catchphrase of Bart Simpson
in *The Simpsons* (TV cartoon, 1989 onwards)

40   **Good morning! . . . And in case I
don't see ya: good afternoon, good
evening and goodnight!**
Andrew Niccol Truman (Jim Carrey) in *The
Truman Show* (film, 1998, directed by Peter
Weir)

41   **One could never make love to a
woman with a glottal stop.**
Brian Sewell *The Times*, 'Quotes of the
Week', 12 September 1998

42   **I can only assume that callers to
Six-o-Six repeatedly ask David
Mellor how he is on the off-chance
that he will reply, 'Terminally ill.'**
Anon. Mellor, the barrister and former Conservative cabinet minister, made an unlikely
host for the football phone-in programme.
Letter to *When Saturday Comes* magazine
1999, quoted in *The Book of Football Quotations*, 'This Supporting Life', ed. Phil Shaw
(1999).

43   **I am in an age group where it is
rude to discuss money, and now it
is all anyone cares about.**
Jack Nicholson *Observer*, 'Sayings of the
Week', 3 January 1999

44   **I remember your name perfectly;
but I just can't think of your face.**
William Archibald Spooner Attributed.
Quoted in *The Penguin Dictionary of Modern*

Humorous Quotations ed. Fred Metcalf (2nd edn 2001).

45 'Good evening.' 'All right?' said the barman, as if querying the mental health of someone who still said that.

Martin Amis *Yellow Dog*, pt 1, ch. 1, sect. 1 (2003)

Speech

1 There was a nun, a Prioress,/ Her way of smiling very simple and coy./ Her greatest oath was only 'By St Loy!'

Geoffrey Chaucer *The Canterbury Tales*, 'The General Prologue' (1387), trans. from medieval to modern English by Nevill Coghill (1951)

2 The sun, the sea, will sooner both stand still/ Than her eternal tongue! Nothing can 'scape it.

Ben Jonson Volpone in *Volpone*, act 3, sc. 2 (1605). He is speaking of the talkative Lady Would-Be.

3 M. JOURDAIN: You mean that when I say: 'Nicole, fetch me my slippers' and 'Give me my nightcap', that's prose?
PHILOSOPHY MASTER: Yes, sir.
M. JOURDAIN: Gracious me! Here I've been, talking prose for forty years, and never knew it!

Molière *The Would-be Gentleman*, act 2, sc. 4 (1671)

4 Faith, that's as well said, as if I had said it myself.

Jonathan Swift *Polite and Ingenious Conversation*, dialogue 2 (1738)

5 Great folks are of a finer mould;/ Lord! How politely they can scold;/ While a coarse English tongue will itch,/ For whore and rogue; and dog and bitch.

Jonathan Swift 'An Epigram on Scolding', first publ. 1746, collected in *Jonathan Swift: Selected Poems* ed. Roland A. Jeffares (1992)

6 Most men make little other use of their speech than to give evidence against their own understanding.

George Savile, 1st Marquess of Halifax *Political, Moral, and Miscellaneous Thoughts and Reflections*, 'Of Anger' (1750).

7 The true use of speech is not so much to express our wants as to conceal them.

Oliver Goldsmith *The Bee*, no. 3 (20 October 1759), 'On the Use of Language'

8 A fool and his words are soon parted.

William Shenstone *Works in Verse and Prose*, vol. 2, 'On Reserve' (1764)

9 Ay, ay, the best terms will grow obsolete. – Damns have had their day.

Richard Brinsley Sheridan Acres in *The Rivals*, act 2, sc. 1 (1774)

10 Speech happens not to be his language.

Madame de Staël Referring to her lover of the moment, a hussar. Attributed remark.

11 The fear of being silent strikes us dumb.

Anon. Quoted by William Hazlitt in 'On the Conversation of Authors', *London Magazine* September 1820, collected in *The Essays of William Hazlitt* ed. Catherine Macdonald Maclean (1949)

12 It is sometimes wonderful to see how a person, who has been entertaining or tiring a company by the hour together, drops his countenance as if he had been shot, or had been seized by a sudden lockjaw, the moment anyone interposes a single observation.

William Hazlitt in ibid.

13 In fact, the difference between nonsense not worth talking, and nonsense worth it, is simply this: the former is the result of a want of ideas, the latter of a superabundance.

Leigh Hunt *The Indicator* 29 November 1820, collected in *Leigh Hunt as Poet and Essayist* ed. Charles Kent (1891)

14 [Of Macaulay] He has occasional flashes of silence, that make his conversation perfectly delightful.

Sydney Smith *A Memoir of the Reverend*

Sydney Smith, vol. 1, ch. 1, by Lady Holland (1855)

15 'Where shall I begin, please your Majesty?' he [the White Rabbit] asked./ 'Begin at the beginning,' the King said, gravely, 'and go on till you come to the end: then stop.'
Lewis Carroll *Alice's Adventures in Wonderland*, ch. 12 (1865)

16 A gentleman talking of the unintelligible exclamations of persons who cry their goods in the streets of London, particularly milk, Caleb Whiteford observed that if it was unintelligible as English, it was very expressive as French – *Mi-eau*; that is, *half water*.
Anon. *The New London Jest Book*, 'Choice Jests', no. 251, ed. W. C. Hazlitt (1871)

17 'Conversation, indeed!' said the Rocket. 'You have talked the whole time yourself. That is not conversation.' 'Somebody must listen,' answered the Frog, 'and I like to do all the talking myself. It saves time, and prevents arguments.'
Oscar Wilde *The Happy Prince and Other Tales*, 'The Remarkable Rocket' (1888)

18 Most English talk is a quadrille in a sentry box.
Henry James *The Awkward Age*, bk 5, ch. 19 (1899)

19 I don't know if women don't like it [swearing] from men: they think it shows vigour.
Alfred, Lord Tennyson *Tennyson and His Friends: Some Recollections of Tennyson's Talk from 1835 to 1853* ed. Hallam, Lord Tennyson (1911)

20 How can I know what I think till I see what I say?
Graham Wallas Quoting 'a little girl' in *The Art of Thought*, ch. 4 (1926)

21 What the oboe does for an orchestra the American accent not used to excess can do for the sound of conversational chatter that one hears

on arriving at a house where a party is in full progress.
Compton Mackenzie *Vestal Fire*, bk 1, ch. 3 (1927)

22 If, with the literate, I am/ Impelled to try an epigram,/ I never seek to take the credit;/ We all assume that Oscar said it.
Dorothy Parker *Sunset Gun*, 'Oscar Wilde' (1928)

23 The human brain starts working the moment you are born and never stops until you stand up to speak in public.
Sir George Jessel *Observer*, 'Sayings of the Week', 7 August 1949, collected in *The Observer Sayings of the Week* ed. Valerie Ferguson (1987)

24 There is an inexorable law which causes one to talk about imbeciles to those who have retarded children, poverty to those on the breadline, and dowdiness to those draped in the fashion of 1950.
Katherine Whitehorn *Whitehorn's Social Survival*, 'Dropped Bricks' (1968)

25 Repartee is something we think of twenty-four hours too late.
Mark Twain *And I Quote*, 'Humour', ed. Ashton Applewhite and others (1992)

26 There's no need to use language. That's what I always say.
Tom Stoppard Thelma in *After Magritte* (one-act play, 1970). Harris has just used the word 'flaming'.

27 I think like a genius, I write like a distinguished author, and I speak like a child.
Vladimir Nabokov *Strong Opinions*, Foreword (1973). Nabokov cited this as the reason he would grant interviews 'only on the understanding they would not be spontaneous'.

28 [Of W. H. Auden] He talks like a driver shooting red lights.
Natasha Spender Quoted in *The Diaries of Kenneth Tynan* ed. John Lahr (2001), entry for 23 February 1973

29 It amuses me in a discouraging way to know I borrow adjectives, nouns, verbs and short phrases from

people I am with and frequently find myself trapped inside their smaller vocabularies like a hamster in a cage.

Joseph Heller *Something Happened*, 'My Wife Is Unhappy' (1974)

30 Isn't it funny how some people will say, 'I'm so hungry I could eat a horse' but never 'I'm so late I could *ride* a horse?'

David Mamet Edmond in *Squirrels*, episode 1 (1974)

31 DON: According to you.
   TEACH: According to me, yes. I am the person it's usually according *to* when I'm talking.

David Mamet *American Buffalo*, act 2 (1975)

32 WAITER: What will you have, sir?
   MAN: Steak and kiddly pie, please.
   WAITER: You mean steak and kidney pie, sir.
   MAN: I said kiddly, diddle I?

Anon. *The Ha Ha Bonk Book*, 'Jokes to Tell Somebody Else's Dog', ed. Janet and Allan Ahlberg (1982)

33 You want to learn the first rule you'd know if you ever spent a day in your life, you never open your mouth till you know what the shot is.

David Mamet Roma in *Glengarry Glen Ross*, act 2 (1983)

34 In a world in which we are constantly assaulted by stimuli – broadcast media, piped-in music, bright lights, bold graphics, exotic scents, indeed, sounds, sights and smells of every kind – there are still moments of quiet, repose and calm. You can get rid of them by talking.

P. J. O'Rourke *Modern Manners*, ch. 9 (1983)

35 As a Trappist monk takes a vow of silence, she had taken a vow of conversation.

Gilbert Adair *The Holy Innocents*, pt 1 (1988)

36 You don't need to listen to his words: the very cadence of Mr Hurd's voice says, 'of course'.

Matthew Parris Of Douglas Hurd. *The Times*

29 June 1993, collected in *I Couldn't Possibly Comment* (1997).

37 Status quo, you know, that is Latin for 'the mess we're in'.

Ronald Reagan At a reception for members of the Associated General Contractors of America, 16 March 1981. *Ronald Reagan: The Wisdom and Humour of the Great Communicator*, 'People Are the Government', ed. Frederick J. Ryan Jr (1995).

38 On the hotel steps I saw Alisdair McNeane . . . a small ruddy Scotsman possessed of such consuming eagerness that he had a habit of reacting to remarks that had not yet been made.

John Preston *Ghosting*, ch. 25 (1996)

39 KEN DODD [as a ventriloquist, addressing his dummy Dickie Mint]: 'I would like to hear you say "Around the rugged rock the ragged rascal ran." '
   DICKIE MINT: 'So would I.'

Ken Dodd On stage at the Empire Theatre, Sunderland, May 2000, quoted in the *Daily Telegraph* 1 July 2000. Dodd, actually quite a decent ventriloquist, delivered Mint's reply in the most mournful of voices.

40 He was the kind of Texan who takes his time telling you to fuck off.

D. B. C. Pierre *Vernon God Little*, act 1, ch. 9 (2003)

Discretion, Indiscretion and Gossip

1 You cannot rely on ready ears to contain a secret,/ and once a word escapes, it flies beyond recall.

Horace *Epistles*, bk 1, no. 18 (c.20 BC), *Horace: Satires and Epistles; Persius: Satires* trans. and ed. Niall Rudd (1973)

2 How hard it is for women to keep counsel!

William Shakespeare Portia in *Julius Caesar*, act 2, sc. 4 (1599)

3 Love, and a cough, cannot be hid.

George Herbert *Outlandish Proverbs*, no. 49 (1640)

4 The harm of an action lies only in its being known. The public scandal is what constitutes the offence: sins committed in private are not sins at all.

Molière Tartuffe in *Tartuffe*, act 4, sc. 5 (1669)

5 'Tis the greatest misfortune in nature for a woman to want a confidant! We are so weak that we can do nothing without assistance, and then a secret wracks us worse than the colic.

George Farquhar Melinda in *The Recruiting Officer*, act 4, sc. 2 (1706)

6 Now that part of his head which nature designed for the reservoir of drink, being shallow, a small quantity of liquor overflowed it, and opened the sluices of his heart; so that all the secrets there deposited ran out.

Henry Fielding Of the school master Partridge in *Tom Jones*, bk 10, ch. 5 (1749)

7 In scandal, as in robbery, the receiver is always thought as bad as the thief.

Lord Chesterfield *Advice to his Son*, 'Rules for Conversation: Private Scandal' (1775)

8 I vow I bear no malice against the people I abuse: when I say an ill natured thing, 'tis out of pure good humour.

Richard Brinsley Sheridan Lady Teazle in *The School for Scandal*, act 2, sc. 1 (1777)

9 Mercy on me, here is the whole set! A character dead at every word, I suppose.

Sir Peter Teazle in ibid., upon seeing the company gathered at Lady Sneerwell's house. Act 2, sc. 2.

10 Bayle says that a woman will inevitably divulge every secret with which she is entrusted, except one – and that is *her own age*.

Anon. *Glasgow Magazine of Wit* (1803)

11 'Kitty has no discretion in her coughs,' said her father: 'she times them ill.'

Jane Austen *Pride and Prejudice*, ch. 2 (1813)

12 'If everybody minded their own business,' the Duchess said in a hoarse growl, 'the world would go round a deal faster than it does.'

Lewis Carroll *Alice's Adventures in Wonderland*, ch. 6 (1865)

13 Confidante: One entrusted by 'A' with the secrets of 'B' confided to herself by 'C'.

Ambrose Bierce *The Devil's Dictionary* (compiled 1881–1906)

14 'It is perfectly monstrous,' he said at last, 'the way people go about nowadays saying things against one behind one's back that are perfectly true.'

Oscar Wilde *The Picture of Dorian Gray*, ch. 15 (1891). Lady Narborough has just said to Lord Henry Wotton: 'Everybody I know says you are very wicked.'

15 Well, this is the story; get your blushes ready.

Dan Leno *Dan Leno Hys Booke*, Chapter Fifth (1899)

16 Questions are never indiscreet. Answers sometimes are.

Oscar Wilde Mrs Cheveley in *An Ideal Husband*, act 1 (1899)

17 My arse contemplates those who talk behind my back.

Francis Picabia *291* magazine, no. 15 (10 July 1921)

18 Mrs Peniston was one of the episodical persons who form the padding of life. It is impossible to believe that she had herself ever been a focus of its activities.

Edith Wharton *The House of Mirth*, ch. 5 (1936)

19 It's terrible to think of all the harm that people cause/ All through opening of their mouths instead of holding of their jaws.

A. P. Herbert *Sip! Swallow!*, ch. 22 (1937)

20 Gossip is the tool of the poet, the shop-talk of the scientist, and the consolation of the housewife, wit, tycoon and intellectual. It begins in

the nursery and ends when speech is past.

Phyllis McGinley *Woman's Home Companion* January 1957

21 If you haven't got anything good to say about anyone come and sit by me.

Alice Roosevelt Longworth Maxim reputedly embroidered on a cushion. Quoted in *Time* 9 December 1966.

22 Discretion is the better part of Valerie.

Roger McGough *Watchwords*, 'Discretion' (1969)

23 Nudge, nudge, wink, wink, say n'more, know what I mean?

Monty Python team Eric Idle as a lewd and insinuating lower-middle-class type in *Monty Python's Flying Circus*, 1st series, episode 3, first broadcast 19 October 1969. Idle later revived the character to advertise Breakaway chocolate bars.

24 'Mind you, I've said nothing' – I wouldn't like that to be my epitaph.

Conor Cruise O'Brien *Observer*, 'Sayings of the Week', 1 June 1969

25 I don't care what anybody says about me as long as it isn't true.

Truman Capote *The Americans*, 'When Does a Writer Become a Star?' by David Frost (1970). Also attributed to Katharine Hepburn.

26 Men have always detested women's gossip because they suspect the truth: their measurements are being taken and compared.

Erica Jong *Fear of Flying*, ch. 6 (1973)

27 Bad taste is simply the truth before it should be said.

Mel Brooks Attributed. Quoted in *Wit and Wisdom of the Movie-Makers* ed. J. R. Colombo (1979).

28 Gossip is what you say about the objects of flattery when they aren't present.

P. J. O'Rourke *Modern Manners*, ch. 9 (1983)

29 Sweetness, I was only joking when I said/ By rights you should be bludgeoned in your bed.

Morrissey 'Bigmouth Strikes Again' (song, 1986, by Johnny Marr and Morrissey)

30 Listen, when I started . . . the only forms of mass communication we had were the Western Union and women.

George Burns *All My Best Friends*, ch. 1 (1989)

31 The idea of strictly minding our own business is moldy rubbish. Who could be so selfish?

Myrtie Barker Quoted in *Women's Wit and Wisdom* (1991)

32 Secrets for her mother still hold their charms. As they trickle in throughout the week, I spend many happy hours gasping, 'No!' into the telephone.

Mary Killen *How to Live with Your Husband*, 'Secrets' (1996)

Charm and Flattery

1 Who will pity a charmer that is bitten by a serpent?

Apocrypha: Ecclesiasticus 12:13, the Bible, Authorized Version (1611)

2 Old praise dies, unlesse you feede it.

George Herbert *Outlandish Proverbs*, no. 699 (1640)

3 There's nothing I hate more than the contortions of your protestation-mongers, the affable exchangers of fatuous greetings, polite mouthers of meaningless words, who bandy civilities with all comers and treat everyone, blockhead and man of sense, alike.

Molière Alceste in *The Misanthropist*, act 1, sc. 1 (1666)

4 A nice man is a man of nasty ideas.

Jonathan Swift *Miscellanies in Prose and Verse*, 'Various Thoughts Moral and Diverting' (1711)

5 In general I do not draw well with Literary men – not that I dislike them but – I never know what to say to them after I have praised their latest publication.

Lord Byron 'Detached Thoughts', no. 53, collected in *Letters and Journals*, vol. 9, *In the*

Wind's Eye (1821–1822), ed. Leslie A. Marchand (1979)

6　Fill a person with love for themselves, and what runs over will be your share, says a certain witty and truthful Frenchman, whose name I can't for the life of me remember.
Jerome K. Jerome *The Idle Thoughts of an Idle Fellow*, 'On Vanity and Vanities' (1889)

7　The advantage of doing one's praising for oneself is that one can lay it on so thick and in exactly the right places.
Samuel Butler *The Way of All Flesh*, ch. 34 (1903)

8　Laudanum: The benumbing effects of excessive praise.
Anon. *The Dictionary of Puns*, 'Laudanum', ed. John S. Crosbie (1977)

9　When a man brings flowers home to his wife for no reason, there is usually a reason.
Anon. Quoted in *Laughter Lines: Family Wit and Wisdom*, 'For Better or Worse', ed. James A. Simpson (1987)

Jealousy

1　The ear of jealousy heareth all things.
Apocrypha: The Wisdom of Solomon 1:10, the Bible, Authorized Version (1611)

2　Your pot broken seems better than my whole one.
George Herbert *Outlandish Proverbs*, no. 270 (1640)

3　This only grant me, that my means may lie/ Too low for envy, for contempt too high.
Abraham Cowley *Essays, in Verse and Prose*, 'Of Myself' (1668)

4　If in a battle you should find One, whom you love of all mankind,/ Had some heroic action done,/ A champion killed, or trophy won:/ Rather than thus be overtopped,/ Would you not wish his laurels cropped?
Jonathan Swift 'Verses on the Death of Dr

Swift, D.S., P.D.' The poem was inspired by reading a maxim of La Rochefoucauld's which translates: 'In the adversity of our best friends we find something that doth not displease us.' Written 1731, collected in *Jonathan Swift: The Selected Poems* ed. Roland A. Jeffares (1992)

5　. . . [William] Goldsmith looked at, considered, public notoriety, or fame, as one great parcel, to the whole of which he laid claim, and whoever partook of any part of it, whether dancer, singer, sleight of hand man, or tumbler, deprived him of his right.
Joshua Reynolds *The Life of Sir Joshua Reynolds*, Vol 1, '1771' by James Northcote (1819)

6　Mary, had Phoebe been dying, you would have called her an angel, but that is ever the way. 'Tis all jealousy to the bride, and good wishes to the corpse.
J. M. Barrie Miss Susan in *Quality Street*, act 1 (1902)

7　The dullard's envy of brilliant men is always assuaged by the suspicion that they will come to a bad end.
Max Beerbohm *Zuleika Dobson*, ch. 4 (1911)

8　Everybody hates me because I'm so universally liked.
Peter De Vries The narrator Joe Sandwich in *The Vale of Laughter*, pt 1, ch. 1 (1967)

Trust

1　What a fool Honesty is! and Trust, his sworn brother, a very simple gentleman.
William Shakespeare Autolycus in *The Winter's Tale*, act 4, sc. 3 (1610–11)

2　It is a folly to expect men to do all that they may reasonably be expected to do.
Richard Whately *Apophthegms* (1854)

3　Put not your trust in money, but put your money in trust.
Oliver Wendell Holmes *The Autocrat of the Breakfast Table*, ch. 2 (1858)

4 **Trust everybody, but cut the cards.**

Finley Peter Dunne *Mr Dooley's Philosophy*, 'Casual Observations' (1900)

5 **To trust people is a luxury in which only the wealthy can indulge; the poor cannot afford it.**

E. M. Forster *Howards End*, ch. 5 (1910)

6 **Never trust a husband too far, nor a bachelor too near.**

Helen Rowland *A Guide to Men*, 'Finale' (1922)

7 **Nobody really trusts anyone – or why do they put 'Tilt' on a pinball machine?**

Steve McQueen Quoted in *McQueen*, ch. 6, by Christopher Sandford (2001). Sandford describes this as McQueen's 'lifelong credo'.

8 **Most people are pretty trustworthy. A telltale sign of people who aren't is that they often say, 'Trust me.'**

Guy Browning *Guardian*, 'How to . . .' column, 23 August 2003

Misanthropy

1 **Man, I can assure you, is a nasty creature.**

Molière Tartuffe in *Tartuffe*, act 5, sc. 6 (1669)

2 **Happily I caught a little cold on Wednesday, the morning we were in Town, which we made very useful; & we saw nobody but our precious, & Mr Tilson.**

Jane Austen Letter to Cassandra Austen of 2 December 1815, collected in *Jane Austen's letters* ed. Dierdre Le Faye (1995)

3 **The sooner every party breaks up the better.**

Jane Austen Mr Woodhouse in *Emma*, ch. 25 (1816)

4 **I have a great deal of company in my house; especially in the morning, when nobody calls.**

Henry David Thoreau *Walden; or, Life in the Woods*, 'Solitude' (1854)

5 **It is easy to find fault, if one has that disposition. There was once a man who, not being able to find** any other fault with his coal, complained that there were too many prehistoric toads in it.

Mark Twain *The Tragedy of Pudd'nhead Wilson*, ch. 9, 'Pudd'nhead Wilson's Calender' (1894)

6 **I wish I loved the human race;/ I wish I loved its silly face;/ I wish I loved the way it walks;/ I wish I liked the way it talks;/ And when I'm introduced to one/ I wish I thought *What jolly fun!***

Sir Walter Raleigh *Laughter from a Cloud*, 'Wishes of an Elderly Man' (1923)

7 **I want to be alone.**

Greta Garbo From the film *Grand Hotel* (1932, screenplay by William A. Drake, directed by Edmund Goulding). In the film *The Single Standard* (1929) she had said: 'I am walking alone because I want to be alone.' The phrase has come to epitomize the Garbo mystique.

8 **The papers are full of the atomic bomb [Hiroshima] which is going to revolutionize everything and blow us all to buggery. Not a bad idea.**

Noël Coward Diary entry for 8 August 1945, *The Noël Coward Diaries* ed. G. Payn and S. Morley (1982)

9 **What've ya got?**

Marlon Brando Johnny (Marlon Brando), on being asked what he is rebelling against, in *The Wild One* (film, 1953, screenplay by John Paxton from a story by Frank Rooney, directed by Laslo Benedek)

10 **I love mankind – it's people I can't stand.**

Charles Schulz Linus in *Go Fly a Kite*, 'Charlie Brown' (1962)

11 **'Get off My Cloud'**

Mick Jagger and Keith Richards Song title, 1965

12 **Beyond the plaza, in the formal vista of the ornamental gardens, solitary pedestrians moved like bedouin, separated from one another by Saharas of empty brown flower-beds and drying tarmacadam. They were so small they seemed to be merely an infestation.**

The authorities should have put human-being powder down and got rid of them.

Michael Frayn *The Russian Interpreter* (1966)

13 In my life why do I smile/ At people who I'd much rather kick in the eye?

Morrissey 'Heaven Knows I'm Miserable Now' (song, 1984, written by Morrissey and Johnny Marr)

14 The art of hospitality is to make people feel at home when you wish they were.

Anon. Quoted in *A Gentleman Publisher's Commonplace Book*, 'Core', by John G. Murray (1996)

15 They are usually a mistake.

Quentin Crisp The subject is other people. Quoted in the *Spectator* 20 November 1999.

16 [On spotting Amis looking grumpy at a party] That's Kingsley Amis, and there's no known cure.

Robert Graves Attributed remark. Quoted in *People on People: The Oxford Dictionary of Biographical Quotations* ed. Susan Ratcliffe (2001).

Shyness

1 The shy man does have some slight revenge upon society for the torture it inflicts upon him. He is able, to a certain extent, to communicate his misery. He frightens other people as much as they frighten him. He acts like a damper on the whole room, and the most jovial spirits become, in his presence, depressed and nervous.

Jerome K. Jerome *Idle Thoughts of an Idle Fellow*, 'On Being Shy' (1889)

2 Shyness is just egotism out of its depth.

Penelope Keith *Daily Mail* 27 June 1988

3 I have always believed in the phrase 'shy bairns get nowt'.

Lara Dixon *The Times*, 'Quotes of the Week', 17 July 1999. Lara, from Whitley Bay, Tyne & Wear, had just won a scholarship to Harvard.

Names

1 And if his name be George, I'll call him Peter.

William Shakespeare Philip the Bastard in *King John*, act 1, sc. 1 (1594–6)

2 Sir, my name is Sir Tunbelly Clumsey, whether you have any business with me or not.

Sir John Vanbrugh *The Relapse*, act 3, sc. 3 (1696)

3 'Violet' is thought a suitable name for the sweetest heroines of romance, on account of its association with the flower; yet add but a letter to it, and that not a harsh one, and it becomes the most unfeminine of characteristics – Violent.

Leigh Hunt *Table Talk*, 'Violet – with a Difference' (1882)

4 Besides, Jack is a notorious domesticity for John! And I pity any woman who is married to a man called John. She would have a very tedious life with him.

Oscar Wilde Gwendolen Fairfax in *The Importance of Being Earnest*, act 1 (1895)

5 She saved a certain amount of time every day by addressing her son as Denry, instead of Edward Henry.

Arnold Bennett *The Card*, ch. 1 (1911)

6 [On being introduced to a Mr Tarrington] 'A very useful kind of name,' said Clovis; 'with a name of that sort no one would blame you if you did nothing in particular heroic or remarkable, would they?'

Saki *The Chronicles of Clovis*, 'The Talking-out of Tarrington' (1911)

7 [On the question of whether to call his son Augustin or Augustus] 'No, it shall be tus,' I said. 'Tus is better than tin.'

Sir Henry Howarth Bashford *Augustus Carp Esq. by Himself*, ch. 19 (1924). This, according to Anthony Burgess in his postscript to the 1966 edition, is one of the quotations that has passed into the private language of lovers of the book.

8 **Higgins was his name, but that was not his fault.**

Mark Twain *Autobiography*, ch. 26 (1924)

9 **I was up in Martinez dickering with a divorced wife of Phil Leach, alias a lot of names.**

Dashiell Hammett *The Dain Curse*, ch. 13 (1929)

10 **GEORGE BURNS: What's your name?**
GRACIE ALLEN: Gracie L. Allen.
GEORGE BURNS: What's the 'L' for?
GRACIE ALLEN: George, watch your language!

George Burns George is examining Gracie in a court of law. Sketch from the US radio sitcom *The George Burns and Gracie Allen Show* (1932–50), collected in *The Golden Age of Comedy: George Burns and Gracie Allen* (CD, 2000)

11 **There is a very beautiful character called Mr Cox at the London Library. You must not make jokes about his name.**

Evelyn Waugh Letter to Lady Mary Langdon of 27 November 1946, collected in *The Letters of Evelyn Waugh* ed. Mark Amory (1980). Mr Frederick Cox (1865–1955) worked for seventy years at the Library.

12 **There was a boy called Eustace Clarence Scrubb, and he almost deserved it.**

C. S. Lewis The opening sentence of *The Voyage of the Dawn Treader* (1955)

13 **Have you noticed how, sooner or later, all doctors are called Mackenzie?**

George Lyttelton Letter of 4 April 1956 to Rupert Hart-Davis, collected in *The Lyttelton–Hart-Davis Letters*, vols 1 and 2, *1955–1957*, ed. Rupert Hart-Davis (1978)

14 **PS: Did you know there's an English family whose name is Hodbod?**

Letter of 19 August 1956 to Rupert Hart-Davis, ibid.

15 **'Leila York's my pen name. I was born Elizabeth Binns. You can't write books if you're a Binns.'**

P. G. Wodehouse *Ice in the Bedroom*, ch. 4

(1961). She is the author of *Heather o'the Hills* and *Sweet Jennie Dean*.

16 **The name of a man is a numbing blow from which he never recovers.**

Marshall McLuhan *Understanding Media*, ch. 2 (1964)

17 **Those girls' names in Numbers! Milcah, Noah, Mahlah, Hoglah, and Tirzah. They sound a bit butch to me. Except for Mahlah maybe. She must have been the dainty one, do you think?**

Joyce Grenfell Letter of 6 September 1973 from Grenfell to Virginia Graham, collected in *Joyce and Ginnie: The Letters of Joyce Grenfell and Virginia Graham* ed. Janie Hampton (1997)

18 **Homer: An American name.**

Beachcomber *Beachcomber: The Works of J. B. Morton*, 'A Dictionary for Today', ed. Richard Ingrams (1974)

19 **I have often wondered what the derivation of my surname was, and I wonder if you can throw light on it? – J. Windowcleaner of Parva Magna, Wilts**

Miles Kington *Moreover*, 'The Moreover Advice Service' (1982)

20 **Agamemnon: Good name for a cat.**

Henry Root *Henry Root's World of Knowledge* (1982)

21 **Readers called Stephen, save time by calling yourself 'Steve'.**

Viz Fake reader's letter, Christmas 2002

22 **Following the debate about women retaining their married names, it occurs to me that if Isla St Clair had married the late Barry White, and then Bryan Ferry, she would now be Isla White Ferry.**

Anon. Letter to the *Daily Telegraph* of 7 August 2003

23 **Q: What's the difference between Tufnell Park and Florence? A: In Tufnell Park there are lots of little girls called Florence, but there are no girls called Tufnell Park in Florence.**

Anon. Joke in circulation in Tufnell Park, North London, in 2003

24 **I am the Smith of my own fortune.**
F. E. Smith Quoted in *Postmaster and the Merton Record* (2003)

Work
Hard Work and Laziness

1 **He that diggeth a pit shall fall into it ...**
Ecclesiastes 10:8, the Bible, Authorized Version (1611)

2 **By much slothfulness the building decayeth; and through idleness of the hands the house droppeth through.**
Ibid. 10:18

3 **Anything for a Quiet Life.**
Thomas Middleton Title of a play, c.1620. In Charles Dickens's *Pickwick Papers*, ch. 51 Sam Weller says: 'Anythin' for a quiet life as the man said wen he took the sitivation [situation] at the lighthouse.'

4 **He that would thrive/ Must rise at five;/ He that hath thriven/ May lie till seven.**
John Clarke *Paraemiologia Anglo-Latina*, 'Diligentia' (1639)

5 **I wish I *could* help you in your Needlework, I have two hands & a new thimble that lead a very easy life.**
Jane Austen Letter to Cassandra Austen of 27–28 December 1808, collected in *Jane Austen's Letters* ed. Dierdre Le Faye (1995)

6 **The shortest way to do many things is to do only one thing at once.**
Samuel Smiles *Self-Help*, ch.9 (1859)

7 **I breakfast after I have done my day's work.**
Anthony Trollope Letter to George Bentley of 9 November 1875, collected in *The Letters of Anthony Trollope* ed. Bradford Allen Booth (1951). In ch. 7 of his *Autobiography* Trollope wrote: 'While I was in Egypt, I finished *Dr Thorne*, and on the following day I began *The Bertrams*. I was moved now by a determination to excel, if not in quality, at any rate in quantity.'

8 **A birdie with a yellow bill/ Hopped upon the window-sill,/ Cocked his shining eye and said:/ 'Ain't you 'shamed, you sleepy-head?'**
Robert Louis Stevenson *A Child's Garden of Verses*, 'Time to Rise' (1885)

9 **It is impossible to enjoy idling thoroughly unless one has plenty of work to do.**
Jerome K. Jerome *Idle Thoughts of an Idle Fellow*, 'On Being Idle' (1886)

10 **I like work; it fascinates me. I can sit and look at it for hours.**
Jerome K. Jerome *Three Men in a Boat*, ch. 15 (1889)

11 **It is awfully hard work doing nothing. However, I don't mind hard work where there is no definite object of any kind ...**
Oscar Wilde Algernon Moncrieff in *The Importance of Being Earnest*, act 1 (1895)

12 **Why, he rides in the Row at ten o'clock in the morning, goes to the Opera three times a week, changes his clothes at least five times a day, and dines out every night of the season. You don't call that leading an idle life, do you?**
Oscar Wilde Mabel Chiltern in *An Ideal Husband*, act 1 (1899)

13 **'Back to Glasgow to do some work for the cause,' I said lightly. 'Just so,' he said, with a grin. 'It's a great life if you don't weaken.'**
John Buchan *Mr Standfast*, ch.5 (1919)

14 **For one person who dreams of making fifty thousand pounds, a hundred people dream of being left fifty thousand pounds.**
A. A. Milne *If I May*, 'The Future' (1920)

15 **It is not real work unless you would rather be doing something else.**
J. M. Barrie Speech to St Andrew's University of 3 May 1922

16 **Idleness is only a coarse name for my infinite capacity for living in the present.**
Cyril Connolly *Journal and Memoir: The Jour-*

nal of Cyril Connolly 1928–1937 ed. David Pryce-Jones (1983)

17 **It is better to have loafed and lost than never to have loafed at all.**

James Thurber *Fables for Our Time*, 'The Courtship of Arthur and Al' (1940). Compare Tennyson, *In Memoriam A. H. H.* (1850): ' 'Tis better to have loved and lost/ Than never to have loved at all.' And Congreve, *The Way of the World*, act 2, sc. 1 (1700): 'Say what you will, 'tis better to be left than never to/ have been loved.'

18 **I believe fully in the Chinese maxim that it is foolish to do anything standing up that can be done sitting, or anything sitting that can be done stretched out.**

H. L. Mencken Entry for 5 May 1945, *The Diary of H. L. Mencken* ed. C. A. Fecher (1989)

19 **As the proverbial Irishman said, I have put my hand to the plough and now I must lie on it.**

Christopher Isherwood Arthur Norris in *Mr Norris Changes Trains*, ch. 4 (1947)

20 **Why should I let the toad *work*/ Squat on my life?/ Can't I use my wit as a pitchfork/ And drive the brute off?**

Philip Larkin 'Toads' (1955). Robert Phillips, interviewing Larkin for the *Paris Review* in 1983, asked: 'How did you arrive upon the image of a toad for work or labour?' Larkin replied: 'Sheer genius.'

21 **I discovered that I was putting on quite a bit of weight and was told that walking was fine for that sort of thing, but, since making the resolution to walk everywhere I go, I find that I just don't *go* anywhere.**

Robert Benchley *Benchley or Else*, 'The Railroad Problem' (1958)

22 **He's been on the dole that long he goes to the staff dances.**

Bernard Manning *Laugh with the Comedians* (LP, 1971)

23 **Being busy is the best excuse for not working.**

Kenneth Tynan Entry for 25 February 1971, *The Diaries of Kenneth Tynan* ed. John Lahr (2001)

24 **Lazy? He used to ride his bike over cobblestones to knock the ash off his ciggie.**

Les Dawson *The Les Dawson Joke Book* (1979)

25 **I could've married a lot of people, but I was busy.**

Mae West Quoted in *the Ultimate Seduction*, 'Mae West', by Charlotte Chandler (1984). West was married once, briefly.

26 **It's not really surprising that I arrived here on a long weekend; you'd be hard pushed to find a way of arriving in Australia on anything else.**

Howard Jacobson *Redback*, ch. 8 (1986)

27 **The parish priest asked young David: 'Which Bible story do you like best, my son?'/ 'The one about the fellow who just loafs and fishes.'**

Anon. Quoted in *The World's Best Fishing Jokes* by John Gurney (1987)

28 **The trouble began with Forster. After him it was considered ungentlemanly to write more than five or six novels.**

Anthony Burgess *Guardian* 24 February 1989

29 **Hard work pays off in the future. Laziness pays off now.**

Steven Wright From his stage act of the 1980s and 90s

30 **We can't stand around here doing nothing. People will think we're working.**

Spike Milligan *And I Quote*, 'Work', ed. Ashton Applewhite and others (1992)

31 **Half-term holiday, family away/ Half wanting to go, half wanting to stay/ Stay in bed for half the day.**

Roger McGough 'Half Term', collected in *The Way Things Are* (1999)

32 **So much time, so little to do.**

Anon. Quoted by Hugo Williams in the *Times Literary Supplement* 26 July 2002. Williams heard somebody say this in connection with what the poets were doing (or not doing) at the Spoleto Poetry Festival in Italy.

33 **Glassback, n.: A person with a poor health record at work. One whose**

constant illnesses keep them from work, but don't prevent them from going to the pub at night or refereeing premiership football matches at the weekend.

Viz Entry in 'Roger's Profanisaurus', September 2003

34 The sooner you fall behind, the more time you have to catch up.

Anon. *Away an' Ask Yer Mother (Your Scottish Father's Favourite Sayings)*, ch. 2, ed. Allan Morrison (2003)

35 They say hard work never hurt anybody, but I figure why take the chance.

Ronald Reagan Attributed

Business Life

1 ... there is boundless theft/ In limited professions.

William Shakespeare Timon in *Timon of Athens*, act 4, sc. 3 (1607–8)

2 Necessity never made a good bargain.

Benjamin Franklin *Poor Richard's Almanac* (1758), entry for April 1735

3 Here's the rule for bargains: 'Do other men, for they would do you.' That's the true business precept.

Charles Dickens The opinion of Mr Jonas in *Martin Chuzzlewit*, ch. 11 (1843–4)

4 It was told to Jekyll that one of his friends, a brewer, had been drowned in his own vat. 'Ah,' he exclaimed, *'floating in his own watery bier.'*

Anon. *The New London Jest Book*, 'Choice Jests', no. 994, ed. W. C. Hazlitt (1871)

5 There's a sucker born every minute.

Phineas T. Barnum Attributed

6 Consult, vb trans.: To seek another's approval of a course already decided upon.

Ambrose Bierce *The Devil's Dictionary* (compiled 1881–1906)

7 He paid some attention to the management of his collieries in the Mid-

land counties, excusing himself for this taint of industry on the ground that the one advantage of having coal was that it enabled a gentleman to afford the decency of burning wood in his own hearth.

Oscar Wilde *The Picture of Dorian Gray*, ch. 3 (1891). The mine owner is Lord Fermor, uncle of Lord Henry Wotton.

8 In modern life margin is everything.

Oscar Wilde Mrs Erlynne in *Lady Windermere's Fan*, act 2 (1893)

9 October. This is one of the peculiarly dangerous months to speculate in stocks in. The others are July, January, September, April, November, May, March, June, December, August and February.

Mark Twain *The Tragedy of Pudd'nhead Wilson*, ch. 13, 'Pudd'nhead Wilson's Calender' (1894)

10 All professions are conspiracies against the laity.

George Bernard Shaw Sir Patrick Cullen in *The Doctor's Dilemma*, act 1 (1906)

11 And remember, dearie, never give a sucker an even break.

W. C. Fields The swindling Professor Eustace McGargle (Fields) in *Poppy* (film, 1936, screenplay by Waldemar Young and Virginia Upp from the play by Dorothy Donnelly, directed by A. Edward Sutherland). This – the last line in the film – became Fields's catchphrase and the title of one of his last films, made in 1941 (called in the UK *What a Man*).

12 A verbal contract isn't worth the paper it is written on.

Sam Goldwyn Attributed. Quoted in *The Great Goldwyn*, ch. 1, by Alva Johnston (1937).

13 No grand idea was ever born in a conference, but a lot of foolish ideas have died there.

F. Scott Fitzgerald *The Crack-Up*, 'Note Books E', ed. Edmund Wilson (1945)

14 Be nice to people on your way up because you'll meet them on the way down.

Wilson Mizner *The Legendary Mizners*, ch. 4

(1953), by Alva Johnson. Also attributed to the comic Jimmy Durante.

15 **Then there is my gambit for the chief executive – having *nothing* on his desk *at all*.**
Stephen Potter *Potter on America*, pt 1, 'Spring 1955' (1955)

16 **Meetings are a great trap. Soon you find yourself trying to get an agreement and then the people who disagree think they have a right to be persuaded. Thus they acquire power; thus meetings become a source of opposition and trouble. However, they are indispensable when you don't want to do anything.**
J. K. Galbraith Entry for 22 April 1961, *Ambassador's Journal*, ch. 5 (1969). Galbraith was US ambassador to India 1961–3.

17 **Chaplin is no businessman – all he knows is he can't take anything less.**
Sam Goldwyn Quoted in *Charles Chaplin: My Autobiography*, ch. 19 (1964)

18 **How dare you involve me in a situation for which no memo has been issued?**
Joe Orton Truscott in *Loot*, act 2 (1966)

19 **Never Mind the Quality, Feel the Width**
Vince Powell and Harry Driver Title of an ITV comedy series (1967–71), which began as a single play for ABC's *Armchair Theatre*

20 **Trading was crisp at the start of the day with some brisk business on the floor. Rubber hardened and string remained confident.**
Monty Python team Eric Idle, portraying a man presenting a stock-market report in *Monty Python's Flying Circus* (BBC TV, 3rd series), episode 1, first broadcast 19 October 1972. He goes on: 'Little bits of tin consolidated although biscuits sank after an early gain and stools remained anonymous.'

21 **Battalions of paper-minded males/ Talking commodities and sales/ While at home their paper wives/ And their paper kids/ Paper the**

walls to keep their gut reactions hid.
Joni Mitchell 'Harry's House – Centerpiece', *The Hissing of Summer Lawns* (LP, 1975)

22 **I am beginning to wonder what I did all the time until I registered for VAT!**
Philip Larkin Letter to Victor Bonham-Carter of 25 April 1977, collected in *Selected Letters of Philip Larkin, 1940–85* ed. Anthony Thwaite (1992)

23 **A camel is a horse designed by a committee.**
Sir Alec Issigonis Attributed. Quoted in the *Guardian* 14 January 1991.

24 **If you think nobody cares you're alive, try missing a couple of car payments.**
Anon. *And I Quote*, 'Self-esteem', ed. Ashton Applewhite and others (1992)

25 **The meek shall inherit the earth, but not the mineral rights.**
J. Paul Getty Attributed. Quoted in *Collins Dictionary of Quotations* ed. A. Norman Jeffares and Martin Gray (1995)

26 **From too much business they didn't close.**
Anon. A waiter at Ratner's Dairy Restaurant in the Lower East Side of New York, explaining why its competitor Rappaport's had gone out of business. Quoted in *The Man Who Ate Everything*, 'Vegging Out', by Jeffrey Steingarten (1997).

27 **People say he's ruthlessly professional. I would say he's professionally ruthless.**
John Lukič Said in 1999 by the one-time Arsenal goalkeeper of his former manager George Graham. Quoted in *The Book of Football Quotations*, 'The Grey Hair and Dreadlocks Club', ed. Phil Shaw (1999).

28 **You should go and see the Millennium Dome. Apparently they've got an exhibition in there that shows you how VAT works.**
Ken Dodd On stage at the Empire Theatre, Sunderland, May 2000. Quoted in the *Daily Telegraph* 1 July 2000. Dodd would refer to the Millennium as 'the aluminium'.

29 **The main advantage of working at**

home is that you get to find out
what cats really do all day.

Lynne Truss Quoted in *Women's Wicked Wit*
ed. Michelle Lovric (2000)

30 **The go-to guy: Refers to the only
person capable of actually making
something happen in a corporate
structure.**

Anon. 'The Jargon Bulletin', a dictionary of
jargon, *Word* magazine June 2003

31 **Sooner or later in life everything
turns into work, including work.**

Alan Bennett *Guardian* 27 September 2003

32 **Of a retired executive, it was said
by his successor that he was his
'sexual consultant': 'When I want
his fucking advice I'll ask for it.'**

Anon. Quoted by Nicholas Lezard in his
review of *Bad Company: The Strange Cult of
the CEO* by Gideon Haigh, *Guardian*,
13 March 2004

33 **Over his shoulder, I watch Ms
Moody shake her head several
times. She's leaning against the
filing cabinet, filing her nails.**

Daren King *Jim Giraffe*, 'Rhinoceros Poo'
(2004)

34 **The codfish lays ten thousand eggs,/
The homely hen lays one./ The codfish never cackles/ To tell you what
she's done./ And so we scorn the codfish,/ While the humble hen we
prize,/ Which only goes to show
you/ That it pays to advertise.**

Anon. 'It Pays to Advertise'; perenially
undated poem

Particular Professions

1 **Let every eye negotiate for itself,
and trust no agent.**

William Shakespeare Claudio in *Much Ado
About Nothing*, act 2, sc. 1 (1600)

2 **Physician, heal thyself.**

Luke 4:23, the Bible, Authorized Version (1611)

3 **Woe unto you, lawyers! for ye have
taken away the key of knowledge.**

Ibid., 11:52

4 **Physicians are like kings, – they
brook no contradiction.**

John Webster Ferdinand in *The Duchess of
Malfi*, act 5, sc. 2 (1623)

5 **Be not a baker, if your head be of
butter.**

George Herbert *Outlandish Proverbs*, no. 321
(1640)

6 **GÉRONTE: It seemed to me that you
got them the wrong way round,
that the heart should be on the
left side, and the liver on the
right.
SGANARELLE: Yes, that was the way
it used to be, but we've changed
all that. Everything's quite different in medicine nowadays.**

Molière *The Doctor Despite Himself*, act 2,
sc. 4 (1667)

7 **Who shall decide, when doctors disagree,/ And sound casuists doubt,
like you and me?**

Alexander Pope *Epistles to Several Persons*,
'To Lord Bathurst' (1733)

8 **To say the truth, every physician
almost hath his favourite disease,
to which he ascribes all the victories obtained over human nature.**

Henry Fielding *Tom Jones*, bk 2, ch. 9 (1749)

9 **[Of advertisers] I cannot but propose
it as a moral question to these
masters of the public ear, whether
they do not sometimes play too
wantonly with our passions.**

Samuel Johnson *The Idler*, 20 January 1759

10 **Well, this is the first time I ever
heard of an innkeeper's philosophy.**

Oliver Goldsmith Sir Charles Marlow in *She
Stoops to Conquer*, act 2, sc. 1 (1773)

11 **No man will be a sailor who has
contrivance enough to get himself
into jail; for being in a ship is being
in a jail, with the chance of being
drowned . . .**

Samuel Johnson *The Life of Samuel Johnson*
by James Boswell, vol. 1, (1791); in G. B. Hill's
edition of 1887, rev. L. F. Powell (1934). In *The
Anatomy of Melancholy*, pt 2, sect. 3 (1621–
51), Robert Burton wrote: 'What is a ship but
a prison?'

12 **A mere antiquarian is a rugged being.**

Ibid. vol. 3, p. 278. Johnson thought there should be 'attention to poetry besides'.

13 **An apothecary in Durham has the following words written in his shop window: '*Dying* stuffs sold here.'**

Anon. *Glasgow Magazine of Wit* (1803)

14 **A stationer, too, on obvious accounts, will excuse us for thinking his concern a very dull and bald-headed business.**

Leigh Hunt 'On the Sight of Shops', *The Indicator* 31 May 1820, collected in *Leigh Hunt as Poet and Essayist* ed. Charles Kent (1891)

15 **Honest William, an easy and good-natured fellow,/ Would a little too oft get a little too mellow;/ Body coachman was he to an eminent brewer,/ No better sat on a box to be sure.**

Anon. 'Brewer's Companion', *Oliver's Comic Songs* (1825?)

16 **In a post-office bred, what a life sure I led,/ As I handled the thoughts of my betters;/ Oh! It was such a scene, that our great public inn/ Might be called a republic of letters.**

'The Post Office', ibid.

17 **I'm jolly Dick the lamplighter,/ They say the sun's my dad;/ And truly I believe it, sir,/ For I'm a pretty lad./ Father and I the world do light,/ And make it look so gay;/ The diff'rence is, I lights by night,/ And father lights by day**

'Jolly Dick the Lamplighter', ibid.

18 **Tho' a barber, I am not ashamed of my trade,/ For by shaving a fortune is easily made;/ From the prince on the throne to the cobbler in stall,/ The principal point's to shave well and shave all.**

'Shave Well and Shave All', ibid.

19 **But of all footmen the lowest class is literary footmen.**

William Hazlitt *Sketches and Essays*, 'Footmen' (1839)

20 **A governess! Better be a slave at once!**

Charlotte Brontë *Shirley*, ch. 13 (1849)

21 **The ugliest of trades have their moments of pleasure. Now, if I were a grave digger, or even a hangman, there are some people I could work for with a great deal of enjoyment.**

Douglas Jerrold *The Wit and Opinions of Douglas Jerrold*, 'Ugly Trades' ed. Blanchard Jerrold (1859)

22 **An American paper spoke of a man who 'died without the aid of a physician'. Such instances of death are very rare.**

Anon. *The New London Jest Book*, 'Choice Jests', no. 114, ed. W. C. Hazlitt (1871)

23 **'Dentist' is an ugly word.**

George Bernard Shaw Philip in *You Never Can Tell*; act 1 (1897). He prefers 'the man of ivory and gold'.

24 **I have no objection to plumbers in the abstract, I just don't like them in my house.**

Dan Leno *Dan Leno Hys Booke*, Chapter Second (1899)

25 **Everybody hates house-agents because they have everybody at a disadvantage. All other callings have a certain amount of give and take; the house-agent simply takes.**

H. G. Wells *Kipps*, bk 3, ch. 1 (1905)

26 **I tell you, Colly, chloroform has done a lot of mischief. It's enabled every fool to become a surgeon.**

George Bernard Shaw Sir Patrick Cullen in *The Doctor's Dilemma*, act 1 (1906)

27 **Henri Deplis was by birth a native of the Grand Duchy of Luxembourg. On maturer reflection he became a commercial traveller.**

Saki *The Chronicles of Clovis*, 'The Background' (1911)

28 **Young Bealby became breathless. 'Why shouldn't I be an engine driver?' he asked./ 'All oily,' said his mother. 'And getting yourself killed in an accident. And got to pay fines. You'd *like* to be an engine driver.'**

H. G. Wells *Bealby*, ch. 1 (1915)

29 Advertising may be described as the science of arresting the human intelligence long enough to get money from it.
Stephen Leacock *The Garden of Folly*, 'The Perfect Salesman' (1924)

30 Yes, yes, the dentist talks a lot; for he's content and you are not.
A. P. Herbert *Sip! Swallow!*, ch. 13 (1937)

31 Ernest Plinlimmon was not one of your butterflies who flit from flower to flower. He was an average adjuster, and average adjusters are like chartered accountants. When they love, they give their hearts for ever.
P. G. Wodehouse *Lord Emsworth and Others*, 'There's Always Golf' (1937)

32 A married man must love his wife, but a navvy can have his pick.
Max Miller 'With the Forces Somewhere in England, Early November 1940', reissued in *Max Miller, The Cheeky Chappie – All His Live Shows in the Late 30s, Early 40s* (CD, 2000)

33 A good farmer is nothing more nor less than a handy man with a sense of humus.
E. B. White *One Man's Meat*, 'The Practical Farmer' (1944)

34 [Query to a tree surgeon] **Have you ever fallen out of a patient?**
Groucho Marx Marx put this question during an episode of the radio version of the game show *You Bet Your Life* (1947–9), over which he presided as quizmaster

35 An advertising agency is 85 per cent confusion and 15 per cent commission.
Fred Allen *Treadmill to Oblivion*, pt 2 (1954)

36 **PRISONER A: Did you never hear of the screw, married a prostitute?**
PRISONER B: No, what happened to him?
PRISONER A: He dragged her down to his level.
Brendan Behan *The Quare Fellow*, act 2 (1956). At another point in the play Warder Regan says of his work: 'It's a soft job, sir, between hangings.'

37 The likes of Healey would take a sup all right, but being a high-up civil servant, he wouldn't drink under his own name.
Dunlavin in ibid., act 1

38 The man at the range, tall and dour like all fish shop proprietors . . .
Keith Waterhouse *Billy Liar*, ch. 12 (1959)

39 I knew a Rouge Dragon Pursuivant once. Then he was promoted Somerset Herald and now when he tells anyone what he is they think he is correspondent of a provincial newspaper. All heralds stammer. Your chum will not rise above pursuivant if he has the full use of his tongue.
Evelyn Waugh Letter to Ann Fleming of 2 September 1959, collected in *The Letters of Evelyn Waugh* ed. Mark Amory (1980)

40 [Of booksellers] **The most agreeable servants of civilization.**
Rebecca West Uttered at a Foyle's Literary Lunch of 1959, quoted in *A Gentleman Publisher's Commonplace Book*, 'Core', by John G. Murray (1996)

41 He soon became a specialist in diseases of the rich.
Tom Lehrer Preamble to 'In Old Mexico', *An Evening Wasted with Tom Lehrer* (LP, 1960)

42 **INTERVIEWER: Aren't you proud of being a doctor?**
DOCTOR HOLLYWOOD: Well, the most . . . because I can park anywhere.
Carl Reiner and Mel Brooks From the sketch 'Psychiatric Society', *Two Thousand and One Years with Carl Reiner and Mel Brooks* (LP, 1961)

43 [Of public relations] **Organized lying**
Malcolm Muggeridge Quoted in *The Anatomy of Britain*, ch. 37, by Anthony Sampson (1962). On the same page Harold Wilson is also quoted on PR: 'A most degrading profession'.

44 [Civil servants] **rise from CMG (known sometimes in Whitehall as 'Call Me God') to the KCMG ('Kindly Call Me God') to – for a select few**

governors and super-ambassadors –
the GCMG ('God Calls Me God').

Anthony Sampson Ibid., ch. 18 (1962)

45 The consumer isn't a moron; she is
your wife.

David Ogilvy *Confessions of an Advertising
Man*, ch. 5 (1963)

46 In that happy time [the 1930s]
when I first became a free-lance
artist, advertising was a disgraceful
trade. The confession that it was
your chosen profession was
received as though you had said
'I'm in burglary.'

Quentin Crisp *The Naked Civil Servant*, ch. 11
(1968). Crisp noted that by the 1960s morality had changed: 'The increased scale of your
operations will lend you respectability. Who,
except possibly the Postmaster General,
would refuse to shake hands with one of the
Great Train Robbers?'

47 Here lies a civil servant. He was
civil/ To everyone, and a servant to
the devil.

C. H. Sisson *The London Zoo*, p. 29 (1969)

48 The astronauts . . . Rotarians in
outer space.

Gore Vidal *Two Sisters*, p. 112 (1970)

49 Our experts describe you as an
appallingly dull fellow, unimagin-
ative, timid, spineless, easily dominated, no sense of humour, tedious
company and irrepressibly drab
and awful. And whereas in most
professions these would be considered drawbacks, in accountancy
they are a positive boon.

Monty Python team *And Now for Something
Completely Different* (film, 1971, screenplay
by the Monty Python team, directed by Terry
Jones)

50 You are invited to the greengrocer's
ball. Dinner at seven thirty. Cabbages at twelve o'clock.

Graeme Garden *I'm Sorry I Haven't a Clue*
(BBC radio series, 1972 onwards), in *I'm Sorry
I Haven't a Clue: Five* (cassette, 1999)

51 You ask me what it is I do./ Well
actually, you know,/ I'm partly a
liaison man and partly P.R.O./
Essentially I integrate the export
drive/ And basically I'm viable from
ten o'clock to five.

John Betjeman 'A Nip in the Air' (1974). An
executive speaking.

52 I assure you that I am a completely
bona fide psychiatrist. Here's my
diploma in psychiatry from the University of Oxford . . . Here's a letter
from another psychiatrist in which
he mentions that I'm a psychiatrist.
I've got a copy of *Psychiatry Today*
in my bag, which I think is pretty
convincing. And a letter here from
my mother in which she asks how
the psychiatry is going . . .

Monty Python team Third Psychiatrist
(Michael Palin) in *Monty Python's Flying
Circus* (4th series, episode 4, first broadcast
21 November 1974)

53 I was overcome with self-loathing
and contemplated suicide again –
this time by inhaling next to an
insurance salesman.

Woody Allen *Without Feathers*, 'Selections
from the Allen Notebooks' (1975)

54 Actually, the more you think about
it, the more attractive the solicitor
idea becomes. It's just as good as
being a doctor because it has the
same advantages inasmuch as the
average person won't know what
you're doing to him.

Ronnie Corbett *Ronnie Corbett's Small Man's
Guide*, 'The Small Man and Work' (1976)

55 WITHENSHAW: You do speed-
    writing, I suppose?
MADDIE: Yes, if I'm given enough
    time.

Tom Stoppard *Dirty Linen* (1976)

56 A press agent is a person who has
hitched his braggin' to a star.

Anon. *The Dictionary of Puns*, 'Brag', ed. John
S. Crosbie (1977)

57 The Civil Service is a self-
perpetuating oligarchy, and what
better system is there?

Lord Armstrong *Observer*, 'Sayings of the
Week', 8 May 1977

58 **Some civil servants are just like my loved ones/ They work so hard and they try to be strong . . .**

David Byrne 'Don't Worry about the Government', *Talking Heads* (LP, 1977)

59 [Of tax collectors] **These dedicated men and women are grossly over-worked and underpaid. I fear that their only effective recourse is immediate STRIKE ACTION. It might be a long struggle lasting months, maybe years. But their cause is just and they would have the nation united behind them.**

Peter Cook *Daily Mail* 4 April 1977, quoted in *Tragically I Was an Only Twin – The Complete Peter Cook* ed. William Cook (2002)

60 **Q: Why are fishmongers so mean? A: Because their job makes them sell fish.**

Anon. *The Crack-a-Joke Book*, 'A Funny Fin Happened', ed. Jane Nissen (1978)

61 **The black hole of Savile Row had taken its toll of some of the finest merchant banking brains of a generation. Luckily, that's not very serious.**

Eric Idle Eric Idle as the narrator in *The Rutles: All You Need Is Cash* (film, 1978, written by Eric Idle, directed by Eric Idle and Gary Weis)

62 **He's not a very good doctor, in fact he's so old-fashioned when he lances a boil he does it on horseback.**

Les Dawson *The Malady Lingers On*, 'The Art of a Pun . . . Or How to Lose an Audience Fast' (1982)

63 **Gynaecologists: All extremely rich. The only people who can afford to visit Covent Garden.**

Henry Root *Henry Root's World of Knowledge* (1982)

64 **Dry-Cleaning, Same Day: 'They'll be ready on Thursday.'**

Ibid.

65 **Had an in-depth talk about O levels with my father, he advised me only to do subjects I'm good at. He said that vets spend half their working life with their hands up cows' bums, and the other half injecting spoiled fat dogs.**

Sue Townsend *The Secret Diary of Adrian Mole Aged 13¾* (1982), entry for Wednesday 13 May

66 **The only time we doctors should accept death is when it's caused by our own incompetence.**

Steve Martin and Carl Reiner Dr Hfuhruhurr in *The Man with Two Brains* (film, 1983, directed by Carl Reiner). The doctor, under time pressure, also says: 'I have two operations, but I can do 'em fast, they're only brain operations.'

67 **Dentistry: Once you sat in a chair, now you lie down on a sort of couch. Nastier for you, producing feelings of helplessness among the old and nervous, but nicer for him because he can sit down. A good textbook example of sod the patient.**

Kingsley Amis *Spectator* 19 October 1985, collected in *The Wit of the Spectator* ed. Christopher Howse (1989)

68 **My friend, the undertaker, the last person on earth to let me down.**

Anon. Quoted in *Bishop's Brew (An Anthology of Clerical Humour)* ed. Ronald Brown, ch. 2 (1989)

69 **Agents? Hell, those guys are just mail drops.**

Robert Mitchum Remark made during negotiations over a TV series in 1990, quoted in *Robert Mitchum: Baby I Don't Care*, 'Big Sleep', by Lee Server (2001). Mitchum, almost uniquely in Hollywood, never used an agent.

70 **Psychiatrist: A Jewish boy who can't stand the sight of blood.**

Anon. *And I Quote*, 'Psychiatrists and Psychiatry', ed. Ashton Applewhite and others (1992)

71 **But surely a hermit who takes a newspaper is not a hermit in whom one can place great confidence?**

Tom Stoppard Lady Croom in *Arcadia*, act 2, sc. 7 (1993). The idea has been mooted of advertising in a newspaper for a hermit.

72 **Someone once said you should**

never trust a doctor whose office plants had died.

Lynne Truss *With One Lousy Packet of Seed*, ch. 1 (1994)

73 [Of Joseph Goebbels] **I wonder, if he had lived, whether he would have gone into advertising.**

Victor Lewis-Smith *Inside the Magic Rectangle*, 'We Have Ways of Making You Think' (1995)

74 **Most barbers have one haircut they can do, and if they suspect you are asking for something different, they panic.**

Hugo Williams *Freelancing*, 'Hair Trouble' (1995)

75 **A Modelizer Glossary: Thing = a model; civilian = women who are not models.**

Candace Bushnell *Sex and the City*, ch. 5 (1996). A modelizer is a man who dates models. The actress Elizabeth Hurley is reported to have used the word 'civilians' to describe the non-famous.

76 **Bric-a-brac bought, antiques sold.**

Anon. Notice inside a West Country shop. Quoted in *A Gentleman Publisher's Commonplace Book*, 'Delightful Oddities', by John G. Murray (1996). From the same book and on the same subject: 'The reason why we can sell our antiques for less is because we buy them direct from the manufacturer' – an advertisement from the *Washington Star*.

77 **Supermarket cashiers: Why not simply have love bites tattooed on your necks. That way there would never be any danger of being without one.**

Viz 'Top Tips', *Viz – The Full Toss (A Corking Compilation of Issues 70 to 75)* (1997)

78 **Learning to care: If you are a doctor or a health visitor, always remember to call breasts boobs.**

Craig Brown *The Little Book of Chaos* (1998)

79 **When you go to see the doctor, you don't see the actual doctor. You must wait in the waiting room. There's no chance of not waiting. That's the name of the room.**

Jerry Seinfeld *I'm Telling You for the Last Time* (CD, 1998)

80 **The models were so nervous backstage they were keeping their food down.**

Jack Dee Quoted in *The Times* 24 February 2001. Dee was compèring the Rover British Fashion Awards.

81 **FIRST SALESMAN: I made some very valuable contacts today. SECOND SALESMAN: I didn't get any orders either.**

Anon. Quoted in *The Penguin Dictionary of Modern Humorous Quotations* ed. Fred Metcalf (2nd edn 2001)

82 **Ninety-nine per cent of the work of the professional bodyguard consisted of one activity: frowning.**

Martin Amis *Yellow Dog*, pt 1, ch. 2, sect. 2 (2003)

83 **There are no doctors who are poor. But there are poor doctors.**

Anon. *Away an' Ask Yer Mother (Your Scottish Father's Favourite Sayings)* ch. 6, ed. Allan Morrison (2003)

84 **What do gardeners do when they retire?**

Bob Monkhouse *Sun* 30 December 2003

Employers and Employees

1 **On rainy days alone I dine,/ Upon a chick, and pint of wine./ On rainy days, I dine alone,/ And pick my chicken to the bone:/ But this my servant much enrages,/ No scraps remain to save board wages.**

Jonathan Swift 'The Author's Manner of Living', collected in *Jonathan Swift. The Selected Poems* ed. A. Norman Jeffares (1992), who dates the poem at somewhere between 1715 and 1718

2 **The highest panegyric, therefore, that private virtue can receive, is the praise of the servants.**

Samuel Johnson *The Rambler* 10 November 1750

3 **To employ women and children unduly is simply to run into debt with Nature.**

Anon. *The Times* 4 March 1867, quoted in

Who Said What ed. John Daintith and others (1988)

4 **A Lecture on the Extreme Folly and Danger of Servants Going on Errands before They Are Sent**

Anon. Title of a book published in 1889, and written by 'a layman'. Quoted in the *Fortean Times*, issue 177 (2003).

5 **Lord Finchley tried to mend the Electric Light/ Himself. It struck him dead: And serve him right!/ It is the business of the wealthy man/ To give employment to the artisan.**

Hilaire Belloc *More Peers*, 'Lord Finchley' (1911)

6 **In a hierarchy every employee tends to rise to his level of incompetence.**

Laurence Peter *The Peter Principle*, ch. 1 (1969)

7 **I don't want loyalty. I want *loyalty*. I want him to kiss my ass in Macy's window at high noon and tell me it smells like roses. I want his pecker in my pocket.**

Lyndon Baines Johnson Discussing what he looks for in an assistant, quoted in *The Best and Brightest*, ch. 20 (1972)

8 **In my department, there are six people who are afraid of me, and one small secretary who is afraid of all of us. I have one other person working for me who is not afraid of anyone, not even me, and I would fire him quickly, but I'm afraid of him.**

Joseph Heller *Something Happened*, 'The Office in Which I Work' (1974)

9 **I don't know what I want, but I want it now.**

Viv Stanshall Sir Henry in *Sir Henry at Rawlinson End* (LP, 1978). Sir Henry utters the cry on waking. His daily woman, Mrs E, replies: 'Fried or fried, Sir Henry?'

10 **I think factories would close down, actually, if it wasn't for working-class people.**

Victoria Wood 'Just an Ordinary School', a sketch from *Victoria Wood as Seen on TV* (TV series, 1985), collected in *Up to You, Porky –*

The Victoria Wood Sketch Book (1985). The speaker, a posh public schoolgirl called Ceal, is explaining why there has to be a working class.

11 **FIRST EMPLOYEE: So is your job secure?**
SECOND EMPLOYEE: Oh yes, it's me they can do without.

Anon. *And I Quote*, 'Status', ed. Ashton Applewhite and others (1992)

12 **A company director who takes a pay rise of £50,000 when the rest of the workforce is getting a few hundred is not part of some general trend. He is a greedy bastard.**

John Edmonds *The Times*, 'Quotes of the Week', 10 September 1998

13 **A boss is a person who's early when you're late and late when you're early.**

Sally Poplin Quoted in *The Penguin Dictionary of Modern Humorous Quotations* ed. Fred Metcalf (2nd edn 2001)

14 **I've created an atmosphere where I'm a friend first and a boss second, probably an entertainer third.**

Ricky Gervais and Stephen Merchant David Brent (Ricky Gervais) as the horripilatingly creepy manager of a paper supplies office in *The Office* (TV sitcom, episode 1, 1st series, 2002)

15 **I don't want any yes men around me. I want everybody to tell me the truth even if it costs them their jobs.**

Sam Goldwyn Attributed

Money
Wealth

1 **Money, wife, is the true fuller's earth for reputations, there is not a spot or a stain but what it can take out.**

John Gay Mr Peachum in *The Beggar's Opera*, act 1, sc. 9 (1728). In *Gone with the Wind* (film, 1939) Rhett Butler (Clark Gable) says: 'Providing you have enough courage – or money – you can do without a reputation.'

2 A large income is the best recipe for happiness I ever heard of. It certainly may secure all the myrtle and turkey part of it.

Jane Austen *Emma*, ch. 22 (1816)

3 We are not here to sell a parcel of boilers and vats, but the potentiality of growing rich, beyond the dreams of avarice.

Samuel Johnson *The Life of Samuel Johnson* by James Boswell, vol. 4, p. 87; in G. B. Hill's edition of 1887, rev. L. F. Powell (1934). Johnson was 'bustling about, with an ink horn and pen in his button hole, like an exciseman' during the sale of Thrale's brewery. · The line 'I am rich beyond the dreams of avarice' had appeared in *The Gamester*, act 2, sc. 2 (1753) by Edward Moore.

4 It is better to have a permanent income than to be fascinating.

Oscar Wilde One of 'the great truths of modern life which Hughie Erskine never realized'. *Lord Arthur Savile's Crime and Other Stories*, 'The Model Millionaire' (1891).

5 'Millionaire models,' remarked Alan [Trevor], 'are rare enough; but, by Jove, model millionaires are rarer still!'

Ibid.

6 Conspicuous consumption of valuable goods is a means of reputability to the gentleman of leisure.

Thorstein Veblen *The Theory of the Leisure Class*, ch. 4 (1899)

7 I am a Millionaire. That is my religion.

George Bernard Shaw Andrew Undershaft in *Major Barbara*, act 2 (1907)

8 Her voice is full of money.

F. Scott Fitzgerald Tom Buchanan speaking of Daisy Baker in *The Great Gatsby*, ch. 7 (1925)

9 Stick with me, kid, and you'll be farting through silk.

Robert Mitchum Promise made by Mitchum in 1935 to Dorothy Spence, who became Dorothy Mitchum on 16 March 1940. They remained married until Mitchum's death in 1992, although he was frequently unfaithful.

10 If all men were rich, all men would be poor.

Mark Twain *Notebook*, ch. 31 (1935)

11 If you can actually count your money, then you are not really a rich man.

J. Paul Getty Quoted in the *Observer* 3 November 1957

12 Wealth is not without its advantages, and the case to the contrary, although it has often been made, has never proved widely persuasive.

J. K. Galbraith *The Affluent Society*, ch. 1 (1958)

13 Loadsamoney!

Harry Enfield Catchprase of one of Enfield's characters, a plasterer overendowed with ready cash by the economic boom of the 1980s, one of his TV creations of the period

Lack of Money

1 Of all that luckless poverty involves,/ Nothing is harsher than the fact that it makes people funny.

Juvenal Satire 3, line 153 (c.AD 100), trans. and ed. Niall Rudd (1991)

2 While I am a beggar, I will rail/ And say there is no sin but to be rich;/ And being rich, my virtue then shall be/ To say there is no vice but beggary.

William Shakespeare Philip the Bastard in *King John*, act 2, sc. 1 (1594–6)

3 Better a bare foote than none.

George Herbert *Outlandish Proverbs*, no. 78 (1640)

4 There is no scandal like rags, nor any crime so shameful as poverty.

George Farquhar Archer in *The Beaux' Stratagem*, act 1, sc. 1 (1707)

5 The mournful truth is everywhere confess'd/ SLOW RISES WORTH, BY POVERTY DEPRESS'D.

Samuel Johnson From his poem 'London' (1738) quoted in *The Life of Samuel Johnson* by James Boswell, vol. 1 (1791); in G. B. Hill's edition of 1887, rev. L. F. Powell (1934)

6 All the arguments which are brought to represent poverty as no evil, show it to be very evidently a

great evil. You never find people labouring to convince you that you may live very happily upon a plentiful fortune.

Ibid. vol. 1, p. 441

7 The most hapless of all things is a poor parson, of an evening, in London in wet weather, without a carriage.

Sydney Smith Letter to Lady Grey of 13 June 1829, quoted in *Twelve Miles from a Lemon: Selected Writings of Sydney Smith*, ch. 4, compiled by Norman Taylor and Alan Hankinson (1996)

8 It is always considered an impertinence in England, if a man of less than two or three thousand pounds a year has any opinions at all upon important subjects.

Sydney Smith *The Works of Sydney Smith*, vol. 1, Preface (1840)

9 How to Live Well on Nothing a Year

William Makepeace Thackeray *Vanity Fair*, title of ch. 36 (1847–8)

10 [Of Mr Micawber] I have known him come home to supper with a flood of tears, and a declaration that nothing was now left but jail; and go to bed making a calculation of the expense of putting bow-windows to the house, 'in case anything turned up', which was his favourite expression.

Charles Dickens *David Copperfield*, ch. 11 (1849–50)

11 Annual income twenty pounds, annual expenditure nineteen pounds six, result happiness. Annual income twenty pounds, annual expenditure twenty pounds ought and six, result misery.

Charles Dickens Mr Micawber in ibid., ch. 12

12 'There's nothing,' said Toby, 'more regular in its coming round than dinner-time, and nothing less regular in its coming around than dinner. That's the great difference between 'em.'

Charles Dickens Toby Veck in *The Chimes*, 'First Quarter' (1852)

13 I have been keeping out of the way, and living cheap, down about the market-gardens; but what's the use of living cheap when you have got no money? You might as well live dear.

Charles Dickens Tony Jobling in *Bleak House*, ch. 20 (1852–3)

14 As a general rule no one has money who ought to have it.

Benjamin Disraeli *Endymion*, ch. 65 (1880)

15 But, though all tramps are leisurely, there are few who can be called gentlemen.

John Buchan *Scholar Gipsies*, 'Gentlemen of Leisure' (1896)

16 PICKERING: Have you no morals, man?

DOOLITTLE: Can't afford them, Governor.

George Bernard Shaw *You Never Can Tell*, act 2 (1897)

17 Years ago, when my capital would occasionally come down to 'what in town the people call a bob', I would recklessly spend a penny of it, merely for the sake of having the change, all in coppers, to jingle. You don't feel nearly so hard up with elevenpence in your pocket as you do with a shilling.

Jerome K. Jerome *The Idle Thoughts of an Idle Fellow*, 'On Being Hard Up' (1889)

18 Like all professional bankrupts, Mr Earp had invariably had belongings which, as he could prove to his creditors, did not belong to him.

Arnold Bennett *The Card*, ch. 3 (1911)

19 I have been working out all about my money. It seems that those who are giving me *money* are not giving me *nearly enough* of it, and those who are taking my money away from me are taking it away from me *much too often* and *much too much* at a time.

Kingsley Amis Letter to Philip Larkin of 15 July 1946, collected in *The Letters of Kingsley Amis* ed. Zachary Leader (2000)

20 Well, I put five bob in the post office savings bank in 1933 and I've never regretted it . . . Even when I lost the book . . . Like I say, *I* can't even get it out, so what chance has anybody else?

Al Read Unnamed stupid character in *The Al Read Show* (BBC Radio series), 25 January 1955

21 In the matter of clothes, I was supported entirely by voluntary contributions, like a hospital.

Quentin Crisp *The Naked Civil Servant*, ch. 21 (1968)

22 I met my wife in Venice. I was broke, you know . . . swimming to my hotel.

Carl Reiner and Mel Brooks '2002-Year-Old Man', *Carl Reiner and Mel Brooks at the Cannes Film Festival* (LP, 1962)

23 It needs to be said that the poor are poor because they don't have enough money.

Sir Keith Joseph *Observer*, 'Sayings of the Week', 1 March 1970

24 When you wish upon a star, makes no difference who you are. If, on the other hand, you apply for a personal loan, all sorts of circumstantial evidence is required.

David Mamet Voice from a TV being watched by Bernard Litko in *Sexual Perversity in Chicago* (1974)

25 Bills are beginning to fall on me like forest giants.

Philip Larkin Letter to Charles Monteith of 5 June 1974, collected in *Selected Letters of Philip Larkin, 1940–85* ed. Anthony Thwaite (1992)

26 Compared to us, poor was already rich.

Walter Matthau Quoted in *All My Best Friends* by George Burns, ch. 1 (1989)

27 Money is better than poverty, if only for financial reasons.

Woody Allen *And I Quote*, 'Money', ed. Ashton Applewhite and others (1992)

28 We were poor when I was young but the difference was that the government didn't come around telling you you were poor.

Ronald Reagan in ibid.

29 Sure, Homer, I'll loan you all the money you need, but since you have no collateral I'm going to have to break your legs in advance.

Matt Groening Moe, proprietor of Moe's Bar, to Homer Simpson in *The Simpsons*, 'Homer vs Patty and Selma', first broadcast 26 February 1995

30 That money talks/ I won't deny./ I heard it once,/ It said, 'Goodbye.'

Richard Armour 'Money', publ. in *The Funny Side: 101 Humorous Poems* ed. Wendy Cope (1998)

31 You're sixty-five today – and it's the first day of the rest of your life savings.

Anon. Quoted in *The Penguin Dictionary of Modern Humorous Quotations* ed. Fred Metcalf (2nd edn 2001)

32 There were times when my pants were so thin, I could sit on a dime and know if it was heads or tails.

Spencer Tracy Quoted in *Halliwell's Who's Who in the Movies* ed. John Walker (2001)

33 At dinner that night Opal Gross reported new developments in her family's difficulties: 'My father's really in trouble. Mum thinks he'll go to prison.'/ 'But he's declared himself bankrupt, hasn't he?' said Pallas. 'That's a great position to be in.'

Muriel Spark *The Finishing School*, ch. 10 (2004)

Meanness and Generosity

1 Can you walk steadily past a coin stuck in the mud/ and not have to gulp down the Lord of Lucre's saliva?

Persius Satire 5 (30s BC), *Horace: Satires and Epistles; Persius: Satires*, trans. and ed. Niall Rudd (1973)

2 My Lady Bountiful

George Farquhar Boniface in *The Beaux' Stratagem*, act 1, sc. 1 (1707), is speaking. Lady

Bountiful is 'an old, civil, Country Gentle-woman'. With her charitable donations she has 'cured more people in and about Lich-field within ten years than the doctors have killed in twenty'.

3 **Is not a Patron, my Lord, one who looks with unconcern upon a man struggling for life in the water, and, when he has reached ground, encumbers him with help?**

Samuel Johnson *The Life of Samuel Johnson*, vol. 1, letter of 7 February 1755 to Lord Chesterfield, p. 262 (1791); in G. B. Hill's edition of 1887, rev. L. F. Powell (1934). A foot-note to this letter records Johnson saying to Garrick: 'I have sailed a long and painful voy-age around the English language; and does he now send out two cock boats to tow me into harbour?' In his *Dictionary of the English Language* (1755) Johnson defines a patron as 'Commonly a wretch who supports with insolence and is paid with flattery'.

4 **Three things I never lends – my 'oss, my wife, and my name.**

R. S. Surtees *Hillingdon Hall*, ch. 33 (1845)

5 **A man, who was asked what sort of wine he preferred, replied 'Other people's.'**

Anon. *The New London Jest Book*, 'Choice Jests', no. 136, ed. W. C. Hazlitt (1871)

6 **Men, married men, young married men, remember that your wives still enjoy chocolates, sweets, per-fume, flowers. Let her see that you haven't forgotten. Mention them occasionally.**

Eric Morecambe and Ernie Wise A line of Eric's from an early 1950s sketch. Quoted in *Eric and Ernie: The Autobiography of More-cambe and Wise*, ch. 6 (1973).

7 **The most dangerous thing in the world is to make a friend of an Eng-lishman, because he'll come sleep in your closet rather than spend ten shillings on a hotel.**

Truman Capote *Observer*, 'Sayings of the Week', 25 March 1966

8 **I would have put £2 in this letter only I have already sealed the envelope.**

Frank Carson Letter to Frank Carson from his mother, which goes on: 'Since you left home

your father has become a sex maniac and tries to make love to me whenever he can. Please excuse the wobbly handwriting.' *Laugh with the Comedians* (LP, 1971).

9 **It's a gorgeous gold pocket watch. I'm proud of it. My grand-father, on his deathbed, sold me this watch.**

Woody Allen *The Nightclub Years, 1965–1968* (LP, 1972)

10 **Jack Warner has oilcloth pockets so he can steal soup.**

Wilson Mizner Quoted in *The Wit and Wis-dom of Hollywood* (1972). This, one hastens to add, is Jack L. Warner of Warner Bros, not the English character actor who played the policeman Dixon of Dock Green in the 1950–70s TV series of that name. Mizner also said: 'Working for Warner Bros is like fucking a porcupine – it's one hundred pricks up against one.'

11 **ROBBER: Quit stalling – I said your money or your life.**
JACK BENNY: I'm thinking it over.

Jack Benny Staple Benny joke

12 **You look so beautiful, I can hardly keep my eyes on the meter.**

Woody Allen *Manhattan* (film, 1979, written by Woody Allen and Marshall Brickman, directed by Woody Allen). Isaac Davis (Woody Allen) and Tracy (Mariel Heming-way) are riding home in a taxi.

13 **The rich hate signing cheques. Hence the success of credit cards.**

Graham Greene Dr Fischer in *Dr Fischer of Geneva; or, The Bomb Party*, ch. 9 (1980)

14 **I was in a stationer's shop where I was buying, on the strict under-standing that it was the poorest and cheapest, a ream of typing paper.**

Robert Robinson *The Dog Chairman*, 'Lost November' (1982)

15 **An old worthy when asked how he was, replied, 'I'm still walking about. It saves funeral expenses.'**

Anon. Quoted in *Laughter Lines: Family Wit and Wisdom*, 'Ills, Pills and Wills', ed. James A. Simpson (1986)

16 **[Jack Benny] was the cheapest man in the country. He was so cheap**

that instead of bringing his date flowers, he brought her seeds.

George Burns *All My Best Friends*, ch. 1 (1989). In fact, Benny was Burns's closest friend.

17 My parents used to take me to Lewis's department store in Argyll Street in Glasgow. They were kind of skinflints, and they'd show me the pet department and tell me it was the zoo.

Billy Connolly Joke told during his twenty-two-night run at the Hammersmith Apollo, London, in 1994

18 He died at ninety . . . I always think he was a hundred and kept ten per cent for himself.

Ken Dodd Quoted in *Inside the Magic Rectangle*, 'Face to Face: Ken Dodd', by Victor Lewis-Smith (1995)

19 I always give homeless people money and my friends yell at me, 'He's only going to buy more alcohol and cigarettes.' And I'm thinking, 'Oh, and like I *wasn't?*'

Kathleen Madigan Quoted in *The Penguin Dictionary of Modern Humorous Quotations* ed. Fred Metcalf (2nd edn 2001)

Accumulating Money

1 Remuneration! O! that's the Latin word for three farthings.

William Shakespeare Costard in *Love's Labour's Lost*, act 3, sc. 1 (1594–5)

2 As the partridge sitteth on eggs, and hatcheth them not; so he that getteth riches, and not by right, shall leave them in the midst of his days . . .

Jeremiah 17:11, the Bible, Authorized Version (1611)

3 Hee that gets out of debt, growes rich.

George Herbert *Outlandish Proverbs*, no. 9 (1640)

4 Pension: Pay given to a state hireling for treason to his country.

Samuel Johnson *A Dictionary of the English Language* (1755)

5 There are few ways in which a man can be more innocently employed than in getting money.

Samuel Johnson *The Life of Samuel Johnson* by James Boswell, vol. 2, p. 323 (1791); in G. B. Hill's edition of 1887, rev. L. F. Powell (1934). Johnson was quoting a Mr William Strahan, who had added: 'The more one thinks of this, the juster it will appear.'

6 I was agreeably surprised to find Louisa Bridges still here. She looks remarkably well (legacies are a very wholesome diet), and is just what she always was.

Jane Austen Letter to Cassandra Austen of 15–17 June 1808, collected in *Jane Austen's Letters* ed. Dierdre Le Faye (1995)

7 Some conjurers say that number three is the magic number, and some say number seven. It's neither, my friend, neither. It's number one.

Charles Dickens Fagin in *Oliver Twist*, ch. 43 (1837–9)

8 We have the highest authority for believing that the meek shall inherit the Earth; though I have never found any particular corroboration of this aphorism in the records of Somerset House.

F. E. Smith *Contemporary Personalities*, 'Marquess Curzon' (1924)

9 Check enclosed.

Dorothy Parker The two most beautiful words in the English language. Attributed.

10 A bank is a place that will lend you money if you can prove that you don't need it.

Bob Hope Quoted in *Life in the Crystal Palace* by Alan Harrington (1959)

11 I have always held the view that the union of two hearts whose incomes are equal is a complete waste of time.

Quentin Crisp *The Naked Civil Servant*, ch. 3 (1968)

12 Security: Shares in something that will go bust sooner or later.

Beachcomber *Beachcomber: The Works of*

J. B. Morton, 'A Dictionary for Today', ed. Richard Ingrams (1974)

13 **Next to being shot at and missed, nothing is quite so satisfying as an income tax refund.**

Anon. And I Quote, 'Taxes', ed. Ashton Applewhite and others (1992)

14 **So what attracted you to million-aire Paul Daniels?**

Caroline Aherne Question asked of Debbie McGee, wife of the magician Paul Daniels, by Caroline Aherne, in character as the little-old-lady chat-show host Mrs Merton. Cited as an outstanding joke in the *Observer* 7 December 2003.

15 **When I was little I got a boy to play doctors with me, but he sent me a bill.**

Joan Rivers Quoted in *Jewish Humour* by Ben Eliezer (2003)

Spending Money

1 **CECIL GRAHAM: What is a cynic? LORD DARLINGTON: A man who knows the price of everything and the value of nothing.**

Oscar Wilde Lady Windermere's Fan, act 3 (1893)

2 **... the time had come to get rid of Henry at any cost. So I decided that the thing that discourages gentle-men more than anything else is shopping.**

Anita Loos Gentlemen Prefer Blondes, ch. 6 (1925)

3 **I like to be in America!/ OK by me in America!/ Everything free in America/ For a small fee in America!**

Stephen Sondheim 'America' (song, music by Leonard Bernstein), *West Side Story* (stage musical, 1957; film, 1961, directed by Robert Wise and Jerome Robbins)

4 **The only way to save money is not to have any.**

Katherine Whitehorn Observations, 'Jane's Economy Kick' (1970)

5 **Schlepper colony = department store.**

Kenneth Tynan Entry for 11 October 1971, *The Diaries of Kenneth Tynan* ed. John Lahr (2000)

6 **Bargain: Any article reduced from ten shillings to eight shillings and worth half a crown.**

Beachcomber Beachcomber: The Works of J. B. Morton, 'A Dictionary for Today', ed. Richard Ingrams (1974)

7 **My problem lies in reconciling my gross habits with my net income.**

Errol Flynn Attributed. Quoted in *Great Lovers of the Movies*, 'Errol Flynn', by Jane Mercer (1975).

8 **There's a particular sort of ache that comes on in my ankles when I've been in a department store for anything longer than about ten minutes. I start to feel like a man who's done a day's manual labour, and long to collapse into one of those bentwood chairs they used to provide for old ladies.**

Robert Robinson The Dog Chairman, 'Sight-seer's Ankle' (1982)

9 **Now back me up on this. Every time you go into one of those cancer research shops ... there's no cancer research going on at all, is there? Just a load of old women standing around selling clothes.**

Harry Hill Quoted in *Loaded* magazine June 1997

10 **A check is like a note from your mother. It says, 'I don't have any money but if you contact these people, they'll stick up for me.'**

Jerry Seinfeld I'm Telling You for the Last Time (CD, 1998)

11 **Manchester United? I don't know them. How much are they?**

Michael Jackson Question asked after watching a football match at Fulham in 1999, quoted in *The Book of Football Quotations*, 'The First XI, Clubs and Themes', ed. Phil Shaw (1999)

12 **The only fetters binding the work-**

ing class today are mock-Rolex watches.

Francis Wheen *Karl Marx*, Introduction (1999)

13 **What every woman knows and no man can ever grasp is that even if he brings home everything on the list, he will still not have got the right things.**

Allison Pearson *I Don't Know How She Does It*, ch. 29 (2002)

14 **The quickest way to stop noticing something may be to buy it.**

Alain de Botton *Status Anxiety*, 'Solutions, Politics' (2004). He adds: 'just as the quickest way to stop appreciating a person may be to marry them.'

People and Places
America and Canada

1 **I would rather ... a nod from an American, than a snuff-box from an Emperor.**

Lord Byron Letter to Joseph Moore of 8 June 1822, collected in *Letters and Journals*, vol. 9, *In the Wind's Eye (1821–22)*, ed. Leslie A. Marchand (1979)

2 **I thought San Francisco was drunk but it's an infant sucking in the night compared to Montana.**

Rudyard Kipling Letter to Alexander Hill of 2 July 1889, *Letters of Rudyard Kipling*, vol. 1 *(1872–89)*, ed. Thomas Pinney (1990)

3 **Many years ago, when all Chicago was afire, the Mayor, watching it from the Lake-Side, exclaimed in a loud voice, 'Who will say now that we are not the finest city in all the world?'**

Max Beerbohm *More*, 'An Infamous Brigade' (1899)

4 **If ever there was an aviary overstocked with jays it is that Yaptown-on-the-Hudson called New York.**

O. Henry 'A Tempered Wind', *Gentle Grafter* (1908)

5 **New York is a large city con-** veniently situated on the edge of America, so that you step off the liner right on to it without an effort.

P. G. Wodehouse *The Man with Two Left Feet*, 'Extricating Young Gussie' (1926)

6 **Long Island represents the American's idea of what God would have done with Nature if he'd had the money.**

Peter Fleming Letter to his brother Rupert of 29 September 1929

7 **There was a young boy of Quebec,/ Who fell into the ice to his neck./ When asked 'Are you friz?'/ He replied 'Yes, I is,/ But we don't call this cold in Quebec.'**

Rudyard Kipling 'The Boy of Quebec', collected in *Home Book of Verse for Young Folks* ed. B. E. Stevenson (1929)

8 **There is nothing the matter with Americans except their ideals. The real American is all right; it is the ideal American who is all wrong.**

G. K. Chesterton *New York Times* 1 February 1931

9 **The Bronx?/ No, thonx!**

Ogden Nash 'Geographical Reflection' (1931)

10 **[Of New Yorkers] I think that your skyline is astounding, and that your women are the most attractive in the world, but that there is a certain amount of exaggeration in the report that your men think of nothing but business, business, business all the time. If it is true, then wherever *did* I get those bruises on my neck?**

Dorothy Parker From a review of *Forty Thousand Sublime and Beautiful Thoughts* compiled by Charles Noel Douglas, *New Yorker* 24 January 1931

11 **California is a fine place to live – if you happen to be an orange.**

Fred Allen *American Magazine* December 1945

12 **I feel most at home in the United States, not because it is intrinsically a more interesting country, but because no one really belongs there**

any more than I do. We are all there together in its wholly excellent vacuum.

Wyndham Lewis *American and Cosmic Man*, 'The Case against Roots' (1948)

13 [Of Los Angeles] **A big hard-boiled city with no more personality than a paper cup.**

Raymond Chandler *The Little Sister*, ch. 26 (1949)

14 **We are all American at puberty; we die French.**

Evelyn Waugh *Diaries*, 'Irregular Notes', entry for 18 July 1961, ed. M. Davie (1976)

15 [Of California] **It was like the Sahara, only dirty.**

Mohammed Mrabet *Look and Move On*, ch. 11 (1967)

16 [On seeing Niagara Falls] **Fortissimo at last!**

Gustav Mahler *Gustav Mahler*, ch. 8, by K. Blaukopf (1973)

17 **Forget it, Jake. It's Chinatown.**

Robert Towne Duffy (Bruce Glover) in *Chinatown* (film, 1974, screenplay by Robert Towne, directed by Roman Polanski). Closing words.

18 **They don't throw their garbage away. They make it into television shows.**

Woody Allen Alvy Singer (Woody Allen) in *Annie Hall* (film, 1977, screenplay by Woody Allen and Marshall Brickman, directed by Woody Allen). Allen does not like LA or, indeed, anywhere really except his home city of New York. In the film *Sleeper* the hero Miles (Woody Allen) is asked what it's like to be asleep for two hundred years. 'It was like a weekend in Beverly Hills,' he replies.

19 **Canada is a country so square that even the female impersonators are women.**

Richard Benner Robin (Richard Benner) in *Outrageous* (film, 1977, written and directed by Richard Benner)

20 **America is a vast conspiracy to make you happy.**

John Updike *Problems*, 'How to Love America and Leave It at the Same Time' (1980)

21 **Canada: Canada's all right, but not for the whole weekend.**

Taki Quoted in *Henry Root's World of Knowledge* (1982)

22 [Of America] ***The Moronic Inferno***

Martin Amis Book title, 1986. In the Introduction Amis wrote that he got the phrase 'from Saul Bellow, who informs me that *he* got it from Wyndham Lewis'.

23 **I *adore* Los Angeles. Think of any way to get rich, think of the most bizarre scam you can and somebody is doing it already. You want to start a hospital for kids' toys? You want to situate Cadillac wrecks on poles two hundred feet in the air? Some guy's already there.**

Richard Rayner *Los Angeles without a Map*, 'Diving' (1989). Said by Chuck, who was 'in A&R at Warner Bros' and had 'staring eyes like chunks of broken sky'.

24 **Flyover states: Derogatory urbanites' term for the bits of America between California and New York, i.e. most of the country.**

Anon. 'The Jargon Bulletin', a dictionary of jargon, *Word* magazine June 2003

25 [Of Texas] **Did you know it's legal there to carry a gun but against the law to own a vibrator?**

Helen Simpson 'The Bloodletter', a short story, *Guardian* 9 April 2003

26 [Of America] **The first attitude isn't suspicion, it's friendliness. 'Have a nice day.' I know it's fucking monotonous, but Christ they mean it.**

John Lydon Quoted in *Mojo* magazine February 2004

Australasia

1 [Of Australia] **It must be so pretty with all the dear little kangaroos flying about.**

Oscar Wilde The Duchess of Berwick in *Lady Windermere's Fan*, act 2 (1893). It is the shape of 'a large packing case', she adds.

2 **Cusins is a very nice fellow, cer-**

tainly: nobody would ever guess that he was born in Australia.

George Bernard Shaw Stephen in *Major Barbara*, act 1 (1907)

3 [On being asked his opinion of New Zealand] **It's hard to say, because when I was there it seemed to be shut.**

Clement Freud BBC radio programme 12 April 1978, quoted in *Who Said What* ed. John Daintith and others (1988)

4 **Q: What's the difference between an Australian wedding and an Australian funeral? A: There's one less drunk at the funeral.**

Anon. Quoted in *Bishop's Brew (An Anthology of Clerical Humour)*, ch. 3, ed. Ronald Brown (1989)

5 **. . . I still felt like an exile in Sydney. I was stranded amongst people who could not even muster the glottal energy to pronounce the 'd' in the name of their own city.**

Barry Humphries *More Please*, 'Sinny' (1992). Humphries was born and raised in Melbourne.

6 **Cultural Centre – Cart Your Arse in Here**

Matt Groening Banner displayed outside an Australian cultural centre in *The Simpsons*, 'Bart vs Australia', first broadcast 19 February 1995

7 **The history of Australia is straightforward. Basically what happened is that Britain sent out a lot of convicts two hundred years ago and, as soon as they had settled down, we sent out a cricket team to bowl very fast at their heads.**

Oliver Pritchett *The Dogger Bank Saga: Writings 1980–95*, '1788 and All That' (1995)

8 **In Australia, not reading poetry is the national pastime.**

Phyllis McGinley Quoted in *The Penguin Dictionary of Modern Humorous Quotations* ed. Fred Metcalf (2nd edn 2001)

9 **Australia is like Jack Nicholson. It comes right up to you and** laughs hard in your face in a highly threatening and ingratiating manner.

Douglas Adams *The Salmon of Doubt*, 'Life', 'Riding the Rays' (2002). 'Every country is like a particular type of person,' Adams said. America 'is like a belligerent adolescent boy. Canada is like an intelligent thirty-five-year-old woman . . .'

10 [Of Australia] **It's as big as the US geographically, with as few people living there as are in this room right now.**

Bill Hicks 'Australia', *Love, Laughter and Truth* (CD, 2002)

Belgium

1 **Brussels: Be sure to visit its internationally famous vegetable market.**

Henry Root *Henry Root's World of Knowledge* (1982)

2 **I refuse to make old cheap jokes about Belgium. It's just too easy to say that when you book into a Bruges hotel and switch on your electric toothbrush the streetlights dim.**

Victor Lewis-Smith *Inside the Magic Rectangle*, 'The Essential History of Europe: Belgium' (1995). 'Or,' he added, 'that Belgium is merely a depot where the French and the Dutch keep their spare citizens.'

Britain and Ireland

1 **England is a paradise for women and a hell for horses: Italy a paradise for horses, hell for women.**

Robert Burton *The Anatomy of Melancholy*, pt 3 (1621)

2 **Lo here I sit at holy head/ With muddy ale and mouldy bread/ All Christian vittles stink of fish/ I'm where my enemyes would wish.**

Jonathan Swift 'Holyhead, Sept. 25, 1727'

3 [Of London] **What temptation can a**

man of my turn and temperament have, to live in a place where every corner teems with fresh objects of detestation and disgust?

Tobias Smollett Letter from Matthew Bramble to Dr Lewis dated 8 June, *The Expedition of Humphry Clinker* (1771)

4 As three to sixteen hundred, so is the proportion of an Englishman to a Frenchman.

Samuel Johnson *The Life of Samuel Johnson* by James Boswell, vol. 1, p. 186 (1791); in G. B. Hill's edition of 1887, rev. L. F. Powell (1934). Dr Adams had wondered how Johnson intended to finish his dictionary within three years, given that the French Academy, consisting of forty members, took forty years to compile their dictionary.

5 BOSWELL: I do indeed come from Scotland, but I cannot help it.
JOHNSON: That, Sir, I find is what a very great many of your countrymen cannot help.

Ibid., vol. 1, p. 392

6 When a man is tired of London, he is tired of life; for there is in London all that life can afford.

Ibid., vol. 3, p. 178

7 Oh, London is a fine town,/ A very famous city,/ Where all the streets are paved with gold,/ And all the maidens pretty.

George Colman the Younger *The Heir at Law* (performed 1797, publ. 1808), act 1, sc. 2

8 One has no great hopes of Birmingham. I always say there is something direful in the sound.

Jane Austen Mrs Elton in *Emma*, ch. 36 (1816)

9 I have been trying all my life to like Scotchmen, and am obliged to desist from the experiment in despair.

Charles Lamb *The Essays of Elia*, 'Mrs Battle's Opinions on Whist' (1823)

10 [Of London] Soon as I got there,/ I ran about quite silly,/ At all the shows to stare,/ In a place call'd Piccadilly./ Oh! Such charming sights!/ Birds in cages thrive, sirs;/ Coaches, fiddles, fights,/ And crocodiles alive sirs.

Anon. 'Lunnan Is the Devil', *Oliver's Comic Songs* (1825?)

11 Mehemet Pacha told me that he did not think I was an Englishman because I walked *so slow*.

Benjamin Disraeli Letter to Benjamin Austen of 18 November 1830, collected in *Benjamin Disraeli: Letters: 1815–1834* ed. J. A. W. Gunn, John Matthews and Donald M. Schurman (1982). Mehemet (or Mohammed) Ali (1769–1849) laid the foundations of the modern Egyptian state; in 1805 the Ottoman Emperor had appointed him pasha.

12 You could not have a softer climate or sunnier skies than this much abused Southend.

Benjamin Disraeli Letter to Sarah Disraeli of Monday 17 February 1834, collected in ibid. 'Here,' he added, 'there are myrtles in the open air in profusion.'

13 Kent, sir – everybody knows Kent – apples, cherries, hops, and women.

Charles Dickens Alfred Jingle in *The Pickwick Papers*, ch. 2 (1837)

14 An acre in Middlesex is better than a principality in Utopia.

Lord Macaulay *Critical and Historical Essays*, vol. 2, 'Francis Bacon' (1843)

15 Whenever he met a great man he grovelled before him, and mylorded him as only a free-born Briton can do.

William Makepeace Thackeray *Vanity Fair*, ch. 13 (1847–8)

16 [Of Oxford] That old monkish place which I have a horror of.

Queen Victoria Letter to Princess Victoria of 31 October 1859

17 London is a roost for every bird.

Benjamin Disraeli *Lothair*, ch. 11 (1870)

18 On a very wet day in the west of Scotland, an English traveller inquired peevishly of a native if it *always rained* in that country. 'No,' replied the Highlander, drily, 'it *snows* sometimes.'

Anon. *The New London Jest Book*, 'Choice Jests', no. 205, ed. W. C. Hazlitt (1871)

19 **Portsmouth is dirty but it is also dull.**
Henry James Observation made after a visit in 1879, quoted by Paul Theroux in *The Kingdom by the Sea*, ch. 4 (1983)

20 [Of the people of Uxbridge] **They will steal the very teeth out of your mouth as you walk through the streets. I know it from experience.**
William Arabin Quoted in *Some Experiences of a Barrister's Life*, vol. 1, ch. 6, by Sir W. Ballantine (1882)

21 **[The English] seem, as it were, to have conquered and peopled half the world in a fit of absence of mind.**
Sir John Seeley *The Expansion of England*, Lecture 1 (1883)

22 **London, the great cesspool into which all the loungers and idlers of the Empire are irresistibly drained.**
Sir Arthur Conan Doyle *A Study in Scarlet*, ch. 1 (1888)

23 **Clunton and Clunbury,/ Clungford and Clun,/ Are the quietest places/ Under the sun.**
A. E. Housman *A Shropshire Lad*, no. 54 (1896)

24 **London is a large village on the Thames, where the principal industries carried on are music-halls and the confidence trick.**
Dan Leno *Dan Leno Hys Booke*, Chapter First (1899)

25 **Very nice sort of place, Oxford, I should think, for people that like that sort of place.**
George Bernard Shaw Straker in *Man and Superman*, act 2 (1903)

26 **I passed through Glasgow on the way here and couldn't help noticing how different it was from Venice.**
Raymond Asquith Letter to Mrs Horner of 28 September 1904, collected in *Raymond Asquith: Life and Letters* ed. John Jolliffe (1980)

27 **There are few more impressive sights than a Scotsman on the make.**
J. M. Barrie *What Every Woman Knows*, act 1 (1906)

28 **I should rather go and live in some cheap place like Bedford Square or even Hampstead than take a farthing of his money.**
George Bernard Shaw Stephen in *Major Barbara*, act 1 (1907)

29 **Englishmen act better than Frenchmen, and Frenchwomen better than Englishwomen.**
Arnold Bennett *Cupid and Commonsense*, Preface (1909)

30 **In these days of rapid and convenient travel . . . to come from Leighton Buzzard does not denote any great strength of character.**
Saki *The Chronicles of Clovis*, 'The Secret Sin of Septimus Brope' (1911). The speaker is Clovis himself.

31 **I remember addressing a coachman by whose side I was sitting as we drove in a coach through that place, and I asked him, 'What sort of place is Winchester?' Answer: 'Debauched, sir, debauched, like all other cathedral cities.'**
Alfred, Lord Tennyson *Alfred Tennyson and His Friends: Fragmentary Notes of Tennyson's Talk* ed. Hallam, Lord Tennyson (1911)

32 **For Cambridge people rarely smile,/ Being urban, squat, and packed with guile.**
Rupert Brooke 'The Old Vicarage, Grantchester' (1915)

33 **Battersea may have its tough citizens, but they do not live in Battersea Park Road. Battersea Park Road's speciality is Brain not Crime.**
P. G. Wodehouse *The Man with Two Left Feet*, 'The Romance of an Ugly Policeman' (1917). Its citizens, Wodehouse continues, 'assault and batter nothing but pianos; they steal nothing but ideas; they murder nobody except Chopin and Beethoven'.

34 **It has been pointed out that if there were higher mountains and more snow in England it would be easier**

to ski there, but it is equally true to
say that if there were more grass
and mangel-wurzels in Switzerland
it would be a better place for feeding sheep.

E. V. Knox 'England: Her Country Homes (a
Warning to American Visitors)', *Punch*
23 March 1927, collected in *Fleet Street* ed.
W. W. Cobbett and Sidney Dark (1932)

35 **Bugger Bognor.**

George V Quoted in *King George V*, ch. 9, by
Kenneth Rose (1983). Possibly said in
response to the suggestion made in 1929
that the seaside town be named 'Bognor
Regis' to mark the King's having recovered
there from an illness. Or his final remark,
made in 1936 as he lay dying, when someone suggested: 'Cheer up, your Majesty, you
will soon be at Bognor again.'

36 **Very flat, Norfolk . . .**

Noel Coward Amanda in *Private Lives*, act 1
(1930)

37 **It is never difficult to distinguish
between a Scotsman with a griev-
ance and a ray of sunshine.**

P. G. Wodehouse *Blandings Castle and Elsewhere*, 'The Custody of the Pumpkin' (1935)

38 **No man should be bored in London,
for at worst there are so many
people and things to avoid in
London.**

Viscount Castlerosse *Sunday Express*, 'The
Londoner's Log', 1 May 1936, repr. in *The Penguin Book of Columnists* ed. Christopher Silvester (1997)

39 **[Denying that he was Irish] Because
a man is born in a stable, that does
not make him a horse.**

Duke of Wellington Attributed. Muriel
Wellesley, great-grandniece of Wellington,
elucidates as follows on the first page of her
biography *The Man Wellington* (1937):
'Though born in Ireland, Arthur Wellesley
was what is known as an English-Irishman,
for in spite of several centuries on Irish soil,
his forebears originally came from England.'
Speaking of his hot temper, Wellesley adds
that sometimes, 'when the English watch-
dog's back was turned, the Irish terrier got
out and laid about him'. Sellars and Yeatman
in *1066 and All That* (1936) wrote: 'The most
important of the great men who at this time
kept Britain top nation was an Irishman

called John Wesley, who afterwards became
the Duke of Wellington (and thus English).'

40 **The flushpots of Euston and the
hanging garments of Marylebone.**

James Joyce *Finnegans Wake*, pt 1 (1939)

41 **An Englishman, even if he is alone,
forms an orderly queue of one.**

George Mikes *How to Be an Alien: A Handbook for Beginners and More Advanced
Pupils*, ch. 1, sect. 14 (1946)

42 **[Of the Lincolnshire Wolds] Sussex
without the stockbrokers.**

John Betjeman *Tennyson as a Humorist* (BBC
radio broadcast, 3 July 1950)

43 **It will be said of this generation
that it found England a land of
beauty and left it a land of beauty
spots.**

C. E. M. Joad *Observer*, 'Sayings of Our Times'
(1953)

44 **It is a great sadness to me that Englishmen dress as though they were
undertakers, and that the pubs
close about four times a day.**

Brendan Behan Interview by Robert Robinson in the *Sunday Graphic* 15 July 1956, repr.
in *The Penguin Book of Interviews* ed. C. Silvester (1993). Behan and Robinson were
standing at the door of a public bar as
Behan said this, watching two men in
bowler hats. Behan 'broke into song as we
entered the pub, and cheered up slightly,'
Robinson reported.

45 **PAT: He was an Anglo-Irishman.
MEG: In the blessed name of God
    what's that?
PAT: A Protestant with a horse.**

Brendan Behan *The Hostage*, act 1 (1958)

46 **There are still parts of Wales where
the only concession to gaiety is a
striped shroud.**

Gwyn Thomas *Punch* 18 June 1958

47 **[Of the Dublin Festival] We have
flower battles just as they do in
Nice. Only here we throw the pots
as well.**

Brendan Behan *Observer*, 'Sayings of the
Week', 10 July 1960

48 In London you waste your time solving the wrong problems.

Arnold Wesker Ada in *I'm Talking about Jerusalem*, act 2 (1960)

49 Blackpool is the *end of the line*. It is the English Siberia. It is pure *torture*. Hateful, tasteless, witless, bleak, boring, dirty tat – *it has nothing*. I loathe every disgusting minute of it.

Kenneth Williams Entry for 27 March 1961, *The Kenneth Williams Diaries* ed. R. Davies (1993), collected in *The Assassin's Cloak* (2000) by Irene and Anne Taylor

50 Cool Britannia/ Britannia take a trip/ Britons ever ever ever will be hip.

Viv Stanshall 'Cool Britannia' (song), *Gorilla* (LP, 1967), by the Bonzo Dog Doo-Dah Band. Thought to be the first use of the term 'Cool Britannia', later used on a *Newsweek* cover and associated with Britain under Tony Blair.

51 I read the news today, oh boy./ Four thousand holes in Blackburn, Lancashire.

John Lennon and Paul McCartney 'A Day in the Life', *Sergeant Pepper's Lonely Hearts Club Band* (LP, 1967)

52 For God's sake bring me a large Scotch. What a bloody awful country.

Reginald Maudling As Conservative Home Secretary, after visiting Northern Ireland, quoted in the *Sunday Times* 1 July 1970. The previous year Britain had sent troops to the province in order to quell sectarian violence.

53 [Of Morecambe, Lancashire] It's a sort of cemetery with lights.

Colin Crompton *Laugh with the Comedians* (LP, 1971)

54 As always there was trouble in other countries, but it was a quiet week domestically.

Clive James *Observer* 25 August 1974

55 [Of England] A soggy little island, huffing and puffing to keep up with Western Europe.

John Updike *Picked-up Pieces*, 'London Life' (1976)

56 Nothing better in its line than Blackpool.

Sir Thomas Beecham *Beecham Stories*, 'Social and Sociological', ed. Harold Atkins and Archie Newman (1978)

57 Balzac describes Lancashire as 'the county where women die of love'. I think this very unlikely.

A. J. P. Taylor *Essays in English History*, Manchester (1976). He continues, 'I have always assumed . . . that Lancashire women are as brisk and businesslike in love-making as in everything else.'

58 . . . As we pull/ out of the station through the dusk and fog,/ there, lighting up, is Durham, dog/ chasing its own cropped tail,/ University, Cathedral, Gaol.

Tony Harrison 'Durham', collected in *Continuous* (1981)

59 [Of a trip to Scotland] There is a loch in front of the cabin and a pine forest and a mountain behind the cabin. There is nothing to do.

Sue Townsend *The Secret Diary of Adrian Mole Aged 13¾* (1982), entry for Sunday 16 August

60 'England resembles a ship in shape,' wrote Ralph Waldo Emerson in *English Traits*. He was wrong . . . It is a hurrying pig; its snout is in the south-west in Wales, and its reaching trotters are Cornwall, and its rump is East Anglia.

Paul Theroux *The Kingdom by the Sea*, ch. 1 (1983). 'The whole of Britain,' he elaborated, 'looks like a witch riding on a pig.'

61 What does the journey seem like to those who aren't British – as they head towards the land of embarrassment and breakfast?

Julian Barnes The journey is the Channel-ferry crossing. *Flaubert's Parrot*, ch. 7 (1984).

62 In summer, London is an old man with bad breath.

Martin Amis *Money* (publ. 1984), p. 85 (1985 Penguin edn)

63 So you're down from Lancashire, where the real people live?

J. L. Carr *The Battle of Pollocks Crossing*, p.3

(1985). The speaker is the clerk of the Anglo-American Goodwill League, and she is addressing George Gidner, who is in fact from Yorkshire.

64 **In Islington you can hardly hurl a brick without hitting three antique shops, an estate agent and a bookshop. Even if you didn't actually hit them you would certainly set off their burglar alarms, which wouldn't be turned off again till after the weekend.**
   Douglas Adams *Dirk Gently's Holistic Detective Agency*, ch. 16 (1987)

65 **The British rather enjoy their position as a people poised between formality and eccentricity.**
   Julian Barnes *New Yorker* September 1991, collected in *Letters from London 1990–1995*, ch. 4 (1995)

66 **[Of Brighton] A town that looks like it's helping police with their enquiries.**
   Keith Waterhouse Quoted in the London *Evening Standard* 9 December 1994

67 **[Of Berwick-on-Tweed] It's a little-known fact . . . that the town is still technically at war with Nazi Germany. Sadly, most of the residents looked as though they were still preoccupied with defeating the Kaiser.**
   Victor Lewis-Smith *Inside the Magic Rectangle*, 'Antiques Roadshow' (1995)

68 **Covent Garden is a place where businessmen dump their wives in order to keep them quiet.**
   Jonathan Miller *The Times* 19 September 1998

69 **The man who is tired of London is tired of looking for a parking space.**
   Paul Theroux Interview in the *Daily Telegraph* 30 November 1998. A refinement of Dr Johnson's famous remark.

70 **I'm Irish. We think sideways.**
   Spike Milligan Quoted in the *Independent on Sunday* 20 June 1999

71 **The English – in England – are the most tolerant bigots on earth.**
   Anon. Introduction to a phrasebook, quoted

in *The Times*, 'Quotes of the Week', 24 July 1999

72 **McTavish's little boy was being questioned by the teacher during an arithmetic lesson. 'If you had five pounds,' said the teacher, 'and I asked you for three, how many would you have then?' 'Five,' said young McTavish.**
   Anon. Quoted in *The Tiny Book of Scottish Jokes* ed. Des MacHale (2000)

73 **Tell someone that you live, or have lived, in Leeds and they are quite likely to say, 'Well, it's easy to get out of.'**
   Alan Bennett *Telling Tales*, 'Days Out' (2000)

74 **And doubtless there is a wing of Soho in Wormwood Scrubs.**
   Keith Waterhouse *Soho*, 'Prelude' (2001)

75 **I've been back to the Isle of Wight about once. I stayed at a hotel where the evening's entertainment was to turn off the lights in the restaurant and watch as a family of badgers played on the lawn.**
   Douglas Adams *The Salmon of Doubt*, 'Life', 'Interview with Virgin.net' (2002)

Crete

1 **The people of Crete unfortunately make more history than they can consume locally.**
   Saki *The Chronicles of Clovis*, 'The Jesting of Arlington Stringham' (1911). This remark – 'not brilliant, but it came in the middle of a dull speech' – was made by Arlington Stringham in a House of Commons debate.

Eastern Europe

1 **There are few virtues that the Poles do not possess – and there are few mistakes they have ever avoided.**
   Winston Churchill Speech, House of Commons, 16 August 1945

2 **A Hungarian is a man who is**

behind you in a revolving door but gets out in front of you.

George Mikes In *Punch* February 1971 George Mikes wrote that, although he had been quoted 'dozens of times' as having said this, he never had.

3 Then we went to Moscow for the weekend (makes a change from the Cotswolds) and when we got back I started telling people it had been like spending four days at a post office with all the positions closed.

Robert Robinson *The Dog Chairman*, 'The Middle-aged Philistine Abroad' (1982)

4 As a global player, Lithuania had been fading since the death of Vytautas the Great in 1430.

Jonathan Franzen *The Corrections*, 'The Generator' (2001)

Europe

1 There is no freedom in Europe – that's certain – it is besides a worn out portion of the globe.

Lord Byron Letter to John Cam Hobhouse of 3 October 1819, collected in *Letters and Journals*, vol. 6, *The Flesh Is Frail (1818–1819)*, ed. Leslie A. Marchand (1976)

France

1 Not a translation – only taken from the French.

Richard Brinsley Sheridan Sneer in *The Critic*, act 1 (1779)

2 Yet, who can help loving the land that has taught us/ Six hundred and eighty-five ways to dress eggs?

Thomas Moore *The Fudge Family in Paris*, letter 8 (1818)

3 Oh how I love Humanity,/ With love so pure and pringlish,/ And how I hate the horrid French,/ Who never will be English!

G. K. Chesterton 'The World State', *Collected Poems* (1933)

4 How can you govern a country that has 246 kinds of cheese?

Charles de Gaulle Speech of 1951, quoted in *Les Mots du Général*, p. 57, ed. Ernest Mignon (1962)

5 There's something Vichy about the French.

Ivor Novello Letter to Edward Marsh of March 1941, quoted in *Ambrosia and Small Beer*, ch. 4, ed. Christopher Hassall (1964)

6 *Chapeau* means hat, *oeuf* means egg. It's like those French have a different word for everything.

Steve Martin *A Wild and Crazy Guy*, 'Language' (LP, 1978). 'See,' he added, 'you never appreciate your language until you go to a country that doesn't have the courtesy to speak English.'

7 When we got to our hundred and eightieth French village, I screamed at the top of my lungs, 'The joke is over!' English, *please*! I couldn't believe that a whole country couldn't speak English.

Mel Brooks Quoted in *Profiles*, 'Mel Brooks', by Kenneth Tynan (1989). Then: 'Every time we passed through a little town, we'd see these signs – "Boulangerie", "Patisserie", and "Rue" this, and "Rue" that.'

8 No accident that debacle is a French word.

John Lanchester *The Debt to Pleasure*, 'Summer', 'A Selection of Cold Cuts' (1996). The narrator Tarquin Winot is quoting his late brother Bartholomew.

Germany

1 But I don't like German. It isn't at all a becoming language. I know perfectly well that I look quite plain after my German lesson.

Oscar Wilde Cecily Cardew in *The Importance of Being Earnest*, act 2 (1895)

2 Now a verb has a hard enough time of it in this world when it's all together. It's downright inhuman to split it up. But that's just what these Germans do. They take a part of a verb and put it down here, like

a stake, and they take the other part of it and put it away over yonder like another stake, and between these two limits they just shovel in German.

Mark Twain Speech on 'The Disappearance of Literature' to the Nineteenth-Century Club at Sherry's, New York, 20 November 1900

3 **Germans are split into two broad categories: those with tall spikes in their hats, and those with briefcases.**

Alan Coren *The Sanity Inspector*, 'All You Need to Know about Germany' (1974)

4 **German is the most extravagantly ugly language. It sounds like someone using a sick bag on a 747.**

Willie Rushton Delivered in 1984, quoted in *The Penguin Dictionary of Modern Humorous Quotations* ed. Fred Metcalf (2nd edn 2001)

5 **I love Germany so dearly that I hope there will always be two of them.**

François Mauriac Quoted in *Newsweek* 20 November 1989

6 **West Germans are tall, pert and orthodontically corrected, with hands, teeth and hair as clean as their clothes and clothes as sharp as their looks. Except for the fact that they all speak English pretty well, they're indistinguishable from Americans.**

P. J. O'Rourke *Rolling Stone* November 1989

7 **[Of German reunification] It's like the Beatles coming together again – let's hope they don't go on a world tour.**

Matt Frei *The Listener* 21 June 1990

8 **There are no such thing as Austrians. All Austrians are Germans.**

Howard Jacobson Marvin Kreitman in *Who's Sorry Now?*, bk 1, ch. 4 (2002). Later he says: 'Germans I can say what I like about. That's their function for the next thousand years – to be the butt of everyone who isn't German.'

Holland

1 **Holland . . . lies so low they're only saved by being dammed.**

Thomas Hood *Up the Rhine*, letter from Martha Penny to Rebecca Page (1840)

Indian Subcontinent

1 **[Of India] It's a fine place to write about but a bad one to live in.**

Rudyard Kipling Letter of 3 May 1866 written from Lahore to Margaret Burne-Jones, collected in *The Letters of Rudyard Kipling*, vol. 1, *(1872–89)*, ed. Thomas Pinney (1990)

2 **Well, India is very *big* and, contrary to the map, not really very pink when you look at it close to. More buff tones really.**

Joyce Grenfell Letter to Virginia Graham of 6 December 1944, collected in *Joyce and Ginnie: The Letters of Joyce Grenfell and Virginia Graham* ed. Janie Hampton (1997)

3 **[Of Pakistan] The sort of place to send your mother-in-law for a month, all expenses paid.**

Ian Botham Remark made during a radio interview of 17 March 1984. It cost Botham a £1,000 fine, levied by the Test and County Cricket Board the following month. When given out against Pakistan in the 1992 cricket world cup, Pakistani fielders taunted, 'Send in your mother-in-law. She couldn't do any worse.'

Iraq

1 **Iraq: Things are going from Iraq to ruin.**

Anon. *The Dictionary of Puns*, 'Iraq', ed. John S. Crosbie (1977)

2 **Baghdad: Always check with Equity before visiting Baghdad.**

Henry Root *Henry Root's World of Knowledge* (1982)

Israel

1 **Can there any good thing come out of Nazareth?**

St John 1:46, the Bible, Authorized Version (1611). The speaker is Nathanael, and he is referring to Jesus. He reveals a snobbery common among pious Jews at the time. The Jewish identity of Galilee, including Nazareth, had been diluted by invasion and occupation over the thousand years before Jesus's birth.

2 **Behold an Israelite indeed, in whom is no guile!**

St John 1:47, the Bible, Authorized Version (1611). Jesus, of Nathanael.

3 **We have always said that in our war with the Arabs we had a secret weapon – no alternative.**

Golda Meir Speech in New York, 3 October 1969

Italy

1 **[Of Italians – after the failure of the Carboneria at an early point in their history] As a pretty woman said to me a few nights ago, with the tears in her eyes, as she sat at the harpsichord, 'Alas! The Italians must now return to making operas.' I fear *that* and macaroni are their forte.**

Lord Byron Letter to Joseph Moore of 28 April 1821, vol. 8, *Born for Opposition (1821)* collected in *Letters and Journals*, ed. Leslie A. Marchand (1978). Byron described the Carboneria as 'the very poetry of politics'.

2 **Everybody meets everybody in Florence every day.**

Anthony Trollope *He Knew He Was Right*, ch. 46 (1869)

3 **They spell it Vinci and pronounce it Vinchy; foreigners always spell better than they pronounce.**

Mark Twain *The Innocents Abroad*, ch. 19 (1869)

4 **Geoffrey of Monmouth: Died 1130. Lived all his life, in Latin.**

O. P. Q. Philander Smiff *Smiff's History of England*, ch. 8, entry under 'Leading Authors under the Norman Kings' (1876)

5 **I found a sort of claustrophobia in Venice and a limited pleasure in sitting in the Piazza San Marco listening to ten bands outside ten different cafés playing selections from *Oklahoma* in ten different tempi.**

John Mortimer *Clinging to the Wreckage*, ch. 15 (1982)

6 **I love the way the Italians park. You turn any street corner in Rome and it looks as if you've just missed a parking competition for blind people.**

Bill Bryson *Neither Here Nor There*, ch. 13 (1991)

7 **The point we will be striving to put across is that Latin is modern, up to date and trendy. It is the 'now' subject. Latin is, as we say in the marketing business, very MCMLXXXVIII.**

Oliver Pritchett *The Dogger Bank Saga: Writings 1980–95*, 'Hail, O Declining Latin Lovers' (1995). The column begins: 'The trouble with Latin as a subject is that it has never been properly marketed.'

Scandinavia

1 **Norway, too, has noble wild prospects; and Lapland is remarkable for prodigious noble wild prospects. But, Sir, let me tell you, the noblest prospect which a Scotchman ever sees, is the high road that leads him to England!**

Samuel Johnson *The Life of Samuel Johnson* by James Boswell, vol. 1, p. 425 (1791); in G. B. Hill's edition of 1887, rev. by L. F. Powell (1934).

2 **Copenhagen is also the only city I've ever been in where office girls come out at lunchtime to sunbathe topless in the city parks. That alone earns it my vote for European City of Culture.**

Bill Bryson *Neither Here Nor There*, ch. 10 (1991)

3 [Peter Cook as Sven, a Norwegian fisherman] **In Norway all we get is this fish stuff going on and on.**

Peter Cook The Sven persona was developed in Cook's late-night calls to Clive Bull, host of a phone-in on the radio station LBC. Sven had two themes: the distressing preponderance of fish in Norwegian life and the motivations of his girlfriend Jutta, who had abandoned him. Sven's dialogues with Bull are quoted in *Tragically I Was an Only Twin – The Complete Peter Cook*, ch. 13, 'Small-Hours Sven', ed. William Cook (2002).

South Africa

1 **I needn't have worried about my figure on South African beaches! You never saw such 'stomicks'.**

Joyce Grenfell Letter of 11 February 1968 from Grenfell to Virginia Graham, collected in *Joyce and Ginnie: The Letters of Joyce Grenfell and Virginia Graham* ed. Janie Hampton (1997)

2 **People in South Africa talk about South Africa, and that's all.**

Jon Ronson *Clubbed Class*, ch. 1 (1995)

Spain

1 **FAITH: Does she like Spain?**
PHILIPPA: She likes the magic and grandeur of the landscape, but she's not keen on the bacon.

Victoria Wood *Barmy: The New Victoria Wood Sketch Book*, 'Spaghetti' (1987)

Switzerland

1 **Switzerland is simply a large, lumpy solid rock, with a thin skin of grass stretched over it.**

Mark Twain *A Tramp Abroad*, ch. 42 (1880)

2 **It is true that a good deal of it reminds one of the drop-scene of a theatre or pictures on the back of chocolate boxes, but that is no more the fault of Switzerland than it is the fault of Shakespeare that**

some of his best lines are hackneyed by quotation.

Raymond Asquith Letter to H. T. Baker of 9 August 1900, collected in *Raymond Asquith: Life and Letters* ed. John Jolliffe (1980)

3 **The Swiss are a neat, industrious people, none of whom is under seventy-five years of age.**

Dorothy Parker From a review of *Forty Thousand Sublime and Beautiful Thoughts* compiled by Charles Noel Douglas, *New Yorker* 24 January 1931. Parker added: 'It's all true about the yodeling and cowbells.'

4 **In Italy for thirty years under the Borgias they had warfare, terror, murder and bloodshed, but they produced Michelangelo, Leonardo da Vinci and the Renaissance. In Switzerland, they had brotherly love; they had five hundred years of democracy and peace – and what did that produce? The cuckoo clock.**

Graham Greene Harry Lime (Orson Welles) in *The Third Man* (film, 1949, directed by Carol Reed, screenplay by Graham Greene). *The Rough Guide to Switzerland* by Matthew Teller (2nd edn 2003) comments: 'Never has one throwaway movie line done so much damage to the reputation of a whole country', adding that Switzerland was 'the most consistently turbulent, war-torn area of Europe' until 1848; that it has in fact produced Hans Holbein, Jean-Jacques Rousseau, Paul Klee, Hermann Hesse, Alberto Giacometti; and that the cuckoo clock was actually invented in Bavaria.

5 **In what language do you think?**

Anon. Question on the Swiss census form, quoted in *The Times*, 'Quotes of the Week', 28 April 2001

Turkey

1 **'Well, it's no use talking about it now,' said Sam. 'It's over, and can't be helped, and that's one consolation, as they always say in Turkey, ven they cuts the wrong man's head off.'**

Charles Dickens Sam Weller in *The Pickwick Papers*, ch. 23 (1837). In ch. 28 he says: 'There;

now we look compact and comfortable, as the father said ven he cut his little boy's head off, to cure him o'squintin'.'

Sense of Identity
Xenophobia

1 French truth, Dutch prowess, British policy,/ Hibernian learning, Scotch civility,/ Spaniard's Despatch, Danes' wit, are mainly seen in/ thee.
Earl of Rochester 'Upon Nothing', st. 10 (1679)

2 The best thing I know between France and England is – the sea.
Douglas Jerrold *The Wit and Opinions of Douglas Jerrold*, 'The Anglo-French Alliance', ed. Blanchard Jerrold (1859)

3 If I were a cassowary/ On the plains of Timbuctoo,/ I would eat a missionary,/ Cassock, band, and hymn-book too.
Samuel Wilberforce Attributed

4 [Of Americans] At bottom he was probably fond of them, but he was always able to conceal it.
Mark Twain *New York World* 10 December 1899, referring to Thomas Carlyle

5 We can trace almost all the disasters of English history to the influence of Wales.
Evelyn Waugh Dr Fagan, who is 'very tall and very old and very well dressed', and English, in *Decline and Fall*, pt 1, ch. 8 (1928)

6 Abroad is unutterably bloody and foreigners are fiends.
Nancy Mitford Uncle Matthew in *The Pursuit of Love*, ch. 15 (1945). He conceded, however, that 'Frogs . . . are slightly better than Huns or Wops.'

7 The main aim of the Englishman abroad is to meet people; I mean, of course, nice English people from next door or from the next street.
George Mikes *How to Unite Nations*, 'Down with Travelling' (1963)

8 I don't hold with abroad and think that foreigners speak English when our backs are turned.
Quentin Crisp *The Naked Civil Servant*, ch. 4 (1968)

9 Abroad is bloody.
George VI Quoted in *A Certain World*, 'Royalty', by W. H. Auden (1970)

10 Gesticulation: Any movement made by a foreigner.
Beachcomber *Beachcomber: The Works of J. B. Morton*, 'A Dictionary for Today', ed. Richard Ingrams (1974)

11 I had just seen a survey in a British paper in which executives had been asked to list their most despised things in the whole universe, and the three top ones were, in this order: garden gnomes, fuzzy dice hanging in car windows, and the French.
Bill Bryson *Neither Here Nor There*, ch. 4 (1991)

Patriotism

1 I fancy your Ladyship hates her own country as some women do their husbands, only for being too near 'em.
Colley Cibber *The Double Gallant*, act 1 (1707)

2 Patriotism is the last refuge of a scoundrel.
Samuel Johnson *The Life of Samuel Johnson* by James Boswell, vol. 2, p. 348 (1791); in G. B. Hill's edition of 1887, rev. L. F. Powell (1934)

3 Self-esteem sometimes takes the guise of patriotism. In one of the western isles of Scotland there is an elderly clergyman who prays every Sunday for himself and his congregation, and 'the neighbouring island of Great Britain'.
J. M. Barrie 'The Modern Peripatetic', first publ. in the *Nottingham Journal* 6 March 1884, repr. in *The Penguin Book of Columnists* ed. Christopher Silvester (1997)

4 'My country right or wrong' is a thing that no patriot would think of saying, except in a desperate

case. It is like saying 'my mother, drunk or sober'.

G. K. Chesterton *The Defendant*, 'Defence of Patriotism' (1901). In 1816 Stephen Decatur, an American naval officer, said: 'Our country! In her intercourse with foreign nations, may she always be in the right; but our country, right or wrong.'

5 **J. L. Carr lives in England.**

J. L. Carr Author biography, as supplied by Carr for his novella *A Month in the Country* (1980)

6 **Straight away you knew you could call the two Welshmen bastards so long as you never, never called the *Welsh* bastards.**

Robert Robinson *Skip All That*, 'Smivvo' (1996)

Parochialism

1 **What e'er you say, I know all beyond High-Park's a desart to you.**

Sir George Etherege Harriet in *The Man of Mode*, act 5, sc.2 (1676)

2 **The French are the *cockneys* of Europe, and have no idea how anyone can exist out of Paris, or be alive without incessant grimace and jabber.**

William Hazlitt 'Merry England', *New Monthly Magazine* December 1825, collected in *The Essays of William Hazlitt* ed. Catherine Macdonald Maclean (1949)

3 **Now if you live in a region, you'll probably be aware of the value of regional broadcasting.**

Chris Morris and Armando Iannucci The news anchor man Chris Morris in *On the Hour* (radio series, 1991)

4 **At the top of page three, there was a piece about a Grimsby-born publisher who had been cleared of fraud charges. The fact that this publisher now lived in Guernsey and had his offices in Gloucestershire didn't deter the *Grimsby Evening Telegraph* one jot.**

Charles Jennings *Up North*, ch. 9 (1995)

5 **A miniature village in Bournemouth caught fire, and the flames could be seen nearly three feet away.**

Bob Monkhouse *The Sun* 30 December 2003

Race

1 **Poor negro say one ting, you take no offence,/ Black and white be one colour a hundred years hence,/ For when massa Death kick him into the grave,/ He no spare negro, buckra, nor massa, nor slave.**

Anon. 'Kickaraboo', *Oliver's Comic Songs* (1825?)

2 **'The Arabs are only Jews upon horseback,' said Baroni.**

Benjamin Disraeli *Tancred*, bk 4, ch. 3 (1847)

3 **The gentleman will please remember that when his half-civilized ancestors were hunting the wild boar in Silesia, mine were princes of the earth.**

Judah Philip Benjamin Response to an anti-Semitic remark made by a US senator of Germanic origin. Attributed.

4 **The so-called white races are really pinko-grey.**

E. M. Forster *A Passage to India*, ch.7 (1924). But Mr Fielding, who made the remark, 'did not realize that "white" has no more to do with a colour than "God save the King" with a god'.

5 **South Africa, renowned both far and wide/ For politics and little else beside.**

Roy Campbell 'The Wayzgoose' (1928)

6 **I have 42,000 children . . . and not one comes to visit me.**

Carl Reiner and Mel Brooks The two-thousand-year-old man, played by Mel Brooks, from *Two Thousand Years with Carl Reiner and Mel Brooks* (LP, 1960). He has been married many hundreds of times and has many Jewish preoccupations.

7 **'You haven't got a chance, kid,' he told him glumly. 'They hate Jews.'/ 'But I'm not Jewish,' answered Clev-**

inger./ 'It will make no difference,' Yossarian promised, and Yossarian was right. 'They're after everybody.'

Joseph Heller *Catch-22*, ch. 8 (1961)

8 All handsome men are slightly sunburned.

Paul Robeson Puckoon, ch. 1, by Spike Milligan (1963). Attributed.

9 It's a great shock at the age of five or six to find that in a world of Gary Coopers you are the Indian.

James Baldwin Speech to the Cambridge Union of 17 February 1965

10 Being a star has made it possible for me to get insulted in places where the average Negro could never hope to go and get insulted.

Sammy Davis Jr *Yes I Can*, pt 3, ch. 23 (1965)

11 You show me a black man who isn't an extremist and I'll show you one who needs psychiatric attention.

Malcolm X *The Autobiography of Malcolm X*, p. 394 (1966)

12 That music was pretty white.

Jack Nicholson Frank Zappa as 'the Critic' to David Jones of the Monkees in *Head* (film, 1968, screen play by Jack Nicholson, directed by Bob Rafelson)

13 A Jewish man with parents alive is a fifteen-year-old boy, and will remain a fifteen-year-old boy until *they die*!

Philip Roth *Portnoy's Complaint*, 'Cunt Crazy' (1969)

14 [Bart, who is black, threatening to shoot himself] Hold it. The next man makes a move, the nigger gets it.

Mel Brooks *Blazing Saddles* (film, 1974, screenplay by Mel Brooks and others, directed by Mel Brooks)

15 When they circumcised Herbert Samuel they threw away the wrong bit.

David Lloyd George *The Listener* 7 September 1978. Attributed.

16 [Reggie (Eddie Murphy) showing his police ID in a bar full of rednecks]

I'm your worst nightmare: a nigger with a badge.

Anon. *48 Hours* (film, 1982), screenplay by Walter Hill and several others (hence 'Anon.'), directed by Walter Hill. Reggie is only impersonating a police officer, which lends an extra tension. Roger Ebert, in his *Video Companion* (1997), writes that this scene made Murphy a star.

17 Gentleman: Always 'coloured'.

Henry Root *Henry Root's World of Knowledge* (1982)

18 'They give you that troll look.'/ 'What troll look?'/ 'The troll look that'/ He finished for her. 'That Jews get in tweeds. Shit, I've really done it. I've married an anti-Semite.'

John Updike *Bech is Back*, 'Macbech' (1982)

19 The Irish are the niggers of Europe, lads. An' Dubliners are the niggers of Ireland . . . An' the northside Dubliners are the niggers o' Dublin. – Say it loud, I'm black an' I'm proud.

Roddy Doyle Jimmy Rabitte in *The Commitments* (1987). He is not black.

20 [Of Asians in Britain] They sell mangoes in our post office – what explanation is there for that?

Alan Bennett Mr Turnbull in *Talking Heads* (TV series, 1988); 'A Chip in the Sugar'

21 I like to think I mowed down as many whites as I did blacks.

Peter Cook As Arthur Streeb-Greebling in *Why Bother?* (radio series, 1994). Streeb-Greebling is a tweedy patrician hell-bent on teaching ravens to fly under water. In this dialogue it emerges that he's 'been involved in racial violence in Los Angeles after the Rodney King incident'. The exchange is transcribed in *The Complete Peter Cook*, ch. 11, 'Sir Arthur Streeb-Greebling', ed. William Cook (2002).

22 How did people ever get the idea that *white* skin was any good at all, let alone the best? White skin was so obviously the worst: carved from the purest Trex.

Martin Amis *The Information*, pt 1 (1995). Trex is a brand of cooking fat.

23 'Black bastard' not racial abuse, says tribunal.

Anon. *Daily Telegraph* headline, quoted in

Cannibal Victims Speak Out, and Other Astonishing Press Cuttings ed. Mat Coward (1995)

24 **Blacks can get into medical school with a lower grade . . . If that's true, a Jew should be able to play basketball with a lower net.**
Jackie Mason *Jackie Mason: An Equal Opportunity Offender* (video, 1995)

25 **He is twenty-five, for God's sake. He was in nappies when I started junior school. He thinks the Bay City Rollers were an American football team. He can't remember Michael Jackson ever being black.**
Meera Syal *Life Isn't All Ha Ha Hee Hee*, ch. 5 (1999)

26 **Everyone's coloured, or you wouldn't be able to see them.**
Captain Beefheart Quoted in *Captain Beefheart*, ch. 16, by Mike Barnes (2000). Barnes also quotes Beefheart as saying: 'Some people think it's hip to have blacks in the band but I've got Jews, man. They know all about suffering.'

27 **Wouldn't it be a helluva thing if this was burnt cork and you folk were being tolerant for nothing.**
Eddie Murphy Quoted in *Halliwell's Who's Who in the Movies*, ed. John Walker (2nd edn 2001)

28 **The Klansman Who Won't Use the N-word**
Jon Ronson Title of ch. 7 of *Them* by Jon Ronson (2001). The Ku Klux Klansman in question is described as 'PR-savvy'.

29 **[Of arranged marriages] I can't wait for my marriage – I'm really looking forward to meeting my husband.**
Shazia Mirza *All You Ever Wanted to Know about Islam but Were Afraid to Ask* (TV programme, 5 November 2002)

30 **What did the Jewish waiter say to the party of Jewish women who were dining in his restaurant one evening?/ Good evening, ladies, is anything all right?**
Anon. Quoted in *Jewish Humour* ed. Ben Eliezer (2003)

31 **They say we Jews are mean, greedy and all we think about is money. I wish I had five pounds for every time I've heard that.**
Ivor Dembina Line used in his stand-up comedy act c.2003

32 **[Of Moses] He led us around the desert for forty years, and he took us to the only part of the region that has no oil.**
Golda Meir Quoted in *Jewish Humour* ed. Ben Eliezer (2003)

Politics
The Nature of Politics

1 **BRABANTIO: Thou art a villain. IAGO: You are – a senator.**
William Shakespeare *Othello*, act 1, sc. 1 (1604)

2 **A little rule, a little sway,/ A sunbeam on a winter's day,/ Is all the proud and mighty have/ Between the cradle and the grave.**
John Dyer *Grongar Hill* (1726)

3 **A little rebellion now and then is a good thing.**
Thomas Jefferson Letter to James Madison of 30 January 1787

4 **France was a long despotism tempered by epigrams.**
Thomas Carlyle *The French Revolution*, pt 1, bk 1, ch. 1 (1837)

5 **A government of statesmen or of clerks? Of Humbug or Humdrum?**
Benjamin Disraeli *Coningsby*, bk 2, ch. 4 (1844)

6 **What is statesmanship but successful crawling and kicking?**
Samuel Palmer Letter to Mrs Julia Robinson of 9 December 1872

7 **I always voted at my party's call,/ And I never thought of thinking for myself at all.**
W. S. Gilbert The Right Hon. Sir Joseph Porter KCB in *HMS Pinafore*, act 1 (1878)

8 **After every election both sides fall**

to explaining the result. It was due to this, it was due to that or the other – there are just as many explanations as there are men who know nothing about it.

Ambrose Bierce 'Prattle', *San Francisco Examiner* 13 November 1898, repr. in *The Penguin Book of Columnists* ed. Christopher Silvester (1997)

9 **Towards the age of twenty-six,/ They shoved him into politics.**

Hilaire Belloc *Cautionary Tales*, 'Lord Lundy' (1907)

10 [Recommended response to political attacks] **Never complain, and never explain.**

Benjamin Disraeli Quoted in *The Life of William Ewart Gladstone*, ch. 1, by J. Morle (1903). Stanley Baldwin gave the same advice to Harold Nicolson in 1943.

11 *Long run* **is a misleading guide to current affairs.** *In the long run* **we're all dead.**

John Maynard Keynes *A Tract on Monetary Reform*, ch. 3 (1923)

12 **The more you read and observe about this Politics thing, the more you got to admit that each party is worse than the other.**

Will Rogers *The Illiterate Digest*, 'Breaking into the Writing Game' (1924)

13 **All Reformers, however strict their social conscience, live in houses just as big as they can pay for.**

Logan Pearsall Smith *Afterthoughts*, 'Other People' (1931)

14 **It is now known that men enter local politics solely as a result of being unhappily married.**

C. Northcote Parkinson *Parkinson's Law*, ch. 10 (1958)

15 **I don't know jokes; I just watch the government and report the facts.**

Will Rogers Quoted in 'A Rogers Thesaurus', *Saturday Review* 25 August 1962

16 **A week is a long time in politics.**

Harold Wilson Attributed, though Wilson could never recall saying it. Possibly a reflection provoked by the sterling crisis of 1964. Quoted in *The New Penguin Dictionary of Modern Quotations*, ed. Robert Andrews (2nd edn 2003)

17 **The people who take no interest in politics should remember that politics takes a strong and continuing interest in them.**

J. B. Priestley *The Edwardians*, pt 2, 'Edwardian Politics' (1970)

18 [Of J. Edgar Hoover] **Better to have him inside the tent pissing out, than outside pissing in.**

Lyndon B. Johnson Quoted in *The Best and Brightest*, ch. 20, by David Halberstam (1972)

19 **I used to say that politics was the second-lowest profession and I have come to know that it bears a great similarity to the first.**

Ronald Reagan Speech in Los Angeles of 2 March 1977

20 **Those who say I am not in agreement with the policy are, rightly or wrongly, quite wrong.**

Willie Whitelaw Quoted in *On the House* by Simon Hoggart, p. 39 (1981). Immigration is the policy in question.

21 **I've learned in Washington that that's the only place where sound travels faster than light.**

Ronald Reagan Speech at the annual convention of the Congressional Medal of Honour Society, New York, 12 December 1983. Quoted in *Ronald Reagan: The Wisdom and Humour of the Great Communicator*, 'People Are the Government', ed. Frederick J. Ryan Jr (1995).

22 **We should not be surprised that backbenchers are such deeply second-rate people when we examine what emerges on the front bench.**

Auberon Waugh *Spectator*, 1 June 1985

23 **Resignation in politics is a bit like creative bankruptcy: if effected in the right way and at the right time, it can restore the fortunes, and even the reputation.**

Julian Barnes *New Yorker* January 1991, collected in *Letters from London 1990–1995* (1995)

24 **I sometimes feel it is only a matter**

of time before the Foreign Secretary, for example, is called Gary.

Brian Thompson *A Half-baked Life*, ch. 17 (1991). The book purports to be the autobiography of an amiable bicycling eccentric with old-fashioned views, namely Claude Lorraine Everitt Jenks (his mother wanted a girl). The true author, named as the writer of the Preface, is Brian Thompson. 'All of us who are truly English can feel it,' argues Jenks, 'the hunger to return our great land to a better future.'

25 Politics is the art of the passable.

Anon. *And I Quote*, 'Politics', ed. Ashton Applewhite and others (1992)

26 Like a glorious tropical sunset, a resigning politician is a beautiful sight.

Matthew Parris *The Times* 26 September 1992, collected in *I Couldn't Possibly Comment* (1997)

27 Being an MP is the sort of job all working-class parents want for their children – clean, indoors and no heavy lifting.

Diane Abbott *Independent* 18 January 1994

28 Running for office is the least aerobic of the socially interactive sports.

Carrie Fisher *Delusions of Grandma*, p. 66 (1994 paperback edn)

29 I see nothing wrong in giving Robert some legal experience as Attorney General before he goes out to practise law.

John F. Kennedy John F. Kennedy on his brother, quoted in *The Law Is a Ass*, 'Lawyers', ed. Ronald Irving (1999)

30 How a minority,/ Reaching majority,/ Seizing authority,/ Hates a minority!

Leonard Robbins 'Minorities'

Particular Politicians

1 Not merely a chip off the old 'block', but the old block itself.

Edmund Burke On the maiden speech of Pitt the Younger, February 1781, quoted in *Historical Memoirs of My Own Time*, pt 2, p. 377, by N. W. Wraxhall (1904)

2 Pitt is to Addington/ As London is to Paddington.

George Canning 'The Oracle', written *c.* 1803. Addington, Prime Minister 1801–4, was sandwiched between two terms served by his political rival Pitt the Younger.

3 [Of Robespierre] O thou seagreen Incorruptible!

Thomas Carlyle *The French Revolution*, pt 3, bk 1, ch. 6 (1837)

4 [Of Sir Robert Peel] He traces the steam engine always back to the kettle.

Benjamin Disraeli Speech, Hansard 11 April 1845

5 If Gladstone fell into the Thames, that would be misfortune; and if anybody pulled him out, that, I suppose, would be calamity.

Benjamin Disraeli Quoted in *The Fine Art of Political Wit* ed. Leon Harris (1965)

6 [Of Gladstone] He has not a single redeeming defect.

Benjamin Disraeli Attributed remark, quoted in *History in Quotations* ed. M. J. Cohen and John Major (2003)

7 [Of Gladstone] He speaks to Me as if I was a public meeting.

Queen Victoria Quoted in *Collections and Recollections*, ch. 14, by G. W. E. Russell (1898)

8 If Kitchener was not a great man, he was, at least, a great poster.

Margot Asquith Remark made in 1914, quoted in *Kitchener: Portrait of an Imperialist*, ch. 14, by Philip Magnus (1958)

9 [Of Sir Oswald Mosley] Tom Mosley is a cad and a wrong 'un and they will find it out.

Stanley Baldwin Remark made 21 June 1929, quoted in *History in Quotations* ed. M. J. Cohen and John Major (2003)

10 [Of Lloyd George] This extraordinary figure of our time, this siren, this goat-footed bard, this half-human visitor to our age from the hag-ridden magic and enchanted woods of Celtic antiquity.

John Maynard Keynes *Essays in Biography*, 'Mr Lloyd George' (1933)

11 **How do they know?**

Dorothy Parker On hearing that the notoriously boring and stilted Calvin Coolidge had died (1933). Quoted in the *Paris Review* summer 1956, repr. in *Writers at Work*, 1st series, ed. Malcolm Cowley (1958). In an attempt to make Coolidge seem more interesting, a reception was arranged in 1924 at which he would be presented to thirty-four filmstars, provoking the *New York Times* to remark: 'The President nearly laughed.'

12 **Why is there all this unrest in India? Because its inhabitants eat only an occasional handful of rice. The day when Mahatma Gandhi sits down to a good juicy steak and follows it up with roly-poly pudding and a spot of Stilton you will see the end of all this nonsense of civil disobedience.**

P. G. Wodehouse *Blandings Castle and Elsewhere*, 'The Juice of an Orange' (1935)

13 **Gladstone ... spent his declining years trying to guess the answer to the Irish Question; unfortunately whenever he was getting warm the Irish secretly changed the Question ...**

W. C. Sellar and R. J. Yeatman *1066 and All That*, ch. 57 (1936)

14 **The *Flying Scotsman* is no less splendid a sight when it travels north to Edinburgh than when it travels south to London. Mr Baldwin denouncing sanctions was as dignified as Mr Baldwin imposing them.**

Lord Beaverbrook Observation made in May 1937, quoted in *People on People: The Oxford Dictionary of Biographical Quotations* ed. Susan Ratcliffe (2001)

15 **[Of Clement Attlee] What can you do with a man who looks like a female llama surprised while bathing?**

Winston Churchill Comment made in 1944, quoted in ibid.

16 **I have never been able to get very far in my exploration of the minds of people who call their dogs Mussolini, Tojo and Adolf, and I suspect the reason is that I am unable to associate with them long enough to examine what goes on in their heads.**

James Thurber *The Beast in Me and Other Animals*, 'How to Name a Dog' (1948)

17 **Dull, duller, Dulles.**

Winston Churchill Speaking in January 1953 of John Foster Dulles, American Secretary of State, whom he found 'obnoxious'. Quoted in *Winston Churchill: A Brief Life*, ch. 12, by Piers Brendon (2001).

18 **[Of Clement Attlee] He is a modest little man who has a good deal to be modest about.**

Winston Churchill Quoted in the *Chicago Sunday Tribune* 27 June 1954. Churchill could never quite believe that he had lost the general election of 1945 to Attlee, whom he found colourless and suburban. 'If you feed a grub on royal jelly,' he remarked of Attlee's ascent to power, 'you may turn it into a queen bee.' He also described Attlee as 'a sheep in sheep's clothing'.

19 **A racing tipster who only reached Hitler's level of accuracy would not do well for his clients.**

A. J. P. Taylor *The Origins of the Second World War*, ch. 7 (1961)

20 **Khrushchev talks for five hours at press conferences, and may even have got it up to ten by the time this survey appears. (Moral: Great oafs from little icons grow.)**

James Thurber *Lanterns and Lances*, 'The Case for Comedy' (1961)

21 **[Of John F. Kennedy] There is something very eighteenth-century about this young man. He is always on his toes during our discussions. But in the evening, there will be music and wine and pretty women.**

Harold Macmillan *New York Journal-American* 21 January 1962

22 **[Of Lloyd George] He did not seem to care which way he travelled as long as he was in the driving seat.**

Lord Beaverbrook *The Decline and Fall of Lloyd George*, ch. 7 (1963)

23 **I caught a glimpse of our future leaders on the telly – people like Mr Callaghan & Mr Healey, & they looked *horrid*, all of them**

enormously fat & flabby with wet mouths & boot-button eyes!

Joyce Grenfell Letter of 18 October 1964 from Grenfell to Virginia Graham, collected in *Joyce and Ginnie: The Letters of Joyce Grenfell and Virginia Graham* ed. Janie Hampton (1997)

24 [Of Sir Harold Macmillan] **His decomposing visage and somehow seedy attire conveyed the impression of an ageing and eccentric clergyman who had been induced to play the part of a Prime Minister in the dramatized version of a Snow novel put on by a village amateur dramatic society.**

Malcolm Muggeridge *Tread Softly for You Tread on My Jokes*, 'England, Whose England?' (1966)

25 [Of Anthony Eden] **As has been truly said in his days as an active politician, he was not only a bore; he bored for England.**

Ibid., 'Boring for England' (1966)

26 [Of de Gaulle] **Not since Napoleon (the Third, I should add, to be truthful) has France had such a leader.**

Ibid., 'What Price Glory?' (1966)

27 Hitler . . . *There* **was a painter! He could paint an entire apartment in one afternoon. Two coats!**

Mel Brooks Franz Liebkind (Kenneth Mars) in *The Producers* (film, 1967, written and directed by Mel Brooks). Liebkind is an apologist for Hitler, maintaining that he was 'better looking' than Churchill and 'a better dresser'.

28 [Of Neville Chamberlain] **He looked less like a banana than an umbrella.**

Maurice Bowra Recalled by Leslie Mitchell in *Maurice Bowra: A Celebration*, 'An Undergraduate's View of the Warden', ed. Hugh Lloyd-Jones (1974)

29 **Never shoot a film in Belgrade, Yugoslavia! The whole town is illuminated by a 20-watt nightlight, and there's nothing to do. You can't even go for a drive. Tito is always using the car.**

Mel Brooks Quoted in *Newsweek* magazine 17 February 1975

30 [Of Gerald Ford] **So dumb he can't fart and chew gum at the same time.**

Lyndon B. Johnson Quoted in *A Ford, Not a Lincoln*, ch. 2 (1975), by Richard Reeves. Gerald Ford was US President 1974–6.

31 **Ernest Bevin was certainly the most remarkable of the politicians I knew. I once referred to him as Britain's only peasant, in that he had a wonderful rural quality.**

Peter Ustinov *Dear Me*, ch. 19 (1977)

32 **It is not necessary that every time he rises he should give his famous impersonation of a semi-house-trained polecat.**

Michael Foot Of the Conservative bruiser Norman Tebbit. Speech, Hansard 2 March 1978

33 **His speech was rather like being savaged by a dead sheep.**

Denis Healey Responding to Geoffrey Howe's attack on his budget of 1978 in the House of Commons, Hansard 14 June 1978. Howe later said of a Healey speech that it was 'like being nuzzled by an old lamb'.

34 **I saw Mr Gladstone in the street last night. I waited and waited but no cab ran him over.**

Eliza Savage Quoted in *Violets and Vinegar*, 'Crown and State', ed. Jilly Cooper and Tom Hartman (1980)

35 [Of Mrs Thatcher] **She is the Enid Blyton of economics. Nothing must be allowed to spoil her simple plots.**

Richard Holme Speech to the Liberal Party Conference of 10 September 1980

36 **Mr Gerry Fitt, the member for West Belfast, used to sit on the wall [of the Terrace of the House of Commons] and salute the passing tourists on the river with his glass of gin and tonic. 'And it's all free!' he would yell at them.**

Simon Hoggart *On the House*, p. 19 (1981). In fact, as Hoggart notes, the alcohol at the Commons is not free, although it *is* cheap.

37 [Of Ronald Reagan] **The acting head of the United States.**

Gore Vidal Remark made *c.* 1981, quoted in

History in Quotations ed. M. J. Cohen and John Major (2003)

38 [Of Hitler] **A really good wife might have made *all* the difference.**

Anon. Quoted in *Smile Please*, 'Blow Hot and Cold' by Arthur Marshall (1982). The remark was made in Aldershot by 'an ancient male of the grandfatherly type' with whom Marshall was billeted in the war.

39 [Of Hitler and Mussolini] **Both of them are top of my shit list.**

Maurice Bowra Quoted in ibid., 'Day by Day'

40 [Of Mrs Thatcher] **For the past few months she has been charging about like some bargain basement Boadicea.**

Denis Healey *Observer*, 'Sayings of the Week', 7 November 1982

41 [Of Ronald Reagan] **A triumph of the embalmer's art.**

Gore Vidal Quoted in the *Observer* 7 February 1982

42 **If you don't stop whining, that Margaret Thatcher will come and get you.**

Anon. Remark overheard from mother to child, publ. in *Word of Mouth*, 'Eavesdroppings', ed. Nigel Rees (1983)

43 [Of Michael Foot] **A good man fallen among politicians.**

Anon. *Daily Mirror* leader 20 February 1983

44 [Of a speech delivered by Michael Foot] **For an audience to whom good words would have been bread, here came a whole cargo of stones.**

Clive James *Observer* 29 May 1983. Reporting on the 1983 election campaign, James also described Foot's speeches as 'sludge without nuggets', adding that he looked like 'a floppy toy on Benzedrine'.

45 [Of Kenneth Clarke] **That podgy life-insurance-risk.**

Alan Clark Entry for 10 April 1984, *Diaries* by Alan Clark (1993). Clarke, who was Minister of State at the Department of Health and Social Security at the time, likes beer, cigars and curries.

46 **The more I think about it, the more convinced I am that Henry Kissinger's most signal achievement is to** have got everyone to call him 'Doctor'.

Christopher Hitchens *Literary Review* September 1985. 'There are literally millions of Ph.D.s and second-rate academics in the United States,' Hitchens continued, 'but he is the only one below the rank of professor to have managed to pull off this trick.'

47 **'Mr Waldheim, are you a Nazi?' 'Well, we had a few beers, next thing we knew we were in Czechoslovakia.'**

Robin Williams *Robin Williams: Live at the Met* (video, 1987)

48 **Let others have the charisma. I've got the class.**

George Bush *Guardian* 3 December 1988

49 [Of Douglas Hurd] ***À deux* he is delightful; clever, funny, observant, drily cynical. But get him anywhere near 'display mode', particularly if there are officials around, and he might as well have a corncob up his arse.**

Alan Clark Entry for 29 January 1988, *Diaries* by Alan Clark (1993). Hurd was Foreign Secretary at the time. Writing in the *New Statesman* on 4 November 2002 Sebastian Shakespeare said: 'How can we ever picture Lord Hurd again without thinking of him with a "corncob up his arse"?'

50 **The finest thoroughbred horses are often accompanied by a favourite donkey, goat or sheep. Some racehorses will travel nowhere without such a beast. Animal psychiatrists report that the pedigree is relaxed by the presence of the plebeian pal./ Sitting behind the junior industry minister, John Redwood, yesterday was his new Parliamentary Private Secretary, David Evans.**

Matthew Parris *The Times* 14 June 1991, collected in *I Couldn't Possibly Comment* (1997)

51 **IF KINNOCK WINS TODAY, WILL THE LAST PERSON IN BRITAIN PLEASE TURN OUT THE LIGHTS**

Anon. *Sun* headline of 8 April 1992, the day of the general election

52 **Out of everybody in the world, I'd like to fuck Colonel Gadaffi.**

Francis Bacon Remark made by Francis Bacon

to Jeffrey Bernard in Wheeler's restaurant in Soho, London – date uncertain. Quoted in *Just the One: The Wives and Times of Jeffrey Bernard*, ch. 4, by Graham Lord (1992). On overhearing this, four American tourists, according to Lord, 'rose and left the restaurant'.

53 [Of Margaret Thatcher] **With my own views on the chintzy, lacquered creature who governs our state I don't wish to burden you.**
Stephen Fry *Paperweight*, 'Thatcher on TV' (1992)

54 **Kinnock always seemed like some downmarket brand of mottled sausage, well past its sell-by date.**
Giles Gordon *Aren't We Due a Royalty Statement?*, ch. 27 (1993)

55 **Given that Mr Blair is fluent, telegenic and young, the first line of attack is to accuse him of lacking ideas.**
Julian Barnes Quoted in the *New Yorker* August 1994, collected in *Letters from London 1990–1995*, ch. 15 (1995)

56 [Of Tony Blair addressing a public meeting] **He absolutely charmed them, but he didn't say a chipolata sausage.**
Julian Barnes Ibid.

57 [Of Richard Crossman] **That goggle-eyed leveller ... remembered for nothing save losing his departmental papers while eating oysters at Prunier's.**
Robert Robinson *Skip All That*, 'Smivvo' (1996). Crossman wore glasses.

58 **Tony Blair is only Bill Clinton with his zip done up.**
Neil Hamilton *The Times*, 'Quotes of the Week', 5 September 1998

59 **Peter Mandelson is someone who can skulk in broad daylight.**
Simon Hoggart *Guardian* 10 July 1998

60 **Like bubonic plague and stone cladding, no one took Margaret Thatcher seriously until it was too late.**
Anon. *Things Can Only Get Better* by John

O'Farrell – first line of the blurb on the cover of the 1999 edition

61 **Clinton is, I can assure you, more sausage than sizzle.**
Peter Mandelson *The Times* 23 December 2000

62 **I am Al Gore, and I used to be the next President of the United States.**
Al Gore Addressing students in Italy, quoted in *The Times*, 'Quotes of the Week', 2001

63 **When George Bush Senior was president, things were tough. The economy was in the dumps, we were warring with Iraq, but now that his son's president ... things are pretty much the same.**
Matt Groening Cartoon character Homer Simpson 'interviewed' in *Q* magazine June 2003

64 [Of President Kennedy] **I mean, I like giving youth a chance, but do we really want a president who rides half fare on the bus?**
Bob Hope Quoted in the *Independent* 16 May 2003

65 **That Tony Blair (as today talking to troops in Basra) will often say 'I honestly believe' rather than just 'I believe' says all that needs to be said.**
Alan Bennett *London Review of Books* 8 January 2004

Politicians as People

1 [On looking at the first House of Commons after the 1832 Reform Act] **I never saw so many shocking bad hats in my life.**
Duke of Wellington Quoted in *Words on Wellington*, ch. 11, by Sir William Fraser (1889)

2 **All reformers are bachelors.**
George Moore *The Bending of the Bough*, act 1 (1900)

3 **If half the people who make speeches would make concrete**

floors they would be doing more good.

Lord Darling *Observer*, 'Sayings of the Week', 15 July 1917, collected in *The Observer Sayings of the Week* ed. Valerie Ferguson (1978)

4 A politician is a person with whose politics you don't agree. If you agree with him, he is a statesman.

David Lloyd George Speech of 2 July 1935, quoted in *The Times* 3 July 1935. In 1973 Georges Pompidou, as President of France, said: 'A statesman is a politician who places himself at the service of the nation. A politician is a statesman who places the nation at his service.'

5 It's so hard to find men of so high type morals that they'll *stay bought*.

Mark Twain Quoting a lobbyist on behalf of a US Senator in *Notebook*, ch. 20 (1935)

6 A statesman is a politician who's been dead ten or fifteen years.

Harry S. Truman *New York World Telegram and Sun* 12 April 1958

7 Greater love hath no man than this, that he lay down his friends for his life.

Jeremy Thorpe Remark of 1962 quoted in *The General Election of 1964*, ch. 1, by D. E. Butler and Anthony King (1965). Prompted by Harold Macmillan's sacking of several members of his cabinet, this is an inversion of the words of Christ in John 15:13: 'Greater love hath no man than this, that a man lay down his life for his friends.'

8 Politician: One who is willing to do anything on earth for the workers except become one.

Leonard Louis Levinson *The Left-Handed Dictionary*, 'Politicians' (1963)

9 Politicians, ugly buildings, and whores all get respectable if they last long enough.

Robert Towne Noah Cross (John Huston) in *Chinatown* (film, 1974, screenplay by Robert Towne, directed by Roman Polanski)

10 My basic rule is that I want people who don't want a job in government.

Ronald Reagan Remark made on 16 November 1980, quoted in *Political Rhu-*

barb, 'From around the World', ed. Adam Shaw (1987)

11 The only safe pleasure for a parliamentarian is a bag of sweets.

Julian Critchley *Listener* 10 June 1982. Critchley called his autobiography (1994) *A Bag of Boiled Sweets*.

12 It's very hard to be in awe of politicians.

Kirsty Wark *The Times*, 'Quotes of the Week', 12 December 1998

13 If, proportionately, as many citizens are gay as MPs are, then homosexuality in Britain is rampant beyond even the wildest calculation of the militant queers.

Matthew Parris *Chance Witness: An Outsider's Life in Politics*, ch. 10 (2002)

Political Ideologies and Parties

1 Let the people think they govern and they will be governed.

William Penn *Some Fruits of Solitude* (1693)

2 I have always said, the first Whig was the devil.

Samuel Johnson *The Life of Samuel Johnson* by James Boswell, vol. 3, p. 326 (1791); in G. B. Hill's edition of 1887, rev. L. F. Powell (1934)

3 Monopoly's long been the rub,/ And from it less harm would ensue,/ If those who monopolized grub,/ Would monopolize appetites too.

Anon. 'Monopoly', *Oliver's Comic Songs* (1825?)

4 There was indeed a considerable shouting about what they called Conservative principles; but the awkward question arose, what will you conserve?

Benjamin Disraeli *Coningsby*, bk 2, ch. 5 (1844)

5 'A sound Conservative government,' said Taper, musingly. 'I understand: Tory men and Whig measures.'

Ibid. bk 2, ch. 6

6 A Conservative government is an organized hypocrisy.

Benjamin Disraeli Speech, Hansard 17 March

1845. Disraeli was attacking Peel for retreating from a defence of the Corn Laws. Robert Blake, in his biography of Disraeli, quotes a journalist of the time reporting that this attack reduced Peel to 'nervous twitching'.

7 **That fatal drollery called a representative government.**

Benjamin Disraeli *Tancred*, bk 2, ch. 13 (1847)

8 **The Conservatives ... being by their law of existence the stupidest party ...**

John Stuart Mill *Considerations on Representative Government*, ch. 7 (1861)

9 **What Socialists are always aiming at is a paternal government under which they are to be the spoilt children.**

Sir Arthur Helps *Thoughts on Government*, ch. 3 (1872)

10 **What is a communist? One who has yearnings/ For equal division of unequal earnings;/ Idler or bungler, or both, he is willing/ To fork out his penny and pocket your shilling.**

Ebenezer Elliott 'Epigram', *The Poetical Works of Ebenezer Elliott* ed. Edwin Elliott (1876)

11 **Every boy and every gal/ That's born into the world alive/ Is either a little Liberal/ Or else a little Conservative!**

W. S. Gilbert 'Chorus of Fairies', *Iolanthe*, act 2 (1882)

12 **All I know is that I am not a Marxist.**

Karl Marx Attributed remark, quoted by Engels in a letter to C. Schmidt of 5 August 1890

13 **Anarchism is a game at which the police can beat you.**

George Bernard Shaw *Misalliance*, p. 85 (1910)

14 **The healthy stomach is nothing if not conservative. Few radicals have good digestions.**

Samuel Butler *The Note-Books of Samuel Butler*, ch. 6, ed. Henry Festing Jones (1912)

15 **He had a peculiar vague horror of**

Socialism, which he regarded as a compound of atheism, republicanism, blight, mildew, measles, and all the worst characteristics of the Continental sabbath.

H. G. Wells Of Lord Chickney in *Bealby*, ch. 8 (1915)

16 **Communism is like Prohibition, it's a good idea but it won't work.**

Will Rogers From a syndicated column of November 1927. Rogers also said: 'Communism is to me one third practice, and two-thirds explanation.'

17 **I belong to no organized party – I am a Democrat.**

Will Rogers Attributed

18 **[Of Bolshevism] Nature has no cure for this sort of madness, though I have known a legacy from a rich relative work wonders.**

F. E. Smith *Law, Life and Letters*, vol. 2, ch. 19 (1927)

19 **Gaiety is the most outstanding feature of the Soviet Union.**

Josef Stalin *Observer*, 'Sayings of the Week', 24 November 1935, collected in *The Observer Sayings of the Week* ed. Valerie Ferguson (1978)

20 **The majority is always in the wrong.**

Mark Twain *Notebook*, ch. 35 (1935)

21 **The radical invents the views. When he has worn them out, the conservative adopts them.**

Ibid., ch. 31

22 **An Englishman has to have a Party, just as he has to have trousers.**

Bertrand Russell Letter to Maurice Amos MP, 16 June 1936

23 **Nine times out of ten a revolutionary is merely a climber with a bomb in his pocket.**

George Orwell *New English Weekly*, 1939

24 **All animals are equal but some animals are more equal than others.**

George Orwell *Animal Farm*, ch. 10 (1945). The animals' commandment as stated at the end of the novel – it had originally been 'All animals are equal.'

25 Democracy means government by discussion, but it is only effective if you can stop people talking.

Clement Attlee Speech in Oxford, 14 June 1957, quoted in *The Times* 15 June 1957

26 Tories, in short, are atrophied Englishmen, lacking certain moral and intellectual reflexes. They are recognizable, homely – even, on occasions, endearing – but liable to turn very nasty at short notice.

Paul Johnson *New Statesman* 18 October 1958. Johnson was not, then, one himself.

27 [Of Soviet Russia] That's one place I'd really like to go to . . . All them cornfields, and ballet in the evenings.

Peter Sellers Remark by Fred Kite (Peter Sellers) in *I'm All Right Jack* (film, 1959, directed by John Boulting, from the novel *Private Life* by Alan Hackney). Kite is a jargon-spouting trade unionist and pedant, who yet has a romantic streak when it comes to communist Russia.

28 An artist must be a reactionary. He has to stand out against the tenor of the age and not go flopping along.

Evelyn Waugh *Writers at Work*, 'Evelyn Waugh', ed. George Plimpton (1967). The interview was conducted at the Hyde Park Hotel in London in 1962, with Waugh in bed smoking a cigar.

29 As a trade unionist, people often ask me why I am voting Conservative. The answer is because I am a stupid cunt.

Peter Cook From a free record issued with *Private Eye* magazine in October 1964. Also performing were Dudley Moore, Richard Ingrams, John Wells and Willie Rushton. Quoted in *Peter Cook: A Biography*, ch. 7, by Harry Thompson (1997).

30 The right to be heard does not automatically include the right to be taken seriously.

Hubert H. Humphrey Speech to the National Student Association, quoted in the *New York Times* 24 August 1965

31 The Labour Party is like a stage coach. If you rattle along at great speed, everybody inside is too exhilarated or too seasick to cause any trouble. But if you stop, everybody gets out and argues about where to go next.

Harold Wilson Remark made c.1971, paraphrased in *The Changing Anatomy of Britain*, ch. 5, by Anthony Sampson (1982)

32 It's not the voting that's democracy, it's the counting.

Tom Stoppard Dotty in *Jumpers*, act 1 (1972). In the *Guardian* of 17 June 1977 Anastasio Somoza (President of Nicaragua 1937–47, 1950–56) was quoted as responding to accusations of electoral malpractice with: 'You won the elections, but I won the count.'

33 I mean, it would be presumptuous to condemn radical ideas simply because they appear to me to be self-evidently stupid and criminal if they do happen to be at the same time radical.

George in ibid., act 1 (1972)

34 Democracy is an interesting, even laudable notion and there is no question but that when compared to communism, which is too dull, or fascism, which is too exciting, it emerges as the most palatable form of government.

Fran Lebowitz *Metropolitan Life*, 'A Few Words on a Few Words' (1978)

35 My political position is based largely on my aversion to large groups, and if there's one thing I know about communism it's that large groups are definitely in the picture.

Ibid., 'Better Read Than Dead: A Revised Opinion'

36 [Of the death of a believer in proportional representation] He has joined what even he would admit to be the majority.

John Sparrow Quoted in *Geoffrey Madan's Notebooks*, 'Phrases and Descriptions', ed. J. A. Gere and John Sparrow (1981)

37 Bleat: Always 'from the left'.

Henry Root *Henry Root's World of Knowledge* (1982)

38 There's a lot of bleeding idiots in this country, and they deserve some representation.

Bill Stones Quoted in the Introduction to *On the House* by Simon Hoggart (1982). Hoggart describes Stone as 'an old mining MP who spent his last years drowning the pain in his lungs with pints of bitter'.

39 Democracy is supposed to give you the feeling of choice, like Painkiller X and Painkiller Y. But they're both just aspirin.

Gore Vidal *Observer* 7 February 1982

40 What is the difference . . . between socialism and capitalism? In capitalism you have the exploitation of man by man; in socialism it is the other way around.

Anon. Quoted by Timothy Garton Ash in the *Spectator* 17 September 1983, collected in *The Wit of the Spectator* (1989)

41 Jesus Christ was not a conservative. That's a racing certainty.

Eric Heffer Quoted in the *Observer* 20 February 1983

42 [Of privatization] First of all the Georgian silver goes, and then all that nice furniture that used to be in the saloon. Then the Canalettos go.

Harold Macmillan Quoted in *The Times* 9 November 1985

43 The [Democratic] government's view of the economy could be summed up in a few short phrases: If it moves, tax it. If it keeps moving, regulate it. And if it stops moving, subsidize it.

Ronald Reagan Remark to State Chairpersons of the National White House Conference on Small Businesses, 15 August 1986. Quoted in *Ronald Reagan: The Wisdom and Humour of the Great Communicator*, 'People Are the Government', ed. Frederick J. Ryan (1995).

44 A liberal is a conservative who has been arrested.

Tom Wolfe *The Bonfire of the Vanities*, ch. 24 (1987)

45 Nikita Khrushchev flew into Los Angeles and he looked down, saw all the swimming pools shining, gleaming in the sun. He said, 'Now I know communism has failed.'

Anon. Quoted by Richard Rayner in *Los Angeles without a Map*, pt 1 (1989). He hears the remark spoken by a bald Greek policeman on a plane from London to Los Angeles.

46 Let's not talk about communism.

Boris Yeltsin Line spoken during a visit to America, quoted in the *Independent* 13 September 1989. 'It was just pie in the sky,' he went on.

47 [Of John Major] It's quite a change to have a Prime Minister who hasn't got any political ideas at all.

Michael Foot *Observer* 24 February 1991

48 The modern conservative is engaged in one of man's oldest exercises in moral philosophy – that is, the search for a superior moral justification for selfishness.

J. K. Galbraith *And I Quote*, 'Conservatives', ed. Ashton Applewhite and others (1992)

49 Channel 4 wants our first show to somehow tie in with their celebration of the birth of democracy two thousand years ago. Democracy may have been born then, I just can't wait until it starts speaking and walking.

Bill Hicks Letter of 1993 to John Lahr, quoted in the *Guardian* 14 February 2004

50 In order to become the master, the politician poses as the servant.

Charles de Gaulle Attributed. Quoted in *Collins Dictionary of Quotations* ed. A. Norman Jeffares and Martin Gray (1995).

51 Equality of opportunity means equal opportunity to be unequal.

Anon. *A Gentleman Publisher's Commonplace Book*, 'Core', by John G. Murray (1996)

52 My known peculiarities and preferences make me a member of what one might call the Millicent Tendency, not just a Champagne Socialist, but a Pink Champagne Socialist to boot.

Stephen Fry Remark made in 1996, quoted in *People on People: The Oxford Dictionary of*

Biographical Quotations ed. Susan Ratcliffe (2001)

53 **I was born in Rotherham. Around where I lived, people thought a Conservative was something you spread on your toast.**
William Hague Quoted in the *Guardian* 11 October 1997

54 **The Conservative Establishment has always treated women as nannies, grannies and fannies.**
Teresa Gorman *The Times* 14 November 1998

55 **I never vote for anyone. I always vote against.**
W. C. Fields *Halliwell's Who's Who in the Movies* ed. John Walker (2nd edn 2001)

56 **Where did the left go wrong? It wasn't anti-Americanism; it was wider than that. It was part of a critique, adopted by left-wing intellectuals, which expresses absolute scepticism about everything from the west – except themselves.**
Nick Cohen Article about the attitude of the British left towards the Second Gulf War, *New Statesman* 5 May 2003

57 **Every night is Burns Night in the SNP.**
Alan Watkins Attributed

Monarchy

1 **Here lies a great and mighty king/ Whose promise none relies on;/ He never said a foolish thing,/ Nor ever did a wise one.**
Earl of Rochester 'The King's Epitaph', publ. 1706. Charles II, the subject of the verse, was given sight of it in his lifetime and responded: 'This is very true, for my words are my own, and my actions are my ministers'.'

2 **I am his Highness' dog at Kew;/ Pray, tell me sir, whose dog are you?**
Alexander Pope 'Epigram Engraved on the Collar of a Dog which I gave his Royal Highness' (1738)

3 **The Right Divine of Kings to govern wrong.**
Alexander Pope *The Dunciad*, bk 4, line 187 (1742)

4 **Courtiers are poor men who got rich by begging.**
Nicolas-Sébastien Roch de Chamfort Written c.1785. Collected in *Chamfort: Reflections on Life, Love and Society*, 'Reflections and Anecdotes', ed. Douglas Parmee (2003)

5 **It was not for me to bandy civilities with my Sovereign.**
Samuel Johnson *The Life of Samuel Johnson* by James Boswell, vol. 2, p. 35 (1791); in G. B. Hill's edition of 1887, rev. L. F. Powell (1934). George III had been complimenting Johnson, who had thought it best to remain silent.

6 **Throughout the greater part of his life, George III was a kind of 'consecrated obstruction'.**
Walter Bagehot *The English Constitution*, 'The Monarchy' (1867)

7 **Henry, like his brother William, had no right to the Crown; accordingly he seized it immediately on hearing of the death of Rufus./ It was the fashion to do this, in those early days.**
O. P. Q. Philander Smiff *Smiff's History of England*, ch. 7 (1876)

8 **Are you a courtier? Come, then, ply your trade,/ Tell me some lies. How do you like your king?**
W. S. Gilbert King Gama to Florian in *Princess Ida*, act 1 (1884)

9 **All kings is mostly rapscallions. All I say is, kings is kings, and you got to make allowances.**
Mark Twain *Huckleberry Finn*, ch. 23 (1884). The opinion of Huckleberry Finn himself, who also says of kings: 'Take them all around, they're a mighty ornery lot.'

10 **The Prince of Wales is really wonderful. I mean even if he was not a prince he would be wonderful, because even if he was not a prince, he would be able to make his living playing the ukulele, if he had a little more practice.**
Anita Loos *Blondes Have More Fun*, ch. 3,

subtitled *London Is Really Nothing* (1925). This is the opinion of Lorelei Lee, American socialite and femme fatale, who is sent to London by her sugar-daddy in order to be 'broadened'.

11 **George the Third/ Ought never to have occurred./ One can only wonder/ At so grotesque a blunder.**

Edmund Clerihew Bentley *More Biography*, 'George the Third' (1929)

12 **Lousy but loyal**

Anon. Grafitto spotted in the East End of London on George V's Jubilee in 1935

13 **SUGARPUSS: Who's 'Richard ill?'**
POTTS: Richard the Third.

Charles Brackett and Billy Wilder *Ball of Fire* (film, 1941, directed by Howard Hawks). Sugarpuss O'Shea, a stripper on the run, was played by Barbara Stanwyck; Professor Bertram Potts, by Gary Cooper.

14 **The whole world is in revolt. Soon there will be only five kings left – the King of England, the King of Spades, the King of Clubs, the King of Hearts and the King of Diamonds.**

King Farouk Quoted in *As I Recall*, ch. 21, by Lord Boyd-Orr (1966). The remark was made in 1948.

15 **As his name implies, George III was the third of the Georges, of whom there were four from 1784 to 1830, or an average of one every twenty-nine years.**

Will Cuppy *The Decline and Fall of Practically Everybody*, 'George III' (1950)

16 **Royalty . . . is the gold filling in a mouthful of decay.**

John Osborne *Declaration*, 'They Call It Cricket', ed. T. Maschler (1957)

17 **I never see any home cooking. All I get is fancy stuff.**

Prince Philip, Duke of Edinburgh *Observer* 28 October 1962

18 **PETE: Did you know we're all in line for succession to the throne?**
DUD: Really?
PETE: Well, if forty-eight million, two hundred thousand, seven

hundred and one people died I'd be Queen.

Peter Cook and Dudley Moore Sketch performed before the Queen at the Royal Variety Performance in November 1965

19 **Her Majesty's a pretty nice girl but she doesn't have a lot to say.**

John Lennon and Paul McCartney 'Her Majesty', *Abbey Road* (LP, 1969): the opening words of the closing track on the last-recorded Beatles album

20 [Of the Duke of Edinburgh on his sixty-fifth birthday] **A snappish OAP with a temper like an arthritic corgi.**

Jean Rook *Daily Express* 10 June 1986

21 [Of Copenhagen] **The city is so safe that Queen Margrethe used to walk from Amalienborg Palace to the shops every morning to buy flowers and vegetables just like a normal citizen. I once asked a Dane who guarded her in such circumstances, and he looked at me with surprise and replied, 'Why, we all do.'**

Bill Bryson *Neither Here Nor There*, ch. 10 (1991)

22 **Shocked to hear on Radio Four that King Olav the Fifth of Norway was buried today. His contribution to the continuing success of the Norwegian leather industry is something that is little appreciated by the majority of the Great British Public.**

Sue Townsend Diary entry for Wednesday 30 January 1991, *Adrian Mole: The Wilderness Years* (1993)

23 **The Queen: popular, respected, thought to be 'good at her job'. Suspected of having a secret sense of humour. As she has got older, she has been less mocked for her tweediness, for her high voice and low dogs.**

Julian Barnes Summary of British opinions on the Queen, *New Yorker* July 1992. Collected in *Letters from London 1990–1995*, ch. 7 (1995). The Duke and Duchess of York did not get off so lightly: 'He a naval officer and couch potato, she an enthusiastic consumer of royalty's perks.'

24 It's all to do with training: you can do a lot if you are properly trained.

Elizabeth II From a TV documentary, 6 February 1992

25 [Of journalists] Some of your lot don't understand. She *likes* being queen.

Anon. Courtier quoted in *Editor*, ch. 13, by Max Hastings (2002)

26 [Of Princess Diana] We heard about her bitter arguments with Charles, her fondness for water sports, and her painful love split which left a yawning chasm that needed to be filled by a succession of men.

Victor Lewis-Smith From a review of a TV programme about Prince Harry, London *Evening Standard* 12 September 2002. While he was about it Lewis-Smith also said that Diana was 'a brood mare crossed with a clothes horse', and that her highest academic attainment was 'a certificate for keeping the hamsters clean'.

27 [Of a type of gruff middle-aged female BBC employee] It was one such who was manning the desk at TV Centre when the King of Norway arrived to visit the director of programmes. She called the office in question, then turned back to the distinguished visitor. 'I'm sorry. Did you say the King of Norway or the King of Sweden?'

Alan Bennett *Guardian* 27 September 2003. Bennett admitted: 'It's a very well-known story.'

Diplomacy and International Relations

1 An ambassador is an honest man sent to lie abroad for the good of his country.

Sir Henry Wotton *Reliquiae Wottonianae: The Life of Sir Henry Wotton* by Izaak Walton (1651)

2 [Of the Schleswig Holstein question] There are only three men who have ever understood it: one was Prince Albert, who is dead; the second was a German professor, who became mad. I am the third – and I have forgotten all about it.

Lord Palmerston *Britain in Europe (1789–1914)*, ch. 11, by R. W. Seton-Watson (1914). Attributed.

3 England seems to have treated Ireland much in the same way as Mrs Brownrigg treated her apprentice – for which Mrs Brownrigg is hanged in the first volume of *The Newgate Calendar*.

Sydney Smith From a review of *Memoirs of Captain Rock, the Celebrated Irish Chieftan*, *Edinburgh Review* 1824, collected in *The Works of Sydney Smith*, vol. 3 (1840)

4 The very phrase 'foreign affairs' makes an Englishman convinced that I am about to treat of subjects with which he has no concern.

Benjamin Disraeli Speech given at Manchester, 3 April 1872

5 English policy is to float lazily downstream, occasionally putting out a diplomatic boathook to avoid collisions.

Lord Salisbury Letter to Lord Lytton of 9 March 1877

6 Consul: In American politics, a person who having failed to secure an office from the people is given one by the administration on condition that he leave the country.

Ambrose Bierce *The Devil's Dictionary* (compiled 1881–1906)

7 Oh! Spies are of no use nowadays. Their profession is over. The newspapers do their work instead.

Oscar Wilde Sir Robert Chiltern in *An Ideal Husband*, act 3 (1899)

8 Diplomacy is to do and say/ The nastiest things in the nicest way.

Isaac Goldberg *The Reflex* October 1927

9 [On being asked his view of Western civilization] I think it would be a good thing.

Mahatma Gandhi Attributed, c.1930

10 The diplomat is smooth and fair/ (I like the way he does his hair),/ But

then he's paid for that;/ You need not hope for high success/ In Foreign Politics unless/ You're well worth looking at.

A. P. Herbert *Wisdom for the Wise*, 'The Diplomat' (1930)

11 America was thus clearly top nation, and History came to a.

W. C. Sellar and R. J. Yeatman *1066 and All That* (1930) – this is the whole of the final chapter

12 GROUCHO: Isn't it true you tried to sell Freedonia's secret war code and plans?

CHICO: Sure. I sold a code and two pairs of plans. At's-a some joke, eh boss?

Groucho Marx *Duck Soup* (film, 1933, screenplay by Bert Kalmar, Arthur Sheekman, Nat Perrin and Harry Ruby, directed by Leo McCarey)

13 To make a United Europe, we need the help of the best Europeans of all – the Americans.

Konrad Adenauer *Observer*, 'Sayings of the Week', 4 December 1949

14 [Of the position of a Foreign Secretary] Forever poised between a cliché and an indiscretion.

Harold Macmillan *Newsweek* 30 April 1956

15 A diplomat these days is nothing but a head-waiter who's allowed to sit down occasionally.

Peter Ustinov The General in *Romanoff and Juliet*, act 1 (1956)

16 The great nations have always acted like gangsters, and the small nations like prostitutes.

Stanley Kubrick *Guardian* 5 June 1963

17 Operating in this country today is one of the finest secret services in the world . . . It belongs to the Russians.

Leslie Bricusse and Anthony Newley Peter Sellers impersonating Harold Macmillan in a sketch called 'The House that Mac Built', from *Fool Britannia* (LP, first issued 1964, re-released as cassette 2002)

18 [Of Anthony Eden] Inevitably he gravitated to the Foreign Office. An astrakhan collar became him.

Malcolm Muggeridge *Tread Softly for You Tread on My Jokes*, 'Boring for England' (1966)

19 There are few ironclad rules of diplomacy but to one there is no exception. When an official reports that talks were useful, it can safely be concluded that nothing was accomplished.

J. K. Galbraith *Foreign Service Journal* June 1969

20 Don't mention the war.

John Cleese Hysterical hotel proprietor Basil Fawlty (John Cleese) counsels discretion as German guests arrive in 'The Germans', *Fawlty Towers* (TV series written with Connie Booth, 1975 and 1979)

21 My favourite cartoon of the last few years was the one – right after we really began rebuilding our military – of two Russian generals. And one of them was saying to the other, 'I liked the arms race better when we were the only ones in it.'

Ronald Reagan Remark made at a White House briefing of 29 June 1987, quoted in *Ronald Reagan: The Wisdom and Humour of the Great Communicator*, 'The Flame of Freedom', ed. Frederick J. Ryan Jr (1995)

22 They're talking about partial nuclear disarmament. It's like talking about partial circumcision.

Robin Williams *Robin Williams: Live at the Met* (video, 1987)

23 The only special thing about a special relationship between two countries, such as America and Britain, is that nobody is aware of its existence except the weaker of the two . . .

Miles Kington *Welcome to Kington*, 'The Wit and Wisdom of Albania' (1989)

24 America is the world's policeman, all right – a big, dumb, mick flatfoot in the middle of the one thing cops dread most, a 'domestic disturbance'.

P. J. O'Rourke *Rolling Stone* August 1990 – with specific reference to the Middle East

25 [Of the European Community] **This is all a German racket, designed to take over the whole of Europe.**

Nicholas Ridley *Spectator* 14 July 1990. After uttering this comment, Ridley was forced to resign as Conservative Trade and Industry Secretary.

26 **I just saw a movie on TV that was so old, France was on our side.**

Anon. *And I Quote*, 'Television', ed. Ashton Applewhite and others (1992)

Economics

1 **Money is like muck, not good except it be spread.**

Francis Bacon *Essays*, 'Of Seditions and Troubles' (1625)

2 **To tax and to please, no more than to love and to be wise, is not given to men.**

Edmund Burke Speech on *American Taxation*, p. 49 (1775)

3 **In this world nothing can be said to be certain except death and taxes.**

Benjamin Franklin Letter to John Baptiste Le Roy of 13 November 1789, *Works of Benjamin Franklin*, vol. 10, ed. John Bigelow (1887). In *History of the Devil*, bk 2, ch. 6 (1726), Daniel Defoe wrote: 'Things as certain as death and taxes, can be more firmly believed.'

4 **The Chancellor of the Exchequer is a man whose duties make him more or less a taxing machine. He is entrusted with a certain amount of misery which it is his duty to distribute as fairly as he can.**

Robert Lowe Speech to the House of Commons, Hansard 11 April 1870

5 **Income Tax has made more liars out of the American people than golf.**

Will Rogers *The Illiterate Digest*, 'Helping the Girls with Their Income Taxes' (1924)

6 **WALL ST LAYS AN EGG**

Anon. Wall Street Crash headline, *Variety* 30 October 1929

7 **When I hear a man talk of Sound Finance, I know him for an enemy of the people.**

Anon. A Hyde Park orator to a heckler, quoted in *Livres sans nom* (Books without a Name; 1930), collected in *Geoffrey Madan's Notebooks* ed. J. A. Gere and John Sparrow (1981)

8 **It's a recession when your neighbour loses his job; it's a depression when you lose yours.**

Harry S. Truman Quoted in the *Observer* 13 April 1953

9 **Let us be frank about it: most of our people have never had it so good.**

Harold Macmillan Speech quoted in *The Times* 22 July 1957. 'You never had it so good' had been the slogan of the Democrats in the 1952 American election, and this is what Macmillan is often assumed to have said.

10 **No one has yet found a way to repeal the law of supply and demand.**

Ronald Reagan Address as Governor of California, 1972, quoted in *Ronald Reagan: The Wisdom and Humour of the Great Communicator*, 'People Are the Government', ed. Frederick J. Ryan Jr (1995)

11 **If I had to give a definition of capitalism I would say: the process whereby American girls turn into American women.**

Christopher Hampton Carlos in *Savages*, sc. 16 (1973)

12 **A news item in the *Daily Telegraph* told how dying is to cost more in Norfolk. Higher burial charges were to be introduced. The report then added, 'The increased cost of living is to blame.'**

Anon. Quoted in *Laughter Lines: Family Wit and Wisdom*, 'Grave Matters', ed. Rev. James A. Simpson (1986)

13 **The economy, stupid!**

Anon. Aide-mémoire for campaigners, prominently displayed in the Clinton headquarters during the 1992 election campaign. Quoted in *Fortune* magazine 19 October 1992.

14 **I'm three hundred per cent against inflation.**

Anon. *And I Quote*, 'Inflation', ed. Ashton Applewhite and others (1992)

15 [Of East Germany] **How the com-
mies managed to make a poor
country out of a nation full of Germans is a mystery.**
P. J. O'Rourke *Daily Telegraph* 10 December
1994

16 **Old people should be taxed to the
hilt. They've spent half their lives
picking fights with Germany,
started two world wars, and then
they expect to sit back and get
cheap central heating while we sort
out the bloody mess they've got the
country into.**
Viz Fake reader's letters, *Viz – The Full Toss*
(A Corking Compilation of Issues 70–75)
(1997)

17 **AT LAST – LARGE SHARE OF
GOVERNMENT CASH TO BE
POURED INTO WORSENING HIGH-
LAND POTHOLES**
Anon. Headline, *Oban Times* 28 February 2002

Political Institutions

1 **One of the great advantages of the
American government is its cheapness. The American king has about
£5000. Per annum, the vice-king,
£1000.**
Sydney Smith *Edinburgh Review* 1818, quoted
in *Twelve Miles from a Lemon: Selected Writings of Sydney Smith*, ch. 3, compiled by Norman Taylor and Alan Hankinson (1996)

2 [Of the House of Commons] **What by
way of jest they call the Lower House.**
Benjamin Disraeli *Coningsby*, bk 3, ch. 4
(1844)

3 **I think . . . that it is the best club in
London.**
Charles Dickens Mr Twemlow, referring to
the House of Commons, in *Our Mutual
Friend*, bk 2, ch. 3 (1864–5)

4 **A severe though not unfriendly
critic of our institutions said that
the cure for admiring the House of
Lords was to go and look at it.**
Walter Bagehot *The English Constitution*,
'The House of Lords' (1867)

5 **There is hardly a single person in
the House of Commons worth painting; although many of them would
be better for a little white-washing.**
Oscar Wilde Lord Henry Wotton in *The Picture of Dorian Gray*, ch. 6 (1891)

6 [Of alcohol] **It makes life bearable to
millions of people who could not
endure their existence if they were
quite sober. It enables Parliament to
do things at eleven at night that no
sane person would do at eleven in
the morning.**
George Bernard Shaw Undershaft in *Major
Barbara*, act 2 (1907)

7 **The House of Lords is like a glass of
champagne that has stood for five
days.**
Clement Attlee Attributed

8 **The House of Lords must be the only
institution in the world which is
kept efficient by the persistent absen-
teeism of most of its members.**
Herbert Samuel *New Review* 5 February 1948

9 **The buck stops here.**
Harry S. Truman Sign on the desk of Harry S.
Truman, thirty-third President of the United
States, quoted in *The Man From Missouri* by
Alfred Steinberg (1962)

10 **The more important the issue, the
duller and more impersonal the
debate. Municipal meetings are
duller than family quarrels; and
normal parliamentary debates are
duller still. By these standards the
debates of the United Nations ought
to be the dullest in the world. And
they are.**
George Mikes *How to Unite Nations*, 'Big and
Small' (1963)

11 **Well, he thought, you can fool some
of the people all the time, and all
the people some of the time, which
is just long enough to be President
of the United States.**
Spike Milligan *Puckoon*, ch. 2 (1963). Compare Abraham Lincoln in a speech of
8 September 1858: 'You can fool some of the
people some of the time, and some of the
people all the time, but you cannot fool all

the people all the time.' US showman Phineas Barnum is sometimes credited with saying much the same.

12 **The House of Lords, an illusion to which I have never been able to subscribe – responsibility without power, the prerogative of the eunuch throughout the ages.**
Tom Stoppard *Lord Malquist and Mr Moon*, pt 4, ch. 1 (1966)

13 **The House of Lords is a perfect eventide home.**
Lady Stocks *Observer*, 'Sayings of the Week', 4 October 1970

14 **Incongruous: Where US laws are made.**
Anon. *The Dictionary of Puns*, 'Incongruous', ed. John S. Crosbie (1977)

15 [Of the House of Commons] **The longest-running farce in the West End.**
Cyril Smith *Big Cyril*, ch. 8 (1977)

16 [Of the House of Lords] **It is, I think, good evidence of life after death.**
Donald Soper *Listener* 17 August 1978

17 **All Presidents want to be Warren Beatty.**
Alec Baldwin Quoted in the *Mail on Sunday* 25 August 1999, when it seemed likely that Beatty might run for the White House

18 **Gasworks, n. pl.: The Houses of Parliament**
Anon. Taxi drivers' slang, quoted in *Taxi!* by Simon Garner and Giles Stokoe (2000)

19 [Of the Scottish Parliament] **A wee, Pretendy Parliament.**
Billy Connolly *The Times*, 9 September 2000

20 **Being President is like being a jackass in a hailstorm. There's nothing to do but stand there and take it.**
Lyndon B. Johnson Attributed. Quoted in *The Penguin Dictionary of Modern Humorous Quotations* ed. Fred Metcalf (2nd edn 2001).

Officialdom

1 **In Germany most human faults and follies sink into comparative insig-** nificance beside the enormity of walking on the grass. Nowhere, and under no circumstances, may you at any time in Germany walk on the grass.
Jerome K. Jerome *Three Men on the Bummel*, ch. 7 (1900). The book is full of such observations about the Germans – for instance: if a German 'can find a notice posted on a tree forbidding him to do something or other, that gives him an extra sense of comfort and security'.

2 **The high official, all allow,/ Is grossly overpaid;/ There wasn't any Board, and now/ There isn't any trade.**
A. P. Herbert 'The President of the Board of Trade' (1922)

3 **If we can't stamp out literature in the country we can at least stop it being brought in from outside.**
Evelyn Waugh Customs officer in *Vile Bodies*, ch. 2 (1930)

4 **Official dignity tends to increase in inverse ratio to the importance of the country in which the office is held.**
Aldous Huxley *Beyond the Mexique Bay*, 'Puerto Barrios' (1943)

5 **A committee is organic rather than mechanical in its nature: it is not a structure but a plant. It takes root and grows, it flowers, wilts and dies, scattering the seed from which other committees will bloom in their turn.**
C. Northcote Parkinson *Parkinson's Law*, 'Directors and Councils' (1958)

6 **You know how in every town in England that one likes there has to be a Society against the Council because the Council wants to pull the town down.**
John Betjeman Speech at the annual dinner of the Royal Academy of Arts, 1 May 1962

7 **There is something about a bureaucrat that does not like a poem.**
Gore Vidal *Sex, Death and Money*, Preface (1968)

8 **No Exit: A sign indicating the most convenient way out of a building.**
Beachcomber *Beachcomber: The Works of*

J. B. Morton, 'A Dictionary for Today', ed. Richard Ingrams (1974)

9 Do you know, I sometimes feel a well-chaired meeting to be an expression of our quintessential humanity.

Howard Jacobson *Redback*, ch. 10 (1986). The speaker is Alex Sneddon, an administrator who thinks like an administrator, eats like an administrator and makes love like an administrator.

10 A committee is a group that takes minutes and wastes hours.

Anon. *And I Quote*, 'Committees', ed. Ashton Applewhite and others (1992)

11 Never believe anything until it has been officially denied.

Claud Cockburn in ibid., 'Propaganda'

12 How to Order a Fridge through Stationery

Lucinda Bredin Title of an imaginary book in a cod magazine mocked up to mark the departure of a colleague at the London *Evening Standard* in 1993

13 One of the Official Monster Raving Loony Party's most coherent policies was to break up the Monopolies and Mergers Commission on the grounds that it was insupportable that such a body should be allowed to operate without competition.

Ross Clark *The Quotable Spectator* (1994)

14 In the old Soviet Union they used to say that anything that wasn't forbidden was compulsory; the trick was to remember which was which.

Douglas Adams *The Salmon of Doubt*, 'Life', 'The Rules' (2002)

The Law
The Legal System and the Law

1 Some say the bee stings: but I say 'tis the bee's wax, for I did but seal

once to a thing and I was never mine own man since.

William Shakespeare Jack Cade in *Henry VI Part 2*, act IV, sc. 2 (1590–91)

2 I am ashamed the law is such an ass.

George Chapman *Revenge for Honour*, act 3, sc. 2 (1654). In *Oliver Twist*, ch. 51 (1838), Mr Bumble says: 'The law is a ass.'

3 Laws are like cobwebs, which may catch small flies, but let wasps and hornets break through.

Jonathan Swift *A Critical Essay upon the Faculties of the Mind* (1709)

4 A fox should not be of the jury at a goose's trial.

Anon. Proverb quoted in *Gnomologia* ed. Thomas Fuller (1732)

5 Laws, like houses, lean on one another.

Edmund Burke *A Tract on the Popery Laws*, pt 1, ch. 3 (*c.* 1765)

6 The art of will-making chiefly consists in baffling the importunity of expectation.

William Hazlitt *Table Talk*, 'On Will-making' (1821–2)

7 The one great principle of the English law is to make business for itself. There is no other principle distinctly, certainly and consistently maintained through all its narrow turnings.

Charles Dickens *Bleak House*, ch. 39 (1852–3)

8 'Give your evidence,' said the king; 'and don't be nervous, or I'll have you executed on the spot.'

Lewis Carroll *Alice's Adventures in Wonderland*, ch. 12 (1865)

9 We have a criminal jury system which is superior to any in the world and its efficiency is only marred by the difficulty of finding twelve men every day who don't know anything and can't read.

Mark Twain Speech on the subject of 'Americans and the English', London 4 July 1872

10 The Common Law of England has been laboriously built about a

mythical figure – the figure of 'The Reasonable Man'.

A. P. Herbert *Uncommon Law*, 'The Reasonable Man' (1935)

11 The Ten Commandments were a very early experiment at legislation – short, clear-cut, unambiguous and universally applicable. They could never stand up in a British court of law.

Miles Kington *Moreover*, 'The Moreover Advice Service' (1982)

12 A jury is composed of twelve persons chosen to decide who has the better lawyer.

Robert Frost Quoted in *The Law is a Ass*, 'In Court', ed. Ronald Irving (1999)

13 This is a court of law, young man, not a court of justice.

Oliver Wendell Holmes Jr Quoted in ibid.

14 The rain it raineth on the just/ And also on the unjust fella/ But chiefly on the just, because/ The unjust steals the just's umbrella.

Lord Bowen Quoted in 'Justice' ibid.

Crime and Punishment

1 Still you keep o' th' windy side of the law.

William Shakespeare Fabian to Sir Toby Belch in *Twelfth Night*, act 3, sc. 4 (1601–2)

2 Many a good hanging prevents a bad marriage.

Feste in ibid., act 1, sc. 5

3 I went out to Charing Cross, to see Major-General Harrison hanged, drawn and quartered; which was done there, he looking as cheerful as any man could do in that condition.

Samuel Pepys Diary entry for 13 October 1660, *Everybody's Pepys*, ed. Henry B. Wheatley (1926). Harrison, the son of a butcher, had been appointed by Cromwell to convey Charles I from Windsor to his trial at Whitehall; he had also signed the warrant for the execution of the King.

4 He that takes what isn't his 'n/ When he's cotched will go to prison/ If you this precious volume bone/ Jack Ketch will catch you for his own.

Anon. 'Hands off' notice scribbled on flyleaves of books in public schools. Jack Ketch was a hangman from 1663 to 1686. Quoted in *The Law is a Ass* ed. Ronald Irving (1999).

5 [Of Paris] Here they hang a man first, and try him afterwards.

Molière *Monsieur de Pourceaugnac*, act 1, sc. 5 (1670)

6 Stolen sweets are best.

Colley Cibber *The Rival Fools*, act 1, sc. 1 (1709)

7 Men are not hanged for stealing horses, but so that horses may not be stolen.

George Savile, 1st Marquess of Halifax *Political, Moral, and Miscellaneous Thoughts and Reflections*, 'Of Punishment' (1750)

8 Depend upon it, Sir, when a man knows he is to be hanged in a fortnight, it concentrates his mind wonderfully.

Samuel Johnson *The Life of Samuel Johnson* by James Boswell, vol. 3, p. 162 (1791); in G.B. Hill's edition of 1887, rev. L. F. Powell (1934). A Dr William Dodd, preacher, author and forger, had produced a better final address than had been expected.

9 The fault is great in man or woman/ Who steals a goose from off a common;/ But what can plead that man's excuse/ Who steals a common from a goose?

Anon. *Tickler* magazine 1 February 1821

10 Murder Considered as One of the Fine Arts

Thomas De Quincey Essay title, *Blackwood's Magazine* February 1827

11 The march of mind has marched in through my back parlour shutters, and out again with my silver spoons, in the dead of night. The policeman, who was sent down to examine, says my house has been broken open on the most scientific principles.

Thomas Love Peacock The Rev. Dr Folliott to

Mr MacQuedy, a defender of 'the march of mind', or progress, who ascribes the intrusion suffered by his friend to poverty. *Crotchet Castle*, ch. 7 (1831).

12 **Criminals have no literary interests.**

Ezra Pound 'A Teacher's Mission', *English Journal* (1934), collected in *Literary Essays of Ezra Pound* ed. T. S. Eliot (1954)

13 **Thou shalt not steal; an empty feat,/ When it's so lucrative to cheat.**

Arthur Hugh Clough 'The Latest Decalogue' (1862)

14 **On account of the great number of suicides, an M. P. moved for leave to bring in a bill to make it a capital offence.**

Anon. *The New London Jest Book*, 'Choice Jests', no. 412, ed. W. C. Hazlitt (1871)

15 **To sit in solemn silence in a dull, dark dock,/ In a pestilential prison, with a life-long lock,/ Awaiting the sensation of a short sharp shock,/ From a cheap and chippy chopper on a big, black block!**

W. S. Gilbert 'All' in *The Mikado*, act 1 (1885)

16 **I shall have to execute somebody at once. The only question is, who shall it be?**

Ko-ko in ibid., act 1. The Emperor of Japan, having noted that nobody has been executed in Titipu for a year, decrees that unless somebody is executed within the month the post of Lord High Executioner, held by Ko-ko, will be abolished.

17 **All crime is vulgar, just as all vulgarity is crime.**

Oscar Wilde Lord Henry Wotton in *The Picture of Dorian Gray*, ch. 19 (1891)

18 **I should fancy, however, that murder is a mistake. One should never do anything that one cannot talk about after dinner.**

Lord Henry Wotton in ibid., ch. 19. He has just expressed the view that 'anything becomes a pleasure if one does it too often'.

19 **We lives and we dies/ In foul dens and styes/ Without any fun or hex-citement/ Like sparrers in cages – / 'Ard work and low wages –/**

Till we figgers vithin a hindictment.

Anon. Last verse of a poem about recent outbreaks of hooliganism. 'Hot Weather and Crime', *The Clarion* 20 August 1898, quoted in *Hooligan: A History of Respectable Fears*, ch. 5, 'Victorian Boys, We Are Here!', by Geoffrey Pearson (1983).

20 **Nothing is easier than to be an incendiary. All you want is a box of matches and a sense of beauty.**

Max Beerbohm *More*, 'An Infamous Brigade' (1899)

21 **Anyone who has been to an English public school will always feel comparatively at home in prison.**

Evelyn Waugh *Decline and Fall*, pt 3, ch. 4 (1928). Former cabinet minister and old Etonian Jonathan Aitken said much the same after completing his own prison sentence for perjury.

22 **I came to the conclusion many years ago that almost all crime is due to the repressed desire for aesthetic expression.**

Sir Wilfred Lucas-Dockery, progressive prison governor, in ibid., pt 3, ch. 1 (1928)

23 **Eaper weaper, chimbley-sweeper/ Had a wife but couldn't keep her,/ Had annover, didn't love her,/ Up the chimbley he did shove her.**

Anon. Collected in *London Street Games* by Norman Douglass (1931)

24 **It ain't no sin if you crack a few laws now and then, just so long as you don't break any.**

Mae West *Every Day's a Holiday* (film, 1937, screenplay by Mae West, directed by Edward A. Sutherland)

25 **There are only about twenty murders a year in London and not all are serious – some are just husbands killing their wives.**

G. H. Hatherhill Quoted in the *Observer* 2 February 1954. Commander Hatherhill was stationed at Scotland Yard.

26 **Did you hear the story of the over-worked law student who confused arson with incest and ended by setting fire to his own sister?**

Rupert Hart-Davis Letter of 13 November

1955 to George Lyttelton, collected in *The Lyttelton–Hart-Davis Letters*, vols 1 and 2, *1955–1957*, ed. Rupert Hart-Davis (1978)

27 **OTHER FELLOW: I can not imagine any crime worse than taking a life, can you?**
PRISONER B: It'd depend whose life.
Brendan Behan *The Quare Fellow*, act 1 (1956)

28 **When I came back to Dublin, I was court-martialled in my absence, and sentenced to death in my absence, so I said they could shoot me in my absence.**
Brendan Behan Pat, on his life in the IRA, *The Hostage*, act 1 (1958)

29 **I'll be glad when dis town gets prison cells with locks on.**
Spike Milligan Sgt MacGillikudie in *Puckoon*, ch. 3 (1963)

30 **You'll have to keep your eyes open now, you know, because they're all alike off that estate. They'll have your breath.**
Barry Hines Mr Porter in *A Kestrel for a Knave*, ch. 1 (1968)

31 **I think crime pays. The hours are good. You travel a lot.**
Woody Allen Social misfit Virgil Starkwell (Woody Allen) in *Take the Money and Run* (film, 1969, written and directed by Woody Allen)

32 **If you want to know who your friends are, get yourself a jail sentence.**
Charles Bukowski *Notes of a Dirty Old Man* (1969)

33 **The priest says [to the man condemned to be hanged] 'Have you got anything to say before we spring this trap?' And the man says, 'Yes, I don't think this damned thing is safe.'**
Anon. Joke told by Groucho, aged eighty-one, at his valedictory performance at Carnegie Hall, New York, on 6 May 1972

34 **VICTOR: What? Really, Mr Castle – blackmail – that's a very ugly word.**

FRED: Ah. I see you know the right dialogue, too.
Ben Travers *The Bed before Yesterday*, act 2, sc. 2 (1975)

35 **Lynching is a trial by fury.**
Anon. *The Dictionary of Puns*, 'Fury', ed. John S. Crosbie (1977)

36 **The working classes may enjoy hanging each other because it is the sort of thing they understand, but we should really not encourage them in case they hang one of us by mistake.**
Auberon Waugh *Spectator* 17 June 1978

37 **ERNIE: I'm going to teach you that crime doesn't pay.**
ERIC: I know it doesn't, but the hours are good.
Eric Morecambe and Ernie Wise *The Morecambe and Wise Jokebook*, skit 23 (1979)

38 **We shall never know the identity of the man who in 1976 made the most unsuccessful hijack attempt ever. On a flight across America, he rose from his seat, drew a gun and took the stewardess hostage./ 'Take me to Detroit,' he said./ 'We're already going to Detroit,' she replied./ 'Oh . . . good,' he said, and sat down again.**
Stephen Pile *The Book of Heroic Failures*, 'The Worst Hijackers' (1979)

39 **One of the many disadvantages of getting murdered is that, in addition to having to put up with the numerous inconveniences connected with premature death, the victim almost always sinks into complete anonymity.**
Arthur Marshall *Smile Please*, 'Murder Most Foul' (1982)

40 **Bystanders: Always 'innocent'.**
Henry Root *Henry Root's World of Knowledge* (1982)

41 **The truth of the matter is that muggers are very interesting people.**
Michael Winner *Daily Express* 11 May 1989

42 **HOMER SIMPSON: How did you get in here?**

BURGLAR: Your door wasn't locked in any serious way.

Matt Groening The Simpsons, 'Homer vs Lisa and the 8th Commandment', first broadcast 7 February 1991

43 Arson is perhaps the most literal-minded of all violent crimes. Who has not, on passing some large public masterpiece of architecture, or glimpsing an exquisitely ordered and human domestic interior through a ground-floor window (the sheet music open on the piano, the steepling bookcases and expectant hearth), felt an uncomplicated urge to set fire to them?

John Lanchester The Debt to Pleasure, 'Autumn', 'A Barbecue' (1996)

44 I have every sympathy for the young lawyer who lost his job simply because he was convicted of rape. He has become the victim of fashion. Nowadays you only have to have sex with a woman against her will and some nutcase will be screaming 'Rape!'

Viz Columnist Charlie Pontoon ('He pulls no punches') in Viz – The Full Toss (A Corking Compilation of Issues 70 to 75) (1997)

45 A kleptomaniac is a person who helps himself because he can't help himself.

Anon. Quoted in The Law is a Ass, 'Crime and Punishment', ed. Ronald Irving (1999)

46 The Australians were the criminal class of Great Britain, and the Brits in order to punish them sent them to Australia, their own prehistoric, Eden-like island continent . . . Bummer!

Bill Hicks 'Australia', Love, Laughter and Truth (CD, 2002)

47 I was never a murderer. I was an honest bank robber. In the Sixties, it was a perfectly respectable occupation.

John McVicar Quoted in the New Statesman 16 December 2002

48 E-dophile: A word for a chat-room nonce.

Viz Entry in 'Roger's Profanisaurus', April 2003

49 Naughty, paughty Jack-a-Dandy,/ Stole a piece of Sugar Candy/ From the Grocer's Shoppy-Shop,/ And away did hoppy-hop.

Henry Carey First verse of 'A Panegyric on the New Versification Address'd to A—P—, Esq.', ridiculing the sing-song verse of Ambrose Philips (1675?–1749)

Police

1 [Of 'the Bow Street men from London'] They stood about the door of the Jolly Bargeman, with knowing and reserved looks that filled the whole neighbourhood with admiration; and they had a mysterious manner of taking their drink, that was almost as good as taking the culprit. But not quite, for they never did it.

Charles Dickens Great Expectations, ch. 6 (1860–1). After the attack on Mrs Joe Gargery.

2 When constabulary duty's to be done,/ A policeman's lot is not a happy one.

W. S. Gilbert Song sung by the Sergeant of Police in The Pirates of Penzance, act 2 (1879)

3 Policeman Peter Forth I drag/ From his obscure retreat:/ He was a merry genial wag,/ Who loved mad conceit./ If he were asked the time of day,/ By country bumpkins green,/ He not unfrequently would say,/ 'A quarter past thirteen.'

W. S. Gilbert 'Peter the Wag', Fifty Bab Ballads (1881)

4 There is nothing more unaesthetic than a policeman.

Sir Arthur Conan Doyle The Sign of Four, ch. 4 (1889). The view of Thaddeus Sholto.

5 The English detectives are really our best friends, and I have always found that by relying on their stupidity, we can do exactly what we like. I could not spare them.

Oscar Wilde Lord Arthur Savile's Crime, ch. 5 (1891). Herr Winckelkopf, manufacturer of explosive clocks, explains why he will not let one of his machines be used for blowing up policemen.

6 **You will remember, Watson, how the dreadful business of the Arbenetty family was first brought to my notice by the depth which the parsley had sunk into the butter on a hot day.**
Sir Arthur Conan Doyle Sherlock Holmes in *The Return of Sherlock Holmes*, 'The Adventure of the Six Napoleons' (1905)

7 **Naturally a detective doesn't want to look like a detective, and give the whole thing away right at the start.**
P. G. Wodehouse *The Man with Two Left Feet*, 'Bill the Bloodhound' (1917)

8 DETECTIVE: **I'm Henderson, plain-clothesman.**
GROUCHO: **You look more like an old-clothes man to me.**
Groucho Marx *A Night at the Opera* (film, 1935, screenplay by George S. Kaufman, Morrie Ryskind and Al Boasberg, directed by Sam Wood)

9 **I'm unmarried because I don't like policemen's wives.**
Raymond Chandler *The Big Sleep*, ch. 1 (1939). The speaker is Philip Marlowe, private detective and former employee of the District Attorney.

10 **There are only two important divisions of the human race. Comes a little trouble, and you can tell them apart./ When this trouble happens members of Division X say: 'I really think we ought to notify the police.' Division Y-men say: 'Whatever happens, for pity's sake let's not get the cops mixed up in this.'**
Claud Cockburn *Nine Bald Men*, 'Answer More or Less' (1956)

11 **We can close the Dick Turpin case now, sir ... We found where he was hiding ... Yes, it was under a gravestone in Highgate cemetery.**
Spike Milligan Unnamed dim policeman in *The Goon Show*, 'The Mysterious Punch-up-the-Conker', first broadcast 7 February 1957

12 **If I ever hear you accusing the police of using violence on a pris-**oner in custody again, I'll take you down to the station and beat the eyes out of your head.
Joe Orton Truscott in *Loot*, act 1, 1966. Truscott is a police inspector masquerading as a representative of the Water Board.

13 **Show business is my main interest, closely followed by crime detection.**
Tom Stoppard Inspector Bones in *Jumpers*, act 1 (1972)

14 **Flying squad: A special contingent of police whose business is to arrive at the scene of a crime shortly after all those connected with it.**
Beachcomber *Beachcomber: The Works of J. B. Morton*, 'A Dictionary for Today', ed. Richard Ingrams (1974)

15 **Q: What happens when you cross a policeman with a ghost? A: You get an Inspectre.**
Anon. *The Crack-a-Joke Book*, 'Funny Fuzz', ed. Jane Nissen (1978)

16 **Branch, Special: 'Look sunshine! You may be Special Branch but that doesn't make you Lord God Almighty!'**
Anon. Typical remark associated with the Special Branch, quoted in *Henry Root's World of Knowledge* (1982)

17 **A white person don't mind if he hears a police car, because he *knows* it ain't coming up *his* ass.**
Richard Pryor *Here and Now* (live video, 1983)

18 **In England, if you commit a crime, the police say 'Stop! Or I'll say "stop" again!'**
Robin Williams *Robin Williams: Live at the Met* (video, 1987)

19 **Police confused by 'absolutely nothing'**
Anon. Headline from the *Holborn Guardian*, quoted in *Cannibal Victims Speak Out! And Other Astonishing Press Cuttings* ed. Mat Coward (1995)

20 **Nice to see the spirit of Sherlock Holmes lives on.**
Anon. *The Times*, 'Quotes of the Week', 1 December 2001. From a letter to *The Times* in response to a police statement describing

the discovery of a woman's body in a suit-case as 'suspicious'.

Lawyers

1 **The first thing we do, let's kill all the lawyers.**
William Shakespeare Dick the butcher in *Henry VI Part 2*, act 4, sc. 2 (1590–1). The spur is Jack Cade's mob-law rebellion.

2 **KENT: This is nothing, fool.**
FOOL: Then 'tis like the breath of an unfee'd lawyer; you gave me nothing for 't.
William Shakespeare *King Lear*, act 1, sc. 4 (1605)

3 **The hungry judges soon the sentence sign,/ And wretches hang that jury-men may dine.**
Alexander Pope *The Rape of the Lock*, canto 3, line 21 (1714)

4 **Oons, sir! Do you say that I am drunk? I say, sir, that I am sober as a judge . . .**
Henry Fielding *Don Quixote in England*, act 3 (1733)

5 **Drunk or sober, bully, I am a justice o' the peace, and know how to deal with strollers.**
Richard Brinsley Sheridan Sir Tunbelly Clumsy in *A Trip to Scarborough*, act V (1777)

6 **Johnson observed, that 'he did not wish to speak ill of any man behind his back, but he believed the gentleman was an *attorney*.'**
Samuel Johnson *The Life of Samuel Johnson* by James Boswell, vol. 2, p. 127 (1791); in G. B. Hill's edition of 1887, rev. L. F. Powell (1934). The reference is to 'a gentleman, who had quitted a company where Johnson was'.

7 **The Americans, we believe, are the first persons who have discarded the tailor in the administration of justice, and his auxiliary the barber – two persons of endless importance in the codes and pandects of Europe.**
Sydney Smith Smith went on to note that in America 'a judge administers justice,

without a calorific wig and particoloured gown'. From the *Edinburgh Review* 1818, quoted in *Twelve Miles from a Lemon: Selected Writings of Sydney Smith*, ch. 3, compiled by Norman Taylor and Alan Hankinson (1996)

8 **A lawyer, quite famous for making a bill,/ And who in good living delighted,/ To dinner, one day, with a hearty good-will,/ Was by a rich client invited;/ But he charged 6s. 8d. for going to dine,/ Which the client he paid, though no ninny;/ And in turn charged the lawyer for dinner and wine,/ One a crown, and the other a guinea!**
Anon. 'Diamond Cut Diamond', *Oliver's Comic Songs* (1825?)

9 **Battledore and shuttlecock's a wery good game, when you an't the shuttlecock and two lawyers the battledores, in which case it gets too excitin' to be pleasant.**
Charles Dickens Sam Weller in *The Pickwick Papers*, ch. 20 (1837)

10 **In Westminster Hall, they have a legend of a litigant who stopped his case because the lawyers said it was 'interesting'. 'Ah,' he remarked afterwards, 'they were going up to the "Lords" with it, and I should never have seen my money.'**
Walter Bagehot *Saturday Review* 1856, collected in *The Complete Works of Walter Bagehot*, vol. 6 p. 81, ed. Norman St John-Stevas (1966–86)

11 **'In my youth,' said his father, 'I took to the law,/ And argued each case with my wife;/ And the muscular strength that it gave to my jaw/ Has lasted the rest of my life.'**
Lewis Carroll *Alice's Adventures in Wonderland* (1865)

12 **An attorney died, and two of his friends meeting, one of them observed that he had left few *effects*. 'I am not surprised at that,' said the other, 'for he had few causes.'**
Anon. *The New London Jest Book*, 'Choice Jests', no. 101, ed. W. C. Hazlitt (1871)

13 But I soon got tired of third-class journeys,/ And dinners of bread and water;/ So I fell in love with a rich attorney's/ Elderly, ugly daughter.

W. S. Gilbert The Learned Judge in *Trial by Jury*, act 1 (1875)

14 You cannot live without the lawyers, and you certainly cannot die without them.

Joseph H. Choate Speech on 'The Bench and the Bar', New York, 13 May 1879

15 If you knew what the address at the head of this sheet meant, it would give a double zest to your pleasures. It means hundreds of dull men sitting in hundreds of dull rooms with hundreds of dull books – men who bear the same relation to real men as pianolas do to pianos.

Raymond Asquith Letter to Aubrey Herbert of 20 March 1906, collected in *Raymond Asquith: Life and Letters* ed. John Jolliffe (1980). The address was 1 Paper Buildings, Temple, London E. C. – in other words, the men were lawyers.

16 Hangover came about through visit of my lawyer Mr Speiser whom I cannot see without the aid and abetment of alcohol.

Ernest Hemingway Letter to Sara Murphy of c.27 February 1936. Hemingway described the hangover as 'like all the tents of Ringling', Ringling being a circus.

17 Lawyers should never marry other lawyers. This is called in-breeding, from which comes idiot children and other lawyers.

Ruth Gordon and Garson Kanin Kip Lurie (David Wayne) to Amanda Bonner (Katharine Hepburn) in *Adam's Rib* (film, 1949, directed by George Cukor)

18 A good cross-exam or even more a summing up gives me intense pleasure. But I hear less well than I did, or else the judges mumble more than they did, and I am often tempted to call out 'Speak up', thereby emulating the bravest man I ever heard of who, as Lord Russell of Killowen began his summing up,

said to him 'Make it snappy, old cock', and evoked a tornado of wrath which would have flattened a forest.

George Lyttelton Letter to Rupert Hart-Davis of 29 March 1956, collected in *The Lyttelton–Hart-Davis Letters*, vols 1 and 2, *1955–1957*, ed. Rupert Hart-Davis (1978)

19 JUDGE WILLIS: What do you suppose I am on the Bench for, Mr Smith?

F. E. SMITH: It is not for me to attempt to fathom the inscrutable workings of Providence.

F. E. Smith Quoted in *F. E.: The Life of F. E. Smith, 1st Earl of Birkenhead*, ch. 9, by 2nd Earl of Birkenhead (1959)

20 For some reason not easy to explain, it nearly always happens that the smaller the ex-magistrate, the louder the dressing gown.

P. G. Wodehouse *Stiff Upper Lip, Jeeves*, ch. 8 (1963)

21 COUNSEL: Counsel for the defence, m'lud. The solicitors appearing for the defendant are Messrs Wealthy, Witty and Wise. I am Witty, m'lud.

JUDGE: That will be for me to judge.

Alan Bennett *Forty Years On*, act 2 (1968)

22 No brilliance is needed in the law. Nothing but common sense, and relatively clean finger nails.

John Mortimer *A Voyage round My Father*, act 1 (1971)

23 I think that a judge should be looked on rather as a sphinx than as a person – you shouldn't be able to imagine a judge having a bath.

Judge H. C. Leon *Observer*, 'Sayings of the Week', 21 December 1975, collected in *The Observer Sayings of the Week* ed. Valerie Ferguson (1987)

24 In a verbal slagging match with the prosecuting counsel she was well ahead on points when the judge interrupted to tell her, 'If you continue to speak like that, Mrs Bernard, I shall have to commit you for contempt of court.' She directed her

attention to him, and replied, 'Make that utter contempt.'

Jeffrey Bernard Recalling his mother. *Spectator* 12 August 1978.

25 The policeman led the accused into the dock and the prisoner bowed his head as the judge thundered to him: 'Is this the first time you've been up before me?' The accused shrugged his shoulders and replied: 'I don't know … what time do you normally get up?'

Les Dawson *The Malady Lingers On*, 'A Literary Interlude' (1982)

26 'Or he may suffer from a bad case of "judgeitis".'/ 'What's "judge-itis"?'/ 'Put briefly, pomposity and self-regard.'

Lord Hailsham Lord Hailsham interviewed by John Mortimer for the *Sunday Times*, collected in *Character Parts: Bollocks to the Bench of Bishops* by John Mortimer (1986)

27 Old lawyers never die, they simply lose their appeals.

John Mortimer Slogan on a coffee mug owned by John Mortimer QC and alluded to in *Murderers and Other Friends*, ch. 13 (1994)

28 … To Gollancz's libel lawyer, John Rubenstein, without whom this book would have been considerably longer.

Victor Lewis-Smith *Inside the Magic Rectangle*, Acknowledgements (1995)

29 Three golden rules for lawyers: Get the money up front/ Make no promises/ Get the money up front.

Anon. American saw, quoted in *The Law is a Ass*, 'Lawyers', ed. Ronald Irving (1999)

30 A man enters law – to get *On*./ He remains there – to get *Oner* (honour)./ He retires from the law – to get *Onest* (honest).

Anon. 'Comparisons of On', *Pearson's Book of Fun*, 'Sundry Siftings', ed. Mr X (n.d.)

31 Perhaps *this* will refresh your memory.

James Thurber Cartoon caption: remark made by a lawyer on producing a kangaroo.

War and Violence
The Nature of War

1 [Of England and France] As you know, these two nations are at war for the sake of a few acres of snow up towards Canada, and are spending on this fine war of theirs more than all Canada is worth.

Voltaire *Candide*, ch. 23 (1759)

2 You can't stop me! I spend thirty thousand men a month.

Napoleon Bonaparte Napoleon to Metternich (the Austrian Foreign Minister) in 1810. Quoted in *History in Quotations* ed. M. J. Cohen and John Major (2003).

3 Jellicoe was the only man on either side who could lose the war in an afternoon.

Winston Churchill *The World Crisis*, vol. 1, ch. 5 (1923)

4 You can't say civilization don't advance, however, for in every war they kill you in a new way.

Will Rogers *New York Times* 23 December 1929

5 We hear war called murder. It is not: it is suicide.

Ramsay MacDonald *Observer*, 'Sayings of the Week', 4 May 1930

6 The Roman Conquest was, however, a Good Thing, since the Britons were only natives at that time.

W. C. Sellar and R. J. Yeatman *1066 and All That*, ch. 1 (1930)

7 We can manage without butter but not, for example, without guns. If we are attacked we can only defend ourselves with guns, not with butter.

Joseph Goebbels Quoted in *Deutsche Allgemeine Zeitung* 18 January 1936. His colleague Hermann Goering also made a speech comparing butter and guns in 1936: 'I ask you – would you rather have butter or guns?' Butter, he concluded, 'merely makes us fat'.

8 War is like love, it always finds a way.

Bertolt Brecht The Chaplain in *Mother Courage and Her Children*, sc. 6 (1939)

9 If it were not for the war,/ This

war/ Would suit me down to the ground.

Dorothy L. Sayers 'London Calling: Lord, I Thank Thee'

10 **We sure liberated the hell out of this place.**

Anon. American soldier, surveying the remains of a village during the Normandy landings in 1944. Quoted in *History in Quotations*, ed. M. J. Cohen and John Major (2003).

11 **I'm all for the atomic bomb, but not to drop it much.**

Joyce Grenfell Letter of 9 August 1945 to Virginia Graham, collected in *Joyce and Ginnie: The Letters of Joyce Grenfell and Virginia Graham* ed. Janie Hampton (1997)

12 **The next war will be fought with atom bombs and the one after that with spears.**

Harold Urey *Observer*, 'Sayings of the Week', 1946

13 **The condition of my feet in those days was quite different to what they are today. Chasing the Hun across Europe, that was what flattened these, mate . . . as far as I'm concerned, my feet represent a war wound.**

Ray Galton and Alan Simpson Tony Hancock in *Hancock's Half Hour*, 'The Reunion Party', first broadcast 4 March 1960

14 **The Falklands thing was a quarrel between two bald men over a comb.**

Jorge Luis Borges *Time* 14 February 1983

15 **Weapons are like money; no one knows the meaning of *enough*.**

Martin Amis *Einstein's Monsters*, Introduction (1987)

16 **I do not have to forgive my enemies. I have had them all shot.**

Ramón Maria Narváez His response, while dying, to the suggestion of a priest that he forgive his enemies. Quoted in *Who Said What* ed. John Daintith and others (1988).

17 **There's no glory in soldiering any more/ we're just nannies to these nukes in a modern sort of war.**

Tony Harrison Guard 2 in *The Common Chorus*, act 1 (1992)

18 **One of the problems about war is that it is not until afterwards that you find out whether it's a four-year war or a six-week war.**

Tom Stoppard *Independent* 23 March 1991

19 **Even the War turns out to be quite dull.**

Alan Bennett *Telling Tales*, 'Our War' (2000) – the Second World War, as viewed from a child's perspective

20 **God created war to teach Americans geography.**

Anon. Quoted by Philip Kerr in the *New Statesman* 25 March 2002. Kerr described it as an 'old joke'.

Terrorism

1 **You all seem to be very worried about how easy it would be for a terrorist to manufacture an atomic bomb. Even the *Daily Express* knows how to do it.**

Peter Cook In the persona of the droning bore E. L. Wisty, *From beyond the Veil*, Mermaid Theatre, London, 1977

2 **When is it all right to shoot a terrorist? – remember if he pulls a gun it might be a toy, if he fires it might be a blank. Answer: when he's blown your head off.**

Kingsley Amis Letter to Robert Conquest of 17 September 1988, collected in *The Letters of Kingsley Amis* ed. Zachary Leader (2000). On 6 March 1988 three unarmed IRA suspects had been shot dead by the SAS in Gibraltar.

3 **Here's my suggestion. We don't rebuild the two towers, we build three. And instead of calling them One World Trade Center and Two World Trade Center, we give them each names: 'Go', 'Fuck', and 'Yourself'.**

Jerry Seinfeld Joke made at a Carnegie Hall benefit held on Monday 8 October 2001 for the relatives of those killed in the Muslim Fundamentalist attacks on the World Trade Center on 11 September. Quoted in the *Daily Telegraph* 10 October 2001.

4 **If everybody flew naked not only**

would you never have to worry about the passenger next to you having explosive shoes, but no religious fundamentalist would ever fly nude or in the presence of women.

Thomas L. Friedman *The Times*, 'Quotes of the Week', 5 January 2002, collected in *The Times Quotes of the Week* introduced by Philip Howard (2002)

5 Hello, my name's Shazia Mirza . . . At least, that's what it says on my pilot's licence.

Shazia Mirza Customary opening to her stage act in the wake of 11 September 2001. Quoted in the *Observer* 7 December 2003.

6 A fruitcake was banned from a plane in Montreal. The airport's scanners could not penetrate the dense cake mixture.

Anon. *Sunday Telegraph* 4 January 2004

Violence in General

1 For sleep a brawl is needed.

Juvenal Satire 3, line 282 (c.AD 100), trans. and ed. Niall Rudd (1991)

2 . . . 'a never broke any man's head but his own, and that was against a post when he was drunk.

William Shakespeare Boy in *Henry V*, act 3, sc. 2 (1599). He is speaking of Nym, a soldier in the King's army.

3 The first blow is half the battle.

Oliver Goldsmith Hardcastle in *She Stoops to Conquer*, act 2, sc. 1 (1773)

4 I'd just as lieve be shot in an awkward posture as a genteel one.

Richard Brinsley Sheridan Acres in *The Rivals*, act 5, sc. 3 (1775)

5 For a slashing article, sir, there's nobody like the Capting.

William Makepeace Thackeray Mr Bungay in *Pendennis*, ch. 33 (1848–50) He is speaking of Captain Costigan.

6 'Let's fight till six, and then have dinner,' said Tweedledum.

Lewis Carroll *Through the Looking Glass*, ch. 4 (1872)

7 Dramatic measures is Latin for a whopping.

F. Anstey (Thomas Anstey Guthrie) *Vice Versa*, ch. 7 (1882)

8 The firing of guns in bedrooms is always a thing that tends to excite the interest of the owner of a country house.

P. G. Wodehouse *Uncle Fred in the Springtime*, ch. 19 (1939)

9 You can get much further with a kind word and a gun than you can with a kind word alone.

Al Capone Attributed

10 My, my. Such a lot of guns around town and so few brains.

Humphrey Bogart Philip Marlowe (Humphrey Bogart) in *The Big Sleep* (film, 1946, screenplay by William Faulkner, Leigh Brackett and Jules Furthman, adapted from Raymond Chandler's novel, directed by Howard Hawks)

11 It is so difficult to make a neat job of killing people with whom one is not on friendly terms.

Robert Hamer and John Dighton Louis Mazzini (Dennis Price) in *Kind Hearts and Coronets* (film, 1949, screenplay by Robert Hamer and John Dighton from the novel *Noblesse Oblige* by Roy Horniman, directed by Robert Hamer)

12 Why do I need a gun licence? It's only for use around the house.

Charles Addams *New Yorker* cartoon caption

13 BLACK KNIGHT (after having his arm sliced off): 'Tis but a scratch. KING ARTHUR: A scratch? Your arm's off ! BLACK KNIGHT: No it isn't.

Monty Python team *Monty Python and the Holy Grail* (film, 1975, directed by Terry Gilliam and Terry Jones, screenplay by the Monty Python team)

14 Mercifully, Henry hit him with the soft end of the pistol.

Viv Stanshall *Sir Henry at Rawlinson End* (LP, 1978)

15 Colin never hurt a fly. Well, only when it was necessary.

Barrie Keeffe Harold Shand (Bob Hoskins) speaking of a dead associate in *The Long*

Good Friday (film, 1980, directed by John Mackenzie, screenplay by Barrie Keeffe)

16 **Who can doubt that the House Full boards went up on Christians v Lions night at the Colosseum?**
Arthur Marshall *Smile Please*, 'Murder Most Foul' (1982)

17 **Instrument: If used to commit a crime always 'blunt', unless 'sharp'.**
Henry Root *Henry Root's World of Knowledge* (1982)

18 **There is only one way to be good at fighting: you have to do it a lot.**
Martin Amis *Money* (publ. 1984), p. 35 (1985 Penguin edn)

19 **In the [US] Constitution, it says you have the right to bear arms, or the right to arm bears. Whatever you want.**
Robin Williams *Robin Williams: Live at the Met* (video, 1987)

20 **A girl was beheaded, chopped into pieces and placed in a trunk, but was not interfered with.**
Anon. 'From a Fleet Street report' quoted in *A Gentleman Publisher's Commonplace Book*, 'Delightful Oddities', by John G. Murray (1996)

21 **I don't have to be careful, I got a gun.**
Matt Groening Homer Simpson in *The Simpsons*, 'The Cartridge Family', first broadcast 2 November 1997

22 **[Of football hooligans] A compliment to the English martial spirit.**
Alan Clark *The Times*, 'Quotes of the Week', 20 June 1998. An official of the German football federation (the trouble occurred in Germany) commented: 'That wasn't hooliganism. It was terrorism.'

23 **Perhaps the predilection of men for rapine and slaughter should be interpreted as meaning that men are premenstrual at all times.**
Germaine Greer Quoted in *Women's Wicked Wit* ed. Michelle Lovric (2000)

24 **You say 'Psycho' like it's a bad thing.**
Anon. Slogan on a T-shirt for sale in Camden Market, London, September 2003

Cowardice and Bravery

1 **SECOND MURDERER: What, shall we stab him as he sleeps?**
FIRST MURDERER: No; then he will say 'twas done cowardly, when he wakes.
William Shakespeare *Richard III*, act 1, sc. 4 (1592–3). They have been sent by the Duke of Gloucester to kill the Duke of Clarence.

2 **Without danger, we cannot get beyond danger.**
George Herbert *Outlandish Proverbs*, no. 1010 (1640)

3 **For all men would be cowards if they durst.**
Earl of Rochester *A Satire against Mankind*, line 158 (1679)

4 **Some have been thought brave because they were afraid to run away.**
Anon. Proverb quoted in *Gnomologia* ed. Thomas Fuller (1732)

5 **Someone having in battle received a wound in his face, was vaunting of it before Augustus, who said to him, *Now this is all your own fault. When you run away you should never look behind.***
Anon. *Glasgow Magazine of Wit* (1803)

6 **Coward: One who, in a perilous emergency, thinks with his legs.**
Ambrose Bierce *The Devil's Dictionary* (compiled 1881–1906)

7 **He had faced death in many forms but he had never faced a dentist. The thought of dentists gave him just the same sick horror as the thought of Socialism.**
H. G. Wells Of the military man Lord Chickney in *Bealby*, ch. 8 (1915)

8 **'There's probably a secret Medal Ring somewhere,' cried the man, delighted at the new idea, 'which encourages wars.'**
A. G. Macdonnell *Lords and Masters*, ch. 3 (1936)

9 **His heart did three somersaults and**

dashed itself against his front teeth.

P. G. Wodehouse *A Few Quick Ones*, 'Oofy, Freddie and the Beef Trust' (1959). Oofy Prosser has just perceived the threat to his person embodied by Porky Jupp and Plug Bosher.

10 **INTERVIEWER: What was the main form of transport in your time? 2000-YEAR-OLD MAN: Well it was mostly fear. An animal would growl, you would go two miles in a minute.**

Carl Reiner and Mel Brooks *The 2000-Year-Old Man* (LP, 1960)

11 **I don't mind giving them a reasonable amount, but a pint – why that's very nearly an armful . . .**

Tony Hancock The line with which Hancock is most readily associated. 'The Blood Donor,' broadcast 23 June 1961, *Hancock's Half-Hour* (BBC TV series written by Ray Galton and Alan Simpson, 1956–61). Hancock re-enacted the routine as a publicity stunt for the Blood Transfusion Service. In *Look-In* magazine January 1994 a strip appeared in which the cowardly cartoon dog Scooby-Doo offers to give blood. When asked for a pint he replies: 'A pint? But that's nearly a pawful.'

12 **There was no established procedure for evasive action. All you needed was fear.**

Joseph Heller *Catch-22*, ch. 5 (1961)

13 **I'm a hero with coward's legs.**

Spike Milligan *Puckoon*, ch. 2 (1963). In Italy in 1944 Milligan, as a young soldier, was reprimanded by an officer for failing to make a delivery to an operations point. He was wounded at the time, and suffering severely from piles.

14 **It was involuntary, they sank my boat.**

John F. Kennedy On being asked how he became a war hero. Quoted in *A Thousand Days*, ch. 4 (1965), by Arthur M. Schlesinger Jr.

15 **I met one of them tonight, down at the House. Everything a hero should be. Handsome, laughing, careless of his life. Rather a bore, and at heart, I suppose, a bit of a Fascist.**

Alan Bennett Hugh in *Forty Years On*, act 1

(1968). He is talking about Battle of Britain pilots.

16 **I was terrified. The referee said, 'You're shaking like a leaf.' I said, 'How do you want me to shake?'**

Eric Morecambe and Ernie Wise The context is boxing. *The Morecambe and Wise Jokebook*, skit 22 (1979).

17 **Okay, I'll make a deal with you. I'll put one up.**

John Cleese and Charles Crichton Otto (Kevin Kline) has just been asked by Archie Leach (John Cleese) to put up his hands in *A Fish Called Wanda* (film, 1988, directed by Charles Crichton)

Service Life

1 **Thou art a soldier, therefore seldom rich.**

William Shakespeare Timon to Alcibiades in *Timon of Athens*, act 1, sc. 2 (1607–8)

2 **[Of England] In this country it is thought requisite now and then to kill an admiral, to encourage the others.**

Voltaire *Candide*, ch. 23 (1759)

3 **Ben Battle was a soldier bold,/ And used to war's alarms:/ But a cannon-ball took off his legs,/ So he laid down his arms!**

Thomas Hood 'Faithless Nelly Gray' (1826)

4 **[Of the British Army] Ours is composed of the scum of the earth – the mere scum of the earth.**

Duke of Wellington Quoted in *Notes of Conversations with the Duke of Wellington*, '4 November, 1831' (1888), by Philip Henry Stanhope

5 **One man asked why a drum was used in wars. It was answered, to stir up valour in the soldiers. 'That is strange,' said the first, 'for wherever the victory falls, the drums are sure to be beaten.'**

Anon. *The New London Jest Book*, 'Choice Jests', no. 43, ed. W. C. Hazlitt (1871)

6 **'Soldiers must be fearfully dishonest,' says Mrs Partington, 'as it**

seems a nightly occurrence for a sentry to be relieved of his watch.'

Anon. Ibid., no. 64

7 A nobleman asked Tarlton what he thought of soldiers in time of peace. 'Why,' quoth he, 'they are like chimneys in the summer.'

Anon. Ibid., no. 830

8 I am the very model of a modern Major-General,/ I've information vegetable, animal and mineral.

W. S. Gilbert Song, sung by Major-General Stanley in *The Pirates of Penzance*, act 1 (1879)

9 The uniform 'e wore/ Was nothin' much before,/ An' rather less than 'arf be'ind.

Rudyard Kipling 'Gunga Din', *Barrack Room Ballads* (1892)

10 You can always tell an old soldier by the inside of his holsters and cartridge boxes. The young ones carry pistols and cartridges: the old ones, grub.

George Bernard Shaw The Man in *Arms and the Man*, act 1 (1898)

11 Foot-foot-foot-foot-sloggin' over Africa – (Boots-boots-boots-boots-movin' up and down again!)

Rudyard Kipling 'Boots' (1903)

12 When the military man approaches, the world locks up its spoons and packs off its womankind.

George Bernard Shaw Don Juan in *Man and Superman* act 3 (1903)

13 Mad, is he? Then I hope he will bite some of my other generals.

George II In response to the Duke of Newcastle who had said that General Wolfe was a madman. Quoted in *Life and Letters of James Wolfe*, ch. 17, by Henry Beckles Wilson (1909).

14 The army ages men sooner than the law and philosophy; it exposes them more freely to germs, which undermine and destroy.

H. G. Wells *Bealby*, ch. 8 (1915)

15 There used to be a limitation to the number of false teeth a recruit could have. I have removed that limitation.

Leslie Hore-Belisha *Observer*, 'Sayings of the Week', 14 November 1937

16 If it moves, salute it,/ If it doesn't move, pick it up./ If you can't pick it up, paint it.

Anon. 'The Sad Sack's Catechism' (1942). A maxim (also anon.) of the Australian outback runs: 'If it moves, shoot it. If it doesn't move, chop it down.'

17 Praise the Lord and pass the ammunition.

Howell Forgy Demanded of sailors handling ammunition. Quoted in the *New York Times* 1 November 1942, and the title of a song by Frank Loesser (1942).

18 The intelligence officers are mostly very unmilitary & no one ever gives an order – They say 'I say would you mind kind of gathering round.'

Evelyn Waugh Letter to Laura Waugh of 20 June 1942, collected in *The Letters of Evelyn Waugh* ed. Mark Amory (1980)

19 Overpaid, overfed, oversexed, and over here.

Tommy Trinder Speaking of American GIs in Britain during the Second World War

20 To-day we have naming of parts. Yesterday,/ We had daily cleaning. And to-morrow morning,/ We shall have what to do after firing. But to-day,/ To-day we have naming of parts. Japonica/ Glistens like coral in all of the neighbouring gardens,/ And to-day we have naming of parts.

Henry Reed *A Map of Verona*, 'Lessons of the War: Naming of Parts' (1946)

21 Four days in a bullock wagon, a hole as big as your fist in my stomach, and maggotty! Happiest time of my life.

Nancy Mitford Uncle Matthew, recalling his time in the Boer War. *Love in a Cold Climate*, ch. 9 (1949).

22 LOU COSTELLO: I joined the navy when I was four years old.
BUD ABBOTT: How did you do that?

LOU COSTELLO: I lied about my age.
Abbott and Costello 'The Story of Moby Dick', vaudeville sketch of the 1940s, collected in *Abbott and Costello: Who's on First?* (CD, 1999)

23 **It is important when you haven't got any ammunition to have a butt on your rifle.**
Winston Churchill *Observer*, 'Sayings of the Week', 31 January 1954

24 **One of the fine things about the army is that it has carried the democratic ideal to its logical conclusion in the sense that not only do they prohibit discrimination on the grounds of race, creed and colour, but also on the ground of ability.**
Tom Lehrer Preamble to singing 'It Makes a Fellow Proud to be a Soldier', *An Evening Wasted with Tom Lehrer* (LP, 1960)

25 **I know there's a war on. I know a lot of people are going to have to suffer for us to win it. But why must I be one of them?**
Joseph Heller Doc Daneeka, 'a very neat, clean man whose idea of a good time was to sulk', in *Catch-22*, ch. 4 (1961)

26 **Some men are born mediocre, some men achieve mediocrity, and some men have mediocrity thrust upon them. With Major Major it had been all three.**
Ibid., ch. 9. A modification of Malvolio's words in *Twelfth Night*, act 2, sc. 5.

27 **Every seven seconds a baby is born in the United States, which means that we produce, every two hours, approximately five companies of infantry.**
James Thurber *Lanterns and Lances*, 'The Darlings at the Top of the Stairs' (1961)

28 **[Of sailors] They returned with their outlook and possibly their anus broadened.**
Quentin Crisp *The Naked Civil Servant*, ch. 13 (1968)

29 **Bally Jerry pranged his kite right in the how's your father. Hairy blighter, dicky-birdied, feathered back his Sammy, took a waspy,** flipped over on his Betty Harper's and caught his can in the Bertie.
Monty Python team Eric Idle as an RAF squadron leader in *Monty Python's Flying Circus*, 4th series, episode 3, broadcast 14 November 1974

30 **'Army cooks don't like tinned food,' says Kidgell. 'Why not?' 'They can't sod it up in tins. They like fresh stuff they can burn the Jesus out of.'**
Spike Milligan *Monty: His Part in My Victory*, 'Carthage' (1976), collected in *The Essential Spike Milligan* compiled by Alex Games (2002)

31 **Q: What is higher than an admiral. A: His hat.**
Anon. *The Crack-a-Joke Book*, 'Rib Ticklers', ed. Jane Nissen (1978)

32 **This foxhole was so deep it was just short of desertion.**
Eric Morecambe and Ernie Wise *The Morecambe and Wise Jokebook*, skit 9 (1979)

33 **I wasn't really what is called officer material and I looked a bit bizarre in uniform (I once, absentmindedly and on a wet day, went on parade with an umbrella).**
Arthur Marshall *Life's Rich Pageant*, Scene 6 (1984)

34 **I think women and seamen don't mix.**
Matt Groening Smithers in *The Simpsons*, 'Treehouse of Horror III' first broadcast 29 October 1992

35 **I'm a centurion, toothbrush on the head.**
Eddie Izzard *Eddie Izzard: Definite Article*, 'The Romans' (CD, 1995)

36 **I am very old-fashioned. I think wars are for men.**
Max Hastings *The Times*, 'Quotes of the Week', 5 January 2002. Caspar Weinberger said: 'I think women are too valuable to be in combat.'

37 **[Of the Swiss army] How butch is an army that has a wine opener on its knife?**
Robin Williams *Robin Williams Live on Broadway* (video, 2003)

Military Incompetence

1 **If you don't want to use the army, I would like to borrow it for a while.**
Abraham Lincoln Letter of 1862 to General George B. McClellan whose lack of activity in the Civil War irritated Lincoln

2 [Of the views of English soldiers in the First World War] **Their faith in newspapers has been sorely shaken for ever by the comparison of accounts with realities. But chiefly by the contrast between the phrase 'mastery of the air' and the reality.**
Ivor Gurney Letter to Marion Scott of June or July 1917

3 **His knowledge of life and ordinary human beings is so hazy, he really deserves some sort of decoration 'For Vaguery in the Field'.**
John Osborne Jimmy Porter in *Look Back in Anger*, act 1 (1956), speaking of Nigel, the 'straight-backed chinless wonder from Sandhurst'

4 **Not so loud, please, do you want to wake up the sentries?**
Spike Milligan Major Bloodnock (Peter Sellers) in 'The Treasure in the Tower', *The Goon Show*, (BBC radio series, 28 October 1957). Bloodnock is on this occasion in charge of the guarding of the Tower of London.

5 **We shall receive four minutes' warning of any impending nuclear attack. Some people have said, 'Oh my goodness me – four minutes? – that is not a very long time!' Well, I would remind those doubters that some people in this great country of ours can run a mile in four minutes.**
Peter Cook *Beyond the Fringe*, 'Whose Finger on the Button?', first performed Monday 22 August 1960. The satirist John Bird called this line 'a joke, which brilliantly clamped its teeth on that era's self-delusion and hopeless nostalgia for power and glory'.

6 **To save the town it became necessary to destroy it.**
Anon. American soldier on the destruction of Ben Tre during the Vietnam War in February 1968. Quoted in *History in Quotations* ed. M. J. Cohen and John Major (2003).

7 **The fastest defeat in any war was suffered in 1896 by Said Khalid, the pretender Sultan of Zanzibar./ On 27 August the British battle fleet arrived to deliver an ultimatum. He declined to vacate the palace at the request of Rear-Admiral Harry Holdsworth Rawson and so fighting broke out at 9.02 am. It reached its peak around 9.15 and was all over by 9.40.**
Stephen Pile *The Book of Heroic Failures*, 'The Fastest Defeat in War' (1979)

8 **A war hasn't been fought this badly since Olaf the Hairy, High Chief of all the Vikings, accidentally ordered eighty thousand battle helmets with the horns on the inside.**
Richard Curtis and Ben Elton Captain Edmund Blackadder in 'Major Star', *Blackadder Goes Forth* (TV series, 1989). He is speaking of the First World War.

9 **Confusion was immediately restored.**
Anon. Described as 'an expression used in the Second World War' in *A Gentleman Publisher's Commonplace Book*, 'Core', by John G. Murray (1996)

10 **Military intelligence is a contradiction in terms.**
Groucho Marx Quoted in *Halliwell's Who's Who in the Movies* ed. John Walker (2nd edn 2001)

11 **The American precision bombing has continued with the use of missiles so accurate they can hit the exact centre of a big, red cross.**
Angus Deayton *Have I Got News for You*, highlights from the BBC TV series (CD, 2003)

Pacifism

1 **There never was a good war, or a bad peace.**
Benjamin Franklin Letter to Josiah Quincy of 11 September 1783, collected in *Works*, vol. 10, ed. John Bigelow (1887)

2 **Nothing justifies war but a box on**

the ear – not a box on the ear by implication but a box on the ear physically corporally actually.

Sydney Smith Smith added: 'Bagdad is oppressed; I do not like the present state of the Delta; Thibet is not comfortable. Am I to fight for all these people?' Letter to George Lamb of 1827, quoted in *Twelve Miles from a Lemon: Selected Writings of Sydney Smith*, ch. 8, compiled by Norman Taylor and Alan Hankinson (1996).

3 **War hath no fury like a non-combatant.**

C. E. Montague *Disenchantment*, ch. 16 (1922)

4 **People who talk about peace are very often the most quarrelsome.**

Nancy Astor *Observer*, 'Sayings of the Week', 11 May 1924

5 **MILITARY TRIBUNAL: What would you do if you saw a German soldier trying to violate your sister?**

LYTTON STRACHEY: I would try to get between them.

Lytton Strachey Quoted in *Good-bye to All That*, ch. 23, by Robert Graves (1929). He was being questioned about his conscientious objection to the First World War. Graves notes that he made his reply while sitting on an air-cushion, 'which he inflated in court as a protest against the hardness of the benches'.

6 **Sometime they'll give a war and nobody will come.**

Carl Sandburg 'The People, Yes', pt 23 (1936). According to Sandburg, this is 'several stories and psalms nobody would want to laugh at'. 'What if they gave a war & Nobody came?' is the first line of a graffito (1972) by Allen Ginsberg.

7 **Pale Ebenezer thought it wrong to fight,/ But Roaring Bill (who killed him) thought it right.**

Hilaire Belloc 'The Pacifist', publ. in *Sonnets and Verses* (2nd edn 1938)

8 **I have never met anyone who wasn't against war. Even Hitler and**

Mussolini were, according to themselves.

David Lowe *New York Times* 10 February 1946

9 **We were driven out to the airport to see Neville Chamberlain return with his little piece of paper by a senior master who impressed us all by saying to me, 'You realize, Lyttelton, that this means peace in your lifetime?' Eton had taught me not to have very profound views on anything, so I just said, 'Oh'.**

Humphrey Lyttelton *I Play As I Please*, ch. 4 (1954)

10 **A very great man once said you should love your enemies, and that's not a bad piece of advice. We can love them, but, by God, that doesn't mean we're not going to fight them.**

Norman Schwartzkopf *Daily Telegraph* 1 February 1991

11 **We all agree that firearms are terrible. In fact, I wrote a song called 'Shoot the Gun.'**

Graham Fellowes Graham Fellowes in the persona of the middle-aged amateur songwriter John Shuttleworth, quoted in *FHM* magazine June 1997

12 **I'd kill for a Nobel Peace Prize.**

Steven Wright Quoted in *The Penguin Dictionary of Modern Humorous Quotations* ed. Fred Metcalf (2nd edn 2001)

13 **Emily is thrilled with the Peacekeeper Barbie I picked up in Stockholm duty free.**

Allison Pearson *I Don't Know How She Does It*, ch. 4 (2002)

14 **Why was all that money wasted on ousting Saddam Hussein from office? He is nearly sixty-five and would have been due for retirement this year anyway.**

Viz Fake reader's letter to *Viz* comic May 2003

3

Knowledge and Education

Education
Historical Perspectives
Science and Technology

Education
Education in General

1 'Tis education forms the common mind,/ Just as the twig is bent, the tree's inclined.
Alexander Pope *Epistles to Several Persons*, 'To Lord Cobham' (1734)

2 Wear your learning, like your watch, in a private pocket: and do not merely pull it out and strike it, merely to show you have one.
Lord Chesterfield *Letters to His Son* (1774), letter of 27 February 1748

3 Let schoolmasters puzzle their brain,/ With grammar, and non-sense, and learning,/ Good liquor, I stoutly maintain,/ Gives genius a better discerning.
Oliver Goldsmith Tony Lumpkin in *She Stoops to Conquer*, act 1, sc. 2 (1773)

4 Leeze me on drink! It gi'es us mair/ Than either school or college.
Robert Burns *The Holy Fair*, st. 19 (1786)

5 He was sent, as usual, to a public school, where a little learning was painfully beaten into him, and from thence to the university, where it was carefully taken out of him.
Thomas Love Peacock *Nightmare Abbey*, ch. 1 (1818)

6 Examinations are formidable even to the best prepared, for the great-est fool may ask more than the wisest man can answer.
Charles Caleb Colton *Lacon* (a book of aphor-isms), vol. 1, no. 183 (1820)

7 Of genius they make no account, for they say that every one is a genius, more or less.
Samuel Butler *Erewhon*, ch. 22, 'The Colleges of Unreason – Continued' (1872), 'they' being the Utopian Erewhonians. The editor of the Penguin English Library version (1970) Peter Mudford states that Butler was much influ-enced by the promotion of the idea of genius by Herder and Kant in Germany, and Coleridge in England.

8 In England at least a university education does one thing – namely, emancipates men from any excess of appreciation of its importance, such as the ablest men who have not passed through it, are inclined to attach to it.

Walter Bagehot 'The Public Bewilderment about Higher Education', *Economist* 1876, collected in *The Complete Works of Walter Bagehot*, vol. 7, p. 447, ed. Norman St John-Stevas (1966–86)

9 Education is an admirable thing. But it is well to remember from time to time that nothing that is worth knowing can be taught.

Oscar Wilde 'A Few Maxims for the Instruction of the Over-educated', *Saturday Review* November 1894. In his *Phrases and Philosophies for the Use of the Young* (1894) Wilde also said: 'In examinations the foolish ask questions that the wise cannot answer.'

10 Fortunately in England, at any rate, education produces no effect whatsoever. If it did, it would prove a serious danger to the upper classes, and probably lead to acts of violence in Grosvenor Square.

Oscar Wilde Lady Bracknell in *The Importance of Being Earnest*, act 1 (1895)

11 In the first place God made idiots. This was for practice. Then he made School Boards.

Mark Twain *Following the Equator*, ch. 61 (1897)

12 It was after I was born. I was three years old just at the moment, and had not quite finished my education.

Dan Leno *Dan Leno Hys Booke*, Chapter Second (1899)

13 There was something admirable – and yet a little horrible – about Henry's method of study. He went after Learning with the cold and dispassionate relentlessness of a stoat pursuing a rabbit.

P. G. Wodehouse *The Man with Two Left Feet*, 'The Man with Two Left Feet' (1926)

14 Education consists mainly in what we have unlearned.

Mark Twain *Notebook*, ch. 31 (1935)

15 More will mean worse.

Kingsley Amis Of universities. *Encounter* July 1960.

16 HEADMASTER: The trouble with you, Franklin, is that you have this unfortunate tendency to put ideas into the boys' heads.
FRANKLIN: I thought that's what education meant.
HEADMASTER: I never liked the word 'education'. I prefer the word 'schooling'.

Alan Bennett *Forty Years On*, act 1 (1968)

17 Language Lab – it's a big name for a room and a tape recorder.

Eddie Izzard *Eddie Izzard: Definite Article*, 'Latin/French' (CD, 1995)

School

1 In fact, Dr Blimber's establishment was a great hothouse, in which there was a forcing apparatus incessantly at work. All the boys blew before their time. Mental green-peas were produced at Christmas, and intellectual asparagus all year round.

Charles Dickens *Dombey and Son*, ch. 11 (1847–8)

2 'That's the reason they're called lessons,' the Gryphon remarked: 'because they lessen from day to day.'

Lewis Carroll *Alice's Adventures in Wonderland*, ch. 9 (1865)

3 He must have known me had he seen me as he was wont to see me, for he was in the habit of flogging me constantly. Perhaps he did not recognize me by my face.

Anthony Trollope On meeting Dr Butler, headmaster of Harrow, in the street. *Autobiography*, ch. 1 (1883).

4 But, good gracious, you've got to educate him first. You can't expect a boy to be vicious till he's been to a good school.

Saki *Reginald in Russia*, 'The Baker's Dozen' (1910)

5 In examinations those who do not wish to know ask questions of those who cannot tell.

Sir Walter Raleigh *Laughter from a Cloud*, 'Some Thoughts on Examinations' (1923)

6 Mr Strong set, for homework, more French than it was convenient for William to learn.

Richmal Crompton *William The Conqueror*, ch. 4 (1926)

7 There will be a prize of half a crown for the longest essay, irrespective of any possible merit.

Evelyn Waugh *Decline and Fall*, pt 1, ch. 1 (1928). Paul Pennyfeather, lately sent down from Oxford, begins his teaching career at Llanabba Castle.

8 I expect you'll be becoming a schoolmaster, sir. That's what most of the gentlemen does, sir, that gets sent down for indecent behaviour.

The university porter in ibid., 'Prelude'. Waugh himself, although not sent down from Oxford (he gained a Third), became a schoolmaster in Wales shortly after leaving the university. 'I was from the first an obvious dud,' he wrote in his autobiography.

9 Educ: during the holidays from Eton.

Sir Osbert Sitwell *Who's Who* entry, 1929

10 Do not attempt to answer this question.

W. C. Sellar and R. J. Yeatman *1066 and All That*, ch. 38 (1930)

11 Every schoolmaster knows that for every one person who wants to teach there are approximately thirty who don't want to learn – much.

W. C. Sellar and R. J. Yeatman *And Now All This*, Introduction (1932)

12 The ape-like virtues without which no one can enjoy a public school.

Cyril Connolly *Enemies of Promise*, ch. 1 (1938)

13 I won't try to explain the intricacies of the form system at Eton beyond saying that Third form was at the very bottom of the school, and Sixth form at the top. I don't know what happened to First and Second form.

Humphrey Lyttelton *I Play as I Please*, ch. 4 (1954)

14 I am glad that I went to the Secondary Modern School, because it was only constructed the year before. Therefore, it was much more hygienic than the Grammar School.

Muriel Spark *Punch* May 1958

15 All Latin masters have one joke./ *Caesar adsum jam forte/* or/ had some jam for tea.

Ronald Searle and Geoffrey Willans *Down with Skool!*, ch. 3, 'Latin Masters' (1958)

16 Give me a girl at an impressionable age, and she is mine for life.

Muriel Spark The credo of Jean Brodie, from *The Prime of Miss Jean Brodie*, ch. 1 (1961)

17 Two kinds of schoolboys often turn out to be artistically gifted. There are those who do impersonations: those are the talented. And there are the ones they are impersonating: these are the geniuses.

Kenneth Tynan Entry for 3 May 1971, *The Diaries of Kenneth Tynan* ed. John Lahr (2000)

18 Von Ribbentrop was the new German Ambassador in London, and as a good Nazi, hoped to send his son to Eton.

Peter Ustinov *Dear Me*, ch. 5 (1977). The boy, Rudolf, was refused a place.

19 TEACHER: I wish you to pay a little attention.
PUPIL: I'm paying as little as I can.

Anon. *The Crack-a-Joke Book*, 'School Rulers', ed. Jane Nissen (1978)

20 Stand firm in your refusal to remain conscious during algebra. In real life, I assure you, there is no such thing as algebra.

Fran Lebowitz *Metropolitan Life*, 'Parental Guidance' (1978)

21 INTERVIEWER: What was life like at Chiswick Grammar?
TOMMY COOPER: Well, they were the happiest days of my life.

INTERVIEWER: Any particular reason?

TOMMY COOPER: It was a girls' school.

Tommy Cooper Excerpt from one of his 1970s TV shows, collected in *Tommy Cooper: Just Like That* (video, 1993)

22 Those who disapprove of public schools may get what comfort they can from the assurance that examination of their past history reveals nothing but spartan living, extremely hard work, minimal amounts of food and regular beatings.

Arthur Marshall *Smile Please*, 'See How They Run' (1982)

23 How do you explain school to a higher intelligence?

Melissa Mathison Elliott (Henry Thomas) to Michael (Robert MacNaughton) in *E. T. the Extra-Terrestrial* (film, 1982, screenplay by Melissa Mathison, directed by Steven Spielberg)

24 TEACHER: You're late! You should have been here at nine o'clock.

BOY: Why? What happened?

Anon. *The Ha Ha Bonk Book*, 'Jokes Not to Tell Your Teacher', ed. Janet and Allan Ahlberg (1982)

25 I came home from school with a headache. All the noise and shouting and bullying is getting me down! Surely teachers should be better behaved!

Sue Townsend *The Secret Diary of Adrian Mole Aged 13¾* (1982), entry for Monday 16 November

26 It is of course a bit of a drawback that science was invented after I left school.

Lord Carrington *Observer* 23 January 1983, quoted in *Who Said What* ed. John Daintith and others (1988)

27 The schoolteacher is certainly underpaid as a childminder, but ludicrously overpaid as an educator.

John Osborne *Observer*, 'Sayings of the Week', 21 July 1985

28 Start at the Prep School where I was dumped at the age of six. They had a sort of initiation ceremony. New boys were made to drink from a loving cup, only it turned out to be a brimming po. I was ill for a year after that. The school said it was because I'd eaten a bad ice cream sundae, but I knew I hadn't.

Alec Guinness Quoted in *Character Parts*, 'The Rope Trick', by John Mortimer (1986)

29 Schoolfriends called 'fatty' never reappear in one's adult life.

Miles Kington *Welcome to Kington*, 'The Wit and Wisdom of Albania' (1989)

30 At Harrow, you could have any boy for a box of Cadbury's milk chocolate.

John Mortimer *Sunday Times* 27 September 1998

31 I quit school in the sixth grade because of pneumonia – not because I had it but because I couldn't spell it.

Rocky Graziano Quoted in *The Daily Telegraph Book of Sports Obituaries* ed. Martin Smith (2000)

32 I vaguely remember my schooldays. They were what was going on in the background when I was trying to listen to the Beatles.

Douglas Adams *The Salmon of Doubt*, 'Life', 'The Voices of All Our Yesterdays' (2002)

33 Q: Why is a man who wears sunglasses like a bad teacher?

A: Because he keeps his pupils in the dark.

Anon. Joke overheard in the Pig's Bise pub, East Prawle, Devon, 16 August 2003

Student Life

1 LATINE: Hey day! Why, were there no women in Oxford?

YOUNG BOOKWIT: No, no; why, do you think a Bedmaker's a woman?

Sir Richard Steele *The Lying Lover*, act 1, sc. 1 (1703)

2 **Sir, we are a nest of singing birds.**
Samuel Johnson Boswell's *Life of Samuel Johnson*, vol. 1, p. 75 (1791); in G. B. Hill's edition of 1887, rev. L. F. Powell (1934). The reference is to graduates or, as Boswell puts it, 'sons of Pembroke College Oxford' – Johnson's own college – and their propensity for poetry.

3 **I spent fourteen months in Magdalen College: they proved the fourteen months the most idle and unprofitable of my whole life.**
Edward Gibbon *Memoirs of My Life* (1796). He prefaced this remark with: 'To the University of Oxford I acknowledge no obligation.'

4 **[Of Oxford dons] Their dull and deep potations excused the brisk intemperance of youth.**
Ibid., ch. 3

5 **[Of student life] Suffice it to say that those parts of the day which are not taken up with eating are spent, by the athletic, in drinking, by the more intellectual in smoking or playing poker.**
Raymond Asquith Letter of October 1897 to Margot Asquith, written from Balliol College, Oxford collected in *Raymond Asquith: Life and Letters* ed. John Jolliffe (1980)

6 **It is bold of you to embark on modern history: even if you can master it it can hardly be a permanent possession and is likely to fade from the mind as rapidly as a second-rate novel.**
Letter to H. T. Baker of 25 September 1900, ibid.

7 **Shakespeare did not write so much in all his life as is written in a single room during one week of examination. Yet some dotards deny progress.**
Sir Walter Raleigh *Laughter from a Cloud*, 'Some Thoughts on Examinations' (1923). Raleigh also wrote: 'The World was made in a week, and its Maker pronounced it good. At that time there were no Examiners.'

8 **You want either a First or a Fourth. There is no value in anything in-between.**
Evelyn Waugh Advice on academic matters

given by his cousin Jasper to Charles Ryder. *Brideshead Revisited*, bk 1, ch. 1 (1945).

9 **I don't think one really 'comes down' from Jimmy's university. According to him, it's not even red brick, but white tile.**
John Osborne *Look Back in Anger*, act 2, sc. 1 (1956)

10 **The close association between gymnastics and philosophy is, I believe, unique to this university.**
Tom Stoppard George in *Jumpers*, act 1 (1972)

11 **A tangled web indeed we weave/ When Adam grants degrees to Eve:/ And much I doubt, had Eve first had 'em,/ If she'd have done as much for Adam.**
A. D. Godley 'Women's Degrees', collected in *The New Oxford Book of Light Verse* ed. Kingsley Amis (1978)

12 **They were famous for being nothing except Oxford characters; once they left their natural habitat in Magdalen or The House they grew faint and dim and ended up down back corridors of Bush House, or as announcers on Radio Monte Carlo.**
John Mortimer *Clinging to the Wreckage*, ch. 7 (1982). 'The House' is Christ Church College.

13 **There is always, in exclusively academic towns such as Cambridge, a detachment of camp-followers and dreamers and has-beens which, while not enjoying any recognized status within the University, closely rivals the official student body as to size, social ambition and intellectual curiosity.**
Howard Jacobson *Redback*, ch. 5 (1986)

14 **College is a storehouse of learning because so little is taken away.**
Anon. *And I Quote*, 'Colleges and Universities', ed. Ashton Applewhite and others (1992)

15 **HANNAH: He's at Oxford, technically.**
BERNARD: Yes, I met him. Brideshead Regurgitated.
Tom Stoppard *Arcadia*, act 1, sc. 1 (1993)

16 Worcester, like most colleges, does not admit dogs. The Dean's dog, Flint, has thus been officially declared a cat by the Governing Body.

Anon. From the Oxford University magazine *Isis*, quoted in *A Gentleman Publisher's Commonplace Book*, 'Core', by John G. Murray (1996)

17 [Of Oxford] Looking back, I have an idea that's what made the place so agreeable: everyone was coming on like Tolstoy or King Arthur because they hadn't learnt to be frightened yet.

Robert Robinson *Skip all That*, 'Going to the Mat with Edith' (1996)

Academics and Academic Disciplines

1 There is nothing so absurd but some philosopher has said it.

Cicero *De Divinatione*, bk 2, sect. 58 (c. 44 BC)

2 [Of historians] What harvest, however, accrues? What crop from the land you/ have tilled?

Juvenal Satire 7, line 103 (c.AD 121), *The Satires*, trans. and ed. Niall Rudd (1994)

3 . . . he that increaseth knowledge increaseth sorrow.

Ecclesiastes 1:18, the Bible, Authorized Version (1611)

4 Whosoever, in writing a modern history, shall follow truth too near the heels, it may happily strike out his teeth.

Alexander Pope *The History of the World*, Preface (1714)

5 Philosophy! The lumber of the schools.

Jonathan Swift 'Ode to Sir W. Temple' (1692)

6 Philosophy's like medicine: lots of drugs, few remedies, and hardly any complete cures.

Nicolas-Sébastien Roch de Chamfort Written c. 1785, collected in *Chamfort: Reflections on Life, Love and Society*, 'Reflections and Anecdotes', ed. Douglas Parmee (2003)

7 Great abilities are not requisite for an historian . . . imagination is not required in any high degree.

Samuel Johnson *The Life of Samuel Johnson* by James Boswell, vol. 1 p. 424 (1791); in G. B. Hill's edition of 1887, rev. L. F. Powell (1934)

8 I know that two and two make four – & should be glad to prove it if I could – though I must say if by any sort of process I could convert 2 & 2 into *five* it would give me much greater pleasure.

Lord Byron Letter to Lady Melbourne of 18 October 1812, collected in *Letters and Journals*, vol. 2, *Famous in My Time (1810–1812)* ed. Leslie A. Marchand (1973). Mathematics, Byron wrote in the same letter, he must be content to admire 'from an incomprehensible distance'.

9 [Of history] The quarrels of popes and kings, with wars or pestilences, in every page; the men all so good for nothing, and hardly any women at all.

Jane Austen *Northanger Abbey*, ch. 14 (1818)

10 [Of political economists] Respectable Professors of the Dismal Science

Thomas Carlyle *Latter-day Pamphlets*, no. 1, 'The Present Time' (1850)

11 No real English gentleman, in his secret soul, was ever sorry for the death of a political economist: he is much more likely to be sorry for his life.

Walter Bagehot 'The First Edinburgh Reviewers', *National Review* 1855, collected in *The Complete Works of Walter Bagehot*, vol. 1, p. 324, ed. Norman St John-Stevas (1966–86). Bagehot himself was (among other things) a political economist.

12 As a philosopher, it's my business to tell other people the truth; but it's not their business to tell it to me.

George Bernard Shaw Charteris in *The Philanderer*, act 2 (1893)

13 But even men of the noblest possible moral character are extremely susceptible to the influence of the physical charms of others. Modern, no less than Ancient History, supplies us with many most painful

examples of what I refer to. If it were not so, indeed, History would be quite unreadable.

Oscar Wilde Gwendolen Fairfax in *The Importance of Being Earnest*, act 3 (1895)

14 It has been said that though God cannot alter the past, historians can; it is perhaps because they can be useful to Him in this respect that He tolerates their existence.

Samuel Butler *Erewhon Revisited*, ch. 14 (1901)

15 I was up till 4 this morning watching Stepney and Cantaur – both drunk – trying to cheat one another at poker; it was a very even match: for tho' Stepney was far more cunning, Cantaur was far less drunk. Such is the All Souls Day.

Raymond Asquith Letter to Mrs Horner of 3 November 1903, collected in *Raymond Asquith: Life and Letters* ed. John Jolliffe (1980). Asquith was a fellow of All Souls College, Oxford.

16 The atmosphere of Oxford is quite the chilliest and least human known to me; you see brains floating about like so many sea anemones, nor have they shape or colour.

Virginia Woolf Letter to Violet Dickinson of December 1907, collected in *Congenial Spirits: The Letters of Virginia Woolf* ed. Joanne Trautmann Banks (1989)

17 History is more or less bunk.

Henry Ford Quoted in the *Chicago Tribune* 25 May 1916. 'The only history that is worth a damn,' he elaborated, 'is the history we make today.'

18 The progress of philosophy consists not so much in solving the old problems and propounding new, as in finding a new and, if possible, a clearer expression of the identical problems that occupied the earliest philosophers.

Sir Walter Raleigh 'The Two Moralities', collected in *Laughter from a Cloud* (1923)

19 If economists could manage to get themselves thought of as humble, competent people on a level with dentists, that would be splendid.

John Maynard Keynes *Essays in Persuasion*, ch. 5 (1931)

20 Without Geography you would be quite lost.

W. C. Sellar and R. J. Yeatman *And Now All This*, pt 4 (1932)

21 I am what is called a *professor emeritus* – from the Latin *e*, 'out', and *meritus*, 'so he ought to be'.

Stephen Leacock *Here Are My Lectures*, ch. 14 (1938)

22 The average Ph.D. thesis is nothing but a transference of bones from one graveyard to another.

J. Frank Dobie *A Texan in England*, ch. 1 (1945)

23 No, he wouldn't be a don, not an English don at least. In Spain of course, it's quite different – dons are somebody there, I believe.

Nancy Mitford Lady Montdore in *Love in a Cold Climate*, ch. 10 (1949)

24 Objectively, our Common Room/ Is like a small Athenian State –/ Except for Lewis: he's all right/ But do you think he's *quite* first rate?

John Betjeman 'A Hike in the Downs', *John Betjeman: Collected Poems* (1958)

25 [Of Sir Richard Jebb, later Professor of Greek at Cambridge] What time he can spare from the adornment of his person he devotes to the neglect of his duties.

William Hepworth Thompson Quoted in *With Dearest Love to All*, ch. 6, by M. R. Bobbit (1960)

26 [Of Napoleon III] He was what I often think is a dangerous thing for a statesman to be – a student of history; and like most of those who study history, he learned from the mistakes of the past how to make new ones.

A. J. P. Taylor *Listener* 6 June 1963

27 If you were in university life you would be familiar with the phrase

'crushing teaching load' – i.e. six hours a week six months a year . . .

Philip Larkin Letter to Barbara Pym of 29 September 1963, collected in *Selected Letters of Philip Larkin (1940–85)* ed. Anthony Thwaite (1992)

28 History gets thicker as it approaches recent times.

A. J. P. Taylor Comment in the bibliography to his *English History 1914–45* (1965)

29 You are the wife of an academic: that means you are twice removed from the centre of events.

Tom Stoppard George to Dotty in *Jumpers*, act 1 (1972)

30 There's nothing colder than chemistry.

Anita Loos *Kiss Hollywood Goodbye*, ch. 21 (1974)

31 THUNDERTHIGHS: You will have a national philosophers' strike on your hands.
COMPUTER: And who exactly will that inconvenience?

Douglas Adams Thunderthighs, a representative of the Amalgamated Union of Philosophers, Sages, Luminaries and Other Professional Thinking Persons, is aggrieved at a computer being given the task of finding out the meaning of life – 'You let the machines get on with the adding up and we'll take care of the eternal verities, thank you very much.' *The Hitchhiker's Guide to the Galaxy* (BBC radio, episode 4, 1st series, 1978)

32 If you're studying geology which is all facts, as soon as you get out of school you forget it all, but if you study philosophy you remember just enough to screw you up for the rest of your life.

Steve Martin *A Wild and Crazy Guy*, 'Language' (LP, 1978)

33 A musicologist is a man who can read music but can't hear it.

Sir Thomas Beecham *Beecham Stories*, 'On Critics and Academics', ed. Harold Atkins and Archie Newman (1978)

34 GIRL: Please, sir, I wish we lived in the olden days.
TEACHER: Why?

GIRL: Then there wouldn't be so much history to learn.

Anon. *The Ha Ha Bonk Book*, 'Jokes Not to Tell Your Teacher', ed. Janet and Allan Ahlberg (1982)

35 Economists: If they're so clever why aren't they rich?

Henry Root *Henry Root's World of Knowledge* (1982)

36 Sociology is a lot of waffle. It is using a lot of words to cover up rather obvious remarks.

Barbara Frances Wootton Observation made in 1984, collected in *Sayings of the Eighties* ed. Jeffrey Care (1989)

37 An economist is someone who sees something that works in practice and wonders if it would work in theory.

Ronald Reagan Remark to business leaders, 13 March 1987, quoted in *Ronald Reagan: The Wit and Wisdom of the Great Communicator*, 'People Are the Government', ed. Frederick J. Ryan Jr (1985). In 1988 Reagan also said: 'I'll tell you the story of a friend of mine who was asked to go to a costume ball a short time ago. He slapped some egg white on his face and went as a liberal economist.'

38 Anthropology is the science which tells us that people are the same the whole world over – except when they are different.

Nancy Banks-Smith *Guardian* 21 July 1988

39 I like history because it's so real, in a long-ago, can't-fucking-believe it, sort of way.

Eddie Izzard *Eddie Izzard: Definite Article*, 'The Romans' (CD, 1995)

40 Economics is extremely useful as a form of employment for economists.

J. K. Galbraith Quoted in *The Penguin Dictionary of Modern Humorous Quotations* ed. Fred Metcalf (2nd edn 2001)

41 To give an accurate and exhaustive account of the period would need a far less brilliant pen than mine.

Max Beerbohm Attributed

Intellect

1 Character without learning has made for excellence and ability more often than learning without character.

Cicero *Pro Archia*, pt 015 (*c.*62 BC), *Cicero: Defence Speeches* trans. D. H. Berry (2000)

2 To endeavour, all one's days, to fortify our minds with learning and philosophy, is to spend so much in armour that one has nothing left to defend.

William Shenstone *Works in Verse and Prose*, vol. 2, 'On Writing and Books' (1764)

3 The world is a comedy to those that think, a tragedy to those that feel.

Horace Walpole Letter to Anne, Countess of Upper Ossory, of 16 August 1776, *Correspondence*, vol. 32 (1973). Maureen Lipman in her book *How Was It For You?* commented: 'I *think* he [Walpole] may be right. I *feel* he could be wrong.'

4 Your intelligence often bears the same relation to your heart as the library of a château does to its owner.

Nicolas-Sébastien Roch de Chamfort Written *c.* 1785, collected in *Chamfort: Reflections on Life, Love and Society*, 'Reflections and Anecdotes', ed. Douglas Parmee (2003)

5 Mr Kremlin was distinguished for ignorance for he had only one idea – and that was wrong.

Benjamin Disraeli *Sybil*, bk 4, ch. 5 (1845)

6 Genius does what it must, and Talent does what it can.

Edward Bulwer-Lytton *Last Words of a Sensitive Second Rate Poet* (1868)

7 I cannot forgive a scholar his homeless despondency.

Ralph Waldo Emerson *Lectures and Biographical Sketches*, 'The Man of Letters' (1883)

8 The world must be rather a rough place for clever people. Ordinary folk dislike them, and as for themselves, they hate each other most cordially.

Jerome K. Jerome *The Idle Thoughts of an Idle Fellow*, 'On Cats and Dogs' (1889)

9 And the mind of the thoroughly well-informed man is a dreadful thing. It is like a bric-a-brac shop, all monsters and dust, with everything priced above its proper value.

Oscar Wilde Lord Henry Wotton in *The Picture of Dorian Gray*, ch. 1 (1891)

10 She is one of those dull, intellectual girls one meets all over the place. Girls who have got large minds and large feet.

Oscar Wilde Algernon Moncrieff in *The Importance of Being Earnest*, act 1 (1895)

11 Dr Chasuble is a most learned man. He has never written a single book, so you can imagine how much he knows.

Cecily Cardew in ibid., act 3

12 The older we grow the greater becomes our wonder at how much ignorance one can contain without bursting one's clothes.

Mark Twain Address 2 February 1901, collected as 'University Settlement Society' in *Mark Twain: Speeches* ed. Shelley Fisher Fishkin (1996)

13 The very best brains in the world take one a very little way if one has not the will to use them; the worst will take one the whole way, if one has.

Raymond Asquith Letter to Mrs A. L. Smith of 28 March 1902, collected in *Raymond Asquith: Life and Letters* ed. John Jolliffe (1980)

14 The dullard's envy of brilliant men is always assuaged by the suspicion that they will come to a bad end.

Max Beerbohm *Zuleika Dobson*, ch. 1 (1911)

15 I have lived over seventy years. I had enough to eat. I enjoyed many things – the comradeship of my wife, my children, the sunsets. I watched the plants grow in the springtime. Now and then the grasp of a friendly hand was mine. Once or twice I met a human being who almost understood me.

Sigmund Freud Quoted in *Glimpses of the Great* (1930) by George Sylvester Viereck.

Freud was suffering from cancer of the jaw; during the interview he spoke of his concern at the growth of anti-Semitism in Germany and Austria. Viereck noted: 'The few years intervening between my last visit and the present had multiplied the wrinkles on his forehead.'

16 **The intelligent are to the intelligentsia what a gentleman is to a gent.**
Stanley Baldwin Quoted in *Stanley Baldwin*, ch. 13, by G. M. Young (1952). Baldwin was apparently 'fond' of saying this.

17 **BLUEBOTTLE: What time is it Eccles?**
ECCLES: Just a minute, I got it written down on this piece of paper.
Spike Milligan *The Goon Show*, 'The Mysterious Punch-up-the-Conker', first broadcast 7 February 1957. The two are working 'in the ground-floor attic' of a clock-repairer's. Eccles explains: 'A nice man wrote the time down for me this morning.'

18 **Is Moby Dick the whale or the man?**
Harold Ross Quoted in *The Years with Ross*, ch. 4, by James Thurber (1959). In a diary entry of 3 January 1940 H. L. Mencken reported Thurber as stating that Ross had just three books: 'One is Mark Twain's *Life on the Mississippi*; the second is a book by a man called Spencer, falsely assumed by Ross to be Herbert Spencer, and the third is a treatise on the migration of eels.' When Dorothy Parker took Ross to see *The Cherry Orchard* he exclaimed: 'Say, this is quite a play!' He'd never heard of it before.

19 **I theenk these must be the intellectuals – nobody stripped.**
George Burns Burns overheard 'the Italian wife of a famous movie star' make this remark at one of his characteristically restrained show business parties of the 1950s. Quoted in *All My Best Friends*, ch. 6 (1989)

20 **To the man in the street, who, I'm sorry to say,/ Is a keen observer of life,/ The word 'Intellectual' suggests straight away/ A man who's untrue to his wife.**
W. H. Auden *Collected Shorter Poems, 1927–1957* (1966)

21 **Though intelligence is powerless to modify character, it is a dab hand at finding euphemisms for its weaknesses.**
Quentin Crisp *The Naked Civil Servant*, ch. 29 (1968)

22 **The nation has been told that Britain and Argentina are not at war, we are at conflict./ I am reading *Scoop* by a woman called Evelyn Waugh.**
Sue Townsend Journal entry for 6 April 1982, *The Secret Diary of Adrian Mole Aged 13¾* (1982). Evelyn Waugh's first marriage was to a woman also called Evelyn. They were known as Hevelyn and Shevelyn.

23 **An amusing anecdote is told of a meeting between [Jorge Luis] Borges and Anthony Burgess in 1972. Though both these polyglots could speak each other's language better than a native, they found it more agreeable on this occasion to converse in ancient Norse.**
Henry Root *Henry Root's World of Knowledge* (1982)

24 **Not many people know that.**
Michael Caine Caine's catchphrase, and the title of his almanac of amazing information (1984). He tends to append the remark after quoting from the *Guinness Book of Records* (a habit of his).

25 **In a bookshop in Ilkley [Yorkshire] – assistant: Is that *Geoffrey* Chaucer?**
Alan Bennett Diary entry for 21 December 1987, *Writing Home: Diaries 1980–1990* (1994)

26 **Now, let me correct you on a couple of things, okay? Aristotle was not Belgian. The central message of Buddhism is not every man for himself.**
John Cleese and Charles Crichton Wanda Gerschwitz (Jamie Lee Curtis) to Otto (Kevin Kline) in *A Fish Called Wanda* (film, 1988, directed by Charles Crichton)

27 **While I am an intellectual (indeed almost a genius), at the same time I am not very clever and so need to study harder than everyone else.**
Sue Townsend *True Confessions of Adrian Albert Mole*, 'Mole on Lifestyle' (1989)

28 In my sex fantasy, no one ever loves me for my mind.
Nora Ephron Quoted in *Women's Wit and Wisdom* (1991)

29 If ignorance is bliss, why aren't more people happy?
Anon. *And I Quote*, 'Ignorance and Stupidity', ed. Ashton Applewhite and others (1992)

Cultural Appreciation and Philistinism

1 O, had I but followed the arts!
William Shakespeare Sir Andrew Aguecheek in *Twelfth Night*, act 1, sc. 3 (1599)

2 Philistinism! – We have not the expression in English. Perhaps we have not the word because we have so much of the thing.
Matthew Arnold *Essays in Criticism*, 1st series, 'Heinrich Heine' (1865)

3 There are two ways of disliking art, Ernest. One is to dislike it. The other is to like it rationally.
Oscar Wilde 'Intentions', *The Critic as Artist*, pt 2 (1891). Gilbert is speaking.

4 There is such a thing as letting one's aesthetic sense override one's moral sense,' said Mrs Panstreppon. 'I believe you would have condoned the South Sea Bubble and the persecution of the Albigenses if they had been carried out in effective colour schemes.'
Saki *The Toys of Peace*, 'Hyacinth' (1919)

5 So Mr Bartlett did not know that I read books, which is quite a co-instance because he reads them too.
Anita Loos *Gentlemen Prefer Blondes*, ch. 2, 'April 14th' (1925)

6 What is a highbrow? He is a man who has found something more interesting than women.
Edgar Wallace *New York Times* 24 January 1932

7 But the one thing you shd. not do is to suppose that when something is wrong with the arts, it is wrong with the arts *only*.
Ezra Pound *Guide to Kulchur*, pt 1, ch. 5 (1938)

8 She said that all the sights in Rome were called after London cinemas.
Nancy Mitford *Pigeon Pie* (1940)

9 In Rome I saw the Forum and I saw the Colosseum where the gladiators died and the slaves were thrown to the lions. A vulgar American remarked to me: 'It looks like a mighty fine quarry.' They talk nasally.
Muriel Spark *The Prime of Miss Jean Brodie*, ch. 3 (1961)

10 It is mainly foreigners, not I, who daily fill the National Gallery. Passing the crowds jostling their way up its steps, it is phrases such as 'Aber, wo ist Elsa?' and 'Dépêche-toi, Marie!' that you hear, rather than 'We seem to have lost your mother.'
Arthur Marshall *Musings from Myrtlebank*, 'In the Picture' (1982)

11 I can't stand that part of the museum with all those old things. No, I go there for the tea.
Anon. Remark made to Peter Cook by a man he met in the street who repeatedly praised the tea served in the British Museum canteen. *Sunday Times*, 'A Life in the Day', 5 August 1984.

12 I went to a museum that had all the heads and arms missing from the statues in the other museums.
Steven Wright *I Have a Pony* (CD, 1986)

13 Well, I think Art and Culture *are* important. *Dead* important.
Sue Townsend *True Confessions of Adrian Albert Mole*, 'Adrian Mole on "Pirate Radio Four"' (1989). Mole continues: 'I therefore feel it incumbent on me to promote artisticness wherever I tread.'

14 Virtually every town around us is now equipped with a vast brown sign, fifteen feet high, headed HISTORIC MARKET TOWN. What a joy

to be an unhistoric market town,
and fall through the net!

Craig Brown *This Is Craig Brown*, 'England,
My England' (2003)

15 [Of America] **I come from a part of
the world where the Egg McMuffin
would be a heritage object.**

Bill Bryson Quoted in the *Daily Telegraph*
29 November 2003

Experts

1 **Too bad that all the people who
know how to run the country are
busy driving taxicabs and cutting
hair.**

George Burns *Life*, December 1979

2 **'Dinosaurs died out on a Tuesday,'
claim experts.**

Chris Morris and Armando Iannucci The
news anchor man Chris Morris in *On the
Hour* (radio series, 1991)

Historical Perspectives
Looking Forward

1 **Suffer and expect.**

George Herbert *Outlandish Proverbs*, no. 702
(1640)

2 **'We are always doing,' says he,
'something for posterity, but I
would fain see posterity do something for us.'**

Joseph Addison *The Spectator* 20 August 1714

3 **The best way to suppose what may
come, is to remember what is past.**

George Savile, 1st Marquess of Halifax *Political, Moral, and Miscellaneous Thoughts and
Reflections*, 'Miscellaneous: Experience' (1750)

4 **The rule is, jam tomorrow and jam
yesterday – but never jam *to-day*.**

Lewis Carroll *Through the Looking Glass*, ch. 5
(1872)

5 **Future, n.: that period of time in
which our affairs prosper, our**

friends are true and happiness is
assured.

Ambrose Bierce *The Devil's Dictionary* (compiled 1886–1906)

6 **Aunt Aida believed that she was terribly psychic. She had warnings, pre-
monitions, and 'feelings'. They
were invariably intimations of
approaching misfortune, sickness,
or death. She never had a premon-
ition that everything was going to
be all right.**

James Thurber *The Middle-Aged Man on the
Flying Trapeze*, 'A Portrait of Aunt Aida'
(1935)

7 **Prophet: Anyone who says that anything will happen.**

Beachcomber *Beachcomber: The Works of
J. B. Morton*, 'A Dictionary for Today', ed.
Richard Ingrams (1974)

8 **Well, it's odd. Heat goes cold. It's a
one-way street. Your tea will end up
at room temperature. What's happening to your tea is happening to
everything everywhere. The sun
and the stars. It'll take a while but
we're all going to end up at room
temperature.**

Tom Stoppard Valentine Coverly in *Arcadia*,
act 2, sc. 7 (1993)

9 **'Always expect the unexpected.' Or
so they say. But if you expect it, it
ceases to be unexpected, thus preventing you from expecting it in
the first place. I think.**

Viz Viz – *The Full Toss (A Corking Compilation
of Issues 70 to 75)* (1997). Purported letter
from a reader.

10 **I don't make predictions, and I
never will.**

Paul Gascoigne Spoken in 1997, quoted in
The Book of Football Quotations, 'Philosophers United', ed. Phil Shaw (1999)

11 **No one called them the middle ages
at the time because the ages afterwards hadn't happened.**

Anon. *The Little Book of Mornington Crescent*, 'Mornington Crescent: A History of the
Game' (2000). This may be a little book, but
it is by at least six authors, all connected

with the BBC radio panel game *I'm Sorry I Haven't a Clue.*

12 **The future ain't what it used to be.**
Yogi Berra Attributed

Looking Back

1 **What all the wise men promised has not happened, and what all the damned fools said would happen has come to pass.**
Lord Melbourne Of the passage of the Catholic Emancipation Act in 1829. Quoted in *Lord Melbourne*, ch. 9, by H. Dunckley (1890). Melbourne supported Catholic emancipation.

2 **'Those darling bygone times, Mr Carker,' said Cleopatra, 'with their delicious fortresses, and their dear old dungeons, and their delightful places of torture, and their romantic vengeances, and their picturesque assaults and sieges, and everything that makes life truly charming! How dreadfully we have degenerated!'**
Charles Dickens Dombey and Son, ch. 27 (1847–8)

3 **It takes a great deal of history to produce a little literature.**
Henry James *Hawthorne*, ch. 1 (1879)

4 **I believe they went out, like all good things, with the Stuarts.**
Benjamin Disraeli *Endymion*, ch. 99 (1880). It is the passing of 'a pottle of strawberries' that is being lamented, by Imogene.

5 **The past is the only dead thing that smells sweet,/ The only sweet thing that is not also fleet.**
Edward Thomas 'Early One Morning' (1916)

6 **It seemed like a good idea at the time.**
Anon. Dates possibly from the film *The Last Flight* (1931), in which its purpose is to explain an American airman's fatal decision to leap into the ring during a bullfight. Quoted in *Cassell's Dictionary of Catchphrases* ed. Nigel Rees (1995).

7 **Things Ain't What They Used to Be**
Ted Persons Song title (1941)

8 **History started badly and hav been getting steadily worse.**
Ronald Searle and Geoffrey Willans *Down With Skool!*, ch. 4, 'Lessons and How to Avoid Them' (1958)

9 **Let us honour if we can/ The vertical man,/ Though we value none/ But the horizontal one.**
W. H. Auden 'Shorts, 1929–31', *W. H. Auden: Collected Poems* ed. Edward Mendelson (1976)

10 **The Past Sure Is Tense**
Captain Beefheart Song title (1982)

11 **I refuse to use the word 'nostalgic'. Nostalgia sounds like neuralgia, and it is a smart new word smacking of psychological slang.**
John Betjeman Quoted by his daughter Candida Lycett-Green in her commentary on *Recollections from the BBC Archives* (cassette, 1998)

12 **We mustn't pre-judge the past.**
Willie Whitelaw Attributed. Quoted in *The Times* 2 July 1999.

13 **We've all passed a lot of water since then.**
Sam Goldwyn Quoted in *Halliwell's Who's Who in the Movies* ed. John Walker (2nd edn 2001)

Particular Eras

1 **One had as good be out of the world, as out of the fashion.**
Colley Cibber *Love's Last Shift*, act 2 (1696)

2 **We live in stirring times – tea stirring times.**
Christopher Isherwood Arthur Norris in *Mr Norris Changes Trains*, ch. 2 (1935). The times are the 1930s.

3 **You don't dictate to a girl now, you use a recording apparatus; no one faints anymore, they have blackouts; in Geneva you don't kill someone by cutting his throat, you blow a poisoned dart through a tube and *zing* you've got him.**
Henry Green *Now Dig This: The Unspeakable Writings of Terry Southern (1950–95),*

'Writers at Work: Henry Green', ed. Nile Southern and Josh Alan Friedman (2001). Said by Green in 1958.

4 **Britain today is suffering from galloping obsolescence.**

Tony Benn Speech 31 January 1963

5 **Dan, these are post-modern times. What do you think this is, *the past*?**

David Mamet Bernard in *Sexual Perversity in Chicago* (1974)

6 **I said to my friend Gore [Vidal], 'I slept through the sixties,' and he said, 'You didn't miss a thing.'**

Gore Vidal *New York Review of Books* 5 February 1976, collected in *The Essential Gore Vidal*, 'Some Memories of the Glorious Bird and an Earlier Self ', ed. Fred Kaplan (1999)

7 **If there's one word that sums up everything that's gone wrong since the War, it's Workshop.**

Kingsley Amis *Jake's Thing*, ch. 14 (1979). In his stand-up shows of the 1990s, Alexei Sayle would sometimes remark: 'Anyone who uses the word "workshop" outside the context of light engineering is a TWAT.'

8 **[One of two old ladies discussing the introduction of decimalization] I think they should have waited until all the old people were dead.**

Anon. Overheard remark quoted in *Word of Mouth*, 'Eavesdroppings', ed. Nigel Rees (1983)

9 **The fifties were ten years of foreplay.**

Germaine Greer *The Late Clive James*, Channel 4, 1984

10 **It's hard for me to get used to these changing times. I can remember when the air was clean and the sex was dirty.**

George Burns *And I Quote*, 'Change', ed. Ashton Applewhite and others (1992)

11 **With children of pre-school age, skirts and long hair are no guide to sex, for both boys and girls were dressed in the same way throughout Edwardian times. The sweet little girl on Great-Grandmother's lap may very well be grandfather.**

Robert Pols *Dating Old Photographs*, 'Dating Early Photographs' (1992)

12 **A TV researcher asked me what I made of Cool Britannia. I told him that to me it meant old people with hypothermia.**

Tony Benn *The Times*, 'Quotes of the Week', 3 October 1998

13 **What can I tell you? It was the Seventies: the joke decade.**

Martin Amis *Experience*, p. 22 (2000)

14 **We are living in an age of mass loquacity.**

Martin Amis *The Times*, 'Quotes of the Week', 13 May 2000

15 **3 May 1979 . . . Coffee is instant. Bread is sliced. Weather is rainy. Car, for Charlie Buck, is a plum-coloured 1973 Triumph Toledo with a starter motor that is always jamming.**

Tim Lott *Rumours of a Hurricane*, ch. 1 (2002)

16 **The late Lionel Bart, composer of *Oliver!*, once told me that he'd done so many drugs in the Seventies he had no memory of the decade at all. As far as he could pin it down, he went to a party in November 1969 and woke up around February 1980. Lucky fellow.**

Mark Steyn *Spectator* 13 March 2004

Science and Technology

Particular Inventions

1 **[Of steam locomotives] I see no reason to suppose that these machines will ever force themselves into general use.**

Duke of Wellington Quoted in *Livres sans nom* (Books without a Name; 1930), collected in *Geoffrey Madan's Notebooks*, ed. J. A. Gere and John Sparrow (1981). In 1830 the Duke attended the opening of the Liverpool to Manchester railway, commonly thought of as the first proper full-scale public railway. He did not enjoy the experience, and saw his cabinet colleague William Huskisson run down by Stephenson's engine the *Rocket*.

2 It's better to be shouted at in English (which is the effect a typed letter always has on me) than to be mumbled at in Chinese, which is what some men write, when they take their pen in their hands.

Rudyard Kipling Letter to Robert Barr of 1 July 1894, *The Letters of Rudyard Kipling*, vol. 2, *1890–99*, ed. Thomas Pinney (1990)

3 [Of the principles of aviation] The airplane stays up because it doesn't have the time to fall.

Orville Wright Attributed

4 The chief point about the gramophone performance was the intense and simple pleasure of the people in it. The two men bent over the instrument smiling as they might have done to a baby that was crooning.

Arnold Bennett Entry for 18 July 1910, *The Journals of Arnold Bennett 1896–1910* ed. Newman Flower (1952)

5 That triumph of the deaf and dumb, the cinematograph.

D. H. Lawrence *Twilight in Italy*, ch. 1 (1916)

6 the typewriter to me has always been a mustery£? And even now that I have gained a perfect mastery over the machine in gront of me i npt the faintest idea hoW it workss%

A. P. Herbert 'A Criminal Type', *Punch* 20 July 1920, collected in *Look Back and Laugh*, 'The Twenties' (1960)

7 [Of a safety razor] A week ago he had bought the thing in a fit of enterprise, and now he shaved in five minutes where before he had taken twenty . . . Calculation revealed to him the fact that in his fifty-five years, having begun to shave at eighteen, he had wasted three thousand three hundred and forty days – or between four and five months – by his neglect of this admirable invention.

John Buchan *Huntingtower*, ch. 1 (1922)

8 The telephone has become as great a boon to bores as the movies are to morons.

H. L. Mencken *Chicago Tribune* 10 April 1927, repr. in *The Penguin Book of Columnists* ed. Christopher Silvester (1997)

9 None of us can ever have as many virtues as the fountain pen, or half its cussedness; but we can try.

Mark Twain *Notebook*, ch. 24 (1935)

10 I've given up the typewriter. I couldn't use it and the noise disgusted me.

Evelyn Waugh Letter to Laura Herbert of 24 August 1935, collected in *The Letters of Evelyn Waugh* ed. Mark Amory (1980)

11 Dictators have only become possible through the invention of the microphone.

Sir Thomas Inskip *Observer*, 'Sayings of the Week', 18 October 1936, collected in *The Observer Sayings of the Week* ed. Valerie Ferguson (1978)

12 I always telephone with my left ear. I could no more telephone with my right ear than I could use a fork in my right hand.

A. P. Herbert *Sip! Swallow!* ch. 21 (1937)

13 Well, if I called the wrong number, why did you answer the phone?

James Thurber Cartoon caption in the *New Yorker* 5 June 1937

14 The thing about hammocks is how uncomfy they are, and the least movement turns one over.

Joyce Grenfell Letter to Virginia Graham of 31 May 1946, collected in *Joyce and Ginnie: The Letters of Joyce Grenfell and Virginia Graham* ed. Janie Hampton (1997)

15 Sirs, I have tested your machine. It adds a new terror to life and makes death a long-felt want.

Herbert Beerbohm Tree Response to a request from a gramophone company for an endorsement, quoted in *Beerbohm Tree*, ch. 19, by Hesketh Pearson (1956)

16 [Of hi-fi] High-frequency range/ Complete with autochange/ All the sharpest notes neither high nor flat/ The ear can't hear as high as

that/ Still I ought to please any passing bat.

Michael Flanders and Donald Swann 'Song of Reproduction', *At the Drop of a Hat* (LP, 1957)

17 String/ Is a very important thing./ Rope is thicker,/ But string,/ Is quicker.

Spike Milligan *Silly Verse for Kids*, 'String' (1963)

18 We don't care. We don't have to. We're the phone company.

Dan Rowan and Dick Martin Ernestine the phone operator (Lily Tomlin) in *Rowan and Martin's Laugh-In* (US TV comedy, shown on BBC TV 1968–71)

19 In modern furniture you find it [the through-leaves feeling] in the most through-leaves form of all: the drawers of a steel filing cabinet which run smoothly on ball bearings. How readily, and how silkily they slide in and out.

Vita Sackville-West From a recording included in 'A Sense of the Past', a radio programme broadcast on 23 August 1968 as part of the *Scenes That Are Brightest* series. 'Through-leaves' was a family phrase derived from the pleasure of walking through fallen leaves. Sackville-West also said: 'It is very through-leaves to run a stick along iron railings.'

20 I could still by telephone pan the suburbs for the last few nuggets of conviviality.

Quentin Crisp Of his recently installed telephone in the 1930s. *The Naked Civil Servant*, ch. 15 (1968).

21 Good hold buttons are hold buttons that hold one silently. Bad hold buttons are hold buttons that hold one musically. When I hold I want to hold silently. That is the way it was meant to be, for that is what God was talking about when he said, 'Forever hold your peace.'

Fran Lebowitz *Metropolitan Life*, 'The Sound of Music: Enough Already' (1978)

22 There are of course many problems connected with life, of which some of the most popular are 'Why are

people born, why do they die, and why do they spend so much of the intervening time wearing digital watches?'

Douglas Adams The Voice of the Book in *The Hitchhiker's Guide to the Galaxy* (BBC Radio series, programme 3, 1st series, 1978)

23 Americans have invented many undesirable things,/ The most notable being mattresses with inner springs/ Developed on the principle that beds should be pliant,/ Mattresses of today are self-reliant./ They not only conform to the shape of *you*/ but to the shape of a couple of other people, too.

E. B. White Collected in *Poems and Sketches of E. B. White* (1981)

24 Completely self-powered, ecologically sound and complying with all noise abatement requirements, carbon paper may well come back into its own as early as 1989.

Miles Kington *Moreover*, 'Dithering Heights' (1982)

25 Staples: As paper fasteners these are more trouble for the recipient than paper-clips but easier for the sender. As ticket fasteners on drycleaned garments they are much more trouble than safety-pins at the receiving end and not that much easier for the people at the shop, but enough to make them worthwhile.

Kingsley Amis *Spectator* 19 October 1985, collected in *The Wit of the Spectator* ed. Christopher Howse (1989)

26 Lavatory bowls: The old design with a steep inside enabled a reasonably careful gentleman to urinate without spilling a drop. The new (newish) one makes it almost impossible not to bounce a couple on to the floor. But it is *new*.

Ibid.

27 The phone is hysterical,/ holding its hands/ over its ears. Screaming.

Craig Raine '1932: Suicide', *History: The Home Movie* (1994). Raine also describes a phone in *A Martian Sends a Postcard Home* (1979): 'In homes, a haunted apparatus sleeps,/ that snores when you pick it up.'

28 **The invention of printing, swiftly followed as it was by the invention of misprints . . .**

Mat Coward *Cannibal Victims Speak Out! And Other Astonishing Press Cuttings*, Introduction, ed. Mat Coward (1995)

29 **I would like to throw an egg into an electric fan.**

Joyce Grenfell When asked her ultimate ambition. Attributed. Quoted in *Collins Dictionary of Quotations* ed. A. Norman Jeffares and Martin Gray (1995).

30 **If you're going to say anything filthy, please speak *clearly* after the tone.**

Viv Stanshall Message on the Stanshall answer machine, quoted in the *Observer* 23 April 1995. Another said he couldn't come to the phone because he was too busy filling in the Channel Tunnel.

31 **[Of the 1930s] Telephones were to be found in some houses, but they were icons, a ritual presence, used mostly in times of crisis.**

Robert Robinson *Skip All That*, 'Hearing the Last of Captain Ferguson' (1996)

32 **Glue CDs together back-to-back. Play one side, then flip it over and play the other. Just like your old vinyl records.**

Viz 'Top Tips', *Viz – The Full Toss (A Corking Compilation of Issues 70 to 75)* (1997)

33 **Remember when cups came out? . . . Oh, the excitement!**

Harry Hill Line used on his national tour of 1997

34 **After a couple of encounters with the Belgian Tourist Board answering-machine my considered opinion was that they would be better off replacing the whole costly system with a simple taped message saying: 'Thank you for telephoning the Belgian Tourist Board. This call has cost you £3.75. Now sod off.'**

Harry Pearson *A Tall Man in a Low Land*, ch. 1 (1998)

35 **If the Nobel Prize was awarded by a woman, it would go to the inventor of the dimmer switch.**

Kathy Lette Quoted in *Women's Wicked Wit* ed. Michelle Lovric (2000)

36 **Dear Sir, I am in possession of a thin circular disc of what seems to be shellac, bearing faint concentric striations and a label reading 'Down Mexico Way with Dame Clara Butt'. Is this a record?**

Kenneth Tynan *The Diaries of Kenneth Tynan* ed. John Lahr (2000)

37 **Now we have the World Wide Web (the only thing I know of whose shortened form – www – takes three times longer to say than what it's short for).**

Douglas Adams *The Salmon of Doubt*, 'The Universe', 'Frank the Vandal' (2002). 'W' is the only non-monosyllable in the English alphabet. In his novel *Yellow Dog* (2003) Martin Amis wrote: 'Scrapping the supposed abbreviation, which has human beings gabbling out nine syllables, and replacing it with three other syllables chosen at random . . . would save global business time half a decade per day . . .'

38 **There's something about the physical thing of the needle in the groove, it's like sex and it's a contact sport.**

Bono Interview in *Mojo* magazine, April 2002. Bono is also quoted as saying: 'I think the digital recordings have a personality but it's the personality of Formica.'

39 **Hell is not other people: hell is trying to get through to other people while listening to seven minutes of Vivaldi played on pan pipes.**

Allison Pearson *I Don't Know How She Does It*, ch. 4 (2002)

40 **London hasn't had any personality to speak of since the tube system, like some mighty course of electroconvulsive therapy, linked node to neighbouring node and shorted them out with hundreds of thousands of volts.**

Will Self *Dr Mukti and Other Tales of Woe*, 'Conversations with Ord' (2004)

Science in General

1 In everything that relates to *science*, I am a whole encyclopaedia behind the rest of the world.

Charles Lamb *The Essays of Elia*, 'The Old and the New Schoolmaster' (1823)

2 A good book about chemistry is as entertaining as a romance.

Anon. Quoted in *Table Talk*, 'Chemistry', by Leigh Hunt (1851). Hunt adds: 'Indeed, a great deal of romance, in every sense of the term, has always been mixed up with chemistry.'

3 The pursuit of science leads only to the insoluble.

Benjamin Disraeli Cardinal Grandison in *Lothair*, ch. 17 (1870)

4 Science is for those who learn; poetry, for those who know.

Joseph Roux *Meditations of a Parish Priest*, pt 1, no. 71 (1886)

5 Science in the modern world has many uses; its chief use, however, is to provide long words to cover the errors of the rich.

G. K. Chesterton *Heretics, Celts and Celto-philes* (1905)

6 [Of scientific terminology] This is the Scylla's cave which men of science are preparing for themselves to be able to pounce out upon us from it, and into which we cannot penetrate.

Samuel Butler *Selections from the Note-Books of Samuel Butler* ed. A. P. Bartholomew (1930)

7 Scientists: There are two classes, those who want to know and do not care whether others think they know or not, and those who do not much care about knowing but care very greatly about being reputed as knowing.

Ibid., ch. 7

8 Science knows only one commandment – contribute to science.

Bertolt Brecht Andrea in *The Life of Galileo*, sc. 14 (1938)

9 Scientists are rarely to be counted among the fun people. Awkward at parties, shy with strangers, deficient in irony – they have had no choice but to turn their attention to the close study of everyday objects.

Fran Lebowitz *Metropolitan Life*, 'Science' (1978)

10 Poor little Tommy Jones/ We'll see him no more,/ For what he thought was H_2O/ Was H_2SO_4

Anon. *Curriculum Vitae*, ch. 2 (1992), by Muriel Spark

11 The big bang, black holes, and the primordial soup turn up every Tuesday in the Science section of the *New York Times*, and as a result my grasp of general relativity and quantum mechanics now equals Einstein's – Einstein Moomjy, that is, the rug seller.

Woody Allen *Sunday Telegraph* 4 January 2004

Technophobia

1 Photography is going to marry Miss Wireless, and heaven help everybody when they get married. Life will be very complicated.

Marcus Adams *Observer*, 'Sayings of the Week', 6 September 1925, collected in *The Observer Sayings of the Week* ed. Valerie Ferguson (1987)

2 Garbage in, garbage out.

Anon. Computing term from the 1960s, quoted in *Cassell's Dictionary of Catchphrases* ed. Nigel Rees (1995)

3 These verses may appear to some/ A teeny bit obscene/ I'm only writing them to test/ This fartarsing machine.

Noël Coward *Oh Dear, Collected Verse* ed. Graham Payne and Martin Tickner (1984). The machine was a typewriter, of which he had just cleaned 'each fucking letter with a pin'.

4 I bought some batteries but they weren't included.

Steven Wright *I have a Pony* (CD, 1986)

5 **Maybe one day we'll travel at the speed of light. They'll have to lose our luggage beforehand.**
Robin Williams *Robin Williams: Live at the Met* (video, 1987)

6 [Computerized voice on out-of-control monorail] **The lever you have pulled – brakes – is not in service. Please make a note of it.**
Matt Groening Homer Simpson, the monorail conductor, is attempting to avert disaster in *The Simpsons*, 'Marge vs the Monorail', first broadcast 14 January 1993

7 **The thing with high-tech is you always end up using scissors.**
David Hockney *Observer* 10 July 1994

8 **Archbishop@demon.net**
Anon. Email address offered to, and rejected by, the Archbishop of Wales. Quoted in *The Times* 19 June 1999.

9 **This information is handwritten in the interest of speeding up our customer service.**
Anon. *The Times*, 'Quotes of the Week', 5 January 2002, collected in *The Times Quotes of the Week* introduced by Philip Howard (2002)

10 [Of his ignorance of computer technology] **A mouse, to me, I put the cat on it.**
Keith Richards *Uncut* magazine, December 2002

11 **'Computers are like buses,' I said cleverly. 'You wait ages for them, then they crash.'**
Daren King Scott Spec in *Jim Giraffe*, 'Stretch Armlong' (2004)

12 **It is my vision that one day every man, woman and child in this country will have a 24-hour computer helpdesk that is not only available for 24 hours a day but is also helpful.**
Oliver Pritchett *Daily Telegraph* 11 February 2004

Architecture

1 **Believe me, that was a happy age, before the days of architects, before the age of builders.**
Seneca *Epistulae ad Lucilium* (Letters to Lucilius), epistle 90 (1st century AD)

2 **For which of you, intending to build a tower, sitteth down first and counteth the cost whether he have sufficient to finish it?**
St Luke, 14:28, the Bible, Authorized Version (1611)

3 **No architecture is so haughty as that which is simple.**
John Ruskin *The Stones of Venice*, vol. 2, ch. 6 (1851–3)

4 **Adrian . . . also built a tremendous wall. This wall, indeed, cost so much that he never got over it.**
O. P. Q. Philander Smiff *Smiff's History of England*, 'The Romans in Britain' (1876)

5 **Sir Christopher Wren/ Said, 'I'm going to dine with some men./ If anybody calls/ Say I'm designing St Paul's.'**
Edmund Clerihew Bentley *Biography for Beginners*, 'Sir Christopher Wren' (1905)

6 **All architecture is great architecture after sunset; perhaps architecture is really a nocturnal art, like the art of fireworks.**
G. K. Chesterton *Tremendous Trifles*, 'The Giant' (1909)

7 **Come, friendly bombs, and fall on Slough!/ It isn't fit for humans now,/ There isn't grass to graze a cow./ Swarm over, Death!**
John Betjeman 'Slough', st. 1, publ. in *Continual Dew* (1937). Betjeman loathed the new towns of southern England, of which Slough was one.

8 **Fortunately a number of the old-fashioned pubs still survive in the less fashionable quarters, but the majority of them are doubtless doomed, and will shortly be replaced by tasteful erections in the**

By-Pass Elizabethan or Brewers'
Georgian styles.

Osbert Lancaster *Pillar to Post*, 'Public House
Classic' (1938)

9 I always say my west window has
the exuberance of Chaucer without,
happily, any of the concomitant vulgarity of the period.

Robert Hamer and John Dighton Bishop
D'Ascoyne (Alec Guinness) in *Kind Hearts and
Coronets* (film, 1949, screenplay by Robert
Hamer and John Dighton from the novel
Noblesse Oblige by Roy Horniman, directed
by Robert Hamer)

10 The physician can bury his mistakes, but the architect can only
advise his client to plant vines.

Frank Lloyd Wright *New York Times*
4 October 1953

11 You get no sun on this side at all.
What you could really do with is
your 'ouse turning right round.

Al Read Al Read as the know-all character in
The Al Read Show (BBC radio series),
25 November 1954

12 There is a French widow in every
room, affording delightful
prospects.

Gerard Hoffnung A sales pitch purportedly
contained in a letter from a Tyrolean landlord and read out by Hoffnung during a
speech to the Oxford Union on 4 December
1958. Collected in *Hoffnung – A Last Encore*
(cassette, 1973).

13 St Paul's indeed! Are they blind to
the beauties of Juxon House? . . . I
am glad to report that the Minister
of Housing is being approached
with a complaint that St Paul's is in
fact obscuring the new office
block's south west front!

Spike Milligan *A Book of Bits*, 'Pull down
St Paul's' (1965), collected in *The Essential
Spike Milligan* ed. Alex Games (2002). Juxon
House is an office block close to St Paul's.

14 I'm a lucky guy to live in my build-
ing/ They all need buildings to help
them along.

David Byrne 'Don't Worry about the Government', *Talking Heads 77* (LP, 1977)

15 Not a remarkable house by any
means – it was about thirty years
old, squattish, squarish, made of
brick, and had four windows set in
the front of a size and proportion
which more or less exactly failed to
please the eye.

Douglas Adams *The Hitchhiker's Guide to the
Galaxy*, ch. 1 (1979)

16 In my experience, if you have to
keep the lavatory door shut by
extending your left leg, it's modern
architecture.

Nancy Banks-Smith *Guardian* 20 February
1979

17 Every child goes to school in a building that looks like a duplicating-
machine replacement-parts world-
wide distribution warehouse.

Tom Wolfe *From Bauhaus to Our House*,
'Introduction' (1981)

18 What a pity they built the Castle so
near the airport.

Anon. Remark overheard at Windsor Castle,
quoted in *Word of Mouth*, 'Eavesdroppings'
ed. Nigel Rees (1983)

19 Most artists, or people who think of
themselves as such, have to get the
public to watch or listen before
they can sod it. The famous pile of
bricks at the Tate Gallery was
powerless against those who never
went to see it, and while still on the
shelf *Finnegans Wake* is impotent.
Architects are different. They have
the unique power of sodding the
consumer at a distance . . .

Kingsley Amis *Spectator* 19 October 1985, collected in *The Wit of the Spectator* ed. Christopher Howse (1989)

20 What I really dislike about buildings like the Pompidou Centre, and
Paris is choking on them, is that
they are just showing off. Here's
Richard Rogers saying to the world,
'Look, I put all the pipes on the *outside*. Am I cute enough to kiss?'

Bill Bryson *Neither Here Nor There*, ch. 4 (1991)

21 We used to have nimbys, but now I
am told that we have a newer, even
tougher generation known as

Bananas: Build Absolutely Nothing Anywhere Near Anything.

Charles, Prince of Wales *The Times* 27 February 1999. 'Nimby' stands for 'Not In My Backyard'.

22 Apparently, if you stand on the top of the Great Wall of China, you can see the moon.

Boothby Graffoe *No Particular Order*, BBC radio programme, 4 March 2004

4

Religion, Philosophy and Morality

Religion and Philosophy

Morality

Religion and Philosophy

Religion in General

1 We have just enough religion to make us hate, but not enough to make us love one another.

Jonathan Swift *Thoughts on Various Subjects* (1711)

2 There is a very good saying that if triangles were to make a god, they would make him three-sided.

Montesquieu *Lettres persanes* (Persian Letters), no. 59 (1721)

3 I am positive I have a soul; nor can all the books with which materialists have pestered the world ever convince me of the contrary.

Laurence Sterne *A Sentimental Journey through France and Italy*, 'Maria Moulines' (1766)

4 Things have come to a pretty pass when religion is allowed to invade the sphere of private life.

Lord Melbourne After hearing an evangelical sermon. Quoted in *Collections and Recollections* by G. W. E. Russell, ch. 6 (1898).

5 The exact number of the Brethren at any given time is always hard to calculate but it can be safely said that a figure of two would be exact; it is our proud claim that we are far more exclusive than our religious competitors.

Peter Cook *Tales of the Seductive Brethren*, a series introduced into *Private Eye* magazine by Peter Cook in 1964. Quoted in *Peter Cook: A Biography* by Harry Thompson, ch. 7 (1997).

6 'God is silent,' he was fond of saying, 'now if we can only get man to shut up.'

Woody Allen *Side Effects*, 'Remembering Needleman' (1980). Needleman is an imaginary philosopher whose theory was that 'Good and just behaviour is not only more moral, but could be done by phone.'

7 Never make a god of your religion.

Sir Arthur Helps Quoted in *Geoffrey Madan's*

Notebooks, 'Extracts and Summaries', ed. J. A. Gere and John Sparrow (1981)

8 **Persecution is when you're forced to join in other people's hymns.**
Howard Jacobson *Roots Schmoots*, ch. 1 (1993)

9 **He didn't love God, he just fancied him.**
Anon. Quoted in *Collins Dictionary of Quotations* ed. A. Norman Jeffares and Martin Gray (1995)

10 [Of the death of Princess Diana] **The cult of a year ago has dwindled and become, as religions tend to, the preserve of children, homosexuals and lonely housewives.**
A. N. Wilson *In the Psychiatrist's Chair* (BBC radio series), 13 September 1998

11 **Religion's okay as long as it doesn't get too lively.**
Captain Beefheart Quoted in *Captain Beefheart*, ch. 16, by Mike Barnes (2000). Beefheart is not religious, although he might have a soft spot for Catholicism, which he describes as 'the glam rock of religions'.

12 **Kindness is the keynote of my sort of – well, what can you call it?**
Robert Robinson *The Club*, ch. 11 (2000)

13 **God was unavailable for comment.**
Anon. *Q* magazine February 2004. Closing remark in an item about the Christian conversion of the 'shock rocker' Alice Cooper.

Particular Religions and Sects

1 **Take heed of *thinking*. The farther you go from the Church of Rome, the nearer you are to God.**
Sir Henry Wotton *Reliquiae Wottonianae: The Life of Sir Henry Wotton* by Izaak Walton (1651)

2 [Of Presbyterianism] **Not a religion for gentlemen.**
Charles II Quoted in *The History of My Own Times* by Gilbert Burnet, vol. 1, bk 2, ch. 2 (1724)

3 **When I mention religion, I mean the Christian religion; and not only the Christian religion, but the Protestant religion; and not only the Protestant religion, but the Church of England.**
Henry Fielding *Tom Jones*, bk 3, ch. 3 (1749). The speaker is the Rev. Thwackum, who 'was for doing justice, and leaving mercy to heaven'.

4 [Of Quakers] **The sedate, sober, silent, serious, sad-coloured sect.**
Thomas Hood *Comic Annual*, 'The Doves and the Crows' (1839)

5 **The Puritan hated bear-baiting, not because it gave pain to the bear, but because it gave pleasure to the spectators.**
Lord Macaulay *A History of England*, vol. 1, ch. 2 (1849)

6 **His Christianity was muscular.**
Benjamin Disraeli *Endymion*, ch. 14 (1880). This is Nigel Penruddock who, 'though a student and devoted to the holy profession for which he was destined, was also a sportsman'.

7 **The Pope, instead of attending to the welfare of the unfortunate people whom he governs, and saving his country from the reproach of being the worst governed state in Europe, is putting up prayers to Heaven for the conversion of England! He might as well come to London, and try to convert Mr Cobden to the corn-laws, or the railway companies to the old roads.**
Leigh Hunt *Table Talk*, 'England and the Pope' (1882). The Pope in question was Gregory XVI.

8 **Scratch the Christian and you find the pagan – spoiled.**
Israel Zangwill *Children of the Ghetto*, bk 2, ch. 6 (1892)

9 **If you are not quite sure about your ever having been christened, I must say I think it rather dangerous your venturing on it now.**
Oscar Wilde Algernon Moncrieff in *The Importance of Being Earnest*, act 3 (1895)

10 [Of Hinduism] **It's a good and gentle religion, but inconvenient.**
Mark Twain *Following the Equator*, ch. 49 (1897)

11 She was one of those people who regard the Church of England with patronizing affection, as if it were something that had grown up in the kitchen garden.

Saki *Reginald*, 'Reginald at the Theatre' (1904)

12 How odd/ Of God/ To choose/ The Jews.

William Norman Ewer *Week-End Book*, p. 117 (1924). In response, Cecil Browne wrote: 'But not so odd/ As those who choose/ A Jewish God,/ But spurn the Jews.' And Leo Rosten: 'Not odd/ of God./ Goyim/ Annoy 'im.'

13 If Christ were here now, there is one thing he would *not* be – a Christian.

Mark Twain *Notebook*, ch. 29 (1935)

14 Beware of the Anglo-Catholics – they're all sodomites with unpleasant accents.

Evelyn Waugh Advice on life at Oxford offered to Charles Ryder by his cousin Jasper. *Brideshead Revisited*, bk 1, ch. 1 (1945).

15 He is a Roman Catholic and I don't see how you can have to do with a man who can't think for himself.

Muriel Spark *The Prime of Miss Jean Brodie*, ch. 6 (1961)

16 It's hard to tell where the MCC ends and the Church of England begins.

J. B. Priestley Quoted in the *New Statesman* 20 July 1962

17 Do you know any *good* Christians?

Joanna Scott Moncrieff Question asked of Joyce Grenfell. Quoted in a letter of 4 September 1964 from Grenfell to Virginia Graham, collected in *Joyce and Ginnie: The Letters of Joyce Grenfell and Virginia Graham* ed. Janie Hampton (1997). Joanna Scott Moncrieff was then working in religious broadcasting for the BBC.

18 dago: any Catholic foreigner.

Beachcomber *Beachcomber: The Works of J. B. Morton*, 'A Dictionary for Today', ed. Richard Ingrams (1974)

19 I'll see him off the premises myself. The hounds are all fagged out from yesterday's Jehovah's Witnesses.

Viv Stanshall Sir Henry in *Sir Henry at Rawlinson End* (LP, 1978)

20 Anagrams of 'evangelicalism': 1. A call is given me/ 2. Sing me 'I've a call.'/ 3. Sell naive magic./ 4. All same vice, gin.

Geoffrey Madan *Geoffrey Madan's Notebooks*, 'Humorous and Memorable', ed. J. A. Gere and John Sparrow (1981)

21 Buddhism: It only works in a pleasant climate, of course.

Henry Root *Henry Root's World of Knowledge* (1982)

22 SCRACKLE: Yes, I have peculiar training methods because I am the current reigning Jehovah's Witness boxing champion.
INTERVIEWER: How do you differ from ordinary boxers?
SCRACKLE: We refrain from violence in the ring.

Spike Milligan Herbert Scrackle (Spike Milligan) in the comedy series *There's a Lot of It About* (1983), collected in *The Essential Spike Milligan* compiled by Alex Games (2002)

23 Time and again in these pages I have pointed out the extraordinarily high proportion of Scots Presbyterians and Calvinists . . . in the Ministry of Health, and the lying propaganda they feed to ministers and press about 'an epidemic of drunkenness'.

Auberon Waugh *Spectator* 14 July 1984

24 It makes you think that Jesus Christ is going to come back, but this time he's not going to look like Ted Nugent, he's going to look like Charles Bronson, and he's going to be pissed off.

Robin Williams *Robin Williams: Live at the Met* (video, 1987)

25 I find it ironic that people who are against sexual thoughts are generally those fundamentalist Christians who also believe you should be fruitful and multiply. It seems like they should *support* sexual thoughts, you know, perhaps even have a centerfold in the Bible.

Bill Hicks At the Vic Theatre, Chicago, November 1990. Quoted in the *Guardian* 14 February 2004.

26 Protestant women may take the pill. Roman Catholic women must keep taking *The Tablet*.

Irene Thomas *Guardian* 28 December 1990

27 Whether I actually believe doesn't really come into it as, to its credit, the Church of England has never particularly bothered itself whether its members are saved or not.

Alan Bennett *Telling Tales*, 'Unsaid Prayers' (2000)

28 Buddhists manage celibacy because they don't have whisky.

Billy Connolly Quoted in *Whisky Wit and Wisdom*, 'Drinking It', ed. Gavin D. Smith (2000)

29 Jesus is coming! Everybody look busy!

Anon. Quoted in *The Penguin Dictionary of Modern Humorous Quotations* ed. Fred Metcalf (2nd edn 2001)

30 If you're in Amish country and you see a man with his hand buried in a horse's ass, remember he's just a mechanic.

Robin Williams *Robin Williams Live on Broadway* (video, 2003)

Clergy and Contemplatives

1 If gold rust, what then will iron do?/ For if a priest be foul in who we trust/ No wonder that a common man should rust . . .

Geoffrey Chaucer *The Canterbury Tales* trans. from medieval to modern English by Nevill Coghill (1951)

2 [Of the clergy] Nothing can render them popular, but some degree of persecution.

Jonathan Swift *Thoughts on Religion* (1765)

3 It was said of one bishop that he'd been created to show how far the human skin can stretch.

Nicolas-Sébastien Roch de Chamfort Written c. 1785, collected in *Chamfort: Reflections on Life, Love and Society*, 'Reflections and Anecdotes', ed. Douglas Parmee (2003)

4 The minister kiss'd the fiddler's wife,/ An' couldna preach for thinkin' o't.

Robert Burns 'My Love She's but a Lassie Yet' (1790)

5 As I take my shoes from the shoemaker, and my coat from the tailor, so I take my religion from the priest.

Oliver Goldsmith Quoted in *The Life of Samuel Johnson* by James Boswell, vol. 2, p. 214 (1791); in G. B. Hill's edition of 1887, rev. L. F. Powell (1934)

6 This merriment of parsons is mighty offensive.

Samuel Johnson Ibid. Johnson made this observation 'by no means in whisper' while in the company of some vicars 'who thought they should appear to advantage by assuming the lax jollity of *men of the world*'.

7 The abbey of Rubygill stood in a picturesque valley, at a little distance from the western boundary of Sherwood Forest, in a spot which seemed adapted by nature to be the retreat of monastic mortification, being on the banks of a fine trout stream, and in the midst of woodland coverts abounding with excellent game.

Thomas Love Peacock *Maid Marian*, ch. 1 (1822)

8 There was an Irish lad,/ Who loved a cloistered nun,/ And it made him very sad,/ For what was to be done?/ He thought it a big shame,/ A most confounded sin,/ That she could not get out at all,/ And he could not get in.

Anon. 'Smalilou', *Oliver's Comic Songs* (1825?)

9 Damn it! Another bishop dead! I believe they die to vex me.

Lord Melbourne Attributed remark, quoted in *Lord M* by Lord David Cecil, ch. 4 (1954). Melbourne must have said this during the years in which he served as Prime Minister: 1834–41.

10 Of late years an abundant shower of curates has fallen upon the North of England.

Charlotte Brontë *Shirley*, ch. 1 (1849)

11 [Of bishops] **In general we observe that those become most eminent in the sheepfold who partake most eminently of the qualities of the wolf.**

Walter Bagehot 'Bishop Butler' in the *National Review* 1854, collected in *The Complete Works of Walter Bagehot*, vol. 1, p. 218, ed. Norman St John-Stevas (1966–86)

12 **Preach not because you have to say something, but because you have something to say.**

Richard Whately *Apophthegms* (1854)

13 **As the French say, there are three sexes – men, women, and clergymen.**

Sydney Smith *A Memoir of the Reverend Sydney Smith*, vol. 1, ch. 9, by Lady Holland (1855)

14 **I don't like bishops; I think there is no use in them.**

Benjamin Disraeli Lord St Aldegonde in *Lothair*, ch. 47 (1870)

15 **The average clergyman, in all countries and of all denominations, is a very bad reader. One would think he would at least learn how to read the Lord's Prayer, by-and-by, but it is not so. He races through it as if he thought the quicker he got it in the sooner it would be answered.**

Mark Twain *A Tramp Abroad*, ch. 36 (1880)

16 **A bishop keeps on saying at eighty what he was told to say at eighteen, and as a natural consequence he always looks absolutely delightful.**

Oscar Wilde Lord Henry Wotton in *The Picture of Dorian Gray*, ch. 1 (1891)

17 **Good in parts – like the curate's egg.**

Anon. From a *Punch* cartoon of 1895, reflecting the wimpishness of curates. A bishop observes: 'I'm afraid you've got a bad egg, Mr Jones', but the curate interjects: 'Oh no, my Lord, I assure you! Parts of it are excellent.' Quoted in *The Cassell Dictionary of Catchphrases* ed. Nigel Rees.

18 **I remember the average curate at home as being something between a eunuch and a snigger.**

Ronald Firbank *The Flower Beneath the Foot*, ch. 4 (1923)

19 **The Bishop of Stortford was talking to the local Master of Hounds about the difficulty he had in keeping his vicars off the incense.**

P. G. Wodehouse *Mr Mulliner Speaking*, 'Unpleasantness at Budleigh Court' (1929)

20 **The cat had that air of portly well-being which we associate with those who dwell in cathedral closes.**

P. G. Wodehouse *Mulliner Nights*, 'The Story of Webster' (1933)

21 **Evangelical vicar/ in want of a portable/ second-hand font/ would dispose/ for the same of a portrait/ in frame/ of the Bishop/ elect of Vermont.**

Ronald Knox Advertisement placed in a newspaper, quoted in *The Lure of the Limerick* by W. S. Baring-Gould, pt 1, ch. 5 (1959)

22 **Them bastards at the monastery let me down again.**

Harold Pinter Davies in *The Caretaker*, act 1 (1960). He has been to a monastery 'just the other side of Luton', in the hope of being given a pair of shoes.

23 **Two archbishops and the Bishop of Durham hold office 'by Divine Providence'; all others by 'Divine Permission'. Hensley Henson added that some bishops do so by Divine Inadvertence.**

Geoffrey Madan *Geoffrey Madan's Notebooks*, 'Beauty, Point and Charm', ed. J. A. Gere and John Sparrow (1981)

24 **Always remember, you can kiss a nun once, or even twice but you must never get into the habit.**

Les Dawson *The Malady Lingers On* 'The Malady Lingers On . . .' (1982).

25 **I had sometimes thought that if there were a single human being able to resist an invitation to appear on a chat show it might turn out to be the Archbishop of Canter-**

bury. But there he was on *Parkinson*.

Robert Robinson *The Dog Chairman*, 'Show Business' (1982)

26 [Of the Vatican] **All human life is here, but the Holy Ghost seems to be somewhere else.**

Anthony Burgess Review of a book about the Vatican, *Observer* 25 May 1986

27 **When I'm sitting I amuse myself by saying, 'Bollocks!' *sotto voce* to the Bishops.**

Lord Hailsham When sitting on the Woolsack in the House of Lords as Lord Chancellor, and feeling bored. Quoted in an interview with John Mortimer, collected in *Character Parts*, 'Bollocks to the Bench of Bishops' (1986).

28 [In response to a vicar who asked whether there was anything he would like his forthcoming sermon to be about] **Yes, about ten minutes.**

Duke of Wellington Attributed. Quoted in *Who Said What* ed. John Daintith and others (1988)

29 [Of Mother Teresa] **She looks like a concertina wrapped in a hankie.**

Jo Brand Line used in her live routine, *c.* 1994

Faith or Lack of It

1 [Of sceptics] **Truth, Sir, is a cow, that will yield such people no more milk, and so they are gone to milk the bull.**

Samuel Johnson *The Life of Samuel Johnson* by James Boswell, vol. 2, p. 444 (1791); in G. B. Hill's edition of 1887, rev. L. F. Powell (1934)

2 **It was here that I suspended my religious inquiries (aged seventeen).**

Edward Gibbon *Memoirs of My Life*, ch. 3 (1796)

3 **God will pardon me, it is His trade.**

Heinrich Heine Spoken on his deathbed, quoted in *Heinrich Heine*, ch. 5, by Alfred Meissner (1856). Compare the following, attributed to Catherine the Great: 'I shall be an autocrat: that's my trade. And the good Lord will forgive me: that's his.'

4 **Well now that we *have* seen each other, if you'll believe in me, I'll believe in you.**

Lewis Carroll The Unicorn to Alice in *Through the Looking-Glass*, ch. 7 (1872)

5 **Irreligion: The principal one of the great faiths of the world.**

Ambrose Bierce *The Devil's Dictionary* (compiled 1881–1906)

6 **No one can be an unbeliever nowadays. The Christian Apologists have left one nothing to disbelieve.**

Saki Lady Caroline in *The Unbearable Bassington*, ch. 13 (1912)

7 **Yet her conception of God was certainly not orthodox. She felt towards Him as she might have felt towards a glorified sanitary engineer; and in some of her speculations she seems hardly to distinguish between the Deity and the Drains.**

Lytton Strachey *Eminent Victorians*, 'Florence Nightingale' (1918)

8 **O God, for as much as without Thee/ We are not able to doubt thee,/ Help us all by Thy grace/ To convince the whole race/ It knows nothing whatever about Thee.**

Ronald Knox Quoted in *The Complete Limerick Book* ed. Langford Reed (1924)

9 **To put one's trust in God is only a longer way of saying that one will chance it.**

Samuel Butler *Selections from the Note-Books of Samuel Butler*, ch. 7, ed. A. T. Bartholomew (1930)

10 **Many people believe that they are attracted by God, or by Nature, when they are only repelled by man.**

William Ralph Inge *More Lay Thoughts of a Dean*, pt 4, ch. 1 (1931)

11 **He was an embittered atheist (the sort of atheist who does not so much disbelieve in God as personally dislike Him).**

George Orwell *Down and Out in Paris and London*, ch. 30 (1933)

12 It ain't necessarily so,/ It ain't necessarily so – / De t'ings that yo' li'ble/
To read in de Bible –/ It ain't necessarily so.

Ira Gershwin 'It Ain't Necessarily So' (song,
1935)

13 An atheist is a man who has no
invisible means of support.

John Buchan Quoted in *On Being a Real
Person*, ch. 10, by H. E. Fosdick (1943)

14 ESTRAGON: Let's go.
VLADIMIR: We can't.
ESTRAGON: Why not?
VLADIMIR: We're waiting for Godot.

Samuel Beckett *Waiting for Godot*, act 1
(1954)

15 I am still an atheist, thank God.

Luis Buñuel Quoted in *Le Monde*
16 December 1959

16 The Lord will provide, but to date
he was behind with his payments.

Spike Milligan *Puckoon*, ch. 2 (1963)

17 God can stand being told by Professor Ayer and Marghanita Laski
that He doesn't exist.

J. B. Priestley *Listener* 1 July 1965. Ayer and
Laski were well-known media sceptics of the
day.

18 Sex is the mysticism of material-
ism. We are to die in the spirit to be
reborn in the flesh, rather than the
other way around.

Malcolm Muggeridge *Tread Softly for You
Tread on My Jokes*, 'The Mysticism of Sex'
(1966)

19 Not only is there no God, but try getting a plumber at weekends.

Woody Allen *Getting Even*, 'My Philosophy'
(1971). Allen is an atheist. He also said, in his
book *Without Feathers* (1976): 'And how can I
believe in God when just last week I got my
tongue caught in the roller of an electric
typewriter?'

20 Socrates was a suicide – or so they
said. Christ was murdered. Nietzsche
went nuts. If there was someone out
there, He sure as hell didn't want
anybody to know about it.

Ibid., 'Mr Big'. Reflections of Kaiser Lupowitz,
a private eye, commissioned to locate God.

21 To ask 'Does God exist?' appears to
presuppose the existence of a God
who may not.

Tom Stoppard George in *Jumpers*, act 1 (1972)

22 The idea that He would take his
attention away from the universe
in order to give me a bicycle with
three speeds on it is just so unlikely
I can't go along with it.

John Updike *Sunday Times* 18 December 1977

23 I guess I wouldn't believe in anything if it weren't for my lucky
astrology mood watch.

Steve Martin *A Wild and Crazy Guy*,
'Religion' (LP, 1978)

24 Do I believe in God?/ I can't say No
and I can't say Yes/ To me it's anybody's guess.

Noël Coward 'Do I Believe?' *Collected Verse*,
ed. Graham Payn and Martin Tickner (1984)

25 I wouldn't put it past God to
arrange a virgin birth if He wanted,
but I very much doubt if He would.

David Jenkins *Church Times* 4 May 1984

26 I am a daylight atheist.

Brendan Behan Quoted by Rae Jeffs, publicist and assistant to Behan, in *Sacred Monsters*, 'Rousting in Dublin', by Daniel Farson
(1988)

27 Episcopal clergyman: 'I don't wear
my collar more than absolutely
necessary now in case I'm taken for
an atheist.'

Anon. *Bishop's Brew (An Anthology of Clerical
Humour)*, ch. 2, ed. Ronald Brown (1989)

28 Ever noticed how creationists look
really unevolved?

Bill Hicks Remark made on stage *c.* 1994

29 God and I have a great relationship,
but we both see other people.

Dolly Parton Quoted in *Women's Wicked Wit*
ed. Michelle Lovric (2000)

30 One of my objections to religion is
that it prevents the search for God.

Arthur C. Clarke *The Times* 6 January 2001

31 Believing in God's one thing, but I
get a wee bit bored of angels. It's a

wee bit in the aromatherapy field for me.

Billy Connolly *The Times*, 'Quotes of the Week', 12 January 2002

Worship

1 I did entertain myself with my perspective glass up and down the church, by which I had the great pleasure of seeing and gazing at a great many very fine women, and what with that and sleeping, I passed away the time till sermon was done.

Samuel Pepys Diary entry for 27 May 1667, *Everybody's Pepys* ed. Henry B. Wheatley (1926)

2 I should be glad to know, what offence it would give to tender consciences, if the house of God was made more comfortable, or less dangerous to the health of valetudinarians.

Tobias Smollett Letter from Matthew Bramble to Dr Lewis dated 4 July, *The Expedition of Humphry Clinker* (1771). He advocates that a church be 'well floored, wainscotted, warmed, and ventilated, and its area kept sacred from the pollution of the dead'.

3 I am afraid he has not been in the inside of a church for many years; but he never passes a church without pulling off his hat. This shows that he has good principles.

Samuel Johnson Speaking of Dr John Campbell. *The Life of Samuel Johnson* by James Boswell, vol. 1, p. 418 (1791); in G. B. Hill's edition of 1887, rev. L. F. Powell (1934).

4 A woman's preaching is like a dog's walking on his hinder legs. It is not done well; but you are surprised to find it done at all.

Ibid., vol. 1, p. 463

5 I remember a Methodist preacher who on perceiving a profane grin to the faces of part of his congregation – exclaimed 'no *hopes* for *them* as *laughs*' . . .

Lord Byron Letter to Augusta Leigh of 19 December 1816, collected in *Letters and Journals*, vol. 5, *So Late into the Night (1816–17)*, ed. Leslie A. Marchand (1976)

6 Religion's in the heart, not in the knees.

Douglas Jerrold *The Devil's Ducat*, act 1, sc. 2 (1830)

7 While I cannot be regarded as a pillar, I must be regarded as a buttress of the church, because I support it from the outside.

Lord Melbourne Attributed. As Prime Minister (1834–41), Melbourne made many frolicsome remarks on religion. According to David Cecil in his book *Lord M.* (1954), Melbourne 'seldom went to church', and when asked by the Archbishop of York to attend an evening service, having been to one earlier in the day he replied, 'No, my Lord, once is orthodox, twice is puritanical.' Melbourne favoured the Church of England, however, as being the 'least meddlesome'.

8 A melting sermon being preached in a country church, all fell a-weeping but one clown, who, being asked the reason of his obduracy, answered, 'Oh! I belong to another parish.'

Anon. *The New London Jest Book*, 'Choice Jests', no. 169, ed. W. C. Hazlitt (1871)

9 Tom turned in without the added vexation of prayers.

Mark Twain *The Adventures of Tom Sawyer*, ch. 3 (1876)

10 We did not over sleep at St Nicholas. The church bell began to ring at 4.30 in the morning, and from the length of time it continued to ring I judged that it takes a Swiss sinner a good while to get the invitation through his head.

Mark Twain *A Tramp Abroad*, ch. 36 (1880)

11 An attempt to warm St Paul's Cathedral Sydney Smith described as useless, saying that one might as well attempt to warm the county of Middlesex.

Sydney Smith *Bon-Mots of Sydney Smith and R. B Sheridan* ed. Walter Jerrold (1893)

12 It was a serious step, but he had been fortified with the experience

previously forced upon him at St James-the-Less, and in less than five months he had become one of the foremost sidesmen at St James-the-Least-of-All, Kennington Oval.

Sir Henry Howarth Bashford *Augustus Carp Esq., by Himself*, ch. 3 (1924). The sidesman is Carp's father.

13 *Hancock's Half Hour* or Church? Difficult decision.

Joyce Grenfell Letter to Virginia Graham of 19 August 1958, collected in *Joyce and Ginnie: The Letters of Joyce Grenfell and Virginia Graham* ed. Janie Hampton (1997)

14 As for the British churchman, he goes to church as he goes to the bathroom, with the minimum of fuss and with no explanation if he can help it.

Ronald Blythe *The Age of Illusion*, ch. 12 (1963)

15 Every week that passes, you can bet your life that, somewhere in this land, there's a first-class row bubbling up about what someone wants in and someone else wants out of a village church.

J. L. Carr *A Month in the Country*, p. 36 (1980)

16 Never read the Bible as if it means something. Or at any rate don't try and mean it. Nor prayers. The liturgy is best treated and read as if it's someone announcing the departure of trains.

Alan Bennett Diary entry for 30 June 1984, publ. in *Writing Home: Diaries 1980–1990* (1994). Bennett had been listening to a reading by Prince Charles at the memorial service for Sir John Betjeman.

17 [At 'a midnight carol service in Tongue [Caithness]'] All the good tunes, and perfectly sensible message of reassurance about the resurrection, a good audience (including some in crew cuts and bomber jackets) and not one mention, from start to finish, of the Third World or the need to 'combat' racism or homelessness or poverty or any of that crap.

Alan Clark Diary entry for Boxing Day 1994,

publ. in *The Last Diaries* ed. Ion Trewin (2002)

18 'Oh, for God's sake, Bridge,' he said. 'You're so obsessed with sex if you saw Mum taking communion you'd think she was giving the vicar a blow job.'

Helen Fielding *Bridget Jones's Diary* (1996), entry for Saturday 18 February

19 [Notice on a synagogue door] Come early if you want to get a seat at the back.

Anon. *Jewish Humour* ed. Ben Eliezer (2003)

Heaven and Hell

1 Oh, one world at a time.

Henry David Thoreau Line purportedly uttered on his deathbed, when asked whether he believed in heaven. Quoted in *Henry D. Thoreau* by F. B. Sanron (1882).

2 When I reflect upon the number of disagreeable people who I know have gone to a better world, I am moved to lead a different life.

Mark Twain *The Tragedy of Pudd'nhead Wilson*, 'Pudd'nhead Wilson's Calender', ch. 13 (1894)

3 My idea of heaven is eating pâté de foie gras to the sound of trumpets.

Sydney Smith Quoted in *The Smith of Smiths*, ch. 34, by H. Pearson (1910)

4 What happens when you die? But what happens when you are born?

Samuel Butler *Selections from the Note-Books of Samuel Butler*, ch. 1, ed. A. T. Bartholomew (1930)

5 Hell is other people.

Jean-Paul Sartre Garcin in *Huis Clos* (No Exit), sc. 5 (1944)

6 DUD: Is this it then? Is this heaven? PETE: Bloody Hell.

Dudley Moore *Not Only . . . But Also* (TV series, episode broadcast 1966). This joke, unlike most in the series, was written by Moore, not Cook. Moore said in 1966: 'I came up with so few jokes that when I invented one I thought, "Son of a gun!"'

7 I don't believe in an afterlife,

although I am bringing a change of underwear.

Woody Allen *Getting Even*, 'Conversations with Helmhotz' (1971). Supposedly one of the insights of Dr Helmhotz. In *Without Feathers* (1975) Allen says: 'I keep wondering if there is an afterlife, and if there is will they be able to break a twenty?'

8 Without you, Heaven would be too dull to bear,/ And Hell will not be Hell if you are there.

John Sparrow From a poem entitled 'C. B. M.' in memory of Maurice Bowra, printed as an appendix to *Maurice Bowra: A Celebration* ed. Hugh Lloyd-Jones (1974)

9 Afterlife? After*shave*. I don't hold with any of it.

Viv Stanshall Sir Henry in *Sir Henry at Rawlinson End* (LP, 1978)

10 What's your rationale for shooting the Pope? I guess the guy figured, hey I want to go to hell, and I don't want to stand in line.

Eddie Murphy *Eddie Murphy* (CD, 1982)

11 Alfred, the assistant editor, was a pillar of St Matthew's, a trendy Anglican Church known as Phipps' fire escape, since it had been built by a local brewer of that name shortly before he died.

Michael Green *Nobody Hurt in Small Earthquake*, ch. 6 (1990)

12 [On being taught at school about hell] Wouldn't you get used to it eventually? Like a hot tub?

Matt Groening Bart in *The Simpsons*, 'Homer vs Lisa and the 8th Commandment', first broadcast 7 February 1991

13 [Of heaven] I've always liked the notion of meeting great figures from history, but then I wonder what if it's like high school and all the cool dead people don't want to hang out with me but with Shakespeare and Lincoln? Mozart will tell me he's too busy, then later I'll see him out with Shakespeare and Lincoln.

Suzanne Martin Niles Crane (David Hyde Pierce) in 'Death of the Dog', 4th series, *Fras-*

ier (TV sitcom, 1993 onwards). Collected in *The Very Best of Frasier* (2001)

14 A minister was comforting a dying highlander when he was disturbed to hear the patient ask him if there was any whisky in heaven. 'Ye ken sir, it's not that I care for it, but it looks well on the table.'

Anon. *Whisky Wit and Wisdom*, 'Dying for it', ed. Gavin D. Smith (2000)

15 I do benefits for all religions: I'd hate to blow the after-life on a technicality.

Bob Hope Quoted in the *Independent* 26 July 2003

16 They figured if heaven was in the sky then everybody had to have wings, they couldn't think of any other way to work it. You can have them if you want, but believe me, there's no actual need. Actually dude, they're pretentious. 'Oh, look at me, I'm an angel in heaven!' You know, that sort of thing.

J. Robert Lennon *Mailman*, pt 9 (2003). The speaker is Jared Sprain, who is dead.

17 Heaven for climate, hell for society.

Mark Twain Attributed

Quasi-philosophical Observations

1 The only certainty is that nothing is certain.

Pliny the Elder *Historia Naturalis* (Natural History), bk 2, ch. 7 (*c.* AD 77)

2 In the country of the blind the one-eyed man is king.

Desiderius Erasmus *Adages*, bk 3, no. 96 (c.1500)

3 There is nothing in this world constant, but inconstancy.

Jonathan Swift *A Critical Essay upon the Faculties of Mind* (1709)

4 The same philosophy is a good horse in the stable, but an errant jade on a journey.

Oliver Goldsmith *The Good-Natured Man*, act 1 (1768)

5 **The best-laid schemes o' mice an' men/ Gang aft a-gley.**
Robert Burns 'To a Mouse' (1786)

6 **Is man an ape or an angel? I am on the side of the angels.**
Benjamin Disraeli Speech of 25 November 1864, quoted in *The Times* 26 November 1864

7 **Well, the way of paradoxes is the way of truth. To test Reality we must see it on the tightrope.**
Oscar Wilde Mr Erskine in *The Picture of Dorian Gray*, ch. 3 (1891)

8 **Nothing that actually occurs is of the smallest importance.**
Oscar Wilde 'Phrases and Philosophies for the Use of the Young', *Chameleon* December 1894

9 **Well, sir, you never can tell. That's the principle in life with me, sir, if you'll excuse my having such a thing, sir.**
George Bernard Shaw The waiter in *You Never Can Tell*, act 2 (1897)

10 **Ah! What is a man? Wherefore does he why? Whence did he whence? Whither is he dithering?**
Dan Leno *Dan Leno Hys Booke*, Chapter First (1899)

11 **I was thinking just what a Rum Go everything is.**
H. G. Wells *Kipps*, bk 3, ch. 3 (1905). Almost the last words of the book.

12 **Sometimes I sits and thinks, and then again I just sits.**
Anon. *Punch*, 24 October 1906. In a cartoon called 'Change of Occupation', this is the response of 'Old Man' (who has a bad leg) to the following inquiry from 'Vicar's Wife': 'Now that you can't get about and are not able to read, how do you manage to occupy the time?'

13 **Life is just one damned thing after another.**
Elbert Hubbard *The Philistine*, December 1909

14 **The world is divided into those who can stop dog-fights and those who cannot.**
P. G. Wodehouse *The Man Upstairs*, 'Ruth in Exile' (1914)

15 **What a queer thing life is! So unlike anything else, don't you know, if you see what I mean.**
P. G. Wodehouse Bertie Wooster in *My Man Jeeves*, 'Rallying round Old George' (1920)

16 **Fate keeps on happening.**
Anita Loos Title of ch. 2 of *Blondes Have More Fun* (1925). Lorelei Lee, heroine of the book, often expresses her belief that a lot of things are 'down to fate'.

17 **She always says, my lord, that facts are like cows. If you look them in the face hard enough they generally run away.**
Dorothy L. Sayers Bunter in *Clouds of Witness*, ch. 4 (1926)

18 **'Tigger is all right, *really*,' said Piglet lazily./ 'Of course he is,' said Christopher Robin./ 'Everybody is *really*,' said Pooh.**
A. A. Milne *The House at Pooh Corner*, ch. 6 (1928)

19 **I yam what I yam.**
E. C. Segar Catchphrase of the cartoon character Popeye, 1929 onwards

20 **Nothing matters very much, and very few things matter at all.**
Arthur Balfour Attributed. This has an end-of-life feel about it, and Balfour died in 1930.

21 **We are like billiard balls in a game played by unskilful players, continually being nearly sent into a pocket, but hardly ever getting right into one, except by a fluke.**
Samuel Butler *Selections from the Note-Books of Samuel Butler*, ch. 1, ed. A. T. Bartholomew (1930)

22 **Life is Just a Bowl of Cherries**
Lew Brown Song title (1931)

23 **It is easier to stay out than to get out.**
Mark Twain *Notebook*, ch. 31 (1935)

24 **It all depends what you mean by . . .**
C. E. M. Joad Habitually began his answer thus when asked a question on *The Brains Trust* (BBC radio series 1941–8)

25 **God made everything out of noth-**

ing. But the nothingness shows through.

Paul Valéry *Mauvaises pensées et autres* (Bad and Other Thoughts; 1942)

26 One should try everything once, except incest and folk-dancing.

Arnold Bax *Farewell, My Youth* (1943). Often recalled, to the irritation of Morris dancers, as 'incest and Morris dancing'. In 2002 Jonathan Meades, while acknowledging the original, entitled his collected journalism thus.

27 My theory is that there are too many people and too many things.

Groucho Marx *Variety* 7 June 1947, quoted in *The Essential Groucho* 'Freelancing', ed. Stefan Kanfer (2000)

28 Life, after all, is one discrepancy after another.

Henry Green Quoted in *Now Dig This: The Unspeakable Writings of Terry Southern (1950–1995)*, 'Writers at Work: Henry Green', ed. Nile Southern and Josh Alan Friedman (2001). This interview with Green first appeared in the *Paris Review* in 1958.

29 Human nature, Mr Allnut, is what we were put on this earth to rise above.

Katharine Hepburn As Rose Sayer, addressing Charlie Allnut (Humphrey Bogart), in *The African Queen* (film, 1951, directed by John Huston, screenplay by James Agee, from the novel by C. S. Forester)

30 Never play cards with a man called Doc. Never eat at a place called Mom's. Never sleep with a woman whose troubles are worse than your own.

Nelson Algren Quoted in *Newsweek* 2 July 1956

31 An empty sack won't stand, as the man said, nor a full one won't bend.

Brendan Behan Warder Regan in *The Quare Fellow*, act 2 (1956)

32 Learn by heart. Never write down a thing. And don't go too near the water.

Harold Pinter Goldberg in *The Caretaker*, act 3 (1958). In act 2 he says: 'I believe in a good laugh, a day's fishing, a bit of gardening.'

33 The people walked about as though they were really going somewhere. I stood for a quarter of an hour at a time, watching them get off the buses and disperse themselves throughout the streets. I was amazed and intrigued that they should all be content to be nobody but themselves.

Keith Waterhouse *Billy Liar*, ch. 9 (1959)

34 Life, you know, is rather like opening a tin of sardines. We are all of us looking for the key.

Alan Bennett Sermon in *Beyond the Fringe* (revue, 1960–62), publ. in *From Fringe to Flying Circus*, ch. 1, by Roger Wilmut (1980). Bennett first wrote the sketch in 1956. 'It took about half an hour to write, and was, I suppose, the most profitable half-hour's work I've ever done. Once I had hit on the form I used to be able to run up sermons for all sorts of occasions.' Bennett himself, when young, thought of becoming a vicar 'for no better reason than that I looked like one'.

35 Life is like a sewer. What you get out of life depends on what you put into it.

Tom Lehrer Preamble to 'We Will All Go Together When We Go' from *An Evening Wasted with Tom Lehrer* (LP, 1960). This remark was made, Lehrer said, by a man who was taken to the Massachusetts Home for the Bewildered immediately afterwards.

36 Apart from the known and the unknown, what else is there?

Harold Pinter Lenny in *The Homecoming*, act 2 (1965)

37 The law of the universe is a law unto itself.

David Mamet Emil in *Duck Variations*, 'Third Variation' (1972)

38 If it ain't broke, don't fix it.

Bert Lance *Nation's Business*, May 1977. Many people wrongly think that Lyndon B. Johnson said this.

39 Is it all right to shout 'Movie!' in a crowded firehouse.

Steve Martin *A Wild and Crazy Guy*, 'Religion' (LP, 1978)

40 One of the oldest of all natural laws

is that seven-eighths of everything remains hidden.

Peter Cook From the Foreword to *Rock Stars in Their Underpants* by Paula Yates (1980)

41 Boxing got me started on philosophy. You bash them, they bash you and you think, what's it all for?

Arthur Mullard Quoted in *ES* magazine, 3 February 1995. Coincidentally, Ludwig Wittgenstein states in *Personal Recollections*, ch. 6, ed. Rush Rees (1981), that 'a philosopher who is not taking part in discussions is like a boxer who never goes into the ring'.

42 Life is like a 'B' movie. You don't want to leave in the middle of it but you don't want to see it again.

Ted Turner *International Herald Tribune* 2 March 1990

43 The way I see it, if you want the rainbow, you gotta put up with the rain.

Dolly Parton Quoted in *Women's Wit and Wisdom* (1991)

44 'Lightning always strikes in the same place twice,' said Mma Ramotswe. 'Whatever people say to the contrary.'

Alexander McCall Smith *The No. 1 Ladies' Detective Agency*, ch. 11 (1998)

45 The world is divided into two sorts of people: those who divide the world into two sorts of people, and those that don't.

Stephen Fry Staple remark of this humorist in the mid-1990s

46 Someone once sent me a marvellous postcard. It said: 'Knock hard, life is deaf.'

Arnold Wesker Quoted in *The Times* 10 February 2001

47 Remembering you set out to drain the swamp is hard when you're up to your ass in alligators.

Anon. An old joke quoted by David Mamet in *Three Uses of the Knife*, ch. 2 (2002)

48 If ye're born tae be hanged, then ye'll no' be drowned.

Anon. *Away an' Ask Yer Mother (Your Scottish Father's Favourite Sayings)*, ch. 2, ed. Allan Morrison (2003)

49 Life is short – only four letters in it. Three-quarters of it is a 'lie', and the half of it is an 'if'.

Anon. *Pearson's Book of Fun*, 'Sundry Siftings', ed. Mr X (n.d.)

Morality
Conscience and Guilt

1 Suspicion always haunts the guilty mind;/ The thief doth fear each bush an officer.

William Shakespeare Gloucester in *King Henry VI Part 3*, act 5, sc. 6 (1590–1)

2 When children stand quiet, they have done some ill.

George Herbert *Outlandish Proverbs*, no. 504 (1640)

3 I never wonder to see men wicked, but I often wonder to see them not ashamed.

Jonathan Swift *Miscellanies in Prose and Verse*, 'Further Thoughts' (1711)

4 In many walks of life, a conscience is a more expensive encumbrance than a wife or a carriage.

Thomas De Quincey *Confessions of An English Opium Eater*, 'Preliminary Confessions' (1822)

5 Conscience and cowardice are really the same things, Basil. Conscience is the trade name of the firm. That is all.

Oscar Wilde Lord Henry Wotton to Basil Hallward in *The Picture of Dorian Gray*, ch. 1 (1891). Hallward replies: 'I don't believe that, Harry, and I don't believe you do either.'

6 An uneasy conscience is a hair in the mouth.

Mark Twain *Notebook*, ch. 35 (1935)

7 One man's remorse is another man's reminiscence.

Ogden Nash *I'm a Stranger Here Myself*, 'A Clean Conscience Never Relaxes' (1938)

8 Show me a woman who doesn't feel guilty, and I'll show you a man.

Erica Jong Quoted in *Women's Wit and Wisdom* (1991)

9 **Conscience gets a lot of the credit that belongs to cold feet.**

Anon. *And I Quote*, 'Conscience', ed. Ashton Applewhite and others (1992)

Good and Evil

1 **Dost thou think, because thou art virtuous, there shall be no more cakes and ale?**

William Shakespeare Sir Toby Belch to Malvolio in *Twelfth Night*, act 2, sc. 3 (1601)

2 **The greatest pleasure I know, is to do a good action by stealth, and to have it found out by accident.**

Charles Lamb *Athenaeum* 4 January 1834

3 **Saint, n.: A dead sinner revised and edited.**

Ambrose Bierce *The Devil's Dictionary* (compiled 1881–1906)

4 **If all the good people were clever,/ And all clever people were good,/ The world would be nicer than ever/ We thought that it possibly could./ But somehow, 'tis seldom or never/ The two hit it off as they should;/ The good are so harsh to the clever,/ The clever so rude to the good.**

Dame Elizabeth Wordsworth 'Good and Clever' (1890), collected in *Poems and Plays* (1931)

5 **Ship me somewheres east of Suez, where the best is like the worst,/ Where there aren't no Ten Commandments an' a man can raise a thirst.**

Rudyard Kipling 'Mandalay' (1892)

6 **It is absurd to divide people into good or bad. People are either charming or tedious.**

Oscar Wilde Lord Darlington in *Lady Windermere's Fan*, act 1 (1893)

7 **I can resist everything except temptation.**

Lord Darlington in ibid., act 1

8 **Wickedness is a myth invented by** good people to account for the curious attractiveness of others.

Oscar Wilde 'Phrases and Philosophies for the Use of the Young', *Chameleon* December 1894

9 **Man is the only Animal that Blushes. Or needs to.**

Mark Twain *Following the Equator*, ch. 27 (1897)

10 **What is virtue but the trade unionism of the married?**

George Bernard Shaw Don Juan in *Man and Superman*, act 3 (1903)

11 **No people do so much harm as those who go about doing good.**

Mandell Creighton *Life*, vol. 2 (1904)

12 **There is something wrong with a man if he doesn't want to break the Ten Commandments.**

G. K. Chesterton *Observer*, 'Sayings of the Week', 12 April 1925

13 **I decline utterly to be impartial as between the fire brigade and the fire.**

Winston Churchill Speech to the House of Commons, Hansard 7 July 1926. Churchill was replying to complaints of bias as editor of the *British Gazette* during the General Strike. Chancellor of the Exchequer at the time, he had referred to the strikers as 'the Enemy'. In a letter to the Prime Minister Stanley Baldwin he had said that, as regarded the strikers, 'A little bloodshed would do no harm.'

14 **Goodness had nothing to do with it.**

Mae West *Night after Night* (film, 1932, screenplay by Vincent Laurence, directed by Archie Mayo). Response to checkroom girl's exclamation, 'Goodness, what beautiful diamonds!'; also the title of West's autobiography (1960).

15 **It is queer how it is always one's virtues and not one's vices that precipitate one into disaster.**

Rebecca West *There Is No Conversation*, ch. 1 (1935)

16 **The quality of moral behaviour varies in inverse proportion to the number of human beings involved.**

Aldous Huxley *The Grey Eminence*, ch. 10 (1941)

17 **I'm a ba-a-a-ad boy!**
Abbott and Costello Catchphrase of Lou Costello to Bud Abbott in their films of the 1940s

18 **They owed me for an incident that happened long ago in the war. Probably the only time I did the right thing quick like a mouse.**
Raymond Chandler *The Long Goodbye*, ch. 53 (1954). The speaker is Terry Lennox.

19 **Very few of the Ten Commandments are accepted by the State. Strange gods and graven images are tolerated, neither swearing nor adultery is forbidden, nobody is required to honour his father or mother. So far as it being a crime to covet one's neighbour's wife, it is generally thought good manners to put up a pretence of coveting her.**
Auberon Waugh *Spectator* 12 February 1983

20 **Of two evils choose the prettier.**
Carolyn Wells Quoted in *Women's Wit and Wisdom* (1991)

21 **You can tell the person who lives for others by the haunted look on the faces of the others.**
Katherine Whitehorn Quoted in *Women's Wicked Wit* ed. Michelle Lovric (2000)

Honesty and Dishonesty

1 **Husband a lie, and trump it up in some extraordinary emergency.**
Joseph Addison *Spectator* 11 October 1712

2 **But if he does really think that there is no distinction between virtue and vice, why, Sir, when he leaves our houses, let us count our spoons.**
Samuel Johnson *The Life of Samuel Johnson* by James Boswell, vol. 1, p. 428 (1791); in G. B. Hill's edition of 1887, rev. L. F. Powell (1934). Under discussion was an 'impudent fellow' from Scotland.

3 **It takes two to speak the truth, – one to speak, and another to hear.**
Henry David Thoreau *A Week on the Concord and Merrimack Rivers*, 'Wednesday' (1849)

4 **Honesty is the best policy, but he who is governed by that maxim is not an honest man.**
Richard Whately *Apophthegms* (1854)

5 **The louder he talked of his honor, the faster we counted the spoons.**
Ralph Waldo Emerson *The Conduct of Life*, 'Worship' (1860). A remark that feels very familiar.

6 **One of the chief causes that can be assigned for the curiously commonplace character of the literature of our age is the decay of Lying as an art, a science, and a social pleasure.**
Oscar Wilde *Intentions*, 'The Decay of Lying' (1891).

7 **Gwendolen, it is a terrible thing for a man to find out suddenly that all his life he has been speaking nothing but the truth.**
Oscar Wilde Jack in *The Importance of Being Earnest*, act 4 (1895). He has been pretending to be Ernest, and this turns out to be his real name.

8 **It is always the best policy to speak the truth, unless of course you are an exceptionally good liar.**
Jerome K. Jerome *The Idler*, February 1892

9 **Truth is the most valuable thing we have. Let us economize it.**
Mark Twain *Following the Equator*, ch. 7 (1897). In 1796, in *Two Letters on Proposals for Peace*, Edmund Burke wrote: 'As in the exercise of all the virtues, there is an economy of truth.' Sir Robert Armstrong, as head of the British Civil Service, said of a document during the 'Spycatcher' trial in the New South Wales Supreme Court: 'It contains a misleading impression, not a lie. It was being economical with the truth' (quoted in the *Daily Telegraph* 19 November 1986).

10 **Matilda told such Dreadful Lies,/ It made one Gasp and Stretch one's Eyes;/ Her Aunt, who, from her Earliest Youth,/ Had kept a Strict Regard for Truth,/ Attempted to Believe Matilda:/ The effort very nearly killed her.**
Hilaire Belloc *Cautionary Tales for Children*, 'Matilda' (1907)

11 **I do not mind lying but I hate inaccuracy.**
Samuel Butler *The Note-Books of Samuel Butler*, ch. 12, ed. Henry Festing Jones (1912)

12 **People ought to start dead and then they would be honest so much earlier.**
Mark Twain *Autobiography*, ch. 55 of the 1959 edn (first published 1924)

13 **There are three kinds of lies: lies, damned lies and statistics.**
Benjamin Disraeli Attributed to Disraeli in ibid.

14 **Truth is more of a stranger than fiction.**
Mark Twain *Notebook*, ch. 31 (1935)

15 **I'm the most terrific liar you ever saw in your life. It's awful. If I'm on my way to the store to buy a magazine, even, and somebody asks me where I'm going, I'm liable to say I'm going to the opera. It's terrible.**
J. D. Salinger Narrator (Holden Caulfield) in *The Catcher in the Rye* (1951)

16 **[On being told that Lord Astor said her allegations concerning himself and his house parties at Cliveden were untrue] He would, wouldn't he?**
Mandy Rice-Davies *Guardian* 1 July 1963

17 **You see, I always divide people into two groups. Those who live by what they know to be a lie, and those who live by what they believe, falsely, to be the truth.**
Christopher Hampton Don in *The Philanthropist*, sc. 6 (1970)

18 **He's not very clever, and he's a very bad liar like most men. If he takes the trouble, like last Saturday, to tell me he's just going down the road to the football match, he might at least choose a day when they're playing at home.**
Alan Ayckbourn Diana speaking of her husband Paul in *Absent Friends*, act 1 (1974)

19 **Marge, it takes two to lie. One to lie, and one to listen.**
Matt Groening Homer Simpson in *The Simpsons*, 'Colonel Homer', first broadcast 26 March 1992

20 **An abomination unto the Lord, but a very present help in times of trouble.**
Anon. A definition of a lie, conflating Proverbs 12:22 and Psalms 46:1. Sometimes attributed to Adlai Stevenson.

Moralizing

1 **'You needn't hurry yourself,' said Squeers; 'there's plenty of time. Conquer your passions, boys, and don't be eager after vittles.' As he uttered this moral precept, Mr Squeers took a large bite out of the cold beef.**
Charles Dickens *Nicholas Nickleby*, ch. 5 (1838–9)

2 **We know no spectacle so ridiculous as the British public in one of its periodic fits of morality.**
Lord Macaulay *Critical and Historical Essays*, vol. 1, 'Moore's Life of Lord Byron' (1843)

3 **Now, I never moralize. A man who moralizes is usually a hypocrite, and a woman who moralizes is invariably plain.**
Oscar Wilde Cecil Graham in *Lady Windermere's Fan*, act 3 (1893)

4 **Moral indignation is jealousy with a halo.**
H. G. Wells *The Wife of Sir Isaac Harman*, ch. 9, sect. 2 (1914)

5

Arts and Culture

Literature
Film
Theatre and Performance
Visual Art
Music
Newspapers, Radio and
Television

Literature
Grammar and Spelling

1 Thou hast most traitorously cor-
rupted the youth of the realm in
erecting a grammar school . . . It
will be proved to thy face that thou
hast men about thee that usually
talk of a noun and a verb, and such
abominable words as no Christian
ear can endure to hear.
William Shakespeare Jack Cade to Lord Say
in *King Henry VI Part 2*, act 4, sc. 7 (1590–1)

2 Grammar, which can govern even
kings.
Molière Philaminte in *Those Learned Ladies*,
act 2, sc. 6 (1672)

3 I will not go down to posterity talking bad grammar.
Benjamin Disraeli Said while correcting the
proofs of his last parliamentary speech,
31 March 1881. Quoted in *Disraeli* by Robert
Blake, ch. 32 (1966).

4 As a matter of fact, there is an English grammar, and one of these
days our schools will recognize the
fact, and it will be taught to our children, penetrating maybe even to literary and journalistic circles.
Jerome K. Jerome *Three Men on the Bummel*,
ch. 6 (1900). He had begun by suggesting
that 'a good many English people' believe
that English has no grammar.

5 I never had any large respect for
good spelling.
Mark Twain *Autobiography*, ch. 40 of the
1959 edn (first published 1924)

6 Damn the subjunctive. It brings all
our writers to shame.
Mark Twain *Notebook*, ch. 26 (1935)

7 I'm thirty-three years old, went to
college once and can still speak English if there's any demand for it.
Raymond Chandler *The Big Sleep*, ch. 1 (1939)

8 This is the sort of English up with
which I will not put.
Winston Churchill Quoted in *The Complete
Plain Words*, 'The Handling of Words', by

Ernest Gowers (1954). Said to be a note scrawled by Churchill against a sentence that seemed too prissily correct regarding a preposition.

9 I have committed an inexcusable solecism in the *Spectator*. 'Anadyomene' for 'Anadyomenos'. What can be more ignominious than to use a rather recondite word and to use it wrong?

Evelyn Waugh Letter to Nancy Mitford of 1 September 1955, collected in *The Letters of Evelyn Waugh* ed. Mark Amory (1980)

10 These are the voyages of the starship *Enterprise*. Its five-year mission ... to boldly go where no man has gone before.

Gene Rodenberry Voice-over introduction to *Star Trek* (TV series, 1966 onwards). Famous as a catchphrase for its split infinitive. In the *Star Trek* films this became 'to boldly go where *no one* has gone before'.

11 [Of Ernie Wise] As for exclamation marks, he has been known to use as many as eight in a row, and even I know five is the limit.

Eric Morecambe Quoted in *Eric and Ernie: The Autobiography of Morecambe and Wise*, ch. 1 (1973)

12 A lifetime's teaching grammar come to this – / Returned as member for Necropolis ...

Tony Harrison *Palladas: Poems*, no. 40 (1975)

13 ERIC: Who was that lady I seen you with last night?
ERNIE: You mean 'I saw'.
ERIC: Sorry. Who was that eyesore I seen you with last night?

Eric Morecambe and Ernie Wise *The Morecambe and Wise Jokebook*, skit 12 (1979)

Literature in General

1 Some hold translations not unlike to be/ The wrong side of a Turkey tapestry.

James Howell *Familiar Letters* (1645–55), 1, letter 6

2 So essential did I consider an Index to be to every book, that I proposed to bring a Bill into parliament to deprive an author who publishes a book without an index of the privilege of copyright; and, moreover, to subject him, for his offence, to a pecuniary penalty.

Baron Campbell Preface to vol. 3 of the *Lives of the Chief Justices* (1876), which included an index to the first two

3 There was things which he stretched, but mainly he told the truth.

Mark Twain *The Adventures of Huckleberry Finn*, ch. 1 (1884)

4 Half past six! What an hour! It will be like having a meat-tea, or reading an English novel.

Oscar Wilde Lord Henry Wotton in *The Picture of Dorian Gray*, ch. 4 (1891) – referring to the time proposed for going to see a play

5 They say the pen is mightier than the sword, but I doubt it; for even in times of peace a sword may come in handy for chopping wood or carving an autumn chicken, and you can't do much in that line with a pen without crossing the nib.

Dan Leno *Dan Leno Hys Booke*, Introductory (1899)

6 A best-seller is the gilded tomb of a mediocre talent.

Logan Pearsall Smith *Afterthoughts*, 'Arts and Letters' (1931)

7 Literature is news that *stays* news.

Ezra Pound *The ABC of Reading*, ch. 2 (1934)

8 If you steal from one author, it's plagiarism; if you steal from many, it's research.

Wilson Mizner *The Legendary Mizners*, ch. 4 (1953)

9 Literature is mostly about having sex and not much about having children. Life is the other way round.

David Lodge Adam Appleby in *The British Museum Is Falling Down*, ch. 4 (1965)

Reading

1 Some books are to be tasted, others to be swallowed, and some few to be chewed and digested; that is, some books are to be read only in parts; others to be read but not curiously; and some few to be read wholly, and with diligence and attention. Some books also may be read by deputy, and extracts made of them by others.
Francis Bacon *Essays*, 'Of Studies' (1625)

2 Reading and marriage don't go well together.
Molière Martine in *Those Learned Ladies*, act 5, sc. 3 (1672)

3 He had read much, if one considers his long life; but his contemplation was much more than his reading. He was wont to say that if he had read as much as other men, he would have known no more than other men.
John Aubrey *Brief Lives* (n.d.). Of Thomas Hobbes.

4 A reader seldom peruses a book with pleasure until he knows whether the writer of it be a black man or a fair man, of a mild or choleric disposition, married or a bachelor.
Joseph Addison *Spectator* 1 March 1711. The first issue of the magazine.

5 The bookful blockhead, ignorantly read,/ With loads of learned lumber in his head.
Alexander Pope *An Essay on Criticism*, line 612 (1711)

6 As we have sometimes great composers of musick, who cannot sing, we have as frequently great writers that cannot read.
Colley Cibber *An Apology for the Life of Mr Colley Cibber, Comedian*, ch. 4 (1739). He instances Dryden, whom he heard reading his play *Amphytrion* to actors 'in so cold, so flat, and unaffecting a manner . . .'

7 Sometimes I read a book with pleasure, and detest the author.
Jonathan Swift *Miscellanies in Prose and Verse*, 'Further Thoughts' (1745)

8 I would go fifty miles on foot, for I have not a horse worth riding on, to kiss the hand of that man whose generous heart will give up the reins of his imagination into his author's hands.
Laurence Sterne *Tristram Shandy*, vol. 3, ch. 12 (1759–67)

9 Madam, a circulating library in a town is an evergreen tree of diabolical knowledge! It blossoms through the year! And depend on it, Mrs Malaprop, that they who are so fond of handling the leaves, will long for the fruit at last.
Richard Brinsley Sheridan Sir Anthony Absolute in *The Rivals*, act 1, sc. 2 (1775)

10 [Of Dr Johnson] He told me, that from his earliest years he loved to read poetry, but hardly read any poem to the end . . .
James Boswell *The Life of Samuel Johnson* by James Boswell, vol. 1, p. 71 (1791); in G. B. Hill's edition of 1887, rev. L. F. Powell (1934). According to Murphy's *Johnson*, 'It may . . . be questioned whether, except his Bible, he ever read a book entirely through. Late in life, if any man praised a book in his presence he was sure to ask, "Did you read it through?" If the answer was in the affirmative, he did not seem willing to believe it.'

11 Women judge of books as they do of fashions or complexions, which are admired only 'in their newest gloss'.
William Hazlitt 'On Reading Old Books', *The London Magazine* February 1821, collected in *The Essays of William Hazlitt* ed. Catherine Macdonald Maclean (1949). Hazlitt himself, by contrast (he states in this essay), 'hate[s] to read new books'.

12 Your *borrowers of books* – those mutilators of collections, spoilers of the symmetry of shelves, and creators of odd volumes.
Charles Lamb *The Essays of Elia*, 'The Two Races of Men' (1823)

13 Read the best books first, or you might not have a chance to read them at all.

Henry David Thoreau *A Week on the Concord and Merrimack Rivers*, 'Sunday' (1849)

14 What a calm and pleasant seclusion the library presents after the bawl and bustle of the newspaper room! There is never anybody here. English gentlemen get up such a prodigious quantity of knowledge in their early life, that they leave off reading as soon as they begin to shave.

William Makepeace Thackeray *Travels in London*, 'The Mr Browns at a Club' (1853)

15 Look at a railway stall; you see books of every colour, blue, yellow, crimson, 'streaked, speckled, and spotted', on every subject, in every style, of every opinion with every conceivable difference, celestial or sublunary, maleficent, beneficent – but all small.

Walter Bagehot 'The First Edinburgh Reviewers', *National Review* 1855, collected in *The Complete Works of Walter Bagehot*, vol. 1, p. 39, ed. Norman St John-Stevas (1966–86)

16 Bentley Drummle, who was so sulky a fellow that he even took up a book as if its writer had done him an injury, did not take up acquaintance in a more agreeable spirit.

Charles Dickens *Great Expectations*, ch. 25 (1860–61)

17 Never read any book that is not a year old.

Ralph Waldo Emerson *Society and Solitude*, 'Books' (1870)

18 The art of reading is to skip judiciously.

P. G. Hamerton *The Intellectual Life*, pt 4, letter 4 (1873)

19 [Of *The Pilgrim's Progress*] The statements was interesting, but tough.

Mark Twain *Huckleberry Finn*, ch. 17 (1884)

20 I never travel without my diary. One should always have some-thing sensational to read on the train.

Oscar Wilde Gwendolen Fairfax in *The Importance of Being Earnest*, act 3 (1895)

21 Child! Do not throw this book about;/ Refrain from the unholy pleasure/ Of cutting all the pictures out!/ Preserve it as your chiefest treasure.

Hilaire Belloc Dedication to *The Bad Child's Book of Beasts* (1896)

22 I am never tired of reading *Paradise Lost*. Perhaps that's because I never start on it; but I really must say I think it is one of Dickens's failures.

Dan Leno *Dan Leno Hys Booke*, Chapter Thirteenth (1899)

23 A classic – something that everyone wants to have read and nobody wants to read.

Mark Twain Addressing the Nineteenth-Century Club at Sherry's, New York, on 'The Disappearance of Literature', 20 November 1900. He had preceded this with: 'Don't believe any of you have ever read *Paradise Lost*.'

24 There is certainly a pleasure to be got from reading a thoroughly mediocre thing by a writer generally esteemed great but whom you don't happen to admire.

Arnold Bennett Journal entry for 12 June 1910, *Journal of Arnold Bennett*, vol. 1, *1896–1910*, ed. Newman Flower (1932). Bennett was reading Tennyson's play *The Promise of May* – 'a masterpiece of tedious conventionality – of no value whatsoever'.

25 I keep my books at the British Museum and at Mudie's.

Samuel Butler *The Humour of Homer and Other Essays*, 'Ramblings in Cheapside' (1913). Mudie's was a bookshop and lending library run by Charles Edward Mudie.

26 When I want to read a novel, I write one.

Benjamin Disraeli Quoted in *The Life of Benjamin Disraeli* by W. Moneypenny and G. Buckle, vol. 6, ch. 17 (1920)

27 I've been drunk for about a week now, and I thought it might sober me up to sit in a library.

F. Scott Fitzgerald *The Great Gatsby* (1925)

28 I decided not to read the book by
Mr Cellini. I mean it was quite
amusing in spots because it was
really quite riskay but the spots
were not so close together.
Anita Loos *Gentlemen Prefer Blondes*, Ch. 1
(1925)

29 The act of reading was in the Out-
laws' eyes inseparable from the
act of imbibing liquid refreshment.
They read aloud in turns, and those
who were listening passed from
hand to hand the bottle of liquorice
water.
Richmal Crompton *William the Conqueror*,
ch. 9 (1926)

30 The ordinary man who is paying
instalments on the *Encyclopaedia
Britannica* is apt to get over-excited
and to skip impatiently to Volume
XXVIII (Vet–Zym) to see how it all
comes out in the end.
P. G. Wodehouse *The Man with Two Left
Feet*, 'The Man with Two Left Feet' (1926)

31 They told me how Gladstone read
Homer for fun, which I thought
served him right.
Winston Churchill *My Early Life*, ch. 2 (1930)

32 Compulsory Preface
W. C. Sellar and R. J. Yeatman *1066 and All
That* (1932). Title of Preface, with '(This
Means You)' printed underneath.

33 That ideal reader suffering from an
ideal insomnia.
James Joyce *Finnegans Wake*, pt 1 (1939)

34 I looked up *effete*. It means primarily 'having given birth'. The dictionary is an endless source of surprise
and pleasure.
Evelyn Waugh Letter to Maurice Bowra of
May 1946, collected in *The Letters of Evelyn
Waugh* ed. Mark Amory (1980)

35 I have noticed that we are inclined
to endow our friends with the stab-
ility of type that literary characters
acquire in their readers' minds. No
matter how many times we reopen
King Lear, never shall we find the
good king banging his tankard in

high revelry, all woes forgotten, at a
jolly reunion with all three daughters and their lapdogs.
Vladimir Nabokov *Lolita*, ch. 27 (1955)

36 I always begin at the left with the
opening word of the sentence and
read toward the right, and I recommend this method.
James Thurber Memo to the *New Yorker* in
1959, publ. in the *New York Times*
4 December 1988

37 You've never read a book in your
life. Don't give me that. You've run
one yes, but you've never read one.
Ray Galton and Alan Simpson Tony Hancock
in *Hancock's Half-Hour*, 'The Missing Page',
first broadcast 26 February 1960

38 You are invited to the dyslexics'
ball. Please sapprpv.
Tim Brooke-Taylor *I'm Sorry I Haven't A Clue*
(radio series, 1972 onwards), from *I'm Sorry I
Haven't A Clue: 5* (cassette, 1999)

39 I love libraries, but I will be
damned if I ever walk into a
'Resource Centre'.
Richard Needham *The Wit and Wisdom of
Richard Needham* (1979)

40 The most overdue book in the history of library services was a copy
of Dr J. Currie's *Febrile Diseases*. It
was taken out of the University of
Cincinnati Medical Library in 1823
by Mr M. Dodd and returned on
7 December 1968 by his great-
grandson.
Stephen Pile *The Book of Heroic Failures*, 'The
Most Overdue Library Book' (1979)

41 I read everything except politics,
philosophy, theology, economics,
sociology, science, or anything to
do with the wonders of nature, anything to do with technology – have
I said politics?
Philip Larkin *Required Writing*, 'An Interview
with the *Observer*' (1983)

42 Books are where things are
explained to you; life is where
things aren't . . .
Julian Barnes *Flaubert's Parrot*, ch. 13 (1984)

43 I never read much because I was too busy living.

Mae West Quoted in *The Ultimate Seduction*, 'Mae West', by Charlotte Chandler (1984)

44 I read biographies backwards, beginning with the death. If that takes my fancy I go through the rest. Childhood seldom interests me at all.

Alan Bennett Diary entry for 3 June 1985, *Writing Home: Diaries 1980–1990* (1994)

45 JEAN: More large-print novels, especially Jackie Collins.
BARBARA: That's for my grandad. He likes smut, and he can't focus.

Victoria Wood *Barmy: The New Victoria Wood Sketch Book*, 'Party Political Broadcast' (1987)

46 Definition of a classic: a book everyone is assumed to have read, and often thinks they have.

Alan Bennett *Independent on Sunday* 27 January 1991

47 I have yet to meet a grown-up reader of comic books who does not also have an affection for tobacco and tattoos.

Bill Bryson *Neither Here Nor There*, ch. 1 (1991)

48 She was far too engrossed in Perdita's *Jackie Collins* . . . round which she'd wrapped the dust jacket of Hilary Spurling's biography of Ivy Compton-Burnett.

Jilly Cooper *Polo*, ch. 1 (1991)

49 I just heard about the greatest book club – you send in $15 a month for a year – and they leave you completely alone.

Anon. *And I Quote*, 'Publishing', ed. Ashton Applewhite and others (1992)

50 Books have body: books (if you are listening) always say what they said last time. Or stay silent when you shut them up.

J. L. Carr *Harpole and Foxberrow, Publishers*, p. 157 (1992). The concluding words of the book.

51 Residents of Stow-on-the-Wold, Glos, took ten days to realize that a new village sign read Stow-the-on-Wold. It has now been removed for repair.

Anon. *Daily Telegraph* headline quoted in *Cannibal Victims Speak Out! And Other Astonishing Press Cuttings* ed. Mat Coward (1995)

52 The main question as to a novel is – did it amuse? Were you surprised at dinner coming so soon? Did you mistake eleven for ten, and twelve for eleven? Were you too late to dress?

Sydney Smith *Twelve Miles from a Lemon: Selected Writings of Sydney Smith*, ch. 7, compiled by Norman Taylor and Alan Hankinson (1996)

53 My favourite writers are Joyce, Tolstoy, Proust and Flaubert, but right now I'm reading *The Little Engine That Could*.

Emo Phillips From his 1990s act

54 If all else fails, read the instructions.

Anon. Observation of the late twentieth century.

55 Please read the titles to yourself. Loud reading annoys your neighbours.

Anon. Generic cinema announcement, quoted in *Cassell's Movie Quotations* ed. Nigel Rees (2nd edn 2002)

56 Folding the top corner of the page over is like marking your territory by peeing on it. You know where you've been, but no one else will ever want to go there.

Guy Browning *Guardian*, 'How to . . .' column, 5 April 2003. In the same column Browning also wrote: 'Never read a large hardback in the bath if your feet don't rest comfortably at the far end. Otherwise, by the end of chapter two, you'll be under water.'

Publishing and the Literary Life

1 He was the first inventor of the art which hath so long lain

dormant, of publishing by numbers; an art even now brought to such perfection, that even dictionaries are divided and exhibited piecemeal to the public; nay, one bookseller hath ('to encourage learning and ease the public') contrived to give them a dictionary in this divided manner, for only fifteen shillings more than it would have cost entire.

Henry Fielding *Joseph Andrews*, bk 2, ch. 1 (1742). 'He' refers to Homer.

2 There is very seldom any thing extraordinary in the appearance and address of a good writer; whereas a dull author generally distinguishes himself by some oddity or extravagance.

Tobias Smollett Letter from Jerry Melford to Sir Watkin Phillips dated 10 June, *The Expedition of Humphry Clinker* (1771)

3 When men write for profit, they are not very delicate.

Horace Walpole Letter to the Rev. William Cole of 1 September 1778, collected in *Correspondence*, Yale edn, vol. 2 (1973)

4 Publish and be damned.

Duke of Wellington Attributed response to a blackmail threat from Harriet Wilson, a Swiss coquette who was one of his mistresses. Quoted in *Wellington: The Years of the Sword*, ch. 10 by Elizabeth Longford (1969).

5 This immortal work which will set all Europe afire and not be forgotten till at least three months has only one fault – it is not written.

Benjamin Disraeli Letter to Henry Colburn of 14 February 1830. Disraeli was in fact halfway through writing his novel *The Young Duke. Benjamin Disraeli: Letters: 1815–1834* ed. J. A. W. Gunn, John Matthews and Donald M. Schurman (1982).

6 'What! Wouldn't you like to be a book-writer?' said the old gentleman./ Oliver considered a little while; and at last said, he should think it would be much better to be a book-seller; upon which the old gentleman laughed heartily, and

declared he had said a very good thing.

Charles Dickens *Oliver Twist*, ch. 14 (1837–9). Mr Brownlow shows Oliver his extensive library.

7 My belief is that if you took the twelve most popular authors in England they would all be beaten [by the Civil Service examination].

Anthony Trollope Letter to George Henry Lewes of 20 July 1860, *The Letters of Anthony Trollope* ed. Bradford Allen Booth (1951)

8 Nine-tenths of existing books are nonsense, and the clever books are the refutation of that nonsense.

Benjamin Disraeli Mr Phoebus in *Lothair*, ch. 29 (1870)

9 An author was reproved by a friend for editing so many volumes: 'My dear sir, you will never reach posterity if you carry so much luggage.'

Anon. *The New London Jest Book*, 'Choice Jests', no. 522, ed. W. C. Hazlitt (1871)

10 Dr Johnson having, in a fit of anger, felled a man with his own dictionary, the other, telling the story with all its circumstances to a friend, concluded by saying, 'He *literally* knocked me down.'

Ibid., no. 315

11 An author who speaks about his own books is almost as bad as a mother who talks about her own children.

Benjamin Disraeli Quoted in *The Times* 20 November 1873

12 To puff and get one's self puffed have become different branches of a new profession.

Anthony Trollope *The Way We Live Now*, ch. 1 (1875). Comment made in a letter from Lady Carbury, who 'spoke of herself in these days as a woman devoted to literature, always spelling the word with a big L'.

13 The annals of law and typography contain the remarkable fact that an edition of the Bible was once printed, in which the word *not*, to the horror and consternation of the

religious world, was left out of the seventh commandment!

Leigh Hunt *Table Talk*, 'Mistakes of the Press'. Some theologians, Hunt noted, thought this was better, since 'in nine cases out of ten the prohibition was the temptation'.

14 **Man is a creature of habit. You cannot write three plays then stop.**

George Bernard Shaw *Plays Pleasant and Unpleasant*, Preface (1898)

15 **One man is as good as another until he has written a book.**

Benjamin Jowett *The Letters of Benjamin Jowett*, vol. 1, p. 248, ed. Evelyn Abbott and Lewis Campbell (1899)

16 **An editor who wanted a free article from me once came along and said, 'You are the greatest writer that ever lived, or *could* live.'**

Arnold Bennett Journal entry for 18 October 1924, quoted in *Arnold Bennett*, ch. 13, by Margaret Drabble (1974). Bennett commented: 'That is the kind of nourishment we require.'

17 **By William Shakespeare, with additional dialogue by Sam Taylor.**

Anon. Credit for *The Taming of the Shrew* (film, 1929, directed by Sam Taylor). Quoted in *Halliwell's Film & Video Guide* ed. John Walker (1998).

18 **The Editor, the Editor,/ I cannot think what he is for –/ I do not like his tone;/ He simply sits and lights his pipe/ With poems much more rich and ripe/ Than his own.**

A. P. Herbert *Wisdom for the Wise*, 'The Editor' (1930)

19 **A third type of woman novelist combined literature and motherhood by writing a good, serious first novel when they were twenty-six; then marrying and having a baby, and, the confinement over, writing articles for the press on 'How I Shall Bring Up My Daughter' by Miss Gwenyth Bludgeon, the brilliant young novelist.**

Stella Gibbons *Cold Comfort Farm*, ch. 6 (1932)

20 **The literary agent was a grim, hardbitten person, to whom, when he called at their offices to arrange terms, editors kept their faces turned so that they might at least retain their back collar studs.**

P. G. Wodehouse *Meet Mr Mulliner*, 'Honeysuckle Cottage' (1932)

21 **Author? Where's your pipe?**

Anon. Customs official's remark, *c.*1933, on looking at the passport of the novelist Anthony Powell. Quoted in the *Times Literary Supplement* 28 February 2003.

22 **The trouble, Mr Goldwyn, is that you are only interested in art and I am only interested in money.**

George Bernard Shaw Quoted in *The Great Goldwyn*, ch. 3, by Alva Johnson (1937). Addressed to Samuel Goldwyn, according to publicity chief Howard Dietz, during talks to engage Shaw as a writer for Hollywood.

23 **Shakespeare describes the poet's eye as rolling in a fine frenzy from heaven to earth, from earth to heaven, and giving to airy nothing a local habitation and a name, but in practice you will find that one corner of that eye is generally glued on the royalty returns.**

P. G. Wodehouse *Uncle Fred in the Springtime*, ch. 12 (1939). 'Poets, as a class,' Wodehouse asserts, 'are business men.'

24 **If my books had been any worse, I should not have been invited to Hollywood, and if they had been any better, I should not have come.**

Raymond Chandler Letter to Charles W. Morton of 12 December 1945, quoted in *Raymond Chandler Speaking*, p. 126, ed. Dorothy Gardiner and Katherine S. Walker (1962)

25 **A freelance writer is a man who is paid per piece or per word or perhaps.**

Robert Benchley Quoted by James Thurber, the *Bermudian* November 1950

26 **Editing is the same as quarreling with writers – same thing exactly.**

Harold Ross *Time* magazine 6 March 1950. His writers would find comments such as 'What mean?', 'Who he?', 'Why in hell?' written in the margins.

27 The trouble with our younger authors is that they're all in their sixties.

Somerset Maugham Said in 1951, quoted in *Collins Dictionary of Quotations* ed. A. Norman Jeffares and Martin Gray (1995)

28 The agent never receipts his bill, puts his hat on and bows himself out. He stays around for ever, not only for as long as you can write anything that anyone will buy, but as long as anyone will buy any portion of any right to anything you did write. He just takes ten per cent of your life.

Raymond Chandler *Atlantic Monthly* February 1952

29 If a writer has to rob his mother, he will not hesitate; the 'Ode on a Grecian Urn' is worth any number of old ladies.

William Faulkner *Paris Review* Spring 1956

30 The most essential gift for a good writer is a built-in, shock-proof shit detector.

Ernest Hemingway Ibid., Spring 1958

31 When I signed my contract with the Devil, bad reviews were not part of the agreement.

Gore Vidal Said in 1958 to Elaine Dundy, quoted in her *Life Itself!*, ch. 21, 'Gore' (2002)

32 A best-seller was a book which somehow sold well simply because it was selling well.

Daniel J. Boorstin *The Image*, ch. 4 (1961)

33 It is my masterpiece, the thing I would like to live after everyone dies.

Carl Reiner and Mel Brooks Warren Balloo, the 'third best poet in America', in the sketch 'The Third Best Poet', *Two Thousand and One Years with Carl Reiner and Mel Brooks* (LP, 1961)

34 Writing a book of poetry is like dropping a rose petal down the Grand Canyon and waiting for the echo.

Don Marquis *O Rare Don Marquis*, p. 146, by E. Anthony (1962)

35 PENELOPE: Read me what you've done today.
BONE: You think in quantities. I am not a typist.

Tom Stoppard *Another Moon Called Earth* (TV play, 1967)

36 There are three reasons for becoming a writer. The first is that you need the money; the second, that you have something to say that you think the world should know; and the third is that you can't think what to do with the long winter evenings.

Quentin Crisp *The Naked Civil Servant*, ch. 24 (1968)

37 I can talk about *not* writing with more passion than they talk about writing.

Kenneth Tynan Diary entry for 22 October 1971, *The Diaries of Kenneth Tynan* ed. John Lahr (2000). He had just spent a flat evening with 'the British journalistic intelligentsia', including Anthony Sampson, Karl Miller, John Gross and David Caute.

38 Writing is turning one's worst moments into money.

J. P. Donleavy *Playboy* May 1979

39 Once, in an excess of irritation with his small son Jean, Camus ordered him from the supper table to bed. 'Good night, minor writer of no importance,' muttered the child as he withdrew.

Christopher Hitchens Quoted in the *New Statesman* 20 July 1979, collected as 'Camus: Un Copain' (Camus: A Friend), *Prepared for the Worst* (1989)

40 Some writers take to drink, other writers take to audiences.

Gore Vidal *New York Times* 12 March 1981

41 O Lord, Let Mine Enemy Write a Book.

Anon. Described as 'the old prayer', and quoted by Christopher Hitchens in a review of *The Years of Upheaval* by Henry Kissinger (who was Hitchens's enemy). *The Nation* 5 June 1982.

42 The reading of proofs: the art of avoiding misprints.

Miles Kington *Moreover*, 'The Moreover Advice Service' (1982)

43 'You want to be a writer?' my father said. 'My dear boy, have some consideration for your unfortunate wife. You'll be sitting around the house all day, wearing a dressing-gown, brewing tea, and stumped for words.'
John Mortimer *Clinging to the Wreckage*, ch. 6 (1982). Mortimer's father recommended law instead: 'That's the great thing about law, it gets you out of the house.'

44 To justify its existence writing has to be extraordinary. If it's ordinary it's less than worthless; it's clutter. Go into any bookshop and try to breathe. You can't. Too many words produced by people working every morning.
John Updike The opinion of Henry Bech in *Bech Is Back*, 'Bech Wed' (1982)

45 It's the most pointless book since *How to Learn French* was translated into French.
Ben Elton and Richard Curtis *Blackadder the Third* (TV, series, 1987), 'Ink and Incapability'

46 The shelf life of the modern hardback writer is somewhere between the milk and the yoghurt.
John Mortimer *Sunday Times* 27 December 1987

47 Of course not everything in the publishing world is fiction, is it Margery? There's non-fiction, for instance.
Victoria Wood Joan in *Barmy: The New Victoria Wood Sketch Book*, Preface (1987)

48 So that's seven books I've written. Not bad for somebody who's only read three.
George Burns *All My Best Friends*, ch. 1 (1989)

49 'Enough about me,' said the newly published woman. 'Have you read my book?'
Anon. *And I Quote*, 'Books and Reading', ed. Ashton Applewhite and others (1992)

50 If I had four fans in every major city in America, I would consider myself to have a readership.
Howard Jacobson *Roots Schmoots*, ch. 7 (1993)

51 If you file your waste-paper basket for fifty years, you have a public library.
Tony Benn *Daily Telegraph* 5 March 1994

52 After writing *The Liar* he maintained that he would not write a second or third novel, but perhaps a fourth.
Stephen Fry Biographical note to *The Hippopotamus* (1995)

53 The trouble with working in publishing is that reading in your spare time is a bit like being a dustman and snuffling through the pig bin in the evening.
Helen Fielding *Bridget Jones's Diary* (1996), entry for Sunday 1 January

54 Most writers sacrifice too much humanity for too little art.
James Cameron Quoted in *Raymond Chandler: A Biography*, ch. 3, by Tom Hiney (1997)

55 I don't do witty off-the-cuff remarks. It's like throwing £5 notes into the gutter.
Keith Waterhouse Quoted in the *Independent* 1 March 1999. Alan Bennett said something similar: that he didn't see why he should go on chat shows and give out all his best lines for free.

56 Just you try doing your VAT returns with a head full of Goblins.
Terry Pratchett On the tendency for his work to take him over. *The Times*, 'Quotes of the Week', 26 February 2000.

57 There have been a couple of books written about me by critics, but I don't read them because I don't want to know what my work is about.
Alan Bennett *The Times*, 'Quotes of the Week', 15 December 2001, collected in *The Times Quotes of the Week* introduced by Philip Howard (2002)

58 I would like to say that my wife, Elaine, possessed all the patience and understanding of a loving wife, etc, but in fact she just said to me: 'Oh, will you just shut up about it, and finish it.'
Jon Ronson *Them* (2001), Preface

59 **A writer without a bottle of whiskey is like a chicken without a goddam head.**

William Faulkner Attributed to the writer (and alcoholic) William Faulkner by Terry Southern in *Now Dig This: The Unspeakable Writings of Terry Southern (1950–1995)*, 'Drugs and the Writer', ed. Nile Southern and Josh Alan Friedman (2001)

60 **How dull the world would be if it were controlled by the omniscient tell-tale blurb writers! 'It's a baby boy!' the blurb-writer midwife would tell the mother. 'He's going to be a moderately successful insurance broker, marry twice, have three children and largely live in Berkshire.'**

Craig Brown *This Is Craig Brown*, 'The Literary Life' (2003)

Genres

1 **A man who is hopeless at field events avoids the equipment,/ keeping his ignorant hands off shot, discus and javelin,/ for fear of giving the crowds of spectators a free laugh./ The fellow who is useless at writing poetry still attempts it.**

Horace *Epistles*, bk 2, no. 3 (*c.*19 BC), from *Horace: Satires and Epistles; Persius: Satires* trans. and ed. Niall Rudd (1973)

2 **'By God,' quod he, 'for pleynly, at a word,/ Thy drasty ryming is nat worth a toord!'**

Geoffrey Chaucer *The Canterbury Tales*, 'The Prologue and Tale of Sir Thopas' (*c.*1387)

3 **For what's a play without a woman in it?**

Thomas Kyd Hieronimo in *The Spanish Tragedy*, act 4, sc. 1 (1592)

4 **No epilogue, I pray you; for your play needs no excuse.**

William Shakespeare Theseus in *A Midsummer Night's Dream*, act 5, sc. 1 (1595–6)

5 **Then Cupid thus: 'This little maid/ Of love shall always speak and write.'/ 'And I pronounce', the satyr**

said,/ 'The world shall feel her scratch and bite.'

Jonathan Swift 'Corinna'. According to A. Norman Jeffares in his *Jonathan Swift: Selected Poems*, this was probably about Mrs Mary Delarivière Manley (1663–1724), mistress to various eminent men, who wrote *The New Atlantis* (1709), an erotic *roman à clef*.

6 **Among all kinds of writing, there is none in which authors are more apt to miscarry than in works of humour, as there is none in which they are more ambitious to excel.**

Joseph Addison *Spectator* 10 April 1711

7 **Unless he were, like Phoebus, young;/ Nor ever nymph inspired to rhyme,/ Unless, like Venus, in her prime./ At fifty-six, if this be true,/ Am I a poet fit for you?**

Jonathan Swift 'Stella's Birthday', written 1725, collected in *Jonathan Swift: Selected Poems* ed. A. Norman Jeffares (1992)

8 **Sir, I admit your gen'ral rule/ That every poet is a fool:/ But you yourself may serve to show it,/ That every fool is not a poet.**

Alexander Pope 'Epigram from the French' (1732)

9 **So, naturalists observe, a flea/ Hath smaller fleas that on him prey;/ And these have smaller fleas to bite 'em,/ And so proceed *ad infinitum*/ Thus every poet, in his kind,/ Is bit by him that comes behind.**

Jonathan Swift 'On Poetry: A Rhapsody', line 337 (1733)

10 **Nothing gives a coxcomb more delight, than when you suffer him to talk of himself; which sweet liberty I here enjoy for a whole volume together.**

Colley Cibber *An Apology for the Life of Mr Colley Cibber, Comedian*, ch. 2 (1739)

11 **While pensive poets painful vigils keep,/ Sleepless themselves, to give their readers sleep.**

Alexander Pope *The Dunciad*, 1, line 93 (1742)

12 ***A novel*** – a small tale, generally of love.

Samuel Johnson *A Dictionary of the English*

Language (1755). Quoted by J. L. Carr at the beginning of his novella *A Month in the Country* (1980).

13 Dull: To make dictionaries is dull work.

Samuel Johnson Definition in *A Dictionary of the English Language* (1755)

14 But these were the dreams of a poet doomed at last to wake a lexicographer.

Samuel Johnson Ibid., Preface (1755). Johnson defines 'lexicographer' as 'a writer of dictionaries, a harmless drudge'.

15 Dictionaries are like watches, the worst is better than none, and the best cannot be expected to go quite true.

Samuel Johnson *The Life of Samuel Johnson* by James Boswell, vol. 1, p. 293; in G. B. Hill's edition of 1887, rev. L. F. Powell (1934)

16 Poetry is – I fear – incurable

Lord Byron Letter to John Murray of 15 October 1816, collected in *Letters and Journals*, vol. 5, *So Late into the Night (1816–17)*, ed. Leslie A. Marchand (1976)

17 The composition of a tragedy requires *testicles*.

Voltaire On being asked why no woman had written a 'tolerable' tragedy. Quoted in a letter from Byron to John Murray of 2 April 1817, collected in ibid.

18 The wives of poets are (for the most part) mere pieces of furniture in the room.

William Hazlitt 'On the Knowledge of Character', *Table Talk* (March 1822), collected in *The Essays of William Hazlitt* ed. Catherine Macdonald Maclean (1949)

19 A novel is a mirror walking along a main road.

Stendhal *The Red and the Black*, ch. 49 (1830)

20 The favourite attitude of the poetical young gentleman is lounging on a sofa with his eyes fixed upon the ceiling, or sitting bolt upright in a high-backed chair, staring with very round eyes at the opposite wall.

Charles Dickens *Sketches by Boz*, 'The Poetical Gentleman' (1836). Dickens adds that the

poetical gentleman 'is fond of quoting passages from his favourite authors, who are all of the gloomy and desponding school'.

21 Poetry's unnat'ral: no man ever talked poetry 'cept a beadle on boxin' day.

Charles Dickens Mr Weller in *The Pickwick Papers*, ch. 33 (1836–7)

22 A well-written Life is almost as rare as a well spent one.

Thomas Carlyle Quoted in *Critical and Miscellaneous Essays* by Jean-Paul Richter (1838)

23 . . . guanoed her mind by reading French novels.

Benjamin Disraeli *Tancred*, bk 2, ch. 9 (1847). This is Lady Constance.

24 That fellow would vulgarize the Day of Judgement.

Douglas Jerrold *The Wit and Opinions of Douglas Jerrold*, 'A Comic Author', ed. Blanchard Jerrold (1859)

25 I often say I am like the pastry cook, and don't care for tarts, but prefer bread and cheese.

William Makepeace Thackeray On why, although a novelist, he preferred non-fiction. Letter to Anthony Trollope of 28 October 1859. Quoted in *The Letters of Anthony Trollope* ed. Bradford Allen Booth (1951).

26 I didn't think this morning there were half so many Scarers in Print.

Charles Dickens Mr Boffin in *Our Mutual Friend*, 'Book the First: The Cup and the Lip', ch. 5 (1864–5)

27 Some men are good for righting wrongs, – / And some for writing verses.

Frederick Locker-Lampson 'The Jester's Plea' (1868)

28 It's awful fun, boys' stories; you just indulge the pleasure of your heart, that's all; no trouble, no strain. The only stiff thing is to get it ended – that I don't see but I look to a volcano.

Robert Louis Stevenson Letter to William Ernest Henley of August 1881, collected in *Great Letters* ed. Wallace Brockway and Bart Keith Winer (1941). The letter is about the writing of *Treasure Island*, the first two chapters of which Stevenson had just finished.

29 **War talk by men who have been in a war is always interesting; whereas moon talk by a poet who has not been on the moon is likely to be dull.**

Mark Twain *Life on the Mississippi*, ch. 45 (1883)

30 **Personally I never cared for fiction or story books. What I like to read about are facts and statistics of any kind. If they are only facts about the raising of radishes, they interest me.**

Mark Twain Interviewed by Rudyard Kipling. Collected in Kipling's *Sea to Sea* (1889). Later in the same interview Twain said: 'Get your facts first, and then you can distort 'em as much as you please.'

31 **A great poet, a truly great poet, is the most unpoetical of all creatures. But inferior poets are absolutely fascinating. The worse their rhymes are, the more picturesque they look.**

Oscar Wilde *The Picture of Dorian Gray*, ch. 4 (1891). The opinion of Lord Henry Wotton, who adds: an inferior poet 'lives the poetry that he cannot write'.

32 **The good end happily, and the bad unhappily. That is what Fiction means.**

Oscar Wilde Miss Prism in *The Importance of Being Earnest*, act 2 (1895)

33 **But I'm going to tell you about my country pleasures in another chapter. I have to be born first.**

Dan Leno *Dan Leno Hys Booke*, Chapter First (1899). Elsewhere in the same work: 'I don't like talking about myself; that's why I'm writing this book.'

34 **The story is just the spoiled child of art.**

Henry James *The Ambassadors*, Preface (1903)

35 **Of course, most of the poets wrote in prose – Rabelais, for instance, and Dickens.**

G. K. Chesterton *Alarms and Discursions*, 'The Three Kinds of Men' (1910)

36 **Immature poets imitate; mature poets steal.**

T. S. Eliot *The Sacred Wood*, 'Philip Massinger' (1920)

37 **Most so-called short stories are not short enough.**

Sir Walter Raleigh Introductory note to some of Raleigh's own *very* short stories, collected in *Laughter from a Cloud* (1923)

38 **With the portion of my life that intervened between my birth and my baptism I do not propose, owing to the exigencies of space, to deal in the fullest detail.**

Sir Henry Howarth Bashford *Augustus Carp Esq., by Himself*, ch. 2 (1924)

39 **People take up a book of short stories and say, 'Oh, what's this? Just a lot of those short things?' and put it right down again.**

Dorothy Parker From a review of *Men without Women* by Ernest Hemingway, *New Yorker* 29 October 1927

40 **Mr Ponderby-Wilkins was a man so rich, so ugly, so cross, and so old that even the stupidest reader could not expect him to survive any longer than Chapter 1.**

E. V. Lucas *The Murder at the Towers: The Most Marvellous Mystery Story in the World*, ch. 1, which appeared in *Punch* May 1929

41 **Hamlet, if written today, would probably be called *The Strange Affair at Elsinore*.**

J. M. Barrie *Observer*, 'Sayings of the Week', 28 April 1929

42 **[Chinese rule of health] One day of the week, if possible, neither read nor write poetry.**

Anon. *Livres sans nom* (Books without a Name) (1930), collected in *Geoffrey Madan's Notebooks* ed. J. A. Gere and John Sparrow (1981)

43 **Broadly speaking, the trouble with every villain of a thriller is that he suffers from a fatal excess of ingenuity. When he was a boy, his parents must thoughtlessly have told him he was clever, and it has**

absolutely spoiled him for effective
work.

P. G. Wodehouse *Louder and Funnier*,
'Thrillers' (1932). 'The ordinary man,' wrote
Wodehouse, 'when circumstances compel
him to murder a female acquaintance,
borrows a revolver and a few cartridges and
does the thing in some odd five minutes of
the day when he is not at the office or the
pictures.'

44 **I always say, keep a diary and some
day it'll keep you.**

Mae West Peaches O'Day in *Every Day's a
Holiday* (film, 1937, screenplay by Mae West,
directed by A. Edward Sutherland)

45 **'Oh son, I wish you hadn't become a
scenario writer!' she sniffed. 'Aw,
now, moms,' I comforted her, 'it's
no worse than playing the piano in
a call house.'**

S. J. Perelman *Strictly from Hunger*, 'Strictly
from Hunger' (1937)

46 **By good rights, great humorists
ought to be gentle, agreeable people
to meet, with a breadth of view and
a kindly tolerance of trifles – such
as they show in print. Mostly they
are not.**

Stephen Leacock *The Boy I Left Behind Me*
(1947)

47 **He has written a lot of poems to me
some of them very beautiful and
quite ethical others not so much.**

Evelyn Waugh *The Loved One* (1948). A PS in
a letter from Aimée Thanatogenos to an
agony page in a local (Californian) newspaper. 'Once, in the days of family piety, it
bore the title Aunt Lydia's Post Bag; now it
was The Wisdom of the Guru Brahmin,
adorned with the photograph of a bearded
and almost naked sage.'

48 **When you put down the good
things you ought to have done, and
leave out the bad ones you did –
well, that's Memoirs.**

Will Rogers *The Autobiography of Will
Rogers*, ch. 16 (1949)

49 **[Of America] In this country the
mystery writer is looked down on
as sub-literary merely because he is
a mystery writer, rather than for**

instance a writer of social signifi-
cance twaddle.

Raymond Chandler Letter to Hamish Hamilton of 10 November 1950, quoted in *Raymond Chandler*, ch. 1, by Tom Hiney (1997)

50 **If you really want to hear about it,
the first thing you'll probably want
to know is where I was born, and
what my lousy childhood was like,
and how my parents were occupied
before they had me, and all that
David Copperfield kind of crap . . .**

J. D. Salinger Narrator (Holden Caulfield) in
The Catcher in the Rye (1951). The opening
lines of the book.

51 **How impossible it is for me to
make regular entries in the diary. I
suddenly remember how I used to
puzzle over that word at school.
Always wondering why diary was
so like Dairy and what the connection was. Never found out.**

Kenneth Williams Entry for 6 January 1953,
The Kenneth Williams Diaries ed. R. Davies
(1993)

52 **Well, as you know, children, I write
lots and lots of books for you and
this is how I set about it. First of all
I go upstairs to my Hidey Hole –
well, this is really just a great big
upstairs work room but I like to call
it my Hidey Hole. I pin a notice on
the door and it says: 'Gone to make-
believe land.'**

Joyce Grenfell 'The Writer of Children's
Stories', *Joyce Grenfell Requests the Pleasure*
(sketch show, 1954), collected in *Turn Back
the Clock* (1977)

53 **I know that poetry is indispensable,
but to what I could not say.**

Jean Cocteau *Observer*, 'Sayings of the
Week', 23 October 1955

54 **We men have got love well weighed
up; our stuff/ Can get by without
it./ Women don't seem to think
that's good enough;/ They write
about it.**

Kingsley Amis 'A Bookshop Idyll' (1956)

55 **One of the myriad traits which
distinguish me from the nation's**

Great Men is my inability to finish a detective story. I can get right up to the last ten pages, but there a galloping indifference sets in and I go to the ice-box.

Robert Benchley *Benchley or Else*, 'Who Killed Alfred Robin?' (1958)

56 The structure of a play is always the story of how the birds came home to roost.

Arthur Miller *Harper's Magazine* August 1958

57 Is Truth stranger than Fiction? . . . Of course in order to settle it, one must know how strange Fiction is. Then, working backward from that, we can see how strange Truth is, and come to some orderly decision satisfactory to both sides. The thing is to avoid hard feelings.

Robert Benchley *Benchley or Else*, 'Fiction Stranger Than Truth' (1958)

58 I promised my mother I would never use that wretched word 'novella'.

Dorothy Parker Article in *Esquire* February 1959

59 [Of Cornelia Fothergill, novelist] She specializes in rich goo for the female trade.

P. G. Wodehouse *A Few Quick Ones*, 'Jeeves Makes an Omelette' (1959). When she later appears, Fothergill turns out to be 'a large spreading woman wearing the horn-rimmed spectacles which are always an occupational risk for penpushers of the opposite sex'.

60 [On writing poetry] It starts as inspiration and ends as a crossword puzzle.

John Betjeman Interviewed by teenagers on *Let's Find Out* (BBC radio programme, 10 August 1962)

61 'But can you?'/ 'Can I what?'/ 'Write an important novel?'/ 'Of course I can. All I have to do is cut out the plot and shove in plenty of misery.'

P. G. Wodehouse *Ice in the Bedroom*, ch. 6 (1964). Freddie Widgeon is interrogating Leila York (aka Elizabeth Binns) authoress of, among others, *Heather o' The Hills* and *Sweet Jennie Dean*.

62 The parody is the last refuge of the frustrated writer. Parodies are what you write when you are associate editor of the Harvard *Lampoon*. The greater the work of literature, the easier the parody. The step up from writing parodies is writing on the wall.

Ernest Hemingway Quoted in *Papa Hemingway*, pt 1, ch. 4, ed. E. Hotchner (1966)

63 The English plays are like their English puddings: nobody has any taste for them but themselves.

Voltaire Quoted in *Anecdotes*, no. 1033, by Joseph Spence, ed. J. M. Osborn (1966)

64 I'd as soon write free verse as play tennis with the net down.

Robert Frost *Interviews with Robert Frost*, p. 203, ed. Edward Lanthern (1966)

65 You're familiar with the tragedies of antiquity, are you? The great homicidal classics?

Tom Stoppard Guildenstern in *Rosencrantz and Guildenstern Are Dead*, act 1 (1967)

66 Most 'serious' American novels are autobiographies, usually composed to pay off grudges.

Gore Vidal *Encounter* December 1967. Collected as 'French Letters: Theories of the New Novel', *The Essential Gore Vidal* ed. Fred Kaplan (1999).

67 He spends most of his time writing, and is currently revising his autobiography to include himself.

Woody Allen *Getting Even*, 'Conversations with Helmholtz' (1971). The 'He' in question is Dr Helmholtz, a contemporary of Freud's, a pioneer of psychoanalysis, 'perhaps best known for his experiments in behavior, in which he proved that death is an acquired trait'.

68 Books can be broken broadly into two classes: those written to please the reader and those written for the greater pleasure of the writer. Subject to numerous and distinguished exceptions, the second class is rightly suspect and especially if the writer himself appears in the story.

David Niven *The Moon's a Balloon*, Introduction (1971)

69 A novelist is, like all mortals, more fully at home on the surface of the present than on the ooze of the past.

Vladimir Nabokov *Strong Opinions*, ch. 20 (1973)

70 The novel was no mere literary form. It was a psychological phenomenon. It was cortical fever. It belonged in the glossary to *A General Introduction to Psychoanalysis*, somewhere between Narcissism and Obsessional Neuroses.

Tom Wolfe *The New Journalism*, ch. 1, 'The Feature Game', ed. Tom Wolfe and E. W. Johnson (1973). The reference is to the American novel of the 1940s, 50s and 60s.

71 I have been the soreheaded occupant of a file drawer labeled 'Science Fiction' . . . and I would like out, particularly since so many critics regularly mistake the drawer for a urinal.

Kurt Vonnegut *Wampeters, Foma and Granfalloons*, 'Science Fiction' (1974)

72 It is a librarian's duty to distinguish between poetry and a sort of belle-litter.

Tom Stoppard Henry Carr in *Travesties* (1975)

73 I don't think anybody should write his autobiography until after he's dead.

Sam Goldwyn *Goldwyn: The Man behind the Myth*, Prologue, by Arthur Marx (1976)

74 A poet's hope: to be,/ like some valley cheese,/ local, but prized elsewhere.

W. H. Auden 'Shorts, 1969–71', *Collected Poems* ed. Edward Mendelson (1976)

75 I've no interest in my autobiography. I've read it.

Jake Thackray *Jake's Progress*, 'Before I Was a Performing Man . . .' (1977). Explaining why he will supply no biographical notes to his book.

76 Book – what they make a movie out of for television.

Leonard Louis Levinson Quoted in *Quotations for our Times* ed. Laurence J. Peter (1977)

77 A beginning, a muddle and an end.

Philip Larkin The 'classic formula' for a novel. *New Fiction*, no. 15 (January 1978).

78 I could not have written this book without the unstinting help of the University of Nebraska, who own many letters written by this wonderful man of letters, or indeed without the assistance of his widow, who burnt far more.

Miles Kington *Miles and Miles*, 'How to Write a Bestseller' (1982). Sample introduction to a biography.

79 case, The: 'You're off the case, George. You're emotionally involved.' 'But Guv . . .' 'That will be all, George.'

Henry Root *Henry Root's World of Knowledge* (1982)

80 Got *Waiting for Godot* out of the library. Disappointed to find that it was a play.

Sue Townsend *The Secret Diary of Adrian Mole Aged 13¾* (1982), entry for Friday 10 April

81 Well, the woman would have to be attractive; women in fiction always were.

John Updike *Bech Is Back*, 'Three Illuminations in the Life of an American Author' (1982). Henry Bech, novelist, is musing about a new female character.

82 Since those days [the Second World War] I haven't attacked a poem and I hope poetry is for my old age, like spending every day in the garden.

John Mortimer *Clinging to the Wreckage*, ch. 7 (1982)

83 She's still writing books. Autobiographies mostly.

Anon. Quoted in *Word of Mouth*, 'Eavesdroppings', ed. Nigel Rees (1983). Remark overheard by the writer Pete Atkin.

84 The first thing I did was my life story. Since I was nine at the time, it was only three-quarters of a page long.

Jack Rosenthal *P'tang, Yang, Kipperbang and Other TV Plays*, Introduction (1984)

85 There is to be a twenty-year ban on

novels set in Oxford or Cambridge, and a ten-year ban on other university fiction.

Julian Barnes Playing at being a 'dictator of literature' in *Flaubert's Parrot*, ch. 7 (1984). Amongst other rulings: 'A quota system is to be introduced on fiction set in South America.'

86 July 10th. I have not written since March, I know, but my felt tip has completely dried up and I

Maureen Lipman *How Was It For You?*, 'Literary Pretenshuns' (1985). Sample diary entry.

87 Surprisingly solid for a showbiz rush-job, Bob Geldof's autobiography could not be more personal if he had written it himself.

Clive James Review of *Is That It?* by Bob Geldof ('helped' by Paul Vallely), *Observer* 11 May 1986

88 A good film script should be able to do completely without dialogue.

David Mamet *Independent* 11 November 1988

89 The business of writing novels is long, lonely, and you get extremely cold.

John Mortimer *Murderers and Other Friends*, ch. 16 (1992)

90 How could this happen? We started out like Romeo and Juliet but it ended up in tragedy.

Mat Groening Milhouse in *The Simpsons*, 'Bart's Friend Falls in Love', first broadcast 7 May 1992

91 [Of screenwriting] It's an opportunity to fly first class, be treated like a celebrity, sit around the pool and be betrayed.

Ian McEwan *Observer*, 'Sayings of the Week', 22 August 1993

92 You didn't have to do much in the literary field, he thought, to merit a biography. So long as you knew how to read and write . . .

Martin Amis *The Information*, pt 3 (1995)

93 'The body lay on the carpet.'/ Well, thought Eric, it's a beginning. I can see a few problems looming, though, Eric old lad. I mean – whose body? That will have to be dealt with.

Joseph Connolly Eric begins his first novel in *This Is It*, ch. 11 (1996)

94 [Of poets] There is no believing a word they say.

Duke of Wellington Quoted in *Wellington – A Personal History*, ch. 27, by Christopher Hibbert (1997). Wellington 'hated the whole race of poets'.

95 There are poems about the internet and about the shipping forecast, but very few by women celebrating men.

Germaine Greer Addressing the Poetry Society. Quoted in *The Times* 27 January 2001.

96 When the curtain goes up we've got your attention, so we dramatists don't *have* to do anything for a while.

David Mamet *Three Uses of the Knife*, ch. 2 (2002)

97 The difference between writing non-fiction and fiction is like sparring with your friends and sparring with someone who's out to beat you.

Norman Mailer Quoted in the *Daily Telegraph* 6 February 2002. A very characteristic image in that Mailer has often hit people – 'Being macho is a bitch,' he said in the same interview.

98 [Of the plight of the satirist] What is the point of bothering to ride into battle if all your enemy are busily falling on their swords?

Craig Brown *This Is Craig Brown*, Introduction (2003). Brown goes on: 'Jokes into reality, reality into jokes: the dividing line grows thinner every year . . .'

99 The poetry world is like the seaside, still going on somewhere, in spite of everything.

Hugo Williams *Times Literary Supplement* 25 July 2003

100 I'm never going to read another novel that doesn't begin with the words 'A shot rang out.'

Kingsley Amis Quoted by Martin Amis in the

Guardian 29 August 2003. Amis Snr had finally lost patience with what he called 'poncey' novelists. 'Nabokov,' his son elaborated, 'for buggering the reader about and Bellow for just babbling.'

Particular Writers and Their Works

1 **Dr Donne's verses are like the peace of God; they pass all understanding.**
James I of England and VI of Scotland Attributed

2 **To the King's Theatre, where we saw *Midsummer Night's Dream*, which I had never seen before, nor shall ever again, for it is the most insipid ridiculous play that ever I saw in my life.**
Samuel Pepys Diary entry for 29 September 1662, *Everybody's Pepys* ed. Henry B. Wheatley (1926)

3 **A brain of feathers, and a heart of lead.**
Alexander Pope *The Dunciad*, bk 2, line 44 (1742). Part of a description of a poet, this is a reference to James Moore Smythe who had once accused Pope of plagiarism.

4 **One of the greatest geniuses that ever existed, Shakespeare, undoubtedly wanted taste.**
Horace Walpole Letter to Christopher Wren of 9 August 1764, collected in *Horace Walpole's Correspondence*, vol. 40 (1973)

5 **I do not think this poem will reach its destination.**
Voltaire Reviewing 'Ode to Posterity' by Jean-Jacques Rousseau. Attributed.

6 [Of Milton] **An acrimonious and surly republican.**
Samuel Johnson *The Lives of the Poets*, 'Milton' (1779–81)

7 [Of Jonathan Swift] **He washed himself with oriental scrupulosity.**
Ibid., 'Swift'

8 **There is no arguing with Johnson; for when his pistol misses fire, he knocks you down with the butt end of it.**
Oliver Goldsmith *The Life of Samuel Johnson* by James Boswell, vol. 2, p. 100 (1791); in G. B. Hill's edition of 1887, rev. L. F. Powell (1934)

9 **It is burning a farthing candle at Dover to shew light at Calais.**
Samuel Johnson Estimating Sheridan's influence upon the English language. Ibid., vol. 1, p. 454. Boswell records Johnson also saying of Sheridan: 'Why, Sir, Sherry is dull, naturally dull; but it must have taken him a great deal of pains to become what we now see him. Such an excess of stupidity, Sir, is not in nature.'

10 **I love Robertson, and I won't talk of his book.**
Ibid., vol. 2, p. 53. The book, by William Robertson, was *A History of Scotland*. Boswell remarked that Johnson's 'prejudice against Scotland appeared remarkably strong at this time'.

11 [Of *Gulliver's Travels*] **When once you have thought of the big men and the little men it is very easy to do all the rest.**
Ibid., vol. 2, p. 319

12 **Burton's *Anatomy of Melancholy*, he said, was the only book that ever took him out of bed two hours sooner than he wished to rise.**
Ibid., vol. 2, p. 121

13 [Of Thomas Gray] **He was dull in a new way, and that made many people think him great.**
Ibid., vol. 2, p. 327

14 [Of the letters of Lord Chesterfield] **They teach the morals of a whore, and the manners of a dancing master.**
Ibid., vol. 1, p. 266

15 [Of Lord Byron] **Mad, bad and dangerous to know.**
Lady Caroline Lamb Remark committed to her journal after meeting Byron at a ball in March 1812. Quoted in *Lady Caroline Lamb*, ch. 6, by Elizabeth Jenkins (1932)

16 [Of Coleridge] **Then a round-faced man in black entered, and dissi-**

pated all doubts on the subject, by beginning to talk. He did not cease while he stayed; nor has he since, that I know of.

William Hazlitt 'My First Acquaintance with Poets', *The Liberal* April 1823, collected in *The Essays of William Hazlitt* ed. Catherine Macdonald Maclean (1949). Towards the end of his life Hazlitt wrote: 'till I became acquainted with the author of *The Ancient Mariner* I could neither write nor speak.'

17 [Of Charles Lamb] **His sayings are generally like women's letters; all the pith is in the postscript.**

William Hazlitt Quoted in *Conversations of James Northcote* (1826–7)

18 [Of Dryden] **His imagination resembled the wings of an ostrich. It enabled him to run, though not to soar.**

Lord Macaulay *Miscellaneous Writings of Lord Macaulay*, 'John Dryden', ed. T. F. Ellis (1828)

19 **There comes Poe with his raven like Barnaby Rudge,/ Three-fifths of him genius, and two-fifths sheer fudge.**

James Russell Lowell *Poe and Longfellow: A Fable for Critics* (1848). In Dickens's novel *Barnaby Rudge* (1841), Rudge wanders about with his raven, Grip. Poe's poem 'The Raven' appeared in 1845.

20 **A wit said of Gibbon's autobiography, that he did not know the difference between himself and the Roman Empire.**

Anon. Quoted by Walter Bagehot in a review of a new edition of Gibbon's *The History of the Decline and Fall of the Roman Empire*, *National Review* 1856, publ. in *The Collected Works of Walter Bagehot*, vol. 1, p. 351, ed. Norman St John-Stevas (1966–86)

21 **Girls, do you know Charlotte has been writing a book, and it is much better than likely?**

Patrick Brontë Quoted in *The Life of Charlotte Brontë* by Elizabeth Gaskell, ch. 16 (1857)

22 [Of Dickens] **He describes London like a special correspondent for posterity.**

Walter Bagehot *National Review* 7 October 1858

23 **Dr Johnson's morality was as English an article as a beefsteak.**

Nathaniel Hawthorne *Our Old Home*, 'Lichfield and Uttoxeter' (1863)

24 **How pleasant to know Mr Lear!/ Who has written such volumes of stuff!/ Some think him ill-tempered and queer,/ But a few think him pleasant enough.**

Edward Lear *Nonsense Songs*, Preface (1871)

25 **It was very good of God to let Carlyle and Mrs Carlyle marry one another and so make only two people miserable instead of four, besides being very amusing.**

Samuel Butler Letter to Miss Savage of 21 November 1884. The Carlyle marriage was a turbulent one.

26 **I can't stand George Eliot, & Hawthorne & those people; I see what they are at, a hundred times before they get to it, & they just tire me to death. And as for *The Bostonians*, I would rather be damned to John Bunyan's heaven than read that.**

Mark Twain Letter to W. D. Howells of 21 July 1885. In the same letter he said of Eliot's works: 'I wouldn't read another of those books for a farm.'

27 **What readers ask now-a-days of a book is that it should instruct and elevate. This book wouldn't elevate a cow. I cannot conscientiously recommend it for any useful purposes whatsoever. All I can suggest is, that when you get tired of reading 'the best hundred books', you may take this up for half an hour. It will be a change.**

Jerome K. Jerome *The Idle Thoughts of An Idle Fellow*, Preface (1889)

28 [Of Robert Louis Stevenson] ***The Black Arrow* is so inartistic as not to contain a single anachronism to boast of, while the transformation of Dr Jekyll reads dangerously like an experiment out of the *Lancet*.**

Oscar Wilde Vivian in *Intentions*, 'The Decay of Lying' (1891)

29 **The rhapsodies of Mr Swinburne,**

again, are so over-whelmingly exuberant in their expression that no ordinary reader can cope with them; the ordinary reader is stunned by them before he is impressed. When he lays down the book and regains consciousness he has forgotten entirely what it was all about.

Max Beerbohm *More*, 'Ouida' (1899)

30 Bernard Shaw is very like his *Saturday Review* articles: he talks too much and keeps on saying that the earth is flat.

Raymond Asquith Letter to H. T. Baker of 12 January 1903, collected in *Raymond Asquith: Life and Letters* ed. John Jolliffe (1980)

31 John Stuart Mill/ By a mighty effort of will/ Overcame his natural bonhomie/ And wrote *Principles of Political Economy*

Edmund Clerihew Bentley *Biography for Beginners*, 'John Stuart Mill' (1905)

32 Remote and ineffectual Don/ That dared attack my Chesterton

Hilaire Belloc 'Lines to a Don' (1910)

33 [Of H. G. Wells] He's like a hat floating on the sea of modern thought; you think that every wave will throw it on the shore, but there it is, still bobbing up and down.

G. K. Chesterton Interview with *Hearth and Home* 17 October 1912, repr. in *The Penguin Book of Interviews* ed. C. Silvester (1993). Chesterton also said: 'You know the sort of pocket-knife that boys love, and I love, too, furnished with every possible implement? Wells is like that knife, except that he hasn't got any nippers.' He believed that Wells's limitation was 'an unlimited mind'.

34 [Of Tennyson] He could not think up to the height of his own towering style.

G. K. Chesterton *The Victorian Age in Literature*, ch. 3 (1912)

35 [Of George Bernard Shaw] A good man fallen among Fabians.

Lenin (Vladimir Ilyich Ulyanov) Quoted in *Russia in 1919*, 'Notes of a Conversation with Lenin', by Arthur Ransome (1919)

36 I always get someone to read *The Faerie Queene* to me when I have neuralgia, and it usually sends me to sleep.

Saki *The Toys of Peace*, 'Louise' (1919)

37 [Of James Joyce's *Ulysses*] Merely the scratching of pimples on the body of the bootboy at Claridge's.

Virginia Woolf Letter to Lytton Strachey of 24th April 1922

38 We do not know when Shakespeare was born nor where he was born. But he is dead.

Stephen Leacock *Winnowed Wisdom*, 'The Outline of Everything' (1926). Leacock's crib for students – in which the bard's name is spelt throughout in different ways – concludes: 'Shakespeare was a very good writer.'

39 When you speak of Disraeli's 'fastidious prose' I start violently. I turn pale, I rise from my seat, and I say, with all submission, 'Then may a tropical jungle be called fastidious.'

Max Beerbohm Letter of 14 January 1928 to H. A. L. Fisher, quoted in *Letters of Max Beerbohm 1892–1956* ed. Rupert Hart-Davis, 1988

40 Tonstant Weader fwowed up.

Dorothy Parker *New Yorker* 20 October 1928. Closing words of a review of *The House at Pooh Corner* by A. A. Milne, in Parker's 'Constant Reader' column. A. A. Milne wrote: 'If I were a critic I should loathe A. A. Milne.'

41 It is not a Life at all. It is a Reticence, in three volumes.

W. E. Gladstone Of *The Life of George Eliot* by J. W. Cross. Quoted in *As We Were*, ch. 6, by E. F. Benson (1930).

42 Among the famous characters of the period was Samuel Pepys, who is memorable for keeping a Diary and going to bed a great deal.

W. C. Sellar and R. J. Yeatman *1066 and All That*, ch. 36 (1930)

43 [Of Dashiell Hammett] He is so hard-boiled you could roll him on the White House Lawn.

Dorothy Parker *New Yorker* 25 April 1931, review of Hammett's novel *The Glass Key*.

She also said he was 'as American as a sawn-off shotgun'.

44 **Shaw's plays are the price we pay for Shaw's prefaces.**

James Agate *Ego* (1935), diary entry for 10 March 1933

45 **Mock on, mock on, Voltaire, Rousseau;/ Mock on, mock on, 'tis all in vain!/ You throw the sand against the wind,/ And the wind blows it back again.**

William Blake MS notebook, p. 7, *The Note-Books of William Blake* ed. Geoffrey Keynes (1935)

46 **If there had been no Voltaire, it would not have been necessary to create one.**

James Thurber *The Middle-Aged Man on the Flying Trapeze*, 'Something to Say' (1935). In his play *Travesties* Tom Stoppard has Henry Carr say: 'If Lenin did not exist, it would be unnecessary to invent him.'

47 **Ben Jonson's position, three hundred years after his death, is more than secure; it might almost be called impregnable. He is still the greatest unread English author.**

Harry Levin *Ben Jonson: Selected Works*, Introduction (1938)

48 **And I'll stay off Verlaine too; he was always chasing Rimbauds.**

Dorothy Parker *Here Lies*, 'The Little Hours' (1939)

49 **Who call him spurious and shoddy/ Shall do it over my dead body.**

Dorothy Parker *The Portable Dorothy Parker*, 'Charles Dickens' (1944)

50 **I am back on Chaucer now. Do you know, I don't believe I like that man very much? There was never anybody who so unswervingly refrained from doing what his admirers are unanimous in declaring he did do.**

Kingsley Amis Letter to Philip Larkin of 13 May 1946, collected in *The Letters of Kingsley Amis* ed. Zachary Leader (2000)

51 [Of P. G. Wodehouse] **English literature's performing flea.**

Sean O'Casey Wodehouse, having quoted

O'Casey's remark, responds: 'I believe he meant it to be complimentary, for all the performing fleas I have met have impressed me with their sterling artistry and that indefinable something which makes the good trouper.' Quoted in *Performing Flea*, 'Huy Day by Day,' by P. G. Wodehouse (1953).

52 [Of Gertrude Stein] **The mama of dada.**

Clifton Fadiman *Party of One*, p. 90 (1955)

53 [Of Virginia Woolf] **I enjoyed talking to her, but thought *nothing* of her writing. I considered her 'a beautiful little knitter'.**

Dame Edith Sitwell Letter to Geoffrey Singleton of 11 July 1955, collected in *Selected Letters of Edith Sitwell (1887–1964)* ed. John Lehmann and Derek Palmer (1970)

54 **I ask you, is anything in life or literature, past or present, in earth, heaven or hell, more devastatingly tedious than D. H. L.'s interest in the human genitalia?**

George Lyttelton Letter to Rupert Hart-Davis of 29 March 1957, collected in *The Lyttelton–Hart-Davis Letters* vols 1 and 2, *1955–1957* ed. Rupert Hart-Davis (1978)

55 **If you are one who likes to give something by Evelyn Waugh, I beg you to hold back, this year, for his *The Ordeal of Gilbert Pinfold* must have been written while he was waiting for the lift to reach his floor.**

Dorothy Parker From a round-up of the year's fiction in *Esquire* December 1957

56 [Of Alexandre Dumas] **He wanted the money, as much of it as he could gouge out of the reading public, but he strongly objected to having to turn out the stuff. So he assigned the rough spadework – the writing of his books – to others.**

P. G. Wodehouse *Cocktail Time*, ch. 23 (1958)

57 **This isn't writing at all – it's typing.**

Truman Capote Quoted in *New Republic* 9 February 1959 – remark made during a TV discussion of the Beat novelists. In 2002 Dr Jonathan Miller, in a TV discussion of Tim Lott's novel *Rumours of a Hurricane*, said: 'This isn't writing – it's word-processing.'

58 [Of Raymond Chandler's novels] **Practically whenever Marlowe calls on a man the man is there all right – but dead. Why do I read him? God knows.**

George Lyttelton Letter to Rupert Hart-Davis of 17 March 1960, collected in *The Lyttelton–Hart-Davis Letters*, vols 5 and 6, *1960–1962*, ed. Rupert Hart-Davis (1981)

59 [Of Noël Coward] **Forty years ago he was Slightly in *Peter Pan*, and you might say that he has been wholly in *Peter Pan* ever since.**

Kenneth Tynan *Curtain*, pt 1 (1961)

60 **Experiment? God forbid! Look at the results of experiment in the case of a writer like Joyce. He started off writing very well, then you can watch him going mad with vanity. He ends up a lunatic.**

Evelyn Waugh Interview in the *Paris Review*, summer/autumn 1963, in response to the suggestion that he experimented in his writing.

61 **The remarkable thing about Shakespeare is that he is really very good – in spite of all the people who say he's very good.**

Robert Graves *Observer* 6 December 1964

62 [Of Max Beerbohm] **As with E. M. Forster, his fame waxed with every book he did not write.**

Malcolm Muggeridge *Tread Softly for You Tread on My Jokes*, 'The Legend of Max' (1966)

63 [Of Evelyn Waugh] **He would so like to have gone to Eton, ridden to hounds, lost enormous sums of money without turning a hair, and so on. Instead, his father was a publisher who lived in Golders Green.**

Ibid., 'My Fair Gentleman'

64 [Of Virginia Woolf] **Of all the honours that fell on Virginia's head, none, I think, pleased her more than the *Evening Standard* award for the Tallest Woman Writer of 1927, an award she took by a neck from Elizabeth Bowen.**

Alan Bennett *Tempest* in *Forty Years On*, act 2 (1968)

65 **Personally, I would rather have written *Winnie the Pooh* than the collected works of Brecht.**

Tom Stoppard Remark made in 1972, quoted in *Double Act: A Life of Tom Stoppard*, ch. 13, by Ira Nadel (2002)

66 [On why *Dante's Inferno* is a classic] **You can read it out of doors.**

Bertolt Brecht Quoted by Kenneth Tynan, diary entry for 3 January 1973, *The Diaries of Kenneth Tynan*, ed. John Lahr (2000)

67 **The Waugh to end Waugh.**

Maurice Bowra Of Evelyn Waugh's *Men at Arms* trilogy, which he didn't like. Quoted by Francis King in *Maurice Bowra: A Celebration*, 'Pray You, Undo This Button', ed. Hugh Lloyd-Jones (1974).

68 **At Ilkley literature festival a woman shrieked and vomited during a Ted Hughes reading. I must say I've never felt like shrieking.**

Philip Larkin Letter to Robert Conquest of 15 June 1975, collected in *Selected Letters of Philip Larkin, 1940–85*, ed. Anthony Thwaite (1992). Larkin continued: 'We had the old crow over at Hull recently, looking like a Christmas present from Easter Island. He's all right when not reading!'

69 **If you still wish to know more about fishing there are various books on the subject, the most famous of which is called *The Compleat Angler* by Izaak Walton. Although how a man who can't even spell 'complete' has got the nerve to write a book, I can't understand.**

Ronnie Corbett *Ronnie Corbett's Small Man's Guide*, 'The Small Man and Hobbies' (1976)

70 [Of Alexander Solzhenitsyn] **Once he came to the West he was under an overriding obligation to speak. Why? Because he was confronted with that most terrible of all temptations, that of being listened to.**

Peter Ustinov *Dear Me*, ch. 19 (1977)

71 **We were put to Dickens as children but it never quite took. That unremitting humanity soon had me cheesed off.**

Alan Bennett *The Old Country*, act 2 (1978)

72 [Of Yeats] **Swish, but always fuggin around with fairies and stuff.**

Julian Barnes *Metroland* pt 1, ch. 1 (1980). The view of the adolescent Christopher, who is forever on the lookout for 'sophisticated tough' writers like Montherlant and Camus.

73 **Burgess went home, did the kitchen, spring-cleaned the flat, wrote two book reviews, a flute concerto and a film treatment, knocked off his gardening column for** *Pravda***, phoned in his surfing page to the** *Sydney Morning Herald***, and then test-drove a kidney machine for** *El Pais* **– before settling down to some serious work.**

Anthony Burgess From a profile of Anthony Burgess, *Observer* 12 October 1980. Quoted in *Anthony Burgess*, Epilogue, by Roger Lewis (2002).

74 **I am all for the plays of Shakespeare being very thoroughly abridged, if not actually altered.**

Arthur Marshall *Musings from Myrtlebank*, 'Scribble Scribble' (1982)

75 [Of D. H. Lawrence] **Not the loudest giggler in class.**

Arthur Marshall *Smile Please*, 'Too Bad to Last' (1982)

76 **Cartland, Barbara (b.1900): You have to admire her. With no background, in an age when background counted for everything, with no money, in an epoch when money was desperately important, and with no natural advantages other than an appetite for hard work, energy, inventiveness and staying power, she has turned herself into a national joke.**

Henry Root *Henry Root's World of Knowledge* (1982)

77 **Ayckbourn, Alan: Thanks to the rapacious activities of philistine property barons, there are now a mere forty-seven theatres in London in which to mount Alan Ayckbourn's agreeable civilized light comedies.**

Ibid.

78 **I started** *Origin of the Species* **today, but it's not as good as the television series.**

Sue Townsend *The Secret Diary of Adrian Mole Aged 13¾* (1982), Friday 16 January

79 **After a depressing visit to the mirror or an unkind word from a girlfriend or an incredulous stare in the street, I say to myself: 'Well.** *Shakespeare* **looked like shit.'**

Martin Amis *Money* (publ. 1984), p. 145 (1985 Penguin edn). Amis refers to 'the beaked and bumfluffed upper lip, the oafish swelling of the jawline, the granny's rockpool eyes'.

80 [Of Dylan Thomas] **Now** *there's* **a chap who read fuck-all BECAUSE HE WASN'T INTERESTED IN FUCK-ALL bar himself.**

Kingsley Amis Letter to Philip Larkin of 14 October 1985, collected in *The Letters of Kingsley Amis* ed. Zachary Leader (2000)

81 [Of Ronald Firbank] **He summed up all the crappy things about novels that Saul Bellow left unsummed up.**

Letter to Philip Larkin of 1 October 1985, ibid. Amis had been asked about Firbank by *Tatler* magazine. His son Martin is known to be a particular fan of Bellow's.

82 [Of James Joyce] **A textbook case of declension from talent to absurdity.**

Philip Larkin *All What Jazz? A Record Diary*, Introduction (2nd edn 1985)

83 **While clearly an impregnable masterpiece,** *Don Quixote* **suffers from one fairly serious flaw – that of outright unreadability.**

Martin Amis From a review of *The Adventures of Don Quixote de la Mancha* by Miguel de Cervantes, *Atlantic Monthly* March 1986. Repr. in *The War against Cliché (Essays and Reviews 1971–2000)* (2001). Amis goes on to say that 'Reading *Don Quixote* can be compared to an indefinite visit from your most impossible senior relative.'

84 [Of a visit to the Finca Vigia, Ernest Hemingway's villa in Cuba] **On the walls are the heads of everything he shot except his own.**

Clive James *Observer* 13 July 1986

85 **DR JOHNSON: Here it is sire. A very cornerstone of English scholar-**

ship. This book contains every word in our beloved language.

BLACKADDER: Every single one, sir?

DR JOHNSON: Every single one, sir.

BLACKADDER: In that case, sir, I hope you will not object if I offer the Doctor my most enthusiastic contrafibularatories.'

Richard Curtis and Ben Elton *Blackadder The Third* (TV series, 1987), 'Ink and Incapability'. 'Dr Johnson' has been boasting about his dictionary before 'Prince George'. Blackadder adds: 'It is a common word down our way.'

86 My next novel out next week. Omens good so far but you know when you're old enough you can get away with piss, cf G. Greene.

Kingsley Amis Letter to Robert Conquest of 17 September 1988, collected in *The Letters of Kingsley Amis* ed. Zachary Leader (2000)

87 My own favourite hero, Biggles, the RFC ace who was hero of the books by W. E. Johns, continued in World War One . . . dodging the ack-ack burst and sending the Fokker triplanes spinning to their doom, the pilots mouthing curses at him in bad German.

Michael Green *The Boy Who Shot Down an Airship*, ch. 6 (1988)

88 Jeffrey Bernard Is Unwell

Keith Waterhouse Title of a stage adaptation of Bernard's *Spectator* columns (1989). These words would appear in the *Spectator* whenever Bernard was unable to file his column which, because he drank too much, was often. When he had his leg amputated the customary formula was departed from in favour of 'Jeffrey Bernard has had his leg off.'

89 [Of Virginia Woolf] Nothing ever happens in her books, does it? And unless something is happening, has happened or is likely to happen, I can't get myself into a book.

J. L. Carr The opinion of Grace Pintle in *Harpole and Foxberrow, Publishers*, p. 101 (1992)

90 I think I am in love with A. E. Housman,/ Which puts me in a worse-than-usual fix./ No woman ever stood a chance with Housman/ *And* he's been dead since 1936.

Wendy Cope *Serious Concerns*, 'An Unfortunate Choice' (1992)

91 Iris Murdoch. I've always admired that name. The iridescent, dilating bloom of 'Iris' and the honest, moral authority of 'Murdoch' inspire such perfect confidence.

Stephen Fry *Paperweight*, 'The Book and the Brotherhood' (1992)

92 It was much like watching the end of a good Shakespeare – characters with swords sticking out of them making long, complicated speeches about metaphor.

Mavis Cheek *Getting Back Brahms*, ch. 5 (1997)

93 I have always relished the idea of my work being not simply misunderstood by readers, but also comprehensively misinterpreted by the professionals.

Will Self *The Times*, 'Quotes of the Week', 9 June 2001

94 Simone de Beauvoir, whom I knew during her Nelson Algren period, worked very well behind absinthe, or its substitute, Pernod, sipping it for hours at the Flore and turning out her typical top-of-the-shelf stuff.

Terry Southern *Now Dig This: The Unspeakable Writings of Terry Southern (1950–1995)*, 'Drugs and the Writer', ed. Nile Southern and Josh Alan Friedman (2001). Southern believed that no serious writer would become an alcoholic, because then he or she would not be working 'behind' the drink, but 'directly in front of it'.

95 And it was all written with a feather!

Sam Goldwyn Supposed exclamation of Samuel Goldwyn on looking into the collected works of Shakespeare for the first time. Quoted by Robert Nye in the *Literary Review* April 2002.

96 My wife recently told a not-very-bookish friend of hers that she was reading a Trollope. 'Which one?' came the reply. 'Jackie Collins?'

Craig Brown *This Is Craig Brown*, 'What Happened Next' (2003)

97 [Of John Braine] **A one-book man, and he's yet to write it.**

Anthony Burgess Remark attributed by Keith Waterhouse to Burgess in Waterhouse's novel *Palace Pier*, ch. 2 (2003)

98 [Of D. H. Lawrence] **A Hitler in a teapot.**

Norman Mailer Quoted in the *Daily Telegraph* 6 March 2003. Mailer said that Lawrence was 'pathetic in all those places he suggests that men should follow the will of a stronger man'.

99 **That J. K. Rowling needs to fucking cheer up. She's about to trouser a cool thirty million quid from the latest *Harry Potboiler*, and she's still got a face like a smacked arse.**

Viz Cod letter, August 2004

Quotation

1 **The devil can cite scripture for his purpose.**

William Shakespeare Antonio in *The Merchant of Venice*, act 1, sc. 3 (1600)

2 **Some for renown, on scraps of learning dote,/ And think they grow immortal as they quote.**

Edward Young *The Love of Fame*, satire 1 (1725–8)

3 **A writer who intermixes great quantity of Greek and Latin with his works, deals by the ladies and fine gentlemen in the same paltry manner with which they are treated by the auctioneers, who often endeavour so to confound and mix up their lots, that, in order to purchase the commodity you want, you are obliged at the same time to purchase that which will do you no service.**

Henry Fielding *Tom Jones*, bk 12, ch. 1 (1749). Fielding also writes: 'To fill up a work with these scraps, may, indeed, be considered a downright cheat on the learned world, who are by no such means imposed upon to buy a second time in fragments and by retail, what they already have in gross.'

4 **Most compilers of anthologies of poetry or of epigrams are like people eating cherries or oysters: they start by picking out the best and end up eating the lot.**

Nicolas-Sébastien Roch de Chamfort Written c.1785, collected in *Chamfort: Reflections on Life, Love and Society*, 'Reflections and Anecdotes', ed. Douglas Parmee (2003)

5 **He lik'd those literary cooks/ Who skim the cream of others' books;/ And ruin half an author's graces/ By plucking bon-mots from their places.**

Hannah More *Florio*, pt 1 (1786)

6 **Classical quotation is the parole of literary men all over the world.**

Samuel Johnson *The Life of Samuel Johnson* by James Boswell, vol. 4, p. 102 (1791); in G. B. Hill's edition of 1887, rev. L. F. Powell (1934). John Wilkes contended that quotation was 'pedantry' but Johnson thought it was 'a good thing'.

7 [Advice to a new Member of Parliament] **Don't quote Latin; say what you have to say, and then sit down.**

Duke of Wellington Attributed. Quoted in *Chambers Dictionary of Quotations* ed. Alison Jones and others (1996).

8 **A book that furnishes no quotations is, *me judice*, no book – it is a plaything.**

Thomas Love Peacock *Crotchet Castle*, ch. 9 (1831). The opinion of the Rev. Dr Folliott. Later, comparing himself to another character who quotes so little that Folliott believes he must have been penalized for doing so at school, he says: 'I could not be abated of a single quotation by all the bumpers in which I was fined.'

9 **I hate quotations. Tell me what you know.**

Ralph Waldo Emerson *Journals and Miscellaneous Notebooks*, vol. 2, entry for May 1849, ed. William H. Gillman and others (1961). Emerson also said, in *Letters and Social Aims*, 'Quotations and Originality': 'Next to the originator of a good sentence is the first quoter of it.'

10 **Quotation, n.: The act of repeating**

erroneously the words of another.
The words erroneously repeated.

Ambrose Bierce *The Devil's Dictionary* (compiled *c.*1881–1906)

11 Of all my verse, like not a single
line;/ But like my title, for it is not
mine./ That title from a better man
I stole;/ Ah, how much better, had I
stol'n the whole!

Robert Louis Stevenson Foreword to
Underwoods (1887)

12 He wrapped himself in quotations –
as a beggar would enfold himself in
the purple of emperors.

Rudyard Kipling *Many Inventions*, 'The Finest
Story in the World' (1893). Of the bank clerk
Charlie Mears who aspires to write 'the
finest story in the world'.

13 George Moore, in his writings,
nearly always attributes to himself
the remarks wherewith other men
have extinguished him in conversation.

Ezra Pound 'Swinburne versus His Biographers', written 1918, collected in *The Literary
Essays of Ezra Pound* ed. T. S. Eliot (1954)

14 JAMISON[(Zeppo Marx), reading
from a letter dictated by Spaulding (Groucho Marx)]: Quotes,
unquotes and quotes.
SPAULDING: That's three quotes . . .
And another quote'll make it a
gallon.

Groucho Marx *Animal Crackers* (film, 1930,
screenplay by Morrie Ryskind and George S.
Kaufman, directed by Victor Heerman)

15 Remarks are not literature.

Gertrude Stein *The Autobiography of Alice B.
Toklas*, ch. 7 (1933)

16 Misquotations are the only quotations that are never misquoted.

Hesketh Pearson *Common Misquotations*,
Introduction (1934)

17 Misquotation is, in fact, the pride
and privilege of the learned. A
widely read man never quotes accurately, for the rather obvious reason
that he has read too widely.

Ibid.

18 There are aphorisms that, like airplanes, stay up only while they are
in motion.

Vladimir Nabokov Koncheyev in *The Gift*,
ch. 1 (1937)

19 I will say to you what Thomas Carlyle once said to a young man who
caught him out in a misquotation:
'Young man, you are heading
straight for the pit of hell!'

Robert Graves Augustine Birrell speaking to
Robert Graves. Graves had just pointed out
to him that Elihu was not one of Job's comforters, and proved the fact with the aid of a
Bible. Quoted in *Goodbye to All That*, ch. 22
(1957).

20 Quotation: Something somebody
said that seemed to make sense at
the time.

Leonard Louis Levinson *The Left-Handed Dictionary* (1963). On a similar theme, Levinson
cites the following definitions of plagiarism:
'One who gives birth to an adopted baby', 'A
literary body-snatcher' and 'A writer of
plays', all of which he attributes to 'that
clever bastard, Anon.' And he quoted Russell
E. Curran, who said that plagiarism was
'Stealing a ride on someone else's train of
thought.'

21 I went through three huge books of
quotations and found them full of
bits like this, 'Be easy.' Now if you
say 'be easy' to anyone, the saying
may not immortalize your name.
But when you learn that Richard
Steele said it in 1771, that adds quite
a bit of lustre to it.

George Mikes *How to Unite Nations*, 'How to
Quote in Self-Defence' (1963). Mikes also
singled out for banality a remark of 1578 by
John Florio: 'After stormes come fayre
weather.'

22 An epigram is only a wisecrack
that's played at Carnegie Hall.

Oscar Levant *Coronet* magazine September
1968

23 Epigram: Any sentence spoken by
anybody who is in the public eye at
the moment.

Beachcomber *Beachcomber: The Works of
J. B. Morton*, 'A Dictionary for Today', ed.
Richard Ingrams (1974)

24 Needlepoint mottos can make your thumb bleed.

Christopher Hampton Dave in *Treats*, sc. 2 (1976)

25 Quotations are useful in periods of ignorance.

Guy Debord *Panegyric*, vol. 1, pt 1 (1989)

26 I've lived a long time, I've been distorted, I've been misrepresented, and I've been quoted accurately, which is perhaps the most appalling.

Peter Cook As the eccentric patrician, Sir Arthur Streeb-Greebling, *Why Bother?* (radio series, 1994). Quoted in *Tragically I Was an Only Twin: The Complete Peter Cook* ed. William Cook (2002)

27 I have always wanted to declare an Ad Libbers' Charter, which would establish that if a good ad lib is only heard by three people then the ad libber is entitled to repeat his ad lib later to a wider audience.

Frank Muir *A Kentish Lad*, ch. 4 (1997). He had in mind a remark he'd made when advised to read a cookbook referred to as being 'by Robert Le Carré' (in fact, by Robert Carrier): 'Oh, didn't he write *The Pie That Came In from the Cold*?' 'Only one lady was in earshot,' he regretfully noted.

28 Silence is not only golden, it is seldom misquoted.

Bob Monkhouse *Sun* 30 December 2003

Literary Style

1 Digressions, incontestably, are the sun-shine; – they are the life, the soul of reading; – – – take them out of this book for instance, – – you might as well take the book along with them; – one cold eternal winter would reign in every page of it; restore them to the writer; – – – – – he steps forth like a bridegroom, – bids All Hail; brings in variety, and forbids the appetite to fail.

Laurence Sterne *Tristram Shandy* (1759–67), vol. 1, ch. 22

2 I open with a clock striking, to beget an awful attention in the audience: it also marks the time, which is four o'clock in the morning, and saves a description of the rising sun, and a great deal about gilding the eastern hemisphere.

Richard Brinsley Sheridan Puff in *The Critic*, act 1, sc. 2 (1779)

3 Tom Birch is as brisk as a bee in conversation; but no sooner does he take a pen in his hand, than it becomes a torpedo to him, and benumbs all his faculties.

Samuel Johnson *The Life of Samuel Johnson* by James Boswell, vol. 1, p. 159 (1791); in G. B. Hill's edition of 1887, rev. L. F. Powell. (1934). Oliver Goldsmith writes in his *Life of Nash*: 'Nash was not a born writer; for whatever humour he might have in conversation, he used to call a pen his torpedo: whenever he grasped it, it benumbed all his faculties.'

4 Read over your compositions, and wherever you meet with a passage that is particularly fine, strike it out.

Ibid., vol. 2, p. 237. Johnson, praising 'plain narrative', was here quoting 'an old college tutor'.

5 We hardly know what to say about this rambling, scrambling book; but that we are quite sure the author, when he began any sentence in it, had not the smallest suspicion of what it was to contain.

Sydney Smith Opening sentence of a review of *Essay on Irish Bulls* by Richard Lovell Edgeworth and Maria Edgeworth. Publ. in the *Edinburgh Review* 1803, collected in *The Works of Sydney Smith*, vol. 1 (1840).

6 Brevity is the sister of talent.

Anton Chekhov Letter to Alexander Chekhov of 11 April 1889, collected in *Anton Chekhov: Letters on the Short Story, the Drama, and Other Literary Topics*, ed. Louis S. Friedland (1965)

7 That is the reason I hate vulgar realism in literature. A man who would call a spade a spade should be compelled to use one. It is the only thing he is fit for.

Oscar Wilde Lord Henry Wotton in *The Picture of Dorian Gray* ch. 17 (1890)

8 As to the Adjective: when in doubt, strike it out.

Mark Twain *The Tragedy of Pudd'nhead Wilson*, ch. 9, 'Pudd'nhead Wilson's Calender' (1894)

9 People think that I can teach them style. What stuff it all is! Have something to say, and say it as clearly as you can. That is the only secret of style.

Matthew Arnold Quoted in *Collections and Recollections* by G. W. E. Russell, ch. 13 (1898)

10 The vocabulary of *Bradshaw* is nervous and terse, but limited.

Sir Arthur Conan Doyle Holmes in *The Valley of Fear*, pt 1, ch. 1 (1915). *Bradshaw* was the national railway timetable of the day. He was trying to find the key to a code in it.

11 I never knew a writer yet who took the smallest pains with his style and was at the same time readable.

Samuel Butler *Selections from the Note-Books of Samuel Butler*, ch. 3, ed. A. T. Bartholomew (1930)

12 You praise the firm restraint with which they write –/ I'm with you there, of course:/ They use the snaffle and the curb all right,/ But where's the bloody horse?

Roy Campbell 'On Some South African Novelists' (1930)

13 Backward ran sentences until reeled the mind.

Wolcott Gibbs *New Yorker* 28 November 1936. A comment on the house style of *Time* magazine.

14 Sir, At the foot of the menu in the restaurant cars of our most up-to-date railway we read that: 'A supplementary portion of any dish will be served on request.' I suppose the first six words mean 'second helpings'. Why not say so?

G. H. Palmer Letter to *The Times* of 2 August 1939, quoted in *The Last Cuckoo: The Very Best Letters to The Times since 1900*, 'The English Language', ed. Kenneth Gregory (1987)

15 This old pub has got to go, they say,/ *'Cos it's redundant.*/ Funny words they use for things today – /

What price 'redundant'?/ Well, what I want to know,/ If a pub has got to go,/ There's no harm is saying so – / *But why 'redundant'?*

A. P. Herbert 'Redundant', *A Book of Ballads* (1949)

16 You are a putter in, and I am a taker out.

F. Scott Fitzgerald From a letter to Thomas Wolfe, quoted in *Lanterns and Lances*, 'The Case for Comedy', by James Thurber (1961)

17 I've had two full-length plays produced in London. The first ran a week and the second ran a year. Of course, there are differences between the two plays. In *The Birthday Party* I employed a certain number of dashes in the text, between phrases. In *The Caretaker* I cut out the dashes and used dots instead.

Harold Pinter From a speech delivered at the National Student Drama Festival in Bristol, 1962, also used as the Introduction to *Pinter Plays: One* (1976). Pinter concluded 'that dots are more popular than dashes'.

18 Good prose is like a window-pane.

George Orwell *Collected Essays*, vol. 1, 'Why I Write' (1968)

19 I'm into language. It's my thing, because language is the most important . . . erm . . .

Steve Martin 'Language', *A Wild and Crazy Guy* (LP, 1978)

20 The word 'meaningful' when used today is nearly always meaningless.

Paul Johnson *Observer* 1982, quoted in *The Penguin Dictionary of Modern Humorous Quotations* ed. Fred Metcalf (2nd edn 2001)

21 Agreeable: A word that sounds well in an article for the *Spectator*.

Henry Root *Henry Root's World of Knowledge* (1982). Another, according to Root, is 'egregious'.

22 Every idiom has its idiot.

Anon. Quoted in *All What Jazz?*, *A Record Diary*, Introduction, by Philip Larkin (1985)

23 The morning menu on British Airways' Super Shuttle from Edinburgh offers '*Selected*' breakfast roll

– which surely takes the biscuit as the year's most fruitless adjective.

Nick Alexander Letter to *The Times* of 7 June 1986, quoted in *The Last Cuckoo: The Very Best Letters to The Times since 1900*, 'The English Language', ed. Kenneth Gregory (1987)

24 It got to be a cliché, because it was true. But if you think about it, if that's its reward, that's a poor reward. Isn't it?

David Mamet Deeny in *The Old Neighbourhood* (1997)

25 If you hear an owl hoot 'To whom' instead of 'To who', you can be certain he was born and educated in Boston.

Anon. Quoted in *The Penguin Dictionary of Modern Humorous Quotations* ed. Fred Metcalf (2nd edn 2001)

26 You must write, when you set your scene, 'The other side of the lake was hidden in mist.' . . . But as you are *setting* the scene, don't make any emphasis as yet. It's too soon, for instance, for you to write, 'The other side of the lake was hidden in the fucking mist.'

Muriel Spark Rowland Mather, tutor in literature, in *The Finishing School*, ch. 1 (2004)

Literary Criticism

1 So let great authors have their due, as time, which is the author of authors, be not deprived of his due, which is further and further to discover the truth.

Francis Bacon *The Advancement of Learning*, bk 1, ch. 4, sect. 12 (1605)

2 Critics are like brushers of noblemen's clothes.

Sir Henry Wotton *Apothegms New and Old*, no. 64 (1625)

3 As learned commentators view/ In Homer more than Homer knew.

Jonathan Swift 'On Poetry: A Rhapsody', line 103 (1733)

4 Though by whim, envy or resent-

ment led,/ They damn those authors whom they never read.

Charles Churchill 'The Candidate' (1764)

5 Every good poet includes a critic; the reverse will not hold.

William Shenstone *Works in Verse and Prose*, vol. 2, 'On Writing and Books' (1764)

6 Until you understand a writer's ignorance, presume yourself ignorant of his understanding.

Samuel Taylor Coleridge *Biographia Literaria*, ch. 12 (1817)

7 Your comedy I have read my friend,/ And like the half you pilfer'd best;/ But, sure, the drama you might mend;/ Take courage, man, and steal the rest.

Anon. *The New London Jest Book*, 'Choice Jests', no. 356, ed. W. C. Hazlitt (1871)

8 Oh I never read a book before reviewing it: it prejudices a man so.

Sydney Smith Quoted in *The Bon Mots of Sydney Smith and R. B. Sheridan* ed. Walter Jerrold (1893)

9 Literary criticism is not your forte, my dear fellow. Don't try it. You should leave that to people who haven't been at a university.

Oscar Wilde Algernon Moncrieff in *The Importance of Being Earnest*, act 1 (1895)

10 A louse in the locks of literature.

Alfred, Lord Tennyson Of John Churton Collins (1848–1908), literary critic and academic. Quoted in *Life and Letters of Sir Edmund Gosse* ed. Evan Charteris, ch. 14 (1931)

11 'Flat.' – the *Intimate Review*./ 'Fizzing.' – the *Daily Express*.

Humphrey Lyttelton Two reviews of Humphrey Lyttelton's first book *I Play As I Please* (1954), quoted in the Introduction to his second, *Second Chorus* (1958)

12 Reviewing novels is a more difficult problem and may even entail actual reading of the first and last chapters.

Stephen Potter *Supermanship*, ch. 3 (1958)

13 From the moment I picked up your book to the moment I put it down I

was convulsed with laughter. Someday I intend reading it.

Groucho Marx Quoted in *Life* 9 February
1962. Referring to *Dawn Ginsbergh's Revenge*
(1929) by S. J. Perelman.

14 **This so-called book . . .**

Anon. Quoted in *Profiles*, 'Graham Greene',
by Kenneth Tynan (1989). A Brighton resident, objecting to Greene's novel *Brighton
Rock*, had written: 'This so-called book is a
gross calumny.' Tynan comments that this
was a case of 'thrashing about in search of
epithets'.

15 **I like reviewing books because it
makes me want to read them.**

Anon. 'Overheard at a literary party'.
A Gentleman Publisher's Commonplace Book,
'Core', by John G. Murray (1996).

Correspondence

1 **Ladies, said a certain philosopher,
always tell their minds in the postscript.**

Horace Walpole Letter of 8 April 1779 to the
Countess of Upper Ossory, collected in *The
Letters of Horace Walpole*, ed. William Hadley
(1926)

2 **An odd thought strikes me: – we
shall receive no letters in the grave.**

Samuel Johnson *The Life of Samuel Johnson*
by James Boswell, vol. 4, p. 413 (1791); in G. B.
Hill's edition of 1887, rev. L. F. Powell (1934)

3 **Expect a most agreeable Letter; for
not being overburdened with subject – (having nothing at all to say)
– I shall have no check to my
Genius from beginning to end.**

Jane Austen Letter to Cassandra Austen of
21–22 January 1801, collected in *Jane Austen's
Letters* ed. Dierdre Le Faye (1995)

4 **Letterwriting is the go.**

John Keats Letter to Charles Dilke of
22 September 1819. He added: 'I have consumed a full Quire at least.'

5 **[Of writing letters] Some folks write
for fun, and some write to dun,/
Some blaming and others contending;/ Some letters are love, and**

others to move/ Soft friends their
odd cash to be lending.

Anon. 'The Post-Office', *Oliver's Comic Songs*
(1825?)

6 **My letters are shorter than Napoleon's, but I love you more than he
did Josephine.**

Benjamin Disraeli Letter to Sarah Disraeli
(his sister) of 26 November 1833, collected in
Benjamin Disraeli: Letters 1815–34 ed. J. A. W.
Gunn, John Matthews and Donald M. Schurman (1982)

7 **I fear my eternal handwriting will
give you no pleasure.**

Benjamin Disraeli Beginning of a letter to
William Pyne of 19 April 1837, collected in
Benjamin Disraeli: Letters, vol. 2, *1835–1837*,
ed. J. A. W. Gunn, John Matthews, Donald M.
Schurman and M. G. Wiebe (1982)

8 **Or don't you like to write letters? I
do because it's such a swell way to
keep from working and yet you feel
you've done something.**

Ernest Hemingway Letter to F. Scott Fitzgerald of 1 July 1925

9 **I notice that employees of the BBC
delight to put 'Dictated by . . . and
signed in his absence by . . .'. To
them I always reply with a letter
signed 'Written by his secretary
and signed in her absence by
J. BETJEMAN.'**

John Betjeman *Spectator* 5 November 1954,
quoted in *John Betjeman: New Fame, New
Love*, ch. 30, 'City and Suburban', by Bevis
Hillier (2002)

10 **Do you know anything about graph-
ology? All I remember from two
expert friends is that when the left-
hand margins of a letter grow wider
as they descend, it shows the writer
is moving ever closer to the person
he is writing to.**

Rupert Hart-Davis Letter to George Lyttelton
of 17 December 1955, collected in *The Lyttelton–Hart-Davis Letters*, vols 1 and 2, *1955–
1957*, ed. Rupert Hart-Davis (1978)

11 **I. T. A. L. Y. (Know what that
means?)**

Evelyn Waugh Letter to the Duchess of
Devonshire, midwinter 1956, collected in *The*

Letters of Evelyn Waugh ed. Mark Amory (1980). Amory explains that it means 'I trust [or treasure] and love you.'

12 **Three gorgeous missiles here from you.**
Joyce Grenfell Letter of 6 April 1960 from Grenfell to Virginia Graham, collected in *Joyce and Ginnie: The Letters of Joyce Grenfell and Virginia Graham* ed. Janie Hampton (1997)

13 **I learnt on the radio today that we can write the date like this: 4–5–67. Neat, eh?**
Letter of 4 May 1967 from Joyce Grenfell to Virginia Graham, ibid.

14 **'No, don't bother to send a post-card,' said one lugubrious mother, 'I'll just listen to the six o'clock news.'**
Katherine Whitehorn *Observations*, 'Keep It Brief' (1970)

15 **If people who design the shape and size of postcards had ever got together with people who design the shape and size of postage stamps, one of them would look very different.**
Miles Kington *Welcome to Kington*, 'The Wit and Wisdom of Albania' (1989)

16 **[Cliff Stern (Woody Allen) as Halley Reed (Mia Farrow) returns his love letters:] It's probably just as well. I plagiarized most of it from James Joyce. You probably wondered about all the references to Dublin.**
Woody Allen *Crimes and Misdemeanors* (film, 1989, directed by Woody Allen)

17 **You don't know a woman until you have had a letter from her.**
Ada Leverson Quoted in *Women's Wit and Wisdom* (1993)

18 **It is surprising that the Impressionists never became involved in the Christmas Card Movement. They remained in a cultural backwater, devoting all their energies towards a form of card known as Blank for Special Messages.**
Oliver Pritchett *The Dogger Bank Saga: Writ-*

ings 1980–95, 'Home Is Where the Art Is' (1995)

19 **Inland Revenue letter of October 1988: 'In spite of continuing heavy arrears of work in this Division we will award this correspondence a sizeable measure of priority.'**
Anon. Sent to John Betjeman, concerning his copyright. Quoted in *A Gentleman Publisher's Commonplace Book*, 'Delightful Oddities', by John G. Murray (1996).

20 **The email of the species is deadlier than the mail.**
Stephen Fry *Sunday Telegraph* 23 December 2001. A play upon the first line of Rudyard Kipling's poem, 'The Female of the Species'.

21 **You have to choose between writing postcards at the end of the holiday, so they arrive home long after you do, or writing them at the start of the holiday, so they arrive home long after you do.**
Guy Browning *Guardian*, 'How to . . .' column, 15 March 2003

The Act of Writing

1 **I have made this letter longer than usual, only because I have not had the time to make it shorter.**
Blaise Pascal *Lettres provinciales* (Provincial Letters), no. 16 (1656)

2 **I should have no objection to this method, but that I think it must smell too strong of the lamp.**
Laurence Sterne *Tristram Shandy*, bk 1, ch. 23 (1759–67). Sterne is referring to the practice of depicting 'a man's character . . . from his evacuations'.

3 **Here is a fact which needs to be remembered more often. Thackeray spent thirty years preparing to write his first novel, but Alexandre Dumas writes two a week.**
Leo Tolstoy Entry for 21 January 1854, *Tolstoy's Diaries* ed. and trans. R. F. Christian (1994)

4 **To begin at the beginning is, next to ending at the end, the whole art of writing; as for the middle you may**

fill it in with any rubble that you choose.

Hilaire Belloc *On Nothing and Kindred Subjects*, 'Getting Respected in Inns and Hotels' (1908)

5 MRS SPOKER: H'm, you don't write very clear.
PETER: I've just had some very thick soup.

Ben Travers *A Cuckoo in the Nest*, act 1, sc. 2 (1926)

6 I am blown like an old flag by my novel.

Virginia Woolf Entry for 23 February 1926, *A Writer's Diary, Being Extracts from the Diary of Virginia Woolf* ed. Leonard Woolf (1953). The novel was *To the Lighthouse*.

7 A woman must have money and a room of her own if she is to write fiction.

Virginia Woolf *A Room of One's Own*, ch. 1 (1929)

8 My notes always grow longer if I shorten them.

Samuel Butler *Selections from the Note-Books of Samuel Butler*, ch. 3, ed. A. T. Bartholomew (1930). He goes on: 'I mean the process of compression makes them more pregnant and they breed new notes.'

9 London, April 13 '97. I finished my book today . . . May 18, '97. Finished the book *again*.

Mark Twain He added thirty thousand words between the first and second entries. *Notebook*, ch. 24 (1935).

10 How to invent names for fictitious characters without fear of prosecution? This morning's *Times* has births to Clague, Fimbel, Futty and Prescott-Pickup.

Evelyn Waugh Entry for 5 May 1963, *The Diaries of Evelyn Waugh* ed. M. Davie (1976)

11 Contrary to what many of you might imagine, a career in letters is not without its drawbacks – chief among them the unpleasant fact that one is frequently called upon to actually sit down and write.

Fran Lebowitz *Metropolitan Life*, 'Writing: A Life Sentence' (1978)

12 I wrote 'The Apple Pie Hubbub', and that was significant for me because I first started using verbs.

Steve Martin 'Language', *A Wild and Crazy Guy* (LP, 1978). 'The Apple Pie Hubbub' is a book existing only in Martin's mind.

13 But then writers who look too much like writers may have to spend as much time doing the looking as the writing . . .

Robert Robinson *The Dog Chairman*, 'Priestley' (1982)

Film
Particular Actors, Directors and Films

1 The man you love to hate.

Anon. Billing for Erich von Stroheim in *The Heart of Humanity* (1918). According to *Halliwell's Who's Who in the Movies*, Stroheim specialized in 'villains and stiff-necked Prussians'.

2 Just tell Stanley that New York does *not* see anything *funny* about the end of the world.

Anon. Columbia Pictures executive to Terry Southern, regarding the film *Dr Strangelove or: How I Learned to Stop Worrying and Love the Bomb* (1953), directed by Stanley Kubrick, co-written by Southern). Quoted in *Now Dig This: The Unspeakable Writings of Terry Southern (1950–95)*, 'Strangelove Outtake: Notes from the War Room', ed. Nile Southern and Josh Alan Friedman (2001).

3 [Of the film *Lawrence of Arabia*] If it had been any prettier, it would have been *Florence of Arabia*.

Noël Coward Attributed. Quoted in *Cassell's Movie Quotations* ed. Nigel Rees (2000). *Lawrence of Arabia* was directed by David Lean in 1962.

4 I've just done a complicated scene with James Coburn. Nice. He was in *The Great Escape* and looks like a slit in an orange.

Joyce Grenfell Letter of 18 November 1963 from Grenfell to Virginia Graham, collected in *Joyce and Ginnie: The Letters of Joyce Grenfell and Virginia Graham* ed. Janie Hampton (1997)

5 [Of Humphrey Bogart] **He was always unsurprised.**
Kenneth Tynan *Playboy* June 1966

6 [Of Louis B. Mayer] **Tsar of all the rushes.**
B. P. Schulberg Quoted in *The Hollywood Tycoons* by Norman Zierold (1969)

7 [Of Julie Andrews] **Working with her is like being hit over the head by a Valentine's Day card.**
Christopher Plummer Quoted in *The Filmgoer's Book of Quotes* ed. Leslie Halliwell (1973). Said after having worked with Andrews on *The Sound of Music*.

8 [Of Clark Gable] **I mostly admired Clark for his lack of vanity . . . One day I happened on him at an outdoor faucet in the alley where he'd stopped to wash off his denture. Clark grinned, pointed to his caved-in mouth, and said with an exaggerated lisp, 'Look, America's thweetheart!'**
Anita Loos *Kiss Hollywood Goodbye*, ch. 6 (1974)

9 **1936. Shirley Temple. I was five and she was eight. My first time sitting there in the dark, I remember her curls so plainly. And could her dimples have been as large as they seemed? If the answer is no, don't tell me.**
William Goldman *Adventures in the Screen Trade*, 'Author's Note' (1983)

10 [Of Robert Redford] **He's just another California blond – throw a stick at Malibu, you'll hit six of him.**
Anon. Observation of unnamed producer prior to casting for *Butch Cassidy and the Sundance Kid*. Quoted in ibid., ch. 1

11 [Of Jessica Lange] **She's like a delicate fawn, crossed with a Buick.**
Jack Nicholson Quoted in *Vanity Fair* October 1984

12 **To Raoul Walsh, a tender love scene is burning down a whorehouse.**
Jack L. Warner Quoted in *Hollywood Anecdotes* ed. P. F. Boller and R. L. Davis (1988)

13 [Of Charlie Chaplin] **I find his films about as funny as getting an arrow through the neck and then discovering there's a gas bill tied to it.**
Richard Curtis and Ben Elton Captain Edmund Blackadder in 'Major Star', *Blackadder Goes Forth* (TV series, 1989)

14 **Never work with children, dogs or Denholm Elliott, British actors are said to advise one another.**
Anon. Quoted in the *Guardian* 29 April 1989. A similar formulation has been applied to many stars.

15 [On being called 'the sexiest man alive'] **Well there are very few sexy ones that are dead.**
Sean Connery Quoted in the *Independent* 15 June 1991

16 **'Dora Bryan drinks practically nothing,' said my father. 'I know because I've seen her on the Brighton train.'**
Andrew Barrow *The Tap Dancer*, ch. 10 (1992). Dora Bryan lives in Brighton, and is teetotal.

17 [Of Kenneth Branagh] **[His] films are fine . . . Not exactly Eisenstein.**
Dillie Keane Song, possibly actually called 'Kenneth Branagh'. Quoted in the London *Evening Standard* 24 March 1994

18 [Of *Forrest Gump*] **This movie is so insistently heartwarming that it chilled me to the marrow.**
Anthony Lane *New Yorker* 25 July 1994

19 **Through it all, I have remained consistently and nauseatingly adorable.**
Meg Ryan Said in 1999, quoted in *People on People: The Oxford Dictionary of Biographical Quotations* ed. Susan Ratcliffe (2001)

20 **Most people seem to think I'm the kind of guy who shaves with a blowtorch. Actually, I'm bookish and worrisome.**
Burt Lancaster Attributed. Quoted in *Cassell's Movie Quotations* ed. Nigel Rees (2nd edn

2002). Another remark concerning Lancaster is attributed to Jeanne Moreau: 'Before he picks up an ashtray he discusses his motivation for an hour or two. You want to say, "Oh, pick up the ashtray and shut up."'

21 **In Mr Phillips's opinion the sexiest film ever made was *The Railway Children*, although he knows you aren't supposed to say that.**

John Lanchester *Mr Phillips*, ch. 13 (2000)

22 **I said I didn't think Chevy Chase could ad-lib a fart after a baked bean dinner. I think he took umbrage at that a little.**

Johnny Carson Attributed. Quoted in *The Penguin Dictionary of Modern Humorous Quotations* ed. Fred Metcalf (2nd edn 2001). For a while in 1993 Chase, actor, was a chat show rival of Carson's on American TV.

23 **[Reviewing *Pearl Harbor*] I hate to think what will happen when these guys get their hands on King Lear.**

Anthony Lane *New Yorker* 4 June 2001

24 **[Of Dean Martin] King Leer.**

Joe E. Lewis Verdict of *Life* magazine. Quoted in *Halliwell's Who's Who in the Movies* ed. John Walker (2001)

25 **[Of Elizabeth Taylor] Is she fat? Her favourite food is seconds.**

Joan Rivers Quoted in *The Penguin Dictionary of Modern Humorous Quotations* ed. Fred Metcalf (2nd edn 2001)

26 **[Of Arnold Schwarzenegger] He looks like a brown condom stuffed with walnuts.**

Clive James Attributed. Quoted in *People on People: The Oxford Dictionary of Biographical Quotations* ed. Susan Ratcliffe (2001)

27 **If you have physical attractiveness, you don't have to act.**

Raquel Welch Quoted in *Halliwell's Who's Who in the Movies* ed. John Walker (2001). In 1968 on *Rowan and Martin's Laugh-In* this joke was made: 'Happiness is bumping into Raquel Welch . . . very slowly.'

28 **Curious name, Edward Woodward, because it sounds like somebody eructating their nates in the bath. Why *does* it have so many d's in it?**

I suppose it's because otherwise he'd be called Ewar Woowar.

Victor Lewis-Smith London *Evening Standard* 28 November 2002

29 **[Of Warren Beatty] At the time I met him, he was still relatively undiscovered as a Don Juan. I felt I was one among thousands at that point – it hadn't reached, you know, the populations of small countries.**

Carly Simon Quoted in the *Daily Telegraph* 30 September 2003. Woody Allen is supposed to have said that if he were reincarnated he would like to come back as 'Warren Beatty's fingertips', but he denies it.

30 **I thought *Deep Throat* was a movie about a giraffe.**

Bob Hope Quoted in the *Independent* 26 July 2003

31 **Am assuming 'The dialogue is "Aramaic"' is a typo for 'American'.**

Steve Martin Stan, a Hollywood producer, responds to Mel Gibson's script for *The Passion of the Christ* in the *New Yorker* 8 March 2004

32 **[Japanese film fan to Hugh Grant] You very handsome but very bad actor.**

Anon. Quoted in Heathrow Express *Big City* in-train magazine January/February 2004. Grant often mentions this remark.

33 **I like to be introduced as America's foremost actor. It saves the necessity of further effort.**

John Barrymore Attributed

34 **Michael Caine can out-act any, well nearly any, telephone kiosk you care to mention.**

Hugh Leonard Attributed

The Industry

1 **The cinema may be described as a cross between a thought-saving machine and a cocktail.**

John Galsworthy *Observer*, 'Sayings of the Week', 5 November 1922

2 **When married men, the heads of households, prefer the flicker of the**

cinematograph to the Athanasian Creed – then it is obviously a task, not to be justifiably avoided, to place some higher example before the world.

Sir Henry Howarth Bashford Augustus Carp, declining to apologize for writing his autobiography, *Augustus Carp Esq., by Himself*, ch. 1 (1924)

3 **The lunatics have taken charge of the asylum.**

Richard Rowland Quoted in *A Million and One Nights*, vol. 2, ch. 79, by Terry Ramsaye (1926). He was referring to the takeover of United Artists by Charlie Chaplin and other filmstars.

4 **I have hardly ever seen a motion picture in which the motion was not too rapid to give any real sense of rapidity.**

G. K. Chesterton *Generally Speaking*, 'On the Movies' (1928)

5 **Bring on the empty horses!**

Michael Curtiz Command made while directing *The Charge of the Light Brigade* (film, 1936). Used by David Niven as the title of the second volume of his autobiography in 1975.

6 **I remembered the story of the last words of George V, or possibly Edward VII, and the debate over whether he said, 'How goes the Empire?' or 'What's on at the Empire?'**

Ian Jack *Granta* magazine, summer 2004. George V died in 1936.

7 **Cecil B. de Mille/ Rather against his will,/ Was persuaded to leave Moses/ Out of *The Wars of the Roses*.**

Edmund Clerihew Bentley Attributed. Quoted in *Clerihews* ed. J. W. Carter (1938).

8 **There's only one thing that can kill the movies, and that's education.**

Will Rogers *The Autobiography of Will Rogers*, ch. 6 (1949)

9 **Hollywood is a place where people from Iowa mistake themselves for movie stars.**

Fred Allen Quoted in *No People Like Show People*, ch. 8, by Maurice Zolotow (1951). The remark dates from *c*. 1941.

10 [Of Hollywood] **A trip through a sewer in a glass-bottomed boat.**

Wilson Mizner Quoted in *The Legendary Mizners* by Alva Johnston (1953). Jimmy Walker (songwriter and flashy Mayor of New York 1926–32) said: 'A reformer is a guy who rides through a sewer in a glass-bottomed boat.'

11 **A wide screen just makes a bad film twice as bad.**

Sam Goldwyn Quoted in *Quote* magazine 9 September 1956

12 [Of the RKO studios] **The biggest electric train set any boy ever had.**

Orson Welles Quoted in *The Fabulous Orson Welles*, ch. 7, by Peter Noble (1956)

13 **Movie music is noise. It's even more painful than my sciatica.**

Sir Thomas Beecham Quoted in *Time* magazine 24 February 1958

14 **KENNETH: You started in silent pictures didn't you?**
   BETTY: Yes. I often appeared in Fatty Arbuckle's shorts. They were the biggest draws in Hollywood at the time.

Marty Feldman and Barry Took Betty Marsden in *Around the Horne* (BBC radio series), 4 April 1965

15 **I wouldn't say when you've seen one Western you've seen the lot; but when you've seen the lot you get the feeling you've seen one.**

Katherine Whitehorn *Sunday Best*, 'Decoding the West' (1976)

16 **In Hollywood, if you don't have happiness you send out for it.**

Rex Reed Quoted in *Wit and Wisdom of the Movie Makers* ed J. R. Colombo (1979)

17 **It would have been cheaper to lower the Atlantic.**

Lew Grade His $40 million film *Raise the Titanic* (1980) having flopped at the box office

18 **In this business we make movies, American movies. Leave the films to the French.**

Sam Shepard Saul in *True West*, act 2, sc. 5 (1980)

19 'Movies should have a beginning, a middle and an end,' harrumphed French film-maker Georges Franju ... 'Certainly,' replied Jean-Luc Godard. 'But not necessarily in that order.'

Jean-Luc Godard *Time* 14 September 1981

20 Cinema: A place where you can get a preview of a television film.

Miles Kington *Moreover*, 'The Moreover Advice Service' (1982)

21 Towards the end of the couple of years I spent being a film critic during the 1960s I was beginning to feel a special sort of fury. The 80 per cent of what I saw that was rubbish didn't seem to *mind* being rubbish, yet I had to treat it as though it were trying to be something else.

Robert Robinson *The Dog Chairman*, 'A Door Opening' (1982)

22 I now formulate a general rule: the best films are the ones nobody's ever heard of.

A. J. P. Taylor *London Review of Books* 18 November 1982. He instanced *Closely Observed Trains* and *The Lady with the Little Dog*.

23 I always held Hollywood at arm's length, like a lover you can't exactly trust.

Mae West Quoted in *The Ultimate Seduction*, 'Mae West' by Charlotte Chandler (1984)

24 If it's a good script, I'll do it. And if it's a bad script, and they pay me enough, I'll do it.

George Burns Quoted in the *International Herald Tribune* 9 November 1988

25 I am seeing if I can shake off this reputation for integrity.

Lindsay Anderson Quoted in the *Independent* 1 April 1989. After Anderson's death Karel Reisz is supposed to have said: 'There was an absoluteness of stance about him, an uncompromising quality that gave him many disciples, but also hundreds of enemies.'

26 If the director said, 'Go in', and I went in, I was a good actor. If he said, 'Go in', and I stayed out in the hall, I was a bad actor.

George Burns *All My Best Friends*, ch. 6 (1989)

27 No one ever went broke in Hollywood underestimating the intelligence of the public.

Elsa Maxwell *And I Quote*, 'The Movies', ed. Ashton Applewhite and others (1992)

28 It is an axiom of cinema history, one admitting of few exceptions, that the longer the film's title, the likelier it is to be an outright dud.

Gilbert Adair Attributed. *The Guinness Book of Movie Facts and Feats* ed. Patrick Robertson (1993)

29 No blow, no show.

Anon. A filmstar's demand for drugs, quoted by Terry Southern in *Now Dig This: The Unspeakable Writings of Terry Southern (1950–1999)*, Epilogue, ed. Nile Southern and Josh Alan Friedman (2000)

30 You get paid the same for a bad film as you do for a good one.

Michael Caine Attributed. Quoted in *Cassell's Movie Quotations* ed. Nigel Rees (2nd edn 2002)

31 For screen writers suffering everywhere (It's what we do).

William Goldman Preface to *Which Lie Did I Tell?* (2000)

32 I sometimes think I shall never view/ A French film lacking Gérard Depardieu

John Updike Quoted in *Cassell's Movie Quotations* ed. Nigel Rees (2nd edn 2002)

33 [On being asked whether he had any advice for his successors as Tarzan] The main thing is, don't let go of the vine when you're swinging through the jungle.

Johnny Weissmuller Quoted in *The Daily Telegraph Book of Sports Obituaries* (2000)

34 Hollywood – an emotional Detroit.

Lillian Gish Quoted in *The Penguin Dictionary of Modern Humorous Quotations* ed. Fred Metcalf (2nd edn 2001)

35 I pity the French cinema because it has no money. I pity the American cinema because it has no ideas.

Jean-Luc Godard Quoted in *Halliwell's Who's Who in the Movies* ed. John Walker (2001)

36 The five stages of an actor's career: 1. Who the hell is Jack Elam? 2. Get

me Jack Elam. 3. Get me a Jack Elam type. 4. Get me a young Jack Elam. 5. Who the hell is Jack Elam?

Jack Elam Quoted in the obituary of Jack Elam, *Daily Telegraph* 23 October 2003

37 **Billy Wilder** was once asked: 'What is an associate producer?' 'Anybody,' he replied, 'who is prepared to associate with a producer.'

Billy Wilder Quoted by John Boorman in the *Guardian* 6 September 2003

38 **Cannes is where you lie on the beach and stare at the stars – or vice versa.**

Rex Reed Attributed

39 [Of Hollywood] **Deep below the glitter, it's all solid tinsel.**

Sam Goldwyn Attributed, like many Goldwynisms. Oscar Levant said: 'Behind the phoney tinsel of Hollywood lies the real tinsel.'

Theatre and Performance
Theatrical Life

1 QUINCE: You can play no part but Pyramus . . .
BOTTOM: What beard were I best to play it in? . . . I will discharge it in either your straw-coloured beard, your orange-tawny beard, your purple-in-grain beard, or your French-crown-colour beard, your perfect yellow.

William Shakespeare *A Midsummer Night's Dream*, act 1, sc. 2 (1595–6)

2 **I'll come no more behind your scenes, David; for the silk stockings and white bosoms of your actresses excite my amorous propensities.**

Samuel Johnson *The Life of Samuel Johnson* by James Boswell, vol. 1, p. 201 (1791); in G. B. Hill's edition of 1887, rev. L. F. Powell (1934). Addressed to David Garrick during the staging of Johnson's play *Irene*. Appendix G notes that the remark was also reported as . . . 'the silk stockings and white bosoms of your actresses do make my genitals to quiver'.

3 When at Chard studied hard,/ When at Louth gave it mouth,/ When at Ware made 'em stare,/ When at Rye made 'em cry,/ When at Lynn made 'em grin,/ When at Hull rather dull/ When at Holt made a bolt/ . . .

Anon. And so on. 'The Country Actor', *Oliver's Comic Songs* (1825?).

4 **It is the custom on the stage, in all good murderous melodramas, to present the tragic and the comic scenes, in as regular alternation, as the layers of red and white in a side of streaky bacon.**

Charles Dickens *Oliver Twist*, ch. 17 (1837–9)

5 'There's genteel comedy in your walk and manner, juvenile tragedy in your eye, and touch-and-go farce in your laugh,' said Mr Vincent Crummles. 'You'll do as well as if you had thought of nothing else but the lamps, from your birth downwards.'

Charles Dickens *Nicholas Nickleby*, ch. 22 (1838–9). Crummles explains why Nicholas would be well advised to go on the stage.

6 **It can hardly improve the reputation of the profession in the eyes of the public when they take up the *Era* and read advertisement after advertisement ending in such lines as 'None but sober people need apply.'**

Jerome K. Jerome *On the Stage and Off*, ch. 18 (1885). The *Era* was the newspaper for 'the show business'.

7 **Theatrical reminiscence is the most awful weapon in the armoury of old age. I am sure that much of the respect we pay to an elderly man is due to our suspicion that he could avenge any slight by describing the late Charles Matthews in *Cool as a Cucumber*.**

Max Beerbohm *More*, 'Actors' (1899). Beerbohm adds: 'It is curiously exasperating to hear about a great actor we have not seen.'

8 **I don't often go to the theatre, but when I do I like one of those plays with some ginger in them which the papers generally cuss. The**

papers say that real human beings don't carry on that way. Take it from me, Mister, they do.

P. G. Wodehouse *The Man with Two Left Feet*, 'The Making of Mac's' (1917)

9 [Of theatrical producers] **Why do they always look like unhappy rabbits?**

Joseph L. Mankiewicz Miss Casswell (Marilyn Monroe) in *All about Eve* (film, 1950, directed by Joseph L. Mankiewicz)

10 **In this Circus, he said, there's only one allowed to drink, and that's the ringmaster.**

Brendan Behan Chief Warder in *The Quare Fellow*, act 2 (1956)

11 **Show business is the best possible therapy for remorse. I've known deserted brides to take fresh interest in life by sweeping up the stage in some godforsaken regional theater.**

Anita Loos *Kiss Hollywood Goodbye*, ch. 13 (1974)

12 **My dressing room was so small, every time I stood up, I hit my head on the chain.**

Eric Morecambe and Ernie Wise *The Morecambe and Wise Jokebook*, skit 25 (1979)

13 **I enjoy travel, and with an act like mine it's a damn good thing I do.**

Les Dawson *The Malady Lingers On*, 'The Malady Lingers On . . .' (1982)

14 **Preview: That part of a theatre run which is not affected by bad reviews.**

Miles Kington *Moreover*, 'The Moreover Advice Service' (1982)

15 **Broadway is the moulting python of strict New York.**

Martin Amis *Money* (publ. 1984), p. 29 (1985 Penguin edn)

16 **I used to be a narrator for bad mimes.**

Steven Wright *I Have a Pony* (CD, 1986)

17 **Billions of years ago, when man made his first faltering efforts to haul himself out of the primordial**

soup, there was precious little in the way of subsidized theatre.

Christopher Douglas and Nigel Planer *I, An Actor*, 'Essential Acting' (1988)

18 **I've been working in show business for eighty-six years, if this keeps up maybe I should consider making it my career.**

George Burns *All My Best Friends*, ch. 1 (1989)

19 **What had Cliff once said to her? 'It's called show business, not show friend.'**

Carrie Fisher *Delusions of Grandma*, p. 139 (1994 paperback edn)

20 **I also do sleight of feet.**

Gerry Sadowitz Stage act in London, 1994

Actors and Acting

1 **The guilds of singing girls, the vendors of drugs, beggars, actresses in farces, buffoons, all that sort of people . . .**

Horace *Satires*, bk 1, Satire 2 (35 BC), *The Works of Horace* ed. and trans. James Lonsdale and Samuel Lee (1887)

2 **All the world's a stage,/ And all the men and women merely players:/ They have their exits and their entrances . . .**

William Shakespeare Jaques in *As You Like It*, act 2, sc. 7 (1599)

3 **. . . suit the action to the word, the word to the action; with this special observance, that you o'erstep not the modesty of nature . . .**

William Shakespeare *Hamlet* to the Players, act 3, sc. 2 (1601–2). He adds: 'And let those that play your clowns speak no more than is set down for them . . .'

4 **A man who has passed above forty years of his life upon a theatre, where he has never appeared to be himself, may have naturally excited the curiosity of the spectators to know what he really was, when in nobody's shape but his own; and whether he, who by his profession had so long been ridiculing his**

benefactors, might not, when the coat of his profession was off, deserve to be laughed at himself.

Colley Cibber *An Apology for the Life of Mr Colley Cibber, Comedian*, ch. 1 (1739)

5 Players, Sir! I look upon them as no better than creatures set upon their tables and joint-stools to make faces and produce laughter, like dancing dogs.

Samuel Johnson *The Life of Samuel Johnson* by James Boswell, vol. 2, p. 404 (1791); in G. B. Hill's edition of 1887, rev. L. F. Powell (1934)

6 You estimate the position of an actor by the time he is late for rehearsal. If he (I don't say a word about ladies, they are always an hour late for everything, bless 'em) is twenty minutes behind, he is most likely mere utility. If a man keeps everybody waiting an hour and a half you may put him down as a star.

Jerome K. Jerome *On Stage and Off*, ch. 5 (1888)

7 I never said all actors are cattle. What I said was that all actors should be treated like cattle.

Sir Alfred Hitchcock Attributed. In his book *Alfred Hitchcock: A Life in Darkness and Light* (2003), Patrick McGilligan writes: 'Nobody has been able to date the origins of that most notorious of Hitchcock's pronouncements', but he quotes the director himself as saying that he 'might first have said something along those lines in the late 1920s'.

8 Actors are only interesting when they go home. *Then the real comedy begins.*

Ivor Brown *Week End Review*, 'The Funny Fellow', 15 March 1930. Collected in *Fleet Street*, ed. W. W. Cobbett and Sidney Dark (1932).

9 DON'T TRY TO BECOME AN ACTOR. FOR EVERY ONE WE EMPLOY, WE TURN AWAY THOUSANDS.

Anon. Sign above the door of Central Casting in the 1930s. Quoted in *Cassell's Movie Quotations* ed. Nigel Rees (2002 edn)

10 Scratch an actor – and you'll find an actress.

Dorothy Parker Attributed. An embellishment of the line from her poem 'Ballade of Great Weariness' (1937): 'Scratch a lover, and find a foe.'

11 The art of acting consists in keeping people from coughing.

Sir Ralph Richardson *The Observer*, 'Sayings of the Week', 19 January 1947

12 The leading man was an amiable ham with a lot of charm, some of it turning a little yellow at the edges.

Raymond Chandler *The Little Sister*, ch. 13 (1949)

13 I mean, the question actors most often get asked is how they can bear saying the same things over and over again night after night, but God knows the answer to that is, don't we all anyway; might as well get paid for it.

Elaine Dundy *The Dud Avocado*, ch. 9 (1958)

14 I am proud to say that in ninety per cent of the plays in which I have performed I have never known what happened at either the end or the beginning.

Michael Green *The Art of Coarse Acting*, ch. 2 (1964). Green elaborates: 'If I am not called early on I am in the bar until the curtain goes up, and if I've finished before the end I'm in the pub when the curtain falls.'

15 How to steal a scene though unconscious.

Michael Green Picture caption in ibid., ch. 2. The picture shows a coarse actor, supposedly knocked out, grimacing horribly.

16 *Any* actress *with a deep voice is* hailed by male critics for her wit, shrewdness, intellectuality – simply because she *sounds like a man*.

Kenneth Tynan Entry for 24 October 1972, *The Diaries of Kenneth Tynan* ed. John Lahr (2002). He had in mind Lauren Bacall, Katharine Hepburn and Marlene Dietrich – 'all of them nice women but by no stretch of the imagination mental giants'.

17 An actor is the kind of guy who if

you ain't talking about him ain't
listening.

George Glass Quoted in *Brando*, ch. 8, by Bob
Thomas (1973), and often attributed to
Brando

18 DOTTY: **How about the words, love?
Am I getting some of them
right?**
LLOYD: **Some of them have a very
familiar ring.**

Michael Frayn *Noises Off*, act 1 (1982). Mrs
Clackett, 'played' in this play within a play
by the character called Dotty Otley,
addresses Lloyd Dallas, the director of the
production.

19 **In the old-fashioned Forties, when
the West End was ruled by homosexual managers, a young actor was
asked in an audition if he wasn't,
perhaps, homosexual. 'Well yes,' he
admitted, and added eagerly, 'but it
doesn't show from the front.'**

John Mortimer *Clinging to the Wreckage*,
ch. 19 (1982)

20 **I can't say this too often: it may be
Hamlet but it's got to be Fun! Fun!
Fun!**

Victoria Wood 'Giving Notes', *Victoria Wood
as Seen on TV* (TV series, 1985), collected in
*Up to You, Porky – The Victoria Wood Sketch
Book* (1985). Alma, 'a middle-aged, sprightly
woman', is addressing her amateur company, the Piecrust Players, after a run-
through of *Hamlet*.

21 **Actresses will happen in the best
regulated families.**

Oliver Herford Quoted in *The Penguin Dictionary of Modern Humorous Quotations* ed. Fred
Metcalf (1st edn 1986)

22 **The only programme I'm likely to
get on is the fucking news.**

Bruce Robinson Withnail (Richard E. Grant)
in *Withnail & I* (film, 1987, written and
directed by Bruce Robinson). Withnail is a
failed actor living in incredible squalor.

23 **Two Christian names is the best
combination; neutral, unintimidat-
ing and conveying to the director a
reassuring sense of dependability. I
wonder if we should have had a
second series of *To the Manor Born***

if the leading lady's stage name had
been Pip Trotsky.

Christopher Douglas and Nigel Planer Her
name was in fact Penelope Keith. *I, An Actor*,
'To the Young Actor' (1988).

24 **Q: How many actors does it take to
change a lightbulb? A: One hundred. One to change the lightbulb,
and ninety-nine to say 'I could have
done that.'**

Anon. *And I Quote*, 'Actors and Acting', ed.
Ashton Applewhite and others (1992)

25 **The scenery was beautiful but the
actors got in front of it.**

Alexander Woollcott Quoted in *Chambers
Dictionary of Quotations* ed. Alison Jones and
others (1996)

26 **Acting is the most minor of gifts.
After all, Shirley Temple could do it
when she was four.**

Katharine Hepburn Quoted in *Halliwell's
Who's Who in the Movies* ed. John Walker
(2001)

27 **Acting is all about honesty. If you
can fake that, you've got it made.**

George Burns Attributed

Audiences

1 **One needs only observe the perpetual loud laughs set up in the pit.
I want nothing else to prove 'tis
good for nothing.**

Molière The Marquis in *The School for Wives*,
act 1, sc. 6 (1663)

2 **Nat that I pretend to be a beau; but
a man must endeavour to look
decent, lest he makes so odious a
figure in the side-box, the ladies
should be compelled to turn their
eyes upon the play.**

Richard Brinsley Sheridan Lord Foppington in
A Trip to Scarborough, act 2, sc. 1 (1777)

3 **In Germany they always hear one
thing at an opera which has never
yet been heard in America, perhaps
– I mean the closing strain of a fine
solo or duet. We always smash into
it with applause. The result is that**

we rob ourselves of the sweetest part of the treat; we get the whisky, but we don't get the sugar in the bottom of the glass.

Mark Twain *A Tramp Abroad*, ch. 10 (1880)

4 You ought never have any part of the audience behind you; you can never tell what they're going to do.

Mark Twain Speech delivered in New York 18 April 1908. Collected as 'Courage' in *Mark Twain: Speeches* ed. Shelley Fisher Fishkin (1996).

5 Long experience has taught me that in England nobody goes to the theatre unless he or she has bronchitis.

James Agate *Ego*, ch. 6 (1935–48)

6 I know two kinds of audience only – one coughing and one not coughing.

Artur Schnabel *My Life in Music*, pt 2, ch. 10 (1961). Schnabel, who disliked playing encores, also said: 'Applause is a receipt, not a bill.'

7 You are the audience. I am the author. I outrank you.

Mel Brooks Franz Liebkind (Kenneth Mars) declining to keep quiet during his own play, *Springtime for Hitler* (*The Producers*, 1968, written and directed by Mel Brooks)

8 Anyone wishing to avoid the crowds when leaving, please wait until the end of the show.

Humphrey Lyttelton *I'm Sorry I Haven't a Clue* (BBC radio series, 1972 onwards), collected in *I'm Sorry I Haven't a Clue: Four* (cassette, 1998)

9 ERNIE: What was the audience like?
ERIC: Well on the first night there was nobody there at all, but on the second night the attendance fell off completely.

Eric Morecambe and Ernie Wise *The Morecambe and Wise Jokebook*, skit 25 (1979)

10 At the Greenwich Theatre once, I was more slept against than sleeping.

Robert Robinson *The Dog Chairman*, 'Sleep Doth Murder Macbeth' (1982). A lady fell asleep on his shoulder. The original, 'I am a

man more sinned against than sinning', is from *King Lear*.

11 I made mistakes in drama. I thought drama was when actors cried. But drama is when the audience cries.

Frank Capra Attributed remark made on French TV February 1983, quoted in *Cassell's Movie Quotations*, ed. Nigel Rees (2nd edn 2002)

12 I hate going to the theatre because you can't smoke and I like to keep to my target of forty a day.

Peter Cook *Sunday Times*, 'A Life in the Day . . .', 5 August 1984

13 Cinemas and theatres are always bigger inside than they are outside.

Miles Kington *Independent* 29 March 1989

14 If I get a hard audience they are not going to get away until they laugh. Those seven laughs a minute – I need them.

Ken Dodd *Daily Telegraph* 20 September 1990

15 I was relieved to hear that your welcome was not excessive.

Peter Ustinov To the audience at the beginning of his one-man show. Quoted in the *San Francisco Chronicle* 25 April 1991

16 [Of films] If my fanny squirms, it's bad. If my fanny doesn't squirm, it's good. Simple as that.

Harry Cohn Attributed remark quoted in *Cassell's Movie Quotations*, ed. Nigel Rees (2nd edn 2002). The screenwriter Herman Mankiewicz responded: 'Imagine the whole world wired to Harry Cohn's ass', and was sacked by Columbia of which Cohn was then head.

17 [Of Chicago audiences of the late 1920s] If they liked you they didn't applaud; they just let you live.

Bob Hope Quoted in his obituary, *Daily Telegraph* 29 July 2003

Particular Plays and Stage Performances

1 He that says he does not like a pantomime, either says what he does

not think, or is not so wise as he fancies himself.

Leigh Hunt *Companion* 9 January 1828

2 'I'm always ill after Shakespeare,' said Mrs Wititterly. 'I scarcely exist the next day; I find the reaction so very great after a tragedy, my lord, and Shakespeare is such a delicious creature.'

Charles Dickens *Nicholas Nickleby*, ch. 27 (1838–9)

3 Mr Clarke played the King all evening as though under constant fear that someone else was about to play the ace.

Eugene Field Of Creston Clarke playing the lead in *King Lear*, Denver 1880. Quoted in *The Portable Woollcott*, 'Capsule Criticism' (1946).

4 [Of Wagner's *Parsifal*] The first act of the three occupied three hours, and I enjoyed that in spite of the singing.

Mark Twain *A Tramp Abroad* (1880). In his *Autobiography* Twain wrote: 'I've been told Wagner's music is better than it sounds.'

5 Sarah Bernhardt was stout last year. This season she is positively obese. But most of the women in her company have waists even larger than hers. Query: Is this an accident?

Arnold Bennett Entry for Monday 5 June 1896, *The Journals of Arnold Bennett 1896–1910* ed. Newman Flower (1932)

6 Oh, for an hour of Herod!

Anthony Hope Reaction to first night of *Peter Pan* in 1904. Quoted in *The Story of JMB*, ch. 17, by Denis Mackay (1941).

7 Musical comedy is the Irish stew of drama. Anything may be put into it, with the certainty that it will improve the general effect.

P. G. Wodehouse *The Man with Two Left Feet*, 'Bill the Bloodhound' (1917). In *Three Men in a Boat* by Jerome K. Jerome, George says that the great advantage of Irish stew is that 'you get rid of such a lot of things'.

8 [Of Katharine Hepburn] She runs the gamut of emotions from A to B.

Dorothy Parker Theatre review of *The Lake*

(1933), quoted in Parker's obituary in *Publishers' Weekly* 19 June 1967

9 Me no Leica.

Walter Kerr Attributed review of *I Am a Camera* (1951), John Van Druten's dramatization of the short story 'Sally Bowles' from *Goodbye to Berlin* (1939) by Christopher Isherwood. Quoted in *No Turn Unstoned*, ch. 5, ed. Diana Rigg (1982).

10 It is about to make me very rich.

Tom Stoppard On being asked what *Rosencrantz and Guildenstern* was about. Attributed, after the play's US opening. Quoted in *Double Act: A Life of Tom Stoppard*, ch. 8, by Ira Nadel (2002).

11 The trouble with nude dancing is that not everything stops when the music stops.

Robert Helpmann Review, 1968, of *Oh! Calcutta!* Quoted in *Collins Dictionary of Quotations* ed. A. Norman Jeffares and Martin Gray (1995)

12 Theatrically speaking, it was Coward who took sophistication out of the refrigerator, and put it on the hob.

Kenneth Tynan *Observer* 1 April 1973

13 Go and see David Copperfield. You'll believe a man can be suspended by wire.

Gerry Sadowitz Remark made on stage in London, 1994. Copperfield, the American magician, performed his famous flying act in London that year.

14 It's a play that after you've been there for a short while, you wonder how long this is going to take.

Garrison Keillor Of *Three Tall Women* by Edward Albee, New York, 2 January 1995

Comedy and Comedians

1 It's an odd job, making decent people laugh.

Molière Dorantes in *The School for Wives*, act 1, sc. 6 (1663)

2 My idea of an ideal programme would be a show where I would have all the questions and some

other bastard would have to figure out the funny answers.

Groucho Marx Letter of 10 October 1940, quoted in *The Oxford Dictionary of Humorous Quotations* ed. Ned Sherrin (1995)

3 The parson may provoke us to yawns with impunity, but the comedian must hold his audience all the time.

A. P. Herbert *A Book of Ballads*, 'Brief Lecture to a Serious Poet' (1949)

4 There is not one female comic who was beautiful as a little girl.

Joan Rivers *Los Angeles Times* 10 May, 1974

5 All comedians must make a financial disclosure. Percentages . . . manager and agent, thirty to thirty-five percent, road expenses ten or twenty percent, development of new material .000 percent.

Steve Martin *A Wild and Crazy Guy*, 'A Wild and Crazy Guy' (LP, 1978)

6 One uses humour to make people laugh . . . The trouble is, it makes them think you aren't being serious. That's the risk you take.

Philip Larkin *Required Writing*, 'An Interview with *Paris Review*' (1983)

7 Maybe [Jimmy] Durante was the only performer who wasn't terrified about working live. I mean, with Jimmy, what could happen? If he said something wrong, how would anybody know?

George Burns As Burns notes: 'Malaprops were an important part of his act, and his writers would always give him two or three in every script, but they'd also put in enough hard words to ensure that he'd mess up a few more. They knew, for example, that Jimmy could always be counted on to ask his orchestra to 'reprieve da music'. *All My Best Friends*, ch. 10 (1989).

8 If Woody Allen were a Muslim he'd be dead by now.

Salman Rushdie Quoted in the *Independent* 18 February 1989

9 I don't think being funny is anyone's first choice.

Woody Allen *Guardian* 23 March 1992

10 Two cannibals are eating a clown. One turns to the other and says, 'Does this taste funny to you?'

Tommy Cooper Quoted in the *Daily Telegraph* 2 December 2000, and described there by Sinclair Mackay as 'a vintage gag that you will hear at least three times a year in the pub'.

11 [Of Tommy Cooper] He had a great rapport with himself.

Russ Abbott *The Times*, 'Quotes of the Week', 3 November 2001, collected in *The Times Quotes of the Week* introduced by Philip Howard (2002)

12 [Of Milton Berle] The thief of bad gags.

Anon. Quoted in the *Daily Telegraph* 28 March 2002. American TV star of the 1940s and 50s and sometime boyfriend of Marilyn Monroe, Berle was reputed to know two hundred thousand jokes, many of which belonged to other people. He once said of a performance he attended: 'I laughed so much I almost dropped my pencil and paper.'

13 Comedians known to be inventive, experimental and challenging invariably come over all conservative when faced with a proper film budget and the sort of film executives who walk around saying things like, 'Where's your third act?' and 'Julia would be perfect for this.'

Tim Dowling *Daily Telegraph* 16 March 2002

14 I'm doing pretty good. Been on the road now doing comedy for ten years so bear with me while I plaster on a fake smile and plough through this shit one more time.

Bill Hicks Preamble to *Love Laughter and Truth* (live CD, 2002)

15 The grin reaper.

Anon. Billing, spotted in October 2003, for a night of comedy at the Blue Posts pub, Rupert Street, London W1

16 Always be one drink behind your audience.

Johnny Vegas Advice to comedians in *Word* magazine, February 2005

Visual Art
Visual Artists as People

1 Every young sculptor seems to think that he must give the world some specimen of indecorous womanhood, and call it Eve, Venus, a Nymph, or any name that may apologize for a lack of decent clothing.
Nathaniel Hawthorne *The Marble Faun*, ch. 14 (1860)

2 It is the process of painting which is repellent: to force from little tubes of lead a glutinous flamboyance and to defile, with the hair of a camel therein steeped, taut canvas, is hardly the diversion of a gentleman.
Max Beerbohm *The Works of Max Beerbohm* 'Dandies and Dandies' (1896)

3 If I could find anything blacker than black, I'd use it.
J. M. W. Turner Quoted in *Dictionary of National Biography* (1917)

4 Cause I'm quick, you know, I don't hang about. Once I've got the inspiration I'm away. I've had a canvas twelve foot by eight filled in, framed and flogged before the first dab had dried.
Ray Galton and Alan Simpson Tony Hancock playing Anthony Hancock, a Home Counties commuter turned successful painter of the Infantile School in *The Rebel* (film, 1961, directed by Robert Day). At the height of his fame, he moves to the Left Bank in Paris, where he orders snails, egg and chips.

5 To me, a painter, if not the most useful, is the least harmful member of society.
Man Ray *Self-Portrait*, ch. 6 (1963)

6 A friend of mine who was young in the same decade as I says that, when he was introduced to an elderly gentleman as an artist, the gentleman said, 'Oh, I know this young man is an artist. The other day I saw him in the street in a brown jacket.'
Quentin Crisp *The Naked Civil Servant*, ch. 3 (1968). The decade was the 1920s.

7 The artist is a lucky dog. That is all there is to say about him. In any community of a thousand souls there will be nine hundred doing the work, ninety doing well, nine doing good, and one lucky dog painting or writing about the other nine hundred and ninety-nine.
Tom Stoppard *Artist Descending a Staircase*, p. 43 (radio play, 1972)

8 An artist is someone who produces things that people don't need to have but that he – for *some reason* – thinks it would be a good idea to give them.
Andy Warhol *From A to B and Back Again*, 'Atmosphere' (1975)

9 Well, I *am* a Sunday painter. It's just that I paint every other day of the week as well.
L. S. Lowry *The Life of L. S. Lowry*, ch. 1, by Allen Andrews (1977)

10 Once when I was fifteen or sixteen years old, I saw a dog peeing and I realized at that moment I was going to die.
Francis Bacon Interview conducted in 1992, publ. in the *Art Newspaper* June 2003

11 I hate flowers – I paint them because they're cheaper than models and they don't move.
Georgia O'Keeffe Quoted in *The Quotable Artist*, ch. 2, ed. Peggy Hadden (2002)

12 It's about time a transvestite potter won the Turner Prize.
Grayson Perry Quoted in the *Daily Telegraph* 8 December 2003

13 Every time I paint a portrait I lose a friend.
John Singer Sargent Attributed

14 [When asked by a young painter to come and look at some of his works] I don't need to – I've seen your tie.
Francis Bacon Attributed

Visual Art in General

1 There are only two styles of portrait painting: the serious and the smirk.

Charles Dickens Miss La Creevy in *Nicholas Nickleby*, ch. 10 (1838–9)

2 A life passed among pictures makes not a painter – else the policeman in the National Gallery might assert himself.

James McNeill Whistler *The Gentle Art of Making Enemies*, 'Whistler v. Ruskin: Art and Critics' (1890)

3 The pictures are all right, in their way; after all, one can always *look* at them if one is bored with one's surroundings, or wants to avoid an imminent acquaintance.

Saki Reginald in *Reginald*, 'Reginald on the Academy' (1904)

4 A product of the untalented, sold by the unprincipled to the utterly bewildered.

Al Capp Speaking of abstract art in the *National Observer* 1 July 1963

5 As an artist he belonged to the ultra-modern school, expressing himself most readily in pictures showing a sardine tin, two empty beer bottles, a bunch of carrots and a dead cat, the whole intended to represent Paris in Springtime.

P. G. Wodehouse *Plum Pie*, 'A Good Cigar Is a Smoke' (1966). This is Lancelot Bingley, 'the rising young artist'.

6 Frankly, these days, without a theory to go with it, I can't *see* a painting.

Tom Wolfe *The Painted Word*, ch. 1 (1975)

7 [Of Modernism] I mean, this is pretty complex stuff: if you want to know how complex, I'm giving a course of ninety-six lectures at the local college, starting next week, and you'd be more than welcome.

Philip Larkin *All What Jazz? A Record Diary*, 'Introduction' (2nd edn, 1985). He added: 'The whole thing's on the rates. You won't have to pay.'

8 The local is the universal. It was a banana to Cezanne.

William Carlos Williams Quoted in *A Dictionary of Art Quotations*, 'Paul Cezanne', ed. Ian Crofton (1988)

9 It can be argued that in an age when religious belief has in supposedly civilized societies fallen into desuetude, the unfathomable mysteries of modern art have become ritual objects of intellectual genuflexion.

Brian Sewell *The Reviews That Caused the Rumpus*, 'Art Criticism' (1994)

10 The avant-garde is to the left what jingoism is to the right. Both are a refuge in nonsense.

David Mamet *Three Uses of the Knife*, ch. 3 (2002)

11 N is for the Nature of art itself. Every significant piece by a modern artist is, apart from anything else, about the Nature of art itself.

Craig Brown *This Is Craig Brown*, 'How to Be a Significant Artist' (2003)

Particular Visual Artists and Their Works

1 Bring my umbrella – I am going to see Mr Constable's pictures.

Henry Fuseli Remark made *c.* 1813. Quoted in *A Dictionary of Art Quotations*, 'John Constable', ed. Ian Crofton (1988). Constable was a close student of precipitation.

2 As for Rubens . . . he seems to me (who by the way know nothing of the matter) the most glaring – flaring – staring – harlotry impostor that ever passed a trick upon the senses of mankind . . .

Lord Byron Letter to John Cam Hobhouse of 1 May 1816, collected in *Letters and Journals*, vol. 5, *So Late into the Night (1816–17)*, ed. Leslie A. Marchand (1976)

3 A Boston newspaper reporter went and took a look at the Slave Ship floundering about in that fierce conflagration of reds and yellows, and

said it reminded him of a tortoise-shell cat having a fit in a platter of tomatoes.

Mark Twain Of *The Slave Ship* by Turner. *A Tramp Abroad*, ch. 21 (1880).

4 [Of the portrait of him by Graham Sutherland] **It makes me look as though I was straining at the stool.**

Winston Churchill Quoted in a letter from Rupert Hart-Davis to George Lyttelton of 20 November 1955, collected in *The Lyttelton –Hart-Davis Letters*, vols 1 and 2, *1955–1957*, ed. Rupert Hart-Davis (1978)

5 **Rembrandt was one of the first to use a roller . . . only for the back-grounds.**

Carl Reiner and Mel Brooks '2002-Year-Old Man', *Carl Reiner and Mel Brooks at the Cannes Film Festival* (LP, 1962)

6 **If people only knew as much about painting as I do, they would never buy my pictures.**

Sir Edwin Landseer Remark made to W. P. Frith, quoted in *Landseer the Victorian Paragon*, ch. 12, by Campbell Lennie (1976)

7 **Ruskin, John (1819–1900): An excellent artist, considering he was an art critic too.**

Henry Root *Henry Root's World of Knowledge* (1982)

8 **Whilst Titian was mixing rose madder,/ His model posed nude on a ladder,/ Her position to Titian/ Suggested coition,/ So he climbed up the ladder and had 'er.**

Anon. Quoted in *The Penguin Book of Limericks* ed. E. O. Parrott (1983)

9 [Of Andy Warhol] **He became the Billy Graham of boredom, and sought to convert us all to the mindless pleasures of the intellectually numb.**

Brian Sewell *Tatler* article of 1983, 'Andy Warhol', collected in *The Reviews that Caused the Rumpus* (1994)

10 **To exhibit Viola's work is an abuse of the purposes of the Whitechapel Gallery – but then, in its proper**

place, the Odeon, it would get the short shrift that it merits.

Brian Sewell Of an exhibition in 1993 by the video artist Bill Viola, ibid., 'Bill Viola' (1994)

11 [On opening an exhibition of Henry Moore's sculptures in Beijing] **He didn't like heads, did he?**

John Prescott *The Times*, 'Quotes of the Week', 21 October 2000

Music
Musicians as People

1 **They say of Greek musicians that the ones who accompany the reed-pipe are the ones who failed with the lyre.**

Anon. *Pro Murena* pt 28 (63 BC). Collected in *Cicero: Defence Speeches* ed. D. H. Berry (2000). Players of the lyre would also sing, the twofold task being considered difficult.

2 **Singers all have the same fault. When asked to perform/ for their friends they never will; when no one asks them they never/ stop.**

Horace *Satires*, bk 1, no. 3 (c.30 BC). *Horace: Satires and Epistles; Persius: Satires* trans. and ed. Niall Rudd (1973).

3 **The singing man keeps a shop in his throat.**

George Herbert *Outlandish Proverbs*, no. 918 (1640)

4 **In came a fiddler – and tuned like fifty stomach aches.**

Charles Dickens *A Christmas Carol*, Stave 2 (1843)

5 **It is clear that the first specification for a composer is to be dead.**

Arthur Honegger *I Am a Composer*, p. 16 (1951)

6 **A [film] musician is like a mortician. He can't bring a body to life, but he can make it look better.**

Adolph Deutsch *British Composers in Interview*, 'Malcolm Arnold', by Murray Schafer (1963)

7 **Well, Norm's got this friend Walter,**

who's a musician. He's a *pro-fessional* musician. I mean, he can do it even when he's not in the mood.

Joyce Grenfell *Shirley's Girl Friend 4*, skit written for the Aldeburgh Festival, 1964. Spoken in the persona of Shirl, a South London girl. Collected in *Turn Back The Clock* (1977).

8 When the reviews are bad I tell my staff they can join me as I cry all the way to the bank.

Liberace *Autobiography*, ch. 2 (1973)

9 Only when you go wrong do you seem to be important.

Jack Brymer Speaking of orchestral players in *From Where I Sit* (1979), collected in *A Dictionary of Musical Quotations*, ed. I. Crofton and D. Fraser (1985)

10 I've suffered for my music, now it's your turn.

Neil Innes From *The Innes Book of Records* (TV series, 1979). Innes was introducing a song in the guise of an earnest protest singer.

11 What is a string quartet? An East German orchestra after a tour of the West.

Anon. Quoted by Timothy Garton Ash in the *Spectator* 17 September 1983, collected in *The Wit of the Spectator* ed. Christopher Howse (1989)

12 I'm conducting . . . in Israel. A young genius is playing. They're all young geniuses now, aren't they?

Sir Edward Heath Interviewed by John Mortimer for the *Sunday Times*, collected in *Character Parts*, 'Three Times Happy', by John Mortimer (1986)

13 Deco's mother worried about him. He'd be eating his breakfast and then he'd yell something like 'Good God Y'Awl' or 'Take It To The Bridge Now'.

Roddy Doyle *The Commitments*, 1988. Deco has just acquired his first electric guitar. The quotes are from 'Get Up I Feel Like Being a Sex Machine' by James Brown.

14 It's curious that *Grove's Dictionary* omits from its pages the musical phrase that best describes the atti-tude of most orchestral players – *moano perpetuo*.

Victor Lewis-Smith *Inside the Magic Rectangle*, 'Omnibus: Everything You Wanted to Know About Conductors but Were Afraid to Ask' (1995)

15 There's a tape/ That we made/ But I'm sad to say/ It never made the grade/ That was me/ Third guitar/ I wonder where the others are.

Randy Newman 'Vine Street' (song), quoted at the beginning of Giles Smith's pop memoir *Lost in Music* (1995)

16 Q: What do you call a musician without a girlfriend? A: Homeless.

Anthony Kiedis Quoted in *Q* magazine March 2003

17 A composer? What the fuck do they do? All the good music's already been written by people with wigs and stuff.

Frank Zappa Attributed

Musicality

1 Musick helps not the tooth-ach.

George Herbert *Outlandish Proverbs*, no. 532 (1640). Martin Amis, in his memoir *Experience* (2000), wrote: 'Bach's "Concerto for Cello" struck me as a faultless *transcription* of a toothache.' The situation is complicated by the fact that Bach did not write a 'Concerto for Cello'.

2 I . . . went to hear Mrs Turner's daughter play on the harpsicon. But Lord! It was enough to make any man sick to hear her; yet I was forced to commend her highly.

Samuel Pepys Diary entry for 1 May 1663, *Everybody's Pepys* ed. Henry B. Wheatley (1926)

3 Sentimentally I am disposed to harmony. But organically I am incapable of a tune.

Charles Lamb *The Essays of Elia*, 'A Chapter on Ears' (1823)

4 The Nightingale Club in a village was held,/ At the sign of the Cabbage and Shears,/ Where the singers, no

doubt, would have greatly excell'd/
But for want of taste, voice and ears.

Anon. 'Nightingale Club', *Oliver's Comic Songs* (1825?)

5 Swans sing before they die – 'twere no bad thing/ Should certain persons die before they sing.

Samuel Taylor Coleridge 'Epigram on a Volunteer Singer', *The Poetical Works of S. T. Coleridge*, vol. 2 (1836)

6 Let a man try the very uttermost to *speak* what he means, before singing is had recourse to.

Thomas Carlyle Quoted, with the note 'Journal, 1843', in *A Dictionary of Musical Quotations* ed. I. Crofton and D. Fraser (1985)

7 Please do not shoot the pianist. He is doing his best.

Oscar Wilde *Impressions of America*, 'Leadville' (1883). Sign above a piano. In 1973 Elton John released an album called *Don't Shoot Me, I'm Only the Piano Player*.

8 Hell is full of musical amateurs. Music is the brandy of the damned.

George Bernard Shaw Don Juan in *Man and Superman*, act 3 (1903)

9 For me the loveliest moments of the evening were enclosed by the opening bars of [Schubert's] 'Du bist die Ruhe'. While I was wiping my eyes at the end of it, a man near me remarked: 'I always think that's a *most* over-rated song.'

Siegfried Sassoon Entry for 30 March 1922, *Siegfried Sassoon: Diaries 1920–22* ed. R. Hart-Davis (1981). Collected in *The Assassin's Cloak* ed. Irene and Alan Taylor (2000).

10 It don't mean a thing/ If it ain't got that swing.

Duke Ellington and Irving Mills Song (1932) – the expression of an Ellington Band member of the 1920s, Bubber Miley

11 The English may not like music, but they absolutely love the noise it makes.

Sir Thomas Beecham Quoted in the *New York Herald Tribune* 9 March 1961

12 My music is best understood by children and animals.

Igor Stravinsky *Observer* 8 October 1961

13 [Of muzak] If we ate what we listened to, we'd all be dead.

Earl Wild Remark made during a TV programme of 1976, *Earl Wild*, and quoted in Clive James's review of it, *Observer* 15 February 1976

14 Singing an entrancingly drab number called 'Mile After Mile', a Norwegian pop singer, Mr Jan Teigan, scored nil in the 1978 Eurovision Song Contest.

Stephen Pile *The Book of Heroic Failures*, 'The Worst Song Entry', by Stephen Pile (1979). Afterwards Mr Teigan said, 'I've got lots of offers for TV appearances, tours and interviews.'

15 The way I write songs is to sit down and play twenty-five great songs by other people, and hope one of mine drops off the end.

Keith Richards Said in 1983, quoted in *Old Gods Almost Dead: The Forty-Year Odyssey of the Rolling Stones*, pt 9, 'World War 3', by Stephen Davis (2001)

16 It's all right letting yourself go, as long as you can let yourself back.

Mick Jagger Quoted in *A Dictionary of Musical Quotations* ed. I. Croft and D. Fraser (1985)

17 I once knew a Norwegian who named his favourite musicians as the Sex Pistols, Thin Lizzy, and Roger Whittaker.

Harry Pearson *The Far Corner*, 'Durham City v. Shildon, Federation Brewery Northern League, Division 1, Saturday 20 November 1993' (1994). Pearson 'protested that it was impossible to like three such disparate musical forms, two of which were also plainly crap'.

18 Harken to the tune within: when all is silent around you, strive to remember a tune that reached number 17 in the charts in 1973. Whistle half the chorus, over and over again, all day long./ As the sun goes down, those of your friends and colleagues who did not know the tune will now know it by heart.

Craig Brown *The Little Book of Chaos* (1998)

19 Singing is the lowest form of communication.

Matt Groening Homer Simpson in *The Simp-*

sons, 'All Singing, All Dancing', first broadcast 4 January 1998

20 **Q: Can you play the violin? A: I don't know, I've never tried.**

Anon. Quoted in *An Introduction to English Poetry* by James Fenton (2002). Fenton describes this as 'the old joke'.

21 **He has Van Gogh's ear for music.**

Orson Welles Attributed to Welles, and appropriated by many

Types of Music

1 **Opera: An exotic and irrational entertainment.**

Samuel Johnson *A Dictionary of the English Language* (1755)

2 **[Of opera] This particularly rapid, unintelligible patter,/ Isn't generally heard, and if it is, doesn't matter!**

W. S. Gilbert *Ruddigore*, act 2 (1887)

3 **Extraordinary how potent cheap music is.**

Noël Coward *Private Lives*, act 1 (1930)

4 **A waltz formed itself dimly on the warm air. A tinsel waltz, but a waltz.**

Raymond Chandler *Trouble Is My Business*, 'I'll Be Waiting' (1946)

5 **Opera is when a guy gets stabbed in the back and, instead of bleeding, he sings.**

Ed Gardner *Duffy's Tavern*, US radio programme of the 1940s

6 **Playing 'bop' is like playing Scrabble with all the vowels missing.**

Duke Ellington *Look* 10 August 1954

7 **Sleep babeling sleep, sleep/ Sleep babeling sleep/ Sleep babeling, sleep, sleep/ Sleep babeling, sleep/ Or thy mother will clout thee.**

Joyce Grenfell Parody of a folksong 'from the Urk mountains of central Europe', where it is known as 'Sloop Boobeling Sloop'. Performed in *Joyce Grenfell Requests the Pleasure*

(sketch show, 1954), collected in *Turn Back the Clock* (1977).

8 **I do not mind what language an opera is sung in so long as it is a language I do not understand.**

Sir Edward Appleton *Observer* 28 August 1955

9 **I guess all songs is folk songs. I never heard no horse sing 'em.**

Louis Armstrong *New York Times* 7 July 1971. But C. Keil, in his book *Urban Blues* (1966), attributes this to Big Bill Broonzy.

10 **It's only rock 'n' roll, but I like it.**

Mick Jagger and Keith Richards Song from *It's Only Rock 'n' Roll* (LP, 1973). Ron Wood of the Stones claims to be the true author.

11 **Down in a cellar in the Boho zone/ I went looking for some sweet inspiration/ Oh well, just another hard time band/ With negro affectations.**

Joni Mitchell 'The Boho Dance', *The Hissing of Summer Lawns* (LP, 1975)

12 **The opera ain't over til the fat lady sings.**

Dan Cook *Washington Post* 3 June 1978

13 **Jazz: A kind of music played by blacks and listened to by whites.**

Miles Kington *Moreover*, 'The Moreover Advice Service' (1982)

14 **Writing contemporary music isn't the problem – anyone can do that; it's *enjoying* it that's so difficult.**

Ibid.

15 **Reggae is one of them stones that was refused by the builders.**

Charlie Ace Quoted in *A Dictionary of Musical Quotations* ed. I. Croft and D. Fraser (1985)

16 **It was a song that sounded sophisticated if you did not listen too carefully – which is probably true of most sophisticated songs.**

Barry Humphries *More Please*, 'Raspberry Ripple' (1992)

17 **With rock and roll, the more you think, the more you *stink*.**

David Briggs Quoted in *Shakey – Neil Young's Biography*, 'The No Men', by Jimmy McDonough (2002)

Types of Instrument

1 **The vile squeaking of the wry-necked fife.**
William Shakespeare Shylock in *The Merchant of Venice*, act 2, sc. 4 (1596–8). The reference is to the flute.

2 **FALSTAFF: . . .'Sblood, I am as melancholy as a gib cat or a lugged bear.**
PRINCE HENRY: Or an old lion or a lover's lute.
FALSTAFF: Yea, or the drone of a Lincolnshire bagpipe.
William Shakespeare *Henry IV Part 1*, act 1, sc. 1 (1597)

3 **The devil rides upon a fiddlestick.**
William Shakespeare Prince Henry in ibid., act 2, sc. 4 (1597)

4 **I have a reasonable ear in music. Let's have the tongs and bones.**
William Shakespeare Bottom in *A Midsummer Night's Dream*, act 4, sc. 1 (1600)

5 **DRYFAT: The organs of the body as some term them.**
MRS PURGE: Organs! Fie, fie, they have a most abominable sound in mine ears; they edify not a whit, I detest 'em. I hope my body has no organs.
Thomas Middleton *The Family of Love*, act 3, sc. 2 (1608)

6 **Give the piper a penny to play, and twopence to leave off.**
Thomas Fuller *Gnomologia* (1732)

7 **Now had Fame's posterior trumpet blown.**
Alexander Pope *The Dunciad*, bk 4, line 71 (1742)

8 **The wedding guest here beat his breast,/ For he heard the loud bassoon.**
Samuel Taylor Coleridge *The Rime of the Ancient Mariner* (1798)

9 **The Piano Forte often talks of you; – in various keys, tunes and expressions I allow – but be it Les-** son or Country dance, Sonata or Waltz, *You* are really its constant Theme.
Jane Austen Letter to Caroline Austen of 23 January 1817, collected in *Jane Austen's Letters* ed. Dierdre Le Faye (1995)

10 **Fiddle, n.: An instrument to tickle human ears by friction of a horse's tail on the entrails of a cat.**
Ambrose Bierce *The Devil's Dictionary* (compiled 1881–1906)

11 **An air played on the bagpipes, with that detestable, monotonous drone of theirs for the bass, is like a tune tied to a post.**
Leigh Hunt *Table Talk*, 'Bagpipes' (1882)

12 **[Of pianos] 'Ours is all wrong about the treble,' said Harris. 'By the way, what *is* the treble?'/ 'It's the shrill end of the thing,' I explained; 'the part that sounds as if you'd trod on its tail.'**
Jerome K. Jerome *Three Men on the Bummel*, ch. 2 (1900)

13 **The saxophone is the embodied spirit of beer.**
Arnold Bennett Attributed

14 **It's organ organ all the time with him.**
Dylan Thomas Mrs Organ Morgan in *Under Milk Wood* (1954)

15 **A confounded box of whistles.**
Christopher Wren Speaking of the organ at St Paul's. Quoted in *A Dictionary of Musical Quotations* ed. I. Croft and D. Fraser (1985).

16 **She wanted a simpler life, the kind you had the time to learn to play the harmonica in.**
Carrie Fisher *Delusions of Grandma*, p. 178 (1994 paperback edn)

17 **[Of bagpipes] The missing link between music and noise.**
Anon. Quoted in *The Tiny Book of Scottish Jokes* ed. Des MacHale (2000)

18 **[Humorous question regularly asked of double bass players] How do you get it under your chin?**
Anon. Quoted in *Spike Milligan: The Biography*, ch. 2, by Humphrey Carpenter (2003)

19 **A typical stroke-job of musical lies,
like everybody grew up with back
then, back when all the tunes had a
trumpet in them, that sounded like
it was played through somebody's
ass.**

D. B. C. Pierre *Vernon God Little*, act 1, ch. 9
(2003). The fifteen-year-old Vernon is listening to his mother's 'Burt Bacharach disc'.

20 **A true gentleman is a man who
knows how to play the bagpipes –
but doesn't.**

Anon. Traditional anti-Scottish joke

21 **'I speak when I'm tolled,' said the
bell,/ 'I am blowed if I do,' said the
organ.**

Anon. 'Be Quiet!', *Pearson's Book of Fun*, 'Sundry Siftings', ed. Mr X (n.d.)

Particular Musicians and Composers

1 **Yes; it was at dear *Lohengrin*. I like
Wagner's music better than any-
body's. It is so loud that one can
talk the whole time without other
people hearing what one says.**

Oscar Wilde Lady Henry Wotton in *The Picture of Dorian Gray*, ch. 4 (1890)

2 **[Of 'Old Man River'] It has never, as
far as one knows, been pointed out
that this song is virtually impossible of proper rendition by a vocalist who is feeling boomps-a-daisy
and on top of the world.**

P. G. Wodehouse *A Few Quick Ones*, 'Big
Business' (1959)

3 **I think Sinatra has the sort of voice
which always sounds as if it will be
better on Wednesday – it is too
thick for my taste.**

Robert Robinson *Inside Robert Robinson*, 'Of
Myth and Men' (1965)

4 **He wasn't even the best drummer
in the Beatles.**

John Lennon Attributed. On being asked
whether Ringo Starr was the best drummer
in the world.

5 **The Beatles are turning awfully
funny, aren't they?**

Elizabeth II Attributed, the remark supposedly having been made to Sir Joseph Lock-
wood, chairman of EMI, *c.* 1967. Quoted in
Lennon and McCartney by Malcolm Doney
(1981).

6 **Tchaikovsky. Was he a tortured
soul who poured out his immortal
longings into dignified passages of
stately music, or was he just an old
poof who wrote tunes?**

Monty Python team Eric Idle as a TV presenter in *Monty Python's Flying Circus*
(programme 2, 3rd series, first broadcast
26 October 1972)

7 **Representing Sweden were Abba, a
two-girl and two-man outfit with a
song called 'Waterloo'. This one,
built on a T-Rex riff and Supremes
phrase, was delivered in a Pikkety
Witch style that pointed up the cretinous lyric with ruthless precision.**

Clive James *Observer* 14 April 1974. Reviewing
the Eurovision Song Contest of that year,
which Abba won, beginning their highly successful career.

8 **Man, I can't *listen* that fast.**

Anon. Unknown jazz musician on hearing
'Shaw Nuff' by Charlie Parker and Dizzy Gil-
lespie. Quoted in *All You Need Is Love* by
Tony Palmer (1976).

9 **[Of Elgar's 'A flat Symphony'] The
musical equivalent of St Pancras
station.**

Sir Thomas Beecham Quoted in *Beecham
Stories*, 'Attitudes to Composers', ed. Harold
Atkins and Archie Newman (1978)

10 **John, Elton: Could he have made
the charts as Reg Dwight? Probably
not, but he might have won a cycle
race.**

Henry Root *Henry Root's World of Knowledge*
(1982)

11 **If Charlie Parker seems a less filthy
racket today than he did in 1950 it
is only because ... much filthier
rackets succeeded him.**

Philip Larkin *All What Jazz? A Record Diary*,
Introduction (2nd edn 1985)

12 **I freely confess that there have**

been times recently, when anything – the shape of a patch on the ceiling, a recipe for rhubarb jam read upside down in the paper – has seemed to me more interesting than the passionless creep of a Miles Davis trumpet solo.

Ibid. '1965'

13 It's a strange world . . . You ever wondered that? You know what I mean, the fact that we live in a world where John Lennon was murdered, yet Milli Vanilli walks the fucking planet.

Bill Hicks Line delivered at the Vic Theatre, Chicago, November 1990. Quoted in the *Guardian*, 14 February 2004. One member of the Milli Vanilli duo died in 1998, however.

14 If anyone has conducted a Beethoven performance, and then doesn't have to go to an osteopath, then there's something wrong.

Simon Rattle *Guardian* 31 May 1990

15 There's this basic rule which runs through all kinds of music, kind of an unwritten rule. I don't know what it is. But I've got it.

Ron Wood *Independent* 10 September 1992

16 I can't listen to too much Wagner, ya know? I start to get the urge to conquer Poland.

Woody Allen Larry Lipton (Woody Allen) in *Manhattan Murder Mystery* (film, 1993, directed by Woody Allen, screenplay by Woody Allen and Marshall Brickman)

17 Every Daz has its Omo, every Bob Dylan his Donovan.

Victor Lewis-Smith *Inside the Magic Rectangle*, 'The Chrystal Rose Show' (1995)

18 [Of Pink Floyd] They are not renowned for snappy, chart-busting singles, but are instead spoken of, in reverent tones, as 'an albums band', a distinction which, during the seventies, one rather generously bestowed on any group that couldn't come up with a decent chorus.

Giles Smith *Lost in Music*, 'Pink Floyd' (1995)

19 I prefer Offenbach to Bach often.

Sir Thomas Beecham Quoted in *A Gentleman Publisher's Commonplace Book*, 'Core', by John G. Murray (1996)

20 I hope I don't die before Harry Secombe. I don't want him singing at my funeral.

Spike Milligan *The Times* 18 July 1998. Milligan died after Secombe, but Secombe sang at his memorial service – on a record.

21 If life was fair, Elvis would be alive and all the impersonators would be dead.

Johnny Carson Quoted in *The Penguin Dictionary of Modern Humorous Quotations* ed. Fred Metcalf (2nd edn 2001)

22 [Of Keith Richards] Keith went over the edge years ago, but when everyone looked down over the edge they saw there was a fucking *ledge*, and he'd landed on it.

Bill Hicks 'Smoking in Heaven', *Love Laughter and Truth* (CD, 2002)

23 The Tremeloes (or 'The Trems' as the chummier disc jockeys would call them) would follow with 'Silence Is Golden' (Gowlden), at which point the Latin master would grunt: 'If only they practised what they preached.'

Craig Brown *This Is Craig Brown*, 'The Summer of Amo, Amas, Amat' (2003). Pop music as listened to in a 'traditional boys' prep school near Basingstoke'.

24 Elvis is just a young, clean-cut American boy who does in public what everybody else does in private.

Bob Hope Quoted in the *Independent* 16 May 2003

25 If a truck could sing, it would sound like Johnny Cash.

Andy Kershaw Remark made during a radio interview, 12 September 2003, the day of the singer's death

26 [Responding to the suggestion that all AC/DC records are the same] You don't go to the butcher for brain surgery.

Angus Young Quoted in *Q* magazine September 2003

27 **We're all Bob Geldof now.**

Simon Hoggart *Guardian* 23 June 2005

The Music Business

1 JOURNALIST: **What do you believe is the reason you are the most popular singing group today?**
JOHN LENNON: **We've no idea. If we did, we'd get four long-haired boys, put them together and become their managers.**

John Lennon *The Q/Omnibus Press Rock 'n' Roll Reader*, 'The Beatles' Press Conferences' (1994). The remark dates from the early 1960s.

2 JOURNALIST: **What do you think you've contributed to the musical field?**
RINGO STARR: **Records.**

Ringo Starr Ibid. Another remark of the early 1960s.

3 **[Of the music business] If you want to call it a business . . . it's more like a knife fight.**

Keith Richards *Uncut* magazine December 2002

Dance

1 **[Of country dancing] If there be but one vicious mind in the set, 'twill spread like a contagion – the action of their pulse beats to the lascivious movement of the jig – the quivering, warm-breathed sighs impregnate the very air – the atmosphere becomes electrical to love.**

Richard Brinsley Sheridan *The Rivals*, act 1, sc. 1 (1774)

2 **As to your studies and school-exercises, I wish you to learn Latin, French and dancing. I would insist upon the last more particularly, both because it is more likely to be neglected, and because it is of the greatest consequence to your success in life.**

William Hazlitt 'On the Conduct of Life; or,

Advice to a School-Boy'. Written in February 1822 for the benefit of Hazlitt's son, who published it in his father's *Literary Remains* (1836).

3 **I daresay you know these Folk Dance people, Corky. They tie bells to their trousers and dance old rustic dances showing that it takes all sorts to make a world.**

P. G. Wodehouse *Lord Emsworth and Others*, 'The Come-Back of Battling Billson' (1937)

4 **Stately as a galleon, I sail across the floor,/ Doing The Military Two-step, as in the days of yore./ I dance with Mrs Tiverton; she's light on her feet, in spite/ Of turning the scale at fourteen stone, and being of medium height.**

Joyce Grenfell 'Stately as a Galleon' (song, 1977, music by Richard Addinsell), collected in *Turn Back the Clock* (1977). A volume of Grenfell's autobiography had the same title.

5 **At least, I assumed she said ballet dancer. But now I come to think of it she does seem rather the wrong shape, and when I asked her where she danced she said Rotherhithe.**

Tom Stoppard Vicar in *The Dog It Was That Died* (radio play, 1982)

6 **Ballet is men wearing pants so tight you can tell what religion they are.**

Robin Williams *Robin Williams: Live at the Met* (video, 1987)

7 **Ballet Performance (the 't' is silent)**

Matt Groening Banner advertising a performance at Springfield Elementary School in *The Simpsons*, 'Homer vs Patty and Selma', first broadcast 2 February 1995

Newspapers, Radio and Television

Journalists and Journalism

1 **It is to be noted that when any part of this paper appears dull there is a design to it.**

Sir Richard Steele *Tatler* 7 July 1709

2 **. . . a newspaper, which consists of just the same number of words,**

whether there be any news in it or not.

Henry Fielding *Tom Jones*, bk 2, ch. 1 (1749)

3 The newspapers! Sir, they are the most villainous – licentious – abominable – infernal. Not that I ever read them – no – I make it a rule never to look into a newspaper.

Richard Brinsley Sheridan Sir Fretful Plagiary in *The Critic*, act 1, sc. 1 (1779)

4 The man must have a rare recipe for melancholy, who can be dull in Fleet Street.

Charles Lamb Letter to S. T. Coleridge of 8 November 1796, *Letters of Charles and Mary Lamb*, vol. 1, ed. E. W. Marrs (1975)

5 Never lay yourself open to what is called conviction: you might as well open your waist-coat to receive a knock-down blow.

Leigh Hunt *The Examiner*, 'Rules for the Conduct of Newspaper Editors', 6 March 1808

6 Lady Middleton . . . exerted herself to ask Mr Palmer if there was any news in the paper./ 'No, none at all,' he replied, and read on.

Jane Austen *Sense and Sensibility*, ch. 19 (1811)

7 '*Pall Mall Gazette*? Why *Pall Mall Gazette*?' asked Wagg./ 'Because the editor was born in Dublin, the sub-editor at Cork, because the proprietor lives in Paternoster Row, and the paper is published in Catherine Street, Strand. Won't that reason suffice you, Wagg?' Shandon said.

William Makepeace Thackeray *The History of Pendennis*, ch. 35 (1848–50)

8 [On working as a parliamentary reporter] Night after night, I record predictions that never come to pass, professions that are never fulfilled, explanations that are only meant to mystify.

Charles Dickens *David Copperfield*, ch. 43 (1849–50)

9 N. B. Willis is stricken with deadly disease, epilepsy and consumption together. The idea of death and of the man who writes editorials for the *Home Journal* are an unnatural combination. Death seems too solemn a matter for him to have any dealings with.

George Templeton Strong Entry for 8 March 1852, *The Diary of George Templeton Strong* ed. A. Nevins and M. Halsey (1952), collected in *The Assassin's Cloak* ed. Irene and Alan Taylor (2000)

10 'I believe that nothing in the newspapers is ever true,' said Madame Phoebus. 'And that is why they are so popular,' added Euphrosyne, 'the taste of the age being decidedly for fiction.'

Benjamin Disraeli *Lothair* (1870). Aneurin Bevan, quoted in *The Times* of 29 March 1960: 'I read the newspapers avidly. It is my only form of continuous fiction.' In *All Things Considered*, 'On the Cryptic and the Elliptic' (1908), G. K. Chesterton wrote: 'Journalism is popular, but it is popular mainly as fiction.'

11 [Of newspapers] It is always the unreadable that occurs.

Oscar Wilde *Intentions*, 'The Decay of Lying' (1891). Vivian is speaking.

12 To edit a lady's paper, even a relatively advanced one, is to foster conventionality and hinder progress regularly once a week.

Arnold Bennett Entry for 12 September 1898, *The Journals of Arnold Bennett*, vol. 1, *1896–1910*, ed. Newman Flower (1932). Bennett was at the time the editor of *Woman*.

13 The ordinary complaint against [Mr] Punch seems to be that he has lost the last two letters of his name.

Max Beerbohm *More*, 'Punch' (1899)

14 Those of you who are journalists put anything funny that they may have to say at the front of their articles, and then start afresh with 'but seriously'. As if – but I could never explain.

Ibid.

15 That's the whole secret of success-

ful interviewing – for the interviewer to talk all the time.

W. T. Stead Interviewed in *The World of
Dress* June 1905, repr. in *The Penguin Book of
Interviews*, ed. C. Silvester (1993). His interviewer, Mrs Maud Churton Braby, noted that
'having delivered himself of this dictum, Mr
Stead proceeded, to my great relief and
delight, to talk steadily for the next twenty-
five minutes.'

16 Journalists can't hit out at the
powerful; they'd lose their jobs. So
they hit the minor poet. It's like a
man who has lost his nerve on the
hunting field, but goes about boasting that he still hunts beetles.

G. K. Chesterton Interview in *Hearth and
Home* 17 October 1912, repr. in ibid.

17 Journalism largely consists in saying 'Lord Jones Dead' to people who
never knew that Lord Jones was
alive.

G. K. Chesterton Mr Finn in *The Wisdom of
Father Brown*, 'The Purple Wig' (1914)

18 Thucydides was a journalist. (It is a
modern folly to suppose that vulgarity and cheapness have the merit of
novelty; they have always existed,
and are of no interest in themselves.)

Ezra Pound 'How to Read', *New York Herald*
(1928), collected in *Literary Essays of Ezra
Pound* ed. T. S. Eliot (1954)

19 Lady X, who was of course Lord X's
third wife, was charming in blue.

Tom Driberg Typical of the *Daily Express*'s
gossip column of the 1920s, 'The Talk of
London'. As given by Driberg, who worked
on the column. Quoted in *Tom Driberg: His
Life and Indiscretions*, 'Tarts and Debs', by
Francis Wheen (1990).

20 [Of the *Daily Mail*] By office boys for
office boys.

Lord Salisbury Quoted in *Northcliffe: An Intimate Biography*, ch. 4, by H. Hamilton Fyfe
(1930)

21 Power without responsibility: the
prerogative of the harlot throughout the ages.

Rudyard Kipling *Journal of Kipling Studies*,
vol. 38, no. 180 (December 1971). Critique of

the position of Lord Beaverbrook, proprietor
of the *Daily Express*, who had told Kipling:
'What I want is power. Kiss 'em one day and
kick 'em the next.' Stanley Baldwin, Kipling's
cousin, obtained permission to use the
phrase in a speech of 18 March 1931.

22 [Gossip columnists] are jackals and
no jackal has been known to live on
grass once he has learned about
meat.

Ernest Hemingway *Esquire* December 1934

23 It's not the world that's got so
much worse but the news coverage
that's got so much better.

G. K. Chesterton Attributed. Quoted in *The
Penguin Dictionary of Modern Humorous Quotations* ed. Fred Metcalf (2nd edn 2001).

24 STICKS NIX HICKS PIX

Anon. Headline in *Variety* 17 July 1935: a
model of (cryptic) concision. Decoded, it
means that rural communities showed
little interest in rustic dramas on the big
screen.

25 I got thirty *Daily Mails* last week
and nearly died of them. I hope you
haven't been trying to read them.

Evelyn Waugh Letter to Laura Herbert of
October 1935 written from Addis Ababa, collected in *The Letters of Evelyn Waugh* ed.
Mark Amory (1980). Waugh was in Ethiopia
to report on the war against the Italians for
the *Mail* – an experience that helped form
Scoop. The job was difficult since the *Mail*
was pro-Italian. When Waugh resigned he
wrote: 'Gradually getting the smell of the
Daily Mail out of my whiskers.'

26 Feather-footed through the plashy
fen passes the questing vole.

Evelyn Waugh From William Boot's 'Lush
Places' column, a backwater of the *Daily
Beast*, in *Scoop*, bk 1, ch. 1, sect. 4 (1938)

27 I trust this is illiterate enough even
for your sheet.

Groucho Marx Note of June 1947 accom-
panying a column submitted to Abel Green,
editor of *Variety*. Although *Variety* regarded
itself as 'the Bible of showbusiness', Groucho
wrote, he considered it 'the Babel of
showbusiness'. Quoted in *The Essential
Groucho*, 'Freelancing', ed. Stefan Kanfer
(2000).

28 At my public school the most

unsympathetic schoolmaster it has ever been my misfortune to come across said to me when returning one of my essays, 'Betjeman, do you want to end up writing little paragraphs in the periodicals?' I said, 'No, sir.'

John Betjeman *Spectator* 27 August 1954, quoted in *John Betjeman: New Fame, New Love*, ch. 30, 'City and Suburban', by Bevis Hillier (2002). The teacher was called A. R. Gidney.

29 [On being telephoned by the *Sunday Express* requiring to know his main wish for 1956] **Not to be telephoned by the *Sunday Express* when I am busy.**

Harold Nicolson Diary entry for 29 December 1955, *Harold Nicolson: Diaries and Letters (1945–62)*, ed. Nigel Nicolson (1968)

30 **So it is that artists of all kinds form part of the battle training of green reporters. 'Don't lounge about the office, lad,' the editors say, 'sit up and insult an artist.'**

Evelyn Waugh *Spectator* 8 July 1955

31 **A single sentence will suffice for modern man: he fornicated and read the papers.**

Albert Camus *The Fall* (1956)

32 **SMALL EARTHQUAKE IN CHILE. NOT MANY DEAD.**

Claud Cockburn *In Time of Trouble*, ch. 10 (1956). With this Cockburn claims to have won a *Times* competition designed to elicit the most boring possible headline.

33 **Probably nobody knows, and certainly nobody cares, when the first newspaper interview with somebody appeared, but what *is* known is that, whenever it was, it was a snoring bore.**

Claud Cockburn *Nine Bald Men*, 'Interview' (1956). Later in the same piece Cockburn writes: 'The listeners haven't revolted yet, and the best bet is that it will be the interviewed people who will be the first to finally pack it in.'

34 **Many interviewers went to the length of describing their particular**

blend of tedium and lie as 'Exclusive'.

Claud Cockburn ibid.

35 **Ain't I seen a picture of your name in the papers?**

Spike Milligan Policeman (Peter Sellers) to Neddy Seagoon (Harry Secombe) in *The Goon Show*, 'The Plasticine Man', broadcast 23 December 1957

36 **Hello, hello. I see the *Titanic*'s sunk again.**

Peter Cook From *Science – Fact or Fiction*, a sketch performed at Cambridge University *c*. late 1959. Quoted in *Peter Cook: A Biography*, ch. 3, by Harry Thompson (1997). In the *Guardian* of 10 January 1995 Jonathan Miller recalled this line as being delivered by Cook as 'some person in a suburban kitchen concealed behind a newspaper'.

37 **The paper looks, somehow, as if it hadn't had a wash,/ The printing must be done with a coal-hammer or a cosh.**

A. P. Herbert 'New Year Resolution'. This poem, about why the author 'would not take the *Sunday Bosom*' any more, appeared in the *New Statesman* of 2 January 1960.

38 **The evening paper rattle-snaked its way through the letter box and there was suddenly a six-o'clock feeling in the house.**

Muriel Spark *The Prime of Miss Jean Brodie*, ch. 2 (1961)

39 **Reading someone else's newspaper is like sleeping with someone else's wife. Nothing seems to be in precisely the right place, and when you find what you are looking for, it is not clear then how to respond to it.**

Malcolm Bradbury Dr Jochum in *Stepping Westward*, bk 1, ch. 1 (1965)

40 **Give us this day our *Daily Express*.**

Malcolm Muggeridge *Tread Softly for You Tread on My Jokes*, 'Where the Viaduct Ends' (1966)

41 **Bob brooded over his book review. 'Mr Berringer knows his New York,' he wrote. A wave of honesty passed over him, and he altered it to 'Mr Berringer appears to know his New**

York.' The wave of honesty was succeeded by a wave of professionalism, and he altered it back to 'Mr Berringer knows his New York.'

Michael Frayn *Towards the End of the Morning*, ch. 1 (1967)

42 ... *Time* magazine, which can't be contradicted, except by its own subsequent issues ...

Quentin Crisp *The Naked Civil Servant*, ch. 29 (1968)

43 Early in life I had noticed that no event is ever correctly reported in a newspaper.

George Orwell *Collected Essays, Journalism and Letters*, ed. Sonia Oswell and Ian Angus (1968)

44 [Of gardening journalism] **The very language is defeating to most of us. There is this use of the passive voice: 'Care must be taken not to allow plants to dry out ...' Imagine yelling 'Care must be taken not to walk on the flower-beds' at your children.**

Katherine Whitehorn *Observations*, 'Their Blessed Plots' (1970)

45 If I peed on paper, they'd print the stain.

Germaine Greer Quoted by Kenneth Tynan in a diary entry for 23 August 1971, *The Diaries of Kenneth Tynan* ed. John Lahr (2000). Greer was speaking of the eagerness of newspapers and magazines to take her writing.

46 **ABSOLUTE CHAOS TONIGHT – OFFICIAL**

Anon. London *Evening Standard* headline quoted by Kenneth Tynan in a diary entry for 7 March 1973, ibid. A railway strike was imminent. Tynan described it as 'the announcement nothing can follow'.

47 I always say that if you've seen one Gentleman of the Press having delirium tremens, you've seen them all.

P. G. Wodehouse *Bachelors Anonymous* (1973)

48 I could spend half my evening, if I wanted,/ Holding a glass of wash-

ing sherry, canted/ Over to catch the drivel of some bitch/ Who's read nothing but *Which*.

Philip Larkin 'Vers de Société', *High Windows* (1974)

49 Freedom of the press in Britain means freedom to print such of the proprietors' prejudices as the advertisers don't object to.

Hannen Swaffer Quoted in *Swaff: The Life and Times of Hannen Swaffer*, ch. 2, by Tom Driberg (1974)

50 If I rescued a child from drowning, the Press would no doubt headline the story 'Benn grabs child.'

Tony Benn Quoted in the *Observer* 2 March 1975. Benn had a bad press for most of the 1970s and 80s, and became so wary of being misrepresented that he tape-recorded every interview he gave.

51 That's what's wrong with this paper. It's produced by the kind of people who read it.

Michael Frayn John in *Alphabetical Order*, act 1 (1975)

52 You may know, if you are a student of the press, or if you have at any time in the last few weeks passed within six feet of a newspaper, that there is no phrase as certain to make a British sub-editor lose his sense of proportion as the phrase 'Mystery woman'.

Tom Stoppard McTeazle in *Dirty Linen* (1976)

53 May I suggest that the number of misprints per page in an English daily newspaper would be a worthy candidate for *The Guinness Book of Records*? Just to establish a claim I nominate page 4 of *The Times* of 12 May which contains 37 misprints.

Graham Greene Letter to *The Times* 24 May 1978, collected in *The Last Cuckoo: The Very Best Letters to The Times since 1900*, ed. Kenneth Gregory (1987). Greene went on to give examples: 'Entertoinment,' he said, 'has a fine cockney ring', and 'rampaign', 'combining in one word the ideas of campaign and rampage', deserves to find a place in the *Oxford Dictionary*.

54 I'm with you on the free press. It's the newspapers I can't stand.

Tom Stoppard Ruth in *Night and Day*, act 1 (1978)

55 The media. It sounds like a convention of spiritualists.

Ibid.

56 The last time I wrote about Sir James Goldsmith at any length I was inhibited by the fact that he was plaintiff in about sixty-five libel actions.

Auberon Waugh *Spectator* 31 March 1979. Waugh confined himself to commenting that he had 'a repulsively ugly face'.

57 Anyone Here Been Raped and Speaks English?

Edward Behr Book title, 1981. Behr overheard this in 1960 shouted 'in a stentorian but genteel BBC voice', from a TV reporter at an airport in the ex-Belgian Congo from which thousands of Belgians were waiting to be airlifted.

58 *Punch* – the official journal of dentists' waiting rooms.

J. B. Priestley *The Times* 7 October 1981

59 With autumn nearly here, summer is nearly over, and that means that gardening correspondents all over the country are getting out the article they wrote this time last year and rephrasing it slightly.

Miles Kington *Moreover*, 'The Moreover Advice Service' (1982)

60 In 1950, the *Daily Mail* found space to tell its readers that Prince Charles had changed his parting ('from left to right'), and the *News Chronicle* revealed that the King owned two tartan dinner jackets. 'For some time he has kept them a close secret,' the *Chronicle* added importantly, in case you hadn't realized it was a scoop.

Robert Robinson *The Dog Chairman*, 'Our Betters' (1982)

61 Worsthorne, Peregrine (b. 1918): The elegant champion of the overprivileged.

Henry Root *Henry Root's World of Knowledge* (1982)

62 If you are Editor [of *The Times*] you can never get away for an evening. It's worse than a herd of dairy cows.

Alan Clark Entry for 6 June 1984, *Alan Clark: Diaries* (1993)

63 *Radio Times*: Nobody is going to stop taking this journal because of disgust at its non-programmatic content, and it exploits this strength by sodding the reader in depth.

Kingsley Amis *Spectator* 19 October 1985, collected in *The Wit of The Spectator* ed. Christopher Howse (1989)

64 Reviewing jazz records in January might be described as scraping the barrelhouse.

Philip Larkin *All What Jazz? A Record Diary*, '1971' (1985)

65 FREDDIE STARR ATE MY HAMSTER

Anon. According to Chris Horrie and Peter Chippindale in their book on the *Sun*, *Stick It Up Your Punter*, this, from February 1986, was 'the *Sun*'s most talked-about front page of all time' with the highest 'Hey Doris! Look at this!' factor. Its only rival in the paper's canon, according to Horrie and Chippindale, is 'Red Jets Buzz Tom Jones'. Needless to say, Starr did not, in fact, eat anybody's hamster.

66 ... I print the sad letter I received from an unknown lady, written the day before she committed suicide – prompted in part, as it would appear, by gloom engendered by reading my articles in the *Spectator*.

Auberon Waugh *Another Voice: An Alternative Anatomy of Britain*, Introduction (1986). When he received the letter (in 1986), he replied, but his letter was returned marked 'deceased'.

67 MAN FOUND DEAD IN CEMETERY

Anon. Quoted in *The Last Cuckoo: The Very Best Letters to The Times since 1900*, 'Finding Wasps' Nests', ed. Kenneth Gregory (1987). Attributed to the *Bath Evening Chronicle* (n.d.).

68 I must tell the story of a daughter of a friend who found a job as a secretary to a couple of 'executives' on the *Daily Mirror*. Asked about

her duties, she replied: 'I have to get them bacon sandwiches when they come back to the office hungry after lunch.'

Alan Watkins *Spectator* 17 January 1987, collected in *The Wit of the Spectator* ed. Christopher Howse (1989)

69 Although a step further down in esteem [from TV critics], writers who preview television programmes have more actual power. They do their best to put the public off stuff that might be bad for it, using phrases like 'routine [non-Anti-American] spy thriller'.

Kingsley Amis *Spectator* 15 October 1988, collected in ibid.

70 CUT OUT LIVER, PREGNANT WOMEN TOLD

Anon. Headline from the *Northern Echo* 19 October 1990, cited in *The Fortean Times*, issue 177 (2003)

71 I am now, like yourself, an elderly gent, overbooked, burdened and committed but I will do everything possible for your magazine. When I hear the literary fire bell ringing I stagger to my feet like an old firehorse.

Saul Bellow Letter to Philip O'Connor of 15 August 1990, quoted in *Quentin and Philip: A Double Portrait*, 'Medieval Gate-Keeper', by Andrew Barrow (2002)

72 Journalism could be described as turning one's enemies into money.

Craig Brown *Daily Telegraph* 28 September 1990

73 He was terrified of getting the paper (and himself) into trouble. In court reports he sprinkled the word 'alleged' with gay abandon and office legend said he once wrote a headline which read MAN'S ALLEGED ALLEGATION.

Michael Green *Nobody Hurt in Small Earthquake*, ch. 1 (1990). Of 'a grey-haired man called Bertie'.

74 He was obsessed by the fact that fifty years ago somebody was described in the paper as having 'pissed peacefully away' and was terrified it would happen again.

Of an underemployed local newspaper journalist called Alfred who 'pored over proofs all day'. Quoted in ibid. ch. 4.

75 The biggest majority of the Debra Chase By Herself series in the Sunday Shocker which I am sposed to of written was a load of rubbish, a virago of lies from start to finish.

Keith Waterhouse *Bimbo*, ch. 1 (1990). Debra Chase is a glamour model given to saying things like 'my first ever holiday abroad was an unquantified success' and 'in he walked, as bald as brass'.

76 This week I will review 1991. Next week I shall offer you my predictions for the forthcoming ... no. Bugger it.

Michael Bywater *Punch* December 1991

77 [*Private Eye*], of course, always thrived on vulgar abuse. But vulgar abuse cannot be indiscriminate. It is irritating to those who have spent time and trouble cultivating the vituperative arts to see what passes for vulgar abuse in the proletarian newspapers.

Auberon Waugh *Will This Do?*, ch. 14 (1991)

78 [Of Bernard Levin] Such impudence in one so not particularly young.

Stephen Fry *Paperweight*, 'Bernard Levin' (1992)

79 If you know somebody is going to be awfully annoyed by something you write, that's obviously very satisfying, and if they howl with rage or cry, that's honey.

A. N. Wilson *Independent on Sunday* 13 September 1992

80 Go out on the front porch of the house, turn the *Washington Post* over with your big toe, and if your name's above the fold, you know you're not going to have a good day.

Bert Lance 'The Bert Lance toe test' as outlined in the *Washington Post* of 6 October 1993

81 **She couldn't edit a bus ticket.**
Kelvin MacKenzie Of Janet Street-Porter who, although chiefly known for her work in television, had been appointed editor of the *Independent on Sunday*. Quoted in *The Times* 3 July 1999.

82 **Many years ago, my first editor in London taught me an essential trick of the trade: when reporting disasters, one should always use the headline 'We name the guilty men' and a graphic captioned 'Arrows point to defective part'.**
Francis Wheen *Hooh-Hahs and Passing Frenzies*, 'Happy, Shiny People' 'The National Cock-Up Syndrome' (2000)

83 **At one point all the TV critics seemed to be women, as it was considered a nice little job for women at home – as Agatha Christie said of murder.**
Nancy Banks-Smith *Guardian* 21 November 2001

84 **I once thought of becoming a political cartoonist because they only have to come up with one idea a day. Then I thought I'd become a sportswriter instead, because they don't have to come up with any.**
Sam Snead Quoted in *The Penguin Dictionary of Modern Humorous Quotations* ed. Fred Metcalf (2nd edn 2001)

85 **POLICEMAN CHASES DOG ON BICYCLE**
Anon. Poster purportedly advertising joke newspaper the *Daily Twit*, spotted in London N8, autumn 2002

86 **The perfect Peterborough piece . . . consisted of one fact, one generalization, and one very slight inaccuracy.**
Hugo Wrotham The opinion of Hugo Wrotham, editor 1934–59 of the 'Peterborough' gossip column in the *Daily Telegraph*. Quoted in a letter to the paper of 1 March 2003 from Lord Bunham. The slight inaccuracy was designed to trigger a follow-up item.

87 **. . . A kindred doctrine in the journalistic process involves the avoidance of making 'that one call too many' in case you learn something that will muddy the clarity of your vision.**
Charles Nevin *Lancashire, Where Women Die of Love*, ch. 4 (2005)

Radio

1 [Of radio] **When a paper announces 'listening-in to the launch of a ship', it might just as well talk about 'smelling a famous statue or eating a symphony or examining a silence with a microscope'.**
G. K. Chesterton *Speaking Generally*, 'On Broadcasting' (1928)

2 **I *adore* switching off the solemn pompous lectures – just extinguishing them.**
J. B. Priestley Betty Whitehouse in *Dangerous Corner*, act 1 (1932). She has just switched off the wireless.

3 **Christ, the blasted wireless is loud. The fag end of the bloody news . . . It's been on for hours. No wonder Dickens and Trollope and Co. could write such enormous books, if this bastard way of rotting the mind hadn't been thought up.**
Philip Larkin Letter to J. B. Sutton of 8 October 1944, collected in *Selected Letters of Philip Larkin, 1940–1985* ed. Anthony Thwaite (2002)

4 **I wish you'd talk to that radio. It sounds like a pretzel being bent.**
Raymond Chandler *Trouble Is My Business*, 'I'll Be Waiting' (1946)

5 **A soap opera is a kind of sandwich, whose recipe is simple enough, although it took two years to compound. Between thick slices of advertising, spread twelve minutes of dialogue, add predicament, villainy, and female suffering in equal measure, throw in a dash of nobility, sprinkle with tears, season with rich announcer sauce, and serve five times a week.**
James Thurber *The Beast in Me*, 'O Pioneers' (1948)

6 **'C-C-C-Christ!' said the one-legged nigger.**

Frank Muir and Denis Norden *A Kentish Lad*, ch 7 (1997). Sentence written in 1950 and designed to breach at least five of the rules for broadcasters laid down in the recently issued in-house document 'The Green Book'.

7 **At last here is a programme for listeners with *three* ears . . .**

Spike Milligan Announcement preceding the first programme in the series *Crazy People*, forerunner of *The Goons*, broadcast 28 May 1951

8 **I had the radio on.**

Marilyn Monroe When asked whether she had posed for a calendar with nothing on. *Time* 11 August 1952.

9 **[Of disc jockeys] They are the hollow men. They are electronic lice.**

Anthony Burgess *Punch* 20 September 1967

10 **All disc jockeys talk like cheeky sons-in-law chatting up mums-in-law.**

Kenneth Tynan Entry for 20 July 1972, *The Diaries of Kenneth Tynan* ed. John Lahr (2000)

11 **Last night's radio play is hardly ever front-page news and I never had to fear 'Mortimer Lays Egg on Third Programme' as a headline in the *Daily Express*.**

John Mortimer *Clinging to the Wreckage*, ch. 3 (1982)

12 **I don't think it is generally known that two hundred feet below Portland Place there is a fully operational studio equipped with enough scripts and actors to continue broadcasting *Afternoon Theatre* for up to fifteen years after a nuclear strike.**

Christopher Douglas and Nigel Planer *I, An Actor*, 'Actor Ergo Sum' (1988). Portland Place is where BBC Broadcasting House is located.

13 **People often wonder how families amused themselves before radio and TV, and the answer is they didn't.**

Michael Green *The Boy Who Shot Down an Airship*, ch. 5 (1988)

14 **This World Service, this little bakelite gateway to the world of Sidney Box, Charters and Caldecott, Mazawattee tea, *Kennedy's Latin Primer* and dark, glistening streets.**

Stephen Fry *Paperweight*, 'The World Service' (1992)

15 **I prefer radio in many ways because the fact is that the radio is easier to look good on than television.**

Peter Cook As the upper-class eccentric Sir Arthur Streeb-Greebling on *Why Bother?* (radio series, 1994)

16 **All popular radio is based on repetition and familiarity. It's almost that the listener knows what you're going to say before you say it . . . If you did it for long enough, you wouldn't have to say anything at all.**

Terry Wogan *Independent on Sunday* 15 March 1998

17 **[Of his former colleagues at Radio 1] They were gormless, but there was an innocence in that gormlessness.**

Andy Kershaw *The Times*, 'Quotes of the Week', 21 April 2001

Television the Medium

1 **Television? The word is half Latin and half Greek. No good can come of it.**

C. P. Scott Attributed, during the early 1930s

2 **The BBC boys are a bit frightening in their pale green corduroys and hatless long hair.**

Joyce Grenfell Letter to Virginia Graham of 9 June 1942, collected in *Joyce and Ginnie: The Letters of Joyce Grenfell and Virginia Graham* ed. Janie Hampton (1997)

3 **Why should people go out and pay money to see bad films when they can stay at home and see bad television for nothing?**

Sam Goldwyn *Observer*, 'Sayings of the Week', 9 September 1956

4 **I hate television. I hate it as much**

as peanuts. But I can't stop eating peanuts.

Orson Welles *New York Herald Tribune* 12 October 1956

5 **So much chewing-gum for the eyes.**

Anon. Small boy's view of certain TV programmes, quoted in *Best Quotes of '50, '55, '56* ed. James Beasley Simpson (1957)

6 **Television has brought back murder into the home – where it belongs.**

Alfred Hitchcock Quoted in the *Observer* 19 December 1965

7 **'It's all in the eyes,' she explained. 'The people with deep sockets do terribly. To project to the camera, you must have eyes set forward in your head. If your eyes turn inward, the viewers turn right off.'**

John Updike Vanessa, a Canadian TV presenter, in *Bech Is Back*, 'Australia and Canada' (1982)

8 **Today television is the fastest way to finish yourself off . . . Too many people see you for nothing.**

Mae West Quoted in *The Ultimate Seduction*, 'Mae West' by Charlotte Chandler (1984). West added: 'They're always wanting me to be on those talk shows, but I don't go.'

9 **I envy people who have the capacity to sit with another human being and find them endlessly interesting. I would rather watch TV.**

Carrie Fisher *Postcards from the Edge*, 'Day Eleven' (1987). She adds: 'Of course, this eventually becomes known to the other person.'

10 **The best that can be said for Norwegian television is that it gives you the sensation of a coma without the worry and inconvenience.**

Bill Bryson *Neither Here Nor There*, ch. 2 (1991)

11 **If you didn't catch it in the theatre, or rent it, or see it some place else, we've got it!**

Matt Groening Boast of the cable TV 'Blockbuster Channel' in *The Simpsons*, 'Homer vs Lisa and the 8th Commandment', first broadcast 7 February 1991

12 **I believe, and I am open to refu-**

tation from those who know better, that I have said the word 'fuck' on television more times in one sitting than anyone of my age and fighting weight in the kingdom.

Stephen Fry *Paperweight*, 'Saying Fuck' (1992). This occurred on a live late-night discussion programme on Central TV, Fry said, but gave no date. He used the word 'about eighteen times in three minutes,' he added.

13 **The TV companies draw lots for us. Like shepherds at sheep-dog trials, they decide how many of us they want in the pen and blow the whistle accordingly. They are helped by the way we associate television with entertainment, just because it has a rectangular screen and happens in the evenings.**

Hugo Williams *Freelancing*, 'Glucovision' (1995)

14 **One of the small but real pleasures of bad television is when an incompetent producer has dubbed on gales of hysterical laughter but has forgotten that the next shot is a reaction shot of the studio audience, and the audience is slumped silently on its seats, half asleep.**

Frank Muir *A Kentish Lad*, Coda (1997)

15 **We are concerned to remind broadcasters that 9pm is a watershed, not a waterfall.**

Anon. Response of the Broadcasting Standards Commission to an increase in viewers' complaints about sex and violence on television. Quoted in *The Times* 12 June 1999.

16 **Half the Beeb is on coke.**

Chris Evans *The Times* 22 May 1999

17 **I must say I find television very educational. The minute somebody turns it on, I go into a library and read a good book.**

Groucho Marx Quoted in *The Essential Groucho*, 'Freelancing', ed. Stefan Kanfer (2000). Kanfer describes this as 'one of the most quoted remarks he ever made'.

18 **I could have endured television**

with more fortitude if they had not laughed so much all the time.

P. G. Wodehouse Quoted in the *Guardian* 17 October 2000

19 **What right-thinking individual would spend hours, *hours* every evening, watching advertisements? Is it not clear that a product which must spend fortunes advertising, drawing attention to itself, is probably not one we need?**

David Mamet *Three Uses of the Knife*, ch. 2 (2002)

20 **Television shrinks its inhabitants. No doubt Florence Nightingale would have emerged with her legend diminished had she appeared on *Parkinson*, swapping anecdotes with Victoria Beckham.**

Craig Brown *Daily Telegraph* 13 March 2003

21 **The attraction of being on the small screen is undeniable and virtually irresistible. Even when I am queuing in my local Victoria Wine, I find my eyes straying up to the small black and white security screen. 'Oooh! That's me!' I think.**

Craig Brown *This Is Craig Brown*, 'There's a Good Boy' (2003)

22 **Channel 5 is all shit, isn't it?**

Adam Faith Reportedly the last words of Adam Faith, watching TV in bed immediately before suffering a heart attack. Channel 5 had a reputation at the time for being slightly tacky in its programme content. Quoted in the *Daily Telegraph* 15 May 2003.

23 **Television . . . That's where movies go when they die.**

Bob Hope Quoted in the *Independent* 16 May 2003

24 **It was while watching a rerun of *The Fly* last week that I realized how much those insects have in common with male television presenters . . . They're both in your face, fascinated with crap and prone to making rapid, pointless movements under hot lights.**

Victor Lewis-Smith London *Evening Standard* 14 April 2003

Particular Television Programmes and Performers

1 **The gift of broadcasting is, without question, the lowest human capacity to which any man could attain.**

Sir Harold Nicolson *Observer*, 'Quotes of the Week', 5 January 1947

2 **Such cruel glasses.**

Frankie Howerd Of the TV inquisitor Sir Robin Day, on *That Was the Week That Was* (BBC TV series, 1962–3)

3 **[Of Joan Bakewell] The thinking man's crumpet.**

Frank Muir Attributed. Bakewell is famous for presenting thoughtful TV programmes like *The Heart of the Matter* and for being good-looking. In her autobiography, *The Centre of the Bed* (2003), Bakewell implies that Muir said this in 1967 when asked by a journalist to sum up the panellists (of whom Bakewell was one) on the arts programme *Late Night Line Up*. Later, she would ask journalists not to use the phrase – 'apologetically, they would explain it was mandatory'.

4 **And now for something completely different.**

Monty Python team A phrase used by various characters throughout *Monty Python's Flying Circus* (TV series, 1969–74) as a link between sketches, and also used by the BBC announcers before the beginning of the show.

5 **Every week I watch Stuart Hall on *It's a Knock-Out* (BBC1) and realize with renewed despair that the most foolish thing I ever did was to turn in my double-O licence and hand back that Walther PPK with the short silencer.**

Clive James *Observer* 17 June 1973. Stuart Hall is a TV presenter and football commentator noted for his very loud laugh. *It's a Knock-Out* was a series of the 1960s and 70s in which regional teams negotiated supposedly amusing obstacle courses.

6 **On BBC2 now, Episode 3 of *George I*, the new 116-part serial about the**

famous English King who hasn't been done yet.

Monty Python team Michael Palin as voice-over in *Monty Python's Flying Circus* (programme 11, 3rd series, 4 January 1973)

7 *Holiday 74* [a BBC TV series] **begins with half a dozen pairs of knockers swaying, rolling or running at you through varying intensities of exotic sunlight. The emphasis on the untrammelled mammary is kept up throughout, handily symbolizing the show's basic assumption that sex is something which happens on holiday.**

Clive James *Observer* 10 January 1974. James added in the same review: 'Cliff Michelmore, as you might expect, flaunts a grin naughty enough to suit the mood, and adds to the air of spontaneity by reading the autocue as if he had never seen a line of it in his life before.'

8 **All my shows are great. Some of them are bad. But they are all great.**

Lew Grade *Observer* 14 September 1975

9 **I think most people know by now that Michael Parkinson hails from Barnsley. I will donate £5 to any charity (unconnected with Barnsley) for every *Parkinson* programme that omits the word 'Barnsley'. I know it will be hard, Michael, but it *can* be done.**

Peter Cook *Daily Mail* 7 February 1977

10 **Our problem is not insanity so much as feeble-mindedness, a refusal to think things out at all. We watch Bruce Forsyth instead.**

Auberon Waugh *Spectator* 2 September 1978. Waugh added: 'Last week's news that [Forsyth] had been signed up to make twelve new programmes for £180,000 ... filled me with unutterable gloom.'

11 [On having saved David Frost from drowning] **I had to pull him out otherwise nobody would have believed I didn't push him in.**

Peter Cook Quoted in *A Year of Stings and Squelches* ed. Nigel Rees (1985). The rescue was effected in 1963 at a house in Fairfield, Connecticut. Cook at the time was known to

be angry with Frost who, he thought, had borrowed some of his ideas for the satirical TV show *That Was the Week That Was* and generally plagiarized his whole comic persona. Cook called him 'the bubonic plagiarist'. He also later said that his one real regret in life was that he had saved David Frost from drowning.

12 **A couple of Sundays ago I was watching *Songs of Praise*, which was coming from Maidstone Prison of all places, when to my amazement I spotted a man in the congregation of the chapel who owes me £50. He was standing there and had the gall to be singing 'Abide with Me'.**

Jeffrey Bernard *Spectator* 8 March 1986, collected in *The Wit of the Spectator* ed. Christopher Howse (1989)

13 **Formaldehyde must be arriving by the lorryload at the BBC's Pebble Mill studios. How else could *Top Gear* (BBC2) have been preserved all these years?**

Victor Lewis-Smith *Inside the Magic Rectangle*, 'Top Gear' (1995). 'Everything about it screams "trapped in the 70s",' Lewis-Smith continued.

14 **As far as I know, Hale and Pace are the world's only double act consisting of two straight men.**

Ibid., 'Hale and Pace'

15 **I love *Songs of Praise*. I watch it religiously every Sunday.**

Vic Reeves and Bob Mortimer *The Smell of Reeves and Mortimer* (BBC TV, 2nd series, 1995)

16 **... Oxford's not what it was – now that Inspector Morse has passed over and through it, like the angel of popular rigor mortis ...**

Howard Jacobson *No More Mister Nice Guy*, ch. 2 (1998)

17 [Of the TV football pundit and ex-player, Mick Channon] **The only man in England who speaks braille.**

Anon. The remark appeared in the football magazine *When Saturday Comes* during the 1990s, and was recalled by Harry Pearson in the *Guardian* 30 August 2003

18 [Of Alan Titchmarsh] **The literary**

giant of the gardening world in everything except physical stature and novel-writing talent.

Viz September 2003

19 [Of *Eastenders*] **There are only two scenes: someone comes in and says 'What's goin' on?', and someone else says, 'Leave it out.'**

Ian Hislop *Have I Got News for You: Highlights from the TV Series* (CD, 2003)

20 **You do not have to occupy much of the moral high ground to do this job. But you do need a few inches.**

Ian Hislop After Angus Deayton, a married man and chairman of the current affairs satire *Have I Got News for You* (on which Hislop is a permanent fixture), was alleged to have taken cocaine with a prostitute. Quoted in the *Observer* 7 December 2003.

On Critics

1 [Of drama critics] **You who scribble, yet hate all who write . . . And with faint praises one another damn.**

William Wycherley Prologue to *The Plain Dealer* (1677)

2 **At ev'ry word a reputation dies.**

Alexander Pope *The Rape of the Lock*, canto 3, line 16 (1714)

3 **The vivacity of our modern criticks is of late grown so riotous, that an unsuccessful author has no more mercy shown him than a notorious cheat, in a pillory . . . The lowest member of the mob, becomes a wit, and will have a fling at him.**

Colley Cibber *An Apology for the Life of Mr Colley Cibber, Comedian*, ch. 5 (1739)

4 **The slanderer of a book is, in truth, the slanderer of the author: for as no one can call another bastard, without calling the mother whore; so neither can any one give the names of sad stuff, horrid nonsense, etc, to a book, without calling the author a blockhead.**

Henry Fielding *Tom Jones*, bk 1, ch. 9 (1749)

5 **Yes, sir, puffing is of various sorts;**

the principal are, the puff direct, the puff preliminary, the puff collateral, the puff collusive, and the puff oblique, or puff by implication.

Richard Brinsley Sheridan The speaker is Puff, 'a practitioner in panegyric, or, to speak more plainly, a professor of the art of puffing', in *The Critic*, act 1, sc. 2 (1779)

6 **A fly, Sir, may sting a stately horse and make him wince; but one is but an insect, and the other is a horse still.**

Samuel Johnson *The Life of Samuel Johnson* by James Boswell, vol 1, p. 263 (1791); in G. B. Hill's edition of 1887, rev. L. F. Powell (1934). The question was whether Thomas Edward's *Canons of Criticism* put Johnson on a par with William Warburton, against whom he had scored 'some smart hits'.

7 **You know who the critics are? The men who have failed in literature and art.**

Benjamin Disraeli Mr Phoebus in *Lothair*, ch. 35 (1870). Coleridge, in Lecture 1 of *Seven Letters on Shakespeare and Milton* (1811–12, publ. 1856), said: 'Reviewers are usually people who would have been poets, historians, biographers, &c., if they could . . .'

8 **The critics have very cleverly taken vulgarity for the note of the attack. You *cannot* combat that charge and it always leaves the critic a little bit above you.**

Rudyard Kipling Letter to Oscar Browning of September 1890. Oscar Wilde had recently written of Kipling's 'superb flashes of vulgarity'. *The Letters of Rudyard Kipling*, vol. 2, *1890–99*, ed. Thomas Pinney (1990).

9 **The lot of critics is to be remembered by what they failed to understand.**

George Moore Quoted in *Impressions and Opinions*, Honoré de Balzac (1891)

10 **I do not believe there is a single drama critic in London who would deliberately set himself to misrepresent the work of any dramatist – unless, of course, he personally disliked the dramatist, or had some play of his own he wished to produce at the same theatre, or had an**

old friend among the actors, or some natural reason of that kind.

Oscar Wilde Interviewed by Robert Ross for the *St James's Gazette* 18 January 1895, repr. in *The Penguin Book of Interviews* ed. C. Silvester (1993). It was in 1895 that Wilde's disgrace would begin. His play *An Ideal Husband* had recently opened, prompting the Scottish drama critic William Archer to write that the cult of Oscar was beginning to overwhelm the artist. Ross asked Wilde: 'How would you define ideal dramatic criticism?', to which he replied: 'As far as my work is concerned, unqualified appreciation.'

11 What is the modern poet's fate?/ To write his thoughts upon a slate;/ The critic spits on what is done,/ *Gives it a wipe* – and all is gone.

Thomas Hood 'A Joke', quoted in *Alfred Lord Tennyson: A Memoir by His Son*, vol. 2, ch. 3, by Hallam Tennyson (1897)

12 You don't expect me to know what to say about a play when I don't know who the author is, do you?

George Bernard Shaw Bannal, on the 'four critics' who have their say in the Epilogue to *Fanny's First Play* (1911). Bannal later adds: 'If it's by a good author, it's a good play, naturally.'

13 Whoso maintains that I am humbled now/ (Who wait the Awful Day) is still a liar;/ I hope to meet my Maker brow to brow/ And find my own the higher.

Frances Cornford 'Epitaph for a Reviewer' (1954)

14 Critics: those who would send Hedda Gabler to the Marriage Guidance Council.

John Osborne Originally written in Osborne's notebook for 1955; quoted in his autobiography, *A Better Class of Person*, ch. 19 (1981)

15 Why do I do this every Sunday? Even the book reviews seem to be the same as last week's. Different books – same reviews.

John Osborne Jimmy Porter in *Look Back in Anger*, act 1 (1956). Opening words of the play.

16 Critics are like eunuchs in a harem: they know how it's done, they've

seen it done every day, but they're unable to do it themselves.

Brendan Behan Attributed. Likely date of utterance: early 1960s.

17 The small girl critic who wrote, 'This book tells me more about penguins than I wanted to know', has a technique of clarity and directness that might well be studied by the so-called mature critics of England and the United States.

James Thurber *Lanterns and Lances*, 'The Darlings at the Top of the Stairs' (1961)

18 Law Ten of Coarse Acting: All critics from the local paper are stupid, but those who praise the actors have had a flash of lucidity.

Michael Green *The Art of Coarse Acting*, ch. 9 (1964)

19 A critic is a man who knows the way but can't drive the car.

Kenneth Tynan *New York Times* 9 January 1966

20 I never had the moral character to pan a friend. I'll rephrase that. I had the moral character never to pan a friend.

Tom Stoppard Spoken in 1972, quoted in *Double Act: A Life of Tom Stoppard*, ch. 5, by Ira Nadel (2002)

21 Odd how [*Private*] *Eye* contributors, like many other right-wing journalists, develop from inky schoolboys into middle-aged schoolmasters without any intervening period of young manhood.

Kenneth Tynan Entry for 28 May 1976, *The Diaries of Kenneth Tynan* ed. John Lahr (2000). Tynan was quite often attacked by the *Eye*.

22 The critic leaves at curtain fall/ To find, in starting to review it,/ He scarcely saw the play at all/ For watching his reaction to it.

E. B. White 'The Critic', collected in *Poems and Sketches of E. B. White* (1981)

23 [Film] critics leave press shows with a faint metallic taste in their mouths, as though the machinery

which processes the fantasies had somehow tainted the product.

Robert Robinson *The Dog Chairman*, 'Movies in the Morning' (1982)

24 [Irving] **Wardle in *The Times* strikes his usual 'Bennett has bitten off more than he can chew' note, just as he did years ago with *Forty Years On*. What he means is that I have bitten off more than he can chew.**

Alan Bennett Diary entry for 24 September 1986, repr. in *Writing Home: Diaries 1980–1990* (1994). The occasion was the opening of Bennett's play *Kafka's Dick* at the Royal Court Theatre in London.

25 **My critics resent everything I represent: sex, wealth and talent.**

Gore Vidal Attributed. Quoted in *The Moronic Inferno*, 'Mr Vidal, Unpatriotic Gore', by Martin Amis (1986)

26 **Personally, I have nothing against critics. I think they have an immensely difficult job which they carry out with great integrity, flair, and when you consider that most of them have been heartbreakingly unsuccessful as playwrights themselves, remarkable lack of bias.**

Christopher Douglas and Nigel Planer Actor Nicholas Craig in *I, An Actor*, 'Actor, Actas, Actat' (1988). Later he says: 'Laziness, ignorance, incompetence and all the charisma of a provincial geography master are one thing, but when the critic oversteps the boundaries of fair comment and enters the realm of personal abuse, the time has surely come to act.'

27 **Critics search for ages for the wrong word which, to give them credit, they eventually find.**

Peter Ustinov Interview in the *Sunday Telegraph* 15 November 1998

28 **Pay no attention to what the critics say; no statue has ever been put up to a critic.**

Jean Sibelius Attributed

6

Sport and Recreation

Sport
Recreation

Sport
Football

1 [Of football grounds] **It's very strange, isn't it, that you can't really tell the difference between the bar and the gents at most clubs?**
Peter Cook 'The Kick I Get Out of Football', *Sunday People* 4 February 1968, repr. in *Tragically I Was an Only Twin: The Complete Peter Cook*, ch. 12, 'Sports Reporter', ed. William Cook (2002)

2 **Soccer in England is a grey game, played on grey days, watched by grey people.**
Rodney Marsh *Observer*, 'Sayings of the Week', 18 September 1977

3 **He's not very good in the air unless he's got lots of space.**
Tom Stoppard Anderson in *Professional Foul* (TV play, 1977). He is speaking of a six-foot-eight Czech footballer.

4 **Hagerty F., Hagerty R., Tomkins, Noble, Carrick, Dobson, Crapper ... Dewhurst, MacIntyre, Treadmore, Davitt.**
Terry Jones and Michael Palin *Ripping Yarns*, 'Golden Gordon' (BBC TV, 1980). Barnstoneworth United is the name of the boy speaking this line; he is named after the little-known football team with which his father Gordon is obsessed, and he has been tutored in the names of the team's players during its far distant glory years in the Yorkshire Premier League.

5 **Wilkins, Ray 'Butch' (b.1956): No one can better his beautifully weighted passes back to the goalkeeper.**
Henry Root *Henry Root's World of Knowledge* (1982)

6 [Of football] **The First Ninety Minutes Are the Most Important**
Bobby Robson Title of a TV documentary, 1983

7 [Of a young Israeli football player] **Israel, the country that gave us the fabulous Jesus Christ, has produced yet another boy wonder.**
Anon. Apparently appeared in the sports pages of the *Daily Mirror*. Quoted by Alan

Watkins in the *Spectator* 4 April 1987, collected in *The Wit of the Spectator* ed. Christopher Howse (1989).

8 **It worries me, the prospect of dying mid-season like that, but of course in all probability I will die sometime between August and May.**

Nick Hornby *Fever Pitch*, 'A Matter of Life and Death' (1992). Hornby has just spotted a man lying dead after a game between Crystal Palace and Liverpool in October 1972.

9 **'Have you heard the news?' the shopkeeper said. 'Keegan's been killed in a freak accident. He was walking across the Tyne and the Shields Ferry hit him.'**

Harry Pearson Of Kevin Keegan, the former Newcastle player who returned to manage the club in 1992. *The Far Corner*, Introduction (1994).

10 **Doubts about Gascoigne's fitness to last ninety minutes persist, and it has been suggested that Taylor might send him out to run the Poles ragged for forty-five minutes. Only a twisted cynic would say that half an oaf is better than none.**

David Lacey *Guardian* 1993, collected in *The Umbro Book of Football Quotations* ed. Peter Ball and Phil Shaw (1996). Taylor was the England manager at the time. His successor Terry Venables said of the brilliant but eccentric Gascoigne: 'There's no nastiness in him. He might just say the wrong thing, or burp at the wrong time.'

11 **[On Britain having invented football] Strictly speaking, under International Law, we are entitled to 1p every time a ball is kicked anywhere in the world. A further 2p is due whenever a player is kicked.**

Peter Cook London *Evening Standard* 16 June 1994

12 **My team talk was very simple. I said: 'Let's just have an old-fashioned match, get the right result and go out for a few drinks afterwards.' It seemed to work better than all the tactical crap.**

Ron Atkinson Speaking as Coventry manager after Coventry had beaten Leeds in 1997.

Quoted in *The Book of Football Quotations*, 'The Beautiful Game' ed. Phil Shaw (1999).

13 **Anyone who uses the word 'quintessentially' in a half-time talk is talking crap.**

Mick McCarthy Responding to a tactical suggestion made by Niall Quinn during half-time in a Republic of Ireland soccer match of 1998. Quoted in ibid, 'Philosophers United'.

14 **Ninety per cent of males are happily married: to eleven men.**

Anon. Slogan of 1999 advertising the Carling Premiership football league. Quoted in ibid., 'This Supporting Life'.

15 **[Football] is what eight-year-olds do. What's the point of kicking a ball all over the place? It's moronic. Even as a small child I realized there was no cultural value to it at all. It's like earthworms.**

A. A. Gill Ibid., 'The Beautiful Game'

16 **On the rare occasions she came across football on TV, it always looked like tropical fish in a tank. First they all went up one end, then they all went down the other end.**

William Sutcliffe *The Love Hexagon*, ch. 34 (2000)

17 **[Of football] If it is the national game, why are we so bad at it?**

Jonathan Meades *Incest and Morris Dancing*, 'Das Volk' (2002)

18 **Professional footballers. Remember, there is plenty of time to get pissed after your playing career has ended.**

Viz 'Top Tips', May 2003

19 **Hamilton: If something's purely academic, as in Hamilton Academicals FC – 'After that, the outcome was just Hamilton.'**

Anon. 'The Jargon Bulletin', a dictionary of jargon, *Word* magazine June 2003

20 **[Of footballers] They require regular exercise, eat a great deal of expensive food, need at least two hours' grooming a day and, particularly when they are younger, can do an**

awful lot of damage to the flowerbeds.

Harry Pearson *Guardian* 20 December 2003

21 From Fairburn came their goal-keeper, a great big man in a flat cap who, like most goalkeepers, swore.

Byron Rogers *The Last Englishman: The Life of J. L. Carr*, ch. 3 (2003)

Cricket

1 I'll be at your Board, when at leisure from cricket.

4th Earl of Sandwich On being appointed a lord commissioner of the Admiralty, June 1745. Quoted in *Who Said What* ed. John Daintith and others (1988).

2 Personally, I have always looked upon cricket as organized loafing.

William Temple Address to parents at Repton School in Derbyshire, 1914

3 A loving wife is better than making a 50 at cricket or even 99; beyond that I will not go.

J. M. Barrie *Observer*, 'Sayings of the Week', 7 June 1925

4 Mr Hodge, having won the toss by a system of his own founded upon the differential calculus and the Copernican theory, sent in his opening pair to bat.

A. G. Macdonell *England Their England*, ch. 7 (1933)

5 If the French noblesse had been capable of playing cricket with their peasants, their châteaux would never have been burnt.

G. M. Trevelyan *English Social History*, ch. 8 (1944)

6 I like that sport where a lot of people are asleep on a lawn, you know ... They sit around on deck chairs ... There's some people in the middle of the lawn and they do something, and there's a chap with a barber's coat on ... And then it starts to rain, you know?

Gerard Hoffnung Said during a series of radio interviews with Charles Richardson in 1951, collected in *Hoffnung – A Last Encore* (cassette, 1973)

7 [Of cricket] It is a tough and terrible, rough, unscrupulous game. No wonder our American friends do not like it. You know how much armour they think it necessary to wear in their special form of football, and even in their rather primitive form of our old beach game – rounders.

A. P. Herbert From a speech made to the Surrey County Cricket Club to celebrate their winning the county championship in 1955. Quoted in *Look Back and Laugh*, 'The Fifties' (1960).

8 When we were children we asked my Uncle Charles what it was like to play cricket with W. G. Grace. 'The dirtiest neck I ever kept wicket behind' was his crisp reply.

Lord Chandos *Observer*, 'Sayings of the Week', 21 June 1959

9 There is one great similarity between music and cricket. There are slow movements in both.

Sir Neville Cardus *Observer*, 'Sayings of the Week', 31 December 1967

10 Cricket – a game which the English, not being a spiritual people, have invented in order to give themselves some conception of eternity.

Lord Mancroft *Bees in Some Bonnets*, p. 185 (1979)

11 My wife had an uncle who could never walk down the nave of his abbey without wondering whether it would take spin.

Alec Douglas-Home *The Twentieth Century Revisited* (BBC TV, 1982)

12 'Middle and leg, please,' said Jack./ 'Find it your flaming self,' said the umpire.

Miles Kington *Moreover*, 'Last Man In' (1982)

13 In the cricket season I learned there was a safe and far-away place called 'deep' which I always chose. When 'over' was called I simply went more and more 'deep' until I was sitting

on the steps of the pavilion reading the plays of Noel Coward.

John Mortimer *Clinging to the Wreckage,* ch. 3 (1982)

14 Mr Sugnett, a Croydon headmaster, c.1893, described as '*a destructive-looking man*', customarily improved his fast underarm grubs by following them down the pitch yelling fiercely, '*That's gotyer!*'

J. L. Carr Entry in *Carr's Illustrated Dictionary of Extra-Ordinary Cricketers* (1983)

15 My own 'thing' was . . . to use the bat the wrong way round and present the triangular side to the ball. The results pass all expectation, the ball ricocheting quite unpredictably, now here, now there, and, as often as not, flying to the boundary.

Arthur Marshall *Life's Rich Pageant,* sc. 2 (1984)

16 [Of Ian Botham] He couldn't bowl a hoop downhill.

Fred Trueman Observation made in 1985. Yet the former England captain Mike Brearley said that Botham was 'the greatest match-winner the game has ever known'.

17 I do love cricket – it's so very English.

Sarah Bernhardt She was watching a game of football at the time. Quoted in *Who Said What* ed. John Daintith and others (1988).

18 My grandfather might have nearly bowled W. G. Grace

Michael Green Subtitle of ch. 1 of *The Boy Who Shot Down an Airship* (1988)

19 His record, take it all in all,/ Was not a very great one;/ He seldom hit a crooked ball/ And never stopped a straight one.

Anon. 'The Rabbit', quoted in *The Wisden Book of Cricket Quotations* ed. David Lemmon (1990)

20 Send fast bowler to play Laertes immediately.

Frank Benson Telegram sent by Benson, the cricket-mad Victorian actor manager. Quoted in *Nobody Hurt in Small Earthquake,* ch. 9, by Michael Green (1990).

21 [Of the experience of being England cricket captain] Like farting against thunder.

Graham Gooch Remark made on his resignation in 1993, quoted in the *Daily Telegraph* 30 July 2003

22 The problem is that, despite appearances, cricket is not a team game. It is a game for highly motivated individuals who recognize that, for a match to take place, other people have to be present at the same time.

Marcus Berkmann *Rain Men,* ch. 4, 'The Village' (1995)

23 Now let's get this straight, shall we? If you wish to run, you shout 'Yes'. If you wish not to run, you shout 'No'. If you're not too sure about it, you shout 'Wait', and pause until your mental processes have caught up with the situation. You do not shout 'Yes, no, yes, no, yes, yes, no' until both men are in the middle of the pitch or are at the same end.

Ibid., ch. 8

24 The world of cricket was rocked to its foundations yesterday by the shock revelation that the captain of the England cricket team had 'taken a catch' in order to change the results of a match.

Anon. Mock news story in *Private Eye,* collected in *The Private Eye Annual* ed. Ian Hislop (2000)

25 The bowler's Holding, the batsman's Willey.

Brian Johnston Famous gaffe supposedly made during a BBC cricket commentary on a test match between England and the West Indies, when the England batsman Peter Willey was facing the fast bowler Michael Holding. But it doesn't exist on any tape, and Barry Johnston, in ch. 23 of his biography of his father *Johnners: The Life of Brian* (2003), wrote: 'I think Brian made it up.'

26 [Of the job of England cricket captain] No sooner do you go on your honeymoon than they order your tombstone.

Martin Johnson *Daily Telegraph* 30 July 2003

Golf

1 The uglier a man's legs are, the better he plays golf. It's almost a law.
H. G. Wells *Bealby*, ch. 3 (1915)

2 . . . the courts decided that the game of golf may be played on Sunday, not being a game within the view of the law, but being a form of moral effort.
Stephen Leacock *Over the Footlights*, 'Why I Refuse to Play Golf' (1923)

3 It was a morning when all nature shouted 'Fore'!
P. G. Wodehouse *The Heart of a Goof*, 'The Heart of a Goof' (1926). Another of Wodehouse's stories, in *Meet Mr Mulliner*, is called 'Those in Peril on the Tee' (1929).

4 And the wind shall say: 'Here were decent godless/ people:/ Their only monument the asphalt road/ And a thousand lost golf balls.'
T. S. Eliot 'The Rock', pt 1 (1934)

5 If you watch a game, it's fun. If you play it, it's recreation. If you work at it, it's golf.
Bob Hope Quoted in *Reader's Digest* October 1958

6 The secret of missing a tree is to aim straight at it.
Michael Green *The Art of Coarse Golf*, ch. 9 (1967)

7 ERNIE: You know what your main trouble is?
ERIC: What?
ERNIE: You stand too close to the ball after you've hit it.
Eric Morecambe and Ernie Wise *The Morecambe and Wise Jokebook*, skit 27 (1979)

8 The City golf club in London is unique among such organizations in not possessing a golf course, ball, tee, caddy or bag . . . 'We had a driving range once,' the commissionaire said, 'but we dropped that years ago.'
Stephen Pile *The Book of Heroic Failures*, 'The Least Successful Golf Club' (1979)

9 Golf is one of the few sports where a white man can dress like a black pimp, and not look bad.
Robin Williams *Robin Williams: Live at the Met* (video, 1987)

10 Loyal wife to callers who wanted the golf-playing Vicar: 'I'm sorry, the Vicar is away on a course.'
Anon. *Bishop's Brew (An Anthology of Clerical Humour)*, ch. 2, ed. Ronald Brown (1989)

11 Danny Kaye was good at almost everything he did, but I don't think he was a great golfer. I will say this for him though, when he hit a bad shot, he threw his clubs much further than anybody else.
George Burns *All My Best Friends*, ch. 7 (1989)

12 I'd give up golf if I didn't have so many sweaters.
Bob Hope Quoted in *Golf Quotations* ed. Helen Exley (1991)

13 Golf acts as a corrective against sinful pride. I attribute the insane arrogance of the later Roman emperors almost entirely to the fact that, never having played a game of golf, they never knew that strange chastening humility that comes from a topped chip shot.
P. G. Wodehouse Quoted in ibid.

14 [Of golf] Standing still is one of the most important parts of the game.
Peter Cook Major Titherly Glibble in *Peter Cook Talks Golf Balls* (video, 1994), quoted in *Tragically I Was an Only Twin: The Complete Peter Cook*, ch. 12, 'Sports Reporter', ed. William Cook (2002)

15 Imagine writing a poem with a sweating, worried-looking boy handing you a different pencil at the end of every word.
John Updike On why caddies put him off his stroke. *Golf Dreams*, 'The Trouble with a Caddie' (1998).

16 Golf is a good walk spoiled.
Mark Twain Attributed. Quoted in any purportedly funny book on golf.

Boxing

1 **The bigger they are, the further they have to fall.**

Robert Fitzsimmons Quoted, before taking part in a boxing match, in the *Brooklyn Daily Eagle* 11 August 1900

2 **Honey, I just forgot to duck.**

Jack Dempsey Quoted in *Dempsey*, ch. 24, by Jack and Barbara P. Dempsey (1977). Accounting for his loss of a world heavyweight title fight to Gene Tunney in 1926. After the attempt on his life in 1981, Ronald Reagan said the same to his wife.

3 **That's your only trouble as a boxer. You don't know how to defend yourself, and you don't know how to attack.**

Harold Pinter Max in *The Homecoming*, act 1 (1965)

4 **TOMMY COOPER: I was in the ring once with Cassius Clay, and I got him worried.**
HENRY COOPER: Oh really.
TOMMY COOPER: He thought he'd killed me.

Tommy Cooper TV exchange of the 1970s, collected in *Tommy Cooper: Just Like That!* (video, 1993)

5 **[He] was so quick he would click off the light and be in bed before the room got dark.**

George Foreman Of Muhammad Ali in 1989. Quoted in *The Penguin Dictionary of Modern Humorous Quotations* ed. Fred Metcalf (2nd edn 2001)

6 **Boxing is just show business with blood.**

Frank Bruno Quoted in the *Guardian* 19 November 1991

7 **I tried shadow boxing, but I lost.**

Anon. *And I Quote*, 'Exercise', ed. Ashton Applewhite and others (1992)

8 **Championship Boxing – Tasteful Attire Prohibited**

Matt Groening Sign outside the Springfield Coliseum in *The Simpsons*, 'The Homer They Fall', first broadcast 10 November 1996

Fishing

1 **[On baiting a hook with a live frog] In so doing, use him as though you loved him.**

Izaak Walton *The Compleat Angler*, pt 1, ch. 8 (1653)

2 **I am, Sir, a Brother of the Angle.**

Ibid., pt 1, ch. 1

3 **As the lone Angler, patient man,/ At Mewry-Water, or the Banne,/ Leaves off, against his placid wish,/ Impaling worms to torture fish.**

George Colman the Younger *The Lady of the Wreck*, canto 2, st. 18 (1813)

4 **Fly fishing may be a very pleasant amusement; but angling or float fishing I can only compare to a stick and a string, with a worm at one end and a fool at the other.**

Samuel Johnson Attributed, in *Instructions to Young Sportsmen*, 'Trout Fishing', by Lieutenant Colonel Peter Hawker (1859). Remark also attributed to Swift in *The Indicator* 27 October 1819.

5 **Douglas said that he caught a fish which escaped before he could draw in his line, but his statement was greeted with open incredulity by the others./ 'A jolly big one too,' said Douglas . . ./ 'Oh, yes,' said William sarcastically, 'so big that none of us could *see* it.'**

Richmal Crompton *William the Conqueror*, ch. 2 (1926)

6 **One particularly maddening commentator on the sport [fishing] multiplied the entities by saying, 'If you're not having much luck, try a grasshopper.'**

Robert Robinson *The Dog Chairman*, 'Try a Grasshopper' (1982)

7 **The ability to tell lies varies with the individual. For example, a short-armed fisherman isn't nearly as big a liar as a long-armed one.**

Anon. Quoted in *The World's Best Fishing Jokes* ed. John Gurney (1987)

8 **If fishing is a religion, fly fishing is high church.**

Tom Brokaw *International Herald Tribune* 10 September 1991

9 **A jerk on one end waiting for a jerk on the other.**

Robert Hughes Described as 'the classic folk definition of fishing' in ch. 1 of *A Jerk on One End* (1999)

Motorsport

1 **Fined ten shillings, and let that be a lesson to you not to go so fast in future, Malcolm Campbell.**

Anon. Magistrate fining Campbell for speeding on his bicycle in 1897. He would go on to set nine water speed records and four land speed records. Quoted in *Donald Campbell: The Man behind the Mask*, ch. 2, by David Tremayne (2004).

2 [Explaining his success in the 1953 Indianapolis 500] **There's no secret. You just press the accelerator to the floor and steer left.**

Bill Vukovich Attributed. The race is run on an oval, and competitors go anticlockwise.

3 **Now you be careful, young man.**

Elizabeth II On presenting an MBE to Barry Sheene, world motorcycle champion, in 1978. Quoted in the London *Evening Standard* 10 March 2003. During the course of his career, Sheene incurred 107 broken bones.

4 [Of Formula One cars] **Those among the spectators who did not already know could now receive valuable training in how to tell the cars apart. They all look like a bobsleigh being humped by a lawnmower but luckily they advertise different things.**

Clive James Report on the Portuguese Grand Prix, *Observer* 21 October 1984

5 **What you've got to remember about Michael [Schumacher] is that under that cold professional Germanic exterior beats a heart of stone.**

Damon Hill Quoted in *People on People: The Oxford Dictionary of Biographical Quotations* ed. Susan Ratcliffe (2001). Schumacher beat

Hill to the world championship in 1994 and 1995, employing, Hill's fans contend, some dubious tactics on the way.

6 **It's simple: get in car, drive car, see what happens.**

Juan Pablo Montoya His philosophy of racing, quoted in *F1 Racing* June 2002. Montoya also commented: 'Mentally prepare? Why? You decide before the race you're gonna pass this guy here, this guy there. Soon as the race starts, he goes the other way.'

7 [Of rallying] **Ever since I had a trial go, up a muddy lane near my parents' house, I've been fascinated by it – the way you can use the hedges to keep your line!**

Eddie Irvine Quoted in *Formula One* magazine November/December 2002

8 **It amazes me – I know drivers who go home at night and play their PlayStation. I think, my God, at ninety years of age, do you really want to say, 'I got to 90,000 on Super Mario 2?'**

Eddie Irvine On the decline of the interesting racing driver. Quoted in the *Mail on Sunday* 4 May 2003.

Tennis

1 **Like a Volvo, Borg is rugged, has good after-sales service, and is very dull.**

Clive James Observation made in June 1980. Quoted in *People on People: The Oxford Dictionary of Biographical Quotations* ed. Susan Ratcliffe (2001).

2 **I should have realized that when English people say they can play tennis they don't mean what Americans mean when they say they can play tennis. Americans mean they can play tennis.**

Martin Amis *Money* (publ. 1984), p. 31 (1985 Penguin edn)

3 **In tennis, love means nothing.**

Anon. *And I Quote*, 'Tennis', ed. Ashton Applewhite and others (1992)

4 [Of doubles tennis] **Nothing can compensate for a partner who knows**

that when you yell 'Mine', you actually mean 'Yours'.

Barbara Toner *Mail on Sunday* 1 June 2003

Rugby

1 The first thing that distinguishes Coarse Rugby from rugger is that neither side is *ever* composed of fifteen men ... An old friend, a converted soccer man who played for one of the coarsest sides in the country, claimed he was twenty-eight before he realized there was supposed to be fifteen on each side. When they told him, he thought for a moment and said: 'Well, I think fifteen a side spoils it.'

Michael Green *The Art of Coarse Rugby*, ch. 1 (1960)

2 [Of some rugby players] I was very much taken with the squareness of their heads, and by the fact that all their eyes were small and set far back, as if Nature had known what they would be about and provided protection.

Howard Jacobson *Redback* ch. 4 (1986)

Swimming

1 Any fool who knows how to swim can swim. It takes a *bird* to fly.

David Mamet George in *Duck Variations*, 'Fourth Variation' (1972)

2 'I wanted to be an Olympic swimmer,' she told her doctor, 'but I had some problems with buoyancy.'

Woody Allen *Side Effects*, 'By Destiny Denied' (1981)

3 There had always seemed to me something uncomfortable and dangerous about public swimming pools. Their tiles had a particularly frightening way of turning a shout into a scream, and this noise and the water and the cold showers and the nakedness could make a swimming pool seem like Auschwitz.

Paul Theroux *The Kingdom by the Sea*, ch. 21 (1983)

4 I swim like a fish – a cooked one.

Maureen Lipman *Thank You for Having Me*, 'Spoilsport' (1990)

5 If swimmin' wis easy, they'd ca it fitba.

Anon. *Away an' Ask Yer Mother* (*Your Scottish Father's Favourite Sayings*), ch. 2, ed. Allan Morrison (2003)

Horseracing

1 [Of jockeys] Those mysterious characters, who with their influence over their superiors and their total want of sympathy with their species are our only match for the oriental eunuch.

Benjamin Disraeli *The Young Duke*, bk 1, ch. 2 (1831)

2 It were not best that we should all think alike; it is difference of opinion that makes horse-races.

Mark Twain *The Tragedy of Pudd'nhead Wilson*, 'Pudd'nhead Wilson's Calender', ch. 19 (1894)

3 A small boy on being asked what were the races that had dominated England since the Romans replied Epsom, Newmarket and Doncaster.

Anon. Edwardian joke

4 People ask me why I like to ride with my bottom in the air. Well, I've got to put it somewhere.

Lester Piggott Interviewed in the *Observer* 7 June 1970. The interviewer, Kenneth Harris, said: 'You remind me of the late Lord Attlee, Mr Piggott: you answer questions as if you were filling in an application for a driving licence.'

5 The way his horses ran could be summed up in one word. Last.

Groucho Marx *Esquire* 1972

6 [Of his bookmaker, Victor Chandler] He greeted me once as I approached him on the rails by turning around

and saying to his workmen, the tic-tac man and his clerk, 'Here comes the lunch money.'

Jeffrey Bernard Bernard spoke of this remark in 1987. Quoted in *Just the One: The Wives and Times of Jeffrey Bernard*, ch. 10, by Graham Lord (1988).

7 **The going at Tavistock today was good but flimsy.**

Chris Morris and Armando Iannucci The news anchor man (Chris Morris) in *On The Hour* (radio series, 1991)

8 **All men are equal on the turf, and under it.**

Anon. Racing maxim, quoted by John Karter in *That's Racing*, 'A Mug is Born', eds. Peter O'Sullevan and Sean Magee (1996)

9 **I backed a horse today, twenty to one. Came in at ten past four.**

Tommy Cooper *The Very Best of Tommy Cooper*, vol. 1 (cassette, 1999)

American Sports

1 **Who is this Babe Ruth? And what does she do?**

George Bernard Shaw Attributed. Quoted in *People on People: The Oxford Dictionary of Biographical Quotations* ed. Susan Ratcliffe (2001). Babe Ruth (1895–1948) played baseball, very well, for the Boston Red Sox and the New York Yankees.

2 **'Babe' Ruth and Old Jack Dempsey,/ Both Sultans of Swat,/ One hits where the other people are,/ The other where they're not.**

Ring Lardner Attributed

3 **'Baseball is a kind of rounders, isn't it, sir?' said cover-point sympathetically./ Donald thought he had never seen an expression change so suddenly as Mr Pollock's did at this harmless, and true, statement.**

A. G. Macdonell *England Their England*, ch. 7 (1933). In the midst of a cricket match Shakespeare Pollock, an American journalist, has just 'thrown down his bat and himself set off at a great rate in the direction of cover-point, momentarily thinking he is playing baseball'.

4 **I saw Joe DiMaggio last night at Chasen's and he wasn't wearing his baseball suit. This struck me as rather foolish. Suppose a ball game broke out in the middle of the night?**

Groucho Marx Letter to Goodman Ace of 18 January 1951, collected in *The Essential Groucho* ed. Stefan Kanfer (2000)

5 **[Of baseball] I don't think I can be expected to take seriously any game that takes less than three days to reach its conclusion.**

Tom Stoppard Quoted in the *Guardian* 24 December 1984. As an amateur cricketer, Stoppard keeps wicket.

6 **Football combines the two worst things about America: it is violence punctuated by committee meetings.**

George F. Will *International Herald Tribune* 7 May 1990

7 **American football? It's just futuristic rugby.**

Peter Baynham, Steve Coogan, Armando Iannucci Steve Coogan as Alan Partridge in *Anglian Lives: Portrait of a Partridge* (ITV programme, 24 March 2003)

8 **[Of baseball] Rounders for cocaine addicts.**

Anon. Quoted in the *Guardian* 30 August 2003. Harry Pearson was recalling humorous remarks that appeared in the football magazine *When Saturday Comes* on the occasion of its two-hundredth edition.

Hunting

1 **If you could runne, as you drinke, you might catch a hare.**

George Herbert *Outlandish Proverbs*, no. 373 (1640)

2 **The world may be divided into people that read, people that write, people that think, and fox hunters.**

William Shenstone *Works in Verse and Prose*, vol. 2, 'On Writing and Books' (1764)

3 **It is very strange, and very melancholy, that the paucity of human**

pleasures should ever persuade us to call hunting one of them.

Samuel Johnson Quoted in *Anecdotes of the Late Samuel Johnson* by Hester Lynch Piozzi (1786)

4 If anything ever endangers the Church, it will be the strong propensity to shooting for which the clergy are remarkable. Ten thousand good shots dispersed over the country do more harm to the cause of religion than the arguments of Voltaire and Rousseau.

Sydney Smith Letter of June 1809 to Lady Holland, quoted in *Twelve Miles from a Lemon: Selected Writings of Sydney Smith*, ch. 4, compiled by Norman Taylor and Alan Hankinson (1996)

5 Like a dog, he hunts in dreams.

Alfred, Lord Tennyson *Locksley Hall*, line 79 (1842). 'He' is the coarse husband of Amy.

6 It ar'n't that I loves the fox less, but that I loves the 'ound more.

R. S. Surtees *Handley Cross*, ch. 16 (1843)

7 But I freely admit that the best of my fun/ I owe it to the horse and hound.

G. J. Whyte-Melville 'The Good Grey Mare', collected in *Songs and Verses* (1869)

8 The English country gentleman galloping after a fox – the unspeakable in pursuit of the uneatable.

Oscar Wilde in *A Woman of No Importance*, Lord Illingworth, act I (1893)

9 I am getting to an age when I can only enjoy the last sport left. It is called 'hunting for your spectacles'.

Sir Edward Grey *The Times* 20 November 1927

10 On Monday morning he read in *The Times* that the second fox had completely let down the North Bucks Hunt. The wretched creature had nipped off at a great rate and in five minutes had dived into a hole from which not even the valiant terriers could extract him. He was, in fact, as *The Times* said, 'a bad fox'.

A. G. Macdonell *England Their England*, ch. 14

(1933). Donald Cameron reads a report of a hunt.

11 They do you a decent death on the hunting field.

John Mortimer *Paradise Postponed*, ch. 18 (1958)

12 Q: Do you hunt bear? A: Not in cold weather.

Anon. *The Dictionary of Puns*, 'Bear', ed. John S. Crosbie (1977)

13 Mr Hemingway said that he shot only lions that were utter strangers to him.

Ernest Hemingway Excerpt from a report in the *New York Herald Tribune*, quoted in *Poems and Sketches of E. B. White* (1981)

14 If God didn't want man to hunt, he wouldn't have given us plaid shirts.

Johnny Carson *And I Quote*, 'Hunting', ed. Ashton Applewhite and others (1992)

15 Jews never go hunting. You *never* see a Jew go hunting ... Who's going to see the outfit?

Jackie Mason Quoted in *Jackie Mason: An Equal Opportunity Offender* (video, 1995)

16 Were foxes good grub, I'd get off the fence on the Jorrocks side.

Jonathan Meades *Incest and Morris Dancing*, 'Matches? No! They're on Order' (2002). Mr Jorrocks was the foxhunting grocer created by R. S. Surtees (1805–64).

17 'The fox kills chickens: he must be punished!' Hel-lo? It's a *beast*. Beasts are meant to behave in a beastly way! If hunters are going to use beastliness to justify their bloodlust, they should go back to the good old days when we put pigs on trial for stepping on mice.

Julie Burchill *Guardian* 12 July 2003

18 The Government's salient commitment to the nation is to pick on a small group of a few thousand eccentrics who like to potter around the countryside on their horses, endlessly breaking their collar-bones, and to tell them that whatever they're doing they mustn't. This is

government of the fox, for the fox, by the fox.

Boris Johnson *The Quotable Spectator* (2004)

Other Sports

1 I saw all sorts of balls; mountains of 'em, to be shot away at churches, and into people's peaceable habitations, breaking the china, and nobody knows what . . . and there's not one of 'em, iron as they are, could do half the mischief of a billiard-ball.

Douglas Jerrold *Mrs Caudle's Curtain Lectures*, Lecture 35 (1846). The complainant, Mrs Caudle, believes her husband plays too much billiards.

2 [Of billiard players] **They've all a yellow and sly look; just for all as if they were first cousins of people who picked pockets.**

Ibid.,

3 'Pall Mall' was the Tudor croquet; and in it boxwood balls were knocked through iron hoops by means of clubs or mallets. We associate Pall Mall with clubs even to this day, which shows how wonderfully history repeats itself, if you only let her alone.

O. P. Q. Philander Smiff *Smiff's History of England*, ch. 36 (1876)

4 [Of steeple-chasing] **It proves nothing except that the chaser is in want of a sensation, and that he has brains not so much worth taking care of as those of other men.**

Leigh Hunt *Table Talk*, 'Steeple-Chasing' (1882)

5 A Frenchman or a Spaniard will seek to persuade you that the bull-ring is an institution got up chiefly for the benefit of the bull. The horse which you imagined to be screaming with pain was only laughing at the comical appearance presented by its own inside.

Jerome K. Jerome *Three Men on the Bummel*, ch. 13 (1900)

6 To play billiards well is a sign of an ill-spent youth.

Herbert Spencer Quoted in *The Life of Herbert Spencer*, ch. 20, by D. Duncan (1908). The remark was actually made to Spencer by 'the late Mr Charles Roupell'.

7 Oxford are ahead. No, Cambridge are ahead. I don't know who's ahead – it's either Oxford or Cambridge.

John Snagge During his boat race commentary for the BBC, 1949

8 You want me to spend good money on a wrestling match? You want me to pay out cash to witness the obscene gyrations of a couple of pot-bellied nitwits who fritter away their time wallowing on mats and behaving like lunatic osteopaths?

P. G. Wodehouse *A Few Quick Ones*, 'Oofy, Freddie and the Beef Trust' (1959)

9 [Of bullfighting] **There is surely nothing more beautiful in this world than the sight of a lone man facing singlehandedly half a ton of angry pot roast.**

Tom Lehrer 'In Old Mexico', *An Evening Wasted with Tom Lehrer* (LP, 1960)

10 Stretch pants – the garment that made ski-ing a spectator sport.

Anon. *Time* magazine 23 February 1961

11 And, whatever happens, after the age of forty-five don't try to jump the net if you win. Especially at badminton.

Michael Green *The Art of Coarse Sex*, ch. 8 (1981). Green also advises that the middle-aged sportsman will probably not impress a young companion by swimming – 'especially if you have to be helped out of the pool'.

12 I have recently taken up two new sports, roller-skating and ankle-spraining, in that order.

Miles Kington *Miles and Miles*, 'The Perils of Roller-Skating' (1982)

13 Point-to-pointing (Peter peeing) is out-and-out Sloane because it's got picnic baskets (Sloanes are the hamper classes); it's connected with hunting (horses have to be 'regularly and fairly' hunted); it's amateurs only,

and it is usually so cold before May no sane person would want to go.

Ann Barr and Peter York *The Official Sloane Ranger Diary*, 'March' (1983)

14 Squash – that's not exercise, it's flagellation.

Noël Coward Quoted in *The Guinness Book of Sports Quotations* ed. Colin Jarman (1990)

15 The simple facts are these. Six greyhounds run around an oval track in pursuit of a mechanical hare. The hare always wins. It is the mystery of what will come second that fascinates those who go to the dogs.

Laura Thompson *The Dogs*, ch. 1 (1994). Opening lines of the book.

16 I like the decathlon. It's great to have an event for people who aren't particularly good at anything.

Jeff Green Quoted in the London *Evening Standard* 28 November 1996

17 I have a problem with that silver medal. Congratulations, you almost won . . . You're the number one loser.

Jerry Seinfeld *I'm Telling You for the Last Time* (CD, 1998)

18 One day someone will run a mile in zero time; thanks to improved diet and training methods they will cross the tape before they've left the blocks.

Howard Jacobson *The Mighty Walzer*, ch. 1 (1999)

19 Ping-pong is airless and cramped and repetitive, and so was I.

Ibid., ch. 2. This is Oliver Walzer, ping-pong prodigy.

20 It's the fate of most ping-pong tables in home basements eventually to serve the ends of other, more desperate games.

Jonathan Franzen *The Corrections*, 'St Jude' (2001)

21 [Of watching the boat race] For one day you can be the blue team, or the other blue team, with no effort and no consequences. It's instant, harmless fanaticism – just add water.

Andy Miller *Tilting at Windmills (Or How I*

Tried to Stop Worrying and Love Sport), ch. 5 (2002)

22 [Of Crown Green Bowling] Who would want to watch a sport where the slow-motion replays are actually faster than the original action?

Jasper Carrott *Daily Telegraph* 17 July 2003

23 The Tour [de France] is a very persuasive argument for the invention of the car.

Giles Smith *Daily Telegraph* 28 July 2003

Sport in General

1 Serious sport has nothing to do with fair play. It is bound up with hatred, jealousy, boastfulness, and disregard of all the rules.

George Orwell *Shooting an Elephant*, 'I Write as I Please' (1950)

2 Phrases like 'the team spirit' are always employed to cut across individualism, love and personal loyalties . . . Cleopatra knew nothing of the team spirit if you read your Shakespeare.

Muriel Spark Jean Brodie in *The Prime of Miss Jean Brodie*, ch. 4 (1961)

3 When it comes to sports I am not particularly interested. Generally speaking, I look upon them as dangerous and tiring activities performed by people with whom I share nothing but the right to trial by jury.

Fran Lebowitz *Metropolitan Life*, 'Modern Sports' (1979)

4 Live sport does smell.

Brian Clough *Cloughie: Walking on Water*, ch. 2 (2002)

Recreation
Gambling

1 He had a system of beating the bank at Monte Carlo which used to make the administration hang out

the bunting and ring the joy-bells when he was sighted in the offing.

P. G. Wodehouse *The Man with Two Left Feet*, 'Extricating Young Gussie' (1917)

2 **GAMBLER**: Say, is this a game of chance?
CUTHBERT J. TWILLIE: Not the way I play it.

W. C. Fields *My Little Chickadee* (film, 1939, screenplay by W. C. Fields and Mae West, directed by Edward Cline)

3 You start out in life a willing, eager sportsman, ready to take anybody on at anything, and then you meet a girl and fall in love, and when you come out of the ether you find not only that you are married but that you have signed on for a lifetime of bridge at threepence a hundred.

P. G. Wodehouse *Uncle Fred in the Springtime* (1939)

4 Don't play with scared money.

Anon. *And I Quote*, 'Gambling', ed. Ashton Applewhite and others (1992)

5 Statistically you stand just as good a chance of winning the Lottery if you don't buy a ticket.

Bob Monkhouse *The Times* 12 December 1998

6 Moth boy, n.: The member of a drinking party who, upon entering a pub, proceeds directly to the bandits, attracted by the flashing lights.

Viz 'Roger's Profanisaurus', April 2003

7 The National Lottery is a tax on stupidity. The more stupid you are, the more you pay.

Daren King *Jim Giraffe*, 'Cops R Tops' (2004)

Hobbies

1 The next time someone says: 'I'm a bit of a bird watcher myself, know what I mean?', say: 'No I *don't* know what you mean.'

Bill Oddie *Bill Oddie's Little Black Bird Book*, 'On Being a Bird Person' (1980)

2 1954: Gave up egg collecting and *instantly* became a better person.

Ibid., 'Bill Oddie's Qualifications'

3 Bird-watching: When referring to this popular pastime in a humorous column, always add: 'Of the feathered variety, of course.'

Henry Root *Henry Root's World of Knowledge* (1982)

4 The group of men were railway buffs. They were always a sure sign that a branch line was doomed. The railway buffs were attracted to the clapped out trains, like flies to the carcass of an old nag.

Paul Theroux *The Kingdom by the Sea*, ch. 20 (1983)

5 If this guy showed me his stamp collections one more time . . . My favorite thing in life, you know, is to look at cancelled postage.

Woody Allen Larry Lipton (Woody Allen) in *Manhattan Murder Mystery* (film, 1993, screenplay by Woody Allen and Marshall Brickman, directed by Woody Allen)

6 Philately will get you nowhere.

Victor Lewis-Smith *London Evening Standard* 10 March 2004

Indoor Games

1 But cards are war, in disguise of a sport.

Charles Lamb *The Essays of Elia*, 'Mrs Battle's Opinions on Whist' (1820–3)

2 Life's too short for chess.

Henry J. Byron Talbot Champneys in *Our Boys*, act 1 (1875)

3 The only athletic sport I ever mastered was backgammon.

Douglas Jerrold *Douglas Jerrold*, vol. 1, ch. 1, by W. Jerrold (1914)

4 It is impossible to win gracefully at chess. No man has yet said 'Mate!' in a voice which failed to sound bitter, boastful and malicious.

A. A. Milne *Not That It Matters*, 'A Misjudged Game' (1919)

5 Whoever called snooker 'chess with balls' was rude but right.

Clive James *Observer* 6 May 1984

6 Cards don't really require that much skill; if you can yell at your partner and reach your wallet, you can play cards.

George Burns *All My Best Friends*, ch. 8 (1989)

7 Chess is ruthless: you've got to be prepared to kill people.

Nigel Short *Observer* 11 August 1991

8 The chances of dropping a tray full of ball-bearings on the floor and their falling in such a way as to spell the phrase 'Little Scrotely welcomes careful drivers' are greater by far than those of two identical [chess] games ever being played.

Stephen Fry *Paperweight*, 'Child of Change' (1992)

9 A computer once beat me at chess. But it was no match for me at kick-boxing.

Emo Phillips Quoted in *The Penguin Dictionary of Modern Humorous Quotations* ed. Fred Metcalf (2nd edn 2001)

Gardening

1 What is a weed? A plant whose virtues have not yet been discovered.

Ralph Waldo Emerson *Fortune of the Republic*, p. 3 (1878)

2 Unkempt about those hedges blows/ An English unofficial rose.

Rupert Brooke 'The Old Vicarage, Grantchester' (1915)

3 Greenfly, it's difficult to see/ Why God, who made the rose, made thee.

A. P. Herbert 'In a Garden', *c.*1948, quoted in *Look Back and Laugh*, 'The Forties' (1960)

4 Are you going to cut that grass, or are you going to wait until it comes in the 'all?

Al Read 'Wife' to 'Husband' in *The Al Read Show* (BBC radio series, 25 November 1954)

5 Perennials are the ones that grow like weeds, biennials are the ones that die this year instead of next and hardy annuals are the ones that never come up at all.

Katherine Whitehorn *Observations*, 'The Disgusting Side of Gardening' (1970)

6 I agree the holiday weekend is angst-producing. I've spent it slaving away in my sodding garden, mowing and scratching up weeds, or what I take to be weeds. Anything that looks bright and positive I take to be a weed.

Philip Larkin Letter to Robert Conquest of 26 May 1974, collected in *Selected Letters of Philip Larkin, 1940–85* ed. Anthony Thwaite (1992)

7 If you are giving your plants food, stop. If you are not feeding them start immediately.

Miles Kington On growing an indoor plant ... 'This is based on the theory that whatever you are doing, it is bound to be the wrong treatment.' *Miles and Miles*, 'Growing Pains' (1982).

8 Yes, I saw her yesterday. She was panic-buying pot plants.

Anon. Overheard remark quoted in *Word of Mouth*, 'Eavesdroppings', ed. Nigel Rees (1983)

9 You know those seed catalogues? I think the pictures are posed by professional flowers getting $50 an hour.

Anon. *And I Quote*, 'Optimism', ed. Ashton Applewhite and others (1992)

10 If you want to be happy for a short time, get drunk; happy for a long time, fall in love; happy for ever, take up gardening.

Arthur Smith *The Times* 7 October 2000

11 For sale: bonsai tree – large.

Jimmy Carr Small-ad purportedly placed by Jimmy Carr. Quoted in the *Daily Telegraph* 4 August 2003.

7

Taken Internally

Intoxicants
Food and Drink

Intoxicants
Alcohol

1 **Take the hair, it is well written/ Of the dog by which you are bitten/ Work off one wine by his brother/ One labour with another.**
Antiphanes Hangover cure (400 BC). Quoted in *Whisky Wit and Wisdom*, 'Drinking It', ed. Gavin D. Smith (2000).

2 **. . . wine maketh merry: but money answereth all things.**
Ecclesiastes 10:19, the Bible, Authorized Version (1611)

3 **At dinner and supper I drank I know not how, of my own accord, so much wine that I was even almost foxed, and my head aked all night.**
Samuel Pepys Diary entry for 29 September 1661, *Everybody's Pepys* ed. Henry B. Wheatley (1926). That night, a Sunday, 'I being now so out of order that I durst not read prayers for fear of being perceived by the servants in what case I was.'

4 **[On drinking] 'Tis a pleasure of decayed fornicators, and the basest way of quenching love.**
William Wycherley Mr Dorilant in *The Country Wife*, act 3, sc. 2 (1675)

5 **I have fed upon ale; I have eat my ale, drank my ale, and I always sleep upon ale.**
George Farquhar Boniface in *The Beaux' Stratagem*, act 1, sc. 1 (1707). He has lived in the town of Lichfield – 'much famed for ale' – 'above eight-and-fifty years, and, I believe, have not consumed eight and fifty ounces of meat'.

6 **Fill it up. I take as large draughts of liquor as I did of love. I hate a flincher in either.**
John Gay Mrs Trapes in *The Beggar's Opera*, act 3, sc. 6 (1728)

7 **Inspiring, bold John Barleycorn,/ What dangers thou canst make us scorn!/ Wi' tippenny, we fear nae evil;/ Wi' usquebae, we'll face the devil!**
Robert Burns *Tam O'Shanter* (1791). 'Usquebae' is whisky.

8 ... Claret is the liquor for boys; port, for men; but he who aspires to be a hero (smiling) must drink brandy.

Samuel Johnson *The Life of Samuel Johnson* by James Boswell, vol. 3, p. 381 (1791); in G. B. Hill's edition of 1887, rev. L. F. Powell (1934). On the same occasion – a dinner at Sir Joshua Reynolds's house – Johnson said of claret that 'a man would be drowned by it before it made him drunk'.

9 Like other parties of the kind, it was first silent, then talky, then argumentative, then disputatious, then unintelligible, then altogethery, then inarticulate, and then drunk.

Lord Byron Letter to Thomas Moore of 31 October 1815, collected in *Letters and Journals*, vol. 4, *Wedlock's the Devil (1814–1815)*, ed. Leslie A. Marchand (1975)

10 They who drink beer will think beer.

Washington Irving *The Sketch Book*, 'Stratford-on-Avon' (1819)

11 Some preachers will tell you, to drink is bad./ I think so too – if there's none to be had.

Anon. 'A Sup of Good Whisky', *Oliver's Comic Songs* (1825?)

12 Champagne certainly gives one werry gentlemanly ideas, but for a continuance, I don't know but I should prefer mild hale.

R. S. Surtees *Jorrocks's Jaunts and Jollities*, ch. 9 (1838)

13 A man praising ale, said it was such an excellent drink, though taken in great quantities it always made him fat. 'I have seen it make you lean,' replied the other. 'When?' inquired the eulogist. 'Why, last night – upon your stick.'

Anon. *The New London Jest Book*, 'Choice Jests', no. 97, ed. W. C. Hazlitt (1871)

14 Licker talks mighty loud w'en it git loose fum de jug.

Joel Chandler Harris *Uncle Remus: His Songs and Sayings*, 'Plantation Proverbs' (1880)

15 If on my theme I rightly think,/ There are five reasons why men drink:/ Good wine, a friend, or being dry,/ Or lest we should be by-and-by,/ Or any other reason why.

Anon. 'Dr Aldrich', quoted in *Table Talk*, by Leigh Hunt (1882)

16 Fifteen men on the dead man's chest/ Yo-ho-ho, and a bottle of rum!/ Drink and the devil had done for the rest –/ Yo-ho-ho, and a bottle of rum!

Robert Louis Stevenson The 'eternal song' of the buccaneer Billy Bones. *Treasure Island*, ch. 1 (1883).

17 By-the-way, we never *eat* anybody's health, always *drink* it. Why should we not stand up now and then and eat a tart to somebody's success.

Jerome K. Jerome *The Idle Thoughts of an Idle Fellow*, 'On Eating and Drinking' (1889)

18 I'm only a champagne teetotaller, not a beer teetotaller.

George Bernard Shaw Proserpine in *Candida*, act 3 (1898). She adds: 'I don't like beer.'

19 'It's a very good whisky,' said Kipps. 'It's what the actor-manager chaps drink in London, I 'appen to know.'

H. G. Wells *Kipps*, bk 2, ch. 4 (1905). To which old Kipps – Kipps's uncle – responds: 'I daresay they do, my boy ... but then they've 'ad their livers burnt out – and I 'aven't.'

20 There are two things that will be believed of any man whatsoever, and one of them is that he has taken to drink.

Booth Tarkington *Penrod*, ch. 10 (1914)

21 Candy/ Is dandy/ But liquor/ Is quicker

Ogden Nash *Hard Lines*, 'Reflections on Ice Breaking' (1931)

22 Drink, and dance and laugh and lie,/ Love the reeling midnight through,/ For tomorrow we shall die!/ (But, alas, we never do.)

Dorothy Parker 'The Flaw in Paganism' (1931)

23 The Laird o' Phelps spent Hogmanay declaring he was sober,/ Counted his feet to prove the fact and found he had one foot/ over.

Louis MacNeice 'Bagpipe Music' (1934)

24 **What two ideas are more inseparable than beer and Britannia?**

Sydney Smith *The Smith of Smiths*, ch. 11
(1934)

25 **It's a naïve domestic Burgundy,
without any breeding, but I think
you'll be amused by its pre-
sumption.**

James Thurber Cartoon caption in the *New
Yorker* 27 March 1937

26 **I'm an occasional drinker, the kind
of guy who goes out for a beer and
wakes up in Singapore with a full
beard.**

Raymond Chandler 'The King in Yellow',
Dime Detective magazine March 1938. The
speaker is Steve Gryce, a Los Angeles hotel
detective and alcoholic.

27 **Why don't you get out of that wet
coat and into a dry Martini?**

Billy Wilder and Charles Brackett Mr
Osborne (Robert Benchley) to Susan
Applegate (Ginger Rogers) in *The Major and
the Minor* (film, 1942, directed by Billy
Wilder). He says this, Mr Osborne comments,
'no matter what the weather'. Mae West
had employed the line in the script for *Every
Day's a Holiday* (1937).

28 **Champagne! I love it. It tastes like
your foot's asleep.**

Hugh Wedlock Joan Davis (Joan Mason) in
George White's Scandals (film, 1945, written
and directed by Hugh Wedlock)

29 **When I die I want to decompose in
a barrel of porter and have it served
in all the pubs in Dublin.**

J. P. Donleavy Sebastian Dangerfield in *The
Ginger Man*, ch. 31 (1955)

30 **I should never have switched from
Scotch to Martinis.**

Humphrey Bogart Bogart's last words (1957).
Quoted in *Whisky Wit and Wisdom*, 'Dying
for It', ed. Gavin D. Smith (2000).

31 **I know more old drunks than I do
old doctors.**

Robert Mitchum Mitchum's response to the
suggestion of a doctor, made during the
filming of *Thunder Road* in 1957, that his
drinking was not doing him any good.
Quoted in *Robert Mitchum: Baby I Don't
Care*, 'Gorilla Pictures' (2001) by Lee Server.

32 **A medium Vodka dry Martini –
with a slice of lemon peel. Shaken
and not stirred.**

Ian Fleming *Dr No*, ch. 14 (1958). Bond further
specifies Russian or Polish vodka, and Dr No
observes: 'You are obviously a man who
knows what he wants.'

33 **Now look, what will you have to
drink? A glass of ale? Curaçao? Fock-
nick Orange? Ginger beer? Tia
Maria? A Wachenheimer Fuschman-
tel Riesling Beeren Auslese? Gin and
it? Châteauneuf-du-Pape? A little Asti
Spumante? Or what do you say to a
straightforward Piesporter Gold-
tropfschen Feine Auslese
(Reichsgraf von Kesselstaff)? Any
preference?**

Harold Pinter Edward in *A Slight Ache* (1959)

34 **I have taken more out of alcohol
than alcohol has taken out of me.**

Winston Churchill Quoted in *By Quentin Reynolds*, ch. 11, by Quentin Reynolds (1964).
Churchill was regarded by some, not least
Hitler, as an alcoholic, but he seldom
seemed the worse for drink.

35 **[An alcoholic] is a man you don't
like who drinks as much as you do.**

Dylan Thomas Quoted in *The Life of Dylan
Thomas*, ch. 6, by Constantine FitzGibbon
(1965). Thomas died after consuming eighteen straight whiskies.

36 **Drink and the world drinks with
you; eat and you eat alone.**

Quentin Crisp *The Naked Civil Servant*, ch. 22
(1968)

37 **Enjoyed it! One more drink and I'd
have been under the host.**

Dorothy Parker On being asked whether she
had enjoyed a party. Quoted in *The Algonquin Wits* ed. Robert E. Drennan (1968).

38 **If he wasn't 'chundering', Barry
might be 'laughing at the ground',
'playing the whale', 'parking the
tiger', enjoying a 'liquid laugh' or a
'technicolour yawn' or simply
'calling'.**

Barry Humphries All euphemisms for being
sick after drinking too much. 'Barry' is Barry
Mackenzie, the hard-living Australian hero of
a strip cartoon scripted by Humphries,

drawn by Nicholas Garland and carried by *Private Eye* in the 1960s.

39 **After Nigeria and Prague I come/ back near to where I started from,/ all my defences broken down/ on nine or ten Newcastle Brown.**

Tony Harrison 'Newcastle Is Peru', *The Loiners* (1970)

40 **I'm only here for the beer.**

Ros Levenstein Advertising slogan for Double Diamond beer, introduced in 1971

41 **[Of Holland] Apart from cheese and tulips, the main product of the country is advocaat, a drink made from lawyers.**

Alan Coren *The Sanity Inspector*, 'All You Need to Know about Europe' (1974)

42 **Q: A barrel of beer fell on a man. Why wasn't he hurt? A: It was light ale.**

Anon. *The Crack-a-Joke Book*, 'Leg Pullers', ed. Jane Nissen (1978)

43 **If I had all the money I'd spent on alcohol . . . I'd spend it on alcohol.**

Anon. Spoken by Sir Henry in *Sir Henry at Rawlinson End* (LP, 1978). But it's an old joke.

44 **Rawlinson motto: omnes blotto.**

Viv Stanshall Sir Henry in ibid. 'There's nothing like a morningcap to start and end the day,' he believes.

45 **I'm bored by all that wine rubbish. There's only one thing in wine that I'm interested in now. *Quantity*.**

Maurice Bowra Quoted in *Smile Please*, 'Be Fruitful and Multiply', by Arthur Marshall (1982)

46 **Only poofs drink rosé.**

John Junor *Brief Lives*, 'Sir John Junor', by Alan Watkins (1982)

47 **Wine that does not come in a bottle, but in a large brown plastic barrel marked BRITISH WINE – GREAT NEW CONTEST! – LOTS OF PRIZES is not a serious wine.**

Miles Kington *Miles and Miles*, 'Vin Extraordinaire' (1982)

48 **Ale, The Campaign for Real: One of the very few good things to have happened in the last twenty-five years.**

Henry Root *Henry Root's World of Knowledge* (1982)

49 **You know it's summer when the offy starts selling Pimm's again. Henry always buys No. 1 (Sloanes are very keen on brand loyalty). And did you know that half the Pimm's produced each year is drunk at Henley? (favourite Sloane statistic)**

Ann Barr and Peter York *The Sloane Ranger Official Diary*, 'May' (1983)

50 **Q: What's . . . a good Jewish wine? A: 'Oh you never take me anywhere.'**

Maureen Lipman *How Was It for You?* (1985)

51 **Maybe there's no devil, maybe it's just God when he's drunk.**

Tom Waits Quoted by Robin Williams in *Robin Williams: Live at the Met* (video, 1987)

52 **I haven't mentioned white wine, which I occasionally enjoy because I'm reminded of my mother's refusal to drink with the explanation: 'No thank you, I don't drink wine. It makes my eyes go small.'**

Maureen Lipman *Thank You for Having Me*, 'Tea Totally' (1990)

53 **I can drink five pints of lager before I need a piss. Can any of your readers beat that?**

Viz *Viz – The Full Toss (A Corking Compilation of Issues 70 to 75)* (1997). Cod reader's letter.

54 **To alcohol! The cause of – and solution to – all of life's problems!**

Matt Groening *The Simpsons*, 'Homer vs the Eighteenth Amendment', first broadcast 16 March 1997. Elsewhere in *The Simpsons* the character Lenny says, of beer: 'Nothing like a depressant to chase the blues away.'

55 **It's a pleasure to be standing up here. It's a pleasure to be standing up.**

George Best Accepting the award of Footballer of the Century, 1999. Quoted in *The Book of Football Quotations* ed. Phil Shaw (1999).

56 **Sure, it goes down your throat like a torchlight procession.**

Anon. Attributed to 'Anonymous Poteen Drinker' in *Whisky Wit and Wisdom*, 'Banning It', ed. Gavin D. Smith (2000)

57 **I'd hate to be a teetotaller. Imagine waking up in the morning, and knowing that's as good as you were going to feel all day.**

Dean Martin Quoted in *Halliwell's Who's Who in the Movies* ed. John Walker (2001). A letter to the *New Statesman* of 8 April 2002 suggested it was Jimmy 'Schnozzle' Durante who first said this. It has also been attributed to Frank Sinatra.

58 **Through the teeth and round the gums,/ Watch out tumtum, here it comes.**

Anon. In *Incest and Morris Dancing* (2002) Jonathan Meades describes this as 'the cry of old dears about to get bevvied on Mackeson or port in Southampton'. It 'might be employed as a straight warning when dining at a Harvester restaurant,' he adds.

59 **Do compromises work? Have you ever tasted rosé?**

Jeff Green *The A–Z of Living Together*, 'Compromise' (2002)

60 **He finished the bottle of wine, that night. He needed a bottle of wine to get him through it: that is to say, he needed a bottle of wine to get him through an evening with only a bottle of wine to get him through it.**

Martin Amis *Yellow Dog*, pt 2, ch. 7, sect. 8 (2003). Xan Meo, this is.

61 **Never drink on an empty stomach . . . Have a few beers first.**

Anon. Advice given on a birthday card widely available in 2003

62 **Abstinence should only be practised in moderation.**

Anon. *Away an' Ask Yer Mother (Your Scottish Father's Favourite Sayings)*, ch. 7, ed. Allan Morrison (2003)

63 ***I* am a character/ *You* are a loose cannon/ *He* is a drunk.**

Craig Brown *This Is Craig Brown*, 'Political Conjugations' (2003)

64 **Cocktails are the liquid interface between alcohol and modern art. At** least, that's the kind of rubbish you come out with when you've had a couple.

Guy Browning *Guardian* 'How to . . .' column, 2 August 2003

65 **Don't mix from different bottles of red wine. Dance with the one that brung ya.**

Christopher Hitchens *Vanity Fair* March 2003. His advice to drinkers also includes: 'Try to eat something . . . at every meal.'

Drugs

1 **[Of snuff] All right-minded people adore it; and anyone who is able to live without it is unworthy to draw breath.**

Molière Sganarelle in *Don Juan*, act 1, sc. 1 (1665)

2 **SIR SIGNAL: Snuff box: why, we take no snuff, signior.**
   PETRO: Then sir, by all means you must learn: for besides the mode and gravity of it, it inviveates the pericranium! That is, sapientates the brain, – that is, inspires wit, through invention, and the like . . .

Aphra Behn *The Feigned Courtesans*, act 2, sc. 1 (1679)

3 **Rob me of money, houses, lands,/ Yea, strip me to the buff;/ Leave me but one of these – my hands,/ Yet leave – my pinch of snuff!**

Anon. First verse of 'A Snuffy Song' *A Pinch of Snuff: Curious Particulars and Original Anecdotes of Snuff-Taking by Dean Snift of Brazen-Nose* (1840)

4 **Cocaine habit-forming? Of course not. I ought to know, I've been using it for years.**

Tallulah Bankhead *Tallulah*, ch. 4 (1952). Actually, she claimed not to have used cocaine 'except medicinally'.

5 **You can't tell a doper well under control from a vegetarian book-keeper.**

Raymond Chandler *The Long Goodbye*, ch. 17 (1954)

6 **This is the main advantage of ether: it makes you behave like the village drunkard in some early Irish novel ... total loss of all basic motor skills: blurred vision, no balance, numb tongue – severance of all connection between the body and brain.**

Hunter S. Thompson *Fear and Loathing in Las Vegas*, pt 1, ch. 6 (1971)

7 **Sex and Drugs and Rock and Roll**

Ian Dury Song title, 1977

8 **I've never had a problem with drugs – only policemen.**

Keith Richards Remark made in 1977, when Richards was under threat of a jail sentence for drugs offences. Quoted in *Old Gods Almost Dead: The Forty-Year Odyssey of the Rolling Stones*, pt 8, 'The Glimmer Twins', by Stephen Davis (2001).

9 **History, having destroyed religion as the opium of the people, now requires that they be given a taste of the real stuff.**

Auberon Waugh *Spectator* 20 October 1984. Complaining about the noise and smells made by proletarian holidaymakers in the West Country, Waugh demanded 'some narcotic which would stop them producing so many goods, earning so much money'.

10 **Got into drugs: marijuana, then cocaine, then Shake 'n' Vac.**

Victoria Wood 'Cleaning', a sketch from *Victoria Wood as Seen on TV* (TV series, 1985), collected in *Up to You, Porky: The Victoria Wood Sketch Book* (1985). The speaker is Kent, a disdainful northerner being interviewed for a job as a cleaner.

11 **Sid said that drugs weren't the problem, *life* was the problem. Drugs were the solution.**

Carrie Fisher *Postcards from the Edge*, 'Day Thirteen' (1987)

12 **There's this thing called freebasing. It's not free, it costs you your home. It should be called 'homebasing'.**

Robin Williams *Robin Williams: Live at the Met* (video, 1987)

13 **Now they're calling taking drugs an epidemic – that's cos white folks are doing it.**

Richard Pryor Line used in his live shows of the 1980s

14 **Cocaine is God's way of saying you're making too much money.**

Robin Williams *Screen International* 15 December 1990

15 **[While smoking crack] Now I tell you the downside of this is you feel awful, but the upside is you feel terrific.**

Peter Cook As Sir Arthur Streeb-Greebling in *Why Bother?* (radio series, 1994). The note in the transcript reads: 'Sir Arthur lights up.' Quoted in *Tragically I Was an Only Twin: The Complete Peter Cook* ed. William Cook (2002).

16 **[Of Bill Clinton's remark, made in 1992 while seeking the Democratic nomination, that he had tried marijuana but had not inhaled] Would you put a pastrami in your mouth if you didn't want to eat it?**

Jackie Mason Quoted in *Jackie Mason: An Equal Opportunity Offender* (video, 1995). Mason called Clinton's statement 'the schmuck lie of all time'.

17 **[Of LSD] I would say that it's an awfully overrated aspirin and very similar to the old people's Disneyland.**

Captain Beefheart Quoted in *Captain Beefheart*, ch. 9 by Mike Barnes (2000). Beefheart also said that marijuana made him feel like 'a fly with a wing trapped in honey'. He claimed that his music came from 'Merely breathing in and out, do you know what I mean?'

18 **As Dr Leary advises, 'Don't just say "No", say "No thanks." '**

Terry Southern *Now Dig This: The Unspeakable Writings of Terry Southern (1950–1995)*, 'Drugs and the Writer', ed. Nile Southern and Josh Alan Friedman (2001)

19 **They tell you pot smoking makes you unmotivated, it's a lie. When you're high you can do everything you normally do just as well. You just realize, it's not worth the fucking effort.**

Bill Hicks 'Drugs Are Bad', *Love Laughter and Truth* (CD, 2002)

20 **Sniggerette, n.: A *tab* containing a quantity of *happy baccy*. A *spliff*.**
Viz 'Roger's Profanisaurus', April 2003

21 **Why should Ben Johnson give up his gold medal from Seoul, for example, when the Beatles remain revered for *Sergeant Pepper* – an album that owed as much to banned substances as anything the Canadian did.**
Harry Pearson *Guardian* 25 October 2003

Smoking

1 **Tobacco is the tomb of love.**
Benjamin Disraeli *Sybil*, bk 2, ch. 16 (1845)

2 **In fact, dear Bob, I must out with it – I am an old smoker. At home I have done it up the chimney rather than not do it.**
William Makepeace Thackeray *Travels in London*, 'The Mr Browns at a Club' (1853). He adds: 'May I die if I abuse that kindly weed which has given me so much pleasure.'

3 **I have a liking old/ For thee, though manifold/ Stories, I know, are told/ Not to thy credit.**
C. S. Calverley 'Ode to Tobacco', *Verses and Translations* (1861)

4 **Hugh Stanbury Smokes Another Pipe**
Anthony Trollope Title of ch. 33 of *He Knew He Was Right* (1869)

5 **All dainty meats I do defy,/ Which fatten men like swine;/ He is a frugal man indeed,/ That on a leaf can dine.**
Anon. *The New London Jest Book*, 'Choice Jests', no. 784, ed. W. C. Hazlitt (1871)

6 **[Upon being awarded the Prussian Order of Merit] Had they sent me ¼lb of good tobacco, the addition to my happiness had probably been suitabler and greater!**
Thomas Carlyle Letter to John Carlyle of 14 February 1874, collected in *New Letters of Thomas Carlyle*, vol. 2, ed. Alexander Carlyle (1904)

7 **A cigarette is the perfect type of a perfect pleasure. It is exquisite, and leaves one unsatisfied.**
Oscar Wilde *The Picture of Dorian Gray*, ch. 6 (1891). Lord Henry Wotton offers a cigarette to Basil Hallward.

8 **It is quite a three-pipe problem, and I beg that you won't speak to me for fifty minutes.**
Sir Arthur Conan Doyle *The Adventures of Sherlock Holmes*, 'Scandal in Bohemia' (1892)

9 **I toiled after it, sir, as some men toil after virtue.**
Charles Lamb Explaining how he came to smoke so much. Quoted in *Memoirs of Charles Lamb*, p. 262, by Thomas Noon Talfourd (1892). Lamb also wrote, in a letter of 26 December 1815 to Robert Southey: 'This very night I am going to leave off tobacco! Surely there must be some other world in which this unconquerable purpose shall be realized.'

10 **There's not a room in this club where I can enjoy a pipe quietly without a woman coming in and beginning to roll a cigaret. It's a disgusting habit in a woman: it's not natural to her sex.**
George Bernard Shaw Cuthbertson in *The Philanderer*, act 2 (1893)

11 **[On how easy it is to give up smoking] I've done it a hundred times!**
Mark Twain Attributed. In an address to St Timothy's School, Catonsville, Maryland, on 10 June 1909 Twain said: 'I am seventy-three and a half years old, and have been smoking seventy-three of them. But I never smoke to excess – that is, I smoke in moderation.'

12 **What this country really needs is a good 5-cent cigar.**
Thomas R. Marshall *New York: Herald Tribune* 4 January 1920

13 **The little glow-worm sits and glows,/ As brilliant as the stars,/ But you are wrong if you suppose/ That he will light cigars.**
A. P. Herbert *Wisdom for the Wise*, 'The Glow-Worm' (1930)

14 **I think cigar bands are hardly necessary in total war.**
Sir Donald Finnemore *Observer*, 'Sayings of the Week', 7 March 1943, collected in *The*

Observer Sayings of the Week ed. Valerie Ferguson (1978)

15 The first twelve months I done [in prison], I smoked my way half-way through the book of Genesis and three inches of my mattress.
Brendan Behan Dunlavin in *The Quare Fellow*, act 1 (1956)

16 I don't inhale because it gives you cancer, but I look so incredibly handsome with a cigarette that I can't not hold one.
Woody Allen Isaac Davis (Woody Allen) to Tracy (Mariel Hemingway) in *Manhattan* (film, 1979, screenplay by Woody Allen and Marshall Brickman, directed by Woody Allen)

17 My beauty routine is a mixture of aerobics, isometrics and a little bit of yoga. To the observer it would look as if I was merely lifting a cup of coffee to my lips and lighting a cigarette.
Peter Cook *Sunday Times* 'A Life in the Day . . .', 5 August 1984

18 Our neighbours were in their mid-forties and smoked so much their front door frame had nicotine stains. Their coughing could have tarmacked a five-a-side pitch.
Harry Pearson *The Far Corner*, Introduction (1994)

19 Cigarettes are the close companions of foreigners: something normal to do with your hands.
Hugo Williams *Freelancing*, 'Did the Manager Notice My Age?' (1995)

20 Smokers: Save £££s every year on matches and cigarette lighters by simply lighting your cigarette with the butt of the previous one.
Viz *Viz – The Full Toss (A Corking Compilation of Issues 70–75)*, 'Top Tips' (1997)

21 The girls pick snouts from the pack as though they're chocolates and it matters which they select.
Howard Jacobson *No More Mister Nice Guy*, ch. 4 (1998)

22 [On smoking] If it's good enough for beagles, it's good enough for me.
Richard Littlejohn *The Times*, 'Quotes of the Week', 21 March 1998

23 Calderstone's pipe was of the curved variety, with a steel stem. What might be called an expert smoker's pipe.
Robert Robinson *The Club*, ch. 10 (2000)

24 I offered Dawn a cigarette. She refused. 'No thanks, I've already got cancer.'
Elaine Dundy *Life Itself !* ch. 30 (2001). Dawn was the writer and wit Dawn Powell. The remark was made in 1965, and she did have cancer, which killed her that year.

Food and Drink
Eating and Drinking

1 Nothing I know calls for less expense than the belly.
Juvenal Satire 5, line 5 (*c*.AD 100), trans. and ed. Niall Rudd (1991)

2 He hath eaten me out of house and home; he hath put all my substance into that fat belly of his.
William Shakespeare Mistress Quickly, of Falstaff, in *Henry IV Part 2*, act 2, sc. 1 (1598)

3 Leave gormandizing; know the grave doth gape/ For thee thrice wider than for other men.
William Shakespeare Henry V to Falstaff in ibid., act 5, sc. 5

4 One should eat to live, and not live to eat.
Molière Valère in *The Miser*, act 3, sc. 1 (1669)

5 I look upon it, that he who does not mind his belly will hardly mind anything else.
Samuel Johnson *The Life of Samuel Johnson* by James Boswell, vol. 1, p. 467 (1791); in G. B. Hill's edition of 1887, rev. L. F. Powell (1934)

6 A good eater must be a good man; for a good eater must have a good digestion, and a good digestion depends upon a good conscience.
Benjamin Disraeli *The Young Duke*, bk 1, ch. 14 (1831)

7 Your piecrust is the unromantic

cause of nine tenths of romantic melancholies in existence.

Leigh Hunt *Wit and Humour from the English Poets*, 'Remedies for the Spleen' (critical note) (1846)

8 Someone was telling an Irishman that a fellow had eaten ten glasses of ice-cream, whereupon Pat shook his head. 'So you don't believe it?' With a nod, Pat answered – 'I belave in the crame, but not in the glasses.'

Anon. *The New London Jest Book*, 'Choice Jests', no. 59, ed. W. C. Hazlitt (1871)

9 Life is with such all beer and skittles;/ They are not difficult to please/ About their victuals.

C. S. Calverley 'Contentment', collected in *Fly Leaves* (1872). He is referring to those who, 'should aught annoy them . . . refuse/ to be annoy'd'.

10 When I am in trouble, eating is the only thing that consoles me. Indeed, when I am in really great trouble, as any one who knows me intimately will tell you, I refuse everything except food and drink.

Oscar Wilde Algernon Moncrieff in *The Importance of Being Earnest*, act 3 (1895)

11 'My aunt never lunches,' said Clovis; 'she belongs to the National Anti-Luncheon League . . . A subscription of half a crown per quarter entitles you to go without ninety-two luncheons.'

Saki *The Chronicles of Clovis*, 'The Talking-out of Tarrington' (1911)

12 I have had no solid food since my elevenses.

Samuel Beckett Mrs Rooney in *All That Fall* (1957)

13 My stomach has got to take what I give it.

Sir John Charles Frederic Sigismund Day Quoted in a letter from George Lyttelton to Rupert Hart-Davis of 9 April 1959, collected in *The Lyttelton–Hart-Davis Letters*, vols 3 and 4, *1958–1959*, ed. Rupert Hart-Davis (1981). In *Our Iron Roads*, 'The Refreshment Room' (1886), F. S. Williams tells of seeing 'a solicitor from St Neots' alighting from a train at Leicester and returning with 'a hunk of Pork Pie and a small flask of sherry'. Williams asked: 'Can you digest that?' to which the solicitor replied: 'Do you think I allow my stomach to dictate to me what I think proper to put into it?'

14 Day one – slice of toast and a finely grated broad bean. Day two – half a fricasséed prune. Day three – one whole starch-reduced grape. Day four – take the pith of one peach and simmer it gently over a low gas. Then throw it away. Day five – summon next of kin.

Marty Feldman and Barry Took Bill Pertwee in *Around the Horne* (BBC radio series, broadcast on 4 April 1965). This is 'fabulous Giovanni's new five-day diet plan'.

15 The French, they say, live to eat. The English, on the other hand, eat to die.

Martin Amis *Money* (publ. 1984), p. 147 (1985 Penguin edn)

16 I have no idea how the rabbit got into Easter: pagan fertility stuff or Walt Disney cuteness? Whatever the reason, my feeling is eat it.

Jennifer Paterson Prelude to a recipe for rabbit with anchovy and capers, *Spectator* 6 April 1985

17 Towards the end of the eighteenth century ladies were using elegant silver 'dunking tongs' to hold the biscuit as they dipped it into their cup.

Oliver Pritchett *The Dogger Bank Saga: Writings 1980–95*, 'Quick Dip into the Art of Dunking' (1995)

18 You cannot eat a bun from the middle.

Anon. Chinese proverb. *A Gentleman Publisher's Commonplace Book*, 'Proverbs', by John G. Murray (1996).

19 'The tragedy is that I've eaten too much crackling,' said Giles, holding his stomach as if wounded.

Mary Killen *How to Live with Your Husband*, 'Bravery in Our Time' (1996)

20 They lunched in the restaurant of the hotel, where all the flavour was in the menu, leaving the actual food tasting of beige.

Robert Robinson *The Club*, ch. 10 (2000)

Eating and Drinking Places

1 There is nothing which has yet been contrived by man, by which so much happiness is produced as by a good tavern or inn.

Samuel Johnson *The Life of Samuel Johnson* by James Boswell, vol. 2, p. 452 (1791); in G. B. Hill's edition of 1887, rev. L. F. Powell (1934). Often seen quoted in pubs.

2 He hurried to a club in which he had been recently initiated, and of which the chief purpose was to prove to mankind that night to a wise man has its resources as well as gaudy day.

Benjamin Disraeli *Lothair*, ch. 30 (1870)

3 Now it happened that there was a refreshment bar in the place. You know what a refreshment bar is, I suppose? Yes, I thought you did.

Dan Leno *Dan Leno Hys Booke*, Chapter Seventh (1899)

4 You've probably noticed about London, mister, that a flock of sheep isn't in it with the nuts, the way they all troop on each other's heels to supper-places. One month they're all going to one place, next month to another.

P. G. Wodehouse *The Man with Two Left Feet*, 'The Making of Mac's' (1917). The speaker is an American waiter.

5 Duff [Hart-Davis] has discovered a new restaurant in Leicester Square called 'Guinea and Piggy'. You pay a guinea each as you go in, and you can eat as much as you like of over a hundred dishes, hot and cold.

Rupert Hart-Davis Letter to George Lyttelton of 9 January 1960, collected in *The Lyttelton –Hart-Davis Letters*, vols 5 and 6, *1960–1962*, ed. Rupert Hart-Davis (1981)

6 My idea is to have the hours altered so that public houses will be permitted to open only between two and five in the morning. This means that if you are a drinking man you'll have to be in earnest about it.

Flann O'Brien *The Best of Myles*, 'A Selection from "Cruiskeen Lawn" ' (1968)

7 [Of Nottingham] The town proudly boasts The Trip to Jerusalem, the oldest pub in England, a unique distinction shared by only 117 others.

Humphrey Lyttelton *I'm Sorry I Haven't a Clue* (radio series, from 1972 onwards), from *I'm Sorry I Haven't a Clue: Five* (cassette, 1999)

8 In the medium-priced restaurant where I go to die . . .

E. B. White First line of 'A Table for One', collected in *Poems and Sketches of E. B. White* (1981)

9 Courteous and efficient self-service.

Anon. Sign in a New York restaurant window. *And I Quote*, 'Quality and Excellence', ed. Ashton Applewhite and others (1992).

10 I . . . found a deeply depressing restaurant just off the Bull Ring. Here, a man at the next table spent five minutes hawking into a handkerchief before sitting back, candidly examining the contents and announcing, 'That's got rid of *that* one.'

Charles Jennings *Up North*, ch 1. (1995). The Bull Ring is in Birmingham.

11 The Horse and Cannon Pub in Holloway, possibly one of the earliest theme pubs in London, pretends to be a World War Two Anderson shelter crossed with a Thai restaurant.

William Sutcliffe *The Love Hexagon*, ch. 2 (2000)

Etiquette of Food and Drink

1 I dined with him, and we were to do more business after dinner. But after dinner is after dinner – an old saying, and true, Much drinking, little thinking.

Jonathan Swift *Journal to Stella*, '26 February, 1712', ed. Sir H. Williams (1948)

2 Is not a bellyful in the kitchen as good as a bellyful in the parlour?
Oliver Goldsmith *She Stoops to Conquer*, act 2, sc. 1 (1773)

3 An indigestion is an excellent common-place for two people that never met before.
William Hazlitt 'The Fight', *New Monthly Magazine* February 1822, collected in *The Essays of William Hazlitt* ed. Catherine Macdonald Maclean (1949)

4 Your thorough waiter has no ideas out of the sphere of his duty and the business.
Leigh Hunt *Leigh Hunt's London Journal*, entry for 13 June 1835

5 I dined yesterday at three on mutton chops and ½ pint of East Indian sherry, and then *tead* and muffined at 8. This is a good regime.
Benjamin Disraeli Letter to Sarah Disraeli of 22 November 1837, collected in *Benjamin Disraeli: Letters*, vol. 2, *1835–37*, ed. J. A. W. Gunn, John Matthews, Donald M. Schurman and M. G. Wiebe (1982)

6 Let me see if Philip can/ Be a little gentleman;/ Let me see, if he is able/ To sit still for once at table.
Heinrich Hoffmann *Struwwelpeter* (Shock-Headed Peter), 'Fidgety Philip' (1848)

7 A fine singer, after dinner, is to be avoided, for he is a great bore, and stops the wine.
William Makepeace Thackeray *Travels in London*, 'On Some Old Customs of the Dining Table' (1853). Described as 'Maxim 4' of 'The Maxims of Sir Morgan O'Doherty'.

8 [The Cannibals' Grace Before Meals] Choo a choo a choo tooth./ Muntch, muntch. Nycey!/ Choo a choo a choo tooth./ Muntch, muntch. Nycey!
Charles Dickens 'Holiday Romance' (1868)

9 [Of the arrival of champagne along with the pudding, after a series of underheated courses at a public dinner] Thank God for something warm at last.
Benjamin Disraeli Attributed remark, perhaps of the early 1870s, quoted in *The Sayings of Disraeli*, 'Gastronomy', ed. Robert Blake (1992)

10 [On ladies carving at dinner] Why doesn't some leader of the fashionable world put an end to this barbarous custom?
Leigh Hunt *Table Talk*, 'Ladies Carving at Dinner' (1882)

11 Oh, no! I can't stand your English house-parties. In England people actually try to be brilliant at breakfast.
Oscar Wilde Mrs Cheveley in *An Ideal Husband*, act 1 (1899)

12 She sprang it on me before breakfast. There in seven words you have a complete character sketch of my aunt Agatha.
P. G. Wodehouse *The Man with Two Left Feet*, 'Extricating Young Gussie' (1917)

13 There, gleaming on the black shiny straw, was a scattering of crumbs, yellow crumbs from a sponge cake, the kind of thing you would expect to find on the hat of a person who had stood on their head to have tea.
P. L. Travers *Mary Poppins Comes Back*, ch. 4 (1935). Mary Poppins and her charges have just visited her cousin Mr Turvy, who was levitating through the air, a condition that proved to be catching.

14 It was M. André Simon (if I recollect aright) who suggested that our lack of culinary tradition was due to the fact that forks were only introduced towards the end of the reign of James I.
Harold Nicolson 'Marginal Comment', *Spectator* 24 February 1939, repr. in *The Penguin Book of Columnists* ed. Christopher Silvester (1997). But Nicolson did not agree: 'Cooking does not really depend on forks.'

15 If it's cold I might have the soup. They give you a good bowl. They give you the slice of bread. They won't do that with tea but they do it with soup.
Harold Pinter 'The Black and White' (monologue, 1954), collected in *Pinter Plays: One* (1976)

16 Nowadays the modern way to eat is to get all your meals in a self-service cafeteria. You slide your tray along the chromium rails past a long line of food, you can choose what you like, and be tucking into it in a matter of seconds . . . Ha, ha, ha!

Al Read *The Al Read Show* (BBC radio programme, 15 November 1955)

17 Eating people is wrong!

Michael Flanders and Donald Swann The Reluctant Cannibal', performed on *At the Drop of a Hat* (LP, 1957). In 1959 Malcolm Bradbury used this as the title of a novel.

18 I am a man more dined against than dining.

Maurice Bowra Adaptation of King Lear's cry in act 3, sc. 2 of *King Lear*, replacing 'sinned' and 'sinning' with 'dined' and 'dining'. Quoted in *Summoned by Bells*, ch. 9, by John Betjeman (1960).

19 MISS KUBELIK: What was this tennis racquet doing in the kitchen?
C. C. BAXTER: I was cooking an Italian dinner.

Billy Wilder and I. A. L. Diamond Miss Kubelik (Shirley MacLaine) to C. C. Baxter (Jack Lemmon) in *The Apartment* (film, 1960, written and directed by Billy Wilder). Baxter eventually adds the further explanation: 'I used it to strain the spaghetti.'

20 Gad, it's hot. Male passengers are going mad with the heat! With my own eyes I actually saw an Englishman *unbutton his dinner jacket at dinner*! He has since been certified.

Spike Milligan Letter to Harry Secombe of 1961, collected in *The Essential Milligan* compiled by Alex Games (2002)

21 At last God caught his eye.

Harry Secombe 'Epitaph for a Head Waiter', *Punch* 17 May 1962

22 I marmaladed a slice of toast with something of a flourish.

P. G. Wodehouse *Stiff Upper Lip, Jeeves*, ch. 1 (1963)

23 The best number for a dinner party is two – myself and a damn good head waiter.

Nubar Gulbenkian *Observer*, 'Sayings of the Week', 19 December 1965

24 Doing abominations is against the law, particularly if the abominations are done while wearing a lobster bib.

Woody Allen *Without Feathers*, 'The Scrolls' (1972)

25 That chap over there is having soup and it sounds delicious.

Eric Morecambe and Ernie Wise *The Morecambe and Wise Jokebook*, skit 18 (1979)

26 Food offers the perfect excuse to use the good dishes.

Fran Lebowitz *Metropolitan Life*, 'Food for Thought' (1979)

27 You can tell a lot about a fellow's character from his way of eating jelly beans.

Ronald Reagan *New York Times* 15 January 1981

28 I eat my peas with honey;/ I've done it all my life./ It makes the peas taste funny,/ But it keeps them on the knife.

Anon. *The Ha Ha Bonk Book*, 'Jokes Not to Tell Your Teacher', ed. Janet and Allan Ahlberg (1982)

29 Then there was a waiter in a restaurant long ago who when I asked for the manager simply stared at me stonily and said, 'He wouldn't come.'

Robert Robinson *The Dog Chairman*, 'Being Rude' (1982)

30 One doesn't like to speak ill of the dead, but I tell you now that Purvis may have liked the odd piece of cheese but he knew nothing about it, nothing at all. Purvis was a man who would melt an Époisses on a slice of Mother's Pride as soon as look at you.

Tom Stoppard Vicar in *The Dog It Was That Died* (radio play, 1982)

31 The decline of the aperitif may well

be one of the most depressing phenomena of our time.

Luis Buñuel *My Last Breath*, ch. 6 (1983)

32 As to those who can find it in them to employ the doubtlessly useful word 'brunch', do they, I wonder, ever upgrade it to 'bruncheon'?

Arthur Marshall *Life's Rich Pageant*, Scene 1 (1984)

33 We want the finest wines known to humanity. We want them here and we want them now.

Bruce Robinson Withnail (Richard E. Grant) in *Withnail & I* (film, 1987, written and directed by Bruce Robinson). In 2003 this came third in a poll of Britain's best-loved lines from cinema. In *On the Razzle*, act 2, by Tom Stoppard 1981, Christopher says: 'We want the best dinner in the house and we want it now.'

34 He smiled rather too much. He smiled at breakfast, you know.

Charles Wheeler Of the spy George Blake. Quoted in the *Independent* 20 September 1990.

35 The table kills more people than war does.

Anon. Catalan proverb, quoted in *The Columbia Dictionary of Quotations* ed. Robert Andrews (1993)

36 Breakfast in bed – there's nothing like it! Nothing like it for making you realize what wonderful inventions the table and chair are.

Michael Frayn *Speak after the Beep*, 'Please Be Seated' (1995)

37 I will not hang donuts on my person.

Matt Groening Bart is seen repeatedly writing this line, as punishment, during the opening sequence of *The Simpsons*, 'Bart vs Australia', first broadcast 19 February 1995

38 [Of people who own soda fountains] God, they're so fucking proud of them, aren't they?

Jack Dee Quoted in the London *Evening Standard* 8 May 1997

39 That's what you do, you go out, you get tanked up on lassi and you go for an English.

Anon. 'The Traditional Bombay Friday Night

Out' sketch, *Goodness Gracious Me* (TV series, 1998–2001, with many credited writers). One of the four young Indians at the restaurant table summons a waiter and imperiously demands: 'What's the blandest thing on the menu?'

40 After supping ale, always show your satisfaction by going 'Warrrgghhhhhh!' and wiping your mouth on your sleeve.

Craig Brown *The Little Book of Chaos*, 'Show Your Satisfaction' (1998)

41 Ye may tak a man tae drink, but ye canna mak him water it.

Anon. Scottish maxim concerning whisky. Quoted in *Whisky Wit and Wisdom*, 'Drinking It', ed. Gavin D. Smith (2000).

42 [After vomiting at a dinner party] It's all right, the white wine came up with the fish.

Herman Mankiewicz Quoted in *Halliwell's Who's Who in the Movies* ed. John Walker (2001)

43 With boiled sweets, you're either a cruncher or a sucker. You can offer some people a boiled sweet and they'll still be sucking it when you next see them a week later.

Guy Browning *Guardian*, 'How to . . .' column, 23 November 2002

44 You don't have to like it, you just have to eat it.

Anon. *Away an' Ask Yer Mother (Your Scottish Father's Favourite Sayings)*, ch. 4, ed. Allan Morrison (2003)

45 The Americans are so disgusted with the French that a national campaign is underway to rename them 'freedom fries'. Wouldn't it be marvellous if the Americans finally saw sense . . . and called them 'chips'?

Boris Johnson The American disgust arose from French resistance to American plans for an attack on Iraq. *Daily Telegraph* 13 March 2003.

46 How does gravity work? And if it were to cease suddenly, would certain restaurants still require a jacket?

Woody Allen *Sunday Telegraph* 4 January 2004

47 Someone at the table, whose order had not yet arrived, said, 'I think "waiter" is such a funny word. It is we who wait.'

Muriel Spark *The Finishing School*, ch. 19 (2004)

Non-alcoholic Drinks

1 Poems written by water drinkers will never enjoy/ long life or acclaim.

Horace *Epistles* bk 1, no. 19 (c.20 BC), *Horace: Satires and Epistles; Persius: Satires* trans. and ed. Niall Rudd (1973)

2 Here's that which is too weak to be a sinner, honest water, which ne'er left man i' the mire . . .

William Shakespeare Apemantus in *Timon of Athens*, act 1, sc. 2 (1607–8)

3 Is there no Latin word for Tea? Upon my soul, if I had known, I would have left the vulgar stuff alone.

Hilaire Belloc *On Nothing*, 'On Tea' (1908). He adds: 'The matter of the Sacrifice must come from China. He that would drink Indian tea would smoke hay.'

4 I like a nice cup of tea with my dinner,/ And a nice cup of tea with my tea,/ And when it's time for bed,/ There's a lot to be said,/ For a nice cup of tea.

A. P. Herbert 'A Nice Cup of Tea' (song, 1937), quoted in *Look Back and Laugh*, 'The Thirties' (1960)

5 Coffee in England is just toasted milk.

Christopher Fry *New York Post* 29 November 1962

6 You know how much nutritive benefits they got in coffee? Zero. Not one thing. The stuff eats [you] up.

David Mamet Don in *American Buffalo*, act 1 (1975)

7 [Of tea bags] I am far from happy about their bogus and clinical and synthetic white appearance before immersion or, after immersion, their depressing and lukewarm brown sogginess and the unaccept-
able feel of them before they find their way into the trash can.

Arthur Marshall *Smile Please*, 'Happy Birthday' (1982)

8 Coca-Cola: You can dissolve a set of false teeth in a glass of Coca-Cola. In the so-called sixties, needless to say, sophomore students on American campuses used Coca-Cola as a spermicide.

Henry Root *Henry Root's World of Knowledge* (1982)

9 [Of Tony Benn] He has a pint mug every hour on the hour, he has one first thing in the morning and last thing at night. Once he accidentally dropped his hearing aid in his night tea, and it worked much better as a result.

Lynn Barber *Independent on Sunday* 30 September 1990. The left-wing politician is, by his own admission, addicted to tea.

10 I sometimes think I'm nothing more than a machine for taking the colour out of strong brown drinks.

Hugo Williams *Freelancing*, 'What about Pleasure? Where Does That Feature in the Freelance Hierarchy?' (1995). He was thinking mainly of coffee.

11 Coffee in England always tastes like a chemistry experiment.

Agatha Christie Quoted in *Women's Wicked Wit* ed. Michelle Lovric (2000)

12 Fish fuck in it.

W. C. Fields On why he never drank water, preferring alcohol. Quoted in *Halliwell's Who's Who in the Movies* ed. John Walker (2nd edn 2001). In *W. C. Fields by Himself* (commentary by Ronald J. Fields, 1974), Fields ascribed his aversion to water to an experience he had aged fourteen, when he and a friend hitched a ride on the baggage wagon of a Philadelphia–New York passenger train. On the bridge over the Delaware River the driver lowered the scoop to collect water, soaking Fields. 'My abhorrence and loathing of water fructified in my receptive adolescent brain.'

13 The water cooler bubbled, perhaps it was boiling?

Will Self *Dr Mukti and Other Tales of Woe*, 'Conversations with Ord' (2004)

Particular Types of Food

1 **Truly, a peck of provender: I could munch your good dry oats. Methinks I have a great desire to a bottle of hay: good hay, sweet hay, hath no fellow.**
William Shakespeare Bottom, wearing the ass's head, in *A Midsummer Night's Dream*, act 4, sc. 1 (1595–6). He means a 'bundle' of hay.

2 **I peseech you heartily, scurvy, lousy knave, at my desires, and my requests and my petitions, to eat, look you, this leek: because, look you, you do not love it, nor your affections and your appetites and your digestions does not agree with it, I would desire you eat it . . . if you can mock a leek, you can eat a leek.**
William Shakespeare Captain Fluellen, who is Welsh, to Pistol in *Henry V*, act 5, sc. 1 (1599)

3 **. . . I am a great eater of beef and, I believe, that does harm to my wit.**
William Shakespeare Andrew Aguecheek in *Twelfth Night*, act 1, sc. 3 (1601)

4 **[Of onions] They make the blood warmer,/ You'll feed like a farmer:/ For this is every cook's opinion,/ No savoury dish without an onion;/ But lest your kissing should be spoiled,/ Your onions must be thoroughly boiled.**
Jonathan Swift *Verses Made for Women Who Cry Apples, etc.*, first publ. 1746, collected in *Jonathan Swift: Selected Poems* ed. A. Norman Jeffares (1992)

5 **Oats: A grain which in England is generally given to horses, but in Scotland supports the people.**
Samuel Johnson *A Dictionary of the English Language* (1755)

6 **Our rabbits are bred and fed in the poulterer's cellar, where they have neither air nor exercise, consequently they must be firm in flesh, and delicious in flavour.**
Tobias Smollett Letter from Matthew Bramble to Dr Lewis, dated 8 June, from Humphry Clinker. *The Expedition of Humphry Clinker* (1771). The reference is to the rabbits available to Londoners.

7 **Hang your prune sauce, say I.**
Oliver Goldsmith Sir Charles Marlow in *She Stoops to Conquer*, act 2 (1773)

8 **. . . a cucumber should be well sliced, and dressed with pepper and vinegar, and then thrown out, as good for nothing.**
Samuel Johnson *The Journal of a Tour to the Hebrides*, James Boswell (1785). In *The Life of Samuel Johnson* also by James Boswell, vol. 4, p. 13 (1791); in G. B. Hill's edition of 1887, rev. L. F. Powell (1934), Johnson says of Gray's *Odes*: 'They are forced plants, raised in a hot-bed; and they are poor plants; they are but cucumbers after all.'

9 **Good apple pies are a considerable part of our domestic happiness.**
Jane Austen Letter to Cassandra Austen of 17–18 October 1815, collected in *Jane Austen's Letters* ed. Dierdre Le Faye (1995)

10 **Indeed, the loaves and fishes are typical of a mixed diet.**
Thomas Love Peacock The Rev. Dr Gaster in *Headlong Hall*, ch. 2 (1816). At issue is the question of whether man is naturally frugivorous or carnivorous.

11 **There's more of gravy than of grave about you, whatever you are!**
Charles Dickens Scrooge in *A Christmas Carol*, Stave 1, 'Marley's Ghost' (1843). Scrooge is attempting to convince himself that there is no ghost, that his senses are deceived. 'A slight disorder of the stomach makes them cheats.'

12 **It *was* a Turkey! He never could have stood upon his hind legs, that bird. He would have snapped 'em off short in a minute.**
Ibid., Stave 5

13 **There is no such passion in nature as the passion for gravy among commercial gentlemen.**
Charles Dickens Mrs Todgers in *Martin Chuzzlewit*, ch. 9 (1843–4)

14 **Don't have nothink to say to the**

cold meat, for it tastes of the stable.

Charles Dickens Betsey Prig in ibid., ch. 25

15 There is no delicacy in the world which Monsieur Francatelli or Monsieur Soyer can produce, which I believe to be better than toasted cheese.

William Makepeace Thackeray *Travels in London*, 'Great and Little Dinners' (1853)

16 Let onion atoms lurk within the bowl,/ And, scarce-suspected, animate the whole.

Sydney Smith *A Memoir of the Reverend Sydney Smith* by Lady Holland, vol. 1, ch. 11, 'Receipt for a Salad' (1855)

17 He was a bold man that first swallowed an oyster

King James I Attributed in *The New London Jest Book*, 'Choice Jests', no. 781, ed. W. C. Hazlitt (1871)

18 Many's the long night I've dreamed of cheese – toasted, mostly.

Robert Louis Stevenson Ben Gunn in *Treasure Island*, ch. 15 (1883)

19 Cauliflower is nothing but cabbage with a college education.

Mark Twain *The Tragedy of Pudd'n head Wilson*, 'Pudd'nhead Wilson's Calender', ch. 5 (1894)

20 And, speaking of the science of Life, have you got the cucumber sandwiches cut for Lady Bracknell?

Oscar Wilde Algernon Moncrieff in *The Importance of Being Earnest*, act 1 (1895)

21 Bread and butter, please. Cake is rarely seen at the best houses nowadays.

Oscar Wilde Gwendolen Fairfax in ibid., act 3 (1895)

22 It is said that the effect of eating too much lettuce is 'soporific'.

Beatrix Potter *The Tale of the Flopsy Bunnies* (1909)

23 Poets have been mysteriously silent on the subject of cheese.

G. K. Chesterton *Alarms and Discursions*, 'Cheese' (1910). But there is 'What a friend we have in cheeses!/ For no food more subtly pleases . . .' by William Cole.

24 [Of oysters] They not only forgive our unkindness to them; they justify it, they incite us to go on being perfectly horrid to them. Once they arrive at the supper table they seem to enter thoroughly into the spirit of the thing. There's nothing in Christianity or Buddhism that matches the sympathetic unselfishness of an oyster.

Saki *The Chronicles Of Clovis*, 'The Match-Maker' (1911)

25 It was one of those exuberant peaches that meet you half way so to speak, and are all over you in a moment.

Ibid., 'The Talking-Out of Tarrington'

26 All millionaires love a baked apple.

Ronald Firbank *Vainglory*, ch. 13 (1915)

27 A corpse is meat gone bad. Well and what's cheese? Corpse of milk.

James Joyce *Ulysses*, ch. 6 (1922)

28 Yes but what about oysters? Unsightly like a clot of phlegm.

Ibid., ch. 8

29 You are offered a piece of bread and butter that feels like a damp handkerchief and sometimes, when cucumber is added, like a wet one.

Compton Mackenzie This occurs 'in most English houses that you visit for tea on Sunday afternoon'. *Vestal Fire*, bk 1, ch. 3 (1927).

30 MOTHER: 'It's broccoli, dear.'
CHILD: 'I say it's spinach, and I say the hell with it.'

E. B. White Caption to *New Yorker* cartoon, 8 December 1928. Quoted in *The Cassell Dictionary of Slang* compiled by Jonathon Green (1998). The slang meaning of spinach in 1920s–40s America is given as 'rubbish, nonsense'.

31 Asparagus, in hours of ease,/ A pleasing substitute for peas,/ When pain and anguish wring the brow/ The *only* vegetable, thou.

A. A. Milne 'Food of the Gods' (1929), collected in *The Hutchinson Book of Essays* ed. Frank Delaney (1990)

32 'Turbot, Sir,' said the waiter, placing

before me two fishbones, two eye-
balls, and a bit of black mackintosh.

Thomas Erle Welby *The Dinner Knell*, 'Birmingham or Crewe?' (1932). This chapter title
comes from the music-hall song that ran:
'Oh, Mr Porter, what shall I do? I wanted to
go to Birmingham and they've sent me off
to Crewe!' The dish in question was served
on a train, together with 'a dollop of trifle or
a trifle of dollop'.

33 Some people think it is cruel to
geese to stuff their livers into pâté
de foie gras, while others think it is
cruel to people to stuff pâté de foie
gras into their livers.

W. C. Sellar and R. J. Yeatman *And Now All
This*, pt 8 (1932)

34 The pig, if I am not mistaken,/ Sup-
plies us sausage, ham, and bacon,/
Let others say his heart is big –/
I call it stupid of the pig.

Ogden Nash 'The Pig' (1933)

35 Some day you'll eat a pork chop,
Joey, and then God help all women.

Mrs Patrick Campbell Said to George Bernard
Shaw, who was a vegetarian. Quoted in
While Rome Burns, ch. 3, by Alexander
Woollcott (1934).

36 I ate cheese gravely.

P. G. Wodehouse *Lord Emsworth and Others*,
'The Letter of the Law' (1937)

37 Occupation is essential. And now
with some pleasure I find that it's
seven; and must cook dinner. Haddock and sausage meat. I think it is
true that one gains a certain hold
on sausage and haddock by writing
them down.

Virginia Woolf Entry for 8 March 1941,
*A Writer's Diary, Being Extracts from the
Diary of Virginia Woolf* ed. Leonard Woolf
(1953). This was the final entry. Four days
later she committed suicide.

38 I scream/ You scream/ We all
scream/ For ice-cream.

Anon. Collected in *A Treasury of American
Folklore* ed. B. A. Botkin (1944)

39 All that you say of *custard* is of
course true, and all really good men
avoid it.

George Lyttelton Letter to Rupert Hart-Davis

of 4 July 1956, collected in *The Lyttelton–
Hart-Davis Letters*, vols 1 and 2, *1955–1957*, ed.
Rupert Hart-Davis (1978). Hart-Davis had
called custard 'a superfluous and taste-
destroying mush'.

40 *Greens* is non-U for U *vegetables*.

Nancy Mitford *Noblesse Oblige*, 'The English
Aristocracy' (1956). Mitford also noted:
'Sweet: non-U for U pudding'.

41 Cheese – milk's leap forward to
immortality.

Clifton Fadiman *Any Number Can Play*, p. 105
(1957)

42 I've just discovered that British eggs
are being stamped with a lion. It's a
fraud! They're not lion's eggs.

Spike Milligan *The Goon Show*, 'The Treasure
in the Tower', first broadcast 28 October
1957. Neddie Seagoon is the speaker.

43 [Of a tin of pilchards] I told them it
was the tomato sauce that's turning
people off. And they should have
taken the heads off. Very unnerving
to open a tin and see six heads
staring up at you.

Ray Galton and Alan Simpson *Hancock's Half
Hour*, 'The Bowmans', first broadcast 2 June
1961

44 Nectarines – I love that fruit. Half a
peach, half a plum. It's a hell of a fruit.

Carl Reiner and Mel Brooks The Two-
Thousand-Year-Old Man (Mel Brooks) in *Two
Thousand Years with Carl Reiner and Mel
Brooks* (LP, 1961). The Two-Thousand-Year-
Old man adds: 'I'd rather eat a rotten nectar-
ine than a fine plum. What do you think
about that?'

45 And then I saw the menu, stained
with tea and beautifully written by
a foreign hand, and on top it said –
God I hated that old man – it said
'Chips with everything'. Chips with
every damn thing. You breed babies
and you eat chips with everything.

Arnold Wesker *Chips with Everything*, act 1,
sc. 2 (1962)

46 If I had a choice between smoked
salmon and tinned salmon, I'd have
it tinned. With vinegar.

Harold Wilson *Observer*, 'Sayings of the
Week', 11 November 1962

47 MR BUN: **What have you got then?**
WAITRESS: **Well there's egg and bacon; egg, sausage and bacon; egg and spam; egg, bacon and spam; egg, bacon, sausage and spam; spam, bacon, sausage and spam; spam, egg, spam, spam, bacon and spam; spam, spam, spam, spam, egg and spam; spam, spam, spam, spam, spam, spam, baked beans, spam, spam, spam, and spam; or lobster thermidor aux crevettes with a mornay sauce garnished with truffle pâté, brandy and a fried egg on top and spam.**

Monty Python team *Monty Python's Flying Circus* (programme 12, 2nd series, first broadcast 15 December 1970). Mr Bun (Graham Chapman) then asks the waitress (Terry Gilliam): 'Have you got anything without spam in it?', and she replies: 'Well, there's spam, egg, sausage and spam. That's not got *much* spam in it.'

48 **Take away that pudding – it has no theme.**

Winston Churchill Quoted in *The Way the Wind Blows: An Autobiography* ch. 16, by Lord Home (1976)

49 **Q: What happened to the man who couldn't tell putty from porridge? A: His windows fell out.**

Anon. *The Crack-a-Joke Book*, 'Nosh-Up', ed. Jane Nissen (1978)

50 **Water chestnuts are supposed to go in a thing, not to be the thing itself.**

Fran Lebowitz *Metropolitan Life*, 'Food for Thought' (1978)

51 [Of a black pudding] **Even the white bits are black.**

Michael Palin Eric Olthwaite in *Ripping Yarns*, 'The Testing of Eric Olthwaite' (BBC TV, 1978)

52 **Tongue sandwich? Eat *what*? But it's been in somebody else's mouth!**

Viv Stanshall Sir Henry in *Sir Henry at Rawlinson End* (LP, 1978)

53 **Why is no food blue?**

Geoffrey Madan *Geoffrey Madan's Notebooks*, 'Humorous and Memorable', ed. J. A. Gere and John Sparrow (1981). This, explains

Madan, was a question asked by 'Jane Asquith (aged 7)'.

54 **Did you know that . . . the Italians can buy pasta in more than 800 different shapes, including butterflies, bow-ties, cog-wheels, ribbons, cufflinks, false teeth, carburettors, mice, fluff, pipe-cleaners, prewar copies of *Oggi*, the staircase of La Scala, the forbidden drawings of Pompeii and roller skates?**

Miles Kington *Moreover*, 'The Moreover Advice Service' (1982)

55 **Imagination ran riot in the salad.**

Robert Robinson *The Dog Chairman* 'Food Talk' (1982). Robinson cites this, which he read somewhere in *The Good Food Guide*, as characteristic of its 'bird-like warble'.

56 **The policeman's favourite meal – Irish stew in the name of the law.**

Anon. Quoted in *The Whizzkid's Handbook 3* by Peter Eldin (1983)

57 **Any part of piggy/ Is quite all right with me.**

Noël Coward *Any Part of Piggy: Collected Verse* ed. Graham Payn and Martin Tickner (1984)

58 [Of papaya] **The only fruit on Earth, in my experience, which actually *tastes* yellow.**

Clive James *Observer* 29 July 1984

59 **Do you know my idea of a good time? Sex and chop suey.**

Mae West Quoted in *The Ultimate Seduction*, 'Mae West' (1984) by Charlotte Chandler. 'Not at the same time,' she stressed to Chandler, 'the chop suey tastes better after.'

60 **My three rules for a long life are regular exercise, hobbies, and complete avoidance of midget gems.**

Victoria Wood 'Kitty: One', *Victoria Wood as Seen on TV* (TV series, 1985), collected in *Up to You, Porky – The Victoria Wood Sketch Book* (1985). Midget gems are very more-ish small wine gums.

61 **Peanut butter has survived everything that has been done to improve it.**

Garrison Keillor Radio broadcast, 29 December 1990

62 The scientists at the Institute thus discovered the driving force behind all change, development and innovation in life, which was this: herring sandwiches. They published a paper to this effect, which was widely criticized as being extremely stupid. They checked their figures and realized that what they had actually discovered was 'boredom' or rather, the practical function of boredom.

Douglas Adams *Mostly Harmless*, ch. 6 (1992)

63 Get yer haggis right here! Chopped heart and lungs, boiled in a wee sheep's stomach! Tastes as good as it sounds.

Matt Groening Willie, the Scottish school janitor, in *The Simpsons*, 'Lisa the Beauty Queen', first broadcast 15 October 1992

64 It's impossible to eat a fucking Toblerone without hurting yourself.

Billy Connolly Joke made during his run of twenty-two nights at the Hammersmith Apollo, London, in 1994

65 At half-time I went down to the snack bar and bought a bag of crisps. I got spring onion because I felt I needed to eat some vegetables.

Harry Pearson *The Far Corner*, 'Gateshead v. Stafford Rangers, GM Vauxhall Conference, Saturday, 4 December 1993' (1994)

66 There is a sinister genius in the very *name* brown Windsor soup.

John Lanchester *The Debt to Pleasure*, 'Winter', 'A Winter Menu' (1996)

67 It gives an epicure the vapours/ To eat boiled mutton without capers.

Ogden Nash Quoted in ibid.

68 Potatoes vary in size even more than human beings.

Jeffrey Steingarten *The Man Who Ate Everything*, 'Totally Mashed' (1997)

69 Here in Flanders we make many different kinds of cheese. Hard cheese, soft cheese, goats' cheese, sheep's cheese. We make orange, white and blue cheeses. Cheeses with herbs and with rinds soaked in beer. Hundreds of cheeses. Great cheeses. But nobody has heard of them. The Dutch make one kind of very tasteless cheese and all the world knows about it.

Anon. A 'Belgian from Limburg', quoted in *A Tall Man in a Low Land*, ch. 4, by Harry Pearson (1998)

70 I had a meal last night, and I said to this waiter, 'This chicken I've got here's cold.' He said, 'Well it should be, it's been dead for two weeks.'

Tommy Cooper *The Very Best of Tommy Cooper*, vol. 1 (cassette, 1999)

71 The world is the perfect place to be born into/ Unless of course, you don't like people/ or trees, or stars, or baguettes.

Roger McGough 'The Perfect Place', collected in *The Way Things Are* (1999)

72 Just Give Me Chocolate And Nobody Gets Hurt

Anon. T-shirt slogan spotted in New York, 1999. Quoted in *The Penguin Dictionary of Modern Humorous Quotations* ed. Fred Metcalf (2nd edn 2001).

73 Salad's on a new footing now.

Alan Bennett *Telling Tales*, 'Eating Out' (2000). Remark made by Alan Bennett's mother in the 1950s after reading in *Ideal Home* about it being permissible to include celery, apple or raisins.

74 The indiscriminate use of tinned sweetcorn was a practice I fondly hoped would not have lasted into the twenty-first century.

Paul Richardson *Cornucopia*, 'Normandy and Sussex' (2000). The cuisine in question is British.

75 I have never known anyone refuse a Smartie.

Nigel Slater *Appetite*, 'Storecupboard – A Shortlist to Save Your Life' (2000). Slater recommends that a store of Smarties be kept at all times.

76 A good fishfinger butty is hard to beat.

Jamie Oliver *The Times*, 'Quotes of the Week', 3 March 2001. In the same week the French chef Raymond Blanc was quoted as saying: 'British people are ignorant of good food.'

77 I stare at a Stilton with blueberries and wonder why the English, with so many fabulous and underrated native cheeses at their disposal, insist on buggering about with them.

India Knight *Don't You Want Me?*, ch. 9 (2002)

78 How come people who buy ready-grated cheese can be arsed to go to the shop in the first place?

Tim Lott Spoken at a party in London, 1 June 2002

79 The baclava tasted like balaclava.

Victor Lewis-Smith The London *Evening Standard* 6 December 2002

80 Hamburger is a word which translates as health risk.

Jonathan Meades *Incest and Morris Dancing*, 'Das Volk' (2002)

81 Q: What's the difference between parsley and pussy? A: Nobody eats parsley.

Anon. Joke told by Steve Tyler, lead singer of the group Aerosmith, in *Q* magazine March 2003

82 What a con this so-called evaporated milk is. I opened a tin of it the other day and it was still completely full.

Viz Fake reader's letter to *Viz* comic May 2003

83 Made from freshly squeezed cows.

Anon. Poster, summer 2003, for Innocent's Fresh Yoghurt Thickie

84 As I always think about pies, if the stuff inside's so nice, why do they want to cover it up?

Julie Burchill *Guardian* 28 June 2003

85 I believe the British people are too mature to need to be told that chewing-gum will taste minty for ever or that the round coconut Allsorts will simply go away.

Oliver Pritchett *Daily Telegraph* 11 February 2004

Cooking

1 'Tis an ill cook that cannot lick his own fingers.

William Shakespeare Second Servant in *Romeo and Juliet*, act 4, sc. 2 (1595–6)

2 Remove the pan into the next room, and place it on the floor. Bring it back again, and let it simmer for three-quarters of an hour. Shake the pan violently till all the Amblonguses have become a pale, purple colour.

Edward Lear 'How to Make an Amblongus Pie', *Nonsense Songs, Stories, Botany and Alphabets* (1871), which begins 'Take 4 pounds (say 4½ pounds) of fresh Amblonguses, and put them in a small pipkin.'

3 Life is too short to stuff a mushroom.

Shirley Conran *Superwoman*, Epigraph (1975)

4 [Of Eric's wife] ERNIE: Couldn't she even boil a pan of water? ERIC: Not without getting lumps in it.

Eric Morecambe and Ernie Wise *The Morecambe and Wise Jokebook*, skit 27 (1979). His wife also asked the butcher for a humpbacked rabbit 'to hold the pie crust up'.

5 If you want to keep your own teeth, make your own sandwiches . . .

Jeanette Winterson *Oranges Are Not the Only Fruit*, 'Deuteronomy: The Last Book of the Law' (1985)

6 Poaching: This is the fancy word for boiling. When somebody suggests, 'Let's have poached fish', say to yourself, 'Let's have boiled fish', and talk them out of it.

P. J. O'Rourke *The Bachelor Home Companion*, ch. 3 (1987)

7 It is no use trying to empty a sugar bag. You will always hear more sugar rattling around inside an empty sugar bag. Just throw it away.

Miles Kington *Welcome to Kington*, 'If You Can't Stand the Kitchen . . .' (1989). Kington adds: 'The same is true of flour, except you cannot hear it.'

8 **Do not trust a cookery writer who has written books about more than three countries.**

Ibid., 'The Wit and Wisdom of Albania'

9 **Soak fourteen pieces of chicken in suggested marinade which only stretches around three thighs, leaving other eleven high and dry. Recipe says, 'Reserve remaining marinade'!**

Maureen Lipman *Thank You for Having Me*, 'The Cook, the Wife, Her Guests and Another' (1990)

10 **She thought that trying to live life according to any plan you actually work out is like trying to buy ingredients for a recipe from the supermarket. You get one of those trolleys which simply will not go in the right direction, you push it and end up having to buy completely different stuff.**

Douglas Adams *Mostly Harmless*, ch. 4 (1992)

11 **You only use that cooker to light your fags off of.**

Jennifer Saunders Saffron (Julia Sawalha) to Edina (Jennifer Saunders) in *Absolutely Fabulous*, 'Birthday' (BBC TV sitcom, 1992)

12 **Punching the air is not just for sportsmen. Accountants do it when the figures add up; others do it when they get a mortgage or complete the *Telegraph* crossword. I have seen people do it when their home-made mayonnaise does not curdle.**

Oliver Pritchett *The Dogger Bank Saga: Writings 1980–95*, 'The Lost Sport of Winning Gracefully' (1995)

13 **Burning dinner is not incompetence but war.**

Marge Piercy *Women's Wicked Wit* ed. Michelle Lovric (2000)

14 **Graham Greene put carrots in a Lancashire hotpot.**

Anthony Burgess *Anthony Burgess*, 'Jack Be Nimble, 1917–37', by Roger Lewis (2002). Burgess often talked about hotpot, which he had eaten a lot of in Manchester as a boy. Lewis describes this remark as part of Burgess's 'familiar bag of tricks' – typical of his conversation. The tone here he describes as 'reproachful'.

15 **I'm not saying my wife's a bad cook, but she uses a smoke alarm as a timer.**

Bob Monkhouse *Sun* 30 December 2003

8

Travel and Transport

Travel
Transport

Travel
Holidays

1 **The traveller with nothing on him sings in the robber's face.**
Juvenal Satire 10, line 23 (c.AD 125), trans. and ed. Niall Rudd (1991)

2 **... 'tis ever common/ That men are merriest when they are far from home.**
William Shakespeare Henry V in *Henry V*, act 1, sc. 2 (1599)

3 **He that traveleth into a country before he hath some entrance into the language, goeth to school, and not to travel.**
Francis Bacon *Essays*, 'Of Travel' (1625)

4 **Travelling is the ruin of all happiness! There's no looking at a building here after seeing Italy.**
Fanny Burney *Cecilia*, bk 7, ch. 5 (1782)

5 **[Of the Giant's Causeway] Worth seeing, yes; but not worth going to see.**
Samuel Johnson *The Life of Samuel Johnson* by James Boswell, vol. 3, p. 410 (1791); in G. B. Hill's edition of 1887, rev. L. F. Powell (1934). Boswell had suggested a trip to Ireland.

6 **There is a certain relief in change, even though it be from bad to worse ... it is often a comfort to shift one's position and be bruised in a new place.**
Washington Irving *Tales of a Traveller*, 'To the Reader' (1824)

7 **The scenery was really painfully sublime. We gazed till our eyes ached and yet dared not withdraw them from the passing wonders.**
Benjamin Disraeli Letter to Isaac Disraeli of 2 September 1826, collected in *Benjamin Disraeli: Letters 1815–1834* ed. J. A. W. Gunn, John Matthews and Donald M. Schurman (1982). The scenery was that of the Rhône Valley and the Alps.

8 **It is because we put up with bad things that hotel-keepers continue to give them to us.**
Anthony Trollope *Orley Farm*, ch. 18 (1862)

9 **The further off from England the nearer is to France.**

Lewis Carroll 'The Lobster Quadrille', *Alice's Adventures in Wonderland*, ch. 10 (1865)

10 **Of all noxious animals, too, the most noxious is a tourist. And of all tourists the most vulgar, ill-bred, offensive and loathsome is the British tourist.**

Francis Kilvert Entry for 5 April 1870, *Selections from the Diary of the Reverend Francis Kilvert* ed. W. Plomer (1938–40)

11 **I don't think we can do better than 'Good old Broadstairs'.**

George Grossmith and Weedon Grossmith Mr Pooter, putting a brave face on things in *The Diary of a Nobody* (1894), entry for 31 July

12 **The difference between Bruges and other cities is that in the latter you look about for the picturesque, while in Bruges, assailed on every side by the picturesque, you look curiously for the unpicturesque, and don't find it easily.**

Arnold Bennett Entry for 23 August 1896, *The Journals of Arnold Bennett*, vol. 1, *1896–1910*, ed. Newman Flower (1932)

13 **Why does the idea of a char-a-banc full of tourists going to see the birthplace of Nelson or the death-scene of Simon de Montfort strike a strange chill to the soul?**

G. K. Chesterton *Alarms and Discursions*, 'The Philosophy of Sight-seeing' (1910)

14 **The landlady of a boarding house is a parallelogram – that is, an oblong figure, which can not be described, but which is equal to anything.**

Stephen Leacock *Literary Lapses*, 'Boarding-House Geometry' (1910)

15 **There's sand in the porridge and sand in the bed,/ And if this is pleasure we'd rather be dead.**

Noël Coward 'The English Lido' (song, 1928)

16 **When setting out on a photographic holiday *always provide yourself with two cameras*, one to leave in** the train going and the other to leave in the cab coming back.

W. C. Sellar and R. J. Yeatman *And Now All This*, pt 9 (1932)

17 **The Victorians had not been anxious to go away for the weekend. The Edwardians, on the contrary, were nomadic.**

T. H. White *Farewell Victoria*, pt 4 (1933)

18 **For heaven's sake don't go too far down the Nile because you'll have to come all the way back up the same old river . . .**

Joyce Grenfell Letter of 28 January 1937 to Virginia Graham, collected in *Joyce and Ginnie: The Letters of Joyce Grenfell and Virginia Graham* ed. Janie Hampton (1997)

19 **Like *Webster's Dictionary*, we're Morocco bound.**

Johnny Burke *The Road to Morocco*, title song of film (1942)

20 **At the age of thirty-five one needs to go to the moon, or some such place, to recapture the excitement with which one first landed at Calais.**

Evelyn Waugh *When the Going Was Good*, Preface (1946)

21 **Later that night I walked H. from the Gladstone to Times Square, so excited that I overdid my running commentary. 'You needn't actually say "gramophone shop" when we see a gramophone shop,' she said.**

Stephen Potter *Potter on America*, pt 1, 'Spring 1955' (1956)

22 **[Advice to tourists visiting Britain for the first time] You will oblige your chamber maid by hanging your mattress out of the window every morning . . . All London brothels display a blue lamp . . . Have you tried the famous echo in the Reading Room of the British Museum?**

Gerard Hoffnung Hoffnung gave this advice during a speech to the Oxford Union, 4 December 1958. Collected in *Hoffnung – A Last Encore* (Cassette, 1973).

23 **'Travel' is the name of a modern disease which became rampant in the**

mid-fifties and is still spreading.
The disease – its scientific name is
travelitis furiosus – is carried by a
germ called prosperity.

George Mikes *How to Unite Nations*, 'Down
with Travelling' (1963)

24 [Of a holiday cottage] 'It's a house in
a place,' said William gloomily. 'I
jus' don't know why people want to
go jus' from one house in one place
to another in another.'

Richmal Crompton William Brown in *William
and the Masked Ranger*, 'William's Summer
Holiday' (1966)

25 I acquiesced in this on the grounds
that the most anyone would expect
from a holiday was a change in
agony.

Quentin Crisp *The Naked Civil Servant*, ch. 12
(1968). The destination was the Isle of
Wight.

26 Exodus: Departure for the seaside.

Beachcomber *Beachcomber: The Works of
J. B. Morton*, 'A Dictionary for Today', ed.
Richard Ingrams (1974)

27 I recall that when I was discussing
this chapter with my publisher I
remarked that holiday camps are
ideal for people with children, to
which he replied, 'Of course they
are, if you don't tell the children
which one you've gone to.'

Ronnie Corbett *Ronnie Corbett's Small Man's
Guide*, 'The Small Man and Holidays' (1976)

28 As a sightseer, what gets you after a
time . . . what destroys the morale,
is the way the actual sight – the
cathedral or the ruin or the stately
home or the collection of Duccios –
goes on making its enormous statements without effort, leaving all
the work to be done by you.

Robert Robinson *The Dog Chairman*, 'Sight-
seer's Ankle' (1982). 'All I want when I trail
around the average stately home,' he adds,
'is a simple typewritten sheet stuck on one
of those wooden bats – it doesn't get
between you and your imagination.'

29 I wouldn't mind seeing China if I
could come back the same day.

Philip Larkin *Required Writing*, 'An Interview

with the *Observer*' (1983). 'Generally speaking,' Larkin added, 'the further one gets from
home the greater the misery.'

30 The English required guests to be
uncomplaining, and most of the
people who ran bed-and-breakfast
places were intolerant of the guest's
moaning, and they thought – with
some justification – that they had
in their lives suffered more than
the guest.

Paul Theroux *The Kingdom by the Sea*, ch. 7
(1983)

31 Imagine please a beautiful small
country from a fairytale, where on
each high cragtop stands an ancient
castello and in fine rustic resi-
dences the traditionally dressed
pheasants of folklore plie away at
their rural trades and practice their
ancient customs, and dances by
pheasants in regional costumes are
regularly performed.

Malcolm Bradbury *Why Come to Slaka?*,
'Geography and History by Professor-
Academician Rom Run (Slakan Academy of
Arts and Sciences)' (1986). The translation is
the work of Dr F. Plitplov (Dozent Extraordin-
arius, Universitet Borism).

32 Slaka is not a very famous country,
and we speak a little language not
many understand, not even us.

Ibid., 'The Languages of Slaka by Katya
Princip (People's Novelist)'

33 We've gone on holiday by mistake.

Bruce Robinson Withnail (Richard E. Grant),
in *Withnail & I* (film, 1987, written and
directed by Bruce Robinson)

34 Please go away.

Anon. Sign on a travel agent's door. Quoted
in *And I Quote*, 'Travel and Vacations', ed.
Ashton Applewhite and others (1992).

35 It is a truism that any holiday only
lasts three – or possibly four – days
before some jarring episode or
reminder changes the atmosphere
and arrests the process of
unwinding.

Alan Clark Entry for Saturday 24 December
1994, *The Last Diaries: In and Out of the Wilderness* ed. Ion Trewin (2002). Clark was holi-

daying in Scotland; the entry goes on to record an attack on a sheep by his dogs.

36 **There's one piece of writing I vow each year to leave behind, but at some relaxed moment I'll reach into my pocket and find it there – No Milk for Next Two Weeks.**

Oliver Pritchett *The Dogger Bank Saga: Writings, 1980–95*, 'The Fine Writing Is on the Wall' (1995)

37 **After breakfast the hours passed in the sickishness, the invalid waiting, of a major holiday.**

Jonathan Franzen *The Corrections*, 'One Last Christmas' (2001)

38 **Coach holidays are divided into three roughly equal parts: motorways, seeing sights and waiting for Colin to find the coach.**

Guy Browning *Guardian*, 'How to . . .' column, 14 September 2002

39 **Matches? No! They're on Order**

Jonathan Meades Title of a chapter on 'the great British hotel', *Incest and Morris Dancing* (2002)

40 **Really, there's nothing worse than going on a family holiday, and your parents are finding things to do in the day that they think'll be fun for you; they're miserable, because they'd much rather be in the pub. You're miserable because you're not that arsed about castles.**

Johnny Vegas Quoted in the *Guardian* 2 November 2002

41 **We're All Going on an Alco-Holiday!**

Viz Cover line, *Viz* comic September 2003

42 *I* **am a traveller/** *You* **are a sightseer/** *He* **is a tourist.**

Craig Brown *This is Craig Brown*, 'A Holiday Primer' (2003)

43 **For spinsters – Isle Of Man./ For invalids – Ealing./ For teetotallers – Freshwater./ For gamblers – Deal./ For chorus girls – Earl's Court./ For bald men – Thatchem./ For the seaside girl – Paignton.**

Anon. 'Some Holiday Resorts', *Pearson's Book of Fun*, 'Sunday Siftings', ed. Mr X (n.d.)

Travel in General

1 **A journeying woman speakes much of all, and all of her.**

George Herbert *Outlandish Proverbs*, no. 279 (1640)

2 **I always love to begin a journey on Sundays, because I shall always have the prayers of the church, to preserve all that travel by land, or by water.**

Jonathan Swift *Polite Conversation*, Dialogue 2 (1738)

3 **I** *wish* **someone would invent a decent way to get to Loughborough from Belfast.**

Philip Larkin Letter to Winifred Arnott of 6 April 1953, collected in *Selected Letters of Philip Larkin (1940–85)* ed. Anthony Thwaite (1992)

4 **Vast Distancemanship for the global traveller: Toronto is slightly nearer to England than it is to Vancouver.**

Stephen Potter *Potter on America*, 2, 'Autumn 1955' (1956)

5 **You can't get there from here.**

Anon. Old joke, quoted in *The Kingdom by the Sea*, ch. 23 (1983), by Paul Theroux

6 **Back at the cottage, our lunch would be followed by a last game of chess before my departure, and further pampering from my aunt./ 'Do you want sugar in your tea as you're going on a journey?'**

Andrew Barrow *The Tap Dancer*, ch. 10 (1992)

7 **It looks to me as if you've done Pyrrhic packing again. It's all very well travelling light, but it's a bit short-sighted to travel so light that you exclude yourself from all activities on arrival through having nothing to wear and none of the equipment.**

Mary Killen The author, to her husband Giles, in *How to Live with Your Husband*, 'Travel Fever' (1996). Giles replies: 'Why would I need a jacket in Northern Ireland?'

Transport

By Water

1 **Oak and triple bronze/ were round the breast of the man who first committed/ a fragile ship to the truculent sea.**

Horace *Odes*, bk 1, no. 3 (c.23 BC), *Horace: The Complete Odes and Epodes* trans. David West (1997)

2 **In every mess I finds a friend,/ In every port a wife.**

Charles Dibdin 'Jack in His Element' (1790), collected in *Songs, Naval and National, of the Late Charles Dibdin* ed. Thomas Dibdin (1841)

3 **I like the sailor's life much, tho' it destroys the toilette.**

Benjamin Disraeli Letter to Isaac Disraeli of 10 October 1830, collected in *Benjamin Disraeli: Letters 1815–1834* ed. J. A. W. Gunn, John Matthews and Donald M. Schurman (1982). Disraeli had lately sailed from Malta to Corfu.

4 **They went to sea in a Sieve, they did,/ In a Sieve they went to sea:/ In spite of all their friends could say,/ On a winter's morn, on a stormy day.**

Edward Lear Opening lines of 'The Jumblies' (1871)

5 **You feel mighty free and easy and comfortable on a raft.**

Mark Twain *The Adventures of Huckleberry Finn*, ch. 18 (1884)

6 **In a boat, I have always noticed that it is the fixed idea of each member of the crew that he is doing everything.**

Jerome K. Jerome *Three Men in a Boat*, ch. 14 (1889)

7 **I mean I always love a ship and I really love the *Majestic* because you would not know it was a ship because it is just like being at the Ritz, and the steward says the ocean is not so obnoxious this month as it generally is.**

Anita Loos *Gentlemen Prefer Blondes*, ch. 2 subtitled 'Fate Keeps On Happening' (1925)

8 **Do not eat the caviar on the Dover–Ostend packet.**

Evelyn Waugh Letter to Christopher Sykes of 16 July 1956, collected in *The Letters of Evelyn Waugh* ed. Mark Amory (1980)

9 **This ship is going much too fast.**

Cary Grant Nickie Ferrante (Cary Grant) to Terry McKay (Deborah Kerr) in *An Affair to Remember* (film, 1957, written by Delmer Daves and Leo McCarey, directed by Leo McCarey). The two are conducting an affair on a transatlantic liner.

10 **Yes – I'm very fond of boats myself. I like the way they're – contained. You don't have to worry about which way to go, or whether to go at all – the question doesn't arise, because you're on a *boat*, aren't you?**

Tom Stoppard Guildenstern in *Rosencrantz and Guildenstern Are Dead*, act 3 (1967)

11 **In Nova Scotia today, Mr Roy Bent of North Walsham in Norfolk became the first man to cross the Atlantic on a tricycle. His tricycle, specially adapted for the crossing, was ninety feet long, with a protective steel hull, three funnels, seventeen first-class cabins and a radar scanner.**

Monty Python team *Monty Python's Flying Circus* (programme 11, 2nd series, first broadcast 8 December 1970)

12 **Once, six miles outside Margate, and this was on the French side, Reggie fell off a hovercraft. You cannot fall off hovercrafts, you cannot. But Reggie has cracked it.**

Jake Thackray *Jake's Progress*, 'Before I Was a Performing Man . . .' (1977). Reggie (Reginald Walter Sedgewick) is a man 'not so much accident-prone . . . as doom-ridden'.

13 **The speedboat ducks and drakes.**

Craig Raine 'The Meteorological Lighthouse at O —', *A Martian Sends a Postcard Home* (1979)

14 **Good morning is often the preliminary to a life-story, and I sometimes think that what makes the idea of a cruise so hideous is that it**

is good morning elevated into a way of life.

Robert Robinson *The Dog Chairman*, 'Good Morning' (1982)

15 INTERVIEWER: Is it true, sir, that the captain goes down with his ship?
2000-YEAR-OLD MAN: Not in a submarine. The captain goes *up* with his ship.

Mel Brooks and Carl Reiner Quoted in the sleeve notes to *The Complete 2000-Year-Old Man* (CD reissue, 1994). This exchange is the sort of adlibbing that produced the skits in which Brooks, in the persona of the long-lived sage, was interviewed by Reiner.

16 Slow down, the sea isn't going to evaporate.

Anon. Sign on French autoroutes to the Mediterranean, quoted in *The Times*, 'Quotes of the Week', 28 July 2001

17 Last night we were talking about the *Titanic*. I said the makers of the ship shouldn't have claimed it was unsinkable. If I built the *Titanic* today I would claim it was sinkable. That way I couldn't lose.

Steve Coogan Steve Coogan, interviewed in the persona of Alan Partridge by *Time Out* magazine 6–13 November 2002

By Road

1 There is an indignant way in which a man sometimes dismounts his horse, which as good as says to him, 'I'll go afoot, Sir, all the days of my life, before I would ride a single mile on your back again.'

Laurence Sterne *Tristram Shandy* (1759–67), vol. 6, ch. 34. Shandy's uncle Toby, however, had not so much dismounted his horse as been flung from it, creating 'a sort of shyness' between himself and the horse.

2 It is a maxim with me that stage-coaches, and consequently stage-coachmen, are respectable in proportion to the distance they have to travel.

William Hazlitt 'The Fight', *New Monthly*

Magazine February 1822, collected in *The Essays of William Hazlitt* ed. Catherine Macdonald Maclean (1949)

3 [Of a London hackney coach driver] The old gentleman saw an extra charge of a shilling in his face.

Leigh Hunt *Companion* 16 January 1828

4 What an interesting book a hackney-coach might produce, if it could carry as much in its head as it does in its body! The autobiography of a broken-down hackney-coach, would surely be as amusing as the autobiography of a broken-down hackneyed dramatist.

Charles Dickens *Sketches by Boz*, 'Scenes', ch. 7, 'A Hackney Coach Passenger' (1836)

5 [On alighting from a cab] We have studied the subject a great deal, and we think the best way is, to throw yourself out, and trust to chance for alighting on your feet. If you make the driver alight first, and then throw yourself upon him, you will find he breaks your fall materially.

Ibid., ch. 17, 'The Last Cab Driver and the First Omnibus Cad'

6 There is no secret so close as that between a rider and his horse.

R. S. Surtees *Mr Sponge's Sporting Tour*, ch. 31 (1853)

7 Many vast vague reputations have been made, solely by taking cabs and going about.

Charles Dickens *Our Mutual Friend*, 'Book the Second: Birds of a Feather', ch. 3 (1867–8)

8 No one who has ever ridden a cycle of any kind but will witness that the things are unaccountably prone to pick up bad habits – and keep them.

H. G. Wells *The Wheels of Chance*, ch. 5 (1896)

9 MELICENT: Aren't bicycle lamps annoying?
MIRIAM (vexatiously): Yes, mine goes out every time I run into anybody!

Jerome K. Jerome *Humours of Cycling*, 'Spokelets' (1905)

10 Cycle tracks will abound in Utopia.

H. G. Wells *A Modern Utopia*, ch. 2, sect. 3 (1905)

11 What is this that roareth thus?/ Can it be a Motor Bus?/ Yes, the smell and hideous hum/ Indicate Motorem Bum!

A. D. Godley 'On the Motor Bus', in a letter to C. R. L. Fletcher of 10 January 1914, collected in *Reliquiae*, vol. 1, p. 292 (1926)

12 The word 'omnibus' is a very noble word with a very noble meaning and even tradition. It is derived from an ancient and adamantine tongue which has rolled it with very authoritative thunders: *quod ubique, quod semper, quod omnibus.*

G. K. Chesterton *The Uses of Diversity*, 'Lamp-Posts' (1920)

13 It is true that some motorists almost live in their motor-cars. But it gratifies me to state that these motorists generally die in their motor-cars too.

Ibid., 'More Thoughts on Christmas'

14 My front bike-lamp, constable? Why, man, the moon! My rear-lamp?/ Shining there ten yards behind me,/ Warm parlour light of the Dish and Spoon!

Robert Graves 'A Vehicle, to wit, a Bicycle', *New Statesman* 16 July 1921

15 An automobile was a new and awesome thing then, and nobody could have it except people who could afford it and people who couldn't.

Mark Twain *Autobiography*, ch. 76 (1924)

16 [There are] only two classes of pedestrians in these days of reckless motor traffic – the quick, and the dead.

Lord Dewar Quoted in *Looking Back on Life*, ch. 28 (1933) by George Robey

17 It is an extraordinary thing that no motorist ever thinks of himself as 'the traffic' or an ingredient of 'the congestion'.

A. P. Herbert *Sip! Swallow!*, ch. 18 (1937)

18 My office-work had taught me to think out a notion in detail, pack it away in my head, and work on it by snatches in any surroundings. The lurch and surge of the old horse-drawn buses made a luxurious cradle for such ruminations.

Rudyard Kipling *Something of Myself*, ch. 4 (1937)

19 BUD ABBOTT: You know, Costello, no matter how you drive, the pedestrians always manage to get out of the way somehow.
LOU COSTELLO: Yeah, sneaky ain't they?

Abbott and Costello Abbott and Costello, supposedly in a car and driving to the Andrews Sisters' ranch. *Abbott and Costello in Alaska*, 1940s radio sketch, collected in *Abbott and Costello: Who's On First?* (CD, 1999).

20 It takes two to make a one-way street.

Ogden Nash *The Private Dining Rooms and Other Verses*, 'Hi-Ho the Ambulance-O' (1952)

21 Her hair was a lovely shade of dark red and she had a distant smile on her lips and over her shoulder she had a blue mink that almost made the Rolls-Royce look just like another automobile. It didn't quite. Nothing can.

Raymond Chandler *The Long Goodbye*, ch. 1 (1954)

22 [Raucous bus conductor] All tickets please. Eh! Sleeping beauty! Did you want to book a return or was it bed and breakfast?

Al Read *The Al Read Show* (radio series), broadcast 25 January 1955

23 There was the strange suspension of life which vehicles exude when they come to a halt and no one has stepped out of them.

Robert Robinson *Landscape with Dead Dons*, ch. 14 (1956)

24 We like to drive in convoys/ We're most gregarious/ That big six-wheeler/ Scarlet-painted/ London transport/ Diesel-engined/ Ninety-seven horsepower/ Omnibus!

Michael Flanders and Donald Swann 'A Transport of Delight', song, *At the Drop of a Hat* (LP, 1957). After Flanders's death, his wife would go on to campaign for disabled access to buses.

25 **Any colour – so long as it's black.**
Henry Ford On the options open to the purchaser of a Model T Ford motor car. Quoted in *Ford* by Allan Nevins, vol. 2, ch. 15 (1957).

26 **Leaving early to catch the bus! Is that living?**
Arnold Wesker Dave in *I'm Talking about Jerusalem*, act 2 (1960)

27 **Motoring in Britain, while it has failed to develop good roads, has been successful in developing many personal rights: the Right to Double Park, for example, was established under Henry VI; taxi cabs gained the Right to Block the Road Absolutely Anywhere they deign to pick up or drop passengers under Richard III.**
George Mikes *How to Unite Nations*, 'How to Be a European' (1963)

28 **It is the overtakers who keep the undertakers busy.**
William Ewart Pitts Said in 1963, quoted in *The Collins Dictionary of Quotations* ed. A. Norman Jeffares and Martin Gray (1995)

29 **Third-class riding's better than first-class walking, any day.**
Barry Hines The milkman to Billy Casper in *A Kestrel for a Knave*, ch. 1 (1968). Billy had been ridiculing his milk float.

30 **Two attitudes are admissible in relation to roads: one, that there are not enough roads in this country and that more should be provided; two, that all existing roads should be ploughed up and wheat sown.**
Flann O'Brien *The Best of Myles*, 'A Selection from "Cruiskeen Lawn" ' (1968)

31 **Why does the loony on the bus always sit next to *me*?**
Jasper Carrott Common complaint of Carrott's in the 1970s and 80s

32 **Island: A small piece of land surrounded on all sides by traffic.**
Beachcomber *Beachcomber: The Works of*

J. B. Morton, 'A Dictionary for Today', ed. Richard Ingrams (1974). Beachcomber also defines 'pedestrian' as 'a person knocked down by a motor car'.

33 **Yellow schools of taxi fishes . . .**
Joni Mitchell 'Harry's House – Centerpiece', *The Hissing of Summer Lawns* (LP, 1975)

34 **The next rainy night you're in a bus queue why not start things going? 'I spy with my little eye something beginning with B.'**
Ronnie Corbett *Ronnie Corbett's Small Man's Guide*, 'The Small Man and Motoring' (1976)

35 [Of taking a driving test] **You will know that your driving was immaculate, but he will fail you on stupid things like, 'Misuse of a shop doorway during the three-point turn'.**
Ibid.

36 **Country bus, north country bus/ Grunting and chuntering, cantankerous/ Country bus, north country bus,/ But no other bus would be good enough for us.**
Jake Thackray 'Country Bus' (song), transcribed in *Jake's Progress* (1977)

37 **The saying that there are two sorts of pedestrians, the quick and the dead, is well matured: but there are also those who choose to be maimed rather than halt.**
Anon. Quoted in *Geoffrey Madan's Notebooks*, 'Humorous and Memorable', ed. J. A. Gere and John Sparrow (1981). Madan credits a *Times* leader of April 1933 with the saying.

38 **A friend reported to me the other day a roadside notice which said, in one long line, LOOSE STONES TRAVEL SLOWLY.**
John Sparrow *Words on the Air*, 'Public Notices' (1981). The answer, continued Sparrow, would be to reverse the order: 'TRAVEL SLOWLY LOOSE STONES.'

39 **I was madly in love with a girl of my age, I had a new bicycle (an Enfield, I remember) with reversible handlebars that could turn into a racer. My first poems were awful,**

but then I reversed the handlebars, and things improved.

Vladimir Nabokov Asked by Robert Robinson to recall 'the earliest stirrings of the impulse to write'. *The Dog Chairman*, 'The Last Interview with Nabokov' (1982).

40 Among the logical and intelligent Japanese, I have been told, it was a defence against any charge of dangerous driving until well into the 1960s to prove that you were drunk at the time, and therefore not responsible for your actions.

Auberon Waugh *Spectator* 14 July 1984

41 The yellow cab shouldered its way through the streets of New York, a caged van taking this mad dog home.

Martin Amis *Money* (publ. 1984), p. 49 (1985 Penguin edn). John Self, 'hero' of the novel, is inside.

42 My Other Car's Also a Volvo.

Peter Freedman Idea for a dull car sticker. Peter Freedman used it in his book *Glad to Be Grey (Or My Other Car's Also a Volvo)* (1985).

43 I have just seen a white van, thickly coated with dirt, on whose side some passing wit has written, 'Also available in white'.

Anon. Graffito quoted by John Grigg in the *Spectator* 25 April 1987, collected in *The Wit of the Spectator* ed. by Christopher Howse (1989)

44 At Holsted an elderly Dane/ Caught his beard in a bicycle chain./ It's hoped if it grows/ Till it reaches his toes,/ He'll be able to cycle again.

Anon. Quoted in a letter to *The Times* following a news report about a man from Holsted getting his beard caught in a bicycle chain. The correspondent, N. R. Davies, said it was a strange coincidence since this rhyme 'was very popular . . . when I was there in [18]92'. Collected in *The Last Cuckoo: The Very Best Letters to The Times since 1900* ed. Kenneth Gregory (1987).

45 Readers under thirty-five may not know what a trolley [bus] looked like. They were electric buses powered by overhead lines, like trams. They were swift, roomy and gave off no fumes, so London Transport got rid of them.

Michael Green *Nobody Hurt in Small Earthquake*, ch. 13 (1990)

46 How could a car be named after a railway station nobody ever got out at – Vauxhall?

Robert Robinson *Prescriptions of a Pox Doctor's Clerk*, 'A Car Called Towser' (1990)

47 **TAXI DRIVER: Where to, bud?**
   JILTED LOVER: Drive off a cliff, I'm committing suicide.

Anon. *And I Quote*, 'Passion', ed. Ashton Applewhite and others (1992)

48 A cousin of mine who was a casualty surgeon in Manhattan tells me that he and his colleagues had a one-word nickname for bikers: Donors. Rather chilling.

Stephen Fry *Paperweight*, 'Bikes, Leather and Aftershave' (1992)

49 Right now Alan's car was charging like a runaway vibrator, towards the very crotch of the flyover.

Will Self *Cock and Bull*, 'Bull', Ch. 4 (1992)

50 We always take the bus to the terminus so you don't have to think.

Gilbert and George Quoted in the London *Evening Standard* 13 May 1993. The speaker is George.

51 Hey – your back wheel's going round!

Anon. Remark made by satirical pedestrians to cyclists. Quoted in *The Cassell Dictionary of Catchphrases* ed. Nigel Rees (1995)

52 'Riding a bike is not necessarily a power move,' said Mr Eccles.

Candace Bushnell *Sex and the City*, ch. 9 (1996)

53 Always put 'pay and display' parking tickets upside down in the centre of your windscreen in the hope that the parking warden will crick his neck trying to read it.

Viz Viz – *The Full Toss (A Corking Compilation of Issues 70 to 75)*, 'Top Tips' (1997)

54 Take time when reading a map: When your partner is driving along

a motorway, wait until the car has just passed the correct exit before stating firmly, 'That was the right one.'

Craig Brown *The Little Book of Chaos* (1998). In the Author's Note, Brown describes himself as someone who 'is careful never to drive anywhere without leaving his right indicator flashing'.

55 I'll tell you what seems to cause a lot of accidents . . . People leaving flowers by the side of the road.

Milton Jones Used in his stage act *c*.1998. It should be mentioned that Jones delivers all his lines in the persona of a dazed halfwit.

56 And how many young people are aware of what happened before the moving bicycle? We are now so used to cycling from A to B that it is hard to imagine the time when bicycles – then known as 'exercise bikes' – were fixed to the ground, often in windowless cells known as health clubs.

Craig Brown *This Is Craig Brown*, 'A Century of Progress' (2003)

57 A Range Rover is like a country cottage on wheels.

Jonathan Glancey *On Inventing the Century* (TV programme, 2003)

58 My dad taught me how to ride a bike by chasing after me with an axe and shouting, 'Come here you bastard!'

Boothby Graffoe Boothby Graffoe in *Boothby Graffoe – In No Particular Order* (Radio 4 series, 2003)

59 Oddly enough, all the bad drivers I have known died peacefully in their beds.

Paul Johnson *The Quotable Spectator* (2004)

By Rail

1 Every fresh accident on the railroads is an advantage and leads to an improvement. What we want is an overturn that would kill a bishop, or at least a dean. This mode of conveyance would then become perfect.

Sydney Smith Letter of September 1842 to Lord Murray. Quoted in *Twelve Miles from a Lemon: Selected Writings of Sydney Smith*, ch. 2, compiled by Norman Taylor and Alan Hankinson (1996).

2 A ticket collector enquired of a woman: 'Is this your boy?' The lady nodded assent. Looking from the boy to the ticket offered him . . . the collector exclaimed, 'He's too big for a half ticket.' Maternal instincts arose as the woman bristled, 'Oh is he? Well, perhaps he is now, but he wasn't when he started. The train is ever so much behind time, and he's a growing lad.'

Anon. Quoted in *Railway Tickets, Timetables and Handbills* by Maurice I. Bray, ch. 2 (1986). The setting for this purported exchange is the Midland Railway, which dates the story between 1844 and 1923.

3 There was even railway time observed in clocks, as if the sun itself had given in.

Charles Dickens *Dombey and Son*, ch. 15 (1847–8). Later in the same passage Dickens notes: 'The very houses seemed disposed to pack up and take trips.'

4 I am the boy at what is called the Refreshment Room at Mugby Junction, and what's proudest boast is that it never yet refreshed a mortal being.

Charles Dickens *Mugby Junction*, 'The Boy at Mugby', in *All the Year Round* magazine, Christmas number, 1866

5 I thunder down to work each morn/ And some historic shrine/ Must have its matchless fabric torn/ To get me there at nine/ And when I gather up my traps/ As sundown sets me free/ A nation's monuments collapse/ To take me home to tea.

Anon. *Punch* poem marking the opening for public service of the Metropolitan Line of what became the London Underground, 10 January 1863, and reflecting unease at the notion of trains going under ground. Quoted in *The Circle Line*, 'Early Days', by Desmond F. Croome (2003).

6 We are often told in our news-papers that England is disgraced by this and by that; by the wretched-ness of our army, by the unfitness of our navy, by the irrationality of our laws, by the immobility of our prejudices, and what not; but the real disgrace of England is the rail-way sandwich.

Anthony Trollope *He Knew He Was Right*, ch. 37 (1869)

7 I cannot read in a railroad, and the human voice is distressing to me amid the whirl and the whistling, and the wild panting of the loosened megatheria who drag us.

Benjamin Disraeli Theodora in *Lothair*, ch. 26 (1870)

8 The idiot who, in railway car-riages,/ Scribbles on window-panes,/ We only suffer/ To ride on a buffer/ In Parliamentary trains.

W. S. Gilbert The Mikado, on how he would make the punishment fit the crime, in *The Mikado*, act 2 (1885)

9 So we went to the high-level plat-form and saw the engine driver, and asked him if he was going to Kingston. He said he couldn't say for certain of course, but he rather thought he was.

Jerome K. Jerome *Three Men in a Boat*, ch. 5 (1889)

10 Come, dear – we have already missed five, if not six, trains. To miss any more might expose us to comment on the platform.

Oscar Wilde Lady Bracknell in *The Impor-tance of Being Earnest*, act 4 (1895)

11 [Of railway termini] They are our gates to the glorious and the unknown. Through them we pass out into adventure and sunshine, to them, alas! we return.

E. M. Forster *Howards End*, ch. 2 (1907). Forster adds: 'In Paddington all Cornwall is latent and the remoter west; down the inclines of Liverpool Street lie fenlands and the illimitable Broads; Scotland is through the pylons of Euston; Wessex behind the poised chaos of Waterloo.'

12 No, take your books of mere poetry and prose, let me read a time-table with tears of pride.

G. K. Chesterton Syme, a self-declared 'poet of law, a poet of order', who believes that the 'Underground Railway' is 'the most poeti-cal thing in the world'. *The Man Who Was Thursday: A Nightmare*, ch. 1 (1908).

13 BARBARA: You think he missed the train on purpose?
MRS BONE: To be quite candid, I think he missed it by appointment.

Ben Travers *A Cuckoo in the Nest*, act 1, sc. 1 (1926)

14 The lamp-and-mop room at the station was a dark and sinister apartment, smelling strongly of oil and porters.

P. G. Wodehouse *Meet Mr Mulliner*, 'The Truth about George' (1927)

15 'Excuse me miss,' said a traveller to the fair custodian of the refresh-ment room, 'but this cup of coffee has a distinct taste of cocoa.' 'I'm very sorry sir,' replied the waitress sweetly, 'I must have given you tea.'

John Aye *Humour on the Rail*, ch. 13 (1931). Also quoted: 'Traveller: "Are these sand-wiches fresh?" Waitress: "I don't know, I've only been working here a fortnight." '

16 DR KIRBY: Sunday tomorrow. Only one train to London. The four-twenty. And a brute.
STELLA: That's nothing. We're used to brutal Sunday trains. They're almost the only kind we know.

J. B. Priestley *Eden End*, act 3, sc. 2 (1934)

17 The next train's gone.

Will Hay *Oh Mr Porter* (film, 1937, directed by Marcel Varnel, written by various). Response of out-of-his-depth rural stationmaster (Will Hay) to passenger's query.

18 The two-forty-five express – Pad-dington to Market Blandings, first stop Oxford – stood at its platform with that air of well-bred reserve which is characteristic of Pad-dington trains.

P. G. Wodehouse *Uncle Fred in the Spring-time*, ch. 8 (1939). In the same chapter Wodehouse observes that, whereas Paddington strikes a note of 'refined calm', Waterloo is all hustle and bustle, 'and the society tends to be mixed'.

19 [Of 'arrival-angst'] **Sensations worse at arriving in the evening than in the morning, and much worse at Victoria and Waterloo, than at Paddington.**

Cyril Connolly *The Unquiet Grave*, pt. 1, 'Ecce Gubernator' (1944)

20 [On being asked why he always travelled third class] **Because there's no fourth class.**

George Santayana Quoted in *Living Biographies of the Great Philosophers* by H. Thomas (1946)

21 **My train was a rapide and God it was slow . . .**

Evelyn Waugh Letter to Nancy Mitford of 15 April 1950, collected in *The Letters of Evelyn Waugh* ed. Mark Amory (1980). Waugh was in Italy; the train stopped 'at every station except two between Modena and Rome'.

22 **There are two kinds of men on tubes. Those who blow their noses and then examine the results in a handkerchief, and those who blow their noses without exhibiting any such curiosity, and simply replace the handkerchief in the pocket.**

Kenneth Williams Entry for 24 January 1953, *The Kenneth Williams Diaries* ed. R. Davies (1993), collected in *The Assassin's Cloak* ed. Irene and Alan Taylor (2000). Williams noted that he himself 'came under the first category'.

23 **The only way to be sure of catching a train is to miss the one before.**

G. K. Chesterton Quoted in *Vacances à tous prix* (Holidays at All Prices) 'Le Supplice de l'heure', by Pierre Daninos (1958)

24 **Everyone is well-behaved on a German train. The Travel-guests are forbidden in a Notsmoker to smoke, in the Wagon out to spit, their Boots on the Bolsters to place, unprotected hatpins to carry, out to lean, the Door before the train halts to open.**

C. Hamilton Ellis *Rapidly Round the Bend*, 'Foreign Railways' (1959)

25 **As we have shown, most of the things that go to make up a railway had been invented by the time of George IV, namely, rails, wheels, locomotives, coaches, wagons and overcrowding.**

C. Hamilton Ellis Ibid., 'Aftermath, Mania, and the Battle of the Gooches' (1959)

26 **'I'm waiting for the train that was due here at sixteen hundred, the time is now nineteen hundred hours, you know what that means?'/ 'Nineteen hundred hours? No, sorry, my watch only goes up to twelve.'**

Spike Milligan Major Stokes to Puckoon stationmaster Donald Feeley in *Puckoon*, ch. 5 (1963)

27 **I sought trains; I found passengers.**

Paul Theroux *The Great Railway Bazaar*, ch. 1 (1975). The book was commended by Graham Greene: 'In the fine old tradition of purposeless travel for fun and adventure . . .'

28 **Q: What goes a hundred miles an hour on the railway lines, and is yellow and white? A: A railwayman's egg sandwich.**

Anon. *The Crack-a-Joke Book*, 'Nosh-Up', ed. Jane Nissen (1978)

29 **Returns, day: Cheaper, paradoxically, than a single fare.**

Henry Root *Henry Root's World of Knowledge* (1982)

30 **Why do 'They' retain absurd distinctions between First and Second Class? Far more helpful if 'They' divided us into, say, talkers and non-talkers, or farters and non-farters.**

Anon. *Notes from Overground: A Commuter's Notebook*, 'Loose Coupling 10', by Tiresias (1984). The author, Tiresias, is described in the book as 'a former commuter and civil servant, currently compiling a modern Greek dictionary'.

31 **Muddled old gentleman to railway porter: 'Tell me, porter, does this train clap at Stopham Junction?'**

Arthur Marshall Quoted in *Life's Rich Pageant*, sc. 3, by Arthur Marshall (1984). Marshall describes this as 'a dear old *Punch* joke of my childhood'.

32 **I wish I could work out how to use the [New York] subway. I've tried. No matter how hard I concentrate I always end up clambering out of a manhole in Duke Ellington Boulevard with a dustbin lid on my head.**

Martin Amis *Money* (publ. 1984), p. 105 (1985 Penguin edn)

33 **The railway station had changed since he had last had call to use it. In the meantime its soot-coated, rentboy-haunted vault of tarry girders and toilet glass had become a flowing atrium of boutiques and croissant stalls and limitless cappuccino.**

Martin Amis *The Information*, pt 2 (1985)

34 **I'm not a fan of the modern railway system. I strongly object to paying twenty-seven pounds fifty to walk the length of the train with a sausage in a plastic box.**

Victoria Wood 'Kitty: One', *Victoria Wood as Seen on TV* (TV series, 1985), collected in *Up to You, Porky – The Victoria Wood Sketch Book* (1985)

35 **A woman travelling in a railway compartment requests a light from a fellow passenger. This passenger lays aside his detective story and proffers his lighter. She thanks him politely; and neither gives the matter another thought. A year later they are married in a small parish church a hundred miles away, still none the wiser.**

Gilbert Adair *The Holy Innocents*, 'First Part' (1988)

36 **Buffet cars: These used to stay open until the train had finished its journey; now they shut in time for the staff to tidy up in slow tempo (and block the corridor with their rubbish) and hit the platform at Paddington or Penzance a couple of strides ahead of you and me.**

Kingsley Amis *Spectator* 15 October 1988, collected in *The Wit of the Spectator* ed. Christopher Howse (1989)

37 **Bombastic brash and over-prone/ To shouting on his mobile phone/ He's cancelling his three-o-clock/ Or booking tickets for Bangkok/ So fellow travellers have no choice/ But hear his self-important voice:/ 'I've godda window, Tuesday. Noon./ Yup. Abso-lootly. Speaktcha soon.'**

Martin Newell From 'Adlestrop Retrieved', *Independent* 10 April 1996. The poem was inspired by the fact that Great Western Railways had made certain carriages mobile-phone-free zones.

38 **On the tube journey home from Stratford East, Jeffrey and I enjoyed asking commuting cockneys if they would kindly direct us to the buffet car.**

Barry Humphries *More Please*, 'Spiked' (1997). 'Jeffrey' is Jeffrey Bernard. A story circulating amongst London Underground staff in the 1980s had it that a Conservative junior transport minister had revealed his lack of experience of public transport by asking to be shown to the buffet car on a tube train.

39 **I believe that trainspotting was just one symptom of an underlying problem which, I fear, is with one to stay. Anoraxia, you might call it.**

Chris Donald *The Oldie* magazine February 2003. He has just described how he labels the backs of his holiday snaps with seven-digit numbers.

40 **Why can the French do it? I was brought up to believe the French can't do anything. But they can run a railway.**

David Hare Passenger 1 in *The Permanent Way*, Prologue (2003)

41 **For years, I thought that *in loco parentis* meant 'my dad's an engine driver'.**

Anon. Quoted by Gyles Brandreth on *Just a Minute* (BBC radio series), 26 January 2004

By Air

1 Take the cylinders out of my kidneys,/ The connecting-rod out of my brain,/ Take the cam-shaft out of my backbone,/ And assemble the engine again.

Anon. 'The Dying Airman', collected in *The Oxford Book of Light Verse* ed. W. H. Auden (1938). The last words of the eponymous hero.

2 Consider the auk;/ Becoming extinct because he forgot how to fly, and/ could only walk./ Consider man, who may well become extinct/ Because he forgot how to walk and learned how to fly/ before he thinked.

Ogden Nash *The Private Dining Room and Other Verses*, 'A Caution to Everybody' (1952)

3 I wish I could write well enough to write about aircraft.

Ernest Hemingway Letter of 3 July 1956 to Harvey Breit, collected in *Ernest Hemingway: Selected Letters 1917–1961* ed. Carlos Baker (1981). He adds: 'Faulkner did it very well in *Pylon* [1935].'

4 NEDDIE SEAGOON: You're back early.
  HENRY CRUN: Yes, we brought the train back on the aeroplane.

Spike Milligan *The Goon Show*, 'The Mysterious Punch-up-the-Conker', first broadcast 7 February 1957

5 I love the dash across the tarmac in the rain, those overnight bags they give you . . . I love those little salt and pepper things you never use . . . it's the flying I can't stand.

Eric Morecambe and Ernie Wise Their first major TV series, *Two of a Kind*, first broadcast 1962, collected in *Two of a Kind*, (video, 1992)

6 Have you noticed the way the wings keep *wagging*? . . . Solid steel. Thick as a bank safe. Flexing like tree branches. It's not natural.

Tom Stoppard Anderson on an aeroplane in *Professional Foul* (TV play, 1977)

7 [Of hang-gliding] Seems a novel enough way to commit suicide.

Viv Stanshall Sir Henry in *Sir Henry at Rawlinson End* (LP, 1978)

8 I get airsick just licking an airmail stamp.

Eric Morecambe and Ernie Wise *The Morecambe and Wise Jokebook*, skit 3 (1979)

9 By the way, is there anybody on board who knows how to fly a plane?

Anon. In-flight announcement made by flight attendant Elaine (Julie Hagerty) in *Airplane!* (film, 1980, directed by Jim Abrahams, screenplay by Jim Abrahams, David Zucker, Jerry Zucker)

10 It can hardly be a coincidence that no language on Earth has ever produced the expression 'as pretty as an airport'.

Douglas Adams *The Long Dark Tea-Time of the Soul*, ch. 1 (1988). The opening line of the book.

11 There is . . . a deliriously vulgar 'caviare bar' at Heathrow Terminal Four, just to the right of the miniature Harrods.

John Lanchester *The Debt to Pleasure*, 'Winter', 'A Winter Menu' (1996)

12 I always sit on the tail end of a plane, because you never hear of a plane backing into a mountain.

Tommy Cooper *The Very Best of Tommy Cooper*, vol. 1 (cassette, 1999)

13 Flying? I've been to almost as many places as my luggage!

Bob Hope Quoted in *The Penguin Dictionary of Modern Humorous Quotations* ed. Fred Metcalf (2nd edn 2001)

14 You know what we need? What we need is an airport.

Martin Amis Captain John Macmanaman, pilot of a failing jet, in *Yellow Dog*, pt 2, ch. 8, sect. 6 (2003)

15 Airline pilots: Encourage your passengers to 'get up and move about a bit' while doing 500mph, 30,000 feet above an ocean, but indignantly insist they 'remain seated with their seatbelts fastened' as you

dawdle the three miles across the tarmac to the arrival gate at 5mph.

Viz 'Top Tips', *Viz* comic, May 2003

16 **But what I want to know is: why don't they make the whole aeroplane out of what the black box recorder's made of?**

Anon. Joke overheard in central London, 2003

17 [Of air hostesses] **They're getting more and more like your mum. One said to me: 'Finish your dinner. There are people starving on Air India.'**

Bob Monkhouse *Sun* 30 December 2003

9

The Natural World

Nature
Man and Nature

Nature
Types of Animals

1 **I am a brother to dragons, and a companion to owls.**
Job 30:29, the Bible, Authorized Version, 1611

2 **A living dog is better than a dead lion.**
Ecclesiastes 9:4, ibid.

3 **Exit, pursued by a bear.**
William Shakespeare Stage direction, *The Winter's Tale*, act 3, sc. 3 (1611)

4 **The man recovered of the bite,/ The dog it was that died.**
Oliver Goldsmith 'Elegy on the Death of a Mad Dog' (1766). Tom Stoppard used this as the title of a radio play of 1982, which begins with a spy jumping off Chelsea Bridge on to a barge and killing a dog.

5 **Sure never were seen two such beautiful ponies;/ Other horses are clowns, but these macaronies:/ To give them this title I am sure can't be wrong./ Their legs are slim, and their tails are long.**
Richard Brinsley Sheridan Poem composed and declaimed by Sir Benjamin Backbite in *The School for Scandal*, act 2, sc. 2 (1777)

6 **Memorandum. In shaving my face this morning I happened to cut one of my moles which bled much, and happening also to kill a small moth that was flying about, I applied it to my mole and it instantly stopped the bleeding.**
James Woodforde Entry for 23 March 1778, *The Diary of a Country Parson*, collected in *The Assassin's Cloak* (2000), ed. Irene and Alan Taylor

7 **Wee, sleekit, cow'rin, tim'rous beastie,/ O what a panic's in thy breastie!/ Thou need na start awa sae hasty,/ Wi' bickering brattle!/ I wad be laith to rin an' chase thee,/ Wi' murd'ring pattle!**
Robert Burns 'To a Mouse' (1786)

8 **He was a vicious man, but very**

kind to me. If you call a dog HER-
VEY I shall love him.

Samuel Johnson *The Life of Samuel Johnson*
by James Boswell, vol. 1, p. 106 (1791); in G. B.
Hill's edition of 1887, rev. L. F. Powell (1934).
Harry Hervey was an army officer who
sometimes invited Johnson to his London
house.

9 The uncommunicating muteness of
fishes.

Charles Lamb *The Essays of Elia*, 'A Quakers'
Meeting' (1823)

10 The mountain sheep are sweeter,/
But the valley sheep are fatter;/ We
therefore deemed it meeter/ To
carry off the latter.

Thomas Love Peacock *The Misfortunes of
Elphin*, ch. 11, 'The War-Song of Dinas Vawr'
(1829)

11 'Extremes meet', as the whiting said
with its tail in its mouth.

Thomas Hood *Comic Annual*, 'The Doves and
the Crows' (1839)

12 Anything like the sound of a rat/
Makes my heart go pit-a-pat!

Robert Browning *The Pied Piper of Hamelin*,
st. 4 (1845)

13 Remember that the most beautiful
things in the world are the most
useless, peacocks and lilies for
instance.

John Ruskin *The Stones of Venice*, vol. 1, ch. 2,
sect. 17 (1851)

14 No human being, however great, or
powerful, was ever so free as a fish.

John Ruskin *The Two Paths*, Lecture 5 (1859)

15 I don't see no p'ints about that frog
that's better 'n any other frog.

Mark Twain 'A feller' in 'The Notorious Jumping Frog of Calaveras County' (1867), collected in *Mark Twain's Library of Humour*
(1888). The book is prefaced by a note from
Twain: 'The selections in this book which are
from my own works were made by my two
assistant compilers, not by me. This is why
there are not more.' The assistants are not
named.

16 [Of the bear] When he wishes to
attack anybody he rises on his hind
legs, as men do in the House of
Commons.

Leigh Hunt *Table Talk*, 'Bears and Their Hunters' (1882)

17 When I meet a dog of my acquaintance, I slap his head, call him oppro-
brious epithets, and roll him over
on his back; and there he lies, gap-
ing at me, and doesn't mind a bit./
Fancy carrying on like that with a
cat! Why, she would never speak to
you again as long as you lived.

Jerome K. Jerome *The Idle Thoughts of an
Idle Fellow*, 'On Vanity and Vanities' (1889)

18 Oh dear, no! lions are only good for
one season. As soon as their manes
are cut, they are the dullest creatures going.

Oscar Wilde *Lord Arthur Savile's Crime and
Other Stories*, 'Lord Arthur Savile's Crime',
ch. 6 (1891). Lady Windermere is speaking.

19 'I wish I owned half that dog.'/
'Why?' somebody asked./ 'Because I
would kill my half.'

Mark Twain *The Tragedy of Pudd'nhead Wilson*, ch. 1 (1894). The one who wants to kill
the dog is David Wilson, who is christened
'Pudd'nhead' by the citizens of Dawson's
Landing on account of this remark.

20 When people call this beast to
mind,/ They marvel more and
more/ At such a little tail behind,/
So large a trunk before.

Hilaire Belloc 'The Elephant', *The Bad Child's
Book of Beasts* (1896)

21 A wonderful bird is the pelican,/
His bill will hold more than his
belican.

Dixon Lanier Merritt 'The Pelican' (1910). It is
often thought that Ogden Nash wrote this.

22 Anything I may have learned at
school or in after life about how to
remove a large ox from a small
garden seems to have escaped from
my memory now.

Saki *Beasts and Super Beasts*, 'The Stalled Ox'
(1914). The speaker is Theophil Ashley.

23 One of Jean Cocteau's jokes. Talking
of a chameleon, he said: 'Its master

put it down on a tartan rug and it died of over-exertion.'

Liane de Pougy Diary entry for 16 July 1919, *My Blue Notebooks* (1986)

24 The hyena is said to laugh: but it is rather in the way in which the M.P. is said to utter 'an ironical cheer'.

G. K. Chesterton *The Uses of Diversity*, 'On Seriousness' (1920)

25 The rabbit has a charming face:/ Its private life is a disgrace./ I really dare not name to you/ The awful things that rabbits do.

Anon. 'The Rabbit', *The Week-End Book* ed. John Gross and others (1925)

26 Standing on his head was the title given to the performance by Jumble's owner. In reality it consisted of rubbing the top of his head on the ground, but William always called it 'Jumble standing on his head', and was inordinately proud of it.

Richmal Crompton *William the Conqueror*, ch. 4, 'William Leads a Better Life' (1926). Jumble is William's dog.

27 If there's a buzzing noise, somebody's making a buzzing noise, and the only reason for making a buzzing noise that *I* know of is because you're a bee.

A. A. Milne *Winnie-the-Pooh*, ch. 1 (1926)

28 I know two things about the horse/ And one of them is rather coarse.

Maude Royden *Weekend Book*, p. 231 (1928)

29 People who count their chickens before they are hatched act very wisely; because chickens run about so absurdly afterwards that it is impossible to count them accurately.

Oscar Wilde Quoted in *Livres sans nom* (Books without a Name; 1930), collected in *Geoffrey Madan's Notebooks* ed. J. A. Gere and John Sparrow (1981). Madan describes this remark as 'unpublished'.

30 A station master completing the form in connection with a cow that had been killed on the line wrote opposite the query, 'Disposition of the carcase', the description, 'Kind and gentle'.

Anon. *Humour on the Rail*, ch. 9, ed. John Aye (1931)

31 Nobody and no animal and no other bird can play a scene so far down as a pigeon can.

James Thurber *The Middle-Aged Man on the Flying Trapeze*, 'There's an Owl in My Room' (1935)

32 Newts need elbow room.

P. G. Wodehouse Gussie Fink-Nottle explaining in *The Code of the Woosters*, ch. 11 (1938), why he put newts into a bathtub

33 The Duke of Dunstable was a nobleman of proud and haughty spirit, swift to resent affronts and institute reprisals – the last person in the world, in short, from whom one could hope to withhold pigs with impunity.

P. G. Wodehouse *Uncle Fred in the Springtime*, 'What This Story Is About' (1939)

34 Why did the chicken cross the road? For some fowl reason.

Max Miller Joke recorded in November 1940, reissued in *Max Miller, the Cheeky Chappie – All His Live Shows in the Late 1930s, Early 40s* (CD, 2000)

35 The song of canaries/ Never varies,/ And when they're moulting/ They're pretty revolting.

Ogden Nash *The Face Is Familiar*, 'The Canary' (1940)

36 If ants are so busy, why do they attend so many picnics?

W. C. Fields Radio broadcast, 1942, with the ventriloquist Edgar Bergen and his dummy Charlie McCarthy. Fields had it in for all animals, especially dogs.

37 The very nastiest grimace/ You make upon the sly,/ Is *choice* beside the hippo's face.

Mervyn Peake *Five Rhymes without Reason*, 'The Hippo's Face' (1944)

38 Giraffes – a People/ Who live between the earth and skies,/ Each in his lone religious steeple,/ Keeping a light-house with his eyes.

Roy Campbell 'Dreaming Spires' (1946)

39 I had been stalking the bluebottle fly for five minutes waiting for him to sit down. He didn't want to sit down. He just wanted to do wing-overs and sing the prologue to Pagliacci.

Raymond Chandler *The Little Sister*, ch. 1 (1949)

40 The Pekinese dog was hurling abuse in Chinese.

P. G. Wodehouse *Nothing Serious*, 'Birth of a Salesman' (1950). In *The Code of the Woosters* (1938), Wodehouse had written: 'The Aberdeen terrier gave me an unpleasant look and said something under its breath in Gaelic.'

41 The Creator, if He exists, has a special preference for beetles.

J. B. S. Haldane Lecture of 7 April 1951 quoted in the *Journal of the British Interplanetary Society* (1951), vol. 10, p. 156. Haldane had noted that there are 400,000 species of beetles but only 8,000 species of animals.

42 I don't even *like* old cars. I mean they don't even interest me. I'd rather have a goddam horse. A horse is at least *human*, for God's sake.

J. D. Salinger Narrator (Holden Caulfield) in *The Catcher in the Rye*, ch. 17 (1951)

43 [Of the duck-billed platypus] I like its independent attitude./ Let no one call it a duck-billed platitude.

Ogden Nash *The Private Dining Room and Other Verses*, 'The Platypus' (1952)

44 There is not much about the hamster/ To stimulate the epigramster./ The essence of his simple story,/ He populates the laboratory.

Ogden Nash Ibid., 'The Hamster'

45 A door is what a dog is perpetually on the wrong side of.

Ogden Nash 'A Dog's Best Friend is His Illiteracy' (1953)

46 I'm a g-nu, I'm a g-nu,/ The g-nicest work of nature in the zoo!

Michael Flanders and Donald Swann Song in *At the Drop of a Hat* (LP, 1957). As Swann explains, his Kensington driveway was often blocked by 'a big flashy car . . . with teeth, you know'. Its registration plate was GNU.

47 OATES: As you know, the snail is a slow mover – sluggish, you might call him.
    TRANTER: Extremely sluggish.
    OATES: The slug, on the other hand, is a speedy creature by comparison.

Peter Cook The President of the Society for the Prohibition of Snail Racing is talking to Lady Tranter, a possible benefactor to the cause. *Pieces of Eight*, Apollo Theatre, London, 1959.

48 And here is *my* bit of swagger – has your robin ever sat on your mowing-machine *as you mowed*?

George Lyttelton Letter to Rupert Hart-Davis, of 15 April 1959, collected in *The Lyttelton–Hart-Davis Letters*, vols 3 and 4, *1958–59*, ed. Rupert Hart-Davis (1981)

49 Daylong this tomcat lies stretched flat/ As an old rough mat, no mouth and no eyes,/ Continual wars and wives are what/ Have tattered his ears and battered his head.

Ted Hughes 'Esther's Tomcat' (1960)

50 This parrot is no more! It has ceased to be! It's expired and gone to meet its maker! This is a late parrot! It's a stiff! . . . *This is an ex-parrot!*

Monty Python team John Cleese in *Monty Python's Flying Circus* (1st series, episode 8, first broadcast 7 December 1969). Cleese plays an exasperated customer in search of a refund for the cost of a parrot that has pretty obviously died. Michael Palin, as the pet shop owner, insists against all the evidence (in particular, the presence of the corpse) that the parrot – a 'Norwegian Blue' – is still alive.

51 You know, the duck's life is not all hearts and flowers. He's got his worries, too. He's got fleas and lice and diseases of the body. Delusions. Wing problems. Sexual difficulties. Many things.

David Mamet George in *Duck Variations*, 'Second Variation' (1972)

52 Suddenly the giant hound pauses in

its headlong flight, spreads its back legs and voids a rancid coil! Another pint of worms for the communal sewer. How much more shit can Britain take before it buckles under the strain and goes down like Atlantis?

Clive James *Observer* 6 July 1975

53 That indefatigable and unsavoury engine of pollution, the dog.

John Sparrow *The Times* 30 September 1975

54 A friend of mine once owned a dog of super intelligence that could understand almost every word said to it, and could perform tricks of amazing complexity. In fact his 'roll over and play dead' was so realistic that when the animal eventually expired they had to get a second opinion before he could be buried.

Ronnie Corbett *Ronnie Corbett's Small Man's Guide*, 'The Small Man and Pets' (1976)

55 CLOUSEAU: Does your dog bite?
HOTEL CLERK: No.
CLOUSEAU: (bending down to pet dog) Nice doggie./ (The dog bites him) I thought you said your dog did not bite!
HOTEL CLERK: That is not my dog.

Blake Edwards and Frank Waldman Peter Sellers as Inspector Clouseau in *The Pink Panther Strikes Again* (film, 1976, directed by Frank Waldman and Blake Edwards, screenplay by Blake Edwards and Frank Waldman)

56 Q: On which side does a chicken have most feathers? A: The outside.

Anon. *The Crack-a-Joke Book*, 'Dumb Clucks', ed. Jane Nissen (1978)

57 Outside, a dog chases its tail/ like a miniature railway . . .

Craig Raine 'Home for the Elderly', *The Onion, Memory* (1978)

58 Herring and ling!/ O herring and ling!/ Of all the fish in the sea/ Is herring the king.

Anon. First verse of 'The Red Herring', collected in *The Faber Book of Nonsense Verse*, ed. Geoffrey Grigson (1979). Grigson notes: 'Folklorists make rather a meal of it.'

59 In town, the Great Dane/ Is kept by the insane.

E. B. White 'Fashions in Dogs', collected in *Poems and Sketches of E. B. White* (1981)

60 Did you know that owls never mate in the rain because it's too wet to woo?

Les Dawson *The Malady Lingers On*, 'The Malady Lingers On . . .' (1982)

61 It is not until you see sheep against snow that you realize that they are, in fact, grey.

Miles Kington *Moreover*, 'Nature Notes' (1982)

62 Guinea-pig: If you hold a guinea-pig upside down by its tail its eyes will fall out.

Henry Root *Henry Root's World of Knowledge* (1982)

63 HOGBIN: I'm *terribly* sorry! I sat on your parrot.
PAMELA: It's not as bad as it looks, he was already dead.

Tom Stoppard *The Dog It Was That Died* (radio play, 1982)

64 A tortoise is, I suppose, a Jewish pet. It knows its place. Out on the lawn. It doesn't bark. It doesn't tear the Dralon.

Maureen Lipman *How Was It for You?*, 'Zuckerman: A Life' (1985)

65 A pelican said to his mate: 'That's a good sort of fish you've caught there.' 'Yes. It fits the bill nicely.'

Anon. Quoted in *The World's Best Fishing Jokes* ed. John Gurney (1987)

66 Cockroaches have been given a bad rap. They don't bite, smell, or get into your booze. Would that all house guests were as well behaved.

P. J. O'Rourke *The Bachelor Home Companion*, ch. 10 (1987)

67 If Noah had been very wise, he would have swatted those two flies.

Anon. *Bishop's Brew (An Anthology of Clerical Humour)*, ch. 4, ed. Ronald Brown (1989)

68 Why do dogs lick their private parts? Because they can.

Anon. *And I Quote*, 'Pets', ed. Ashton Applewhite and others (1992)

69 I was in love with a female man-
drill before I met my wife . . . Very
high style with a rainbow across
the nose. Beautiful.

Captain Beefheart Quoted on the sleeve of
*A Carrot Is as Close as a Rabbit Gets to a Dia-
mond* (CD, 1993)

70 Possibly the most dangerous
element of the stay, as I recall it,
were the bears, because strictly
speaking they're not vegetarians.

Peter Cook As Sir Arthur Streeb-Greebling,
remembering being abandoned by his father
in forests near Toronto, *Why Bother?* (radio
series, 1994). Quoted in *Tragically I Was an
Only Twin: The Complete Peter Cook* ed. William Cook (2002).

71 If you were a pigeon you could fuck
forty times a day. It's something to
bear in mind when filling out the
form for reincarnation.

A. A. Gill *Rising Sap*, ch. 1 (1996)

72 Who can say whether the man is
playing with the cat or the cat is
playing with the man, eh?

Simon Gray Brownlow in *The Late Middle
Classes*, act 1, sc. 2 (1999)

73 If you cannot escape, your only
option is to run alongside the stam-
pede to avoid getting trampled.
Bulls are not like horses, and will
not avoid you if you lie down – so
keep moving.

Joshua Piven and David Borgenicht *The
Worst-Case Scenario Survival Handbook*, 'How
to Deal with a Charging Bull' (1999)

74 I once heard a koala keeper at
London Zoo say, 'I have a soft spot
for marsupials. Nothing that stupid
should be allowed to survive on the
planet. But they come from Australia.'

Nancy Banks-Smith *Guardian* 21 September
2000

75 Cats are intended to teach us that
not everything in nature has a
purpose.

Garrison Keillor Quoted in *The Penguin Dictionary of Modern Humorous Quotations* ed.
Fred Metcalf (2nd edn 2001)

76 'What exact type of rhinoceros are
we discussing here?', he asked./
. . . 'Dunno . . . I can only tell you
that it's one of the big, grey type,
you know, with the horn.'

Douglas Adams *The Salmon of Doubt*, 'The
Salmon of Doubt', ch. 11 (2002)

77 A camel can go without a drink for
eight days. But who wants to be a
camel?

Anon. Inscription on a sign in the Ship Inn,
Dunwich, Suffolk (and probably many
others). Spotted December 2002.

78 Cats: The simple rule is that, like
exclamation marks, more than two
signifies complete nutcase.

Jeff Green *The A–Z of Living Together*, 'Cats'
(2002)

79 Flies he hunted down: the fatter
and hairier they were, the worse he
needed to see them dead. Some
were armoured: they looked like
the attack aircraft of the twenty-
second century.

Martin Amis *Yellow Dog*, pt 1, ch. 5, sect. 1
(2003)

80 Dogs – they're smarter than us.
They never tread in dog muck.

Bob Monkhouse *Sun* 30 December 2003

81 [Of giraffes] They've got really long
necks and they only eat certain
leaves at the top of trees, which is a
stroke of luck, isn't it?

Boothby Graffoe *Boothby Graffoe – In No Particular Order* (radio programme, 4 March
2004)

Vegetation

1 Won't you come into the garden? I
would like my roses to see you.

Richard Brinsley Sheridan Suggested to a
young lady. Attributed.

2 [In Australia] Earth here is so kind,
that just tickle her with a hoe and
she laughs with a harvest.

Douglas Jerrold *The Wit and Opinions of
Douglas Jerrold*, 'A Land of Plenty', ed.
Blanchard Jerrold (1859)

3 A toadstool – that vegetable which springs to full growth in a single night – had torn loose and lifted a mass of pine needles and dirt of twice its own bulk into the air . . . Ten thousand toadstools, with the right purchase, could lift a man, I suppose, but what good would it do?

Mark Twain In a German forest. *A Tramp Abroad*, ch. 12 (1880).

4 The position of the rose among flowers is like that of the dog among animals. It is not so much that both are domesticated as that we have some dim idea that they were always domesticated.

G. K. Chesterton *Alarms and Discursions*, 'The Wrath of the Roses' (1910)

5 I think that I shall never see/ A Poem lovely as a tree . . .

Joyce Kilmer 'Trees', *Trees and Other Poems* (1914). The poem continues: 'Poems are made by fools like me,/ But only God can make a tree.' A remarkably popular poem in America.

6 You stupid woman, if rationality were the criterion for things being allowed to exist, the world would be one gigantic field of soya beans!

Tom Stoppard George to Dotty in *Jumpers*, act 1 (1972)

7 Vegetables are interesting but lack a sense of purpose when accompanied by a good cut of meat.

Fran Lebowitz *Metropolitan Life*, 'Food for Thought' (1978)

8 France is the only country I know where drivers are warned about beetroot on the road: BETTERAVES, I once saw in a red warning triangle, with a picture of a car slipping out of control.

Julian Barnes *Flaubert's Parrot*, ch. 7 (1984)

9 Plants use up too much oxygen.

Mae West Quoted in *The Ultimate Seduction*, 'Mae West' (1984) by Charlotte Chandler. West was explaining why there were no house plants in her apartment.

10 Everything's Coming Up Rhubarb

Keith Waterhouse Subheading of ch. 13, *Bimbo* (1990)

11 One cannot get bored by a bluebell.

David Attenborough *The Times*, 'Quotes of the Week', 22 April 2000

12 No one puts flowers on a flower's grave.

Tom Waits 'Flower's Grave', *Alice* (LP, 2002)

Natural Phenomena

1 All the rivers run into the sea; yet the sea is not full.

Ecclesiastes, 1:7, the Bible, Authorized Version (1611). Written on a bridge in Stockton-on-Tees.

2 Pour some salt water on the floor –/ Ugly I'm sure you'll allow it to be:/ Suppose it's extended a mile or more,/ [That's] very like the Sea.

Lewis Carroll *Phantasmagoria*, 'A Sea Dirge' (1869)

3 BRICK: Well, they say nature hates a vacuum, Big Daddy.

BIG DADDY: That's what they say, but sometimes I think that a vacuum is a hell of a lot better than what nature replaces it with.

Tennessee Williams *Cat on a Hot Tin Roof*, act 2 (1955)

4 The North Wall is a sheer glass-like face of ice broken only by rock, snowfields, ice-pinnacles, crevasses, bergschrunds, ridges, gulleys, scree, chimneys, cracks, slabs, gendarmes, Dames, Anglaises, needles, strata, gneiss and gabbro.

W. E. Bowman The North Wall of Rum Doodle, that is. *The Ascent of Rum Doodle*, ch. 6 (1956).

5 I realized the car wasn't having problems; the *ground* was having problems.

Anon. Said by a driver on the San Francisco–Oakland Bay Bridge during the 1989 earthquake. Quoted in *The Penguin Dictionary of Modern Humorous Quotations* ed. Fred Metcalf (2nd edn 2001)

6 There is one thing, I concede, that

the countryside does very well and that is dew.

Stephen Fry *The Hippopotamus*, ch. 3, pt 3 (1995)

7 [Of the sea] It comes in, it goes out. Anything else and it would be called shilly-shallying.

Alan Bennett Miss Plunkett in *Two in Torquay*, radio play publ. in the *London Review of Books* 10 July 2003

Outer Space

1 You have a foolish saying, that such a one knows no more than the man in the moon: I tell you, the man in the moon knows more than all the men under the sun. Don't the moon see all the world?

George Farquhar Kite in *The Recruiting Officer*, act 4, sc. 3 (1706)

2 There was a man lived in the moon, lived in the moon, lived in the moon,/ There was a man lived in the moon,/ And his name was Aiken Drum.

Anon. Opening lines of 'Aiken Drum'. According to *The Oxford Dictionary of Nursery Rhymes*, a version of this appeared in James Hogg's *Jacobite Relics* (1821).

3 Prometheus is reaching out to the stars with an empty grin on his face.

Arthur Koestler *New York Times* 21 July 1969. Of the first moon landing.

4 Can we actually 'know' the universe? My God, it's hard enough finding your way around in Chinatown.

Woody Allen *Getting Even*, 'My Philosophy' (1971)

5 Of course, to somebody *on* it, the moon is always full.

Tom Stoppard Dotty in *Jumpers*, act 1 (1972)

6 Space isn't remote at all. It's only an hour's drive away if your car could go straight upwards.

Fred Hoyle *Observer* 9 September 1979,

quoted in *Who Said What* ed. John Dalntith and others (1988)

7 If they could put one man on the moon, why couldn't they put them all?

Anon. Quoted in *Women's Wicked Wit* ed. Michelle Lovic (2000)

8 All women hate space.

Martin Amis Karla White, aka Cora Susan, in *Yellow Dog*, pt 3, ch. 9, sect. 3 (2003)

9 Space is like my refrigerator after I get through it – cold and empty.

Matt Groening Cartoon character Homer Simpson, 'interviewed' in *Q* magazine June 2003

10 My advice to anyone has always been to avoid black holes because, once inside, it's extremely hard to climb out and still retain one's ear for music.

Woody Allen *Sunday Telegraph* 4 January 2004. He continued: 'If, by any chance, you do fall all the way through a black hole and emerge from the other side, you'll probably live your entire life over and over but will be too compressed to go out and meet girls.'

Weather

1 He that is warme, thinkes all so.

George Herbert *Outlandish Proverbs*, no. 80 (1640)

2 Walk fast in snow,/ In frost go slow,/ And still as you go,/ Tread in your toe:/ When frost and snow are both together,/ Sit by the fire and spare shoe-leather.

Anon. 'A good proverb the Devonshire people have', quoted by Jonathan Swift in *Journal to Stella*, entry for 21 January 1711, ed. Sir H. Williams (1948)

3 Some are weather-wise and some are otherwise.

Benjamin Franklin *Poor Richard's Almanac* (1758), entry for February 1735

4 The best sun we have is made of Newcastle coal, and I am determined never to reckon upon any other.

Horace Walpole Letter of 15 June 1768 to

George Montague, collected in *The Letters of Horace Walpole* (1766–71), vol. 8, ed. Mrs Paget Toynbee (1904)

5 **What dreadful Hot weather we have! – It keeps one in a continual state of Inelegance.**

Jane Austen Letter to Cassandra Austen of 18 September 1796, collected in *Jane Austen's Letters* ed. Dierdre Le Faye (1995)

6 **I have often observed that if one writes about the Weather, it is generally completely changed before the Letter is read.**

Letter to James-Edward Austen of 9 July 1816, ibid.

7 **The English winter – ending in July./ To recommence in August.**

Lord Byron *Don Juan*, canto 13 (1819–24)

8 **The evening grew more dull every moment, and a melancholy wind sounded through the deserted fields, like a distant giant whistling for his house dog.**

Charles Dickens *The Pickwick Papers*, ch. 2 (1837)

9 **'A pleasant evenin',' said the voice of Mrs Gamp, 'though warm, which, bless you, Mr Chuzzlewit, we must expect when cowcumbers is three for twopence.'**

Charles Dickens *Martin Chuzzlewit*, ch. 51 (1843–4)

10 **Let no man boast himself that he has got through the perils of winter till at least the 7th of May.**

Anthony Trollope *Doctor Thorne*, ch. 47 (1858)

11 **Ninety degrees at four in the morning is not fair.**

Rudyard Kipling Letter to Edmonia Hill, written from Lahore, of 28 May 1888, *The Letters of Rudyard Kipling*, vol. 1, *1872–89*, ed. Thomas Pinney (1990)

12 **It all comes of being so attractive, as the old lady said when she was struck by lightning.**

Jerome K. Jerome *The Idle Thoughts of an Idle Fellow*, 'On the Weather' (1889)

13 **Pray don't talk to me about the weather, Mr Worthing. Whenever people talk to me about the weather, I always feel quite certain that they mean something else. And that makes me so nervous.**

Oscar Wilde Gwendolen Fairfax in *The Importance of Being Earnest*, act 1 (1895)

14 **Everybody talks about the weather, but nobody does anything about it.**

Mark Twain Attributed to Twain by Charles D. Warner in the *Hartford Courant* 27 August 1897

15 **Think it's going to rain if it doesn't stay dry?**

Dan Leno Typically vacuous barber's question, *Dan Leno Hys Booke*, Chapter Eighth (1899)

16 **We were wakened up in the night by a very heavy thunderstorm. The thunder really was dramatic; quite as good as Drury Lane.**

Arnold Bennett Entry for 15 July 1910, *The Journals of Arnold Bennett*, vol. 1, *1896–1910*, ed. Newman Flower (1932)

17 **For my part I will praise the English climate till I die – even if I die of the English climate.**

G. K. Chesterton *Alarms and Discursions*, 'The Glory of Grey' (1910). He adds: 'There is also an insulting speech about "one grey day just like another". You might as well talk about one green tree like another.'

18 **'Correct me if I am wrong,' he said, 'but am I right in supposing that it is a very Blusterous day outside?'**

A. A. Milne *The House at Pooh Corner*, 'A Very Grand Thing' (1928)

19 **It rained. It nearly always rained – just as it does now.**

Winston Churchill *My Early Life*, ch. 1, 'Childhood' (1930). It is hard to say whether he is speaking generally, or specifically about Ireland, where he spent his early years.

20 **Summer afternoon – summer afternoon . . . the two most beautiful words in the English language.**

Henry James Quoted in *A Backward Glance* by Edith Wharton, ch. 10 (1934)

21 **The glass is falling by the hour, the glass will fall for ever,/ But if you**

break the bloody glass you won't
hold up the/ weather.

Louis MacNeice 'Bagpipe Music' (1937). The
closing lines of the poem.

22 **In Hampshire, Hereford and Hert-**
ford, hurricanes hardly ever
happen.

George Bernard Shaw *Pygmalion* (film, 1938,
screenplay by Anatole de Grunwald, W. P. Lip-
scomb, Cecil Lewis and Ian Dalrymple, from
the play by George Bernard Shaw, directed
by Anthony Asquith and Leslie Howard).
Shaw himself approved the introduction of
this saw into the script as an elocution test.

23 **The rain in Spain stays mainly on**
the plain.

Alan Jay Lerner *My Fair Lady*, 'The Rain in
Spain' (1956)

24 **What, in the last resort, is there to**
be said for February?

George Lyttelton Letter to Rupert Hart-Davis
of 23 February 1956, collected in *The Lyttelton
–Hart-Davis Letters*, vols 1 and 2, *1955–1957* ed.
Rupert Hart-Davis (1978)

25 **It is more important to know**
whether there will be weather than
what the weather will be.

Norton Juster The Whether Man in *The Phantom Tollbooth*, ch. 2 (1961)

26 **There are holes in the sky/ Where**
the rain gets in,/ But they're very
small/ That's why rain is thin.

Spike Milligan *Silly Verse for Kids*, 'Rain'
(1963)

27 **Don't need a weather man to say**
which way the wind blows.

Bob Dylan 'Subterranean Homesick Blues',
Bringing It All Back Home (LP, 1965)

28 **There's one thing. The weather is as**
perfect as it always is when the
world is quaking.

Alan Bennett Franklin (playing Hugh in the
play-within-the-play) in *Forty Years On*, act 1
(1968). The occasion is the outbreak of the
Second World War. Later in the play Moggie
points out that 'during the Home Rule crisis
it was 97 degrees'.

29 **As I took a seat on the upper deck, a**
stranger said, 'Too wet even for you?'

Quentin Crisp *The Naked Civil Servant*, ch. 24
(1968)

30 **the sun likes horses/ but hates cats/**
that is why it makes hay/ and heats
tin roofs

Roger McGough *After the Merrymaking*, 'a
cat, a horse and the sun' (1971)

31 **The gutters leaked like secrets and**
the rain rained like rain at Rawlin-
son End.

Viv Stanshall *Sir Henry at Rawlinson End* (LP,
1978)

32 **Come on, it's an electrical storm, do**
you want to wind up in an ashtray?

Woody Allen *Manhattan* (film, 1979, written
by Woody Allen and Marshall Brickman,
directed by Woody Allen). Isaac Davis
(Woody Allen) to Mary Wilke (Diane Keaton).

33 **Whether we are able to give you the**
weather tomorrow depends on the
weather.

Anon. Said on an Arab news programme in
January 1979 after severe flooding in Jeddah.
The station relied on weather reports from
an airport, which was closed. Quoted in *The
Book of Heroic Failures*, 'The Least Successful
Weather Report', by Stephen Pile (1979).

34 **FIRST LADY: Isn't the weather**
    dreadful?
   SECOND LADY:Yes, but it's better
    than nothing.

Anon. Overheard remark in *Word of Mouth*,
'Eavesdroppings', ed. Nigel Rees (1983)

35 **A very still, sultry evening: perhaps**
rain is on the way – I hope so, for
the sake of England's batsmen.

Philip Larkin Letter to Judy Egerton of 30 July
1984, collected in *Selected Letters of Philip Larkin, 1940–85* ed. Anthony Thwaite (1992)

36 **March is the month designed to**
show people who don't drink what
a hangover is like.

Garrison Keillor Radio broadcast, 1 December
1991

37 **[Of New York] In winter the tempera-**
ture falls well below the legal
minimum.

Douglas Adams *Mostly Harmless*, ch. 2 (1992)

38 **London had this ability, Naomi now**
knew, to take spring and turn it

into autumn, just by tweaking the air quality, raising its contrast.

Will Self *Cock and Bull*, 'Bull', ch. 4, 'Pursuit' (1992)

39 **There was a man standing next to me. He was one of those guys who turn up everywhere and say, 'You think it's cold today? You should have been here yesterday.'**

Billy Connolly Recalling a visit to Oslo. Joke told during his twenty-two-night run at the Hammersmith Apollo, London, in 1994.

40 **Spring bustled in late to London, full of excuses and panting slightly.**

Meera Syal *Life Isn't All Ha Ha Hee Hee*, ch. 5 (1999)

41 **I did a picture in England one winter and it was so cold I almost got married.**

Shelley Winters Quoted in *Halliwell's Who's Who in the Movies* ed. John Walker (2nd edn 2001). She has a fitting name for this quote, of course.

42 **It was the rain forest, so guess what, it pissed down.**

Simon Armitage First line of 'The Wood for the Trees', *The Universal Home Doctor* (2002)

43 **What a miserable day, eh? It's the sort of day you get your dog put down.**

Dick Clement and Ian La Frenais Dennis Patterson (Tim Healy) looking at a grey Teesside sky in *Auf Wiedersehen, Pet* (TV series, 2002)

44 **It is in our nature to dramatize. At least once a day we reinterpret the weather – an essentially impersonal phenomenon – into an expression of our current view of the universe. 'Great. It's raining. Just when I'm blue. Isn't that just like life?'**

David Mamet *Three Uses of the Knife*, ch. 1 (2002)

45 **As he climbed from the car a boob-job of a raindrop gutflopped on his baldspot.**

Martin Amis *Yellow Dog*, pt 3, ch. 9, sect. 1 (2003). The victim of this affront is Xan Meo.

46 **You may speak as you like of the weather,/ You may speak of the birds as they sing,/ But if you sit on a red-hot poker,/ It's a sign of an early spring.**

Anon. Weather forecast, *Pearson's Book of Fun*, 'Capital Verses', ed. Mr X (n.d.)

Man and Nature

Man's Relationship with Nature

1 **God made the country, and man made the town.**

William Cowper *The Task*, bk 1, 'The Sofa' (1785)

2 **The Views of an Erewhonian Philosopher Concerning the Rights of Vegetables**

Samuel Butler *Erewhon*, title of ch. 27 (1872). The philosopher – also a Professor of Botany – is quoted as saying: 'When we call plants stupid for not understanding our business, how capable do we show ourselves of understanding theirs?'

3 **Nothing helps scenery like ham and eggs.**

Mark Twain *Roughing It*, ch. 17 (1872)

4 [Of vivisection] **Between ourselves, you know, it's horribly cruel: you must admit that it's a deuced nasty thing to go ripping up and crucifying camels and monkeys. It must blunt all the finer feeling sooner or later.**

George Bernard Shaw Craven in *The Philanderer*, act 2 (1873)

5 **Nature is usually wrong.**

James McNeill Whistler *Mr Whistler's Ten o'Clock*, p. 14 (1885)

6 **But Nature is so uncomfortable. Grass is hard and lumpy and damp, and full of dreadful black insects. Why, even Morris's poorest workman could make you a more comfortable seat than the whole of nature can.**

Oscar Wilde *Intentions*, 'The Decay of Lying' (1891). The allusion is to William Morris.

7 **Wiv a ladder and some glasses,/**

You could see to 'Ackney Marshes,/ If it wasn't for the 'ouses in between.

Edgar Bateman and George Le Brunn 'If It Wasn't for the 'Ouses in Between' (song, 1894)

8 You will find that the woman who is really kind to dogs is always one who has failed to find sympathy in men.

Max Beerbohm *Zuleika Dobson*, ch. 6 (1912)

9 I have a good, deep voice, due to the hound strain in my pedigree, and at the public house, when there was a full moon, I have often had people leaning out of the windows and saying things all down the street.

P. G. Wodehouse *The Man with Two Left Feet*, 'The Mixer – 1' (1917). The narrator is a dog.

10 Because it's there.

George Mallory On being asked why he wanted to climb Mount Everest. Quoted in the *New York Times* 18 March 1923.

11 human wandering through the zoo/ what do your cousins think of you?

Don Marquis *archy and mehitabel*, 'archy at the zoo' (1927)

12 The next moment the day became very bothering indeed, because Pooh was so busy not looking where he was going that he stepped on a piece of the Forest which had been left out by mistake.

A. A. Milne *The House at Pooh Corner*, ch. 3 (1928)

13 The quality of Mersey is not strained.

Anon. *Sunday Graphic* 14 August 1932, referring to pollution in the River Mersey

14 You can't have any cherries in summer 'cause the birds have got 'em all ... Talk about gratitude! Feed 'em all winter on coco-nuts an' crumbs and then soon as we've got a bit of something to eat ourselves they start pinchin' it.

Richmal Crompton *William the Detective*, 'William the Rat-Lover' (1935)

15 There is precious little in civilization to appeal to a Yeti.

Edmund Hillary *Observer*, 'Sayings of the Week', 3 June 1960

16 A dog teaches a boy fidelity, perseverance, and to turn around three times before lying down.

Robert Benchley *Artemus Ward, His Book*, Introduction (1964)

17 De Selby has some interesting things to say on the subject of houses. A row of houses he regards as a row of necessary evils. The softening and degradation of the human race he attributes to a waning interest in the art of going outside and staying there.

Flann O'Brien *The Third Policeman*, ch. 2 (1967)

18 [On why he hated animals] I have enough dumb friends without them.

Quentin Crisp *The Naked Civil Servant*, ch. 4 (1968)

19 Arrived to find Helmholtz trimming some rose bushes. He was quite eloquent on the beauty of flowers, which he loves because 'they're not always borrowing money'.

Woody Allen *Getting Even*, 'Conversations with Helmholtz' (1971)

20 Mind where you're putting your feet. This field's in a disgusting state.

Alan Bennett Mr Shorter (James Cossins) in *A Day Out* (TV film, 1972, directed by Stephen Frears). The pompous Mr Shorter is pushing his bike through a Yorkshire field along with other members of a cycling club. It is 1911.

21 I think that I shall never see/ A billboard lovely as a tree./ Indeed, unless the billboards fall/ I'll never see a tree at all.

Ogden Nash *Happy Days*, 'Song of the Open Road' (1973). A development of the opening lines of 'Trees', a poem of 1914 by Joyce Kilmer.

22 The trouble with fresh air is that you can't control the temperature.

Eric Morecambe and Ernie Wise Remark

made in 1973 'by a man spiking up leaves in Central Park'. Morecambe had just commented that it was nice to be out in the fresh air. Quoted in *Eric and Ernie: The Biography of Morecambe and Wise*, ch. 13, by Graham McCann (1998).

23 **Remote: A place with only one big modern hotel. See also 'off the beaten track'.**

Beachcomber *Beachcomber: The Works of J. B. Morton*, 'A Dictionary for Today', ed. Richard Ingrams (1974)

24 **The Atlantic Ocean was something then. Yes, you should have seen the Atlantic Ocean in those days.**

Burt Lancaster Lou (Burt Lancaster) to Dave (Robert Joy) in *Atlantic City* (film, 1981, screenplay by John Guare, directed by Louis Malle)

25 **Animals, wild: How ironic that wild animals should behave so much better than so-called Homo sapiens! Rape is unheard of in the jungle. To say nothing of social security frauds and the whole range of inner-city crimes!**

Henry Root *Henry Root's World of Knowledge* (1982)

26 **I am at two with nature.**

Woody Allen Quoted in *Woody Allen*, pt 1, by Eric Lax (1991). Lax says that Allen wrote this 'early in his career', and quotes Mia Farrow as saying of Allen's visits to her country house in Connecticut: 'Within half an hour of arriving he's walked around the lake and is ready to go home. He gets very bored.'

27 **All our pets are flushable.**

Matt Groening Sign outside the Springfield pet shop in *The Simpsons*, 'Two Dozen and One Greyhounds', first broadcast 9 April 1995

28 **A cat has got nine lives – which makes them ideal for experimentation.**

Jimmy Carr Quoted in the *Daily Telegraph* 4 August 2003. One of his most complained-about jokes.

29 **No one likes to admit that they like London parks pure and simple, so thousands have traditionally relied on a canine alibi.**

Will Self *Dr Mukti and Other Tales of Woe*, 'Conversations with Ord' (2004)

Environmentalism

1 **These days, anyone who loves nature is accused of living in a world of pure fantasy.**

Nicolas-Sébastien Roch de Chamfort Written c. 1785. Collected in *Chamfort: Reflections on Life, Love and Society*, 'Reflections and Anecdotes', ed. Douglas Parmee (2003).

2 **I prefer the philosophy of bricks and mortar to the philosophy of turnips.**

G. K. Chesterton *Alarms and Discursions*, 'The Surrender of a Cockney' (1910). He adds: 'Nature-worship is more morally dangerous than the most vulgar man-worship of the cities.'

3 **It is exciting to have a real crisis on your hands, when you have spent half your political life dealing with humdrum issues like the environment.**

Margaret Thatcher Speech to the Scottish Conservative Party Conference, 14 May 1982

4 **People against people for nuclear energy.**

Matt Groening Slogan of the Springfield anti-nuclear group in *The Simpsons*, 'Homer's Odyssey', first broadcast 21 January 1990

5 **One green bottle,/ Drop it in the bank./ Ten green bottles,/ What a lot we drank./ Heaps of bottles/ And yesterday's a blank/ But we'll save the planet,/ Tinkle, tinkle clank!**

Wendy Cope *Serious Concerns*, 'Kindness to Animals' (1992)

6 **JOHN SHUTTLEWORTH: Alternative energy . . . Is it the way forward, Ken?**
   KEN WORTHINGTON: I'm sorry, me mind's gone blank.

Graham Fellowes Sketch quoted in the London *Evening Standard* 10 October 1994

7 **We are getting away from the leather sandals and lentils approach.**

Anon. Sainsbury's spokesman, after the launch of organic gin and tonic. Quoted in *The Times* 11 September 1999.

8 I was recently ear-bashed by my flatmate for leaving the tap running as it wastes water. In the next breath he explained that because of global warming, everywhere will eventually be flooded. If this is the case, surely the best thing to do is to leave the tap on so all of this water goes down the drains.

Viz Spoof letter, *Viz* comic October 2002

9 It's Leaves and It's Grass, and It's Outta Your Class

Neil Young Title of early obscure Neil Young song, quoted in *Shakey – Neil Young's Biography*, 'A Big Blur of Images', by Jimmy McDonough (2002)

10 Sellafield is almost silent. It hums with quiet menace. As my mum says, it's the quiet ones you have to watch.

Ian Marchant *Parallel Lines*, 'Lancaster: The Pretty Way' (2003)

Author Biographies

Abbott and Costello US Comedians
Bud Abbott and Lou Costello. Levered their vaudeville routines into films such as *Buck Privates* (1941) and *Lost in a Harem* (1944). Abbott was tall, cross and always wore a hat, Costello was chubby and gullible. 1895–1974 and 1906–59

Diane Abbott UK Politician
Labour MP since 1987; Britain's first black woman MP. 1953–

Russ Abbott UK Comedian
Tall, amiable comedian. Broke through when he inherited *Freddie Starr's Variety Madhouse*, which became *Russ Abbott's Madhouse* in 1980. Amongst his characterizations are C. U. Jimmy, a potentially violent Scotsman, the suave Basildon Bond and Cooperman, a cross between a superhero and Tommy Cooper. 1947–

Charlie Ace Jamaican Musician
Reggae performer and entrepreneur. Produced tracks for Bunny Lee and Lee Perry, but operated on a small scale, selling his own records from a converted van labelled the 'Swing-A-Ling Record Shack'. 1945–

Goodman Ace US Broadcaster
Radio presenter. Also author of works such as *The Book of Little Knowledge* (1957). 1899–1982

Gilbert Adair UK Novelist, Journalist
His journalism is at the intellectual end of the market; his elegant novel of 1988, *The Dreamers*, was filmed in 2003 by Bertolucci.

Douglas Adams UK Novelist, Scriptwriter
Succeeded more or less immediately with *The Hitchhiker's Guide to the Galaxy* (1979), in which a bewildered Englishman, Arthur Dent, goes into outer space and through time armed with little more than the eponymous guidebook. In it, the weirdest phenomena are described in drolly matter-of-fact terms. The novel was adapted for radio, television, the stage and film. It also became a computer game. 1952–2000

Marcus Adams UK Photographer
Son of the photographer Walton Adams, he is known for photographs of children and royalty. 1875–1959

Charles Addams US Cartoonist
Drew morbid, funny cartoons for the *New Yorker* (from 1932). His sepulchral Addams Family inspired a TV series (1964 onwards), then films. Collected instruments of torture and replied to fan mail using the address The Gotham Home for Mental Defectives. 1912–88

Joseph Addison English Writer
Poet, playwright, Whig politician; founded the *Spectator* in 1711 with Sir Richard Steele. 1672–1719

Konrad Adenauer German Politician
President of the Prussian State Council 1920–33, then ousted by the Nazis; returned as first Chancellor of the Federal Republic of Germany 1949–63. 1876–1967

James Agate UK Journalist
Drama critic for the *Manchester Guardian* and, from 1923, the *Sunday Telegraph*. *Ego* (1935–48) is an autobiography in nine parts. 1877–1947

Caroline Aherne UK Comedian
Secretary at Granada TV who graduated to character comedy in *The Fast Show* (from 1994) and in her own chat show, here albeit in the guise of the geriatric Mrs Merton. 1963–

Nick Alexander UK Businessman, Entrepreneur
Also a noted collector of transport memorabilia. 1955–

Nelson Algren US Writer
Chronicler of Chicago low-life in *The Man with the Golden Arm* (1949) and other novels. Sometime lover of Simone de Beauvoir. 1909–81

Fred Allen US Comedian
Vaudeville, then radio, then TV comic with a mordant style much appreciated by James Thurber among others. His autobiography is *Treadmill to Oblivion* (1954). 1894–1956

Woody Allen US Comedian, Writer, Film Director
Born Allen Stewart Konigsberg. Began as a successful stand-up and TV gag-writer. Started directing films with *Take the Money and Run* (1969), which was near-slapstick. At his artistic and commercial peak with *Annie Hall* (1977) and *Manhattan* (1979) – which were mainly funny and neurotic, but also elegant and romantic. 1935–

Robert Altman US Film Director
Hollywood maverick; broke through in 1970 with the manic *M*A*S*H*; *Gosford Park* was a big hit of 2001. David Thomson wrote, 'No one else alive is as capable of a dud, or a masterpiece.' 1925–

Kingsley Amis English Novelist, Poet
Had great success with his first novel *Lucky Jim* (1953), a satire on provincial university life that has a status equivalent in fiction to that of John Osborne's *Look Back in Anger* (1956) in drama: it pits a representative of a new, young, democratized Britain against the old order. His later novels include *The Old Devils* (1986), for which he won the Booker Prize. By then Amis was a determined foe of liberalism and political correctness. 1922–95

Martin Amis English Writer
Son of Kingsley Amis, his mimetic prose is a mixture of high style and street talk, ever at the service of a very dry wit. Amis's novels from *The Rachel Papers* (1973) onwards made him the most talked-about and influential English literary novelist of his time. 1949–

Diane Amos US Painter and Writer

Lindsay Anderson UK Film Director
Intellectual, known particularly for the harrowing class-studies films *This Sporting Life* (1963) and *If . . .* (1968). 1923–94

F. Anstey English Humorist
Born Thomas Anstey Guthrie. Barrister and exuberantly imaginative contributor to *Punch*. In his novel *Vice Versa* (1882) Mr Bultitude and his son magically exchange identities. 1856–1934

Antiphanes Greek Poet
Of the Middle Comedy period, *c.*400–*c.*323 BC. Much of his work has been lost, and Antiphanes himself is an obscure figure. 4th century BC

Sir Edward Appleton UK Physicist
Nobel Prize winner in 1947; identifed electrically charged particles in the atmosphere, without which radio wouldn't work. 1892–1965

William Arabin English Judge
1773–1841

Louis Aragon French Poet, Novelist, Journalist
Leading surrealist and, from 1930, a communist activist. 1897–1982

Simon Armitage UK Poet
The most important British poet of the 1990s who could reasonably be called 'young', Armitage has won many prizes for his volumes such as *The Universal Home Doctor* (2002), in which he combines modern colloquialisms with a timeless elegance. Also writes novels and reportage; is particularly associated with his home county of Yorkshire. 1963–

Richard Armour US Humorist
Author of, for example, *The Adventures of Egbert the Easter Egg* (1965). 1906–

Lord Armstrong UK Civil Servant
Head of the Civil Service 1983–7. During the government's attempt to halt publication of the book *Spycatcher*, by Peter Wright, Armstrong admitted that he had been 'economical with the truth', thereby achieving immortality in an instant. 1927–

Louis Armstrong US Jazz Musician
Sent to a 'coloured waifs'' home in 1912 after firing a pistol in the air. There he learnt to play the cornet. Armstrong went on to become the biggest name in jazz, famous for his improvisatory solos and, latterly, for a gravelly vocal style as employed in the songs 'Hello Dolly' (1964) and 'What a Wonderful World' (1968). 1901–71

Matthew Arnold English Poet, Critic
Son of the educationalist Thomas Arnold, Matthew Arnold was an inspector of schools for over thirty years and a pessimistic observer of British society in general, which he believed was suffering spiritual decline – a theme reflected in his poem 'Dover Beach' (1867). The *Daily Tele-*

graph called him 'an elegant Jeremiah' and 'the high-priest of kid-gloved persuasion'. 1822–88

Daisy Ashford English Writer

Author of the misspelt, highly comic social satire *The Young Visiters* (1919). In his preface to the book, J. M. Barrie vouched for the fact that Daisy had written it in her ninth year. She later became Mrs George Norman. 1881–1972

Margot Asquith Scottish Salonnière

Witty hostess, founder of the free-thinking 'Souls'; wife of Herbert Asquith, Liberal Prime Minister 1908–16. 1864–1945

Raymond Asquith UK Barrister, Soldier

Fellow of All Souls College, Oxford, from 1902, intellectually brilliant society figure; son of the Prime Minister Herbert Asquith. A prime exemplar of the 'golden youth' lost to England in the First World War, he was killed at the Somme in 1916. 1878–1916

Mary Astell English Writer

Proto-feminist, yet strongly Anglican. 1668–1731

Nancy Astor UK Politician

Viscountess Astor of Hever Castle. American-born, she was the first woman to sit in the House of Commons, succeeding her husband as Conservative MP for Plymouth in 1919. 1879–1964

Mustapha Kemal Atatürk Turkish Politician

Leader of Turkish nationalism from 1909. He forged the identity of Turkey as an independent secular state. 1881–1938

Ron Atkinson UK Footballer, Manager

Played for Oxford United; has managed Manchester United and Aston Villa. Famous for his jewellery and bouffant hair as much as for his tactical nous. As a TV football pundit he employed an array of strange phrases – a good pass, for example, would be 'the Hollywood ball'. His career was checked in 2004 when he blurted out a racist remark, for which he has apologized. 1939–

David Attenborough UK Naturalist, Broadcaster

Ever since *Zoo Quest* which began in 1954, he has presented wildlife programmes for the BBC. Controller of BBC2 1965–8. Brother of the actor Richard; knighted in 1985. 1926–

Clement Attlee UK Politician

Labour Prime Minister 1945–51. His government laid the foundations of the Welfare State. In style, he was the opposite of his bombastic rival Churchill. George VI observed: 'I gather they call the Prime Minister "Clem". Clam would be more appropriate.' 1883–1967

John Aubrey UK Writer

Biographer. His *Brief Lives* is regarded as unmethodical but useful as a chronicle of the seventeenth century. 1626–97

W. H. Auden UK Poet

Leading light of a left-wing set that included Stephen Spender, Cecil Day-Lewis, Louis MacNeice and Christopher Isherwood. Auden established himself with *Look Stranger!* (1936); in 1939 he emigrated to America, where he was awarded the Pulitzer Prize for *The Age of Anxiety* (1947). His eccentric habits and crumpled face exerted an increasing fascination as he got older; Stravinsky called him 'the dirtiest man I have ever liked'. 1907–73

Jane Austen UK Novelist

Depicted a narrow middle-class circle with great insight, subtlety and dry wit. Has been credited with bringing to maturity the English novel as an art form, contributing to its flowering in the nineteenth century. 1775–1817

Tex Avery US Animator

Created wild and funny (and violent) cartoons for MGM. Many comedians appreciated, and may have been influenced by, his work – notably all the Goons. 1907–80

Alan Ayckbourn UK Playwright

Author of more than sixty plays; the most performed living playwright – and yet he lives in Scarborough. Ayckbourn began with domestic farce, later moving into darker territory. He has said, 'I have a theory that to be genuinely respectable as a so-called comic writer, on a par with an equivalent "serious" writer, you need to have been dead preferably for a century.' 1939–

John Aye UK Writer

Pseudonym of Lieutenant-Colonel John Atkinson. He produced compilations of humorous anecdotes for particular professions, such as *Humour in the Civil Service* (1928).

Francis Bacon English Writer, Philosopher, Politician

1st Baron Verulam and Viscount St Albans. Mainly concerned with classification of the branches of learning, but since the mid-nineteenth century a strain of scholarship has contended that he wrote the plays attributed to Shakespeare. 1561–1626

Francis Bacon Irish Painter

Mainly depicted nightmarishly distorted human figures, and by the 1980s was commonly regarded as the greatest living painter. He was also revered in Soho as a drinker and sybarite. Julian Barnes wrote that 'the biggest influence on Francis Bacon has been his own surname'. 1909–92

Arthur 'Bugs' Baer US Writer

Sacked from his first proper job as an artist on the *Philadelphia Public Ledger*, for accidentally boarding a ship that took him to Delaware. Moving on to the *Washington Times*, he drew a cartoon involving an insect shaped like a base-ball – hence his nickname. Graduated to writing a humorous column for the *New York World* called 'One Word Leads to Another', which was eventually syndicated widely via Hearst's King Features. Baer had a beguiling, cryptic style. 'His whole work is a cable language of his own,' wrote the critic Gilbert Seldes. 1886–1969

Walter Bagehot UK Economist, Constitutional Historian

The English Constitution (1867) remains a standard introduction to the study of English politics, and is much wittier than it sounds. He also wrote on literature. 1827–77

David Bailey UK Photographer

As the most exciting British fashion photographer of the 1960s and 70s, he had the cachet and the looks of a pop star. 1938–

Alec Baldwin US Actor

Sex symbol. Credits include *Married to the Mob* (1988) and *Notting Hill* (1999). His brothers Stephen, William and Daniel are also actors – and also sex symbols. 1958–

James Baldwin US Novelist

His novels deal with being black in America and with homosexuality. Titles incude *Go Tell It on the Mountain* (1953) and *Just above My Head* (1979). 1924–87

Stanley Baldwin UK Politician

Conservative statesman; Prime Minister 1923, 1924–9 and 1935–7. Regarded as humane, decent and liberal, but George Orwell wrote: 'One could not even dignify him with the name of a stuffed shirt. He was simply a hole in the air.' 1867–1947

Arthur Balfour UK Statesman

Conservative; First Earl of Balfour. As Prime Minister 1902–5, he exhibited the same melancholic pragmatism as his predecessor, and uncle, Lord Salisbury. 1848–1930

Pierre Balmain French Couturier

Opened his fashion house in 1945; unpretentious in style. 1914–82

Tallulah Bankhead US Actress

Remembered for her wild personal life – 'she was a woman who lived without boundaries', according to her biographer Joel Lobenthal – as much as for her fifty-year career on stage, screen and radio. 1902–68

Nancy Banks-Smith UK Journalist

The *Guardian*'s funniest and longest-serving TV critic. She said of her own name: 'I have lived too long with Nancy Banks-Smith to find it funny, though Ernie Wise said it reminded him of someone falling off a horse at Hickstead.'

Lynn Barber UK Journalist

Has spent much of her career as the most respected (and feared) newspaper interviewer in Britain; associated in turn with the *Sunday Express*, the *Independent on Sunday* and the *Observer*. She has said: 'I am nervous of showing how much I care about interviewing. It's only journalism, after all.' 1944–

Myrtie Barker US Columnist

1910–

Ronnie Barker UK Actor

Highly rated comedian. In the 1970s and early 80s he was paired with Ronnie Corbett in the inventive sketch show *The Two Ronnies*. Played the old lag Fletcher in the sitcom *Porridge*. According to Peter Hall, Barker 'completely inhabited what it was he was being, even if it was a North Country charlady'. Barker has written much of his own sketch material under the name Gerald Wiley. 1929–

Julian Barnes UK Novelist

His first book *Metroland* (1981) established him as a writer of witty, elegant novels, less ferocious in style than most of his peers. In *Flaubert's Parrot* (1984) his Francophilia came out into the open. 1946–

Phineas T. Barnum US Showman

Hyberbolical character. From 1871 he began running a three-ring circus he called 'The Greatest Show on Earth'. In 1881, he and James Anthony Bailey founded the Barnum and Bailey Circus. 1810–91

Ann Barr and Peter York UK Journalists

Social observers who captured an era and a type with *The Official Sloane Ranger Handbook* (1982).

An important sub-section of the category was the Hooray Henrys.

J. M. Barrie UK Writer

James Matthew Barrie. Scottish-born, the son of a weaver. *Quality Street* (1901) and *The Admirable Crichton* (1902) were successful plays, but his fame rests on his children's play *Peter Pan* (1904). He said: 'We are all failures – at least, all the best of us are.' But he was made a baronet, and much lauded in his lifetime. 1860–1937

Andrew Barrow UK Writer

As a journalist he has chronicled high society with an amused eye; his autobiographical novel *The Tap Dancer* (1992) has often been described as a comic masterpiece. 1945–

John Barrymore Jnr US Actor

Larger than life, ultra-handsome leading man, and alcoholic. His parents were actors, and his daughter is the actress Drew Barrymore. 1932–

Sir Henry Howarth Bashford UK Doctor, Writer

Private physician to George VI. It was not discovered until after his death that he was the writer of the comic classic *Augustus Carp Esq. by Himself* (1924), the life story of a sanctimonious Victorian. 1880–1961

Kim Basinger US Actress

'Often in over-sexed roles', according to *Halliwell's Who's Who in the Movies*. 1953–

Thomas Bastard English Writer

1566–1618

Edgar Bateman and George Le Brunn UK Songwriters

Their output was popular in the music halls, where Bateman was known as 'the Shakespeare of Aldgate pump'.

Arnold Bax English Composer

Influenced by the Celtic revival; also wrote short stories with an Irish setting under the name Dermot O'Byrne, but chiefly famous for saying what he did about folk dancing. 1883–1953

Peter Baynham UK Writer and Comedian

Among many other credits, he wrote and performed with Armando Iannucci in *The Saturday Night Armistice* (1995) and with Chris Morris in *Brass Eye* (1997).

Beachcomber UK Humorist

J. B. Morton. Booming, exuberant Catholic convert and opponent of modernity who in 1923 inherited the 'Beachcomber' column from D. B. Wyndham Lewis (known to the Sitwells as 'the wrong Wyndham Lewis'). Under Morton the column portrayed in a wild, surreal style the doings of various strangely named recurring characters such as Mr Justice Cocklecarrot, along with other one-off comic excursions. Evelyn Waugh described Beachcomber as having 'the greatest comic fertility of any Englishman'. 1893–1979

Aubrey Beardsley UK Artist

Made his name by supplying sinuous, fantastical, erotic illustrations for an edition of *Le Morte d'Arthur*, Oscar Wilde's *Salome* and the art quarterly the *Yellow Book*. A leading figure of the Aesthetic movement. His biographer Matthew Sturgis noted that 'people were struck by how closely he resembled his drawings: elongated, monochromatic and unhealthy'. 1872–98

Warren Beatty US Actor

Good-looking actor whose love life became an American epic. Among his best films are *Bonnie and Clyde* (1967) and *The Parallax View* (1974). 1937–

Lord Beaverbrook UK Newspaper Proprietor

William Maxwell Aitken, 1st Baron Beaverbrook. Made a fortune in cement in Canada, then moved to England where he acquired the *Daily Express* in 1916 and began to intimidate and inspire a generation of journalists. Also a Conservative minister in both wars. 1879–1964

Margaret Beckett UK Politician

Cabinet minister under Tony Blair. 1943–

Samuel Beckett Irish Playwright

Author of bleak, gnomic plays. After the great success of *Waiting for Godot* (1955) he became associated with the Theatre of the Absurd. Awarded the Nobel Prize for Literature in 1959. 1906–89

Duke of Bedford UK Aristocrat

John Robert Russell, 13th Duke of Bedford. Born, as he puts it in the Preface to his *Book of Snobs*, into 'one of the most aristocratic families in England', but he was estranged from that family from an early age. Sometime estate agent, writer and farmer in South Africa. 1917–2002

Sir Thomas Beecham UK Conductor

Worked with the London Philharmonic and the Royal Philharmonic Orchestras. Liked to be seen as a 'card'. Neville Cardus described him as 'a complex character – Falstaff, Puck, Malvolio all mixed up'. But he always bowed to the orchestra first. 1879–1961

Captain Beefheart US Musician
Don van Vliet. Grew up in the Mojave Desert; attended the same school as Frank Zappa. From *Safe as Milk* (1967), he began producing his own avant-garde version of R 'n' B. A dozen albums followed, including *Trout Mask Replica*, which, according to *The Penguin Encyclopedia of Popular Music*, 'teetered between genius and madness'. Of late, Beefheart has confined himself to painting. A musical colleague said, 'Weird was cool, and he had a headlock on weird.' 1941–

Max Beerbohm UK Writer, Caricaturist
A tiny dandy; the author of many witty essays and of the novel *Zuleika Dobson* (1911), a satire on Oxford undergraduate life. 1872–1956

Brendan Behan Irish Writer
His time spent in Borstal for association with the IRA gave rise to the book *Borstal Boy* (1958). Behan, who drank himself to death, was a humorist with a tragic edge. 'Message? Message? What the hell do you think I am, a bloody postman?' he once said. 1923–64

Aphra Behn English Playwright, Novelist
Thought of as the first professional female writer in the country. Her tombstone reads: 'Here lies proof that wit can never be/Defence against mortality.' 1640–89

Edward Behr US Foreign Correspondent and Writer

Hilaire Belloc UK Writer
French-born workaholic and combative Catholic, best remembered today for his darkly funny children's poems *Cautionary Tales* (1907). Belloc and his fellow Catholic controversialist and friend G. K. Chesterton were once referred to as 'two buttocks of one bum'. 1870–1953

Saul Bellow US Novelist
Awarded the Nobel Prize for Literature in 1997. Works include *The Adventures of Augie March* (1953) and *Humboldt's Gift* (1975). The critic James Wood described him as 'the greatest of American prose stylists in the twentieth century', while Martin Amis said that his first name was a mistake, that he ought to have been called Soul Bellow. 1915–2005

Robert Benchley US Humorist
His output of humorous writings has been eclipsed by this remark: 'It took me fifteen years to discover that I had no talent for writing, but I couldn't give it up because by that time I was too famous.' 1889–1945

Judah Philip Benjamin US Lawyer, Politician
Born in South Africa into a Jewish family. Moved to America, attended Yale, became a lawyer, and a Senator 1853–61; served the Confederacy as Attorney General, then Secretary of State for War. Subsequently fled to England where from 1866 he forged a successful career as a barrister. 1811–84

Tony Benn UK Politician
Labour MP 1950–2001; held ministerial office under Harold Wilson and James Callaghan. The socialist scourge of middle England and, indeed, of Labour governments – or so he has been presented. In his diaries his idealism is tempered by an attractive dry wit. 1925–

Richard Benner Canadian Film Director
His films include *Outrageous* (1977), about a Toronto drag queen.

Alan Bennett UK Playwright, Actor
In the celebrated Oxbridge revue team of the early 1960s the Leeds-born Bennett was, like George Harrison of the Beatles, 'the quiet one'. Gradually abandoned the idea of becoming a medieval historian and began to write a series of dramas for television and the stage which, as Alex Games noted in his Introduction to his biography of Bennett in 2001, have earned him half a column in the *Oxford Companion to the Theatre*. His writing is often melancholic, but a delicious strain of recognizably northern drollery runs through it all. 1934–

Arnold Bennett UK Writer
Prolific novelist, playwright, diarist and critic. His stories set in 'the five towns' of the Potteries in the Midlands are the most read. He drew much snobbish criticism for writing entertaining books about ordinary people (his favourite word was 'quotidian'), especially from Virginia Woolf. His biographer Margaret Drabble wrote: 'He was a great writer from a stony land, and he was also one of the kindest and most unselfish of men.' 1867–1931

Jack Benny US Comedian
Starred in vaudeville, on radio and in film, beginning with *Hollywood Revue* (1929). He played the violin badly on purpose and affected a persona of extreme stinginess. 1894–1974

Frank Benson UK Actor Manager
Also obsessed with sport, cricket especially. Became a company manager at twenty-five; relentlessly toured productions of Shakespeare

thereafter. Max Beerbohm found his Henry V excellent 'as a branch of university cricket' but not so good 'as a form of acting'. Benson was knighted in 1916. 1858–1939

Edmund Clerihew Bentley UK Writer
Gave his middle name to the 'clerihew', which the *Concise Oxford Dictionary* defines as 'a short, witty, comic, or nonsensical verse, usually in two rhyming couplets with lines of unequal length'. 1875–1956

Marcus Berkmann UK Writer
Humorous journalist, and author of non-fiction books including *Rain Men* (1995) about cricket, and *Brain Men* (1999) about pub quizzes. 1960–

Jeffrey Bernard UK Journalist
Chronicled his 'Low Life' in a funny, bleak *Spectator* column of that name. Market research showed that most readers turned to it before anything else. Keith Waterhouse wrote a play about him, *Jeffrey Bernard is Unwell*, titled after the words that explained the column's frequent absence from the magazine. Philip Howard described him as 'our street-corner Socrates'. Bernard himself said: 'I am a cunt but not a shit, there's a big difference.' He drank himself to death. 1932–97

Lord Berners UK Novelist, Composer
Gerald Hugh Tyrwhitt-Wilson; well-connected aesthete; novels include *Far from the Madding War* (1941). 1883–1950

Sarah Bernhardt French Actress
Legendary tragedienne. 1844–1923

Yogi Berra US Baseball Player and Coach
1925–

George Best UK Footballer
Many say one of the best ever. The heart-throb of Manchester United in the 1960s, but subsequently best known for his playboy lifestyle. Admitted to spending 90 per cent of his money on women, fast cars and booze. The rest, he said, he'd wasted. 1946–

John Betjeman UK Poet
His first collection, *Mount Zion*, appeared in 1930; his *Collected Poems* were published in 1958. Betjeman was also an admirer of Victorian architecture, and wrote and campaigned for its conservation. He became poet laureate in 1972. His nostalgic concerns and traditional style attracted criticism, and one of his (mock) regrets on the eve of his death was that he was 'not taken seriously by the *TLS*'. He had his heavy-

weight defenders though, notably Philip Larkin. 1906–84

Mark Bevan UK Poet
Author of, for example, *Lays for the Days and Other Verses* (1956)

Ambrose Bierce US Writer
Came to notice after having been hired by William Randolph Hearst as a columnist on the *San Francisco Examiner* (1897–1901). Covered military, political and cultural matters with an acerbic style. Bierce, who disappeared in Mexico in 1914, is best remembered today for his *Devil's Dictionary* (compiled 1881–1906), which had a complicated origin, beginning under various names in various columns. David E. Schultz and S. T. Joshi claim in *The Unabridged Devil's Dictionary* (2000) that Bierce's life is summarized in one of his definitions: 'Cynic, n. A blackguard whose faulty vision sees things as they are, not as they ought to be.' The editors note that it was lodged between 'curse' and 'damn' in the first edition of the work. 1842–1914

William Blake UK Artist, Poet
Self-educated eccentric and mystic whose poetry and engravings are associated with the beginnings of Romanticism. 1757–1827

Ronald Blythe UK Writer
Mainly known for *Akenfield: Portrait of an English Village* (1969), which falls somewhere between oral history and a work of art. 1922–

Humphrey Bogart US Actor
His many well-known films include *Casablanca* and *The Big Sleep*. Always played the tough guy, but with grace and restraint. 'Bogart,' wrote Raymond Chandler, 'can be tough without a gun.' 1899–1957

Erma Bombeck US Humorist
1927–96

Napoleon Bonaparte French Emperor
Formidable military tactician who established an empire that in 1807 covered most of continental Europe. Ruled France 1799–1814, and for the 'hundred days' in 1815. 1769–1821

Bono Irish Rock Singer
Leader of the stadium-filling band U2; also active in humanitarian causes. 1960–

Daniel J. Boorstin US Historian
The Americans (1958–73) was Pulitzer Prize-winning. 1914–

David Borgenicht *see* Joshua Piven

Jorge Luis Borges Argentinian Writer
Author of fiction and poetry, frequently of a fantastical strain, making him the father of magical realism; blind from 1955. 1899–1986

James Boswell UK Biographer
Scottish lawyer and rake, who produced one of the classics of English literature in his *Life of Samuel Johnson* (1791). Stanley Baxter, reflecting on Boswell, sighed: 'To be so randy . . . and so literate.' 1740–95

Ian Botham UK Cricketer
Rambunctious all-rounder, frequently at odds with the cricket establishment; won the 1981 Test series for England against Australia practically single-handedly. Botham has raised fortunes for leukaemia research. His motto is 'Life: be in it.' 1955–

Dion Boucicault Irish Actor, Playwright
Born Dionysius Lardner Boursiquot. 1820–90

Lord Bowen UK Judge
Also a classicist and melancholy wit. In 1903, during a negligence action, he said: 'We must ask ourselves what the man on the Clapham omnibus would think?' thus popularizing that benchmark of reasonableness. 1835–94

W. E. Bowman UK Writer, Engineer
Author of *The Ascent of Rum Doodle* (1956), a deadpan account of an inept and gentlemanly mountain ascent. According to Miles Kington: 'it did for mountaineering what *Three Men in a Boat* did for Thames-going.' 1911–

Maurice Bowra UK Literary Critic
Arthur Marshall wrote: 'His numerous academic and administrative distinctions – Warden of Wadham [College] and Vice-Chancellor [of Oxford University], among others – sat very lightly upon him and he remained in many ways the brilliantly clever and funny and pugnacious Cheltenham schoolboy that he had once been.' He was small and round, and it is said that when, after he had been knighted by the Queen, Her Majesty said, 'Arise, Sir Maurice', he gruffly replied, 'I *have* risen.' 1898–1971

Charles Brackett US Film Writer-Producer
Highly rated; often collaborated with Billy Wilder. 1892–1969

Malcolm Bradbury UK Novelist
Associated with 'the campus novel': *Eating People Is Wrong* (1959) is one such. Associated with the campus also in that from 1970 he ran the creative writing programme at the University of East Anglia. 1932–2000

Lord Melvyn Bragg UK Writer, Broadcaster
Has presented mainly arts programmes, especially the long-running ITV *South Bank Show*. He has also headed Border Television, written TV films and a string of novels, many with a northern setting. It is very much part of Bragg's persona that he comes from Cumbria. 1939–

Jo Brand UK Comedian
Brand's droll stand-up routines often concern her size – she was alternatively billed as 'the Sea Monster' early in her career. She has moved into television with, for example, her own series *Jo Brand: Like It or Lump It*. 1957–

Marlon Brando US Actor
Emblem of rebellion in *The Wild One* (1953), and retained his dark mystique as his girth increased in films such as *The Godfather* (1972) and *Apocalypse Now* (1977). 1924–2004

Gyles Brandreth UK Politician, Writer, Entertainer
Conservative MP 1992–7; also TV presenter (in trademark garish jumper), features writer, author of over a hundred books, including seventy for children, holder of the record for the longest after-dinner speech (twelve hours, thirty minutes in 1982) and founder of the National Scrabble Championships. 1948–

Bertolt Brecht German Playwright, Poet
Important figure in twentieth-century theatre. His austere and stylized works were influenced by Expressionism and Marxism. *The Threepenny Opera* (1928) was inspired by *The Beggar's Opera* by John Gay. 1898–1956

Lucinda Bredin UK Journalist
Has worked on the London *Evening Standard* and the *Week*. Specializes in witty observation of the arts. 1960–

Leslie Bricusse UK Lyricist, Composer
Credits include *Doctor Dolittle* (1967), and *Willie Wonka and the Chocolate Factory* (1971). 1931–

Alan Brien UK Journalist, Novelist
Sometime columnist with *Punch*, and many other publications; *Sunday Times* film critic. Records, among his hobbies in *Who's Who*, 'sleeping in libraries'. 1925–

David Briggs US Record Producer
Began by producing comedians, making, he

claims, 'the first record that ever said "fuck" on it'. Subsequently associated with Neil Young, whose suspicion of technology he shared. 1944–

Tom Brokaw US Broadcaster
TV news anchor man, and NBC correspondent during the Watergate episode. 1940–

Charlotte Brontë English Novelist
Sister of Anne and Emily, her masterpiece is *Jane Eyre* (1847). 1816–55

Patrick Brontë English Clergyman
Of Irish descent. Father of the Brontë sisters. 1777–1861

Rupert Brooke UK Poet
Of the pastoral 'Georgian' group. With his dashing good looks and, as F. R. Leavis slightingly had it, his 'middle-class accent', he symbolized the gilded generation sacrificed in the First World War. 1887–1915

Tim Brooke-Taylor UK Comedian, Writer
A product of the Cambridge Footlights and the satire boom of the 1960s, he found television fame in the 70s in *The Goodies* – he was the prissy, patriotic one. A regular panellist on the radio game show *I'm Sorry I Haven't a Clue*. 1940–

Mel Brooks US Writer, Film Director
Brooks wrote jokes for Sid Caesar's *Your Show of Shows* (1950–4), and was acclaimed by his friends for his ability to be spontaneously funny about almost anything for almost ever. Carl Reiner exploited this talent when he initiated the dialogues that became the recorded interviews with Brooks as the 2000-Year-Old Man. Brooks went on to make films, beginning with *The Producers* (1968). His friend Joseph Heller admitted that he put many of Brooks's lines into his novel *Something Happened* (1974). 1926–

Shirley Brooks English Journalist
Humorist, and a *man*, incidentally. Contributor to *Punch* 1851–, and its editor 1870–. Also assisted Henry Mayhew with his social surveys. 1816–74

Pierce Brosnan Irish Actor
In 1995 he took over as James Bond, beginning with *Goldeneye*. 1959–

Craig Brown UK Journalist
Prolific columnist. Rated the best parodist of his time. His alter egos include Bel Littlejohn, earnest liberal and conceptual artist, and the reactionary Wallace Arnold, who was granted 'the great honour in 1986 of being invited to accompany their Royal Highnesses the Duke and Duchess of York on their honeymoon'. 1957–

Ivor Brown UK Journalist, Writer
Drama critic, and sometime editor of the *Observer*. 1891–1971

Lew Brown US Songwriter
Born Louis Brownstein. Wrote the lyrics for 'The Best Things in Life Are Free'. 1893–1958

Guy Browning UK Humorist
Author of a funny, purportedly instructional column in the *Guardian*, 'How to . . .'; also a broadcaster and consultant on business creativity. 1964–

Robert Browning UK Poet
Made his name in 1842 with *Dramatic Lyrics*, which contained 'The Pied Piper of Hamelin'. 1812–89

Frank Bruno UK Boxer
Became the WBC World Heavyweight Champion in 1995, but lost the title to Mike Tyson in 1996. He kept the ring in which he won in his back garden. 1961–

Jack Brymer UK Musician
Invited to join the Royal Philharmonic Orchestra as principal clarinettist by Sir Thomas Beecham; stayed 1947–63. He played on the Beatles track *A Day in the Life* and shared a birthday with his favourite composer, Mozart. 1915–2003

Bill Bryson US Writer
Anglophile, bestselling author of humorous travel books. In 2003, however, he said: 'I think it's time for more serious travel books, much more serious than mine.' 1951–

John Buchan UK Novelist
Baron Tweedsmuir; MP, and Governor General of Canada 1935–40. Author of brisk adventure stories, notably *The Thirty-Nine Steps* (1915). 1875–1940

Charles Bukowski US Writer
German-born poet and novelist. Chronicler of low-life in spare prose. 1920–94

Luis Buñuel Spanish Film Director
Surrealist, who moved on to social, especially anti-religious, satire. 1900–1983

Julie Burchill UK Journalist, Writer
Began by writing about pop music, and was the pouting leather-jacketed star of the *New Musical Express* at the time of punk. Went on to

write novels and funny, bile-filled columns for a succession of national papers. 1960–

Anthony Burgess UK Novelist

Late starter who became almost preposterously fecund after the brilliant *A Clockwork Orange* (1962). Also a critic, journalist, composer, librettist, screenwriter. 1917–93

Edmund Burke Irish Politician, Writer

MP, polemicist. *Reflections on the Revolution in France* (1790) argues for the organic, evolutionary development of society as opposed to the severe ideological approach of the French revolutionaries. Matthew Arnold called Burke 'our greatest English prose writer'. 1729–97

Johnny Burke US Songwriter

Wrote the words for 'Pennies from Heaven' and 'Swinging on a Star'. 1908–64

Fanny Burney English Novelist

Aristocratic socialite, courtier to Queen Charlotte and protégée of Dr Johnson's. Starting with *Evelina* (1778), Burney wrote lively social satires. 1752–1840

George Burns US Comedian

Born Nathan Birnbaum. Droll comic who began working a double act with the scatter-brained Gracie Allen, who became his wife. Later she said: 'My husband will never choose another woman; he's too fine, too decent, too old.' 1896–1996

Robert Burns Scottish Poet

The son of a poor farmer, but decently educated. His Scots dialect poems are celebrated around the world on Burns Night, 25 January, when it is traditional to drink a lot, as Burns himself was fond of doing. Tennyson called him 'a great genius, but very coarse sometimes'. 1759–96

Mike Burton UK Comedian

Robert Burton English Writer

Author of the sprawling work *The Anatomy of Melancholy* (appearing from 1621), a frequently amusing compendium of information on the condition. He was also a clergyman. 1577–1640

George Bush US Statesman

Republican; President 1989–93. 1925–

Candace Bushnell US Writer

New York journalist who, in 1996, published *Sex in the City*, chronicling the sexual adventures of a group of worldly women in late youth. It transferred to television in 1998, becoming one of the very few American series to employ the word

'fuck'. Indeed, in 1999 the word appeared in an episode title: 'The Fuck Buddy'.

Samuel Butler UK Novelist

Satirist who attacked the strictures of Victorian life in *Erewhon* (1872) and *The Way of All Flesh* (1903); the direct descendant, in literary terms, of Jonathan Swift. 1835–1902

David Byrne US Rock Musician

The creative force behind Talking Heads, wittiest of the American New Wave bands. As their singer and songwriter, he had a nerdy, faux-naïf persona. 1952–

Henry J. Byron UK Writer

1835–84

Lord Byron English Poet

His tempestuous life, embracing numerous affairs and great fame as well as aid to insurgents in oppressed Greece, became a motivating myth for the Romantic movement. Enoch Powell speculated in 1988 that Byron was 'always looking at himself in mirrors to make sure he was sufficiently outrageous'. 1788–1824

Michael Bywater UK Journalist

From the mid eighties he wrote the 'Bargepole' column in *Punch*, so called because it was 'about all the stuff you wouldn't want to touch with one . . . TV personalities, jerk politicians, spanner-faced businessmen'. He currently writes a column in similar Swiftian vein for the *Independent on Sunday*.

James Branch Cabell US Writer

He ranged from fiction to genealogy. 1879–1958

Michael Caine UK Actor

Born Maurice Micklewhite. A laid-back, drawling anti-hero with a glottal stop who has appeared in such films as *The Ipcress File* (1965) and *Alfie* (1966). Later, he ranged more widely in his roles. 'In England, I was a cockney actor. In America I was an actor,' he has said. He has interests in six restaurants. 1933–

C. S. Calverley English Writer

Barrister, light versifier. 1831–84

James Cameron UK Journalist

Morally engaged yet witty current affairs reporter. He also wrote and presented TV programmes such as *Men of Our Time* (1963). Later turned to writing drama. 1911–85

Baron Campbell UK Barrister, Writer of Legal Books
John Campbell. Lord Chancellor of Ireland 1841. 1779–1861

Mrs Patrick Campbell UK Actress
Born Beatrice Stella Tanner. A friend of Shaw; he created the part of Eliza Doolittle for her in *Pygmalion* (1914). Yeats said she had 'an ego like a raging tooth'. 1865–1940

Roy Campbell South African Poet
A swashbuckling Catholic right-winger, Campbell fought for Franco in the Spanish Civil War. He celebrated nature in much of his poetry, and was anti-gentility. Attacked the Bloomsbury set in *The Georgiad* (1931). In his book *Four Absentees* (1960) Raymond Heppenstall wrote that Campbell 'was inclined to hit people'. 1901–57

Albert Camus French Writer
Algerian born; philosophically convinced that life was absurd. *The Outsider* (1942) made his name and associated him with Existentialism. He won the Nobel Prize for Literature in 1957. 1913–60

George Canning UK Politician
A Conservative with a reputation for intellectual brilliance, Canning was Prime Minister in 1827, having served twice as Foreign Secretary. 1770–1827

Al Capone US Criminal
Archetypal American gangster of Prohibition-era Chicago. 1899–1947

Truman Capote US Writer
Socialite, celebrity author. *Breakfast at Tiffany's* (1958) was later filmed. The murder tale *In Cold Blood* (1966) was a 'nonfiction novel' and his highest achievement before block set in. 1924–84

Al Capp US Cartoonist
Drew the bucolic Li'l Abner and friends for the *New York Mirror* (from 1934). 1909–79

Frank Capra US Film Director
Creator of humane comedies that (usually) stopped short of sentimentality, chiefly *It's a Wonderful Life* (1946). 1897–1991

Sir Neville Cardus UK Journalist
Joined the *Manchester Guardian* in 1916, where he wrote about cricket and music in an elegant high style. For example (from 1930): 'Now is the time of the cricketer's plenty – June and July. Let him cherish every moment as it passes; never will he be so young again.' 1889–1975

Henry Carey English Comic Writer
Introduced the word 'namby-pamby' as a term of abuse. Wrote, about 1734, *Chrononhotonthologos*, a burlesque of current drama, 'the Most Tragical Tragedy that ever was Tragediz'd by any company of Tragedians'. *c*.1681–1743

George Carlin US Comedian
A touring stand-up since, as he puts it, 'the counter-culture' became the 'over-the-counter culture' (late 1960s); author of the bestselling *Brain Droppings* (1997), which includes such pithy remarks as 'What year did Jesus Christ think it was?'

Thomas Carlyle UK Historian, Political Philosopher
Essayist, thinker, a product of the Scottish Enlightenment. His *History of the French Revolution* (1837) established his reputation – once he had rewritten it, the first draft having been used by J. S. Mill to light a fire. Carlyle became 'the sage of Chelsea' (where he lived). Turned increasingly away from democracy and towards authoritarianism. A. N. Wilson, an admirer of Carlyle, has said: 'It is probably impossible for me to persuade [anyone] that Carlyle is worth another try.' 1795–1881

Art Carney US Comedian, Actor
Stooge, or 'second banana', to many stars of American TV, notably Jackie Gleason with whom he was paired in *The Honeymooners*, one of the most popular sitcoms of the 1950s. He later acted in films. 1918–2003

J. L. Carr UK Author
Headmaster, publisher, novelist. Resident of Kettering and, according to Byron Rogers, 'the last Englishman' (it was the title of his biography of Carr). Carr wrote exquisite short comic novels in the main, such as *How Steeple Sinderby Wanderers Won the FA Cup* (1975), but his masterpiece, *A Month in the Country* (1980), was a tragedy. 1912–94

Jimmy Carr UK Comedian
According to the *Daily Telegraph*, he 'likes making people laugh at things they know they shouldn't laugh at'. 1973–

Lord Carrington UK Politician
Peter Carrington; Conservative. Held ministerial posts under Churchill, Eden and Macmillan; an urbane and gentlemanly Foreign Secretary 1979–82; resigned over the Falklands War, accepting responsibility for security shortcomings that allowed the Argentinian invasion. Secretary General of NATO 1984–88. 1919–

Lewis Carroll English Writer

Charles Lewis Dodgson. Maths lecturer at Christ Church, Oxford, who produced *Alice's Adventures in Wonderland* (1865) and its successor *Through the Looking Glass* (1871). Both are funny, dreamlike, frightening, reflecting Carroll's interest in logic chopping and the activities of pretty young girls. 1832–98

Jasper Carrott UK Comedian

Born Robert Davis. Appeared on TV throughout most of the 1980s and 90s. The *Daily Telegraph* has written: 'Carrott's scrawny tortoise face emerging from his pipe-cleaner body is perfectly formed to express indignation at the follies of the world.' 1945–

Frank Carson UK Comedian

Irrepressible Ulsterman, came to prominence on the ITV show of the early 1970s *The Comedians*. His catchphrase: 'It's the way I tell 'em', or (sometimes) 'You've heard 'em all before but it's the way I tell 'em.' 1926–

Johnny Carson US Talk Show Host

Urbane host of *The Tonight Show* 1962–92. He would perform a monologue, then interview celebrities. 1925–2005

Viscount Castlerosse Irish Journalist

Valentine Charles Browne. Gossip columnist, socialite, friend of the famous, author. He was painted by Sickert. 1891–1943

Nicolas-Sébastien Roch de Chamfort French Writer

Society figure and failed playwright who shot himself rather than be captured by the Jacobins during the French Revolution. He died, eventually, of his wounds, leaving behind a large number of insightful and witty maxims that were first published in the year after his death. 1741–94

Charlotte Chandler US Journalist

Specializes in interviewing the very famous. At the age of nineteen she gave up telling people her age, according to Christopher Silvester in *The Penguin Book of Interviews* (1992).

Raymond Chandler US Writer

Born in Chicago and raised in England, along with Dashiell Hammett Chandler brought literary respectability to the mystery genre. His best works such as *Farewell My Lovely* (1940) and *The Long Goodbye* (1953) feature the soulful, hard-drinking detective Philip Marlowe, and chronicle the low-life of Los Angeles. As Chandler wrote in 1944: 'Down these mean streets a man must go . . .' 1888–1959

Lord Chandos UK Publisher

Anthony Alfred Lyttelton, second Viscount Chandos. 1920–80

George Chapman English Playwright

It is to Chapman's *The Whole Works of Homer: Prince of Poets* (1611) that Keats's poem 'On first looking into Chapman's *Homer*' refers. Among Chapman's plays is the comedy *The Gentleman Usher* (c.1602). The tragedy *Revenge for Honour* was ascribed to him after his death, possibly wrongly. c.1559–1634

Charles, Prince of Wales Heir to the British Throne

Prince of Wales; heir to Elizabeth II – and has been for a famously long time. Speaks out strongly on rural life and architecture. 1948–

Charles II King of England, Scotland and Ireland 1660–85

Religious arguments dominated his reign, and he was persistently suspected of Catholic sympathies. 1630–85

Geoffrey Chaucer English Poet

Also senior public official, initially under Edward III. His masterpiece *The Canterbury Tales* was begun in the late 1380s, when his career in royal service was declining. Through its depiction of a group of pilgrims of varying degrees of immorality, it offers a panorama of medieval life. c.1345–1400

Mavis Cheek UK Novelist

Starting with *Pause between Acts* (1988) she has written novels of relationships, done with wry humour. 1948–

Anton Chekhov Russian Writer

Main works are *Uncle Vanya* (1896), *The Three Sisters* (1901) and *The Cherry Orchard* (1904); he also wrote short stories. 1860–1904

Lord Chesterfield English Politician, Writer

Philip Dormer Stanhope, 4th Earl of Chesterfield. Whig MP 1716–26, twice ambassador to Holland, ameliorative and reforming Lord Lieutenant of Ireland 1745–6. As a writer, best known for his shrewd and amusing *Letters to His Son* (1774). 1694–1773

G. K. Chesterton UK Writer

Wrote poetry, fiction, social and literary criticism and, after his conversion to Catholicism in 1922, upon religious matters. An exuberant Falstaffian figure, he is best remembered for the stories of his priest-detective Father Brown (1911–35). The journalist and writer Hugh Lunn wrote in 1912 that at Oxford, Shavians and Chestertonians were common types. The Chestertonians were not so brilliant as the Shavians, but welcomed 'a writer who defends old modes of thought with humour, and attacks modern thinkers on the ground that they are antiquated bores in disguise'. 1874–1936

Joseph H. Choate US Lawyer

Tax lawyer; ambassador to Britain 1899–1905. 1832–1917

Agatha Christie Writer

The most prolific and bestselling crime writer ever. Wrote over three hundred books. 1890–1976

Charles Churchill English Poet

Satirist; a feisty, combative figure from a humble background. *The Prophecy of Famine* (1763) attacks the Scots; *The Ghost* (1762–3) was aimed at Samuel Johnson (Boswell, though, admired Churchill). 1731–64

Winston Churchill UK Statesman, Writer

Credited by Sir Henry 'Chips' Channon with being 'the saviour of the civilized world', he led the coalition government during the Second World War. Lost the general election of July 1945 to Clement Attlee, leader of the Labour Party, but became Prime Minister for the second time in 1951. Among his writings are *A History of the English-Speaking Peoples* (1956–8) and *My Early Life* (1930), a compelling account of his aristocratic childhood and *Boys' Own*-style escapades during the Boer War. Awarded the Nobel Prize for Literature in 1953. He was a great wit, and highly eloquent in print and vocally, as his morale-boosting wartime broadcasts proved. When Attlee was asked what Churchill had done to win the war, he replied: 'Talk about it.' 1874–1965

Colley Cibber English Playwright

The brusque and showy Cibber became the hero of the third edition of Pope's *Dunciad*, and his comedies were praised by Smollett and Walpole. His autobiography *An Apology for the Life of Mr Colley Cibber, Comedian* was published in 1740. 1671–1757

Cicero Roman Soldier, Statesman, Lawyer, Writer

The most prolific of Roman authors whose works survive. His writings, in a variety of genres (letters, speeches, philosophy), were long considered models of elegance. Cicero was murdered in the faction fighting of the late Republic. 106–43 BC

Alan Clark UK Politician, Diarist

The most considerable literary figure to emerge from British politics since ... well, for a very long time. An Old Etonian right-wing Conservative, Clark was a junior minister under Margaret Thatcher and John Major but will be remembered for his *Diaries*, especially the first volume (1993) in which he is by turns skittish, moody and – above all – lustful. When asked whether he had any skeletons in the closet, Clark replied: 'Dear boy, I can hardly close the door.' 1928–99

Ross Clark UK Journalist

Contributes to the *Sunday Telegraph*, *Spectator* and the *Mail on Sunday*. Has also written a history of Cambridgeshire, where he lives. 1966–

Arthur C. Clarke UK Writer

As a boy he became addicted to the pulp stories for sale in his local Woolworth's in Taunton, especially those in a magazine called *Astounding Stories*. After the Second World War, he took a first in maths and physics at London University and then began writing science fiction, from *The Sands of Mars* (1951) onwards. He also writes non-fiction with a scientific theme. His novel *2001: A Space Odyssey* was filmed, magisterially, by Stanley Kubrick. Clarke lives in Sri Lanka. 1917–

John Clarke English Poet
d. 1658

John Cleese UK Comic Actor, Writer

Performer with a manic style, particularly good at portraying middle-class men coming unravelled. Cleese was a member of the *Monty Python* team whose surreal TV programmes ran from 1969 to 1974. He later co-wrote and starred in the BBC TV series *Fawlty Towers*, rated by many as the finest ever sitcom; more recently he has concentrated on films. 1939–

Dick Clement and Ian La Frenais UK Scriptwriters

After achieving great success on British TV with sitcoms such as *Porridge* (1974–7) and *Auf Wiedersehen Pet* (1983–6), the pair moved to LA, where they became film script doctors (*The Rock*, 1996) and scriptwriters (*The Commitments* (1991) *Still Crazy* (1998)). 1937– and 1938–

Hillary Clinton US Politician

Wife of Bill, Democratic Senator from 2001. More likely than anyone else to be America's first female president. 1947–

Arthur Hugh Clough English Poet
Protégé of Dr Arnold at Rugby School; much of his poetry arose from his personal crises of religion. 1819–61

Brian Clough UK Footballer, Manager
His successful playing career was cut short by injury. As manager of Nottingham Forest (1964–75), a theoretically small club, he won the League Championship once, the League Cup four times and the European Cup twice. Logically, he should have managed England, but was too opinionated and undiplomatic. Clough was known as 'Ol' Big Head'. Asked whether he considered himself the best manager of his time, he replied: 'I'd say I was in the top one.' 1935–2004

Claud Cockburn UK Journalist
Described by Malcolm Muggeridge as 'the most perfect specimen of the genus [journalist] ever to exist'. He wrote funnily about serious subjects. Originally a communist. 1904–81

Jean Cocteau French Polymath
Actor, film director, novelist, artist, critic, and brilliantly successful at all. Cecil Beaton wrote: 'As silent as Jean's mouth is talkative, the dilated pupils of his bulging fishy eyes, anguished and tortured, aghast and helpless, seem to be looking into another existence.' 1889–1963

Nick Cohen UK Journalist
Prolific, pugnacious, left-wing, and equally adept at polemic and investigation. Consistently against Tony Blair until the Second Gulf War in 2003, which Cohen supported, thus himself becoming a target for the left. 1962–

Harry Cohn US Film Executive
For a long time head of Columbia Pictures, Cohn was a formidable operator. 'I don't get ulcers, I give them,' he once said. 1891–1958

Frank Moore Colby US Critic
Editor of the *New International Encyclopedia* 1900–1903 and 1913–15. 1865–1925

Samuel Taylor Coleridge UK Poet, Critic, Philosopher
Lyrical Ballads (1798), written with William Wordsworth, contains his best-known poem *The Rime of the Ancient Mariner* and signifies the start of English Romanticism. 1772–1834

Colette French Novelist, Music-Hall Artiste
Sidonie Gabrielle Colette. In the music halls she was a dancer and mime artist; as a writer she was good on nature and childhood, and is best known in England for *Gigi* (1944). 1873–1954

Joan Collins UK Actress
Starred in *The Stud* (1979) and *The Bitch* (1980), based on books written by her sister Jackie Collins, and as the glamorous but vicious Alexis Carrington in *Dynasty* (1981–9). Famous for the longevity of her looks. 1933–

George Colman the Elder English Playwright
Also barrister and friend of Garrick, with whom he wrote *The Clandestine Marriage* (1766); author of comedies in his own right, including *The Jealous Wife* (1761) and *Tit for Tat* (1786). His son George Colman the Younger was also a playwright. 1732–94

George Colman the Younger English Playwright
Comedy specialist, son of George Colman the Elder. 1762–1836

Charles Caleb Colton English Clergyman, Writer
Best remembered for his collection of aphorisms, *Lacon* (from 1820), which included: 'Imitation is the sincerest form of flattery.' He committed suicide over gambling debts. 1780–1832

Pat Condell UK Comedian

William Congreve English Playwright
Contemporary of Swift's at Trinity College, Dublin. *Love for Love* (1695) is considered his richest play. He died in a coach accident. 1670–1729

Sean Connery Scottish Film Actor
Played James Bond from *Dr No* (1962) to *Never Say Never Again* (1983), and is usually thought of as the best Bond. Subsequently came out as bald, and won an Academy Award for his performance in *The Untouchables* (1987). Knighted in 2000. 1930–

Billy Connolly Scottish Comedian
Highly successful – formerly a welder. Henry Root, in *Henry Root's World of Knowledge*, said his insouciance 'is such that even his constant references to "big jobbies" seldom give offence'. 1947–

Cyril Connolly UK Critic
Known mainly for his witty, aphoristic *Enemies of Promise* (1938), which set out his rules for writers. With Stephen Spender he founded the literary magazine *Horizon* (1939–50). He also enjoyed, and wrote about, food and wine. Ken

Tynan described Connolly as 'either a bon viveur with a passion for literature, or a littérateur with a passion for high living'. 1903–74

Joseph Connolly UK Writer

Hirsute and dapper bookseller turned comic novelist. Titles include *This Is It* (1993) and *The Works* (2003). His style has been described as a felicitous combination of Kingsley and Martin Amis's. 1950–

Shirley Conran UK Writer

The first female editor of the *Observer* magazine. Her Superwoman series of books (1974–7, 1990) were bestsellers written for harassed working wives. Was married (1955–62) to Terence Conran. 1932–

Steve Coogan UK Actor, Character Comedian

On the radio news satire of the early 1990s *The Day Today* he created the character of Alan Partridge, a vain sports reporter with a suburban mindset. Partridge grew into his own television chat show, *Knowing Me, Knowing You . . . with Alan Partridge*, followed by *I'm Alan Partridge*. Coogan also acted in films, and is often compared to Peter Sellers for the subtlety of his observation. 1965–

Dan Cook US Sports Journalist

Peter Cook UK Comedian, Writer

As the de facto leader of the Oxbridge quartet in *Beyond the Fringe* (revue, from 1960), the founder of the Establishment Club and the magazine *Private Eye*, Cook was at the heart of the 1960s 'satire boom'. In fact, he *was* it, although his humour soared far above the earnestness that is often associated with satire. He wrote the TV series *Not Only . . . But Also* (1965–71) in which he starred with Dudley Moore. He also acted in several films, but Cook's entrepreneurial flare waned and he spent much of his last two decades sitting at home in Hampstead drinking and smoking too much – which only added to his romantic allure, especially since his humour was undiminished. 1937–1995

Jilly Cooper UK Novelist

Highly successful author of racy, effervescent novels such as *Riders* (1985) and *Polo* (1991). 1937–

Tommy Cooper UK Comedian

A shambling, deliberately malcoordinated comic magician, highly respected for his timing. Made his name on the London variety circuit and progressed to several TV series of his own. Cooper collapsed during a televised stage performance;

Harry Secombe commented: 'I knew he'd died because he fell gracefully.' 1922–84

Wendy Cope UK Poet

A schoolteacher until the publication of *Making Cocoa for Kingsley Amis* in 1986. Other collections of 'seriously funny' poetry followed. She has said: 'I think it's a question which particularly arises over women writers: whether it's better to have a happy life or a good supply of tragic plots.' 1945–

Ronnie Corbett UK Comedian, Actor

Small. From 1971, worked with Ronnie Barker on the TV comedy series *The Two Ronnies*. 1930–

Alan Coren UK Humorist

Editor of *Punch* 1978–87, and was one of the funny ones. Writes numerous articles, which are then collected into books. 1938–

Frances Cornford UK Poet

Known for 'To a Fat Lady Seen from a Train', described by Margaret Drabble as 'curiously memorable though undistinguished'. 1886–1960

Mat Coward UK Writer

Prolific author. Writes journalism, crime fiction, children's books, among other genres. Interests include left-wing politics, vintage comedy, cats and gardening. He is considering compiling *The Bumper Book of Not Terribly Funny Jokes.*

Noël Coward UK Playwright, Actor, Composer

His *Hay Fever* (1925), *Private Lives* (1930) and *Blithe Spirit* (1941) are classic comedies. He wrote the film *Brief Encounter* (1946), among others. His selling point was wit. Kenneth Tynan said: 'His sense of humour is as ebullient as a paying oilwell.' Coward said that when he died 'there [would] be lists of apocryphal jokes I never made and gleeful misquotations of words I never said'. 1899–1973

Abraham Cowley English Poet

Wrote the poem 'Pyramus and Thisbe' when he was ten. *The Puritan and the Papist* (1643) was a satire, and an attempt to ingratiate himself with the Royalist cause in the Civil War, in which he was never quite successful. Known for the clarity of his style. 1618–67

William Cowper English Poet

Contributed hymns to John Newton's *Olney Hymns* (1779) that are still enjoyed today; forerunner of Wordsworth as a nature poet. 1731–1800

Mandell Creighton UK Prelate

Rose to become Bishop of London; also a historian and author of *The Shilling History of England* (1879), among other historical works. 1843–1901

Pat Crerand UK Footballer

Won the European Cup in 1968, among other trophies in his nearly four hundred games with Manchester United. 1939–

Charles Crichton UK Film Director

Associated with Ealing Comedies. Among his credits are *The Lavender Hill Mob* (1951) and *The Titfield Thunderbolt* (1952). 1910–99

Quentin Crisp UK Writer, Raconteur

Born Denis Pratt. In youth he was 'not merely a self-confessed homosexual but a self-evident one'. At a time when 'men searched themselves for vestiges of effeminacy as though for lice', he walked about in full makeup and with hennaed hair. One of the great camp epigrammatists. He gave one-man shows, and his scabrous art reached its height in his autobiography *The Naked Civil Servant* (1968), which became a celebrated TV film in 1975 and enabled him to move to New York. 1908–99

Julian Critchley UK Politician, Writer

Conservative MP for Aldershot 1970–97. A maverick on the left of his party, Critchley wrote several irreverent books on political life including *Palace of Varieties: An Insider's View of Westminster* (1989). 1930–2000

David Croft and Jimmy Perry UK Writers

Co-creators of the exemplary sitcom *Dad's Army* (from 1968) about a socially variegated Home Guard unit whose members varied from the merely incompetent to the near-senile. The pair also wrote *Are You Being Served?* and *'Allo 'Allo*, among other sitcoms characterized by large ensemble playing. Perry had actually been in the Home Guard. 1922– and 1923–

Colin Crompton UK Comedian

Sometime bank clerk who rose to a moderate degree of fame on the TV show *The Comedians* (from 1971), which showcased the talent from the northern clubs. Crompton is gloomy and consumptive-looking, with wonderful deadpan timing.

Richmal Crompton UK Writer

Born Richmal Crompton Lamburn. Her main creation is the anarchic schoolboy William Brown, who appeared in thirty-eight books (starting

with *Just William* in 1922) that are still considered funny. 1890–1969

Barry Cryer UK Comedian

Reliable jokesmith; has written scripts for Morecambe and Wise, George Burns and many others. Presented the TV series *Jokers Wild* in the 1970s, and is a regular on the BBC radio spoof panel game *I'm Sorry I Haven't a Clue*. 1935–

Will Cuppy US Humorist

His best-known work, *The Decline and Fall of Almost Everybody*, appeared posthumously in 1950. It is sometimes sold as a companion to *1066 and All That*. 1884–1949

Richard Curtis UK Screenwriter

Co-wrote with Ben Elton and Rowan Atkinson the 'historical' BBC TV sitcom *Blackadder*. His films, including *Four Weddings and a Funeral* (1994) and *Notting Hill* (1999), are polished romantic comedies. 1956–

Michael Curtiz Hungarian Film Director

Born Mihaly Kertesz. Highly efficient director of over sixty films; moved to Hollywood in the 1920s. 1888–1962

Lord Curzon UK Politician

George Nathaniel Curzon, Conservative. Viceroy of India 1898–1905 and Foreign Secretary 1919–24. 1859–1925

Salvador Dali Spanish Painter

Highly egotistical surrealist, best known for his work of 1931 *The Persistence of Memory* (or *Limp Watches*). 1904–89

Lord Darling UK Politician

George Darling; Labour MP 1950–74; also a journalist. 1905–85

Clarence Darrow US Lawyer

Defended Leopold and Loeb in the sensational murder trial of 1924; determined opponent of the death penalty. 1857–1938

Miles Davis US Jazz Trumpeter

Innovative musician who played with Charlie Parker in the early days of bebop, then pioneered 'cool jazz' with the arranger Gil Scott-Heron. Davis was acclaimed for his plangent tone and feared by some on account of his acerbic personality. 1926–91

Sammy Davis Junior US Singer, Entertainer

A versatile star since the 1950s, Davis could sing,

dance, act, do impersonations and tell jokes, often about having only one eye (he lost the other in a car crash in 1954). He would boast, or complain, of being the world's only 'one-eyed Jewish nigger'. 1901–78

Les Dawson UK Comedian
Rubber-faced Lancastrian (he could put his nose into his mouth) who in vocal style was a classic northern droll. From *Sez Les* (1969–76), he was a TV success. A considerable wordsmith, he also wrote several novels and comic books. 1934–93

Sir John Charles Frederic Sigismund Day UK Judge
Queen's Bench Division. 1826–1908

Alain de Botton UK Writer
In his books, which include *The Consolations of Philosophy* (2000) and *The Art of Travel* (2002), de Botton shows how the writings of great thinkers apply to the difficulties of everyday life, while supplying his own learned interjections. 1967–

Charles de Gaulle French General, Statesman
Effectively the leader of the French Resistance during the Second World War, and President of France 1958–69. 1890–1970

Liane de Pougy French Socialite
Folies Bergere dancer, reputedly the most beautiful courtesan in Paris. She married Prince Georges Ghika of Romania in 1920; later became a nun. 1869–1950

Thomas De Quincey UK Essayist
The Confessions of An English Opium Eater recounts his time living in London with a prostitute called Anne, and was first published as a serial in *The London Magazine* in 1821. 1785–1859

Madame de Staël French Writer
Anne-Louise-Germaine Necker, daughter of Jacques Necker, the Genevan statesman. Intellectual of the Enlightenment and a liberated woman before her time, famous for her many affairs. De Staël wrote a lot of books, notably *De l'Allemagne* (1810) in which she pioneered the use of the word 'Romanticism'. 1766–1817

Peter De Vries US Writer
Associate of James Thurber and, like him, a witty regular in the *New Yorker*; his twenty novels include *Tunnel of Love* (1954). 1910–93

Angus Deayton UK Comedian, Actor
The enjoyably sardonic chairman of the topical quiz show *Have I Got News for You*, until in

2002 an alleged sexual indiscretion made him the show's main target. He was then fired. He appeared as Patrick in the long-running sitcom *One Foot in the Grave*. 1956–

Guy Debord French Writer
1931–94

Jack Dee UK Comedian
Dee, who once applied to train as a vicar, is a saturnine comic with a perpetually curled lip. Has presented his own TV series including *Jack Dee's Saturday Night* (1995–6); also performs as a straight actor. 1961–

Daniel Defoe English Writer
Often thought of as the first true English novelist in that his work was of an unprecedented realism. *Robinson Crusoe* (1719) was his first novel, published after Defoe had made his name as a political writer. 1660–1731

Ivor Dembina UK Comedian
Highly rated stand-up based in London. He addresses tricky subjects such as prostitution and anti-Semitism. 1951–

Jack Dempsey US Boxer
Nicknamed the Manassa Mauler, he won the world heavyweight title in 1919. When he lost it in 1926 he set up as a restaurateur. 1895–1983

Adolph Deutsch UK Composer, Conductor
Composed and arranged for many Hollywood films, including *Some Like It Hot* (1959). 1897–1980

Lord Dewar UK Businessman
Distiller, raconteur, author of books of funny sayings. 1864–1930

I. A. L. Diamond US Screenwriter
Romanian born; frequently collaborated with Billy Wilder. 1920–88

Charles Dibdin English Songwriter, Playwright
Originally an actor; wrote a hundred sea songs including 'Poor Jack' and 'Tom Bowling'. 1745–1814

Thomas Dibdin English Bibliographer
Nephew of Charles Dibdin. 1776–1847

Charles Dickens English Writer
Fanatically driven writer of fiction and journalism, his industry perhaps deriving from childhood poverty; he was the best of his time, and possibly of any time. His first novel was *The Pick-*

wick Papers (1836); his own favourite, and the most autobiographical, was *David Copperfield* (1849). Dickens excelled at comedy, but Thomas Carlyle found in his work, 'hiding amid dazzling of the sun, the elements of death itself'. 1812–70

John Dighton UK Screenwriter
Scripted *The Happiest Days of Your Life* from his own play (1949); co-wrote *Kind Hearts and Coronets* (1949). 1909–

Phyllis Diller US Writer, Actress
Wild and strange-looking comedienne, seen on TV and, less successfully, in films. 1917–

Isak Dinesen Danish Writer
Karen Blixen. Highly regarded since *Seven Gothic Tales* (1934). 1885–1962

Benjamin Disraeli UK Politician
Disraeli, later 1st Earl of Beaconsfield, was Conservative Prime Minister 1868 and 1874–80, and the nearest Britain has ever come to having an Oscar Wilde in the top seat. Remarkably, he was witty, dandified, sexually mysterious, impecunious and Jewish, and had not been to private school or university. As a politician he is associated with emollient one-nation Conservatism. Gladstone, his political foe, described him as a 'sophisticated rhetorician inebriated by the exuberance of his own verbosity'. His biographer Robert Blake wrote: 'The wits and aphorists are not qualified to govern their country simply because of those gifts, but it adds to the gaiety of nations when they do. And Disraeli and Churchill did it rather well.' 1804–81

Lara Dixon UK Scholar
In 1999 won a scholarship worth £64,000 to read Economics at Harvard, having been turned down by Oxford. 'I screamed with delight,' she said. 1981–

J. Frank Dobie US Writer
Texan folklorist. Temporarily thwarted in his academic career by the lack of a PhD, he nonetheless became a full professor at the University of Texas. During the Second World War he taught literature at Cambridge. 1888–1964

Ken Dodd UK Comedian
Regularly seen on TV in the 1960s, but latterly the sole perpetuator of the music-hall tradition in that he constantly tours the provincial theatres of England. Famous enough for a 'Ken Dodd' to be cockney rhyming slang for a wad of banknotes. 1927–

Chris Donald UK Humorist
Co-founder with his brother Simon in 1979 of the brilliantly funny X-rated parody of a children's comic, *Viz*. Notoriously keen on trains and lives in a converted railway station. *See also Viz.*

William Donaldson UK Humorist
Has also written under the name Henry Root. 'Root' wrote letters to well-known people eliciting their support for his bigoted causes; *The Henry Root Letters* became a bestseller. Also produced *Henry Root's World of Knowledge*, 'the first and most comprehensive one-volume encyclopaedia of British common sense ever to be published'. A very funny man. 1935–2005

J. P. Donleavy Irish-American Novelist
Born in New York of Irish parents; associate, while at Trinity College, Dublin, of Brendan Behan. His picaresque, bawdy first novel *The Ginger Man* (1955) was regarded as a comic masterpiece. He also paints. 1926–

Christopher Douglas UK Humorist
Co-writer, with Nigel Planer, of *I, An Actor* (1988), the cod biography of a very actorly actor. Another amusing alter ego of Douglas's is Dave Podmore, acquisitive, cliché-spouting county cricketer.

Sir Alec Douglas-Home UK Statesman
Baron Home of the Hirsel; Conservative. Prime Minister in 1963, succeeding Macmillan. Lost the 1964 election to Harold Wilson. Home, according to the mantra of the time, was pronounced Hume. 1903–95

Tim Dowling UK Journalist, Humorist
American-born. Also the author of *The Inventor of Disposable Culture: King Camp Gillette* and *Not the Archer Prison Diary*. 1963–

Sir Arthur Conan Doyle UK Writer
Creator of the most fascinating and popular detective in crime fiction, the preternaturally observant Sherlock Holmes who figured in his stories 1887–1905. Doyle arranged for Holmes to be killed at the hands of his arch-enemy Professor Moriarty, but was required by overwhelming public demand to resurrect him. 1859–1930

Roddy Doyle Irish Novelist
His palette is working-class Dublin. *Paddy Clarke Ha Ha Ha* won the Booker Prize in 1993. 1958–

Tom Driberg UK Politician, Journalist
Combined left-wing socialism, high Anglicanism and high spirits. Also a skilful journalist who rose to become Chairman of the Labour Party in 1957. Driberg, who died Lord Bradwell, was the

first person to be described as homosexual in a *Times* obituary. 1905–76

Harry Driver and Vince Powell UK Scriptwriters
Co-wrote *Bless This House* and *Nearest and Dearest*, among other sitcoms. Harry Driver died in 1973.

Alexandre Dumas French Writer
Romantic storyteller, best known for *The Count of Monte Cristo* and *The Three Musketeers*, both published in 1844. 1802–70

Elaine Dundy US Actress, Writer
Born Rita Brimberg. In 1950 she met Ken Tynan, who said, 'I am the illegitimate son of Peter Peacock. I have X amount of pounds. I will either kill myself or die at the age of thirty, because I will have said all there is to say . . . Will you marry me?' Dundy reflected, 'Well, I just might', and she did. Her book *The Dud Avocado* appeared in 1958. 1921–

Nell Dunn UK Writer
Middle-class connoisseur of working-class life, and author of the vivid demotic novel *Poor Cow* (1967). Her plays include *Steaming* (1981), set in a women-only Turkish bath. 1936–

Finley Peter Dunne US Humorist
Often spoke in the persona of his fictional Irish publican and philosopher Mr Dooley. 1867–1936

Ian Dury UK Singer, Songwriter
Highly literate lyrics-writer for, and lead singer of, the Blockheads, who were associated with New Wave and came to prominence with their album *New Boots and Panties* (1977). 1942–2000

John Dyer Welsh poet
An appreciator of the countryside, who became a clergyman. 1699–1757

Bob Dylan US Singer, Songwriter
Born Robert Zimmerman. Through his free-associating poetic lyrics, his connection with radicalism in the 1960s – epitomized by the song 'Blowin' in the Wind' (1962) – and his enigmatic persona, Dylan transcended the folk scene to become one of the giants of rock music. George Harrison said: 'He makes William Shakespeare look like Billy Joel.' 1941–

Jake Eberts Canadian Film Producer
Founder of Goldcrest Films, the production company whose biggest success was *Chariots of Fire* (1981). 1941–

Jenny Éclair UK Comedian, Writer
At first remarkably foul-mouthed, Éclair won the Perrier Award at the Edinburgh Festival in 1995 and went on to feature in many TV shows, to write scripts and, in 2000, a novel, *A Camberwell Beauty*.

Thomas Alva Edison US Inventor
Invented, amongst a thousand other things, the gramophone (1877) and the incandescent light bulb. 1847–1931

John Edmonds UK Trade Unionist
General Secretary of the GMB from 1986 to 2003; staunch defender of the public sector. 1944–

Blake Edwards US Film Director
Also a screenwriter. Associated from 1963 with the Pink Panther series, which he wrote and directed. 1922–

Jack Elam US Actor
Tall, gaunt, with a wild and rolling left eye, Elam was well equipped to play the baddie in Westerns, and this he did in *High Noon* (1952), *Gunfight at the OK Corral* (1957) and *Once Upon a Time in the West* (1969). 1918–2003

George Eliot English Novelist
Born Mary Ann Evans. From *Adam Bede* (1859) onwards, she was a success. Her reputation declined after her death, but was revived in the 1940s by the critic F. R. Leavis. 1819–80

T. S. Eliot Anglo-American Poet
Thomas Stearns Eliot. One of the most important poets of the twentieth century. *The Waste Land* (1924) is a cynical account of the postwar world that has been much imitated and parodied. Eliot himself called it 'a piece of rhythmical grumbling'. Awarded the Nobel Prize for Literature in 1948. 1888–1965

Elizabeth I Queen of England and Ireland 1558–1603
1533–1603

Elizabeth II Queen of Great Britain and Northern Ireland 1952–
1926–

Duke Ellington US Jazz Musician
Edward Kennedy Ellington. Endlessly inventive pianist and band leader who came to prominence in the 1930s. One of the first jazz musicians to write long pieces. 1899–1974

Ebenezer Elliott English Poet
A master-founder in Sheffield, author of the

anti-Corn Law *Corn Law Rhymes* of 1830. 1781–1849

C. Hamilton Ellis　UK Writer

Wrote at least thirty-six books on railways. His main interest was locomotives, but the *Oxford Companion to British Railway History* lists as his most notable publication *Railway Carriages in the British Isles 1830–1914* (1965). His writing was lively and anecdotal, with a visual flair – he was also a painter. 1909–87

Ben Elton　UK Comedian and Writer

Made his name as the leading 'alternative' comedian of the 1980s with routines combining descriptions of domestic neuroses and political themes. His successful sitcoms include *Blackadder* (initially with Richard Curtis) and *The Young Ones* (with Rik Mayall and Lise Mayer); and Elton did not falter when he turned to writing novels, plays and stage adaptations. A website about him refers to 'the Ben Elton comedy shelf' at Amazon.co.uk 1959–

Ralph Waldo Emerson　US Philosopher, Poet

Having resigned as a Unitarian pastor in Boston, he went on to promote individualism and spiritual independence. An associate of Thomas Carlyle. 1803–82

Dick Emery　UK Comedian

His eponymous TV series began in 1963 and ran for twenty years. Emery – skilled in characterization – portrayed a gallery of grotesques, much as Harry Enfield would in the following decade. 1917–83

Harry Enfield　UK Comedian, Actor

In his comic characterizations for TV, Enfield captured many archetypes of the 1980s and early 90s. He has said that in private life he is 'always the second-funniest person in the room'. 1961–

Nora Ephron　US Screenwriter, Director

Adept at witty romantic comedy, as witness *When Harry Met Sally* (1989) and *Sleepless in Seattle* (1993); also wrote and directed *You've Got Mail* (1998). 1941–

Desiderius Erasmus　Dutch Humanist

Priest who became attracted to Christian humanism; his criticisms of the Church anticipated Luther. Author of many popular books on philosophy. c.1466–1536

Sir George Etherege　English Playwright

A rakish figure. Influenced by Molière, he wrote comedies of manners. The best is *The Man of Mode* (1676). 1636–91

Chris Evans　UK Broadcaster

'Bad boy' disc jockey of the mid-1990s, with Radio 1 and then Virgin Radio; also a TV presenter, and owner of Ginger Productions. 1966–

William Norman Ewer　UK Writer

1885–1976

Clifton Fadiman　US Writer, Broadcaster

Literary critic who chaired the NBC radio programme *Information Please* (1938–52), in which members of the public could earn two dollars if a question they submitted was put to a panel of witty intellectuals. 1904–99

Adam Faith　UK Singer, Actor

Born Terence Nelhams. A pop star with an insouciant style, before becoming an actor. Successful on TV in the 1970s, playing a cockney rogue in *Budgie* (1971–2), written by Keith Waterhouse and Willis Hall. In his later years he owned a personal finance TV channel. 1940–2002

King Farouk　King of Egypt 1936–52

His extravagant lifestyle, and his defeat by Israel in 1948, led to the coup of 1952 by which he was ousted. 1920–65

George Farquhar　Irish Playwright

Originally an actor. Accidentally stabbed another actor at the Dublin Smock Alley Theatre during the duel scene of Dryden's *Indian Emperor*. Gave up acting, and Dublin, moving to London to write such vigorous comedies as *The Recruiting Officer* (1706) and *The Beaux' Stratagem* (1707), but died destitute. 1677–1707

William Faulkner　US Writer

Masterpieces include *The Sound and the Fury* (1929), which established his fraught, stream-of-consciousness style. Faulkner, who was known to write while drunk, was awarded the Nobel Prize for Literature in 1949. 1897–1962

Marty Feldman　UK Writer, Comedian

With Barry Took wrote the radio series *Round the Horne* (1966–9). Went on to star in his own TV shows and in the Mel Brooks films *Young Frankenstein* (1973) and *Silent Movie* (1976). With his bulging eyes, caused by an overactive thyroid, he was thought early on to be unsuitable for mainstream viewing. The thyroid problem may have made him restless, accounting for the frequent changes of direction in his career. 1933–82

Graham Fellowes　UK Comedian

While a drama student, in 1978 had a punk hit

as 'Jilted John'. In 1985 he created the persona of John Shuttleworth, a mild-mannered, middle-aged retired security guard and aspiring pop star. 'Shuttleworth' has appeared in radio and TV series. Typical of his songs is 'Mary Had a Little Lamb', about a trip with his wife to a local carvery. 1960–

Sir Alex Ferguson UK Football Manager

Fiery Scotsman, not a good loser. As manager of Manchester United he won the League Championship, the FA Cup and the European Championship in 1999, and many competitions besides. 1941–

Eugene Field US Writer

Wrote the column 'Sharps and Flats' for the *Chicago Morning News* 1883–95; and poetry for children, including 'Little Boy Blue' (1888). 1850–95

Helen Fielding UK Writer

BBC producer turned novelist. Her first book was *Cause Celeb* (1994) but she is best known for *Bridget Jones's Diary* (1997), which arose out of a newspaper column and chronicles the life of a lovelorn single woman in her thirties, eternally pursuing inner poise and meanwhile drinking and smoking to excess.

Henry Fielding English Writer

Wrote 'comic epics in prose', effectively the first 'modern' English novels; as a lawyer he also co-founded the Bow Street Runners, the beginnings of the police force. *His Apology for the Life of Mrs Shamela Andrews* (1741) was a parody of Samuel Richardson's *Pamela*, which he considered pompous; in 1749 *Tom Jones* was an instant success. 1707–54

W. C. Fields US Actor

His trademarks on screen were misanthropic wisecracks, stovepipe hat, pelican-headed cane and above all his bulbous red nose. This was taken to be the result of drinking, but although Fields did drink a lot – his only known poem was about Martinis – his nose was deformed by a skin condition unrelated to alcohol. He played Micawber in *David Copperfield* (1934) and wrote many of the comedies he appeared in, including *My Little Chickadee* (with Mae West, 1940). 1879–1946

Sir Donald Finnemore UK Judge

County Court 1940–47; High Court thereafter. 1889–1974

Ronald Firbank UK Writer

Author of amusing, mannered novels; specialist in dialogue; his style influenced Evelyn Waugh, who said, 'I think there would be something wrong with an elderly man who could enjoy Firbank.' 1886–1926

Carrie Fisher US Actress, Writer

Daughter of Eddie Fisher and Debbie Reynolds. Married for a while to Paul Simon. Played Princess Leia in *Star Wars* (1977); also a scriptwriter, script doctor and acerbic novelist. 1956–

F. Scott Fitzgerald US Novelist

Chronicler, in such books as *The Great Gatsby* (1925), of moneyed hedonism in the Jazz Age. Later a martyr to the Hollywood scriptwriting process. 1896–1940

Robert Fitzsimmons US Boxer

Scored 40 victories with 32 knockouts, 11 losses. Won three world titles at the turn of the nineteenth and twentieth centuries; known as Bob. 1862–1917

Michael Flanders and Donald Swann UK Musicians

Met at Westminster School. Donald Swann wrote the lyrics, Michael Flanders the words of their comic songs. Fame came in 1956 with the LP *At the Drop of a Hat*. They performed in dinner jackets, and Flanders, who had contracted polio in 1943, in a wheelchair (which he considered 'the perfect mask for constitutional laziness'). 1922–75, 1923–94

Ian Fleming UK Writer

Creator, starting with *Casino Royale* (1952), of the suave British secret agent James Bond. The books were admired by some for their terse style, damned by others for their sadism. Bond's afterlife in blander films has been commercially unstoppable. 1908–64

Peter Fleming UK Writer

Prolific journalist associated with the *Spectator*; also known for his travel books, including *Brazilian Adventure* (1933); brother of Ian. 1907–71

Errol Flynn US Actor

At his swashbuckling peak in *The Adventures of Robin Hood* (1938). A wayward character. David Niven said of him: 'You always knew precisely where you stood with him because he *always* let you down.' 1909–59

Marshal Foch French Soldier

Ferdinand Foch; became Allied Commander-in-Chief in 1918. 1851–1929

Michael Foot UK Politician

Originally a political journalist with radical views, he led the Labour Party 1980–83. Widely considered the product of a more bookish age, with his long sentences and rather scruffy attire. 1913–

Henry Ford US Industrialist

Founder of the Ford motor company in 1903; pioneer of the production line. 1863–1947

George Foreman US Boxer

Won the world heavyweight championship in 1973, lost it the following year to Muhammad Ali, then regained the title in 1994. Foreman said: 'I want to keep fighting because it is the only thing that keeps me out of the hamburger joints.' On retirement he endorsed the 'lean mean fat-reducing grilling machine', of which fifty million have been sold. He has ten children. 1948–

Howell Forgy US Naval Chaplain

1908–83

E. M. Forster UK Writer

Wrote subtle, insightful novels of emotionally 'muddled' English middle-class life, such as *A Room with a View* (1908), *Howards End* (1910). 1879–1970

Redd Foxx US Actor

Born John Elroy Sanford. Star of *Sanford and Son* (1972–7). 1922–91

Benjamin Franklin US Statesman, Scientist, Writer

Also printer and public official in Pennsylvania; inventor of the lightning rod (Franklin proved that lightning was an electrical discharge); inventor of the bifocal lens; negotiator of peace with Britain after the American Revolution. Writer, often humorously, on public affairs, and energetic correspondent. 1706–90

Jonathan Franzen US Novelist

Made it big with *The Corrections* (2001), about a family falling apart – it was widely considered a masterpiece. 1959–

Michael Frayn UK Journalist, Novelist, Dramatist

First known for his humorous columns in the *Guardian* newspaper. Among his fiction is *Towards the End of the Morning* (1967), usually regarded as the only Fleet Street novel to compete with Evelyn Waugh's *Scoop*. Frayn's plays range from the near-slapstick (*Noises Off*, 1982) to the highly cerebral (*Copenhagen*, 1998). 1933–

Peter Freedman UK Journalist, Marketing Consultant

Founder of the bright-ideas consultancy Thinkinc; sometime leader of the 'Campaign for Shorter Plays'. 1958–

Matt Frei UK Broadcaster

BBC Journalist since 1987. Born in East Germany, he reported on the fall of the Berlin Wall. 1963–

Clement Freud UK Politician, Broadcaster

Grandson of Sigmund, brother of Lucian. Baleful wit of radio and TV, sometime celebrity chef, one-time jockey and, for a *long* time, a Liberal MP. 1924–

Sigmund Freud Austrian Neurologist, Founder of Psychoanalysis

Traced neurosis to infant sexuality, and would quote with approval Walt Whitman: 'Yet all were lacking, if sex were lacking.' 1856–1939

Thomas L. Friedman US Writer

Pulitzer Prize-winning foreign affairs correspondent for the *New York Times*; an expert on the Middle East. 1953–

Robert Frost US Poet

Much garlanded, the unofficial poet laureate of America. His imagery owed a lot to his boyhood on a New England farm. 1874–1963

Christopher Fry UK Playwright

Author of free-verse plays with religious themes, including *The Lady's Not for Burning* (1949) and *Venus Observed* (1950). Film scripts include *Ben Hur* (1959). 1907–

Stephen Fry UK Writer, Actor

A very prolific performer and brilliant wit. Came to prominence working with Hugh Laurie in the TV shows *A Bit of Fry and Laurie* (1989–94) and *Jeeves and Wooster* (1991–3). His writings include the novels *The Liar* (1991) and *The Stars' Tennis Balls* (2000). In 1994 he played his hero Oscar Wilde in the film *Wilde*. His epigrams – fruity and often scatological – have enlivened many game shows. 1957–

Thomas Fuller English Clergyman, Writer

Chaplain to Charles II; author of whimsical works such as *The History of the Worthies of England* (1622). 1608–61

Henry Fuseli English Artist

Swiss-born priest, turned romantic history painter and teacher of art. Keeper of the Royal

Academy 1804–25. Fuseli was irascible and could swear in seven languages. 1741–1825

Zsa Zsa Gabor US Actress

Born Sari Gabor in Hungary, she was Miss Hungary in 1936. Her fame grew perhaps more on account of her eight marriages than her films. Oscar Levant said: 'Her face is inscrutable, but I can't vouch for the rest of her.' 1919–

Serge Gainsbourg French Singer, Songwriter

Romantic figure in France, with his eternal cigarette and glass of wine. His songs were often explicitly sexual, especially 'Je t'aime', which was basically a transcribed orgasm, performed by Gainsbourg's lover, the English actress Jane Birkin. 1929–91

J. K. Galbraith US Economist

Epigrammatic Keynesian, adviser to J. F. Kennedy. His books such as *The Affluent Society* (1958) have reached a wide audience. 1908–

John Galsworthy UK Writer

From 1906 onwards wrote the volumes of *The Forsyte Saga*, which dissected English upper-middle-class life before and after the First World War. Galsworthy fell out of fashion later in the 1920s, when a new generation of writers found him too preoccupied with society, too little with human nature. He also wrote thirty plays. 1867–1933

Ray Galton and Alan Simpson UK Comedy Scriptwriters

The two met while convalescing from TB. Wrote the radio and TV scripts for Tony Hancock, helping to forge his persona as a wistful romantic stuck in East Cheam, and making him the biggest comedian in Britain for the duration of the shows (1954–61). They had great success with another sitcom, *Steptoe and Son*. 1930– and 1929–

Mahatma Gandhi Indian Politician

Leader of the Indian National Congress, in which capacity he orchestrated the campaign of civil disobedience against British rule. After independence he tried to mediate between Hindus and Muslims in Bengal, and was killed by a Hindu militant. 1869–1948

Lowell Ganz US Screenwriter

Comedy specialist. 1948–

Greta Garbo Swedish Actress

Cultivated an aura of remoteness and enigma in films such as *Flesh and the Devil* (1927) and *Grand Hotel* (1932). But Herbert Kretzmer said:

'Boiled down to essentials, she is a plain, mortal girl with large feet . . .' 1905–90

Graeme Garden UK Comedian, Writer

Best known as one of the TV show trio of the late 1970s, *The Goodies*. He played a crazed professor-type, a characterization suggested by his medical training at Cambridge. Has written comedy scripts for many artists and is a regular on the radio comedy series *I'm Sorry I Haven't a Clue*. 1943–

Ed Gardner US Comic

His radio show *Duffy's Tavern* became a film in 1945, in which he starred. *Halliwell's Film & Video Guide* called it 'flat'. 1901–63

David Garrick English Actor

Also theatre manager and playwright. His performance as Richard III in 1741 established him. Known for his pioneering naturalism; for fidelity to Shakespeare texts as originally written (and also for cutting them heavily). He wrote *The Clandestine Marriage* with George Colman the Elder, but they fell out over it. Garrick was by far the dominant thespian of his time. Dr Johnson said, 'His profession made him rich and he made his profession respectable.' 1717–79

Paul Gascoigne UK Footballer

Known as 'Gazza' and generally thought to be, as the title of an early biography had it, 'daft as a brush'. A brilliant player, though, with Newcastle, Tottenham and, to a lesser extent, Lazio and Glasgow Rangers. 1967–

Elizabeth Gaskell English Novelist

Best known for *Cranford* (1853). Lived in Manchester; associated with 'the condition of England' novel. 1810–65

John Gay English Poet, Playwright

Remembered for *The Beggar's Opera* (1728), an amusing depiction of low-life written at the suggestion of Swift. It is said to have made Gay rich and John Rich, the producer, gay. A genial, impecunious man, Gay is buried in Westminster Abbey. 1685–1732

George II King of Great Britain and Ireland 1727–60
1683–1760

George V King of Great Britain and Northern Ireland 1910–36
1865–1936

George VI King of Great Britain and Northern Ireland 1936–52
1894–1952

Ira Gershwin US Songwriter

Lyricist. Co-wrote smash musicals with his brother George. By himself he wrote the lyrics for the *Ziegfeld Follies* (1936), among others. 1896–1983

Ricky Gervais UK Comedian

Creator of *The Office*, a comedy of embarrassment which, according to the *Observer*, 'proved that British sitcom does not necessarily need to be not funny'. It purports to be a fly-on-the-wall documentary of life in a paper-distributing office tyrannized by the ingratiating David Brent, played by Gervais. 1962–

J. Paul Getty US Billionaire

Yet, wrote Bernard Levin, he looked like someone who 'cannot quite remember whether he remembered to turn the gas off before leaving home'. 1892–1976

Edward Gibbon English Historian

Author of *The Decline and Fall of the Roman Empire*, which appeared in six volumes 1776–88. 1737–94

Stella Gibbons UK Novelist

Remembered for *Cold Comfort Farm* (1932), a parody of torrid country novels as written by D. H. Lawrence among others. 1902–89

Wolcott Gibbs US Critic

1902–58

W. S. Gilbert UK Poet, Librettist

Sir William Schwenck Gilbert. Failed barrister who turned to comic poetry, then found his perfect outlet as the librettist for the comic operas of Arthur Sullivan, beginning with *Trial by Jury* (1875). Sullivan called his technique 'topsy-turveydom': that is, proceeding logically from an absurd premise. He died attempting to save a young woman from drowning. 1836–1911

Gilbert and George UK Artists

Gilbert Proesch and George Passmore. Modern art double act. Performed as Singing Sculptures in the 1960s, went on to work with manipulated photographs. Turner Prize-winners in 1986. They have often declared: 'We are an artist.' 1942–, 1943–

A. A. Gill UK Journalist, Novelist

Amusing star critic (restaurants and TV) of the *Sunday Times*, where he combines a high style and frequently swingeing abuse.

Lillian Gish US Actress

Beautiful silent-film star who graduated to talk-ies, notably as the eccentric matriarch in *Night of the Hunter* (1955). 1917–83

William Ewart Gladstone UK Statesman

Prime Minister 1868–74, 1880–85, 1886, 1892–4. Entered Parliament as a reactionary Conservative, but joined the Liberals in 1867 as he came to see politics as a series of moral crusades, culminating in his unsuccessful mission to 'pacify Ireland'. The long-standing adversary of the more flippant Disraeli, he died much loved, the Grand Old Man of British politics. 1809–1903

Jonathan Glancey UK Writer, Journalist

Specializes in architecture and design; associated with the *Guardian*; author of many books, including, for example, *New British Architecture* (1989).

George Glass US Film Producer

1910–84

Jean-Luc Godard French Film Director

Associated with the New Wave. His films are often experimental, and open to being called pretentious. 'You don't make a movie, the movie makes you,' he has said. 1931–

A. D. Godley English Classicist

Also a writer of light verse. 1856–1925

Joseph Goebbels German Politician

Nazi propaganda minister under Adolf Hitler, with whom he committed suicide. 1897–1945

Isaac Goldberg US Writer

1887–1938

William Goldman US Screenwriter

His credits include *Butch Cassidy and the Sundance Kid* (1969). In 1984 he told the truth about Hollywood in his book *Adventures in the Screen Trade*, after which his telephone went very quiet. 1931–

Oliver Goldsmith Anglo-Irish Writer

A hack who transcended that status with the novel *The Vicar of Wakefield* (1766) and the play *She Stoops to Conquer* (1773). 1730–74

Sam Goldwyn US Film Producer

Born Samuel Goldfish. A tough negotiator with a trenchant style, he was at the top of his profession from 1913 onwards. He said: 'I was always an independent, even when I had partners.' 1882–1974

Graham Gooch UK Cricketer

Batsman; captained Essex and England. 1953–

Giles Gordon UK Literary Agent

Novelist, editor and, primarily, agent, in which capacity he represented amongst others Sue Townsend and members of the royal family. His waspish wit was revealed in his autobiography, whose title, *Aren't We Due a Royalty Statement?*, was a question once asked of him by the Prince of Wales. 1940–2003

Ruth Gordon and Garson Kanin US Scriptwriters

Ruth Gordon was an eminent actress who also wrote scripts with her husband Garson Kanin, including *A Double Life* (1948), and *Adam's Rib* (1949). 1896–1985 and 1912–98

Al Gore US Politician

Democrat. Vice President under Clinton. Lost the 2000 election to George W. Bush by a very narrow margin. 1948–

Teresa Gorman UK Politician

Outspoken Conservative MP for Billericay 1987–2001; a minister under John Major. She campaigned against European integration and in favour of women's rights. Her book titles are characteristic: *The Amarant Book of HRT* (1989), *The Bastards: Dirty Tricks and the Challenge to Europe* (1993) and *No, Prime Minister* (2001). 1931–

Lew Grade UK TV and Film Entrepreneur

Born Louis Winogradsky in Ukraine; ended as Baron Grade of Elstree. Indefatigable champion of mainstream family entertainment. 1906–98

Boothby Graffoe UK Comedian

Born James Rogers; borrowed his stage name from a Lincolnshire village. He is a tall, spaced-out-looking comedian who has fronted several BBC radio shows, including *The Big Booth* and *Boothby Graffoe in No Particular Order*. He frequently performs live, and has written two stage plays.

Kenneth Grahame UK Writer

Sometime Bank of England clerk, author of the children's classic *The Wind in the Willows* (1908). 1859–1932

Cary Grant US Actor

Born in Bristol, which forever skewed his accent; expert at comedy, but made good use of by Hitchcock in the thrillers *Suspicion* (1941) and *Notorious* (1946). 1904–86

Robert Graves UK Poet

Particularly celebrated as a love poet; he also wrote non-fiction, including his autobiography *Goodbye to All That* (1929) and novels such as *I Claudius* (1934). He 'bred show dogs in order to be able to afford a cat,' he said. The dogs were prose; the cat, poetry. 1895–1985

Alasdair Gray Scottish Novelist, Painter

After a career as a painter, he began writing late – in 1981 – with *Lanark*. 1934–

Simon Gray UK Playwright

Writes witty plays of middle-class life. 1936–

Rocky Graziano US Boxer

World middleweight champion in 1947 and 1948. Born in New York's Little Italy, he was a juvenile delinquent: 'We stole everything that began with "a" – a piece of fruit, a bicycle, a watch, anything that wasn't nailed down.' In retirement, he took up painting. 1919–

Henry Green UK Novelist, Industrialist

A restless experimental writer. *Living* (1929) attempts to evoke working-class life, observed by Green at the family firm, through a stylized form of colloquial language; *Nothing* (1950) and *Doting* (1952) are mainly dialogue. 1905–73

Jeff Green UK Comedian

The London *Evening Standard* said: 'He brings on that delicious deliquescent feeling of knowing you're going to laugh at anything he says.' 1963–

Matthew Green English Poet

A Quaker, and a Customs House employee. According to Leigh Hunt, he was 'subject to low spirits'. 1696–1737

Michael Green UK Writer

Journalist turned author of books of amazingly durable comedy. Many are to do with how to be good (or bad) at sport, from *The Art of Coarse Rugby* (1960) onwards. A connoisseur of amateurishness, Green used to 'play football with a man who would lean on my shoulder while he turned blue during a game, asking "Am I foaming much, Mike?" ' 1927–

Graham Greene UK Writer

A Catholic convert, one of the leading novelists of his time. His works examine moral questions within milieux invariably described by his fans and detractors alike as 'seedy'. 1904–91

Germaine Greer Australian Feminist, Writer

The Female Eunuch (1970) galvanized a generation of women. She is an academic and a regular broadcaster. 1939–

Joyce Grenfell UK Humorist

First came to notice in *The Little Revue* (1939); became a successful theatrical comedian thereafter. Her one-woman show, *Joyce Grenfell Requests the Pleasure*, went to New York in 1955. In style, Grenfell was a gentle but highly observant satirist of the middle classes. Her catchphrase was 'George, don't do that', an admonition to an unseen child – and also the title of her autobiography (1977). 1910–79

Sir Edward Grey UK Politician

A Liberal; Foreign Secretary for eleven years, until 1916. At the start of the First World War, while watching the street lights coming on through the Foreign Office windows, he commented: 'The lamps are going out all over Europe; we shall not see them lit again in our lifetime.' He was a keen birdwatcher. 1862–1933

Matt Groening US Cartoonist

Comic-strip artist who struck gold in 1987 when he created the animated comedy series *The Simpsons*, depicting a raucous but loving working-class family. With Groening presiding, a remarkably high standard has been maintained by various writers over hundreds of episodes. *The Simpsons* is the longest-running cartoon sitcom in history, and almost universally approved of: Dr Rowan Williams, the Archbishop of Canterbury, has called it 'One of the most subtle pieces of propaganda around in the cause of sense, humility and virtue', and when Barbara Bush called it 'the dumbest show I have ever seen' it was considered politically expedient for her to apologize, which she did. According to Zoë Williams: 'The Simpsons is . . . cast-iron proof that whatever people tell us about the mainstream palate . . . even at our lowest common denominator we are extremely sophisticated.' 1954–

George and Weedon Grossmith UK Writers

Brothers, and authors of *The Diary of a Nobody* (1892), satirizing the aspirations of the pompous lower-middle-class Mr Pooter. Weedon also illustrated the book; George sang in the comic operas of Gilbert and Sullivan. 1847–1912, 1854–1919

Alec Guinness UK Actor

Famously 'faceless' actor, who could disappear into any role. Notable films include *The Ladykillers* (1955) and *The Bridge on the River Kwai* (1957); also a Catholic convert and waspish diarist. Knighted in 1959. 1914–2000

Nubar Gulbenkian Armenian Tycoon

Oil magnate and art dealer, and known as 'Mr Five Percent'. 1896–1972

Ivor Gurney UK Composer, Poet

Gassed in the First World War, he produced two volumes of war poetry in the aftermath; musically, his high point was 'Five Elizabethan Songs' (1920). He lived in a mental institution from 1922. 1890–1937

William Hague UK Politician

Aged sixteen, he made a Churchillian speech at the 1977 Conservative Party Conference, and was on the fast track thereafter. Became the party leader in 1997, and resigned after being trounced in the election of 2001. 1961–

Earl Haig UK Soldier

1st Earl Haig of Bemersyde; Commander-in-Chief of the British army in France, December 1915–1918. 1861–1928

Lord Hailsham UK Politician

Quintin McGarel Hogg. Barrister; Conservative. Lord of the Admiralty 1956–7, Lord Chancellor 1970–74 and 1979–87; and held various ministerial posts in between. 1907–2001

J. B. S. Haldane Anglo-Indian Mathematical Biologist

Oxford-born; adopted Indian nationality while at the Indian Statistical Institute in Calcutta from 1957 onwards; author of numerous books of popular science. 1892–1964

Jerry Hall US Model

Texan, always described as 'leggy'. Married Mick Jagger, although his lawyers later denied that. 1956–

Professor Albert Henry Halsey UK Sociologist

Educationalist. Publications include *Traditions of Social Policy* (1976) and *A History of Sociology in Britain* (2004). 1923–

Margaret Halsey US Writer

1910–

Robert Hamer UK Film Director

Before succumbing to alcoholism, a meticulous and highly rated director, notably of *Kind Hearts and Coronets* (1949) which he also co-wrote. 1911–63

P. G. Hamerton UK Artist

Also a writer, and founder of the art periodical *The Portfolio* in 1869. 1834–94

Neil Hamilton UK Entertainer

From 1983 to 1997 Hamilton, a barrister, was a waspish Conservative MP, latterly a minister. His career was ruined by a failed libel action against Mohamed Al Fayed, who had stated that he had accepted bribes. Since then Hamilton and his wife Christine (always described as 'redoubtable') have seemingly done almost anything for publicity and money. Thus he is credited in *Who's Who* with appearing in *Jack and the Beanstalk* at Guildford in 2002, yet also as having been, in his earlier life so to speak, the editor of *The Land Development Encyclopedia* (1981). 1949–

Dashiell Hammett US Novelist
Hard-drinking crime writer, known for his terse style and mind-bending plots; he actually had worked as a detective. Julian Symons called *The Glass Key* (1931) 'the peak of the crime writer's art in the twentieth century', but noted that Hammett's drinking was explicable (according to one of his friends) 'only by an assumption that he had no expectation of being alive much beyond Thursday'. 1894–1961

Christopher Hampton UK Playwright
Began in the radical setting of the Royal Court Theatre, London, where he was the first writer in residence. His greatest success was *Les Liaisons Dangereuses* (1985, filmed 1998), an adaptation of the novel by Pierre Choderlos de Laclos (1741–1803). 1946–

Tony Hancock UK Comedian
As the pompous yet glum hero of the radio series *Hancock's Half Hour* (began in 1954, written by Ray Galton and Alan Simpson), Hancock became the number one comedian in Britain. The series transferred to television in 1956. In 1963 he sacked Galton and Simpson and began an increasingly neurotic quest to develop as a performer, which led, via alcoholism and depression, to his suicide. Bob Monkhouse said: 'Hancock tried to control his own talent, when he should have let it control him.' 1924–68

E. Y. Harburg US Poet, Librettist
Poet who turned librettist after hearing *HMS Pinafore* by Gilbert and Sullivan. He ran an electrical business to fund his efforts, but it failed in the stockmarket crash. He wrote 'Brother, Can You Spare a Dime?' (1932) and, with Harold Arlen, 'Over the Rainbow' (1939). Killed in a car accident. 1898–1981

Oliver Hardy US Comedian
The supposedly sophisticated one of the film comedy duo, Laurel and Hardy. From 1926 onwards, they appeared in over two hundred films. 1892–1957

David Hare UK Playwright
Author of polemical social critiques, dissecting

the Church of England in *Racing Demon* (1990) and the privatized railways in *The Permanent Way* (2003). 1947–

W. F. Hargreaves UK Songwriter
1846–1919

Joel Chandler Harris US Writer
A journalist who digested the black speech rhythms and folklore of his native Georgia to produce the stories of *Uncle Remus: His Songs and His Sayings* (1880); *Nights with Uncle Remus* followed (1883). 1848–1908

Tony Harrison UK Poet, Playwright
A classicist, but galvanized by a working-class background and a sense of social injustice. 1937–

Rupert Hart-Davis UK Publisher, Writer
From an aristocratic background, Hart-Davis became a true twentieth-century man of letters. His publishing company, Rupert Hart-Davis Ltd, was important in promoting science fiction; Hart-Davis edited volumes of letters by Oscar Wilde, Siegfried Sassoon and others, and wrote a biography of Hugh Walpole (1952). His correspondence with his former schoolmaster in Eton, George Lyttelton, was successfully published as *The Lyttelton–Hart-Davis Letters* (1978 onwards). 1907–99

Max Hastings UK Journalist, Writer
Gangly, cigar-smoking war reporter; then edited the *Daily Telegraph* and the London *Evening Standard* from a relatively liberal standpoint. 1945–

G. H. Hatherhill UK Police Officer

Nathaniel Hawthorne US Novelist
A highly rated writer, scion of an eminent Puritan family, concerned with sin and redemption in such novels as *The Scarlet Letter* (1850). 1804–64

Ian Hay Scottish Writer
Pseudonym of John Hay Beith, novelist and playwright. Collaborated with P. G. Wodehouse on the plays *Damsel in Distress* (1928) and *Leave it to Psmith* (1930). 1876–1952

Will Hay UK Actor
Comedy performer who began in music hall playing a harassed headmaster; appeciated for the subtlety of his characterizations in films such as *Oh Mr Porter* (1938). 1888–1949

William Hazlitt English Writer
Essayist, protégé of Coleridge, who found the poet 'brow hanging, shoe contemplative,

strange . . .' Hazlitt wrote on radical politics and literature. He was associated with the *Edinburgh Review*; friend of Charles Lamb and Leigh Hunt. 1778–1830

Denis Healey UK Politician
Labour statesman. Chancellor of the Exchequer 1974–9, Deputy Leader 1980–83. A communist in his youth, he later became a figurehead of the party's right wing. Brusque but cultured, he prides himself on having 'hinterland' – that is, interests outside politics. 1917–

Sir Edward Heath UK Politician
Conservative Prime Minister 1970–74. Replaced as leader by Margaret Thatcher in 1975, then grumbled from the back benches as the party moved away from his style of social democracy in subsequent years. Also a skilled yachtsman and musician. Tony Benn said, 'Ted Heath is left of New Labour.' 1916–2005

Eric Heffer UK Politician
Labour MP for Walton, Liverpool, from 1964. A plain-speaking socialist and, unexpectedly, a Christian in the Anglo-Catholic tradition. 1922–91

Heinrich Heine German Poet
Many of his poems were set to music by Schubert and Schumann. 1797–1856

Joseph Heller US Novelist
Experience as a bombardier in the Second World War lay behind his sprawling black comedy of military life, *Catch-22*, which has overshadowed his other books. He has said: 'When I read something saying I've not done anything as good as *Catch-22*, I'm tempted to reply, "Who has?" ' 1923–99

Robert Helpmann Australian Dancer, Choreographer
1908–86

Sir Arthur Helps UK Historian
1813–75

Ernest Hemingway US Writer
The Sun Also Rises (1926) established Hemingway as a novelist. His concerns with violence and manliness are reflected in his terse prose style. He committed suicide. 1899–1961

O. Henry US Writer
William Sydney Porter; wrote mannered short stories, from *Cabbages and Kings* (1904) onwards. 1862–1910

Katharine Hepburn US Actress
Feisty, independent-minded, and she played that kind of woman on screen. 1907–

A. P. Herbert UK Writer
Sir Alan Patrick. Humorous author, light versifier and librettist; often, from 1924, to be read in *Punch*; Independent MP for Oxford University 1935–50. Behind his jokes about marriage, notably in the novel *Holy Deadlock* (1934), lay a record of campaigning for easier divorce. 1890–1971

George Herbert English Poet
Metaphysical poet from an aristocratic background, who spurned opportunities for worldly success in favour of the life of a country priest. 1593–1633

Oliver Herford US Poet, Illustrator
All-round wit, and contributor to many publications. 1863–1935

Herodotus Greek Historian
Wrote of the Greco-Persian Wars from 500 to 497 BC. Known as 'father of history'. c.484 BC–c.425 BC

Bill Hicks US Comedian
Lugubrious stand-up comic who railed against most forms of American moralizing. Died of pancreatic cancer, aged thirty-two. In 1997, according to his instructions, two CDs of his material were released: *Arizona Boy* and *Rant in E-Minor*. 1962–94

Benny Hill UK Comedian
Began in variety; TV debut in 1949; practitioner of broad comedy in sketch shows; admired, oddly enough, by Ben Elton. But seaside postcard bawdiness was increasingly frowned on in the politically correct 1980s. 1925–92

Damon Hill UK Formula One Racing Driver
Level-headed son of the more flamboyant Graham Hill. At Melbourne, in the deciding race of the 1994 Championship, he was taken off the track by a chopping move from Michael Schumacher. Won the World Championship in 1996. 1960–

Harry Hill UK Comedian
Born Matthew Hall. Doctor turned nerdy-looking surreal comic whose material mixes British nostalgia, non-sequiturs and slapstick; his staccato style has been compared to the effect of turning the dial on the radio. Hill has appeared regularly in his own TV shows, starting with *Harry Hill's Fruit Fancies* (1994). 1964–

Edmund Hillary New Zealand Mountaineer
Climbed Everest in 1953, the first man (along with Sherpa Tenzing Norgay) to do so. 1919–

James Hilton UK Novelist
Best known for *Lost Horizon* (1933) and *Goodbye Mr Chips* (1934); later a screenwriter in Hollywood. 'Tempted by Hollywood, a writer must decide whether he would rather say a little less exactly what he wants, to millions, or a little more exactly, to thousands,' he once said. 1900–54

Barry Hines UK Writer
Born in Barnsley and associated with the North; best known for *A Kestrel for a Knave* (1968), set in a Yorkshire mining village and filmed as *Kes* by Ken Loach (1969). Hines played football for Barnsley before turning to writing. 1939–

Ian Hislop UK Writer, Broadcaster
Took over the editorship of the satirical magazine *Private Eye* in 1986; has written many TV scripts and appears regularly on *Have I Got News For You*, in which he gives unflinching opinions on the conduct of those in the news. 1960–

Sir Alfred Hitchcock UK Film Director
Films include *The Thirty-Nine Steps* (1939), *Dial M for Murder* (1945), *Psycho* (1960). Technically innovative, a 'master of suspense' (which he sharply differentiated from 'mystery'), Hitchcock had many disciples, including the ostensibly more artistic film-makers of the French Nouvelle Vague. 1899–1980

Christopher Hitchens UK Writer
An Englishman settled in America, Hitchens is a columnist on *Vanity Fair* and *The Nation*. A figure of eighteenth-century wit and feistiness, he has written polemical books against Henry Kissinger, Mother Teresa of Calcutta and President Clinton, and in favour of George Orwell. Being a figure of the left, he perplexed some by writing in favour of the invasion of Iraq in 2003. 1949–

David Hockney UK Artist
Originally a painter associated with the Pop Art movement, he moved on to experiment with photography and computers. 1937–

Heinrich Hoffmann German Doctor, Writer
Author of *Shock-Headed Peter* (1848), a series of cautionary tales in verse about children who come to a bad and violent end. 1809–94

Gerard Hoffnung UK Humorist
Rotund tuba player, cartoonist, broadcaster and writer. 1925–59

Simon Hoggart UK Journalist
At the start of the Thatcher era, he began writing a humorous political column in *Punch*. Went on to become a feature writer for the *Observer* and parliamentary sketch writer of the *Guardian*. P. J. O'Rourke has described him as 'the P. G. Wodehouse of Westminster'. He is the son of the literary critic and sociologist Richard Hoggart. 1946–

Richard Holme UK Politician
Liberal Democrat peer since 1990 and businessman. 1936–

Oliver Wendell Holmes Jr US Lawyer
1841–1935

Arthur Honegger Swiss composer
Wrote *Pacific 231* (1924), a musical evocation of a locomotive. 1892–1955

Thomas Hood English Poet
Journalist and humorist. His *Comic Annuals* (1830–39) were highly popular. A specialist in puns, but called a 'half-Hogarth' by Lamb for not being biting enough. 1799–1845

Anthony Hope UK Writer
Name under which the barrister Sir Anthony Hope Hawkins wrote *The Prisoner of Zenda* (1894). He also wrote, in more humorous vein, *The Dolly Dialogues* (also 1894). 1863–1933

Bob Hope US Comedian
British-born, Hope spoke in wisecracks, his familiar themes being his meanness and, as he got older, his longevity. He starred in a series of successful comedy films in the 1940s, often alongside the more sensible Bing Crosby. 1903–2003

Horace Roman Poet
A humorous, humane and quotable writer, all of whose works survive. The *Odes* represent the zenith of his achievement. 65–8 BC

Leslie Hore-Belisha UK Politician
1st Baron Hore-Belisha. In 1931 became Chairman of the National Liberal Party. As Minister of Transport in 1934 he gave his name – the last part of it – to the orange beacons that flash at zebra crossings; he also introduced driving tests. A reforming Secretary of State for War 1937–40. 1893–1957

Nick Hornby UK Writer

Fever Pitch (1992) viewed the serious events of his childhood through the prism of football, thereby inaugurating a new genre of biography mediated through an ostensibly trivial subject. Highly popular novels have followed, featuring amusingly immature male heroes. 1957–

A. E. Housman UK Poet

Best known for *A Shropshire Lad* (1896). 1859–1936

James Howell English Writer

While imprisoned for Royalist sympathies under Cromwell, he wrote letters describing political intrigue, which were later published many times over. 1593–1666

Frankie Howerd UK Comedian

Camp comic with a stutter, which gave rise to his interestingly disjointed delivery. His catchphrase was 'Titter ye not.' 1922–92

Fred Hoyle UK Astronomer

Taught maths and astronomy at Cambridge; his works on astronomy include *The Nature of the Universe* (1952); also wrote science fiction and children's fiction. 1915–2001

Elbert Hubbard US Writer

A successful businessman who established a craft community in homage to the philosophy of William Morris. The community made art nouveau furniture and was served by a journal called *The Philistine*. 1856–1915

Kin Hubbard US Humorist

Born F. Mckinney Hubbard. 1896–1930

Robert Hughes Australian Art Critic

Has written about art for *Time* magazine since 1970. Presented the series *The Shock of the New* on BBC TV in 1980; keen fisherman. 1938–

Ted Hughes UK Poet

Craggy-looking writer of frequently violent nature poetry, in such as *Hawk in the Rain* (1957) and *Lupercal* (1960). Married to Sylvia Plath; Poet Laureate from 1984. 1930–98

Hubert H. Humphrey US Politician

Democrat. Vice-President to Lyndon B. Johnson from 1964, when he suffered politically as a defender of the Vietnam War; beaten to the presidency by Nixon in 1968. 1911–78

Barry Humphries Australian Comedian

A figure on the fringes of satirical London in the 1960s, Humphries came into his own through his alter ego Dame Edna Everage, a loud, lurid magnification of a typical Melbourne housewife. Dame Edna received her first sustained TV exposure on *The Barry Humphries Show* in 1976. 1934–

Leigh Hunt English Essayist

And self-educated poet, remembered today for 'Jenny Kissed Me' (1844), but primarily an amusing and high-spirited essayist for publications he also founded such as *The Examiner*, *The Indicator*, *The Liberal*, *The Companion*. A staunch defender of Hazlitt and Keats, with whom he was bracketed by snobbish castigators of the 'cockney' school of literature. Of a radical bent, he was sentenced in 1913 to two years in prison for libelling the Prince Regent, having refused to apologize or mitigate the offence in any way. 1784–1859

Norman Hunter UK Children's Writer

Creator of the mad, or at least absent-minded, Professor Branestawm, in a series of books from 1933 onwards. Hunter was also a magician. 1899–1995

Aldous Huxley UK Novelist

Huxley, who was almost blind, began as a satirist and turned to mysticism. In between these phases came *Brave New World* (1932), which warned of scientific brainwashing. 1894–1963

Armando Iannucci UK Writer

Ph.D. student turned TV producer, who helped create the radio news satire *On the Hour* with Chris Morris, and its successor on TV *The Day Today* (1994); he and his writing partner Peter Baynham also provided scripts for Steve Coogan in his role as the crass interviewer Alan Partridge.

Eric Idle UK Comedian, Actor

Proud to be known as 'the third tallest member of Monty Python'. Associate of pop singers. His main post-Python project was the Beatles parody, *The Rutles: All You Need is Cash* (1978), in which he played Dirk McQuickly in a way that apparently caused some coolness between him and the character's model, Paul McCartney. 1943–

William Ralph Inge UK Writer, Cleric

Dean of St Paul's 1911–34; referred to as 'the gloomy Dean' for his downbeat remarks, which often figured in articles for the London *Evening Standard*. 1860–1954

Neil Innes UK Musician, Comedian

A founding member of the Bonzo Dog Doo-Dah Band, and unique among them in that he could read music. He has combined music and comedy ever since, notably in his TV series *The Innes Book of Records* (1979–81) and in the spoof Beatles documentary *The Rutles: All You Need Is Cash* (1978), for which Innes wrote the songs and in which he played Ron Nasty (John Lennon). He has also been the in-house *Monty Python* musician. 1944–

Sir Thomas Inskip UK Politician, Lawyer
First Viscount Caldecote, Lord Chancellor 1939–40; Lord Chief Justice 1940–46. 1876–1947

Eddie Irvine UK Racing Driver
Northern Irish driver of the old school – that is, a playboy as well. Retired from Formula One in 2002. 1965–

Washington Irving US Writer
Considered the first American man of letters. Wrote a five-volume biography of George Washington; also, in comic vein and in the persona of his invented Dutch-American scholar Diedrich Knickerbocker, *A History of New York*. The tales in *The Sketch Book* (1819), which he wrote as Geoffrey Crayon, include 'Rip Van Winkle' and 'The Legend of Sleepy Hollow'. 1783–1859

Christopher Isherwood UK Novelist
His best-known book, *Goodbye to Berlin* (1939), was set in Germany on the eve of Hitler's rise; part of it was adapted to become the musical, then film, *Cabaret*. Isherwood wrote verse plays with W. H. Auden, and emigrated to America with him in 1939. 1904–86

Sir Alec Issigonis UK Car Designer
Turkish-born amateur racing driver who went on to design the Morris Minor and the Mini, the outstanding classic of British motor car design. 1906–88

Eddie Izzard UK Comedian
Born in the Yemen, raised in Wales and Northern Ireland. His TV show *Eddie Izzard: Dressed to Kill* was a hit of 2000. His performances feature stream-of-consciousness monologues, animal impressions and transvestism. He has acted in films since 1996. 1962–

Ian Jack UK Journalist
Reporter on the *Sunday Times*, then co-founder of the *Independent on Sunday*, which he edited 1991–5. Has edited the literary journal *Granta* since 1995. Jeremy Paxman has called him 'the best features writer in Britain'. 1945–

Michael Jackson US Singer, Songwriter
Performed with his brothers as the Jackson Five, then the Jacksons; from 1986, went on to

unprecedented solo success. Usually portrayed as deeply eccentric, with a Peter Pan complex. 1958–

Howard Jacobson UK Writer
One-time Cambridge don turned cerebral and humorous novelist. His main concerns are Jewishness and sex. 1942–

Mick Jagger UK Singer, Songwriter
Leader of the Rolling Stones; co-writer, with Keith Richards, of most of their material; a glamorous enigma. 'There is no connection between the public midnight-rambler image of Jagger and the man himself,' Terry Southern wrote. 'On the contrary he is its antithesis – quiet, generous and sensitive. What this suggests, then, is an extraordinary potential for *acting*.' 1943–

James I of England 1603–25 and VI of Scotland 1567–1625
1566–1625

Clive James Australian Writer, TV Presenter
As the learned but droll TV critic of the *Observer* in the 1970s, he made television reviewing a respectable job for a writer. He has a particularly good ear for the inanities of sports commentaries and a sharp eye for the strangeness of winter sports, especially as conducted by the British. He has also written novels, poems and song lyrics, and presented his own TV shows. 1939–

Henry James US Writer
In his densely written novels, plot is subordinated to psychology and the development of character. He became a British subject in 1915. 1843–1916

Randall Jarrell US Poet, Critic
The collection *Blood for a Stranger* (1942) describes his experience in the war, with which he was preoccupied thereafter. Wrote a highly regarded novel of academic life, *Pictures from an Institution* (1954), and children's books including *The Animal Family* (1965). His death in a road accident may have been suicide. 1914–65

Thomas Jefferson US Statesman
Third US President, 1801–9, and principal drafter of the Declaration of Independence; also an architect and a scholar. 1743–1826

David Jenkins UK Cleric
Bishop of Durham 1984–94; caused controversy with his left-wing views and apparent scepticism. 1925–

Charles Jennings UK Writer
Witty author of observational feature articles and books. *Up North* annoyed a lot of people in the North of England when it appeared in 1995. 1959–

Jerome K. Jerome UK Writer
The son of a failed ironmonger, he was an actor, then a journalist – experiences which made him a connoisseur of shabby gentility and pretension. In 1892 he founded *The Idler* magazine. His novel *Three Men in a Boat* (1889) is routinely cited as one of the funniest ever. 1859–1927

Douglas Jerrold English Playwright, Journalist
Wrote plays including *Black-Eyed Susan* (1829), developed from the ballad by John Gay. Jerrold later wrote for *Punch*, most notably monologues of a hectoring wife entitled *Mrs Caudle's Curtain Lectures*. 1803–57

Sir George Jessel English Judge
Lucid Master of the Rolls from 1873. 1824–83

C. E. M. Joad UK Philosopher
A civil servant who became head of philosophy at Birkbeck College, University of London. Best known for his appearances on the BBC radio series *The Brains Trust*, in which intellectuals were asked questions in a strongly *de-haut-en-bas* atmosphere. 1891–1953

Boris Johnson UK Politician, Journalist
Conservative MP for Henley; editor of the *Spectator*. Johnson also writes on politics, often in jocular vein, for the *Daily Telegraph*. 1964–

Lyndon Baines Johnson US Politician
Texan Democrat, President 1963–9 following the assassination of President Kennedy. Johnson, who had a trenchant style, prosecuted the Vietnam War and made significant reforms in the field of civil rights. 1908–73

Martin Johnson UK Journalist
Formerly cricket commentator with the *Independent*, turned sports feature writer for the *Telegraph*. 1949–

Pamela Hansford Johnson UK Writer
Author of twenty-five novels, depicting complex social interaction with satirical overtones and luxurious language. Her model, to some extent, was Proust. *The Unspeakable Skipton* (1959) was recently republished as a comic classic. She was married to C. P. Snow. 1912–81

Paul Johnson UK Writer
Prolific: his many books include *A History of the American People* (1997) and *A History of the Jews* (2001). Used to edit the *New Statesman*, but is now a columnist on the *Spectator* – a move reflecting his political shift from left to right. 1928–

Philander Chase Johnson US Humorist
1866–1939

Samuel Johnson English Writer
Focal point of Augustan literature, and the archetypal man of letters. His early poetry includes *The Vanity of Human Wishes* (1749); while writing essays for *The Rambler* he compiled his *Dictionary of the English Language* (1755), and his *Lives of the Poets* appeared in 1781. Johnson's large-hearted, opinionated, humorous nature is captured, along with a fund of his epigrams, in *The Life of Samuel Johnson* (1791) by James Boswell. All that said, George Bernard Shaw believed that Johnson had 'wasted his life trifling with literary fools in taverns' instead of 'shaking England with the thunder of his spirit'. 1709–84

Brian Johnston UK Broadcaster
After education at Eton and Oxford and winning the Military Cross in the Second World War, Johnston joined the BBC, gravitating to cricket commentary on first television, then radio. Known to listeners as 'Johnners', an amiable Bertie Woosterish figure, even in his seventies. 1912–94

Milton Jones UK Comedian
Tousled, dazed-looking performer, at his best expressing bewilderment. Won the Perrier Best Newcomer award at the Edinburgh Fringe in 1997; has appeared on TV in, for example, *Planet Mirth* (1997), and on radio in the ongoing sketch show *The Very World of Milton Jones*.

Terry Jones UK Comedian, Film Director
Member of the *Monty Python* comedy team who, post-*Python*, has directed films, promoted real ale and written books reflecting his interest in medieval history. 1942–

Vinnie Jones UK Footballer, Actor
Played for Wimbledon from 1986, gaining a reputation as a hard man in a hard team. Retired from football in 1999 to play hard men in films. 1965–

Erica Jong US Poet, Novelist
Has said that she writes 'out of a naked female consciousness'. With her novel *Fear of Flying* (1973), she also acquired a reputation for sexual frankness. 1942–

Ben Jonson English Playwright
After a turbulent and violent youth, he produced his first important play in *Every Man in His Humour* (1598). Shakespeare – whom Jonson loved 'on this side of idolatry' – appeared in it. The masterpieces that followed included *Volpone* (1606), *The Alchemist* (1610) and *Bartholomew Fair* (1614). His posthumous reputation suffered as Shakespeare's increased. 1573–1637

Janis Joplin US Singer
Rebellious white blues singer. 1943–70

Sir Keith Joseph UK Politician
Cabinet minister under Margaret Thatcher, and her chief intellectual ally; an important ideological buttress of Thatcherism. 'We need inequality to eliminate poverty,' he said. 1918–94

Benjamin Jowett English Scholar
Professor, and Master of Balliol College, Oxford (1870–93). Translator of Plato, Aristotle, Thucydides. 1817–93

James Joyce Irish Writer
Foremost novelist of Modernism. *Ulysses* (1922) follows the streams of consciousness of three ordinary Dubliners; *Finnegans Wake* (1939) is more like a stream of *unconsciousness*: the transcribed dream of a publican, full of neologisms. *Ulysses*, especially, was greeted with acclaim, but also with derision. 1882–1941

John Junor UK Journalist
Trenchant political columnist who rose to become editor of the *Sunday Express*. His catchphrase as a columnist was 'I do not know the answer to this, but I think we should be told.' 1919–97

Norton Juster US Writer
Author, in 1962, of the children's classic *The Phantom Tollbooth*; also an architect. 1929–

Juvenal Roman Writer
The foremost satirist of Imperial Rome. From Juvenal come the Latin tags 'a healthy mind in a healthy body' and 'bread and circuses'. C.AD 60–140

Garson Kanin *see* Ruth Gordon

Jeffrey Katzenberg US Film Executive
Head of Walt Disney Films 1985–94. 1951–

Danny Kaye US Actor
Born David Daniel Kaminsky. A madcap, ginger-haired whirlwind on stage and film. His best films include *Hans Christian Andersen* (1952) and *The Court Jester* (1956). 1913–87

Dillie Keane UK Musician
Sometime newspaper columnist; leader of the witty female singing trio Fascinating Aida, who look genteel but are not.

John Keats English Romantic Poet
Lamia . . . and Other Poems (1820) encapsulates his genius. 1795–1821

Barrie Keeffe UK Playwright
Writer of hard-hitting, socially concerned plays beginning with *Only a Game* (1973). Wrote the screenplay for *The Long Good Friday* (1984), regularly cited as the best British thriller. 1945–

Garrison Keillor US Novelist, Humorist
His radio show *The Prairie Home Companion* presents humorous, folksy tales from the fictional town of Lake Wobegon (1974 onwards). Several books stemmed from the broadcasts, including *Lake Wobegon Days* (1985). Keillor is a regular contributor to the *New Yorker*. 1942–

Penelope Keith UK Actress
Plays snooty women, most notably Margot Leadbeatter in the sitcom *The Good Life* (1975–8). The voice of the bear in *Teletubbies*. 1939–

John F. Kennedy US Statesman
Democratic President from 1960 until his assassination in 1963, an event which cast a permanent shadow over American history. Kennedy was the youngest man ever to be elected to the office. 1917–63

Nick Kent UK Rock Journalist
Has something of the profile of a rock star himself, being a pale and, at one time, drug-fuelled bohemian. The definitive collection is *The Dark Side: Selected Writings on Rock Music 1972–1995*. Elvis Costello wrote a song called 'Waiting for the End of the World' after spotting Kent on an Underground train.

Jean Kerr US Playwright
Wife of the drama critic Walter Kerr, an alliance that may have inspired the plotline of the 1963 film *Critic's Choice*, which is about a critic who gives a bad review to his wife's play. 1923–

Walter Kerr US Theatre Critic
Won a Pulitzer Prize for Dramatic Criticism in 1978; husband of Jean Kerr, the playwright. 1913–

Andy Kershaw UK Broadcaster
Disc jockey who, in a pronounced Lancastrian accent, conveys his enthusiasm for World Music. 1959–

John Maynard Keynes UK Economist
Elegant in style; proponent of state intervention to create full employment. 1883–1946

Anthony Kiedis US Musician
Lead singer with the Red Hot Chili Peppers, who became famous with the LP *Blood Sugar Sex Magik* (1991). 1962–

Mary Killen UK Humorist
Funny journalist, author of the 'Dear Mary' column (among others) in the *Spectator*, which deals with questions of etiquette arising largely from her own imagination.

Aline Kilmer US Poet
1888–1941

Joyce Kilmer US Poet
Actually a man; best known for his poem 'Trees' of 1914. 1886–1918

Francis Kilvert English Clergyman, Diarist
His diary, dating from 1870 but not published until 1938, recorded rural life in mid-Victorian Wales. 1840–79

Benjamin Franklin King US Poet
His poetry often appeared in newspapers and journals such as *The Century*. Popular in his time, but little information on his career survives. 1857–94

Daren King UK Novelist
Author of *Boxy an Star* and *Jim Giraffe*. His writing has been said to resemble 'some delirious encounter between P. G. Wodehouse and William S. Burroughs'. 1972–

Hugh Kingsmill English Writer
Critic, novelist, biographer, anthologist. 1889–1949

Miles Kington UK Humorist
Writer of genuinely humorous articles for, successively, *Punch*, *The Times*, the *Independent*. Often, as he admits, referred to as 'Miles Kingston'. 1941–

Rudyard Kipling English Writer
Born in India, educated in England, then returned to India as a journalist. He provokes extreme reactions, having a trenchant yet flamboyant style – Kingsley Amis said that to read Kipling was to be 'bombarded with felicities' – and being associated with the defence of imperialism. *The Jungle Books* (1894–5), *Kim* (1901) and the *Just So Stories* (1902) are all children's classics. His collections of poetry and autobio-

graphical works were also highly popular. Awarded the Nobel Prize for Literature in 1907. 1865–1936

Henry Kissinger US Diplomat
Secretary of State under Nixon from 1973; exponent of intensive 'shuttle diplomacy' between the US and both China and Russia, and between the Arabs and the Israelis. 1923–

India Knight UK Writer
Author of the semi-autobiographical comic novels *My Life on a Plate* and *Don't You Want Me?* 1965–

E. V. Knox UK Humorist
Contributed to *Punch* as 'Evoe', and edited the magazine 1932–49. 1881–1971

Ronald Knox UK Writer, Priest
Catholic convert who produced books on theology; also light verse. Evelyn Waugh wrote his biography in 1959. 1888–1957

Arthur Koestler UK Writer
Born in Budapest, a communist until the eve of the Second World War. His best-known book is *Darkness at Noon* (1940), an allegory of Stalinism. 1905–83

Stanley Kubrick US Film Director, Screenwriter
Noted for his monomaniacal approach to making such visually extravagant films as *Dr Strangelove* (1963), *A Clockwork Orange* (1971) and *Full Metal Jacket* (1987). Julia Phillips wrote: 'To me, there has always been chocolate cake and all other kinds of cake, Stanley Kubrick and all other directors . . .'. 1928–2001

Thomas Kyd English Playwright
Chiefly remembered for *The Spanish Tragedy* (c. 1587), which was extremely popular in its time. 1558–94

Ian La Frenais *see* Dick Clement

David Lacey UK Sports Journalist
Wrote about football on the *Guardian* staff from 23 November 1964 (Coventry City v Crystal Palace) to the final of the 2002 World Cup (Brazil v Germany). He once wrote that David Batty 'would doubtless get himself booked playing Handel's Largo'.

Lady Caroline Lamb English Writer
Wife of William Lamb, 2nd Viscount Melbourne, she became obsessed with Lord Byron, and consequently unstable. Her novel *Glenarvon* (1816) depicted herself and Byron. 1785–1828

Charles Lamb English Writer
Devoted his life to caring for his sister Mary, who had stabbed their mother in an attack of mania. He and Mary wrote *Tales from Shakespeare* (1807), but Lamb is best known for his *Essays of Elia* (1823–33). 1775–1834

Burt Lancaster US Actor
Hollywood leading man. His notable films include *Gunfight at the OK Corral* (1957), *The Swimmer* (1967) and *Atlantic City* (1981). 1913–94

Osbert Lancaster UK Writer, Cartoonist
Drew a pocket cartoon in the *Daily Express* that starred Maudie, Countess of Littlehampton. In the words of Alan Watkins: 'He was also an illustrator of books, a designer of stage-sets, an historian of architecture, an underestimated writer of English prose, a dandy, a compulsive clubman and, as he freely admitted, a most tremendous snob.' 1908–86

Bert Lance US Government Official
White House Budget director for nine months under Jimmy Carter. 1931–

John Lanchester UK Writer
His first novel *The Debt to Pleasure* (1996), narrated by a sinister gourmand, won the Whitbread First Novel Prize; *Mr Philips* followed in 2000, *Fragrant Harbour* in 2002. 1962–

Ann Landers US Journalist
Born Esther Pauline Friedman. Wrote a widely syndicated agony column. Divorced in 1975, she referred freely to this event in the advice she gave others. 1918–

Sir Edwin Landseer UK Animal Painter
He modelled the lions at the foot of Nelson's Column. 1802–73

Anthony Lane UK Journalist
Film critic of the *New Yorker* from 1993.

Ring Lardner US Writer
Sports journalist who also produced wry, streetwise short stories. 1885–1933

Philip Larkin English Poet, Novelist
Larkin's poetry appeared in collections from *The North Ship* (1945) to *High Windows* (1964). He came to prominence in the 1950s as part of the Movement group, who reacted against the intellectualism of the likes of Auden and Eliot. Larkin was humorous, downbeat, the foe of pretension. 1922–85

D. H. Lawrence UK Novelist
Remembered for lyrical, and frank, treatment of sex in *Women in Love* (1921) and *Lady Chatterley's Lover*, which was published in Italy in 1928, but did not appear in Britain until 1960. 1885–1930

George Le Brunn *see* Edgar Bateman

Stephen Leacock British-born Canadian Writer
Part-time humorist, Professor of Economics at McGill University, biographer of Dickens and Mark Twain. His more surreal writings influenced Spike Milligan. 1869–1944

Edward Lear English Artist, Humorous Poet
Engaged by the Earl of Derby in 1832 to sketch the animals in his menagerie, Lear began to entertain the Earl's children with nonsense limericks, poems and drawings. This led to *A Book of Nonsense* (1846) and others in similar vein. 'Children swarmed to him like settlers', wrote Auden. 'He became a land.' 1812–88

Fran Lebowitz US Humorist
Her elegantly sarcastic observations appear in the collections *Metropolitan Life* (1978) and *Social Studies* (1981). Edmund White described Lebowitz as being 'for the eternal verities of sleep, civilized conversation and cigarette smoking'. 1951–

Laurie Lee UK Writer
Nature poet, author of the bucolic and autobiographical *Cider with Rosie* (1959). 1914–97

Tom Lehrer US Songwriter
Harvard maths postgraduate who, in the late 1950s, began writing and performing darkly humorous songs, often with a left-wing theme. After his greatest success, with the album *That was the Year That Was* (1965), he reverted to academia, encouraging rumours of his own death in order, he said, to reduce the volume of junk mail he received. A characteristic song title is *Poisoning Pigeons in the Park*. Lehrer reflected, 'If, after hearing my songs, just one human being is inspired to say something nasty to a friend, or perhaps strike a loved one, it will all have been worth the while.' 1929–

Lemmy UK Pop Musician
Ian 'Lemmy' Kilminster. Leader, from 1975, of the heavy metal band Motorhead, who play faster than most heavy metal bands, and even louder. *The Penguin Encyclopedia of Popular Music* sums up: 'No musical progress in ten years, but the fans love it.' 1945–

Vladimir Ilyich Ulyanov Lenin Russian Revolutionary
Prime mover of the Bolshevik Revolution; leader of Soviet Russia 1917–24. 1870–1924

J. Robert Lennon US Novelist
Author, to date, of five fiction works, all highly praised. 1970–

John Lennon UK Musician
Driving force – at least in their early years – of the Beatles. He and Paul McCartney wrote their hits in a spirit of cooperation, or competition. Lennon was the most astringent of the four, both musically and personally. Pursued a solo career until assassinated in New York. 1940–80

Dan Leno UK Comedian
A music-hall performer since the age of three, he could sing, tell jokes, dance and do contortions. In 1897 he was billed as the 'funniest man on earth' during an American tour. In 1901 he was given a diamond cravat pin by Edward VII. He had soulful eyes and a gently pessimistic worldview. 'You can't get away from facts' he would say. 1860–1904

H. C. Leon UK Lawyer, Writer
County Court Judge and author of at least forty books under the name Henry Cecil. 1902–76

Hugh Leonard Irish Writer
Playwright, and sometime screenwriter. 1926–

Leonardo da Vinci Italian Artist, Engineer
Renaissance genius. 1452–1519

Alan Jay Lerner US Songwriter
Collaborated with Frederick Loewe on Broadway musicals such as *Paint Your Wagon* (1951) and *Gigi* (1958); also scripted the film *An American in Paris* (1951). 1918–86

Kathy Lette Australian Writer
Wrote her first novel, *Puberty Blues*, as a teenager. Half a dozen more have followed – epigrammatic accounts of women's travails. 1958–

Oscar Levant US Musician, Actor
A notoriously crotchety man who played particularly the music of Gershwin, and was paid very large sums for doing so; Levant also wrote the film *An American in Paris* (1951). 1906–72

Ros Levenstein UK Advertising Copywriter
'It beats as it sweeps as it cleans' (for Hoover vacuum cleaners) is among his famous slogans.

Ada Leverson UK Writer
Made her name as a humorist parodying her friend Oscar Wilde in *Punch*. He praised her wit. Her novels, featuring strong women, include *The Twelfth Hour* (1907) and *Love's Shadow* (1908). 1865–1936

Harry Levin US Literary Critic
Noted stylist; expert on the Elizabethans. 1912–94

Leonard Louis Levinson US Humorist
Specializes in collecting definitions, as in 'comedian: a guy with a good memory who hopes nobody else has'. These are collected in *The Left-Handed Dictionary* (1963). Also wrote screenplays, and once worked in a circus, where he said, he cleaned out the lions' cages.

C. S. Lewis UK Writer
English literature don at Oxford, then Cambridge. The author of numerous books on the practice of the Christian faith, and of the seven 'Narnia' stories (1950–56), children's classics that can be read as Christian allegory. 1898–1963

Joe E. Lewis US Comedian
1901–71

Wyndham Lewis UK Writer, Painter
Son of an American father and an English mother. On the eve of the First World War he founded the Vorticist movement with Ezra Pound. In terms of painting, it was harsh and angular; or, as Lewis later said, it comprised 'what I, personally, did and said at a particular period'. A sometime Hitler sympathizer, Lewis also wrote the satires *The Apes of God* (1930) and *The Childermass* (1928). 1882–1957

Victor Lewis-Smith UK Journalist, Broadcaster
Postgraduate student of music at York University, who presented a witty, eclectic and often obscene local radio programme in the city. In 1990 he was given his own show on Radio 1, which involved sound collage and hoax phone-calls to celebrities; a surreal TV comedy series, *Inside Victor Lewis-Smith*, followed in 1993. He writes ribald, highly entertaining television reviews for the London *Evening Standard*. 1961–

Liberace US Pianist
Born Wladziu Valentino. An unbelievably camp and flamboyant – though classically trained – pianist. 1919–87

Abraham Lincoln US Statesman
President of the United States 1860–65; oppon-

ent of slavery; led the North to Republican victory in the American Civil War. 1809–65

Derek (Deacon) Lindsay UK Writer
Under the name of A. E. Ellis, he wrote *The Rack*, a well-received novel about life in a TB hospital. Friend of Ken Tynan. 1926–

Maureen Lipman UK Actress, Writer
Prefers comedy roles, and in 1978 she was given her own series, *Agony*, in which she played agony aunt Jane Lucas. She is also known for her stage tribute to Joyce Grenfell, *Re: Joyce!*, for being married to the comedy scriptwriter Jack Rosenthal, for her characterization of the stereotypical Jewish mother Beattie in advertisements for BT, and for her humorous journalism. 1946–

Mary Wilson Little US Writer
1875–1952

Richard Littlejohn UK Journalist
Outrageous libertarian columnist of the *Sun*, he pursued many of his favourite themes in his novel *To Hell in a Handcart* (2001) which, according to the *Guardian*, was about 'a salt-of-the-earth former policeman pushed over the edge by thuggery, burglary and the proliferation of speed cameras'. 1954–

David Lloyd George UK Statesman
1st Earl of Dwyfor. Prime Minister 1916–22. A progressive Liberal and canny operator; as Chancellor of the Exchequer 1908–15 he implemented important social reforms. Took over the leadership of the wartime coalition government from H. H. Asquith. 1863–1945

Frederick Locker-Lampson English Poet
1821–95

David Lodge UK Novelist
Comic novelist of Catholicism and academia. 1935–

Alice Roosevelt Longworth US Political Hostess
Witty daughter of Theodore Roosevelt. 1884–1980

Anita Loos US Writer
Successful screenwriter, and author of *Gentlemen Prefer Blondes* (1925), ostensibly narrated by a semi-literate femme fatale. Winston Churchill is reputed to have kept this book on his bedside table, and James Joyce read it repeatedly. 1893–1981

Tim Lott UK Novelist
His debut, *The Scent of Dried Roses* (1996), chronicling the suicide of his mother, is regarded as a classic of modern biography. Its successor *White City Blue* (1999) won the Whitbread First Novel Award. Lott writes drolly about Londoners on the cusp of the working and middle classes. 1956–

David Lowe UK Cartoonist
Born in New Zealand. Drew cartoons for British newspapers from 1919 onwards. Created Colonel Blimp as a mouthpiece for ridiculous reactionary views. 1891–1963

Robert Lowe UK Politician
1st Viscount Sherbrooke; a Liberal. 1811–92

James Russell Lowell US Writer, Diplomat
1819–91

L. S. Lowry UK Artist
Painted Lancashire industrial scenes in a naive style. Worked as a rent collector and property clerk for fifty years. 1887–1976

E. V. Lucas UK Humorist
Wrote books in many genres; regular contributor to *Punch*; author of the 'Wanderer's Notebook' column in the *Sunday Times*; very keen on cricket. Chairman of the publishers Methuen & Co. from 1924. 1868–1938

John Lukič UK Footballer
Played for Leeds, Arsenal, Leeds, Arsenal – in that order. 1960–

John Lydon UK Musician
Alias Johnny Rotten, front man of the Sex Pistols; and icon of punk, which he later resented: 'I haven't lived this life to end up in an art gallery.' Left the Pistols in 1978, formed the group Public Image Ltd, to make more introspective, experimental music, and settled in California. 1956–

George Lyttelton UK Schoolteacher, Writer
Assistant master at Eton, whose correspondence with a former pupil, Rupert Hart-Davis, was published from 1978 onwards as *The Lyttelton–Hart-Davis Letters*. Lyttelton's letters reveal an elegant, dry sense of humour. He was a descendant of the politician and poet George, the first Lord Lyttelton, and is the father of Humphrey Lyttelton, the jazz trumpeter, writer and broadcaster. 1883–1962

Humphrey Lyttelton UK Jazz Trumpeter, Writer, Broadcaster

From an aristocratic background – he is the son of George Lyttelton – he taught himself trumpet at Eton. After the Second World War he became premier revivalist trumpeter in Britain or, according to Louis Armstrong, 'the top trumpet man in England today'. When he lost his trumpet, the story was headline news in the *Daily Mail*. Since 1954 he has produced volumes of autobiography, in the second of which he wrote: 'The Press critics who asked, in effect, "What's so odd about a viscount's nephew becoming a jazz man?" may have a valid point. I suppose the only remarkable thing about it is that it has never been done before.' Since 1972 Lyttelton has also been the unusually droll, and lugubrious, radio game show host *I'm Sorry I Haven't a Clue*. In that capacity he is said to have uttered the obscenest remark ever made on Radio 4. 1921–

Lord Macaulay English Historian

Thomas Babington, 1st Baron Macaulay. His *History of England from the Accession of James II*, published in five volumes 1848–61, has the great virtue of readability. Lord Melbourne said: 'I wish I was as cocksure of anything as Tom Macaulay is of everything.' 1800–59

Ed McBain US Crime Writer

Alias Evan Hunter, author of *Blackboard Jungle* (1954). Has also written, as Ed McBain, a series of crime novels set in the 87th Precinct of an imaginary city. 1926–

Alexander McCall Smith UK Writer, Lawyer

His series of novels featuring Botswana's only female private detective, Mma Ramotswe, began in 1998. McCall, who was born in Zimbabwe, is Professor of Medical Law at the University of Edinburgh. 1948–

Mick McCarthy UK Footballer, Manager

Played largely for Barnsley; has managed the Republic of Ireland and Sunderland. 1959–

Paul McCartney UK Musician

Rivalled John Lennon for leadership of the Beatles. His songs and public utterances suggested a more emollient personality than Lennon's. His solo career has helped him climb ever higher up Britain's rich list. 1942–

Ramsay MacDonald UK Politician

Prime Minister in 1924 of the short-lived first-ever Labour government; Labour Prime Minister again 1929–31; then, 1931–5, of a predominantly Conservative coalition. A pacifist by original conviction. 1866–1937

A. G. Macdonell UK Writer

Author of the comic novel *England, Their England* (1933), about an observant Scotsman at large in England after the First World War. Tom Stoppard read it as a schoolboy: 'For years afterwards my sentence structure was consciously and unconsciously based on that book,' he said. 1895–1941

Ian McEwan UK Novelist

Began with shocking, macabre short stories in *First Love, Last Rites* (1975); other fictions in a similar vein followed, but by the time of *Atonement* (2001), he had adopted a mellower, more lyrical style, though still with the sinister element. In 2005 his publishers confidently billed him as 'the country's unrivalled literary giant'. 1948–

Phyllis McGinley US Poet

1905–78

Roger McGough UK Poet

One of the wry Pop Art-oriented 'Liverpool Poets' of the 1960s; a member of the humorous pop group Scaffold 1962–73. 'I feel like a poet when I'm writing a poem. Otherwise I feel that I'm on the outside of things.' 1937–

Compton Mackenzie UK Writer

Prolific novelist, director of the Aegean Intelligence Service in Syria during the First World War; founder in 1923 of *The Gramophone* magazine. 1883–1972

Kelvin MacKenzie UK Journalist

Flamboyant, provocatively coarse editor of the *Sun* newspaper 1981–94. 'The *Sun* was me,' he has said. Latterly, Chairman and Chief Executive of the Wireless Group. 1946–

Marshall McLuhan Canadian Communications Theorist

In *The Gutenberg Galaxy* (1962) and *Understanding Media* (1964) he conveyed views which might be summed up by his remark that 'all media work us over completely'. 1911–80

Harold Macmillan UK Statesman

1st Earl of Stockton. Conservative Prime Minister 1957–63. Aristocratic, self-deprecating. An unlikely Prime Minister in increasingly demotic times. 1894–1986

Louis MacNeice UK Poet

His poetry, according to Edward Lucie-Smith,

combines 'an underlying gravity' with 'a flippant, glittering surface'. 1907–63

Steve McQueen US Actor
Graduated from juvenile delinquency and a broken home to stardom in the 1960s and 70s. For all the millions of dollars he made, he preserved an aggrieved outlook on life, forever accusing people of trying to manipulate him, or 'twisting my melon'. 1930–80

John McVicar UK Ex-Criminal, Writer
Scottish armed robber in the 1960s, labelled by the police as 'Public Enemy Number 1'. 'It was a bad year for criminals, so my antics got over-billed,' he has said. On release from prison in 1978 he forged a successful career as a writer and journalist. According to his website, 'Even his mother admits he is "difficult".'

Candida McWilliam UK Novelist
Voted one of Britain's top twenty young writers in *Granta* magazine, 1993, her novels include *A Case of Knives* and *A Little Stranger*. 1955–

Geoffrey Madan UK Bibliophile
Bacon, Milton and Locke recorded snippets of their reading in commonplace books. Geoffrey Madan, whose *Notebook* was published in 1981, has been described as the last of the line. 1895–1947

Kathleen Madigan US Comic
Journalist who turned comedian in 1990. Many TV appearances have ensued.

Gustav Mahler Austrian Composer
1860–1911

Norman Mailer US Writer
Pugnacious anti-establishment character. His first novel was *The Naked and the Dead* (1948); also the writer of iconoclastic non-fiction, including *The Executioner's Song*, which won the Pulitzer Prize in 1979. 1923–

George Mallory UK Mountaineer
An academic who died during his third attempt to climb Mount Everest. 1886–1924

David Mamet US Writer
As a playwright he came to prominence with *American Buffalo* (1975); he has also written essays, novels and many first-rate film scripts. He specializes in droll, gnomic dialogue, and frequently deals with questions of masculinity in a tough, politically incorrect way. 1947–

Lord Mancroft UK Conservative Politician
Served as Minister without Portfolio 1957–8; Chairman of the Tote 1972–6. Author of *A Chinaman in My Bath* (1974) and other humorous works. 1914–87

Babaloo Mandel US Screenwriter
Mark Mandel. Often collaborates with Lowell Ganz. 1949–

Peter Mandelson UK Politician
Co-architect of Blairism, but has benefited only fitfully from its success. Twice a minister, but resigned both times over minor scandals. Currently a European Commissioner. 1953–

Herman J. Mankiewicz US Screenwriter, Playwright
Rakish son of a Columbia University professor; thought to have written most of *Citizen Kane*. 1897–1953

Joseph L. Mankiewicz US Filmwriter, Producer, Director
Wrote and directed *A Letter for Three Wives* (1949) and *All about Eve* (1950). A full list of his credits would be voluminous. 1909–1993

Bernard Manning UK Comedian
Outspoken Mancunian. Manning (who began in showbusiness as a resident vocalist with the Oscar Rabin band at the London Lyceum) is a living symbol of political incorrectness, which tends to get in the way of the fact that he possesses a near-perfect sense of comic timing. 1930–

Ian Marchant UK Author
Amusing novelist and writer of non-fiction, also sometime bookseller and comedian. 1958–

Don Marquis US Poet, Journalist
Wrote satirical columns in the New York *Sun* and New York *Herald Tribune*. His mouthpieces were archy, a cockroach, who wrote in free verse, and mehitabel the cat, whose motto was '*toujours gai*'. 1878–1937

Frederick Marryat English Writer
Naval officer turned novelist of maritime themes, including *Peter Simple* (1833); in 1847 he published *The Children of the New Forest*, for children. 1792–1848

Rodney Marsh UK Footballer
Flamboyant long-haired player who made his name with Queen's Park Rangers. Not to be confused with the Australian wicket-keeper of the same name. 1944–

Arthur Marshall UK Writer, Broadcaster
Schoolteacher; humorous journalist, well known for writing about, and parodying, schoolgirl stories. From 1979 he was a regular panellist on the BBC TV series *Call My Bluff*. His father, a stern engineer, would frequently ask: 'Where does Arthur get it from?' 1910–89

Thomas R. Marshall US Politician
A Democrat; notably loyal Vice-President to Woodrow Wilson 1913–21. 1854–1925

Martial Roman Poet
Marcus Valerius Martialis. His books of epigrams appeared from AD 86. c.AD 40–c.AD 104

Dean Martin US Actor, Singer
Born Dino Paul Crocetti. Appeared as a foil to Jerry Lewis in comedy films such as *Hollywood or Bust* (1956); also an ultra-relaxed TV crooner. To put it bluntly, he always looked slightly pissed. 1917–95

Dick Martin *see* Dan Rowan

Steve Martin US Comedian, Actor
As a manic stand-up comic he would frequently lapse into the persona of the 'wild and crazy guy', a lubricious foreigner with a very strange accent. Translated successfully into films, receiving particular acclaim for *Roxanne*, which he produced, wrote and starred in. 1945–

Suzanne Martin US Scriptwriter
Has written episodes of *Frasier*; also a TV producer.

Andy Marx
Grandson of Groucho. 1960–

Chico Marx US Comedian
One of the Marx Brothers. S. J. Perelman called him 'a jaunty coxcomb who carried the love interest'. 1891–1977

Groucho Marx US Comedian
Wisecracking mainstay of the Marx Brothers, a family of Jewish-American comics whose zany energy took them from childhood vaudeville, to Broadway, to films like *Duck Soup* (1933) and *A Night at the Opera* (1935). His painted moustache, large eyebrows, crouching walk and machine-gun delivery have been a gift to bad impersonators everywhere. 1895–1977

Karl Marx German Sociologist
Chief begetter of the *Communist Manifesto* (1848); began his major work *Das Kapital* in 1867, arguing that class attrition would inevitably result in the overthrow of capitalism. 1818–83

Jackie Mason US Comic
Born Jacob Moshe Maza. Son of a rabbi who trained as a rabbi himself, then realized that fast, deadpan humour was his forte. 1939–

Melissa Mathison US Screenwriter
Also, sometime wife of Harrison Ford. 1949–

Walter Matthau US Actor
Walter Matasschanskayasky. Hangdog demeanour, lugubriously comic, notably in *The Odd Couple* (1968). 1920–2000

Reginald Maudling UK Politician
Conservative. Chancellor of the Exchequer 1962–4, Home Secretary 1970–72. 1917–79

W. Somerset Maugham UK Writer
Prolific author of novels and short stories, poised between high- and middlebrow. Many of his writings reflect his travels in South East Asia. 1874–1965

François Mauriac French Writer
Wrote novels with Roman Catholic themes and psychological orientation. Won the Nobel Prize for Literature in 1952. 1885–1970

Elsa Maxwell US Journalist
Described in *Halliwell's Who's Who in the Movies* as 'a dumpy American columnist and party-giver'. She was also an actress. 1883–1963

Rik Mayall UK Comedian
Manic, saucer-eyed performer. He made his name, from 1982, as the alternately arrogant and craven Rick in the cartoonish sitcom *The Young Ones*, which Mayall co-wrote. 1958–

Jonathan Meades UK Writer, Broadcaster
Ferociously learned, Meades specializes in architecture, topography and food. Restaurant critic of *The Times* since 1986. Christopher Biggins said: 'I first met Meades in Salisbury where we were both sporting grey shorts. I knew then he would be a great restaurant critic: he had wonderful calves.' 1947–

Golda Meir Israeli politician
Prime Minister of Israel 1969–74. 1898–1978

Lord Melbourne UK Statesman
William Lamb, 2nd Viscount Melbourne. Languid, eccentric, humorous; 'the fine flower of Whig agreeability', according to his biographer David Cecil. He was Prime Minister 1834,

1835–41, in which capacity he became an avuncular mentor to the young Queen Victoria, who was both amused and perplexed by his remarks, such as 'people who talk much of railways and bridges are generally Liberals' and 'shopping is very demonstrative'. She earnestly remarked to him, 'There are not many good preachers' and he replied, 'But there are not many good anything', which she delightedly agreed was 'very true!' Melbourne was married, agonizingly, to Lady Caroline Lamb. 1779–1848

George Melly UK Writer and Musician
Journalist, libertine, connoisseur of Surrealist art and a zoot-suited jazz singer with John Chilton's Feetwarmers. His volumes of autobiography, starting with *Owning Up* (1965), tell the story. 1926–

H. L. Mencken US Writer
Editor, founder of magazines, cynical anti-populist writer. Son of a prosperous cigar manufacturer, Mencken lived his whole life in Baltimore. *Newspaper Days 1899–1906* (1941) is a memoir of his early career on the *Baltimore Morning Herald*. He was a columnist on that paper, and later on the *Baltimore Sun*, from which he was sacked for defending the sinking of the *Lusitania*. Also supplied columns to the *New York Evening Mail* and the *Chicago Tribune*. Among his targets were puritanism and political humbug. Many of his essays and reviews were collected in six volumes of *Prejudices* (1919–27). 1888–1956

Johnny Mercer US Songwriter
The Penguin Encyclopedia of Popular Music noted 'nearly every lyric intelligent, optimistic, memorable'. Mercer wrote over a thousand songs, including *Moon River*. Also a singer. 1909–76

Stephen Merchant UK Writer
Former radio executive who co-wrote the sitcom *The Office* with Ricky Gervais. He is six feet seven inches tall.

George Meredith UK Poet, Novelist
Known chiefly for *The Egoist* (1879) and *Diana of the Crossways* (1885). Greatly eminent in his time, his florid style ensures he is not much read today. 1828–1909

Dixon Lanier Merritt US Poet
1879–1972

Lise Meyer UK Writer
Co-creator from 1982 of the sitcom *The Young Ones*.

Thomas Middleton English Playwright
Son of a bricklayer, albeit a prosperous one. Middleton was a versatile writer whose works include *A Mad World, My Masters* (1608) and *Women Beware Women* (c. 1625). c.1580–1627

George Mikes UK Humorist
Hungarian-born writer who viewed England from the perspective of an amused foreigner. The *Times Literary Supplement* described him as 'the man with the heavy accent in the corner taking notes'. 1912–87

John Stuart Mill English Philosopher
Supported Jeremy Bentham in espousing utilitarianism, a major concern being the promotion of birth control. A progressive liberal in Parliament from 1865. 1806–73

Andy Miller UK Writer
Journalist; author, in 2002, of *Tilting at Windmills (Or How I Tried to Stop Worrying and Love Sport)*. 1966–

Arthur Miller US Playwright
His poignant play *Death of a Salesman* (1949) is an American classic; *After the Fall* (1964) is thought to be based on his four-year marriage to Marilyn Monroe. 1915–2005

Jonathan Miller UK Writer, Director
Progressed from a medical training at Cambridge to the *Beyond the Fringe* revues (1961–4) with Peter Cook, Dudley Moore and Alan Bennett. Went on to produce TV programmes, direct films and plays, and direct operas with the English National Opera. In 1977 he presented the TV series *The Body in Question*. In 2003 he exhibited sculptures he'd made from bits of rubbish. It is obligatory to describe Miller as 'a polymath'. 1934–

Max Miller UK Comedian
Leading comic of the variety era, he topped the bill at the Holborn Empire in London for three decades from 1926 onwards. Always saucy, to say the least. 1895–1963

Spike Milligan Irish Comedian, Humorous Writer
'Wrote *The Goon Show* – died.' That is how Milligan feared he would be remembered. The show ran on BBC radio 1951–60, trepidatiously billed as 'a rather extravagant form of humour'. To some it was a collage of silly voices, to many more its wildness and madcap imaginativeness made most other broadcast comedy seem tame. From 1969 Milligan's *Q* series brought a similar logic-defying style to television. He made many stage, film and TV appearances; wrote poetry

and one novel, *Puckoon* (1963); and his war memoirs, beginning with *Adolf Hitler, My Part in His Downfall* (1971). 'Milligan is the great God of us all,' said John Cleese. Milligan took his father's nationality after a run-in with the Passport Office in the 1960s, saying he would rather be a member of the Hackney Empire than the British one. 1918–2002

Irving Mills US Jazz Impresario
Managed Duke Ellington between 1926 and 1939 and successfully promoted other deserving jazzmen as well. Also a composer and lyricist. 1884–1985

A. A. Milne UK Writer
Alan Alexander Milne. Veteran of the Somme, who was inspired by the stuffed toy animals of his son Christopher Robin to create (from 1926) the character of Winnie-the-Pooh and his associates. They were charmingly anthropomorphized to display familiar human failings. Tom Stoppard said that he would rather have written *Winnie-the-Pooh* than the complete works of Bertolt Brecht. 1882–1956

Shazia Mirza UK Comic
Billed as 'the first female Muslim stand-up in Britain', she came to prominence after 11 September 2001, a subject she did not shy away from. 1976–

Joni Mitchell Canadian Singer, Songwriter
Writer of melancholic, minor-key tunes and sophisticated, emotionally complicated lyrics. Amongst her most highly praised albums are *Blue* (1971) and *The Hissing of Summer Lawns* (1975). According to the *Penguin Encyclopedia of Popular Music* she, along with Bob Dylan and Van Morrison, 'showed pop music how to become an art form'. 1943–

Julian Mitchell UK Playwright
Experimental novelist turned author of plays, including *Another Country* (1981), which was concerned with the attraction of communism to English public schoolboys of the 1930s. 1935–

Robert Mitchum US Actor
Laid-back and rakish, he starred in many films from the 1940s to the 90s, including *Night of the Hunter* (1955), *Ryan's Daughter* (1971), *Farewell My Lovely* (1975). His chief quality was languor. Asked how he kept fit, he said: 'I lie down a lot.' 1917–97

Nancy Mitford UK Writer
One of the six Mitford sisters, daughters of Lord Redesdale. Witty novelist of upper-class life:

Love in a Cold Climate (1949), *The Blessing* (1951), for example. *Noblesse Oblige* (1956) divided the world into 'U' and 'Non-U' phenomena, meaning those acceptable to the upper classes and those not. 1904–73

Wilson Mizner US Writer
Cardsharp, prize fighter and prospector for gold in the Klondike who turned to playwrighting and screenwriting. 1876–1933

Molière French Playwright
Born Jean-Baptiste Poquelin, Molière was also an actor. Progressed from writing farces to comedies rich in social satire and in the study of character. *Tartuffe* (1669) offended the Church. *The Misanthropist* (1666) is his most performed play. 1622–73

Bob Monkhouse UK Comedian
The English Bob Hope, in that he had at his command a seemingly endless stream of slick one-liners – too slick for some, and Monkhouse was often criticized for being smarmy on TV. He presented quiz and game shows, but considered himself 'a born club comic'. 1928–2003

Marilyn Monroe US Actress
Born Norma Jean Mortenson or Baker. The archetype of the dumb blonde in such films as *Gentlemen Prefer Blondes* (1953) and *Some Like It Hot* (1959), she was something much more complicated off screen, and died from a drug overdose. 'To put it bluntly,' she said, 'I seem to be a whole superstructure with no foundation.' 1926–62

C. E. Montague UK Writer
Drama critic. Also wrote novels, including *Disenchantment* (1922), based on his experiences in the First World War. 1867–1928

Montesquieu French Philosopher
Charles-Louis de Secondat, baron de Montesquieu. *Lettres persanes* (Persian Letters) was a satire on French society. His most influential work was *De L'esprit des lois* (The Spirit of the Law, 1750). 1689–1755

Juan Pablo Montoya Colombian Racing Driver
Champ Car champion in America in 1999; then graduated to the Williams team in Formula One. Apparently fearless; often described as having 'balls of steel' and so on. *Autosport* said he was 'about as predictable as a cat in a bath'. 1975–

Monty Python UK Comedy Team
Created the ground-breaking, surreal mimetic TV series that ran from 1969 to 1974. The troupe

comprised Graham Chapman (1941–89), John Cleese (b. 1939), Terry Gilliam (b. 1940), Eric Idle (b. 1943), Terry Jones (b. 1942), Michael Palin (b. 1943). All except Gilliam, who is American, are British and Oxbridge-educated. They have gone on to make films.

Keith Moon UK Pop Musician
Drummer with the Who. Moon, who pioneered a dynamic, restless style of rock drumming, was described in *Q* magazine as 'the world's greatest drummer, bon viveur, practical joker and hotel demolition expert'. 1947–78

Dudley Moore UK Comedian, Musician
Comic partner of Peter Cook, first in the revue *Beyond the Fringe* from 1960 onwards. From an idea for a Dudley Moore show grew the Cook and Moore series *Not Only . . . But Also* (1964 onwards). Cook wrote most of the material, but Moore was a great foil, not least because he was his physical opposite. Cook called their partnership 'ideal'. Later, when Moore became a Hollywood filmstar, relations between them became strained. Cook said that Moore had 'gone from being a subservient little creep, a genial serf, to become an obstinate bastard who asserted himself'. 1935–2002

George Moore Anglo-Irish Writer
Influenced by the French naturalism of Émile Zola and others, and an influence in turn on Arnold Bennett. Best known for *Esther Waters* (1894), but unfashionable today. 1852–1933

Thomas Moore Irish Poet
Originally a lawyer. His *Selection of Irish Melodies*, produced 1807–34, were a great success in Ireland. *The Fudge Family in Paris* (1818) satirized the banal observations of pompous English people abroad. 1779–1852

Hannah More English Writer
Novelist, poet and writer of tracts; a prominent member of the proto-feminist Blue-Stocking Circle of the late eighteenth century. 1745–1833

Eric Morecambe and Ernie Wise UK Comedy Duo
Born Eric Bartholomew and Ernest Wiseman. North of England comedy duo who, after a stuttering career in variety, found from the early 1960s onwards that their subtle interactions translated wonderfully to television. Eric was mercurial: alternately dreamy, dim, cutting; Wise was stolid, pompous, boasting of 'the plays what I wrote', of which, apparently, he would produce dozens in a day. 1926–84; 1925–99

Chris Morris UK Comedian
An extremist of black comedy, Morris targets the pomposity of broadcasters and the moralizing of celebrities, and is known for making jokes about things not normally considered the province of humour such as September 11th, which he said had left Al Qaeda with 'second-album syndrome' – that is, not knowing how to follow it up. Morris was the prime mover behind *On the Hour* (BBC radio, 1991) and its TV successor *The Day Today* (1994). His TV series *Brass Eye* (1997) was still more macabre. 1962–

Morrissey UK Rock Musician
Born Steven Morrissey. Lugubrious and fey but very witty lyricist and lead singer with the highly rated Mancunian group the Smiths. When they split up in 1987 Morrissey moved to LA and recorded solo albums. Has often been accused of not being able to sing, to which he responded in the song 'Frankly Mr Shankly': 'That's nothing, you should hear me play piano.' Has been described as 'the first openly celibate rock star'. 1959–

Bob Mortimer *see* Vic Reeves

John Mortimer UK Lawyer, Writer
Creator of, and probably not unlike, the notably unpompous, liberal, anti-pc barrister Horace Rumpole, who has featured in novels and a TV series (*Rumpole of the Bailey*). Mortimer wrote a portrait of his intimidating father in the play *A Voyage round My Father* (1970), and novels satirizing English upper-middle-class life. When asked by the *Guardian* in 2003 to say when his prime was, he replied: 'Oh, I've had a few.' 1923–

Mohammed Mrabet Moroccan Writer
1940–

Malcolm Muggeridge UK Journalist, Broadcaster
Restless iconoclast who, beginning on the *Manchester Guardian*, gravitated to Roman Catholicism, ending up with the nickname 'Saint Mug'. Edited *Punch* 1953–7, which prompted in him much agonizing about the nature of humour. 1903–90

Frank Muir UK Scriptwriter
Dapper, bow-tie-wearing humorist. His writing partner from 1947 was Denis Norden, their first project being the radio series, *Take It from Here*. His charming speech impediment (couldn't say his Rs) helped ensure his success as a team captain opposing Patrick Campbell (who stuttered) on the television panel game *Call My Bluff*. 1920–98

Arthur Mullard UK Comic Actor

Cockney rag-and-bone man and sometime boxer who became a TV and film actor specializing in the portrayal of pugnacious, dim men. 1910–95

Eddie Murphy US Comedian, Actor

Livewire star who made his name with *48 Hours* (1982) and *Beverly Hills Cop* (1985). 1961–

Vladimir Nabokov US Novelist

Born in Russia to aristocratic parents, he and his family became émigrés in Europe after the Revolution. Nabokov took American citizenship in 1945. His first novels were in Russian, but by the time of the scandalous *Lolita* (1958) he'd switched to English, in which, many would contend, he wrote more lucidly than any native speaker of the time. 1899–1977

Ramón Maria Narváez Spanish Soldier, Politician

Autocratic ruler of Spain 1850s and 60s. 1800–68

Ogden Nash US Humorist

A regular in the *New Yorker*, author of many collections of polished, tricksy light verse. 1902–71

Richard Needham Canadian humorist

Winner, in 1967, of the Stephen Leacock Medal for Humour. 1912–

Lord Nelson UK Admiral

Hero of the naval battles against Napoleon. Lost his eye in battle in 1794, his arm in 1796. Ennobled after his victory over the French at the Battle of the Nile in 1798. Won the Battle of Copenhagen in 1801, and defeated the French and Spanish fleets at Trafalgar, but died from his wounds. 1758–1805

E. Nesbit UK Writer

Author of charming children's stories, such as *Five Children and It* (1902) and *The Railway Children* (1906). 1858–1924

Charles Nevin UK Writer

'Half-northern' humorist, who began in journalism on a graduate trainee course with the *Liverpool Daily Post and Echo*. On his first day, a piece of paper in his typewriter read 'NO GRADS HERE'.

Martin Newell UK Musician, Poet

Author of very English pop songs. Took to poetry in the early 1990s. Founder of the group the Cleaners from Venus. Has a cult following. 1953–

Anthony Newley UK Singer and Songwriter

Child-actor turned singer of novelty pop songs and (in partnership with Leslie Bricusse) songwriter. Newley was born in the East End and came full circle in that one of his last acting roles was as a used-car dealer in *EastEnders* 1931–99

Paul Newman US Actor

Broke through in *The Hustler* (1961), achieved superstardom with *Butch Cassidy and the Sundance Kid* (1979). Specialized in cussed types; keen on motorsport, and still raced cars in his seventies. 1925–

Randy Newman US Singer, Songwriter

Author of plaintive, funny songs; has collaborated with many of the West Coast rock aristocracy. In 1977 he was in trouble over the lyrics of 'Short People', in which he expressed the view that short people 'don't deserve to live'. 1944–

Andrew Niccol New Zealand-born Scriptwriter

1964–

Jack Nicholson US Actor

Has played drawling, rakish/diabolic figures in films from *Easy Rider* (1969) onwards. According to John Huston, he's 'a lovely man to drink with'. 1937–

Harold Nicolson UK Diplomat, Politician, Writer

Diplomat 1909–29; National Liberal MP 1935–45; author of biographies, histories, political works and, notably, his *Diaries and Letters 1930–62* (1968). Was married to Vita Sackville-West. 1886–1968

David Niven UK Actor

Leading man, despite strange looks; inextricably connected to the word 'debonair'. 1909–83

Denis Norden UK Humorist

Wrote radio comedy with Frank Muir; latterly has presided in avuncular fashion over a series of TV shows, *It'll Be Alright on the Night*, in which celebrities and others are shown making mistakes on camera. 1922–

Lord Northcliffe UK Newspaper Proprietor

Alfred Charles William Harmsworth, 1st Viscount Northcliffe. Invented English popular journalism via the *Daily Mail*. *The Times* and the *Daily Mirror* also came within his empire. Liked to be called 'the Napoleon of Fleet Street', and was ennobled in 1905. 1865–1922

Ivor Novello UK Songwriter
Born David Ivor Davies. Author of 'Keep the Home Fires Burning' (1915), among many others; also a playwright. 1893–1951

Simon Nye UK Writer
Scored a hit with the exuberantly laddish TV sitcom *Men Behaving Badly* (1994–8), which he developed from his own novel of that name. 1958–

Conor Cruise O'Brien Irish Diplomat, Writer
Member of the Irish Parliament 1969–77; bold critic of the IRA; regular contributor to the *Observer*. 1917–

Flann O'Brien Irish Writer
An author with three names. Christened Brian O'Nolan, he wrote three fantastical comic novels, including *At Swim-Two-Birds* (1939), under the name Flann O'Brien. From 1940 he supplied a column to the *Irish Times* as Myles na Gopaleen. Graham Greene was an early mentor. 1911–66

Sean O'Casey Irish Playwright
Wrote overwrought dramas of working-class life in Dublin, such as *Shadow of a Gunman* (1923) and *Juno and the Paycock* (1924). 1884–1964

Philip O'Connor UK Tramp, Writer
Eccentric, raised by a stranger with an artificial leg. Sometime vagrant, poet broadcaster, father of nine children at least. His *Memoirs of a Public Baby* (1958) is a classic of autobiography. Andrew Barrow wrote of him, 'His reputation as a madman is considerable.' 1916–98

Bill Oddie UK Comedian
A member of the 1970s TV comedy trio *The Goodies* (he was the scruffy, bolshy one); also a scriptwriter and keen birdwatcher. He is, as he once wrote, 'the only proper "show-biz" bird person'. 1941–

John O'Farrell UK Writer
Political researcher turned comedy scriptwriter (for *Spitting Image* and *Have I Got News for You*, among others). His first book, *Things Can Only Get Better*, chronicled his time spent 'helping the Labour party lose elections at every level'. 1962–

David Ogilvy UK Advertising Executive
Sometime tobacco farmer who founded the advertising agency Hewitt, Ogilvy, Benson & Mather. His campaign for Schweppes Tonic Water is often cited as one of the finest ever. 1911–99

Georgia O'Keeffe US Artist
Early modernist; tended to paint flowers in a near-abstract style. Married, from 1924, to the photographer Alfred Stieglitz. 1887–1986

Jamie Oliver UK Chef
Began cooking, aged eight, in his father's pub. Author of cookbooks, presenter of TV cookery programmes. His fame reflects the newfound importance of food in early twenty-first-century Britain, and his successful campaign of 2005 to improve the quality of school meals prompted a letter to the *Guardian*, contending that if Jamie had come out against the second Gulf War then it wouldn't have happened. 1976–

Sir Laurence Olivier UK Actor, Director
Imperious. The most celebrated Shakespearian actor of his time and the first director of the National Theatre, 1963–73. 1907–89

P. J. O'Rourke US Journalist
Besuited, cigar-smoking right-wing humorist whose exuberantly politically incorrect articles, often for *Rolling Stone*, have appeared in collections such as *Give War a Chance* (1992). He has said: 'Jest, ignorance, or substance abuse have been the excuse, reason or rationale for my entire existence.' 1947–

Joe Orton UK Playwright
Started his literary career by defacing and amending library books in company with his boyfriend Kenneth Halliwell. Went on to write bad-taste farces such as *Entertaining Mr Sloane* (1964) and *Loot* (1966). Halliwell then murdered him. 1933–67

George Orwell UK Writer
His early books were reportage from a socialist angle: *Down and Out in Paris and London* (1933) and *The Road to Wigan Pier* (1937). Went on to write a series of social-realist novels, then celebrated allegory of the failure of communism *Animal Farm* (1945) and the totalitarian dystopia *Nineteen Eighty-Four* (1949). V. S. Pritchett called him 'the wintry conscience of a generation'. 1903–50

John Osborne UK Playwright
Best known for the momentous *Look Back in Anger* (1956), which established him as the 'angry young man' of British theatre and introduced a new working-class realism to British drama. Also acted, wrote film scripts and three volumes of autobiography, all in the shadow of that great early success. 1929–94

Peter O'Toole UK Actor
Roistering Shakespearian who became a star

after playing the title role in *Lawrence of Arabia* (1962). According to the film critic David Thomson: 'He has a voice like a rapier that has been used to stir cream.' 1932–

Michael Palin UK Comedian

A member of the Monty Python comedy team. After the collective began to function only part time, he scripted with Terry Jones the two wonderful TV series of *Ripping Yarns* (1978, 1980), which parodied *Boys' Own* adventure stories. Has also acted in films and, beginning with *Around the World in Eighty Days* (1988), has presented popular, and lucrative, travel programmes for the BBC. Described by John Cleese as 'a very, very, very, very, very, very, very, very, very, very, very, very, nice chap'. 1943–

G. H. Palmer *Times* Reader, Railway Traveller

Wrote a letter to *The Times* on 2 August 1939.

Samuel Palmer English Painter

A watercolourist mainly, interested in the mystical, along with his friend and inspiration William Blake. 1805–81

Lord Palmerston UK Prime Minister

Henry John Temple. Tory turned Whig. A womanizing practitioner of gun-boat diplomacy, according to myth; the true picture was more complex. Twice a Foreign Secretary concerned with containment of Russia, Prime Minister 1855–8, and 1859–65. 1784–1865

Dorothy Parker US Writer

Came into her own as a contributor to the *New Yorker*. A member in the 1920s of the Algonquin Hotel Round Table lunch group, a forum for waspish wit. Wrote reviews, poetry, short stories and film scripts. Such was her epigrammatic gift that George S. Kaufman remarked: 'Everything I've ever said will be credited to Dorothy Parker.' But she lost momentum later in life, and died a depressed alcoholic. 1893–1967

C. Northcote Parkinson UK Humorist

Academic historian who achieved fame with his saturnine critique of bureaucracy, *Parkinson's Law: The Pursuit of Progress* (1957). 1909–93

Norman Parkinson UK Photographer

Of the upper-class fashion and society worlds. 1913–90

Matthew Parris UK Writer

Conservative MP turned political journalist. Since 1988 he has written the parliamentary sketch in *The Times*, in which capacity he is usually droll and urbane, but he can shock. 1949–

Dolly Parton US Singer, Songwriter

The most famous country singer of the 1970s and 80s. A very talented musician, but probably best known for her breasts. She has said, 'I enjoy the way I look, but it's a joke.' 1946–

Blaise Pascal French Philosopher, Physicist, Theologian

Laid the groundwork for probability theory and integral calculus, and for the invention of the barometer and the syringe. A philanthropist, he is also credited with organizing the first ever (horse-drawn) public bus service. A proto-socialist, yet subject to religious visions. His *Lettres provinciales* (Provincial Letters) are a defence of Antoine Arnauld, a proponent of Jansenism. 1623–62

Jennifer Paterson UK Food Writer

The *Spectator*'s lunch cook, then food columnist, who became a television personality thanks to the cookery programme *Two Fat Ladies*, in which she appeared with Clarissa Dickson-Wright. 1928–99

James Payn English Writer

Poet, essayist, journalist (he edited *Chambers's Journal* 1859–74). Also wrote a hundred novels. 1830–98

Thomas Love Peacock English Novelist, Poet, Essayist

Author of satirical novels such as *Headlong Hall* (1816), *Melincourt* (1817) and *Nightmare Abbey* (1818), in which proponents of the dogmas that Peacock disliked (such as those of political economy) are assembled in picturesque surroundings. 1785–1866

Mervyn Peake UK Writer, Illustrator

Author, chiefly, of the macabre *Gormenghast* trilogy (1946–59), concerning a society of grotesques in a vast castle. 1911–68

R. Pearsall UK Writer

Literary critic. 1927–

Allison Pearson UK Writer, Broadcaster

A prolific and talented journalist (as columnist, critic and interviewer). In 2002 wrote *I Don't Know How She Does It*, a logistical comedy of the modern career woman's attempt to reconcile work and family. 1962–

Harry Pearson UK Writer

Unusually tall author of surrealistic and humorous articles and books; interested in football, the North of England and, in *A Tall Man in a Low Land* (1998), Belgium. 1961–

Hesketh Pearson UK Actor, Biographer
Originally a member of the acting company of
Beerbohm Tree, whose biography he wrote,
along with many others. His earlier works
tended to flirt with libel. 1887–1964

William Penn English Quaker, Col-
onialist
Campaigned against the persecution of
Quakers; from 1681 founded Pennsylvania as a
haven for them. 1644–1718

Samuel Pepys English Diarist
Naval administrator who flourished in the Restoration and whose frank and vivid diary, cover-
ing the years 1660–69, provides the best
first-hand accounts of the Plague (1665–6), the
Great Fire of London (1666) and much else.
Robert Louis Stevenson wrote that he was
known 'to his remote descendants with an
almost indecent familiarity, like a tap-room companion'. 1633–1703

S. J. Perelman US Humorist
His prose, much of it originally for the *New
Yorker*, appears in collections such as *Crazy Like
a Fox* (1944). He also wrote scripts for, among
others, the Marx Brothers. 1904–79

Grayson Perry UK Artist
Transvestite potter who won the Turner Prize in
2003. The *Daily Telegraph* called the result 'surprising on a number of levels': Perry, who has
regularly worn women's clothing since childhood, has been praised for breathing new life
into pottery. 1960–

Jimmy Perry *see* David Croft

Persius Latin Poet
Stoic of reserved temperament, whose six surviving satires are modelled on Horace's. AD 34–62

Ted Persons US Songwriter

Laurence Peter Canadian Sociologist
Skewered in history as identifier of 'the Peter
principle'. 1919–90

Prince Philip, Duke of Edinburgh Con-
sort of Queen Elizabeth II
Duke of Edinburgh. Born in Greece, he adopted
British nationality in 1947 when he married the
future Queen. Famous for saying the wrong
thing. 1921–

Emo Phillips US Comic
Came to prominence on *Saturday Night Live* in
the early 1980s; delivers blackly comic one-liners
in the persona, according to the *Guardian*, of an
'overgrown remedial child'.

Francis Picabia French Artist
Gravitated from Impressionism to Surrealism.
The magazine he edited, *291*, was in provocative
surrealist vein. 1879–1953

Marge Piercy US Novelist
Feminist. Novels include *Going Down Fast* (1969)
and *Gone to Soldiers* (1987). Raised as a Jew by
her mother and grandmother, she is 'passion-
ately interested in the female lunar side of Juda-
ism'. 1936–

D. B. C. Pierre Mexican-Australian
Novelist
Pseudonym of the enigmatic author born Peter
Finlay, who won the Booker Prize in 2003 with
his debut *Vernon God Little*. D. B. C. stands for
'dirty but clean'. 1961–

Lester Piggott UK Jockey
Monosyllabic and partly deaf, Piggott is known
as 'the long fellow' because, at five feet nine,
he's tall for a jockey. Nonetheless he's arguably
the best the twentieth century produced. 1935–

Stephen Pile UK Humorist
Founder, he says, of the Not Terribly Good Club
of Great Britain; author, in 1977, of the very successful *Book of Heroic Failures*, true tales of inep-
titude. Also a restaurant critic and television
reviewer. 1949–

Arthur Pinero UK Playwright
Author of about fifty plays, and the most
commercially successful playwright of late-
nineteenth-century England. Reached his artistic
peak with *The Second Mrs Tanqueray* (1893).
1855–1934

Harold Pinter UK Playwright
Author, from *The Birthday Party* (1959) onwards,
of brilliant, ambiguous plays full of sinister,
gnomic dialogue and, famously, pauses – for
which the term 'Pinteresque' has emerged. In
the 1990s the ambiguity and humour diminished as he became more explicitly political. Has
also written many highly rated film scripts.
1930–

William Ewart Pitts UK Chief Constable
1900–1980

Joshua Piven and David Borgenicht US
Humorists
Joint authors of *The Worst-Case Scenario Survival*

Handbook (1999). Borgenicht also wrote *The Little Book of Stupid Questions* (1999).

Nigel Planer UK Actor, Writer

Best known for his portrayal of the gormless hippy Neil in the BBC TV comedy series *The Young Ones* (1982–4). Also an amusing writer.1955–

Ken Platt UK Comedian

Sceptical Lancastrian; popularized the phrase 'daft as a brush'. 1922–

Pliny the Elder Roman Scholar, Soldier

Historia Naturalis, the very broad-ranging compendium of knowledge and speculation, is his sole surviving work. Killed while observing an eruption of Vesuvius. AD 23–79

Christopher Plummer Canadian Actor

Leading man with many credits, but best known as Captain Von Trapp in *The Sound of Music* (1965). 1927–

Robert Pols UK Historian

Expert on the interpretation of old photographs, author of several books on the subject during the 1990s.

Alexander Pope English Poet

Of the Augustan school; satirist; intimate of Joseph Addison and Jonathan Swift. *The Rape of the Lock* (1712) established him. In 1715 he translated Homer's *Iliad* into heroic couplets. *The Dunciad* (1728) is an attack on his detractors and on literary iniquities in general. Pope was four feet six tall, which is thought to help explain his choleric disposition. 1688–1744

Sally Poplin US Humorist

Cole Porter US Songwriter

Peruvian-born Harvard law graduate who wrote successful musical comedies and many of the classics of American song, including *Night and Day* (1932) and *Ev'ry Time We Say Goodbye* (1944). Known for his subtle, literate style and frequently cited as the greatest songwriter of the twentieth century. 1891–1964

Beatrix Potter UK Writer, Illustrator

Wrote about, and drew, anthropomorphized but not sentimentalized animals, from *The Tale of Peter Rabbit* (1900) onwards. 1866–1943

Stephen Potter English Humorist, Radio Producer, Critic

Best known for a series of short, funny books of pastiche self-help, with the theme of getting on in society and titles ending in 'ship'. The first was *The Theory and Practice of Gamesmanship; or The Art of Winning Games without Actually Cheating* (1947). 1900–69

Ezra Pound US Poet, Critic

Prophet of Modernism, credited by T. S. Eliot with being the wellspring of modern poetry, but others see him as teetering on the brink of humbug. His *Cantos*, from 1917, are a series of poems revealing Chinese and classical influences. After broadcasting Fascist propaganda from Italy at the start of the Second World War he was confined to an asylum in America until 1958. 'Ezra was right half the time,' said Hemingway, 'and when he was wrong, he was so wrong you were never in any doubt about it.' 1885–1972

Dawn Powell US Writer

Novelist and playwright. Powell's preferred subject was small-town life, and she said, 'I contend that the writer's business is minding other people's business . . . all the vices of the village gossip are the virtues of the writer.' 1896–1965

Vince Powell *see* Harry Driver

Terry Pratchett UK Novelist

His *Discworld* series is science fiction written in the tone of P. G. Wodehouse. A. S. Byatt has observed: 'He writes extraordinary sentences.' 1948–

John Prescott UK Politician

Cabinet minister under, and Deputy Prime Minister to, Tony Blair from 1994. By virtue of his bluff manner, working-class origins and left-wing track record, Prescott serves as the conscience of the Labour Party, counteracting Blair's more metropolitan persona. 1938–

John Preston UK Novelist

Comic novelist with a languorous, dry humour; titles include *Kings of the Roundhouse* (2004). Also the TV critic of the *Sunday Telegraph*. 1953–

J. B. Priestley UK Writer

Born in Bradford, educated at Cambridge. His reputation was established with his novel of music-hall life, *The Good Companions* (1929); among his fifty plays is *An Inspector Calls* (1947). Priestley was preoccupied with 'Englishness', and while a fêted man of letters, liked to present a Yorkshire down-to-earthness. 1894–1984

Oliver Pritchett UK Humorist

Pritchett's career has been described as 'a struggle to free himself from facts', in that he has progressed from serious journalism to the writing of humorous columns for the London

Evening Standard, the *Sunday Telegraph*, the *Daily Telegraph*. Son of the writer V. S. Pritchett and father of the cartoonist Matt. 1939–

V. S. Pritchett UK Writer
As a novelist – from *Clare Drummer* (1929) – he opposed zealotry with humour; also a literary critic. 1900–1997

Richard Pryor US Comedian, Actor
Manic and edgy, often teamed with Gene Wilder. 1940–

Craig Raine UK Poet
Chief exponent of 'Martian' poetry – looking at commonplace things as if for the first time. *A Martian Sends a Postcard Home* (1979) remains his best-known volume. 1944–

Sir Walter Raleigh English Courtier
Favourite of Queen Elizabeth until he began an affair with one of her maids; also an explorer who attempted to colonize parts of America, and brought tobacco and potatoes to England. Executed by James I. 1552–1618

Sir Walter Raleigh UK Academic
From 1904, the holder of the first Chair of English Literature at Oxford. Descended from the eminent Elizabethan of the same name. 1861–1922

Arthur Ransome UK Writer
Covered the Russian Revolution for the *Manchester Guardian*, then fled Russia with Lenin's secretary, whom he married. With *Swallows and Amazons* (1930) he embarked on a series of novels featuring two families of wholesome children and their adventures in the great outdoors. 1884–1967

Terence Rattigan UK Playwright
Plays include *French without Tears* (1936), *The Winslow Boy* (1946). His subject was English repression and he wrote, as he self-deprecatingly admitted, for the Aunt Ednas of the world. 1911–77

Simon Rattle UK Conductor
Chief Conductor of numerous orchestras, most recently the Berlin Philharmonic. 1955–

Man Ray US Artist
Emanuel Rabinovitch. Painter, sculptor, photographer, film maker. Early Dadaist with Marcel Duchamp and Francis Picabia. 1890–1976

Richard Rayner UK Writer
Born in 'soot-caked' Bradford in Yorkshire, he came to notice with his novel/memoir *Los*

Angeles without a Map (1989), a young Englishman's take on LA. 1956–

Al Read UK Comedian
Baleful northerner, originally head of a sausage-making firm. *The Al Read Show* (BBC radio) drew audiences of thirty-five million in the 1950s and 60s. 1909–87

Ronald Reagan US Actor, Statesman
Acted in fifty films before turning to Republican politics (originally a Democrat). Elected President in 1980 and, by a record margin, in 1984. Believed in strong defence and laissez-faire economics. Castigated by opponents for lack of intellectual depth, but even they couldn't fault his timing of a joke. 1911–2004

Henry Reed UK Poet, Playwright
Best known for the poem 'Naming of Parts' based on his army experiences; wrote many radio plays. 1914–86

Rex Reed US Journalist, Actor
Best known as a gossip columnist; played the transsexual Myra Breckinridge in the film of that name. 1938–

Vic Reeves and Bob Mortimer UK Comedians
In the early 1990s Reeves (born Jim Moir), a sometime farmworker, established with the former solicitor Bob Mortimer a TV comedy duo representing an advance even on the strangeness of *Monty Python*. 1959– and 1959–

Carl Reiner US Writer, Film Director
Comic partner of Mel Brooks in the early 1960s. Later a writer of comic films such as *The Man with Two Brains* (1983), and a director of such as *Oh God* (1977). 1922–

Burt Reynolds US Actor
Sinewy, self-deprecating leading man, seen to good effect in *Deliverance* (1972) and *Boogie Nights* (1997). 1936–

Joshua Reynolds English Artist
Mainly a portrait painter. Associate of Samuel Johnson and his circle; first President of the Royal Academy (from 1768). Sir Edward Burne-Jones said: 'Reynolds is all right. He's got no ideas, but he can paint.' 1723–92

Lady Rhondda UK Journalist
Margaret Haig Thomas. A suffragette, sent to prison for attempting to destroy a postbox with a chemical bomb. A founder, in 1920, of the political magazine *Time and Tide*. 1883–1958

Mandy Rice-Davies UK Model, Showgirl

Performed at Murray's Cabaret Club in London, and became caught up in the sexual and political scandal of the Profumo affair (1963). Described her life after giving evidence at the ensuing trial as 'one long descent into respectability'. 1944–

Keith Richards UK Rock Musician

Originally Keith Richard. Rhythm guitarist and renegade-in-chief of the Rolling Stones; also the writer, along with Mick Jagger, of most of the group's material. It is a puzzle to many that he's still alive, in light of his reported drug and alcohol intake. 1943–

Paul Richardson UK Writer

Specializes in writing amusingly about food; he also *grows* food on his farm in Spain. 1960–

Sir Ralph Richardson UK Actor

Regarded as the most comedically gifted of the great British postwar triumvirate, Gielgud and Olivier being the other two. 1902–83

Nicholas Ridley UK Politician

Laid-back, chain-smoking right-winger, son of Viscount Ridley. Held various ministries under Margaret Thatcher. 1929–93

Joan Rivers US Comic

Acid-tongued New Yorker. Broke through on *The Tonight Show*, then graduated to her own programmes starting with *That Show Starring Joan Rivers* (1968). In 1983 recorded an album called *What Becomes a Semi-Legend Most*. 1933–

Leonard Robbins US Writer

1877–1947

Paul Robeson US Singer, Actor

Black singer who performed on stage and in numerous films; as an actor, often played Othello. 1898–1976

Bruce Robinson UK Film-Maker

Wrote the screenplay for *The Killing Fields* (1984); wrote and directed the cult comedy *Withnail & I* (1987). 1946–

Edward Arlington Robinson US Poet

Unknown until praised by Theodore Roosevelt in 1905. Thereafter celebrated for his irony and psychological insight. 1869–1935

Robert Robinson UK Writer, Broadcaster

Hosted the programme on which the word 'fuck' was uttered on air for the first time. It

was Kenneth Tynan who said it, and Robinson responded coolly with 'It's an easy way to make history.' His measured, epigrammatic speech has infuriated some, but one reviewer said that on Robinson's programmes 'words are measured by the ounce rather than the job lot'. Programmes have included, from 1967, *Call My Bluff*, among other literate TV game shows, and the incestuous but amusing radio show *Stop the Week* in which he and his friends discussed minute subjects such as 'Does it matter if people say "different to"?' Has also produced witty collections of his journalism and a series of entertaining novels. 1927–

Bobby Robson UK Football Player and Manager

Played for Fulham, West Bromwich Albion and England; has managed Ipswich, PSV Eindhoven and England – and with remarkable success, despite his mangled speech patterns. 1933–

Earl of Rochester English Poet

John Wilmot. Aristocratic libertine, philosophically pessimistic – and important – poet located between the Metaphysical poets and the Augustans. 1647–80

Gene Rodenberry US Screenwriter

Texas-born; sometime pilot and songwriter; creator of *Star Trek*. 1921–91

Byron Rogers UK Journalist

A features writer of the old school, in that he writes beautifully observed pieces about obscure eccentrics, often ones who live in the Midlands or Wales. His articles are collected in books such as *An Audience with an Elephant* (2001), of which he wrote in the preface: 'In the following pages you will not meet anyone with a press agent or a publicist, or with a film or pop tour to promote.'

Will Rogers US Actor, Humorist

Cowboy comedian who espoused a homespun philosophy in the *Ziegfeld Follies* (1916–25), the *New York Times* (from 1922) and films such as *State Fair* (1933). 1879–1935

James Rolmaz US Songwriter

Jon Ronson UK Writer, Broadcaster

As writer and documentary-maker Ronson interacts, to humorous effect, with eccentrics. His bestselling book *Them* (2001) depicts, according to one reviewer, 'insane views held in humdrum surroundings'. 1967–

Jean Rook UK Journalist

Striking-looking columnist who stood in judgement over celebrities, mainly for the *Daily Express*. Once described as 'a sort of cross between Lynda Lee-Potter and a wolf. 1931–61

Henry Root See William Donaldson

Jack Rosenthal UK Scriptwriter
Known for his humorous, affecting TV plays, including *Bar Mitzvah Boy* (1976) and *P'Tang, Yang, Kipperbang* (1984). Was married to Maureen Lipman. 1931–2004

Alan S. C. Ross UK Professor of Linguistics
His paper on 'Upper-Class English Usage', published in the *Bulletin de la Société Neo-Philologique de Helsinki*, inspired Nancy Mitford to write her book on the English class system *Noblesse Oblige* (1956), to which Ross contributed a chapter. 1907–80

Harold Ross US Editor
Founder in 1925, and guiding spirit, of the *New Yorker*. Yet although he presided over this most literary of magazines, he was apparently not a big reader. 1892–1951

Edmond Rostand French Playwright, Poet
Author of the play *Cyrano de Bergerac* (1897), whose eponymous hero has the usual romantic attributes but also an enormous nose. The work popularized the word 'panache' in Britain. 1868–1918

Philip Roth US Novelist
Came to notice as a satirist of the sort of middle-class Jewish life in which he himself was raised, specifically in *Portnoy's Complaint* (the complaint is masturbation). His other novels include *Zuckerman Unbound* (1981) and *American Pastoral* (1997). 1933–

Joseph Roux French Writer
Quotable priest and man of letters. 1834–86

Dan Rowan and Dick Martin US Comedians
Hosts of *Rowan and Martin's Laugh-In*, fast-moving, satirical sketch show of the 1960s. It popularized the phrase 'sock it to me'. 1922–87 and 1923–

Helen Rowland US Writer
Wrote funny non-fiction on problems of courtship and marriage: for example, *A Guide to Men* (1922). 1875–1950

Richard Rowland US Film Executive
d. 1947

Maude Royden UK Social Worker, Writer
Suffragette who went into social work in London and published books on women in society. 1876–1956

Damon Runyon US Writer
Journalist who wrote poetry, then racy stories of New York street life. *Guys and Dolls* (1932) was turned into a musical in 1952. 1884–1946

Salman Rushdie UK Novelist
Born in Bombay; originally associated with the magical realist school. His brilliant Indian epic *Midnight's Children* (1981) won the Booker Prize and made his name. *The Satanic Verses* (1988) was judged blasphemous towards Islam by Ayatollah Khomeini, and a fatwa was issued sentencing Rushdie to death. He is quite often seen at parties, nonetheless. 1947–

Willie Rushton UK Comic, Cartoonist
Droll regular on many game shows. Upper-class, countrified persona (he always looked dressed for fishing). Co-founder of the satirical magazine *Private Eye*. 1937–96

John Ruskin English Art Critic, Writer
First Slade professor of fine arts at Oxford (from 1869). A considerable philanthropist, Ruskin allied his aesthetic theories to proposals for social reform. Osbert Lancaster said he expressed 'in prose of incomparable grandeur thought of an unparalleled confusion'. 1819–1900

Bertrand Russell UK Philosopher
3rd Earl Russell. *Principia Mathematica* (1910–13) is considered a landmark in philosophy. Thereafter, while still publishing important philosophical works, he gravitated towards politics and populism. A pacifist in the First World War, a proponent of nuclear disarmament after the Second. He had secondary reputations as a wit and a womanizer. 1872–1970

Meg Ryan US Actress
Winsome leading lady, best known for *When Harry Met Sally* (1989). 1961–

Vita Sackville-West UK Writer
Very aristocratic author of poetry – *The Land* (1926) won the Hawthornden Prize – and non-fiction. At Sissinghurst in Kent she and her husband Harold Nicolson created a famous garden. She was a close friend of Virginia Woolf. 1892–1962

Gerry Sadowitz UK Comedian
Thoughtful though foul-mouthed comic and

magician. Typically, he greeted an audience in Canada with: 'Hello, moose-fuckers.' He has had various late-night TV incarnations – notably, from 1998, *The People vs Gerry Sadowitz*. 1960–

Saki UK Writer

Born Hector Hugh Munro. From *Reginald* (1904) onwards, he specialized in volumes of short stories taking the form of blackly humorous morality tales. He was shot during the First World War while resting in a crater. 1870–1916

J. D. Salinger US Writer

Catcher in the Rye (1951) is a classic of adolescent gaucherie. Salinger also wrote slim volumes of masterful, drily amusing short stories about the awkwardnesses of youth. Since the mid-1960s he has lived as a recluse – a rich one, since *Catcher in the Rye* sells a quarter of a million copies annually. 1919–

Lord Salisbury UK Politician

3rd Marquess of Salisbury. A Conservative; Prime Minister 1855–6, 1889–92, 1895–1902. Imbued with Christian pessimism concerning the utility of politics. 1830–1903

Anthony Sampson UK Author

Beginning with *Anatomy of Britain* (1962), he wrote a series of books dissecting British society and exposing its formal and informal power structures. 1926–2004

Herbert Samuel UK Politician

A Liberal; the first unconverted Jew to serve in a British cabinet; as the first High Commissioner for Palestine, 1920–25, he was, in the words of the Jewish Virtual Library, 'the first Jew to govern the land of Israel in two thousand years'. 1870–1963

Carl Sandburg US Poet

His poetry appeared mainly in the 1920s and was experimental, frequently colloquial in style. 1878–1967

4th Earl of Sandwich English Politician

John Montagu. Incompetent First Lord of the Admiralty 1748–51, 1771–82. Had no good ideas for how to deal with the American Revolution. Said to have invented the sandwich. 1718–92

George Santayana Spanish Philosopher, Writer

A sceptic and a Platonist, he was also a respected literary critic and novelist. 1863–1952

John Singer Sargent US Painter

Society portraitist inspired by the Old Masters, especially Velazquez. Once described as 'an American born in Italy, educated in France, who looks like a German, speaks like an Englishman and paints like a Spaniard.' 1856–1925

Jean-Paul Sartre French Philosopher, Writer

Left-winger; existentialist; archetypal chain-smoking Parisian intellectual. Novels include *Nausea* (1938); plays include *No Exit* (1946). *Being and Nothingness* (1956) is his main philosophical statement. 1905–80

Siegfried Sassoon UK Writer

Experiences in the trenches inspired harrowing war poetry, collected in *The Old Huntsman* (1917). *Memoirs of a Fox-Hunting Man* (1928) was also informed by the horrors of the First World War. 1886–1967

Jennifer Saunders UK Comedian

From the early 1980s, comic partner of Dawn French in *French and Saunders*, from which grew their series *Absolutely Fabulous* (1992 onwards) in which Saunders plays the neurotic, spoilt fashion industry PR Edina Monsoon. 1958–

Eliza Mary Anne Savage UK Writer, Artist

Friend of, and literary adviser to, Samuel Butler. She corresponded with him and is the model for the subtly benign Alethea Pontifex in *The Way of All Flesh* (1903). They became acquainted after Butler had offered her a cherry in a London street. 1836–85

George Savile, 1st Marquess of Halifax English Politician, Writer

George Savile, known as 'the Trimmer' for advocating to Charles II that he suppress his politically problematic pro-Catholic instincts. Author of many worldly essays. 1633–95

Dorothy L. Sayers UK Writer

Creator – beginning with *Whose Body?* (1923) – of the aristocratic detective Lord Peter Wimsey, who was generally accompanied by his deferential but verbose butler, Bunter. Sayers also wrote *The Man Born to Be King* (1942–3), a series of radio plays about the life of Christ. 1893–1957

Artur Schnabel Austrian Pianist, Composer

Beethoven and Mozart specialist; lived in America from 1939. 1882–1951

B. P. Schulberg US Film Publicist

1892–1957

Charles M. Schulz US Cartoonist

Starting in 1950, his *Peanuts* cartoon strip, featuring the wistful child Charlie Brown, became the most widely syndicated in history. 1922–

Norman Schwartzkopf US General
Leader of the coalition forces in the Gulf War of 1990. Known as 'Stormin' Norman'. 1934–

C P. Scott UK Editor
Editor 1872–1929 of the *Manchester Guardian*, the voice of liberalism in Britain. 1846–1932

Joanna Scott Moncrieff UK Broadcaster
Vicar's daughter who produced *Woman's Hour*, then moved into religious broadcasting. 1920–78

Ronald Searle and Geoffrey Willans Cartoonist and Humorous Writer (Respectively)
In the 1940s Willans, a former teacher, wrote skits on school life at St Custard's for *Punch*, where Searle worked as a cartoonist creating the anarchic, violent schoolgirls of St Trinian's who would feature in books and films written by others. The two collaborated to produce *Down with Skool!* in 1958, the first of a series of comic books purportedly written by Nigel Molesworth, a prep school boy with poor spelling. 1920– and 1911–58

Harry Secombe UK Comedian
Army entertainer who developed, postwar, a variety act in which he shaved in various styles. Such was his manic energy in those days that Spike Milligan described him as 'someone from Mars'. Secombe performed in *The Goons* (1951–60) along with Peter Sellers and Milligan, always playing the amiable chump Neddie Seagoon. He was thereafter successful in film and on stage, and presented the religious TV series *Highway* in the 1980s. He recorded many LPs and had a good voice, but this was always eclipsed by his sparkling comedy. Knighted in 1981. 1921–2001

Sir John Seeley English Historian
1834–95

E. C. Segar US Cartoonist
In 1919 began writing a syndicated strip called *Thimble Theatre*, in which (in 1929) appeared the aggressive, spinach-fuelled sailor Popeye, animated in cartoons from 1933. 1894–1938

Jerry Seinfeld US Comedian
Stand-up comic, a regular on *Late Night with David Letterman* and the *Tonight* show in the late 1980s. From 1990 he and Larry David created *Seinfeld*, a sitcom about 'nothing' – in fact, tiny episodes in the lives of a group of forty-something New Yorkers. 1954–

Will Self UK Writer
Bad boy of English letters, who in the run-up to the 1997 election was reportedly discovered to be smoking heroin on a plane carrying the Prime Minister, John Major. His books, from *The Quantity Theory of Insanity* (1991) onwards, show a saturnine humour and an interest in psychological strangeness and drugs. Also a prolific journalist and broadcaster. 1961–

W. C. Sellar and R. J. Yeatman, UK Writers
A schoolteacher and an advertising manager respectively, they wrote *1066 and All That* (1930), enshrining schoolboy misunderstandings of history to brilliant comic effect. Follow-ups like *Garden Rubbish* (1932) were not as good. 1898–1951, 1897–1968

Peter Sellers UK Actor
Uncannily good mimic, as demonstrated in the *Goon Show*. Sellers went on to become the best comic actor of his time in films such as *Dr Strangelove* (1962) and *Being There* (1979). It has been contended that he had no personality of his own. 1925–80

Seneca Roman Stoic Philosopher
Son of Lucius Annaeus Seneca. Known as Seneca the Younger. c.4 BC–c.AD 65

Dr Seuss US Children's Writer, Illustrator
Theodor Seuss Giesel. His stories such as *The Cat in the Hat* (1958) feature simple rhymes and hairy, anarchic creatures, and sell by the million. 1904–91

Brian Sewell UK Art Critic
Writes for the London *Evening Standard*, known for his rarefied accent, elegance of style and intolerance of most modern art. In 1994 supporters of contemporary art presented a petition to the editor of the *Standard* asking that Sewell be fired, alleging philistinism and 'social and sexual hypocrisy'. Two months later he was named Critic of the Year at the Press Awards. Andrew Barrow (a fan of the man) has written: 'Is Brian Sewell an old queen? Frankly, who gives a fuck?' 1931–

Anne Sexton US Poet, Children's Writer
Originally a fashion model. Her collection *Live or Die* (1966) won a Pulitzer Prize. She suffered from mental illness and committed suicide at the peak of her career. 1928–74

William Shakespeare English Playwright, Poet

The source of many, if not most, of the world's dramatic masterpieces. Alfred, Lord Tennyson described him as 'the man one would have wished to introduce to another planet as a sample of our kind'. 1564–1616

George Bernard Shaw Irish Playwright

In 1876 Shaw moved from Dublin to London, where he established himself as a critic. In 1885 he began writing plays that bristled with epigrammatic wit but were also concerned with social reform and progressive thought. These include *Arms and the Man* (1894), *Candida* (1897), *Man and Superman* (1905) and *Pygmalion* (1913; adapted as the musical *My Fair Lady*, 1956; filmed, 1964). He was awarded the Nobel Prize for Literature in 1935. 'He was a good man fallen among Fabians,' said Lenin. Shaw was known for his vegetarianism and general austerity, his feminism, his lack of interest in sex, his height and, towards the end, his great age. When he referred to himself in his seventies, as 'seven-eighths dead', he was in turn described as 'straight as a pine tree and brimful of pep'. 1856–1950

William Shenstone English Poet

Wrote in a variety of styles, and was a landscape gardener. 1714–63

Sam Shepard US Playwright, Actor

Social-commentating writer who won a Pulitzer for his play *Buried Child* in 1978. His film appearances include *The Right Stuff* (1983). 1943–

Richard Brinsley Sheridan English Playwright

Exuberant comedies *The Rivals* (1775) and *The School for Scandal* (1777) brought social success, and in 1780 he became the MP for Stafford. But his ownership of the Drury Lane Theatre brought mounting debts (especially after it burnt down in 1809). 1751–1816

Nigel Short UK Chess Player

Became a Grand Master at the dramatically early age of nineteen. 1965–

Clement King Shorter UK Journalist

Founded several magazines 'on less serious lines', including the *Sphere*, which he edited from 1900 until his death. 1857–1926

Jean Sibelius Finnish Composer

A Finnish nationalist; composer of seven symphonies. 1865–1957

Carly Simon US Singer, Songwriter

Well known for her song 'You're So Vain' (1972), which might have been about Mick Jagger, or Warren Beatty . . . 1945–

Neil Simon US Playwright

Highly successful author of comedy plays, including *The Odd Couple* (1965) and *California Suite* (1976), both of which were filmed. 1927–

Alan Simpson *see* Ray Galton

Helen Simpson UK Writer

Author of beautifully turned stories, first collected in *Four Bare Legs in a Bed* (1990). 1962–

N. F. Simpson UK Playwright

Writer of comedies; associated with the Theatre of the Absurd. 1919–

C. H. Sisson UK Poet

Established his reputation from *The London Zoo* (1961) onwards; also a civil servant. 1914–2003

Dame Edith Sitwell UK Poet

Formidable, aristocratic, vulpine Modernist, sister of Osbert and Sacheverell. 1887–1964

Sir Osbert Sitwell UK Writer

Brother of Edith and Sacheverell. Wrote satirical poetry arising from his experiences in the First World War; also a novelist, but best remembered for his autobiography, in five volumes, from *Left Hand! Right Hand!* (1945) onwards. 1892–1969

John Skelton English Poet

Writer of comic vernacular poetry. c.1460–1529

Nigel Slater UK Food Writer

Promoter of brisk cookery. His cookbooks include *Real Fast Food*, *Real Cooking* and *Appetite*. Author of a weekly cookery column in the *Observer*. His engaging autobiography *Toast* appeared in 2003, avoiding all mention of dates.

O. P. Q. Philander Smiff UK Writer

Pseudonym of Aglen A. Dowty, under which he wrote *Smiff's History of England* (1876).

Samuel Smiles Scottish Social Reformer

North of England railway official who wrote *Self-Help* (1859), a book often given as a prize in Victorian schools. 1812–1914

Arthur Smith UK Comedian, Writer

South Londoner who likes to style himself 'Mayor of Balham'; sometime dustman. His play

An Evening with Gary Lineker became a TV film; he broadcasts frequently. 1954–

Cyril Smith UK Politician
Fluent, overweight spring-manufacturer and Liberal MP for Rochdale 1972–92. 1928–

Dodie Smith UK Writer
Originally a playwright, but best known for her novel *I Capture the Castle* (1949) in praise of the exuberance of youth, and the children's book *The Hundred and One Dalmatians* (1956). 1896–1990

F. E. Smith UK Politician, Lawyer
1st Earl of Birkenhead. A barrister and loose cannon, he entered Parliament in 1906, rising to become Lord Chancellor 1919–22; also, Secretary of State for India 1924–8. Known for his wit and general irreverence. 1872–1930

Giles Smith UK Journalist
A humorous columnist, interested in sport and pop music, Smith has been associated with the *Independent*, the *Daily Telegraph* and *The Times*. His memoir *Lost in Music* appeared in 1995. Sometime member of the pop group The Cleaners from Venus. 1962–

Logan Pearsall Smith US Writer
Published some fiction, but mainly literary criticism and epigrams. Took British citizenship in 1913; described in *The Cambridge Dictionary of American Biography* as 'essentially an appreciator'. 1865–1946

Mark E. Smith UK Rock Musician
Mainstay, and sometimes sole member, of the Manchester cult group The Fall. Sings weird lyrics in a declamatory style over repetitious backing. 1957–

Stevie Smith UK Poet, Novelist
Florence Margaret Smith – nicknamed after the jockey Steve Donoghue, because she was short. *Novel on Yellow Paper* (1936) was followed by verse collections including *Not Waving But Drowning* (1957). Her style is whimsical, dreamy, alternately funny and sad. 1902–71

Sydney Smith English Clergyman, Writer
Also, wit. In 1802 he co-founded the *Edinburgh Review*, to which he contributed regularly. Strong proponent of Catholic emancipation and of other social reforms. He once occupied a house in Combe Florey, Somerset, that was later owned by Evelyn Waugh. 1771–1845

Tobias Smollett Scottish Writer
Satirist, best known for *Travels through France and Italy* (1766), in which he was rude about foreigners, and the misanthropic novel *The Expedition of Humphry Clinker* (1771). Smollett was once regarded alongside Defoe, Richardson, Fielding and Sterne as a pioneer of the English novel, but is seldom read today. 1721–71

John Snagge UK Broadcaster
Commentated on the Oxford and Cambridge boat race from 1931 to 1980. 1904–96

Sam Snead US Golfer
Won the US Open in 1946; won both the Masters and the PGA Championship three times. 1912–2002

Stephen Sondheim US Composer, Lyricist
Wrote the lyrics for the musical *West Side Story* (1957), and both words and music for *A Little Night Music* (1973) and *Sweeney Todd the Demon Barber of Fleet Street* (1979). Known for his sophisticated, intricate style. 1930–

Donald Soper UK Methodist
Socialist; created a life peer in 1965. 1903–98

Terry Southern US Writer
Once described as 'the secret genius of the counter-culture', Southern combined sharp wit with an interest in all things psychedelic. Co-wrote the scripts for *Dr Strangelove* (1964) and *Easy Rider* (1969), among others. 1924–99

Thomas Southerne Irish Playwright
Wrote comedies and tragedies. A friend of Dryden's. 1659–1746

Muriel Spark UK Novelist
Born in Edinburgh, but has lived mainly in Italy and New York; a Catholic convert, like Evelyn Waugh, who appreciated the combination in her work of the comic and the sinister. *The Prime of Miss Jean Brodie* (1961) was filmed in 1969. 1918–

John Sparrow UK Academic
Lawyer, who wrote on literature. Warden of All Souls College, Oxford, 1952–77. Provocative character. 1906–92

Britney Spears US Pop Singer
Groomed for stardom at seventeen with the single '. . . Baby One More Time', and successful thereafter. Craig Brown said: 'She has a slight look of Nancy Reagan.' 1981–

Johnny Speight UK Writer
Sometime milkman who in 1965 created Alf Gar-

nett, foul-mouthed bigot (in fact, he was limited to 'bloody') of the sitcom *Till Death Us Do Part*. One of Garnett's adversaries was Mike, 'a randy scouse git' and wastrel husband of his daughter. Mike was played by Anthony Booth, father of Cherie Blair. 1921–98

Herbert Spencer UK Philosopher, Naturalist
Promoter of Darwinism. 1820–1903

Natasha Spender UK Author
Married the poet Stephen Spender in 1941.

Stephen Spender UK Poet
Co-founded the literary magazine *Horizon* with Cyril Connolly, and was its editor 1939–41. Spender's poetry is political, socially engaged, and originally written from a hard-left perspective. *Poems from Spain* (1939) and *The Edge of Darkness* (1949) record his experiences in the Spanish Civil War and the Second World War. A friend of Auden, Isherwood and many other writers. 1909–95

Edmund Spenser English Poet
Author of *The Shepheardes Calender* (1579), regarded as the start of Elizabethan poetry, and *The Faerie Queen* (1590 and 1596), a panegyric to Elizabeth I. *c.*1552–99

William Archibald Spooner UK Clergyman
Dean, then Warden, of New College, Oxford, at the turn of the eighteenth and nineteenth centuries. He would accidentally transpose the initial letters of words, or parts of words, or entire words. 'Let us drink to the queer old dean' is one of many attributed to him. 1844–1930

Josef Stalin Soviet Leader
Authoritarian ruler of Soviet Russia 1924–53. 1879–1953

Viv Stanshall UK Musician, Comedian
Lyricist, singer and tuba player with the Bonzo Dog Doo Dah Band, which broke up in 1969. The highlight of Stanshall's erratic solo career was the creation (from 1978) of Sir Henry of Rawlinson End, a cracked, apoplectic toff, proud of the 'small but daunting prisoner-of-war camp' in his grounds. Sir Henry cropped up on radio, record and film. Mike Oldfield described Stanshall as 'rock 'n' roll's answer to Peter Cook', which probably took account of Stanshall's drinking as well as his comic genius. 1943–95

Ringo Starr UK Musician, Actor
Born Richard Starkey. Plucked from Rory Storm and the Hurricanes to join the Beatles. The least musically gifted of the four, but the best actor. 1940–

Christina Stead Australian Novelist
Writer of strongly left-wing opinions, chiefly known for *The Man Who Loved Children* (1940), a scathing view of family life. 1902–83

W. T. Stead UK Writer
Edited the *Pall Mall Gazette* 1883–8. A spiritualist. His investigative article 'The Maiden Tribute of Modern Babylon' (1885) led Parliament to raise the age of consent to sixteen. Drowned in the *Titanic*. 1849–1912

Sir Richard Steele English Playwright, Journalist
Holder of various public offices, author of comedies including *The Lying Lover* (1703) and *The Tender Husband* (1705). Founded the *Tatler* in 1711; co-founded the *Spectator*, with Addison, also in 1711. Denigrated the bawdy excesses of Restoration drama. 1672–1729

Gertrude Stein US Writer
Experimental, perverse. *The Autobiography of Alice B. Toklas* (1933) is in fact Stein's own life story. 1874–1946

Gloria Steinem US Feminist, Writer, Social Reformer
Books include *Outrageous Acts and Everyday Rebellions* (1983) and *Revolution from Within: A Book of Self-Esteem* (1992). 1934–

Jeffrey Steingarten US Food Writer
Restaurant critic of American *Vogue*, who has admitted that he is able to keep on eating long after others have finished. His book *The Man Who Ate Everything* (1997) is a food classic.

Stendhal French Novelist
Pen-name of Henri Beyle. *Le Rouge et le Noir* (1830) is considered his masterpiece. 1783–1842

Laurence Sterne Irish Writer
Ordained in 1738. Published in four volumes, 1759–67, *The Life and Opinions of Tristram Shandy, Gentleman* – a comic novel composed of multiple digressions on apparently trivial subjects. 1713–68

Adlai Stevenson US Politician
Intellectually distinguished Democrat who helped found the United Nations. 1900–65

Robert Louis Stevenson Scottish Writer
Known for romantic adventure stories – notably *Treasure Island* (1883) and *Kidnapped* (1886) –

and the horror story *The Strange Case of Dr Jekyll and Mr Hyde* (1886); also, for suffering throughout his life from what was probably tuberculosis. 1850–94

Mark Steyn Canadian Journalist

Combines right-wing politics with an interest in pre-rock era popular music, and contributes to publications on both sides of the Atlantic. His witty, fulminatory articles are galvanizing or infuriating, depending on one's views. Steyn was very pro the invasion of Iraq; Chris Patten, the European Commissioner, said: 'It's wonderful to find a Canadian warmonger, isn't it?'

Lady Stocks UK Academic

Mary Danvers Stocks. Economist and historian; works include *A Hundred Years of District Nursing* (1960). In *Who's Who* she listed 'attending the House of Lords' among her recreations. 1891–1975

Mervyn Stockwood UK Prelate

Camp, amusing, left-wing Bishop of Southwark 1959–80. 1913–95

Bill Stones UK Politician

Miner turned mines inspector, Labour MP for Consett 1955–66. 1904–69

Tom Stoppard UK Playwright

Born in Czechoslovakia and raised in India. *Rosencrantz and Guildenstern Are Dead* opened in London in 1967, and Stoppard, like Byron, became instantly famous. He has pursued ever since his vision of 'the perfect marriage between the play of ideas and farce'. Ken Tynan once noted that 'you have to be foreign to write with that kind of hypnotized brilliance'. Stoppard was knighted in 1997. 1937–

Lytton Strachey UK Biographer

A foppish member of the Bloomsbury set and a conscientious objector during the First World War, Strachey sensationally undermined several reputations in *Eminent Victorians* (1918). 1880–1932

Igor Stravinsky US Composer

Russian born; in 1913 his music for the ballet *Rite of Spring* caused a riot when first played, such was its startling newness. 1882–1971

George Templeton Strong US Lawyer

Kept a diary that totalled four million words, and revealed much about late-nineteenth-century New York. 1820–75

Sir John Suckling English Writer

Playwright, and highly rated poet of the witty

Cavalier group (supporters of Charles I). As a leading Royalist he fled to France, where he committed suicide. He may have invented cribbage. 1609–41

R. S. Surtees English Writer

Lawyer, and author of humorous sporting tales. *Jorrocks's Jaunts and Jollities* (1838) depicted episodes in the life of a sporting club and directly inspired *The Pickwick Papers*, which did the same. *Handley Cross* (1843) is a classic of fox-hunting. 1805–64

William Sutcliffe UK Writer

Author of humorous novels: *New Boy* (1996); *Are You Experienced?* (1997). 1971–

Hannen Swaffer UK Journalist

One of the most famous of his time, reputed to have written four million words a year. Associated particularly with the *Daily Mirror*. Swaffer was both a socialist and a spiritualist. 1879–1962

Donald Swann *see* Michael Flanders

Jonathan Swift Anglo-Irish Satirist, Clergyman

The chief exemplar of the word 'satirist', Swift is the author of increasingly highly regarded verse and, among many other prose works, *Gulliver's Travels* (1726), a fable satirizing political and religious bickering which gradually becomes suffused with a wider misanthropy. As a supporter of the Tories, Swift suffered a political reverse on the succession of George I and was effectively banished to Dublin where he served as Dean of St Patrick's Cathedral. His epitaph, written (in Latin) by himself, translates as: 'Where fierce indignation can no longer pierce his heart.' Swift said that he only ever laughed twice in his whole life. 1667–1745

Meera Syal UK Writer, Actress

Co-writer of the comedy series *Goodness Gracious Me* (1998–2001); also writes screenplays, including *Bhaji on the Beach* (1993), and novels, including *Life Isn't All Ha Ha Hee Hee* (1999). She mines the cultural contradictions of British Asians. 1964–

Taki Greek Journalist

Pen-name of Taki Theodoracopoulos. The son of a Greek shipping millionaire, he was a professional tennis player before becoming a writer. Since 1978 he has contributed the 'High Life' column to the *Spectator*, an unabashed celebration of his playboy existence.

Booth Tarkington US Writer

Author of humorous plays and novels and now

completely out of fashion. His novel *The Magnificent Ambersons* (1918) was filmed by Orson Welles in 1942. 1869–1946

A. J. P. Taylor UK Historian
Known for his puckish, provocative and terse style. His major work is *The Struggle for Mastery in Europe 1848–1918* (1954). 1906–90

Bert Leston Taylor US Writer
Humorist and writer of mystery stories. 1866–1921

Jeremy Taylor English Theologian
Chaplain to Charles I; upon the Restoration, became Bishop of Down and Connor in Ireland. Known for *The Rule and Exercises of Holy Living* (1650) and *The Rule and Exercises of Holy Dying* (1651). 1613–67

William Temple UK Horseracing Entrepreneur
Born Phil Bull. As the more elegantly named Temple, he supplied information on the form of racehorses through his firm Timeform, founded in Halifax. 1910–89

Alfred Tennyson UK Poet
Known as Alfred, Lord Tennyson after he became a baron in 1884. Poet Laureate in 1850, succeeding Wordsworth. His Romantic and yet formally structured poems reflect the pride of Victorian Britain as well as its anxieties in the face of rapid change. Indeed, he came to epitomize the age through works such as *In Memoriam A. H. H.* (1850), 'The Charge of the Light Brigade' and 'Maude' (both 1854), and he died the most famous Englishman in the world. A later poet, John Betjeman, argued that Tennyson was more amusing than is generally realized, not least in his private conversation. 1809–92

William Makepeace Thackeray English Writer
Early hack work blossomed into the great social satire *Vanity Fair* (1848), which put him, as he said, at 'all but the top of the tree, having a great fight there with Dickens if truth be known'. 1811–63

Jake Thackray UK Singer, Songwriter
Romantic-looking Yorkshire-born folksinger in thrall to the French *chansonniers*. In the 1970s his maudlin, topical songs were for many the highlight or indeed the only redeeming feature of the consumer affairs TV show *That's Life*. David Hepworth, reviewing *The Very Best of Jake Thackray* in 2003, wrote: '[his work] is at once a celebration of unfashionable opinion and an invitation to a Tuesday afternoon sag-off for adults

with the promise of three pints in a darkened pub, a mooch round the public library and then some sex in broad daylight'. 1939–2002

Margaret Thatcher UK Politician
Baroness Thatcher of Kesteven. Became Conservative Party leader in 1975, then first woman Prime Minister 1979–90. Strident opponent of trade union power, high government spending and liberal-left 'consensus government'. T. E. Utley said that she was 'not by temperament averse to the Messianic role'. 1925–

Paul Theroux US Writer
Novels began with *Waldo* (1969); *The Great Railway Bazaar* (1975) established him as a connoisseur of railway journeys and a highly marketable travel writer. 1941–

Brandon Thomas UK Playwright
Author of the durable farce *Charley's Aunt* (1892). 1856–1914

Dylan Thomas Welsh Poet
The best of his rhythmic and emotional poems are contained in *Deaths and Entrances* (1946). Thomas, an alcoholic legend, was an antidote to the dryness and scepticism of Eliot and Auden. 1914–53

Edward Thomas UK Poet
Killed in the First World War. His 'Adlestrop' (1914), about a country railway station and the landscape beyond, has gained great poignant force as a symbol of tranquillity about to be shattered. 1878–1917

Elizabeth Thomas English Poet
1675–1731

Gwyn Thomas UK Writer
Welsh novelist and raconteur. Once described as 'the greatest talker in the world'. A star of *The Brains Trust* on BBC Radio Four. ?–1981

Irene Thomas UK Broadcaster
Former chorus girl who won the *Brain of Britain* radio quiz in 1961 after recuperating from a mastectomy. As she once said: 'The loss of the breast was partly compensated for by the discovery of a brain.' From 1968, she was a regular panellist on another radio quiz show, the highly recondite *Round Britain Quiz*. 1920–81

Brian Thompson UK Writer
Historian and biographer. Also author of the beautiful comic novel *A Half-Baked Life* (1991), which is purportedly the autobiography of an unwordly, puncture-prone bicyclist called Claude

Jenks, and stands as one of the lost classics of humorous prose. 1935–

Caroline Thompson US Scriptwriter, Director
Wrote the script for *Edward Scissorhands* (1990), for example; and has directed *Buddy* (1997), among others. 1956–

Hunter S. Thompson US Writer
Intoxicated hero of the counter-culture; practitioner of New Journalism, most notably in *Fear and Loathing in Las Vegas* (1971). He shot himself, leaving one misspelt word on a typewritten sheet: 'counselor'. 1939–2005

Laura Thompson UK Writer
Made her name writing with rare style and humour about sport. Her book on greyhound racing, *The Dogs* (1994), won the Somerset Maugham Award. 1965–

William Hepworth Thompson UK Classicist
From 1866, Master of Trinity College, Cambridge. 1810–86

Henry David Thoreau US Writer
Wrote about nature in both prose and poetry. His classic is *Walden; or, Life in the Woods* (1854), written when he was cut off from the world at Walden Pond, Concord, Massachusetts. In his book *Status Anxiety* Alain de Botton describes Thoreau as 'one of the most renowned bohemians of nineteenth-century America'. 1817–62

Jeremy Thorpe UK Politician
A dandyish barrister who was leader of the Liberal Party from 1967 until his resignation in 1976. In 1979 he was tried for conspiracy to murder, of which he was found not guilty. 1929–

James Thurber US Humorist
From 1927 he worked on, then for, the *New Yorker*, where many of his best essays and cartoons first appeared. Created the character of Walter Mitty, who in his daydreams performed heroic feats. 1894–1961

Paul Tillich US Theologian, Philosopher
Lutheran minister and academic; fled Nazi Germany in 1933. In his works, he sought to meet the challenge of a sceptical age. Died America's best-known theologian. 1886–1965

Sandi Toksvig UK Comedian, Writer
Born in Copenhagen; her family then settled in America. An academic high-flyer at Cambridge,

she went on to act, broadcast and write comedy scripts, children's books and novels. 1958–

Leo Tolstoy Russian Writer
Also philosopher and Christian mystic. *War and Peace* (1863) and *Anna Karenina* (1874) combine social sweep and psychological insight. 1828–1910

Barbara Toner Australian Writer
Columnist, associated with the *Mail on Sunday*; also the author of six novels.

Barry Took UK Comedian, Scriptwriter
Author, with Marty Feldman, of the hit radio comedy *Round the Horne*, starring Kenneth Horne and described in the *Daily Telegraph* as 'an orgy of double entendres'. Later wrote for *Rowan and Martin's Laugh-In* and became head of light entertainment at London Weekend Television. An expert on theatrical comedy. 1928–2002

Robert Towne US Screenwriter
Credits include *Chinatown* (1974), *Shampoo* (1975) and *Days of Thunder* (1990). Also a director. 1936–

Sue Townsend UK Author
The Secret Diary of Adrian Mole, Aged 13¾ established her as Britain's best selling author of the 1980s. Mole, a sort of adolescent Pooter, returned in several sequels, gaucherie intact. 1946–

Spencer Tracy US Actor
Specialized in playing wry, stoical figures in films such as *Bad Day at Black Rock* (1955). 1900–67

Ben Travers UK Playwright
Writer of farces, mainly in the 1920s, including *Rookery Nook* and *A Cuckoo in the Nest* (1926), but also (in 1975) *The Bed before Yesterday*. 1886–1980

P. L. Travers Australian Writer
A very private woman, remembered for her eight books featuring the eccentric (and magical) London nanny, Mary Poppins. 1899–1996

Sir Herbert Beerbohm Tree English Actor-Manager
Half-brother of Sir Max Beerbohm, Tree ran and built theatres, founded the Royal Academy of Dramatic Art in 1904, and was a fine character actor. 1852–1927

G. M. Trevelyan UK Historian
More interested in the substructure of society

than in the superstructure. Most famous work: *English Social History* (1944). 1876–1962

Tommy Trinder UK Comedian

A cockney who described himself as the 'Mr Woolworth of Showbusiness'. Acted in films, played indefatigably in concerts for the troops during the Second World War, and compèred the TV show *Sunday Night at the London Palladium* during the late 1950s. 1909–89

Anthony Trollope English Writer

Author of forty-seven novels including the *Barchester* series, which began with *The Warden* (1855); and, from *Can You Forgive Her?* (1864), the *Palliser* series. Trollope was a less pyrotechnical, but still droll and socially insightful, alternative to Dickens. As an official at the Post Office, he introduced the pillar box. 1815–82

Fred Trueman UK Cricketer

Fast bowler. Played for Yorkshire 1949–68, and in sixty-seven Tests. Thereafter a broadcaster, and a living symbol of Yorkshireness. 1931–

Harry S. Truman US Statesman

Democrat; down-to-earth character; unexpectedly dynamic President 1945–52. 1884–1972

Lynne Truss UK Writer, Broadcaster

Author of three comic novels and many radio plays. Her book on bad punctuation, *Eats, Shoots and Leaves*, was the Christmas book sales phenomenon of 2003. 1955–

J. M. W. Turner English Painter

Supreme painter of landscapes. Lived an uncouth and furtive private life, frequenting inns. In such works as *The Shipwreck* (1805) and *Frosty Morning* (1813) he showed a profound interest in the mutability of light, and his dying words are said to have been 'The sun is God'. 1775–1851

Ted Turner US TV Executive

In 1996 the merger of Time Warner and the Turner Broadcasting System created the biggest media company in the world. Turner was married to Jane Fonda 1999–2001. 1938–

Mark Twain US Writer

Pen-name of Samuel Langhorne Clemens. 'Mark Twain' means 'two fathoms', reflecting the fact that Twain was a Mississippi riverboat pilot before turning to journalism and book-writing. His masterpiece is the vernacular novel *The Adventures of Huckleberry Finn* (1884), which draws on his own boyhood on the banks of the Mississippi. Twain was a fount of humorous epigrams, of which his *Autobiography*, which has appeared in various forms, is something of a compendium. 'All modern American literature comes from one book by Mark Twain called *Huckleberry Finn*,' said Ernest Hemingway. 1835–1910

Steve Tyler US Singer, Songwriter

Lascivious lead singer of Aerosmith, a group frankly in thrall to the Rolling Stones. They hit the big time with *Toys in the Attic* (1975), and *Pump* (1989) was considered a return to form after years of drug abuse. 1948–

Kenneth Tynan UK Critic

The most influential theatre critic of his time, and a dandyish epicure more celebrated than most of the writers he reviewed. Also the literary manager of the National Theatre when Laurence Olivier was director. He created the erotic revue *Oh Calcutta!* 1927–80

John Updike US Writer

At the core of his many novels in the Rabbit series is Harry 'Rabbit' Angstrom, confused ex-basketball champion, car salesman and American Everyman. But Updike's range encompasses most of American society. 1932–

Harold Urey US Scientist

In 1932 he discovered heavy water, a crucial ingredient of the atomic bomb. He said at the time he thought it might have an application in neon signs. He later advocated banning nuclear weapons. In 1934 Urey was awarded the Nobel Prize for Chemistry. 1893–1981

Peter Ustinov UK Performer, Writer

Born in London of White Russian parents, the multilingual Ustinov was famous as much for being able to do a lot of things as for actually doing any particular one of them. He was actor, comedian, director, novelist, playwright, journalist and, in Britain, an all-purpose symbol of internationalism. He had serious concerns, but was also good at silly voices. His autobiography *Dear Me* (1977) was a great success. 1921–2004

Amanda Vail UK Novelist

1921–66

Paul Valéry French Poet, Philosopher

The collections *La Jeune Parque* (The Young Fate, 1917) and *Charmes* (1922) made his name. Latterly he wrote on philosophy and art. 1871–1945

Sir John Vanbrugh English Playwright, Architect

High-spirited writer of 'Restoration comedies' such as *The Relapse* (1696) and *The Provok'd Wife* (1697); also, the architect (along with Nicholas Hawksmoor) of Castle Howard (1702) and Blenheim Palace (1705). 1664–1726

Thorstein Veblen US Economist
Eccentric both professionally and personally, Veblen was disparaging of modern industrial society in works such as *The Theory of the Leisure Class* (1899). Invented the phrase 'conspicuous consumption'. 1857–1929

Johnny Vegas UK Comedian
Boozy, blustering, emotional alter ego of Michael Pennington, first seen in stand-up routines, then given a TV showcase on *The Johnny Vegas Television Show* (1998). Pennington/Vegas is also a skilled potter, and was probably the first man to feature a potter's wheel within a comedy performance. 1970–

Terry Venables UK Football Player, Manager
Played for Chelsea, Tottenham and England; managed Crystal Palace, Barcelona, Tottenham and England with success. Undoubted tactical nous, but business ventures sometimes landed him in trouble. He responded: 'Everyone says I should stick to coaching, but if you've got something about you, you want to do different things.' Venables co-wrote the TV detective series *Hazell* from 1974. 1943–

Victoria Queen of the United Kingdom 1837–1901
H. G. Wells said: 'Queen Victoria was like a great paper-weight that sat on men's minds, and when she was removed their ideas began to blow about all over the place haphazardly.' 1819–1901

Gore Vidal US Writer
Dapper, tart, strongly pro-Democrat American novelist and social commentator. Victoria Glendinning has called him 'the most Swiftian writer we have . . .' 1925–

King Vidor US Film Director
At his best on a bombastic scale; works include *Billy the Kid* (1930) and *Northwest Passage* (1939). 1894–1982

Tim Vine UK Comedian
Known for his speedy delivery. Averages ten jokes a minute.

Viz UK Publication
Parody of a children's comic, with adult content. Founded in a Newcastle bedroom in 1979 by Chris and Simon Donald, it has fluctuated between minor cult and commercial success, but has remained the funniest 'top-shelf' publication in Britain. *See also* Chris Donald.

Voltaire French Writer
François Marie Arouet; historian, tragedian, satirist, wit. *Candide* (1759) satirizes the philosophical optimism of Leibnitz and others. 1694–1778

Kurt Vonnegut US Novelist
Writer of darkly droll novels concerned with the dehumanizing effects of war and technology. *Slaughterhouse Five* (1969) is concerned with the destruction of Dresden. Vonnegut was originally bracketed as a science-fiction writer. 1922–

Bill Vukovich US Racing Driver
Died racing in the Indianapolis 500, which he had won in the two previous years. 1918–55

Tom Waits US Singer, Songwriter
Chronicler of low-life, with a gravel-voiced, guttural style. Albums include *Heartattack and Vine* (1980), and *Swordfishtrombones* (1983). Originally, he drank too much like the characters in his songs, but then he realized: 'The guy who writes murder mysteries doesn't have to be the murderer.' 1949–

Frank Waldman US Screenwriter
Wrote the later *Pink Panther* films starring Peter Sellers. 1919–

Edgar Wallace UK Writer
Thriller-writer, author of possibly about five hundred novels. 1875–1932

Graham Wallas UK Political Scientist
1858–1932

Horace Walpole English Writer
4th Earl of Orford, son of Sir Robert Walpole (first English Prime Minister 1721–42). Horace Walpole was a pioneer of the Gothic style both at his home at Strawberry Hill, Twickenham, and in *The Castle of Otranto* (1764), regarded as the first Gothic novel. His letters are more widely read today, however. 1717–97

Izaak Walton English Writer
An ironmonger who befriended John Donne and is celebrated as the author of *The Compleat Angler*, a book on fishing and much more besides, which has been called 'the story of a lad and a bass'. 1593–1683

Andy Warhol US Artist
A leading figure of Pop Art who held court at his New York studio, the Factory, where he turned out repetitive images of, for example, Campbell's soup cans (in 1960) and of celebrities such as Marilyn Monroe and Elvis Presley. His work

echoed the blandness of mass production and he cultivated a blank personal style to match. He left over a hundred million dollars at his death, and was described by Gore Vidal as 'a genius with the IQ of a moron'. 1928–87

Kirsty Wark UK TV Presenter

A regular presenter of *Newsnight* and other current affairs programmes. She has said: 'I don't think I have ever been patronized, except by Jeffrey Archer, who called me "love".' 1954–

Jack L. Warner US Film Producer

Youngest of the four Warner Brothers. 1892–1978

Keith Waterhouse UK Writer

Made his name with *Billy Liar* (1959), about a young fantasist in Bradford; it was subsequently a play (written by Waterhouse with his frequent collaborator Willis Hall) and a musical. Many comic and satirical novels followed; also successful plays. Waterhouse observes the inanities of the modern world in his *Daily Mail* newspaper column; his recreation, according to *Who's Who* is 'lunch'. 1927–

Alan Watkins UK Journalist

Political correspondent and sometime script-writer for the satirical programme *BBC3*; then amusing political columnist, first for the *Observer* (from 1976) and latterly for the *Independent on Sunday*. Has also written several books. 1933–

Auberon Waugh UK Writer

Elder son of Evelyn Waugh. Accidentally shot himself while on National Service in Cyprus, losing his spleen as a result – which is odd, since, as a journalist for the *New Statesman*, the *Spectator* and *Private Eye*, the word that best describes Waugh might be 'splenetic'. He combined surrealism with great personal ferocity towards certain left-wingers. As editor of the *Literary Review* (1986–2000), he encouraged many young writers. He also wrote five novels. 1939–2001

Daisy Waugh UK Writer, Journalist

Daughter of Auberon Waugh, granddaughter of Evelyn. Her books include the novels *What Is the Matter with Mary Jane?*, *Ten Steps to Happiness*, and *A Small Town in Africa*, her account of six months spent teaching in Kenya. 1967–

Evelyn Waugh UK Novelist

Decline and Fall (1928) proclaimed a comic genius, with an Augustan elegance of style. Other comedies followed, but with *Brideshead Revisited* (1945) his writing took on a more

elegiac tone. His diaries (published in 1976) and his letters (1980) bear further testimony to the brilliance of his comic timing and to his increasing misanthropy. Waugh converted to Catholicism in 1930. 1903–66

John Webster English Playwright

Known chiefly for *The White Devil* (1612) and *The Duchess of Malfi* (1623), violent tragedies which are continually revived. He was also a coach-maker. c.1578–c.1623

Hugh Wedlock US Screenwriter

Wrote comedy for films and TV, 1940s–80s. 1908–93

Johnny Weissmuller US Athlete, Actor

As an Olympic swimmer turned actor, he played Tarzan in nineteen films from 1932 onwards. 1903–84

Thomas Erle Welby UK Writer

1881–1933

Raquel Welch US Actress

She had a thoughtful approach to her status as the number one sex symbol of the late 1960s. 1940–

Orson Welles US Film Director, Actor

Directed *Citizen Kane* (1941), commonly picked as the best film ever. Dwindled somewhat thereafter, of course, but with many successes on the way, such as his performance as Harry Lime in *The Third Man* (1949). 1915–85

Duke of Wellington British Soldier, Statesman

Arthur Wellesley. Scourge of Napoleon, whom he defeated decisively at Waterloo in 1815. As a national hero (and amusing with it), he served as Prime Minister 1827–30. A thoroughgoing reactionary, he nevertheless enacted Catholic emancipation. 1769–1852

Carolyn Wells US Writer

Author of many crime novels – *The Deep-Lake Mystery* (1928), for example – and editor of anthologies of humorous writing. She was deaf from the age of six. 1872–1942

H. G. Wells UK Writer

Prolific, and associated with many strains of progressive thought. His books range from *The Time Machine* (1895), which founded science fiction, to the social comedy *Kipps* (1905). 1866–1946

Arnold Wesker UK Playwright

His best-known play is *Chips with Everything*

(1962). His East End Jewish background informs in his work. 1932–

Mae West US Actress
Epigrammatic leading lady and sex symbol. West, who wrote plays, as well as many of her own film scripts, excelled at the lewd double entendre in a theoretically non-permissive film era. 1892–1980

Rebecca West UK Writer
Suffragette, and a novelist in a feminist vein; lover of H. G. Wells; prolific and feisty journalist. 1892–1983

Edith Wharton US Novelist
Writer who dissected the brittle upper-class society into which she was born. Known for her wit although her most-read book, *The House of Mirth* (1905), is a tragedy. c.1861–1937

Richard Whately English Theologian
Professor of Political Economy, ultimately Archbishop of Dublin. 1787–1863

Charles Wheeler UK Broadcaster
Authoritative presenter of the TV programmes *Panorama* and *Newsweek*. Journalist of the Year, 1988. 1923–

Francis Wheen UK Broadcaster, Writer
Began on newspapers as a diarist, which he concedes is 'the polite term for a gossip columnist'. Unusual in that profession in being markedly left-wing. Has gone on to become a regular broadcaster and the author of books including *Tom Driberg: His Life and Indiscretions* (1990) and *How Mumbo-Jumbo Conquered the World* (2003). 1957–

James McNeill Whistler US Painter
Though American-born, he worked mainly in Paris, then London; sometimes bracketed with the Impressionists; flamboyant character; friend of Oscar Wilde. Richard Ellmann described Whistler as 'short but formidable'. 1834–1903

E. B. White US Humorist
White, whose journalism helped set the urbane, witty tone of the *New Yorker*, is famous for his droll and charming children's stories including *Stuart Little* (1945) and *Charlotte's Web* (1952). 1899–1985

Jack White US Singer, Songwriter
He and his 'sister' (they cultivate speculation about their relationship) comprise the rock group White Stripes. Minimalist in outlook, they play bluesy rock with just guitar and drums, and always dress in red and white. Their album *Elephant* was voted the best of 2003 in many magazines. 1975–

T. H. White UK Novelist
An outdoorsman, interested in nature; wrote the children's classic *The Sword in the Stone* (1937). 1906–64

Katherine Whitehorn UK Journalist
For many years a columnist on the *Observer*, she writes humorously, mainly on domestic themes. 1926–

Willie Whitelaw UK Politician
William Whitelaw, 1st Viscount. A cabinet minister under Edward Heath who unexpectedly – because he was on the opposite side of the party – became a firm supporter of, and Deputy Prime Minister to, Margaret Thatcher. 'Every Prime Minister needs a Willie,' she archly said. 1918–99

Charlotte Whitton Canadian Politician
Mayor of Ottawa 1951–6 and 1960–64; first female to serve as mayor of a Canadian city. 1896–1975

G. J. Whyte-Melville English Novelist
Of aristocratic origins; a great proponent of fox-hunting in his novels, from *Digby Grand* (1853) onwards. Having survived many an encounter with hedges and fences, Whyte-Melville met his end while galloping contentedly over a flat field. 1821–78

Samuel Wilberforce English Prelate
Third son of William Wilberforce. Bishop of Oxford, then of Winchester. His mercurial personality was reflected in his nickname 'Soapy Sam'. 1805–73

Earl Wild US Musician
Distinguished virtuoso pianist. 1915–

Oscar Wilde Anglo-Irish Writer
Flamboyant aesthete and brilliant wit; the supreme epigrammatist of English literature; infinitely quotable. Author of one novel, *The Portrait of Dorian Gray* (1891), poems and plays, including his masterpiece *The Importance of Being Earnest* (1895). Imprisoned for homosexual offences in 1895. Rudyard Kipling said: 'I've never cared for his work, too scented.' 1854–1900

Billy Wilder US Film Director, Scriptwriter
Born Samuel Wilder, in Austria. His highly successful films include *Sunset Boulevard* (1950),

The Seven-Year Itch (1955) and *Some Like It Hot* (1959). A perfectionist, he directed – as Shirley MacLaine once said – 'to the eyelash'. The actor Robert Philips, who worked with him on *The Secret Life of Sherlock Holmes* (1970), said Wilder was 'as witty as Oscar Wilde'. 1906–2002

George F. Will US Journalist
Widely syndicated columnist. In 1990 he published *Men at Work*, on baseball. 1941–

Geoffrey Willans *see* Ronald Searle

Hugo Williams UK Writer
Conspicuously good-looking old-Etonian poet. His first collection, *Symptoms of Loss* (1965), was inspired by the 'tough tone' of Thom Gunn. Williams's stylish column, 'Freelance', appears fortnightly in *The Times Literary Supplement*. It has been described as a 'clearing house for whatever is happening in his head'. He plays rock music – often heavy metal – while writing and chronicles his life in a scrapbook running to over sixty volumes. 1942–

Kenneth Williams UK Comedian
A broadly comic foil to Tony Hancock in *Hancock's Half Hour*, and a star of the saucy *Carry On* series of films from *Carry On Sergeant* (1958) onwards. Adept at a wide range of funny voices, and a brilliant timer of jokes. But his diaries, published in 1994, showed the sad complexity of the man underneath. It is possible that he committed suicide. 1926–88

Robin Williams US Actor
Stand-up comedian who gravitated, via the sitcom *Mork and Mindy*, to starring roles in films such as *Popeye* (1980), *Mrs Doubtfire* (1993) and *Good Will Hunting* (1997). Alternately manic and lachrymose in style; a brilliant mimic, as many interviewers have been disconcerted to discover. 1951–

Tennessee Williams US Playwright
Born Thomas Lanier. *The Glass Menagerie* made his name in 1945; *A Streetcar Named Desire* and *Cat on a Hot Tin Roof* followed in 1948 and 1955. Lovelorn characters expressed themselves in lyrical yet demotic language. 1911–83

William Carlos Williams US Writer, Poet
Author of poems and novels. Modernist. His masterpiece was *Paterson*, a portrait of a real American town, which appeared in five volumes between 1946 and 1958. His watchword was 'No ideas but in things'. 1883–1963

A. N. Wilson UK Writer
Determinedly controversial journalist, associated with the *Spectator*, the *Daily Telegraph* and the London *Evening Standard*. Also an elegant novelist, starting with *The Sweets of Pimlico* (1977), and a biographer and historian. Deals particularly with literature and religion. Early in his career he was the embodiment of the Young Fogey movement, with his parsonical manner and his bicycle with a basket on the front. 1950–

Harold Wilson UK Statesman
Labour Prime Minister 1964–70, 1974–6. Currently regarded as having been too pragmatic, Wilson's career ended with a rather mysterious resignation. 1916–95

Larry Wilson US Screenwriter
Credits include *The Addams Family* and *Beetlejuice*

Michael Winner UK Film Director
Flamboyant character, best known for the revenge drama *Death Wish* (1974); also a restaurant critic. He said, 'Success has gone to my stomach.' 1935–

Shelley Winters US Actress
Character actress with many credits. She said: 'In *A Patch of Blue*, I thought I was lousy, and I won the Oscar.' 1920–

Jeanette Winterson UK Novelist
Came to prominence with *Oranges Are Not the Only Fruit* (1985), an account of lesbianism flowering in spite of parental religious oppression. It won the Whitbread Prize, and was turned into a TV serial. 1959–

Ernie Wise *see* Eric Morecambe

P. G. Wodehouse UK Novelist, Short-story Writer
Highly regarded humorist; author of more than a hundred escapist comedies of upper-class life, often featuring the apparently buffoonish Bertie Wooster and his learned butler, Jeeves. Wodehouse became an American citizen in 1955. Aged eighty, he said: 'I've always been a recluse. I've never seen any sort of life – I got it all from the newspapers.' 1881–1975

Terry Wogan Irish Radio and TV Presenter
Former bank clerk and one of the original disc jockeys on Radio 1, he has never looked back. Described by Jeff Evans in *The Penguin TV Companion* as '*the* TV personality of the 80s'. 1938–

Tom Wolfe US Writer
Witty, dandified essayist who in the late 1960s pioneered 'the new journalism', which borrowed some of the techniques of fiction, novel-writing seeming to be in abeyance at the time. His first novel was *The Bonfire of the Vanities* (1987). 1931–

Ron Wood UK Rock Musician
Famously convivial (and, until recently, bibulous) guitarist, first with the Faces and, from 1976, the Rolling Stones. 1947–

Victoria Wood UK Comedian, Actress, Songwriter
Began her career on the talent show *New Faces* in 1975. Specializes in satirical songs and impersonations of ebullient northern women. 1953–

James Woodforde English Writer, Vicar
His *Diary of a Country Parson* (published in five volumes from 1924) is full of quotidian charm, though not considered literature. 1740–1803

Virginia Woolf UK Writer
Neurotic novelist, at the heart of the Bloomsbury group. Developed a loosely associative, lyrical style in *Mrs Dalloway* (1925), *To the Lighthouse* (1927) and *The Waves* (1931). Prone to depression, she drowned herself. Germaine Greer wrote, 'There was not much wrong with Virginia Woolf except that she was a woman.' 1882–1941

Alexander Woollcott US Journalist, Theatre Critic
Sparring partner of Dorothy Parker's at the Algonquin Hotel Round Table. Described in *Life* magazine as 'testy as a wasp, and much more poisonous'. 1887–1943

Barbara Frances Wootton UK Social Scientist
Baroness Wootton (of Abinger). Best remembered for her book *Testament for Social Science* (1958); created a life peer in 1958. 1897–1988

Dame Elizabeth Wordsworth UK Educationalist
Grand-niece of Wordsworth; founding Principal 1879–1909 of Lady Margaret Hall, Oxford. 1840–1932

Sir Henry Wotton English Poet, Diplomat
Ambassador to James I, later Provost of Eton. As a young man he was a friend of John Donne and, later, of Izaak Walton. 1568–1639

Christopher Wren English Architect
Built more than fifty churches in London after the Great Fire of 1666. His monument is the biggest of them, St Paul's. 1632–1723

Frank Lloyd Wright US Architect
Charismatic pioneer of a rustic modern style. Perhaps the only architect to have been celebrated, or even mentioned, in a pop song – 'Frank Lloyd Wright' by Paul Simon. 1867–1959

Orville Wright US Aviator
On 17 December 1903 he and his brother Wilbur (1867–1912) achieved the first flight in a machine heavier than air. 1871–1948

Steven Wright US Comedian
A stand-up comic since 1979; has frequently appeared on *Saturday Night Live*, *Late Night with David Letterman* and *The Tonight Show* with Johnny Carson. His act constitutes a stream of unrelated one-liners. He has said: 'People say I use one-liners, I talk in a monotone, I'm deadpan – I agree with all that, but it's how I think.' 1955–

Hugo Wrotham UK Journalist

William Wycherley English Playwright
Author of comedies including *The Gentleman Dancing Master* (1672) and *The Country Wife* (1675). c.1640–1716

Malcolm X US Black Activist
Born Malcolm Little. Muslim convert, eloquent spokesman for Black Power in the 1950s and early 60s. Assassinated by black extremists as a consequence of tempering his views on black and white coexistence. 1925–65

R. J. Yeatman *see* W. C. Sellar

Boris Yeltsin Russian Statesman
Ally of the reformer Gorbachev; President of Russia 1991–9. 1931–

Peter York *see* Ann Barr

Angus Young UK Rock Musician
Lead guitarist of AC/DC, a heavy metal band formed in Australia in 1974 (Young's family having emigrated there), and considered very good at what they do. Always performs dressed as a schoolboy. 1959–

Edward Young English Playwright, Poet
Author of tragedies, a series of satires called *The Love of Fame* (1725–8) and, particularly, the long poem *The Complaint: or, Night-Thoughts on Life,*

Death and Immortality (1742–5), which contains lugubrious but often whimsically amusing epigrams. 1683–1765

Neil Young Canadian Singer, Songwriter

Began with the psychedelic country band Buffalo Springfield, then briefly added his surname to the bestselling group Crosby, Stills and Nash; thereafter solo. His many albums include *After the Gold Rush* (1970) and *Rust Never Sleeps* (1979). Known for his loose, spontaneous style, quavery voice and cussed attitude. 1945–

Scott Young Canadian Writer

Father of Neil Young, though divorced from Neil's mother Rassy. Scott Young has written sports journalism and many books including a series featuring an Inuit detective, and is almost as famous in Canada as his son. 1918–

Henny Youngman US Humorist
1906–98.

Israel Zangwill UK Writer

Editor of *Ariel*, a humorous journal; wrote novels on Zionism, including *Children of the Ghetto* (1892). 1864–1926

Frank Zappa US Musician

Intelligent, opinionated songwriter, composer and guitar virtuoso. His work stretched from the risqué pop he produced with the Mothers of Invention to avant-garde orchestral pieces. According to Matt Groening he had 'the best moustache ever'. 1940–93

Author Index

Mamet, David 375
Clothes and Fashion 11.58; Family 83.40; Genres
222.88, 222.96; Lack of Money 115.24; Literary Style
234.24; Non-alcoholic Drinks 300.6; Particular Eras
182.5; Quasi-philosophical Observations 201.37;
Speech 95.30, 95.31, 95.33; Swimming 280.1;
Television the Medium 268.19; The Body and Its
Functions 62.38, 62.39; Types of Animals 326.51;
Visual Art in General 250.10; Weather 333.44
Mancroft, Lord 375
Cricket 275.10; Happiness 41.6
Mandel, Babaloo 375
Lust and Promiscuity 25.22
Mandelson, Peter 375
Particular Politicians 140.61
Mankiewicz, Herman J. 375
Boastfulness and Modesty 47.7; Etiquette of Food
and Drink 299.42
Mankiewicz, Joseph L. 375
Theatrical Life 243.9
Manning, Bernard 375
Hard Work and Laziness 103.22
Marchant, Ian 375
Environmentalism 336.10
Marquis, Don 375
Man's Relationship with Nature 334.11; Optimism
and Pessimism 34.12; Publishing and the Literary
Life 214.34
Marryat, Frederick 375
Anger 46.3
Marsh, Rodney 375
Football 273.2
Marshall, Arthur 376
By Rail 319.31; Cricket 276.15; Crime and
Punishment 155.39; Cultural Appreciation and
Philistinism 179.10; Death 75.35; Etiquette of Food
and Drink 299.32; Family 83.33; Non-alcoholic
Drinks 300.7; Particular Writers and Their Works
228.74, 228.75; School 172.22; Service Life 166.33;
The Body and Its Functions 63.46; Violence in
General 163.16
Marshall, Thomas R. 376
Smoking 293.12
Martial 376
Town and Country 88.1
Martin, Dean 376
Alcohol 291.57
Martin, Dick 387
Particular Inventions 184.18
Martin, Steve 376
Academics and Academic Disciplines 176.32;
Comedy and Comedians 248.5; Death 75.34; Faith
or Lack of It 196.23; France 127.6; Friendship and
Enmity 78.22; Literary Style 233.19; Marriage 17.59;
Particular Actors, Directors and Films 239.31;
Particular Professions 110.66; Quasi-philosophical
Observations 201.39; Sexual Perversion 27.4; The
Act of Writing 237.12; The Artistic Mind 59.7
Martin, Suzanne 376

Heaven and Hell 199.13
Marx, Andy 376
Old Age 73.12
Marx, Chico 376
Sleep and Dreams 58.6; The Sex Act 25.4
Marx, Groucho 376
American Sports 281.4; Beauty and Ugliness 2.23;
Class and Snobbery 88.36; Comedy and
Comedians 247.2; Death 75.22; Diplomacy and
International Relations 148.12; Festive Occasions
84.5; Horseracing 280.5; Intelligence and Stupidity
54.20; Journalists and Journalism 260.27; Literary
Criticism 234.13; Men on Women 20.13; Military
Incompetence 167.10; Particular Professions
108.34; Police 157.8; Quasi-philosophical
Observations 201.27; Quotation 231.14; Television
the Medium 267.17; The Body and Its Functions
61.21
Marx, Karl 376
Political Ideologies and Parties 142.12
Mason, Jackie 376
Drugs 292.16; Hunting 282.15; Race 134.24
Mathison, Melissa 376
School 172.23
Matthau, Walter 376
Lack of Money 115.26
Maudling, Reginald 376
Britain and Ireland 125.52
Maugham, W. Somerset 376
Accidents 38.5; Death 75.29; Humour 43.22; Love
13.30; Publishing and the Literary Life 214.27
Mauriac, François 376
Germany 128.5
Maxwell, Elsa 376
The Industry 241.27
Mayall, Rick 376
Battle of the Sexes 19.19
Meades, Jonathan 376
Class and Snobbery 88.46; Football 274.17;
Holidays 311.39; Hunting 282.16; Particular Types
of Food 306.80
Meir, Golda 376
Israel 129.3; Race 134.32
Melbourne, Lord 376–7
Beauty and Ugliness 1.8; Clergy and
Contemplatives 193.9; Looking Back 181.1; Religion
in General 190.4; Worship 197.7
Melly, George 377
Old Age 73.17
Mencken, H. L. 377
Battle of the Sexes 19.25; Hard Work and Laziness
103.18; Love 13.25; Marriage 16.34, 18.67; Particular
Inventions 183.8; Pregnancy and Contraception
26.3
Mercer, Johnny 377
Optimism and Pessimism 34.18
Merchant, Stephen 377
Employers and Employees 112.14
Meredith, George 377

More, Hannah 379
　Quotation 230.5
Morecambe, Eric 379
　Audiences 246.9; By Air 321.5, 321.8; Clothes and
　Fashion 10.40; Cooking 306.4; Cowardice and
　Bravery 164.16; Crime and Punishment 155.37;
　Etiquette of Food and Drink 298.25; Festive
　Occasions 84.10; Golf 277.7; Grammar and Spelling
　207.11, 207.13; Man's Relationship with Nature
　334.22; Meanness and Generosity 116.6; Memory
　57.18; Service Life 166.32; Size 4.16; Sleep and
　Dreams 58.9; Theatrical Life 243.12
Morris, Chris 379
　Experts 180.2; Horseracing 281.7; Parochialism
　132.3
Morrissey 379
　Discretion, Indiscretion and Gossip 97.29; Family
　83.34; Misanthropy 100.13; The Single Life 30.6
Mortimer, Bob 379
　Particular Television Programmes and Performers
　269.15
Mortimer, John 379
　Actors and Acting 245.19; Cricket 275.13; Genres
　221.82, 222.89; Homosexuality and Bisexuality
　23.9; Hunting 282.11; Italy 129.5; Lawyers 159.22,
　160.27; Publishing and the Literary Life 215.43,
　215.46; Radio 266.11; School 172.30; Student Life
　173.12
Morton, J. B. see Beachcomber
Mrabet, Mohammed 379
　America and Canada 120.15
Muggeridge, Malcolm 379
　Diplomacy and International Relations 148.18;
　Faith or Lack of It 196.18; Homosexuality and
　Bisexuality 23.7; Humour 43.28; Journalists and
　Journalism 261.40; Particular Politicians 138.24,
　138.25, 138.26; Particular Professions 108.43;
　Particular Writers and Their Works 227.62, 227.63
Muir, Frank 379
　Particular Television Programmes and Performers
　268.3; Quotation 232.27; Radio 266.6; Television
　the Medium 267.14
Mullard, Arthur 380
　Quasi-philosophical Observations 202.41
Murphy, Eddie 380
　Accidents 39.12; Heaven and Hell 199.10; Race
　134.27

Nabokov, Vladimir 380
　Accidents 38.9; By Road 315.39; Genres 221.69;
　Quotation 231.18; Reading 210.35; Speech 94.27
Narváez, Ramón Maria 380
　The Nature of War 161.16
Nash, Ogden 380
　Alcohol 288.31; America and Canada 119.9; By Air
　321.2; By Road 314.20; Conscience and Guilt 202.7;
　Fame 36.13; Man's Relationship with Nature
　334.21; Middle Age 71.6; Particular Types of Food
　303.34, 305.67; The Body and Its Functions 61.23;

The Generation Gap 71.9; Types of Animals 325.35,
326.43, 326.44, 326.45
Needham, Richard 380
　Reading 210.39
Nelson, Lord 380
　The Body and Its Functions 60.9
Nesbit, E. 380
　The Generation Gap 71.7
Nevin, Charles 380
　Journalists and Journalism 265.8
Newell, Martin 380
　By Rail 320.37
Newley, Anthony 380
　Diplomacy and International Relations 148.17
Newman, Paul 380
　Success and Failure 31.12
Newman, Randy 380
　Musicians as People 252.15
Niccol, Andrew 380
　Manners, or Lack of 92.40
Nicholson, Jack 380
　Manners, or Lack of 92.43; Old Age 73.22;
　Particular Actors, Directors and Films 238.11;
　Pornography 29.4; Race 133.12; States of Mind 55.8
Nicolson, Harold 380
　Etiquette of Food and Drink 297.14; Health and
　Illness 65.16; Journalists and Journalism 261.29;
　Particular Television Programmes and Performers
　268.1
Niven, David 380
　Genres 220.68
Norden, Denis 380
　Middle Age 72.9; Radio 266.6
Northcliffe, Lord 380
　Class and Snobbery 88.39
Novello, Ivor 381
　France 127.5
Nye, Simon 381
　Death 76.50

O'Brien, Conor Cruise 381
　Discretion, Indiscretion and Gossip 97.24
O'Brien, Flann 381
　By Road 315.30; Eating and Drinking Places 296.6;
　Growing Up 70.10; Humour 43.32; Man's
　Relationship with Nature 334.17
O'Casey, Sean 381
　Particular Writers and Their Works 226.51
O'Connor, Philip 381
　Childishness 51.2; Fame 37.34; Intelligence and
　Stupidity 54.24
Oddie, Bill 381
　Hobbies 285.1, 285.2
O'Farrell, John 381
　Battle of the Sexes 19.23
Ogilvy, David 381
　Particular Professions 109.45
O'Keeffe, Georgia 381
　Visual Artists as People 249.11

Thematic Index

to d. is bad 288.11
what will you have to d.? 289.33
who d.s as much as you do 289.35
wouldn't d. under his own name 108.37
ye may tak a man tae d. 299.41
drinking, if you are a d. man 296.6
much d., little thinking 296.1
drive, d. off a cliff 316.47
driver, all the bad d.s I know 317.59
I know d.s who go home at night 279.8
like a d. shooting red lights 94.28
make the d. alight first 313.5
driving, your d. was immaculate 315.35
dropped, not wish to be d. by 77.5
drowned, better d. than duffers 51.4
then ye'll no' be d. 202.48
drugs, calling d. an epidemic 292.13
d. were the solution 292.11
never had a problem with d. 292.8
sex and d. and rock and roll 292.7
they're both on d. 71.11
drummer, best d. in the Beatles 256.4
drums, the d. are sure to be beaten 164.5
drunk, and then d. 288.9
d. for about a week now 209.27
he is a d. 291.63
just God when he's d. 290.51
more old d.s than I do old doctors 289.31
prove that you were d. at the time 316.40
when d., gentlemen often become amorous 87.29
drunkard, makes you behave like the village d.
  292.6
drunkenness, an epidemic of d. 192.23
dry-cleaning, d., same day 110.64
Dublin, all the references to D. 236.16
duchess, see the d. lay a foundation stone 88.44
duck, d.'s life is not all hearts and flowers 326.51
I just forgot to d. 278.2
duffers, if not d. won't drown 51.4
duke, a fully equipped d. 86.18
d.s are just as great a terror 86.18
forgot to tell you I was made a d. 46.4
included a d. 88.47
separating the d. from his horny-palmed
  employees 88.38
the misfortune to be a d. 86.11
dull, d., duller, Dulles 137.17
d. in a new way 223.13
Dumas, Alexandre, A.D. writes two a week 236.3
dumb, I guess you think I'm d. 54.22
so d. he can't fart 138.30
strikes us d. 93.11
dumps, we're all in the d. 40.8
dunces, the d. are all in confederacy 52.4
dunking, elegant silver 'd. tongs' 295.17
Durante, Jimmy, I can't overlook J.D.'s nose 7.17
maybe D. was the only performer 248.7
Durham, there, lighting up, is D. 125.58
duties, devotes to the neglect of his d. 175.25

dying, death must be distinguished from d. 74.21
d. is a very dull, dreary affair 75.29
d. is to cost more 149.12
d. of nothing 66.35
d. stuffs sold here 107.13
if this is d. 75.27
rural England has been d. 90.20
the prospect of d. mid-season 274.8
Dylan, Bob, every B.D. his Donovan 257.17
dyslexics, invited to the d.' ball 210.38

eagerness, such consuming e. 95.38
ear, a box on the e. 167.2
e. may be a dust-trap 62.40
e.s too big 7.22
for listeners with three e.s 266.7
have tattered his e.s 326.49
I always telephone with my left e. 183.12
little flaps to close the e.s 62.26
points out to accentuate his e.s 11.58
they used to be my e.s 62.29
early, late when you're e. 112.13
earth, e. here is so kind 328.2
how long the meek can keep the e. 46.5
keeps saying that the e. is flat 225.30
princes of the e. 132.3
put on this e. to rise above 201.29
scum of the e. 164.4
the meek shall inherit the e. 105.25
earthquake, small e. in Chile 261.33
earwax, not so much brain as e. 52.1
East Anglia, its rump is E.A. 125.59
eat, e. to die 295.15
e. to live 294.4
my feeling is e. it 295.16
never e. at a place called Mom's 201.30
the great ones e. up the little ones 32.2
you just have to e. it 299.44
eaten, e. me out of house and home 294.2
eater, a good e. must be a good man 294.6
eating, e. is the only thing that consoles me 295.10
e. people is wrong! 298.17
people e. cherries or oysters 230.4
echo, the famous e. in the Reading Room 309.22
economics, e. is extremely useful 176.40
the Enid Blyton of e. 138.35
economist, a form of employment for e.s 176.40
an e. is someone 176.37
e.s: if they're so clever 176.35
if e.s could manage 175.19
sorry for the death of a political e. 174.11
economy, the e., stupid! 149.13
edit, couldn't e. a bus ticket 265.81
editing, e. is the same thing 213.26
editor, e.s kept their faces turned 213.20
if you are e. 263.62
my first e. 265.82
the e., I cannot think what he is for 213.18
education, a university e. does one thing 170.8

what on earth is this l. 13.19
when he fell in l. at first sight 13.24
when they l. 108.31
women who l. the same man 13.21
loved, *absence of l. ones* 82.22
as though you l. him 278.1
better to have l. and lost 13.20
invite your l. ones outside 85.19
lovely, *you look both l. and desirable* 26.13
lover, *a l. you can't exactly trust* 241.23
a pressing l. 24.7
greatest l. that I have ever had 29.4
scratch a l. 13.22
we that are true l.s 12.2
loving, *l. alone* 14.7
loyal, *lousy but l.* 146.12
loyalty, *I want l.* 112.7
lozenges, *Koffnot l.* 65.11
Lucan, Lord, *L.L. is merely 'missing'* 88.42
luck, *l. is always important* 33.11
seven years' bad l. 33.14
lucre, *the Lord of L.'s saliva* 115.1
luggage, *as many places as my l.* 321.13
lose our l. beforehand 187.5
lump, *a l. bred up in darkness* 80.1
lunatics, *the l. have taken charge of the asylum* 240.3
lunch, *hungry after l.* 263.68
sharpening the appetite for l. 75.35
start having l. and actually eating it 13.32
luncheon, *national anti-l. league* 295.11
lung, *actually afraid of his l.s* 60.7
said to affect the l.s 66.25
worst thing about a l. transplant 66.37
luxury, *l. the accomplish'd sofa* 79.3
lying, *I do not mind l.* 205.11
organized l. 108.43
the decay of l. as an art 204.6
lynching, *l. is trial by fury* 155.35
lyric, *pointed up the cretinous l.* 256.7

mac, *have you got a light m.?* 11.54
macaroni, *m. and memorial services* 72.7
that and m. are their forte 129.1
McGrath, Paul, *P.M. limps on water* 66.28
machine, *I have tested your m.* 183.15
these m.s will ever force themselves 182.1
this fartarsing m. 186.3
mad, *everyone is more or less m.* 54.3
I am not m. 54.5
m., bad and dangerous to know 223.15
m., is he? 165.13
mental: non-U for m. 55.6
never go to bed m. 46.7
people who were a little m. 6.10
the world said I was m. 55.2
when a heroine goes m. 8.7
madman, *one difference between a m. and me* 54.5
magazine, *do everything possible for your m.* 264.71

Magdalen College, *I spent fourteen months at M.C.* 173.3
magic, *number three is the m. number* 117.7
magistrate, *the smaller the ex-m.* 159.20
mail, *deadlier than the m.* 236.20
Majesty, *Her M.'s a pretty nice girl* 146.19
Major-General, *model of a modern M.-G.* 165.8
majority, *the contented m.* 88.45
the m. is always in the wrong 142.20
would admit to be the m. 143.36
make-up, *a m. man with a spray gun* 3.36
maker, *meet my m. brow to brow* 271.13
male, *battalions of paper-minded m.s* 105.21
more deadly than the m. 20.12
Malibu, *throw a stick at M.* 238.10
malice, *I bear no m. against the people* 96.8
m. is of a low stature 77.3
malignant, *only part of Randolph that was not m.* 78.18
man, *a bit of a ladies' m.* 62.32
a good m. fallen among politicians 139.43
a m. in his eightieth year 72.8
a m. is designed to walk three miles in the rain 19.20
a m. is nobody 35.7
a m. is . . . so in the way 79.7
a m. of less than two or three thousand pounds 114.8
a m. who can't think for himself 192.15
a m. who is slovenly and untidy 80.23
a m. who moralizes 205.3
a modest m. is such a nuisance 47.6
a nice m. is a m. of nasty ideas 97.4
a one-book m. 230.97
a self-made m. 33.10
an elderly m. of forty-two 71.5
between the m. and his knocker 79.5
buy it like an honest m. 88.39
consider m. 321.2
foot-in-the-grave young m. 69.3
he was a vicious m. 323.8
I never hated a m. enough 19.13
if they could put one m. on the moon 330.7
if we can only get m. to shut up 190.6
is m. an ape or an angel? 200.6
it is the entire m. 61.13
looking as cheerful as any m. could 153.3
m. has his will 18.6
m., I can assure you, is a nasty creature 99.1
m. is a creature of habit 213.14
m. is the only animal that blushes 203.9
m. sometimes succeeds in a library 79.6
never mine own m. since 152.1
no m. can ever grasp 119.13
no m. is so boring 23.12
no m. wanted me 30.10
no m. would be old 72.3
not a year or two shows us a m. 18.1
repelled by m. 195.10

no one has m. who ought to have it 114.14
poor because they don't have enough m. 115.23
put not your trust in m. 98.3
rude to discuss m. 92.43
than take a farthing of his m. 123.28
the only way to save m. 118.4
when you don't have m. 40.17
where his m. used to be 83.44
will lend you m. if you can prove that you don't
need it 117.10
working out all about my m. 114.19
your m. or your life 116.11
monkeys, *crucifying camels and m.* 333.4
monogamy, *m. is the same* 25.18
m. leaves a lot to be desired 17.55
monopoly, *m.'s long been the rub* 141.3
Montana, *compared to M.* 119.2
months, *one of the peculiarly dangerous m.* 104.9
monument, *a nation's m.s collapse* 317.5
their only m. the asphalt road 277.4
moo, *you silly m.* 19.16
moon, *don't the m. see all the world* 330.1
if they could put one man on the m. 330.7
the m. is always full 330.5
there was a man lived in the m. 330.2
we walked on the m. 92.29
you can see the m. 189.23
moonlight, *sunbathe by m.* 38.37
Moore, George, *G.M., in his writings* 231.13
moral, *m. indignation* 205.4
much of the m. high ground 270.20
override one's m. sense 179.4
moralitee, *good-bye m.!* 59.3
morality, *Dr Johnson's m.* 224.23
for our best m. 89.6
one of its periodic fits of m. 205.2
moralize, *I never m.* 205.3
morals, *have you no m., man?* 114.16
so high type m. 141.5
more, *m. will mean worse* 170.15
mores, *o tempora, o m.!* 90.1
morning, *ninety degrees at four in the m.* 331.11
spent the m. going to Africa 59.4
Morocco, *we're M. bound* 309.19
moron, *I wish I were a m.* 53.19
the consumer isn't a moron 109.45
Morris, William, *even M.'s poorest workman* 333.6
morsels, *all his m. are not his owne* 68.1
Moscow, *went to M. for the weekend* 127.3
Moses, *leave M. out of* The Wars of the Roses 240.7
moth, *kill a small m.* 323.6
m. boy 285.6
mother, *a m. who talks about her own children*
212.11
as the summer riot ends, is m.'s 69.8
either my father or my m. 68.2
gave her m. forty whacks 81.13
if a writer has to rob his m. 214.29
keeps your m. from hitting you 83.35

like a note from your m. 118.10
m.'s eyes and teeth handed around 48.5
my m., drunk or sober 131.4
off your living m. 25.7
tell my m. I'm a lesbian 85.18
we seem to have lost your m. 179.10
when his m. feels chilly 10.50
mother-in-law, *a m. is not a simple idea* 82.18
given pleasure to my m. 81.3
I haven't spoken to my m. 83.39
I knew it was the m. 82.25
marvellous place to drop one's m. 82.19
sort of place to send your m. 128.3
watching your m. drive over a cliff 83.40
when his m. died 81.11
motherhood, *the most sublime is m.* 27.1
motion, *the m. was not too rapid* 240.4
motor, *these days of reckless m. traffic* 314.16
motorcars, *generally die in their m. too* 314.13
Triumph Sodomite m. 92.31
see also car
motoring, *m. in Britain* 315.27
motorist, *no m. ever thinks of himself* 314.17
mottos, *needlepoint m. can make your thumb bleed*
232.24
mountaineer, *the real m. has a tremendous*
advantage 87.33
mouse, *a m., to me, I put the cat on it* 187.10
not much bigger than a m. 4.12
moustache, *a man who didn't wax his m.* 61.15
big chap with small m. 6.9
cultivate a handlebar m. 7.20
mouth, *in somebody else's m.* 304.52
never open your m. 95.33
through opening of their m.s 96.19
whispering in her m. 25.4
wiping your m. on your sleeve 299.30
moved, *if we m. in next door* 80.28
moves, *if it m., salute it* 165.16
movie, *a m. about a giraffe* 239.30
American m.s 240.18
as the m.s are to morons 183.8
life is like a 'B' m. 202.42
m. music is noise 240.13
m.s should have a beginning 241.19
one thing that can kill the m.s 240.8
shout 'm.' in a crowded firehouse 201.39
this m. is so insistently heartwarming 238.18
what they make a m. out of 221.76
where m.s go when they die 268.23
Mozart, Wolfgang Amadeus, *M. will tell me he's*
too busy 199.13
when M. was my age 31.14
you cannot enjoy M. 11.55
MP, *being an M. is the sort of job* 136.27
Mr Toad, *they answered, 'M.T.'* 47.5
much, *how m. are they?* 118.11
muddle, *a beginning, a m. and an end* 221.77
muggers, *m. are very interesting people* 155.41

mum, *getting more and more like your m.* 322.17
   they fuck you up, your m. and dad 68.4
murder, *as Agatha Christie said of m.* 265.83
   brought back m. into the home 267.6
   m. considered as one of the fine arts 153.10
   m. is a mistake 154.18
   m. one another in 'youth centres' 9.38
murdered, *many disadvantages of getting m.* 155.39
murderer, *mass m. suffering from an ingrowing*
   toenail 69.5
Murdoch, Iris, *I.M.. I've always admired the name*
   229.91
museum, *can't stand that part of the m.* 179.11
   missing from the statues in the other m.s 179.12
mushroom, *life is too short to stuff a m.* 306.3
music, *a man who can read m.* 176.33
   a reasonable ear in m. 255.4
   all the good m.'s already been written 252.17
   danceth without m. 33.2
   how potent cheap m. is 254.3
   I like Wagner's m. better than anybody's 256.1
   I've suffered for my m. 252.10
   missing link between m. and noise 255.17
   movie m. is noise 240.13
   m. helps not the tooth-ach 252.1
   my m. is best understood 253.12
   similarity between m. and cricket 275.9
   that m. was pretty white 133.12
   the English may not like m. 253.11
   Van Gogh's ear for m. 254.21
   when the m. stops 247.11
   writing contemporary m. 254.14
musical, *contributed to the m. field* 258.2
musician, *a m. is like a mortician* 251.6
   a m. without a girlfriend? 252.16
   he's a professional m. 251.7
   named his favourite m.s 253.17
   they say of Greek m.s 251.1
musicologist, *a m. is a man* 176.33
Muslim, *if Woody Allen were a M.* 248.8
mutton, *boiled m. without capers* 305.67

nails, *filing her n.* 106.33
naked, *if everybody flew n.* 161.4
name, *a very useful kind of n.* 100.6
   Agamemnon: good n. for a cat 101.20
   alias a lot of n.s 101.9
   and if his n. be George 100.1
   Higgins was his n. 101.8
   Homer: an American n. 101.18
   if your n.s above the fold 264.80
   Leila York's my pen n. 101.15
   my 'oss, my wife and my n. 116.4
   n. I can't for the life of me remember 98.6
   n. mentioned as one of the great authors 35.9
   not make jokes about his n. 101.11
   remember your n. perfectly 92.44
   retaining their married n.s 101.22
   stage n. had been Pip Trotsky 245.23

the n. of a man is a numbing blow 101.16
the n.s of all these places 59.1
they can spell your n. in Karachi 36.21
those girls' n.s in Numbers 101.17
two Christian n.s is the best combination 245.23
two n.s have melted into one 37.30
'Violet' is thought a suitable n. 100.3
whose n. is Hodbod 101.14
wouldn't drink under his own n. 108.37
naming, *today we have n. of parts* 165.20
narcissism, *between n. and obsessional neuroses*
   221.70
narcissist, *a n. is someone better looking* 11.7
nastiest, *the n. thing in the nicest way* 147.8
nasty, *man, . . . is a n. creature* 99.1
   turn very n. at short notice 143.26
nation, *have the n. united behind them* 110.59
   small n.s like prostitutes 148.16
nature, *anyone who loves n.* 335.1
   at two with n. 335.26
   attracted by God, or by n. 195.10
   human n., Mr Allnut 201.29
   most irrelevant thing in n. 81.6
   n. has no cure for this sort of madness 142.18
   N. is so uncomfortable 333.6
   N. is usually wrong 333.5
   N.'s way of telling you 75.25
   one of n.'s gentlemen 86.12
   run into debt with N. 111.3
   the g-nicest work of n. 326.46
   the modesty of n. 243.3
   the n. of art itself 250.11
   the only link between Art and N. 8.19
   they say n. hates a vacuum 329.3
   what God would have done with N. 119.6
   when all n. shouted 'fore!' 277.3
naughty, *n., paughty Jack-a-Dandy* 156.49
navvy, *a n. can have his pick* 108.32
navy, *I joined the n. when I was four* 165.22
Nazareth, *any good thing come out of N.* 129.1
Nazi, *are you a N.?* 139.47
   as a good N. 171.18
necessity, *n. invented stools* 79.3
   n. never made a good bargain 104.2
   n. with her imperial law 32.1
neck, *really long n.s* 328.81
   the back of a young man's n. 10.49
   the dirtiest n. I ever kept wicket behind 275.8
   wherever did I get those bruises on my n.? 119.10
nectarines, *n. – I love that fruit* 303.44
need, *will you still n. me* 73.11
negro, *he no spare n. . . . nor massa* 132.1
   where the average n. 133.10
   with n. affectations 254.11
neighbours, *irritability of your n.* 80.25
   to make sport for our n. 32.4
net, *don't try to jump the n.* 283.11
neurosis, *a n. is a secret* 56.13
   n. is the way of avoiding non-being 55.4